¡Así se dice! Glencoe Spanish 2

More than just a textbook!

W9-BQT-845

QuickPass

Use your chapter-specific Web code for quick and easy navigation. Access the Online Student Edition, extra practice, and self-check quizzes with QuickPass at glencoe.com.

Download the entire audio program to your MP3 player.

Not online? No problem! Access your Student Edition, Audio Program, and Workbook with StudentWorks™ Plus CD-ROM.

VIDEO

Enrich your Spanish skills with videos tailored to your learning needs: vocabulary, grammar, dialogue, and culture.

¡Así se dice!

Glencoe Spanish ②

Conrad J. Schmitt

McGraw Hill Glencoe

Information on featured companies, organizations, and their products and services is included for educational purposes only and does not present or imply endorsement of the ¡**Así se dice!** program. Permission to use all business logos has been granted by the businesses represented in this text.

The *McGraw-Hill* Companies

 Glencoe

Copyright © 2009 The McGraw-Hill Companies, Inc. All rights reserved. No part of this publication may be reproduced or distributed in any form or by any means, or stored in a database or retrieval system, without the prior written consent of The McGraw-Hill Companies, Inc., including, but not limited to, network storage or transmission, or broadcast for distance learning.

Send all inquiries to:
Glencoe/McGraw-Hill
8787 Orion Place
Columbus, OH 43240-4027

ISBN: 978-0-07-877783-7
MHID: 0-07-877783-6

Printed in the United States of America.

1 2 3 4 5 6 7 8 9 10   071/055   14 13 12 11 10 09 08 07

About the Author

Conrad J. Schmitt

Conrad J. Schmitt received his B.A. degree magna cum laude from Montclair State University, Upper Montclair, New Jersey. He received his M.A. from Middlebury College, Middlebury, Vermont, and did additional graduate work at New York University. He also studied at the Far Eastern Institute at Seton Hall University, Newark, New Jersey.

Mr. Schmitt has taught Spanish and French at all academic levels—from elementary school to graduate courses. He served as Coordinator of Foreign Languages for the Hackensack, New Jersey, public schools. He also taught courses in Foreign Language Education as a visiting professor at the Graduate School of Education at Rutgers University, New Brunswick, New Jersey.

Mr. Schmitt has authored or co-authored more than one hundred books, all published by The McGraw-Hill Companies. He was also editor-in-chief of foreign languages, ESL, and bilingual education for The McGraw-Hill Companies.

Mr. Schmitt has traveled extensively throughout Spain and all of Latin America. He has addressed teacher groups in all fifty states and has given seminars in many countries including Japan, the People's Republic of China, Taiwan, Egypt, Germany, Spain, Portugal, Mexico, Panama, Colombia, Brazil, Jamaica, and Haiti.

Contributing Writers

Louise M. Belnay
Teacher of World Languages
Adams County School District 50
Westminster, Colorado

Reina Martínez
Coordinator/Teacher of World Languages
North Rockland Central School District
Thiells, New York

Contenido

Student Handbook

Student Handbook

GeoVistas
Explorando el mundo hispanohablante... SH42

Repaso

Capítulo **1** En avión

Objetivos

You will:
- talk about packing for a trip and getting to the airport
- tell what you do at the airport
- talk about being on an airplane
- discuss air travel in South America

You will use:
- verbs that have **g** in the **yo** form of the present tense
- the present progressive tense

Capítulo 2 ¡Una rutina diferente!

Objetivos

You will:
- identify more parts of the body
- talk about your daily routine
- talk about backpacking and camping

You will use:
- reflexive verbs
- commands with **favor de**

Capítulo 3 En tren

Objetivos

You will:
- use vocabulary related to train travel
- discuss interesting train trips in Spain, Peru, and Mexico

You will use:
- the preterite of irregular verbs
- the verb **decir**
- prepositional pronouns

Capítulo 4 En el restaurante

Objetivos

You will:
- order and pay for a meal at a restaurant
- identify more foods
- identify eating utensils and dishes
- discuss restaurants in Spain and Latin America

You will use:
- stem-changing verbs in the present and preterite
- adjectives of nationality
- the passive voice with **se**

Capítulo 5 ¿Qué se celebra?

Objetivos

You will:
- talk about several Hispanic holidays
- compare holidays that you celebrate with those in some Spanish-speaking countries

You will use:
- regular and irregular forms of the imperfect tense

Capítulo 6 Tecnomundo

Objetivos

You will:
- talk about computers, the Internet, and e-mail
- talk about a digital camera and an MP3 player
- make and receive phone calls
- discuss technology in Hispanic countries

You will use:
- the preterite and imperfect tenses

Capítulo 7 En el hotel

Objetivos

You will:
- check into a hotel or hostel
- ask for things you may need while at a hotel or hostel
- discuss hotel stays in Latin America and Spain

You will use:
- the present perfect tense
- double object pronouns

Capítulo 8 Ciudad y campo

Objetivos

You will:
- describe life in the city
- describe life in the country
- discuss the differences between the city and the country in Latin America

You will use:
- the future tense
- object pronouns with infinitives and gerunds

Capítulo 9 ¿Vas en carro?

Objetivos

You will:
- talk about cars and driving
- give directions
- discuss the Pan American Highway

You will use:
- **tú** affirmative commands
- the conditional

Capítulo 10 Cocina hispana

Objetivos

You will:
- talk about foods and food preparation
- talk about a Spanish recipe

You will use:
- the subjunctive
- formal commands
- negative informal commands

Capítulo 11 ¡Cuídate bien!

Objetivos

You will:
- identify more parts of the body
- talk about exercise
- talk about having a little accident and a trip to the emergency room
- discuss physical fitness

You will use:
- the subjunctive with impersonal expressions
- **ojalá, quizás, tal vez**
- the subjunctive of stem-changing verbs
- the comparison of like things

Literary Reader

Student Resources

Guide to Symbols

Throughout **¡Así se dice!** you will see these symbols, or icons. They will tell you how to best use the particular part of the chapter or activity they accompany. Following is a key to help you understand these symbols.

 Audio link This icon indicates material in the chapter that is recorded on compact disk.

 Recycling This icon indicates sections that review previously introduced material.

 Paired activity This icon indicates activities that you can practice orally with a partner.

 Group activity This icon indicates activities that you can practice together in groups.

 Critical thinking This icon indicates activities that require critical thinking.

InfoGap **InfoGap** This icon refers to additional paired activities at the end of the book.

 ¡Bravo! This icon indicates the end of new material in each chapter. All remaining material is recombination and review.

Literary Reader This icon lets you know that you are prepared to read the indicated literature selection.

Why Learn Spanish?

¡Viva el español!

Spanish is currently the fourth-most-spoken language in the world. Studying Spanish will help you explore other cultures, communicate with Spanish speakers, and increase your career possibilities.

It's fascinating!

Culture Hispanic culture is full of diverse expressions of music, art, and literature. From dancing the tango or salsa to admiring a modern painting by Salvador Dalí, your studies will introduce you to an array of what the culture has to offer. You'll learn about the various customs, traditions, and values in Latin America and Spain. From food and family to school and sports, you'll learn all about life in the Hispanic world.

▲ **Dancers of the tango on the streets of Argentina**

It's all around us!

Communication The United States is home to more than forty-four million Hispanics or Latinos. Whether on the radio, in your community or school, or in your own home, the Spanish language is probably part of your life in some way. Understanding Spanish allows you to sing along with Latin music on the radio or chat with Spanish speakers in your school, community, or family. No matter who you are, Spanish can enrich your life in some way.

If you plan to travel outside the United States, remember that Spanish is the official language of twenty-one countries. Experiencing another country is more fun and meaningful when you can understand restaurant menus, read newspapers, follow street signs, watch TV, and better yet converse with the locals.

◄ **Singer Shakira performs.**

A Spanish-speaking dentist

It's a lifelong skill!

Career Do you know what career you plan to pursue? Medicine, business, social work, teaching? What will you do if you have a Spanish-speaking patient, client, or student? Speak Spanish, of course! Whatever your career, you will be able to reach more people if you are able to converse in Spanish. After all, it's spoken by 13 percent of the U.S. population. You will also be open to many more career opportunities if you know Spanish. Businesses, government agencies, and educational institutions are always looking for people with the ability to speak and read more than one language.

It's an adventure!

Challenge When you study a language, you not only learn about the language and its speakers but also about yourself. Studying a language requires that you challenge yourself and more fully develop your skills. When you know about the customs and values of another culture, you are better able to reflect upon your own. Language is a means of self-discovery. Enjoy!

▼ Fans of Enrique Iglesias

Reading in a New Language

Following are skills and strategies that can help you understand what you read in a language you have just begun to learn. *Reading and Succeeding* will help you build skills and strategies that will make it easier to understand what you are reading in your exciting new language.

The strategies you use frequently depend on the purpose of your reading. You do not read a textbook or standardized testing questions the same way you read a novel or a magazine article. You read a textbook for information. You read a novel or magazine article for fun.

In the early stages of second-language learning, your vocabulary is, of course, very limited in comparison to the vast number of words you already know in English. The material presented to you to read in the early stages must accommodate this reality. Your limited knowledge of the language does not have to deter you from enjoying what you are reading. Most of what you read, however, will come from your textbook, since original novels and magazine articles are not written for people who have limited exposure to the language.

As you develop your reading ability in Spanish, you will encounter basically two types of readings.

Intensive Readings

These readings are short. They are very controlled, using only language you have already learned. You should find these readings easy and enjoyable. If you find them difficult, it means you have not sufficiently learned the material presented in the chapter of the textbook. The vast majority of these informative readings will introduce you to the fascinating cultures of the Spanish-speaking world.

A very important aspect of reading in Spanish is to give you things to "talk about" in the language. The more you read, speak, and use the language, the more proficient you will become. Whenever you finish reading one of the intensive reading selections, you should be able to talk about it; that is, you should be able to retell it in your own words.

Extensive Readings

Since it is unrealistic to assume that you will never encounter new words as you branch out and read material in Spanish, you will also be presented with extensive readings. The goal of these extensive readings is to help you develop the tools and skills you need in order to read at some future date an original novel or magazine article. They do indeed contain some words and structures that are unfamiliar to you. In this *Reading and Succeeding* section, you will learn to develop many skills that will enable you to read such material with relative ease.

Use *Reading and Succeeding* to help you:

- adjust the way you read to fit the type of material you are reading
- identify new words and build your vocabulary
- use specific reading strategies to better understand what you read
- improve your ability to speak by developing strategies that enable you to retell orally what you have read
- use critical thinking strategies to think more deeply about what you read

Identifying New Words and Building Vocabulary

What do you do when you come across a word you do not know as you read? Do you skip the word and keep reading? You might if you are reading for fun. If it hinders your ability to understand, however, you might miss something important. When you come to a word you don't know, try the following strategies to figure out what the word means.

Reading Aloud

In the early stages of learning a second language, a good strategy is to sit by yourself and read the selection aloud. This can help you understand the reading because you once again hear words that you have already practiced orally in class. Hearing them as you read them can help reinforce meaning.

Identifying Cognates

As you read you will come across many cognates. Cognates are words that look alike in both English and Spanish. Not only do they look alike but they mean the same thing. Recognizing cognates is a great reading strategy. Examples of cognates are:

cómico	nacionalidad	entra
popular	secundaria	clase
cubano	matemática	prepara
video	blusa	televisión

Identifying Roots and Base Words

The main part of a word is called its root. From a root, many new words can be formed. When you see a new word, identify its root. It can help you pronounce the word and figure out its meaning.

For example, if you know the word **importante,** there is no problem determining the meaning of **importancia.** The verb **importar** becomes a bit more problematic, but with some intelligent guessing you can get its meaning. You know it has something to do with importance so it means *it is important,* and by extension it can even carry the meaning *it matters.*

Identifying Prefixes

A prefix is a word part added to the beginning of a root or base word. Spanish as well as English has prefixes. Prefixes can change, or even reverse, the meaning of a word. For example, the prefixes **in-, im-,** and **des-** mean *not.*

estable/inestable   posible/imposible
honesto/deshonesto

Using Syntax

Like all languages, Spanish has rules for the way words are arranged in sentences. The way a sentence is organized is called its syntax. Spanish syntax, however, is a bit more flexible than English. In a simple English sentence someone or something (its subject) does something (the predicate or verb) to or with another person or thing (the object). This word order can vary in Spanish and does not always follow the subject/verb/object order.

Because Spanish and English syntax vary, you should think in Spanish and not try to translate what you are reading into English. Reading in Spanish will then have a natural flow and follow exactly the way you learned it. Trying to translate it into English confuses the matter and serves no purpose.

Example

English always states: *John speaks to me.*
Spanish can state: *John to me speaks. or*
To me speaks John.

The latter leaves the subject to the end of the sentence and emphasizes that it is John who speaks to me.

Using Context Clues

This is a very important reading strategy in a second language. You can often figure out the meaning of an unfamiliar word by looking at it in context (the words and sentences that surround it). Let's look at the example below.

Example

The glump ate it all up and flew away.

You have no idea what a *glump* is. Right? But from the rest of the sentence you can figure out that it's a bird. Why? Because it flew away and you know that birds fly. In this way you guessed at the meaning of an unknown word using context. Although you know it is a bird, you cannot determine the specific meaning such as a robin, a wren, or a sparrow. In many cases it does not matter because that degree of specificity is not necessary for comprehension.

Let's look at another example:
The glump ate it all up and phlumped.

In this case you do not know the meaning of two key words in the same sentence—*glump* and *phlumped.* This makes it impossible to guess the meaning and this is what can happen when you try to read something in a second language that is beyond your proficiency level. This makes reading a frustrating experience. For this reason all the readings in your textbook control the language to keep it within your reach. Remember, if you have studied the vocabulary in your book, this will not happen.

Understanding What You Read

Try using some of the following strategies before, during, and after reading to understand and remember what you read.

Previewing

When you preview a piece of writing, you are looking for a general idea of what to expect from it. Before you read, try the following.

- Look at the title and any illustrations that are included.
- Read the headings, subheadings, and anything in bold letters.
- Skim over the passage to see how it is organized. Is it divided into many parts? Is it a long poem or short story?
- Look at the graphics—pictures, maps, or diagrams.
- Set a purpose for your reading. Are you reading to learn something new? Are you reading to find specific information?

Using What You Know

Believe it or not, you already know quite a bit about what you are going to read. Your own knowledge and personal experience can help you create meaning in what you read. There is, however, a big difference in reading the information in your Spanish textbook. You already have some knowledge about what you are reading from a United States oriented base. What you will be reading about takes place in a Spanish-speaking environment and thus you will be adding an exciting new dimension to what you already know. Comparing and contrasting are important critical skills to put to use when reading material about a culture other than your own. This skill will be discussed later.

Visualizing

Creating pictures in your mind about what you are reading—called visualizing—will help you understand and remember what you read. With the assistance of the many accompanying photos, try to visualize the people, streets, cities, homes, etc., you are reading about.

Identifying Sequence

When you discover the logical order of events or ideas, you are identifying sequence. Look for clues and signal words that will help you find how information is organized. Some signal words are **primero, al principio, antes, después, luego, entonces, más tarde, por fin, finalmente.**

Determining the Main Idea

When you look for the main idea of a selection, you look for the most important idea. The examples, reasons, and details that further explain the main idea are called supporting details.

Reviewing

When you review in school, you go over what you learned the day before so that the information is clear in your mind. Reviewing when you read does the same thing. Take time now and then to pause and review what you have read. Think about the main ideas and organize them for yourself so you can recall them later. Filling in study aids such as graphic organizers can help you review.

Monitoring Your Comprehension

As you read, check your understanding by summarizing. Pause from time to time and state the main ideas of what you have just read. Answer the questions: **¿Quién?** *(Who?)* **¿Qué?** *(What?)* **¿Dónde?** *(Where?)* **¿Cuándo?** *(When?)* **¿Cómo?** *(How?)* **¿Por qué?** *(Why?)*. Summarizing tests your comprehension because you state key points in your own words. Remember something you read earlier: reading in Spanish empowers your ability to speak by developing strategies that enable you to retell orally what you have read.

Thinking About Your Reading

Sometimes it is important to think more deeply about what you read so you can get the most out of what the author says. These critical thinking skills will help you go beyond what the words say and understand the meaning of your reading.

Compare and Contrast

To compare and contrast shows the similarities and differences among people, things, and ideas. Your reading experience in Spanish will show you many things that are similar and many others that are different depending upon the culture groups and social mores.

As you go over these culturally oriented readings, try to visualize what you are reading. Then think about the information. Think about what you know about the topic and then determine if the information you are reading is similar, somewhat different, or very different from what you know.

Continue to think about it. In this case you may have to think about it in English. Determine if you find the similarities or the differences interesting. Would you like to experience what you are reading about? Analyzing the information in this way will most certainly help you remember what you have read.

- Signal words and phrases that indicate similarity are **similar, semejante, parecido, igual.**
- Signal words and phrases that indicate differences are **diferente, distinto, al contrario, contrariamente, sin embargo.**

Cause and Effect

Just about everything that happens in life is the cause or the effect of some other event or action. Writers use cause-and-effect structure to explore the reasons for something happening and to examine the results of previous events. This structure helps answer the question that everybody is always asking: Why? Cause-and-effect structure is about explaining things.

- Signal words and phrases are **así, porque, por consiguiente, resulta que.**

Using Reference Materials

In the early stages of second-language learning, you will not be able to use certain types of reference materials that are helpful to you in English. For example, you could not look up a word in a Spanish dictionary as you would not be able to understand many of the words used in the definition.

You can, however, make use of the glossary that appears at the end of your textbook. A glossary includes only words that are included in the textbook. Rather than give you a Spanish definition, the glossary gives you the English equivalent of the word. If you have to use the glossary very frequently, it indicates to you that you have not studied the vocabulary sufficiently in each chapter. A strategy to use before beginning a reading selection in any given chapter is to quickly skim the vocabulary in the **Vocabulario 1** and **Vocabulario 2** sections of the chapter.

Expand your view of the Spanish-speaking world.

¡Así se dice! will show you the many places where you will be able to use your Spanish.

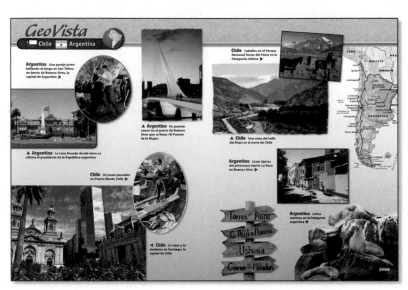

Cultural and geographic information is at your fingertips with GeoVistas, your virtual field trip to the Spanish-speaking countries.

Start your journey into language and culture.

Opening photo provides a cultural backdrop for the chapter.

Aquí y Allí introduces you to the chapter theme and invites you to make connections between your culture and the cultures of Spanish-speaking countries.

Objectives let you know what you will be able to do by the end of the chapter.

Access your eBook with QuickPass at glencoe.com.

Get acquainted with the chapter theme.

Explore each chapter's theme with vivid cultural photos and informative captions.

Introducción al tema

¿Qué se celebra?

Mira las fotos para familiarizarte con el tema de este capítulo—un tema de alegría—fiestas, festivales y celebraciones. El mundo hispano es famoso por sus fiestas. A mucha gente le gusta participar en las festividades en la plaza de su ciudad o pueblo o en su propio barrio.

▲ **México** Aquí vemos a una joven chiapaneca vestida en un traje tradicional durante la Fiesta de Enero. Durante todo el mes de enero hay festivales en Chiapas.

México Estas figuras del Día de los Muertos son de un cuadro de la artista mexicana Dolores Olmedo Patiño. ▶

▶ **México** Celebraciones navideñas en una plaza de Oaxaca

▲ **Perú** Unas danzarinas vestidas en trajes tradicionales bailan en una calle de Ollantaytambo durante el festival de Ollantay Raymi en junio.

◀ **Cuba** Unos jóvenes se divierten en La Habana durante el Carnaval. El Carnaval de La Habana es uno de los más famosos del mundo.

Colombia Todo el mundo se divierte durante el Carnaval. Las comparsas desfilan por las calles como aquí en Barranquilla. Los días de alegría y festejo terminan con el Miércoles de Cenizas cuando empieza la Cuaresma—cuarenta días de abstinencia. ▶

Ecuador El festival de la Mamá Negra tiene lugar en Latacunga en noviembre. Hay un desfile de personajes que representan las diferentes herencias étnicas del país—española, indígena, africana. ▼

España Los fuegos artificiales iluminan el cielo durante las festividades en la plaza de la Cibeles para celebrar el Año Nuevo en Madrid. ▼

España Sevillanas vestidas en los trajes tradicionales para la Feria de Sevilla en el mes de abril ▼

▲ **Ecuador** Aquí vemos a unos niños en disfraz en Cotacachi durante unas festividades para celebrar la Navidad.

136

See how the theme relates to different countries in the Spanish-speaking world.

Talk about the chapter theme with your new vocabulary.

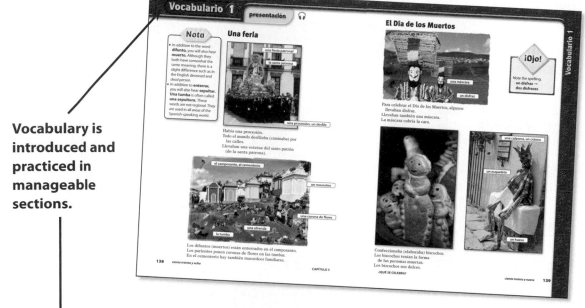

Vocabulary is introduced and practiced in manageable sections.

Recorded presentation ensures proper pronunciation.

Watch video clips to experience the diversity of the Spanish-speaking world while reinforcing the language you have learned and improving your listening and viewing skills.

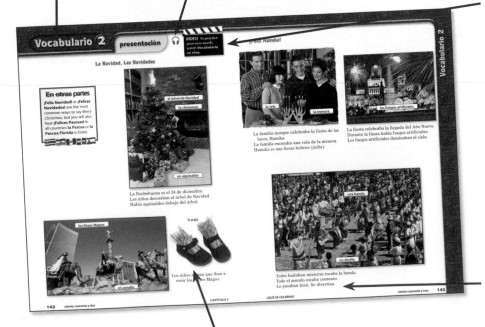

New words are used in a meaningful context.

Photos and illustrations aid comprehension and vocabulary acquisition.

Practice and master new vocabulary.

Practice and master your new vocabulary with your **Workbook and StudentWorks™ Plus.**

Use QuickPass to easily access additional vocabulary practice at glencoe.com.

Practice authentic communication with InfoGap activities.

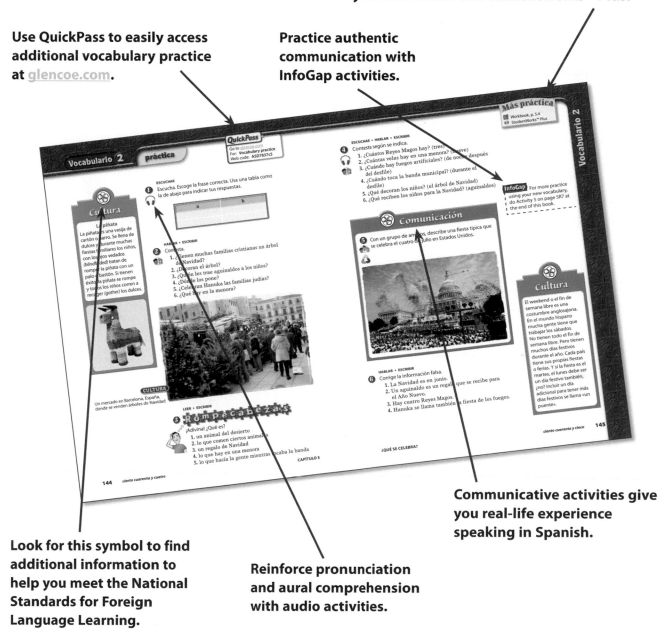

Communicative activities give you real-life experience speaking in Spanish.

Look for this symbol to find additional information to help you meet the National Standards for Foreign Language Learning.

Reinforce pronunciation and aural comprehension with audio activities.

Learn grammar within the context of the chapter theme.

Useful tips help you avoid language pitfalls.

New grammar is presented in simple terms with familiar vocabulary.

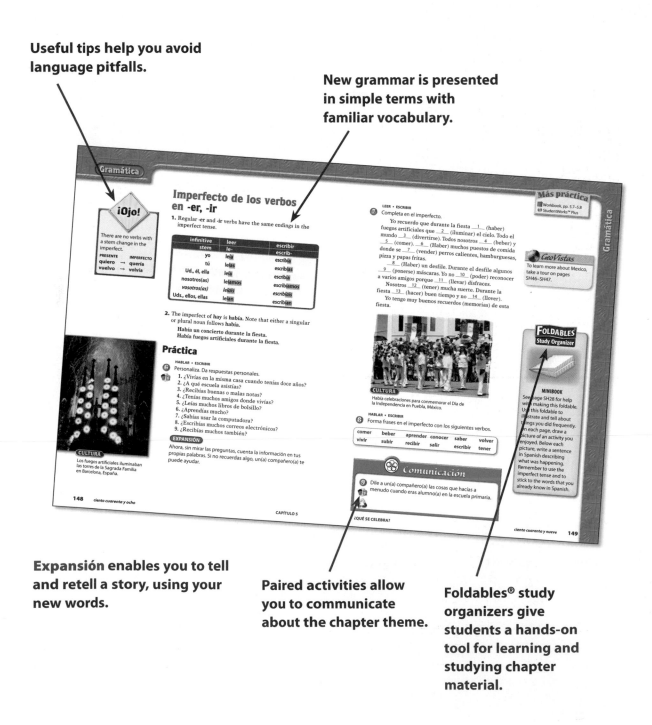

Expansión enables you to tell and retell a story, using your new words.

Paired activities allow you to communicate about the chapter theme.

Foldables® study organizers give students a hands-on tool for learning and studying chapter material.

Build on what you already know.

You will build confidence as you complete activities that progress from easy to more challenging.

Cultural photos are explained by captions that use grammar and vocabulary that you can understand.

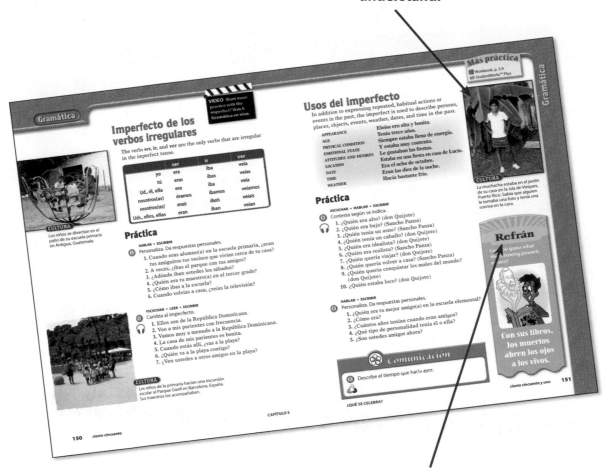

Have fun using your Spanish to figure out the meaning of Spanish proverbs.

Engage classmates in real conversation.

Use QuickPass to access the Conversation online at glencoe.com.

You will have a sense of accomplishment when you are able to comprehend the conversation.

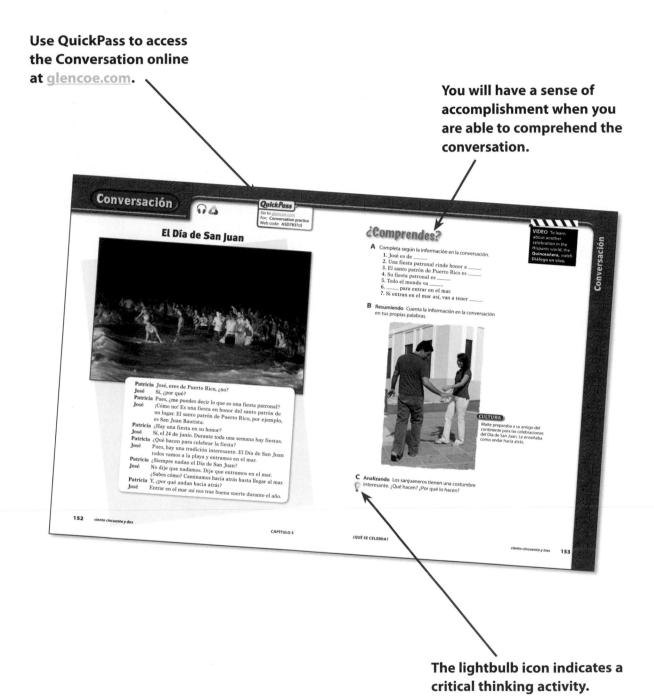

The lightbulb icon indicates a critical thinking activity.

Heighten your cultural awareness.

Step-by-step reading strategies help to develop your reading skills.

Cultural reading uses learned language to reinforce chapter theme.

Recorded reading online and on CD provides options for addressing various skills and learning styles.

Verify your comprehension throughout the selection with Reading Checks.

Un poco más reading reinforces the chapter theme and expands your understanding of the Spanish-speaking world.

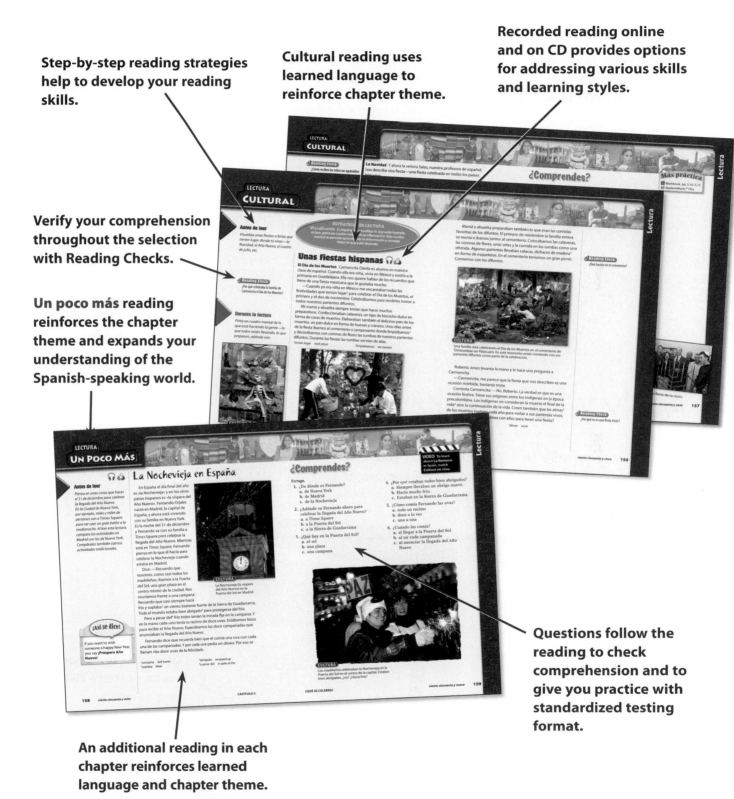

Questions follow the reading to check comprehension and to give you practice with standardized testing format.

An additional reading in each chapter reinforces learned language and chapter theme.

Show what you know!

Review what you have learned and prepare for your chapter test.

Reference notes direct you to the correct pages for review.

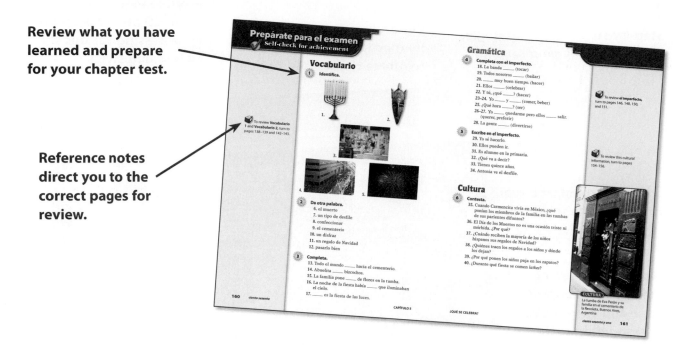

Apply what you have learned!

Use your new skills to communicate orally in meaningful, open-ended activities.

Practice what you have learned while improving your written Spanish.

Writing Strategy gives you the tools you need to develop better writing skills.

Graphic organizers make practice clear and easy.

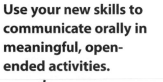
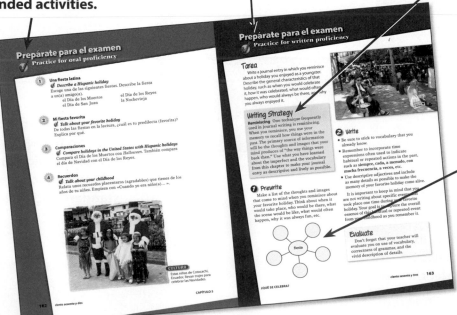

Review grammar and vocabulary at a glance.

Succinct grammar notes help you efficiently review chapter material.

Use this vocabulary list to review the vocabulary you have learned in this chapter.

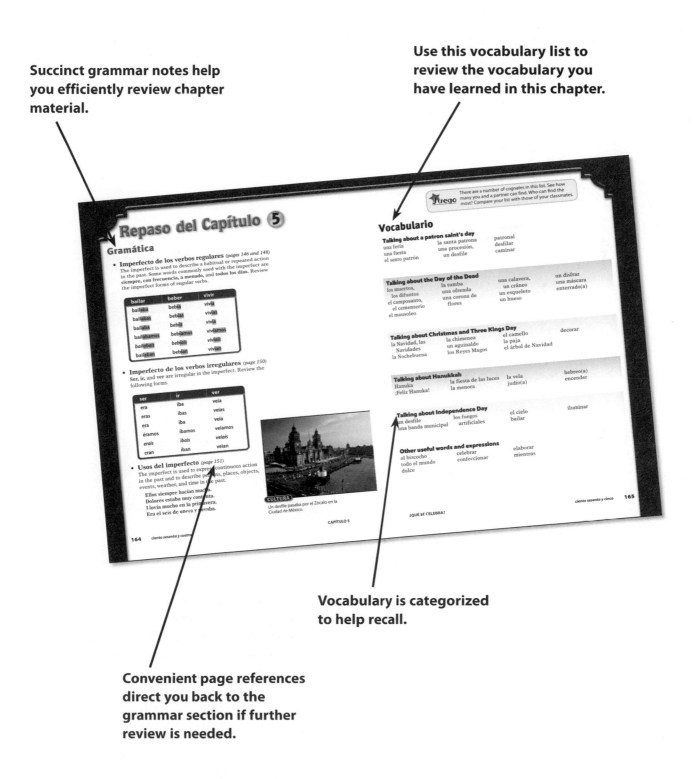

Repaso del Capítulo 5

Gramática

- **Imperfecto de los verbos regulares** *(pages 146 and 148)*
  The imperfect is used to describe a habitual or repeated action in the past. Some words commonly used with the imperfect are **siempre, con frecuencia, a menudo,** and **todos los días.** Review the imperfect forms of regular verbs.

bailar	beber	vivir
bailaba	bebía	vivía
bailabas	bebías	vivías
bailaba	bebía	vivía
bailábamos	bebíamos	vivíamos
bailabais	bebíais	vivíais
bailaban	bebían	vivían

- **Imperfecto de los verbos irregulares** *(page 150)*
  Ser, ir, and ver are irregular in the imperfect. Review the following forms.

ser	ir	ver
era	iba	veía
eras	ibas	veías
era	iba	veía
éramos	íbamos	veíamos
erais	ibais	veíais
eran	iban	veían

- **Usos del imperfecto** *(page 151)*
  The imperfect is used to express continuous action in the past and to describe persons, places, objects, events, weather, and time in the past.

  Ellos siempre hacían mucho.
  Dolores estaba muy contenta.
  Llovía mucho en la primavera.
  Era el seis de enero y nevaba.

CULTURA
Un desfile pasaba por el Zócalo en la Ciudad de México.

CAPÍTULO 5

164 ciento sesenta y cuatro

Vocabulario

Juego There are a number of cognates in this list. See how many you and a partner can find. Who can find the most? Compare your list with those of your classmates.

Talking about a patron saint's day
una feria / la santa patrona / patronal
una fiesta / una procesión, / desfilar
el santo patrón / un desfile / caminar

Talking about the Day of the Dead
los muertos, / la tumba / una calavera, / un disfraz
los difuntos / una ofrenda / un cráneo / una máscara
el camposanto, / una corona de / un esqueleto / enterrado(a)
el cementerio / flores / un hueso
el mausoleo

Talking about Christmas and Three Kings Day
la Navidad, las / la chimenea / el camello / decorar
Navidades / un aguinaldo / la paja
la Nochebuena / los Reyes Magos / el árbol de Navidad

Talking about Hanukkah
Hanuka / la fiesta de las luces / la vela / hebreo(a)
¡Feliz Hanuka! / la menora / judío(a) / encender

Talking about Independence Day
un desfile / los fuegos / el cielo / iluminar
una banda municipal / artificiales / bailar

Other useful words and expressions
el bizcocho / celebrar / elaborar
todo el mundo / confeccionar / mientras
dulce

¿QUÉ SE CELEBRA?

165 ciento sesenta y cinco

Vocabulary is categorized to help recall.

Convenient page references direct you back to the grammar section if further review is needed.

Practice what you have learned so far in Spanish.

Cumulative activities allow you to practice what you have learned so far in Spanish class.

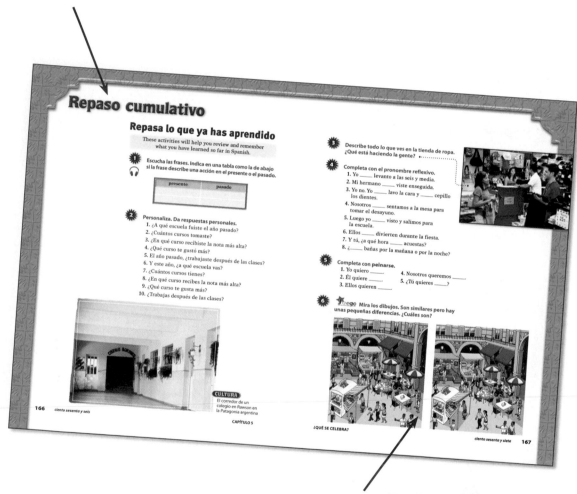

Illustrations recombine material to remind you what you have already learned in Spanish. Use the illustration as a prompt to demonstrate how much you can say or write.

Enhance your appreciation of literature and culture.

Literary Reader gives you another opportunity to apply your reading skills in Spanish.

Literary selections present another view of Hispanic culture.

Literary Reader

Contenido

The literary selections in the pages that follow will introduce you to Hispanic literature while helping you to develop reading skills and a better understanding of Hispanic culture. These selections have been carefully adapted to match your developing language skills. As you draw on your knowledge of Spanish grammar and vocabulary and apply the reading strategies you have learned, you will discover that you are able to comprehend and enjoy the selections. ¡A leer!

356 *trescientos cincuenta y seis*

Level-appropriate literature selections make reading fun.

Foldables

Dear Student,

Foldables are interactive study organizers that you can make yourself. They are a wonderful resource to help you organize and retain information. Foldables have many purposes. You can use them to remember vocabulary words or to organize more in-depth information on any given topic, such as keeping track of what you know about a particular country.

You can write general information, such as titles, vocabulary words, concepts, questions, main ideas, and dates, on the front tabs of your Foldables. You view this general information every time you look at a Foldable. This helps you focus on and remember key points without the distraction of additional text. You can write specific information—supporting ideas, thoughts, answers to questions, research information, empirical data, class notes, observations, and definitions—under the tabs. Think of different ways in which Foldables can be used. Soon you will find that you can make your own Foldables for study guides and projects. Foldables with flaps or tabs create study guides that you can use to check what you know about the general information on the front of tabs. Use Foldables without tabs for projects that require information to be presented for others to view quickly. The more you make and use graphic organizers, the faster you will become able to produce them.

To store your Foldables, turn one-gallon freezer bags into student portfolios which can be collected and stored in the classroom. You can also carry your portfolios in your notebooks if you place strips of two-inch clear tape along one side and punch three holes through the taped edge. Write your name along the top of the plastic portfolio with a permanent marker and cover the writing with two-inch clear tape to keep it from wearing off. Cut the bottom corners off the bag so it won't hold air and will stack and store easily. The following figures illustrate the basic folds that are referred to throughout this book.

Good luck!

Dinah Zike
www.dinah.com

Category Book

Los números Use this *category book* organizer as you learn dates and numbers.

Step 1 **Fold** a sheet of paper (8½" x 11") in half like a *hot dog*.

Step 2 On one side, **cut** every third line. This usually results in ten tabs. Do this with three sheets of paper to make three books.

Step 3 **Write** one Arabic number on the outside of each of the tabs. On the inside write out the respective number. As you learn more numbers, use *category books* to categorize numbers in this way.

Other Suggestions for a *Category Book* Foldable

You may wish to use *category book* foldables to help remember numbers. As you learn numbers, make two *category book* foldables. One will have the numerals on the outside and the numbers written out on the inside. The other will have the numbers written out on the outside and the numerals on the inside. This is a good way for you to practice your numbers on your own. You may also wish to make one foldable containing even numbers and one containing odd numbers.

A *category book* foldable may be used to practice conjugating Spanish verbs. On the top tab, write the infinitive form of a verb. On the following tabs, write the subject pronouns: **yo, tú, él, ella, Ud., nosotros(as), ellos, ellas, Uds.** Then open each tab and write the corresponding form of the verb.

Forward-Backward Book

Las estaciones Use this *forward-backward book* to compare and contrast two seasons of your choice.

Step 1 **Stack** three sheets of paper. On the top sheet, trace a large circle.

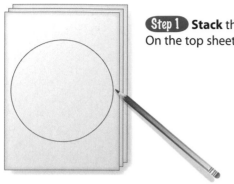

Step 2 With the papers still stacked, **cut out** the circles.

Step 3 **Staple** the paper circles together along the left-hand side to create a circular booklet.

Step 4 **Write** the name of a season on the cover. On the page that opens to the right list the months of the year in that particular season. On the following page draw a picture to illustrate the season.

front

inside

El invierno

Step 5 **Turn the book upside down** and write the name of a season on the cover. On the page that opens to the right list the months of the year in that particular season. On the following page draw a picture to illustrate the season.

back

inside

El verano

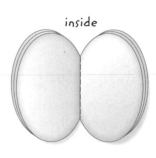

Other Suggestions for a *Forward-Backward Book* Foldable

You may wish to use a *forward-backward book* foldable to organize vocabulary pertaining to the city and the country. On the front cover write **la ciudad.** Open your book. On the right-hand page list words you have learned that pertain to the city. On the next right-hand page, draw a picture illustrating the words on your list. Close your book and flip it over. On the back cover write **el campo** and do the same.

It may be helpful to use a *forward-backward book* foldable to organize the food groups. You could use the name of a food group in Spanish (meat, vegetable, fruit, etc.) as the title. On the inside, list as many foods in this food group as you can on the right-hand page and illustrate these foods on the opposite page. Give the same information for a second food group by reversing the book.

Pocket Book

La geografía Use this *pocket book* organizer in your ongoing study of all the countries in the Spanish-speaking world.

Step 1 **Fold** a sheet of paper (8½" x 11") in half like a *hamburger*.

Step 2 **Open** the folded paper and fold one of the long sides up two inches to form a pocket. Refold the *hamburger* fold so that the newly formed pockets are on the inside.

Step 3 **Glue** the outer edges of the two-inch fold with a small amount of glue.

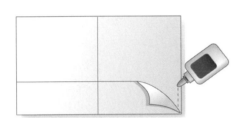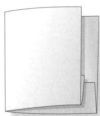

Step 4 **Make a multipaged booklet** by gluing six pockets side-by-side. Glue a cover around the multipaged *pocket book*.

Step 5 **Label** five pockets with the following geographical areas: **Europa, la América del Norte, la América del Sur, la América Central,** and **Islas del Caribe.** Use index cards inside the pockets to record information each time you learn something new about a specific country. Be sure to include the name of the country (in Spanish, of course) and its capital.

Other Suggestions for a *Pocket Book* Foldable

You may wish to use a *pocket book* foldable to organize masculine and feminine nouns or singular and plural forms. You can make an index card to put in the correct pocket each time you learn a new word.

A *pocket book* foldable may be used to organize information about several subjects. For example, to organize information about airplane travel, label pockets with topics such as *preparing for a trip, getting to the airport, at the airport,* and *on the airplane* in Spanish.

Make cards for all the words and phrases you know that go with each topic.

If you wish to organize what you are learning about important people, works of art, festivals, and other cultural information in countries that speak Spanish, a *pocket book* foldable may be helpful. You can make a card for each person, work of art, or event that you study, and you can add cards and even add categories as you continue to learn about cultures that speak Spanish.

Vocabulary Book

Sinónimos y antónimos Use this *vocabulary book* to practice your vocabulary through the use of synonyms and antonyms.

Step 1 **Fold** a sheet of notebook paper in half like a *hot dog*.

Step 2 On one side, **cut** every third line. This usually results in ten tabs. Do this with two sheets of paper to make two books.

Step 3 **Label** the tops of the *vocabulary books* with the word **Sinónimos** on one and **Antónimos** on the other. As you learn new vocabulary in each unit, try to categorize words in this manner. Remember also to think of words you have previously learned to fill in your books.

Other Suggestions for a *Vocabulary Book* Foldable

You may wish to use a *vocabulary book* foldable to help you practice your informal commands. On the front of each flap, write the infinitive form of a verb. Then open each flap and write the informal (**tú**) command of the verb.

You can use a *vocabulary book* foldable to help remember any verb conjugation in Spanish. Write the infinitive at the top. If you know several tenses of a verb, you should also write what tense or tenses are being practiced. On the outside of the foldable, write the pronouns, and on the inside, write the corresponding verb form. You can use this as a quick study and review tool for any verb. At a more advanced level, you may wish to write many verbs down the outside and entire conjugations on the inside.

You may wish to use a *vocabulary book* foldable to help organize different kinds of clothing. Come up with categories in Spanish to list on the outside, such as *school, casual, men's, women's, summer, winter,* etc. On the inside, list as many articles of clothing fitting the category as you can in Spanish.

You can use *vocabulary book* foldables to practice adjective forms. Create two *vocabulary book* foldables, one for singular forms and the other for plural forms. On the singular book, write either masculine or feminine singular adjective forms on the outside and the other forms on the inside. To make this more challenging, write a mix of masculine and feminine forms on the outside, with the corresponding form on the inside. Repeat this process on the second book for the plural forms.

Tab Book

Preguntas Use this *tab book* to practice asking and answering questions.

Step 1 **Fold** a sheet of paper (8½" x 11") like a *hot dog* but fold it so that one side is one inch longer than the other.

Step 2 On the shorter side only, **cut** five equal tabs. On the front of each tab, **write** a question word you have learned. For example, you may wish to write the following.

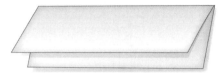

Step 3 On the bottom edge, **write** any sentence you would like.

Step 4 Under each tab, **write** the word from your sentence that answers the question on the front of the tab.

Other Suggestions for a *Tab Book* Foldable

You may also use a *tab book* foldable to practice verb conjugations. You would need to make six tabs instead of five. Write a verb and a tense on the bottom edge and write the pronouns on the front of each tab. Under each tab, write the corresponding verb form.

You may wish to use a *tab book* foldable to practice new vocabulary words. Leave extra space on the bottom edge. Choose five or six vocabulary words and write each one on a tab.

You may also use a *tab book* to practice the subjunctive. On the top of each tab, write an expression that requires the subjunctive, for example **Es imposible que... .** Then open each tab and write a sentence using that expression with the subjunctive.

Miniature Matchbook

Descripciones Use this *miniature matchbook* to help communicate in an interesting and more descriptive way.

Step 1 **Fold** a sheet of paper (8½" x 11") in half like a *hot dog*.

Step 2 **Cut** the sheet in half along the fold line.

Step 3 **Fold** the two long strips in half like *hot dogs,* leaving one side ½" shorter than the other side.

Step 4 **Fold** the ½" tab over the shorter side on each strip.

Step 5 **Cut** each of the two strips in half forming four halves. Then cut each half into thirds, making twelve *miniature matchbooks.*

Step 6 **Glue** the twelve small *matchbooks* inside a *hamburger* fold (three rows of four each).

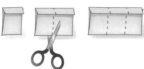

Step 7 On the front of each *matchbook,* **write** a subject you are going to tell or write about, for example, **la escuela.** Open up the tab and list any words you think you could use to make your discussion more interesting. You can add topics and words as you continue with your study of Spanish. If you glue several sections together, this foldable will "grow."

Other Suggestions for a *Miniature Matchbook* Foldable

You may use a *miniature matchbook* foldable to test each other on your knowledge of the vocabulary. Work in pairs with each partner making a blank *miniature matchbook* foldable. Each partner writes a topic related to the subjects you have just studied on the front of each *matchbook.* You may use categories of vocabulary, verbs you have recently learned to conjugate, or the subject of a reading. Your partner then writes as much as he or she can about that topic under the flap. This can alert you if you need to go back and review a topic.

A *miniature matchbook* foldable may help you organize and remember information you have read. After doing a cultural or literary reading, write down a concept presented in the reading on the front of each *matchbook.* Open up each tab and write down supporting details that support the idea.

Single Picture Frame

Dibujar y escribir Use this *single picture frame* to help you illustrate the stories you write.

Step 1 **Fold** a sheet of paper (8½" x 11") in half like a *hamburger*.

Step 2 **Open** the *hamburger* and gently roll one side of the *hamburger* toward the valley. Try not to crease the roll.

Step 3 **Cut** a rectangle out of the middle of the rolled side of paper, leaving a ½" border and forming a frame.

Step 4 **Fold** another sheet of paper (8½" x 11") in half like a *hamburger*.

Step 5 **Apply** glue to the picture frame and place it inside the *hamburger* fold.

Variation:
- Place a picture behind the frame and glue the edges of the frame to the other side of the *hamburger* fold. This locks the picture in place.
- Cut out only three sides of the rolled rectangle. This forms a window with a cover that opens and closes.

Other Suggestions for a *Single Picture Frame* Foldable

You may wish to write about a shopping trip using a *single picture frame* foldable. Before you begin, organize what you will say by drawing your path through the shops at the market, through the supermarket, or through the mall. You can then write about the shopping trip using your drawings as a guide.

Work in small groups. Each student should create a *single picture frame* foldable with a picture glued into it. You may either cut out a magazine picture or draw your own, although it should be fairly complex. Then give your foldable to another member of the group who will write sentences about what is in the picture and what people in the picture are doing. That student will pass it on to a third student who will write sentences about what is not in the picture and what people in the picture are not doing. The foldables can be passed to additional students to see if they can add more sentences.

Minibook

Mi autobiografía Use this *minibook* organizer to write and illustrate your autobiography. Before you begin to write, think about the many things concerning yourself that you have the ability to write about in Spanish. On the left pages, draw the events of your life in chronological order. On the right, write about your drawings.

Step 1 **Fold** a sheet of paper (8½" x 11") in half like a *hot dog*.

Step 2 **Fold** it in half again like a *hamburger*.

Step 3 Then **fold** in half again, forming eight sections.

Step 4 **Open** the fold and **cut** the eight sections apart.

Step 5 **Place** all eight sections in a stack and fold in half like a *hamburger*.

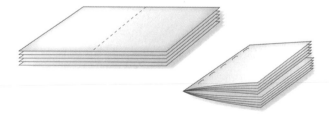

Step 6 **Staple** along the center fold line. **Glue** the front and back sheets into a construction paper cover.

Other Suggestions for a *Minibook* Foldable

Work in pairs to practice new verbs and verb forms using a *minibook* foldable. Illustrate different verbs on the left pages. If it is not clear what pronoun is required, you should write the pronoun under the drawing, for instance to differentiate between *we* and *they*. Then trade *minibooks* and write sentences to go with each picture on the right pages, using the new verb and the pronoun illustrated or indicated.

A *minibook* foldable can be used to help practice the imperfect tense. On each page, draw a picture of an activity that you enjoyed doing frequently. Below each picture, write a sentence describing what was happening. Remember to use the imperfect and to stick to the words you already know in Spanish.

Paper File Folder

Las emociones Use this *paper file folder* organizer to keep track of happenings or events that cause you to feel a certain way.

Step 1 **Fold** four sheets of paper (8½" x 11") in half like a *hamburger*. Leave one side one inch longer than the other side.

Step 2 On each sheet, **fold** the one-inch tab over the short side, forming an envelope-like fold.

Step 3 **Place** the four sheets side-by-side, then move each fold so that the tabs are exposed.

Step 4 Moving left to right, **cut** staggered tabs in each fold, 2⅛" wide. Fold the tabs upward.

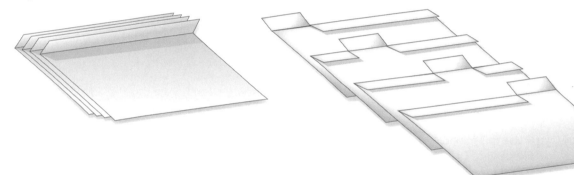

Step 5 **Glue** the ends of the folders together. On each tab, write an emotion you sometimes feel. Pay attention to when it is that you feel happy, sad, nervous, etc. Describe the situation in Spanish and file it in the correct pocket.

Other Suggestions for a *Paper File Folder* Foldable

You may use a *paper file folder* organizer to keep track of verbs and verb forms. You should make a folder for each type of regular verb and for each type of irregular verb. Write the conjugations for some important verbs in each category and file them in the *paper file folder* organizer. Add new tenses to the existing cards and new verbs as you learn them.

A *paper file folder* organizer can be useful for keeping notes on the cultural information that you will learn. You may wish to make categories for different types of cultural information and add index cards to them as you learn new facts and concepts about the target cultures.

Envelope Fold

Un viaje especial Use this *envelope fold* to make a hidden picture or to write secret clues about a city in the Spanish-speaking world you would like to visit.

Step 1 Fold a sheet of paper into a *taco* to form a square. Cut off the leftover piece.

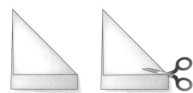

Step 2 Open the folded *taco* and refold it the opposite way, forming another *taco* and an X-fold pattern.

Step 3 Open the *taco fold* and fold the corners toward the center point of the X, forming a small square.

Step 4 Trace this square onto another sheet of paper. Cut and glue it to the inside of the envelope. Pictures can be drawn under the tabs.

Step 5 Use this foldable to **draw** a picture of the city you would like to visit. Or if you prefer, **write** clues about the city and have your classmates raise one tab at a time until they can guess what city the picture represents. Number the tabs in the order in which they are to be opened.

Other Suggestions for an *Envelope Fold* Foldable

An *envelope fold* can be useful for practicing vocabulary related to airports, trains, technology, or driving. Draw a scene that depicts many of the vocabulary words. Then write on each of the four flaps the new words that are represented under that flap. You could also give the picture to a partner and have the partner fill in the words.

You may want to use an *envelope fold* to review a selection you have read. Depict a scene from the selection on the paper covered by the tabs. Number the tabs in the order they are to be opened and have a partner open the tabs one at a time to guess what scene is illustrated. The partner should then write a description of the scenes.

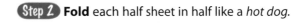

Large Sentence Strips

El presente y el pasado Use these *large sentence strips* to help you compare and contrast activities in the past and in the present.

Step 1 Take two sheets of paper (8½" x 11") and **fold** into *hamburgers*. Cut along the fold lines, making four half sheets. (Use as many half sheets as necessary for additional pages to your book.)

Step 2 **Fold** each half sheet in half like a *hot dog*.

Step 3 Place the folds side-by-side and **staple** them together on the left side.

Step 4 About one inch from the stapled edge, **cut** the front page of each folded section up to the top. These cuts form flaps that can be raised and lowered.

Step 5 To make a half-cover, use a sheet of construction paper one inch longer than the book. **Glue** the back of the last sheet to the construction paper strip, leaving one inch on the left side to fold over and cover the original staples. Staple this half-cover in place.

Step 6 With a friend, **write** sentences on the front of the flap, either in the present tense or in the past tense. Then switch your books of sentence strips and write the opposite tense inside under the flaps.

Other Suggestions for a *Large Sentence Strips* Foldable

You may work in pairs to use *large sentence strips* to practice using direct and/or indirect object pronouns. On the front of each flap, write full sentences that have direct or indirect objects or both. Then trade sentence strips. You and your partner will each write sentences under the flaps replacing the direct or indirect objects with object pronouns.

Large sentence strips can help you contrast summer and winter activities. On the front of each flap, write sentences about activities that you do in either summer or winter. Under each flap, you should write that in the other season you do not do that activity, and you should tell what you do instead. This may be done as an individual or a partner activity.

You may use *large sentence strips* to practice using verbs that can be used reflexively and nonreflexively. Write a sentence using a reflexive verb on the outside of each flap. Under the flap, write a sentence using the same verb nonreflexively.

Project Board With Tabs

Diversiones favoritas Use this *project board with tabs* to display a visual about your favorite movie or event. Be sure to make it as attractive as possible to help convince others to see it.

Step 1 **Draw** a large illustration, a series of small illustrations, or write on the front of a sheet of paper.

Step 2 **Pinch** and slightly fold the sheet of paper at the point where a tab is desired on the illustrated piece of paper. Cut into the paper on the fold. Cut straight in, then cut up to form an L. When the paper is unfolded, it will form a tab with the illustration on the front.

Step 3 After all tabs have been cut, **glue** this front sheet onto a second sheet of paper. Place glue around all four edges and in the middle, away from tabs.

Step 4 **Write** or draw under the tabs. If the project is made as a bulletin board using butcher paper, tape or glue smaller sheets of paper under the tabs.

Think of favorite scenes from a movie or cultural event that you enjoyed and draw them on the front of the tabs. Underneath the tabs write a description of the scene or tell why you liked it. It might be fun to not put a title on the project board and just hang it up and let classmates guess the name of the movie or event you are describing.

Other Suggestions for a *Project Board With Tabs* Foldable

You may wish to use a *project board with tabs* to practice your formal commands. Think of the food words you know in Spanish and use them to create a recipe of your own. Draw a small picture of each ingredient in the order you will use it in your recipe. Next, lift each tab and write instructions about how to prepare each ingredient for your recipe using formal commands. For a more complex recipe, combine two or more *project boards with tabs.*

You may also use a *project board with tabs* to illustrate a party, museum, sport, or concert. Draw one aspect of it on the outside of the tab and write a description of your drawing under the tab.

You may work in pairs to practice the comparative and superlative. Each of you will make a *project board with tabs.* On the outside of each tab, draw a different comparison or superlative. Then trade with your partner and under each tab write a sentence describing the other's illustrations.

You may also wish to use a *project board with tabs* to practice the use of object pronouns. Draw a series of scenes involving two or more people on the outside of the tabs. Write sentences using object pronouns describing the people's conversations.

Sentence Strip Holder

Para practicar más Use this *sentence strip holder* to practice your vocabulary, your verbs, or anything else you might feel you need extra help with.

Step 1 **Fold** a sheet of paper (8½" x 11") in half like a *hamburger*.

Step 2 **Open** the *hamburger* and fold the two outer edges toward the valley. This forms a shutter fold.

Step 3 **Fold** one of the inside edges of the shutter back to the outside fold. This fold forms a floppy L.

Step 4 **Glue** the floppy L tab down to the base so that it forms a strong straight L tab.

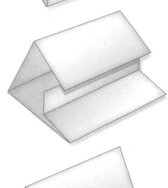

Step 5 **Glue** the other shutter side to the front of this L tab. This forms a tent that is the backboard for the flashcards or student work to be displayed.

Step 6 **Fold** the edge of the L up ¼" to ½" to form a lip that will keep the sentence strips from slipping off the holder.

Vocabulary and verbs can be stored inside the "tent" formed by this fold.

Other Suggestions for a *Sentence Strip Holder* Foldable

You may wish to practice new or irregular verbs using a *sentence strip holder*. Work in pairs. Make flash cards showing the infinitives of the verbs to practice in Spanish. You should each take half of the cards and take turns setting one verb on the *sentence strip holder*. One partner will then say as many sentences as possible using different forms of that verb, and the other will write down the subject and conjugated verb form (or just the verb form) for each sentence. Partners should check to make sure each verb form is spelled correctly. You can repeat this activity for each verb.

You may practice food vocabulary working in small groups and using a *sentence strip holder*. Groups may make flash cards containing the names of local restaurants that everyone will be familiar with, making sure to include different types of restaurants. Put the cards up on the *sentence strip holder* one at a time. Students will spend several minutes writing about what they like to eat at that restaurant. After writing about each restaurant on the list, share your favorite foods with the group.

El alfabeto español

a *a*vión

b *b*ebé

c *c*esta

d *d*edo

e *e*lefante

f *f*oto

g *g*emelas

h *h*amaca

i *i*glesia

j *j*abón

k *k*ilo

l *l*ago

m *m*ono

n *n*ariz

ñ *ñ*ame

o *o*so

p *p*elo

q *q*ueso

r *r*ana

s *s*ala

t *t*é

u *u*va

v *v*aca

w *W*ashington, D.C.

x e*x*amen

y *y*eso

z *z*apato

---

ch chicle

ll lluvia

rr guitarra

Ch, ll, and **rr** are not letters of the Spanish alphabet. However, it is important for you to learn the sounds they represent.

▼ México

Spanish is the language of almost 400 million people around the world. Spanish had its origin in Spain. It is sometimes fondly called the "language of Cervantes," the author of the famous novel and character, *Don Quijote*. The Spanish **conquistadores** and **exploradores** brought their language to the Americas in the fifteenth and sixteenth centuries. Spanish is the official language of almost all the countries of Central and South America. It is the official language of Mexico and several of the larger islands in the Caribbean. Spanish is also the heritage language of more than forty-four million people in the United States.

Perú ▶

▲ Puerto Rico

▲ España

OCÉANO ÁRTICO

GROE

Mar de Beaufort

Bahía de Baffin

Mar de Bering

Bahía de Hudson

Golfo de Alaska

CANADÁ

Mar del Labrador

AMÉRICA DEL NORTE

ESTADOS UNIDOS

OCÉANO ATLÁNTICO

MÉXICO

Golfo de México

C

CA VE

OCÉANO PACÍFICO

MAR CARIBE

VENEZUELA
GUYANA
SURINAM
GUAYANA FRANCESA

GA C

SIEF

COS

COLOMBIA

ECUADOR

AMÉRICA DEL SUR

PERÚ

BRASIL

SAMOA

POLINESIA FRANCESA

BOLIVIA

PARAGUAY

TONGA

URUGUAY

CHILE ARGENTINA

GOLFO DE MÉXICO

BAHAMAS

TURCAS Y CAICOS (R.U.)

OCÉANO ATLÁNTICO

CUBA

PUERTO RICO (EE.UU.)
ISLAS VÍRGENES (EE.UU. y R.U.)

MÉXICO

HAITÍ REPÚBLICA DOMINICANA

ANTIGUA Y BARBUDA

BELICE

JAMAICA

SAN CRISTÓBAL-NEVIS

GUADALUPE (FR.)

GUATEMALA

DOMINICA
MARTINICA (FR.)

HONDURAS

MAR CARIBE

SANTA LUCÍA

EL SALVADOR

SAN VICENTE Y GRENADINES

BARBADOS

NICARAGUA

ARUBA

GRANADA

TRINIDAD Y TOBAGO

COSTA RICA

PANAMÁ

VENEZUELA

GUYANA

OCÉANO PACÍFICO

COLOMBIA

SURINAM

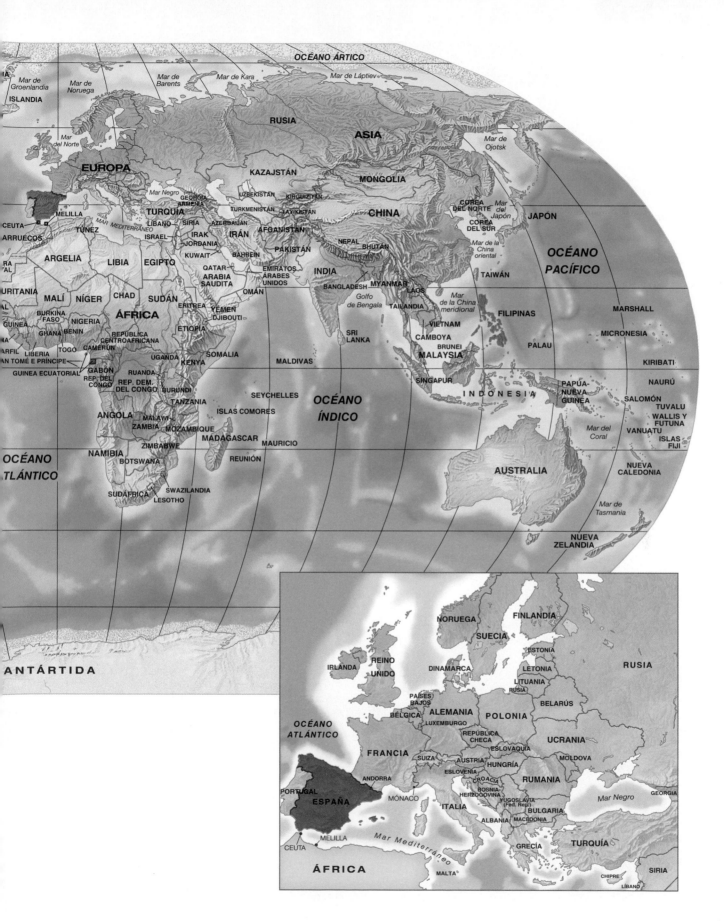

OCÉANO ÁRTICO

Mar de Groenlandia
ISLANDIA
Mar de Noruega
Mar de Barents
Mar de Kara
Mar de Láptiev

RUSIA

ASIA

Mar de Ojotsk

EUROPA

Mar del Norte

KAZAJSTÁN

MONGOLIA

Mar Negro
GEORGIA
ARMENIA
UZBEKISTÁN
KIRGUIZITÁN
TURKMENISTÁN
TAXIKISTÁN

COREA DEL NORTE
Mar del Japón
JAPÓN

TURQUIA
LÍBANO
SIRIA
AZERBAIJÁN
AFGANISTÁN
COREA DEL SUR

CEUTA
MELILLA
ISRAEL
IRAK
JORDANIA
IRÁN
NEPAL
BHUTÁN
Mar de la China oriental

ARRUÉCOS
TÚNEZ
KUWAIT
PAKISTÁN
CHINA

OCÉANO PACÍFICO

ARGELIA
LIBIA
EGIPTO
BAHREIN
QATAR
EMIRATOS ÁRABES UNIDOS
INDIA
TAIWÁN

ARABIA SAUDITA
OMÁN
BANGLADESH
MYANMAR
LAOS
Mar de la China meridional

URITANIA
MALÍ
NÍGER
CHAD
SUDÁN
ERITREA
YEMEN
DJIBOUTI
Golfo de Bengala
TAILANDIA
FILIPINAS
MARSHALL

ÁFRICA
ETIOPÍA
VIETNAM
MICRONESIA

BURKINA FASO
NIGERIA
SRI LANKA
CAMBOYA
PALAU

GHANA
BENIN
REPÚBLICA CENTROAFRICANA
BRUNEI
MALASYA
KIRIBATI

ARFIL
LIBERIA
TOGO
CAMERÚN
UGANDA
SOMALIA
MALDIVAS
NAURÚ

AN TOMÉ E PRÍNCIPE
GABÓN
KENYA
SINGAPUR
PAPÚA-NUEVA GUINEA
SALOMÓN
TUVALU

GUINEA ECUATORIAL
REP. DEL CONGO
RUANDA
REP. DEM. DEL CONGO
BURUNDI
SEYCHELLES
INDONESIA
WALLIS Y FUTUNA

ANGOLA
TANZANIA
ISLAS COMORES
OCÉANO ÍNDICO
Mar del Coral
VANUATU
ISLAS FIJI

MALAWI
ZAMBIA
MOZAMBIQUE
MADAGASCAR
MAURICIO

NAMIBIA
ZIMBABWE
REUNIÓN
NUEVA CALEDONIA

OCÉANO ATLÁNTICO
BOTSWANA
AUSTRALIA

SUDÁFRICA
SWAZILANDIA
LESOTHO
Mar de Tasmania

ANTÁRTIDA
NUEVA ZELANDIA

NORUEGA
FINLANDIA
SUECIA

IRLANDA
REINO UNIDO
DINAMARCA
ESTONIA
LETONIA
LITUANIA
RUSIA

PAÍSES BAJOS
RUSIA

OCÉANO ATLÁNTICO
BÉLGICA
ALEMANIA
POLONIA
BELARÚS

LUXEMBURGO
REPÚBLICA CHECA
UCRANIA

FRANCIA
SUIZA
ESLOVAQUIA
MOLDOVA

AUSTRIA
HUNGRÍA
ESLOVENIA
CROACIA
RUMANIA

ANDORRA
BOSNIA-HERZOGOVINA
YUGOSLAVIA (Fed. Rep.)
GEORGIA

PORTUGAL
MÓNACO
ITALIA
BULGARIA
Mar Negro

ESPAÑA
ALBANIA
MACEDONIA

MELILLA
CEUTA
Mar Mediterráneo
GRECIA
TURQUÍA

ÁFRICA
MALTA
CHIPRE
SIRIA
LÍBANO

EL MUNDO HISPANOHABLANTE

OCÉANO ATLÁNTICO

FRANCIA

MAR CANTÁBRICO

Golfo
de Vizcaya

La Coruña

Santander

San
Sebastián

ANDORRA

Oviedo

Asturias

Cantabria

Bilbao

Roncesvalles

Santiago de
Compostela

*País
Vasco*

Pamplona

LOS PIRINEOS

Galicia

CORDILLERA CANTÁBRICA

Navarra

León

Burgos

Rioja

Río Ebro

Cataluña

Castilla y León

Zaragoza

Barcelona

Valladolid

Río Duero

Aragón

Menorca

Salamanca

Segovia

Islas baleares

Ávila

SIERRA DE GUADARRAMA

Río Tajo

Palma

Madrid

Madrid

*Comunidad
Valenciana*

Mallorca

PORTUGAL

ESPAÑA

Valencia

Ibiza

Formentera

Castilla-la Mancha

Lisboa

Río Guadiana

Extremadura

Alicante

MAR
MEDITERRÁNEO

Murcia

Murcia

Río Guadalquivir

Córdoba

Cartagena

Sevilla

Granada

Andalucía

SIERRA NEVADA

Jerez de la
Frontera

Málaga

COSTA DEL SOL

Cádiz

Marbella

Estepona

Gibraltar (R.U.)

Estrecho de Gibraltar

Ceuta (Esp.)

Tánger

OCÉANO
ATLÁNTICO

Melilla (Esp.)

ARGELIA

Islas Canarias

La Palma

Santa Cruz
de Tenerife

Lanzarote

Gomera

Fuerteventura

Las Palmas

MARRUECOS

Tenerife

Hierro

*Gran
Canaria*

ÁFRICA

MARRUECOS

OCÉANO ATLÁNTICO

SAHARA
OCCIDENTAL

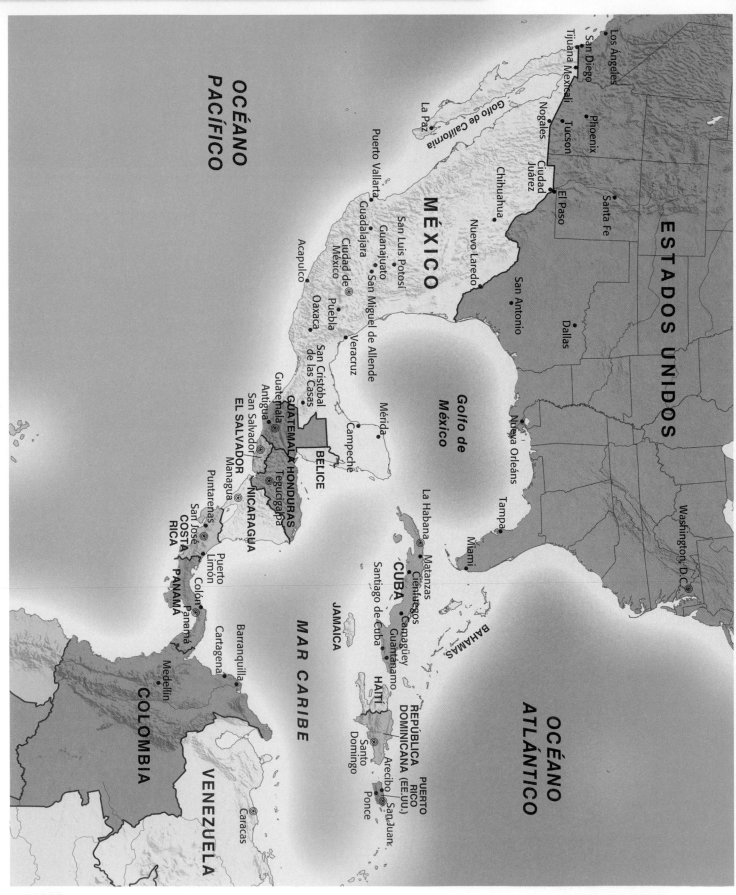

OCÉANO PACÍFICO

OCÉANO ATLÁNTICO

ESTADOS UNIDOS

MÉXICO

Golfo de California

Golfo de México

MAR CARIBE

COLOMBIA

VENEZUELA

Los Angeles
Tijuana
San Diego
Mexicali
Nogales
Tucson
Phoenix
Santa Fe
La Paz
Ciudad Juárez
El Paso
Chihuahua
Nuevo Laredo
San Antonio
Dallas
Puerto Vallarta
Guadalajara
Guanajuato
San Luis Potosí
San Miguel de Allende
Ciudad de México
Acapulco
Oaxaca
Puebla
Veracruz
San Cristóbal de las Casas
Mérida
Campeche
Nueva Orleáns
Tampa
Miami
Washington, D.C.
Guatemala
Antigua
San Salvador
EL SALVADOR
Managua
Puntarenas
San José
COSTA RICA
Puerto Limón
Colón
Panamá
PANAMÁ
GUATEMALA
HONDURAS
Tegucigalpa
NICARAGUA
BELICE
La Habana
Matanzas
Cienfuegos
CUBA
Santiago de Cuba
Camagüey
Guantánamo
JAMAICA
BAHAMAS
HAITÍ
REPÚBLICA DOMINICANA
Santo Domingo
PUERTO RICO (EE.UU.)
Arecibo
San Juan
Ponce
Barranquilla
Cartagena
Medellín
Caracas

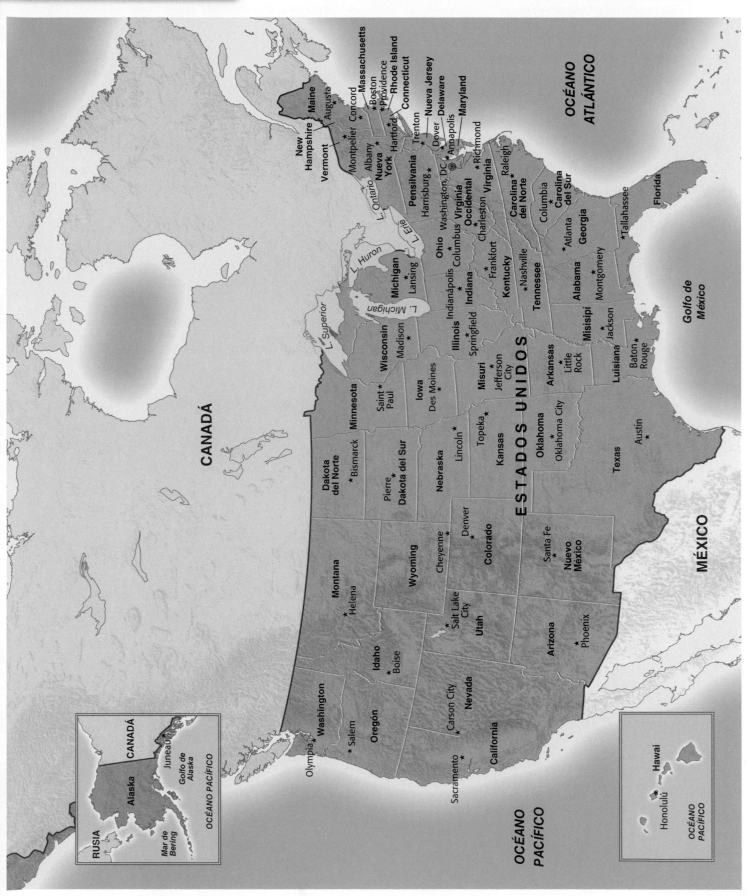

OCÉANO ATLÁNTICO

OCÉANO PACÍFICO

CANADÁ

MÉXICO

Golfo de México

RUSIA

CANADÁ

Alaska

Juneau ★

Golfo de Alaska

Mar de Bering

OCÉANO PACÍFICO

Hawai

Honolulú ★

OCÉANO PACÍFICO

Maine
Augusta ★
New Hampshire
Concord ★
Massachusetts
Boston ★
Providence ★
Rhode Island
Connecticut
Hartford ★
Nueva Jersey
Delaware
Trenton ★
Dover ★
Maryland
Annapolis ★
Richmond ★
Vermont
Montpelier ★
Albany ★
Nueva York
Pensilvania
Harrisburg ★
Washington, DC ◉
Virginia Occidental
Charleston ★
Virginia
Raleigh ★
Carolina del Norte
Columbia ★
Carolina del Sur
Florida
Tallahassee ★

L. Ontario
L. Erie
L. Huron
L. Superior
L. Michigan

Ohio
Columbus ★
Indianápolis ★
Indiana
Frankfort ★
Kentucky
Nashville ★
Tennessee
Atlanta ★
Georgia
Alabama
Montgomery ★
Misisipi
Jackson ★
Luisiana
Baton Rouge ★

Michigan
Lansing ★
Illinois
Springfield ★
Wisconsin
Madison ★
Iowa
Des Moines ★
Misuri
Jefferson City ★
Arkansas
Little Rock ★

Minnesota
Saint Paul ★
Dakota del Norte
Bismarck ★
Dakota del Sur
Pierre ★
Nebraska
Lincoln ★
Kansas
Topeka ★
Oklahoma
Oklahoma City ★
Texas
Austin ★

ESTADOS UNIDOS

Montana
Helena ★
Wyoming
Cheyenne ★
Colorado
Denver ★
Santa Fe ★
Nuevo México

Idaho
Boise ★
Utah
Salt Lake City ★
Arizona
Phoenix ★

Washington
Olympia ★
Oregón
Salem ★
Nevada
Carson City ★
California
Sacramento ★

Golfo de México

GeoVistas

El lago Titicaca en la frontera entre Perú y Bolivia

Explorando el mundo hispanohablante

GeoVista

Palacio de Telecomunicaciones en la plaza de la Cibeles en Madrid, la capital de España ▶

▲ Mezquita de Córdoba

La costa del Atlántico en la Coruña en Galicia

Un pueblo típico en las montañas de Andalucía en el sur de España ▼

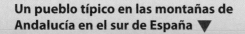

◀ Una muchacha en un traje típico de Ibiza, una isla en el mar Mediterráneo

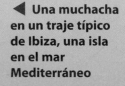

▲ Molinos de viento en La Mancha, una región en el centro de España

Una escena de la famosa novela *El Quijote* de Cervantes ▼

La del alba sería cuando Don Quijote salió de l'venta, tan contento, tan gallardo, tan alboro zado por verse ya ar-mado caballero que el gozo le reventaba por las cinchas del caballo.

(Don Quijote de la Mancha, cap. IV)

▲ Naranjas de Valencia

◄ Dos niños de Galicia en el norte de España

Un lince ibérico ▼

Golfo de Vizcaya

FRANCIA

Mar Cantábrico

La Coruña

San Sebastián
Bilbao
Pamplona

LOS PIRINEOS

Santiago de Compostela

Río Ebro

Río Duero

Zaragoza

Barcelona

Salamanca   Segovia

SIERRA DE GUADARRAMA

★ Madrid

Río Tajo

Islas Baleares

PORTUGAL

ESPAÑA

Valencia

Mérida

Mar Mediterráneo

Río Guadiana

Córdoba

SIERRA NEVADA

Río Guadalquivir

Sevilla

Granada

Cádiz

Marbella

Estepona

Estrecho de Gibraltar

Ceuta

Melilla

Islas Canarias

MARRUECOS

GeoVista

▲ El lago de Chapala al sur de Guadalajara

Durante el invierno, miles y miles de mariposas monarca emigran del Norte a los estados de México y Michoacán. ▶

El balneario de Cancún en la península de Yucatán en la costa del Caribe ▶

Un café al aire libre en Puebla ▶

Una máscara típica para el Día de los Muertos ▼

▲ Edificios modernos en la Ciudad de México

ESTADOS UNIDOS

Tijuana
Mexicali
Ciudad Juárez

DESIERTO DE SONORA

Golfo de California

DESIERTO DE CHIHUAHUA

Chihuahua

Río Grande
Río Bravo

SIERRA MADRE OCCIDENTAL

SIERRA MADRE ORIENTAL

Nuevo Laredo

Golfo de México

La Paz

Monterrey
Matamoros

MÉXICO

San Luis Potosí

Río Grande de Santiago

Guanajuato
San Miguel de Allende

Cancún

Puerto Vallarta
Río Lerma

Campeche

Guadalajara
Lago Chapala

México, D.F. ⭐
Puebla

Veracruz

OCÉANO PACÍFICO

Volcán Pico de Orizaba

Oaxaca

Mar Caribe

BELICE

SIERRA MADRE DEL SUR

Acapulco

GUATEMALA

▲ Un puesto de frutas en Cabo San Lucas, Baja California

◀ Tejidos bonitos del estado de Guerrero

El monumento de la Independencia en el famoso Paseo de la Reforma en la Ciudad de México, la capital ▶

Ruinas famosas de varias civilizaciones indígenas de México en Monte Albán en el estado de Oaxaca en el sur de México ▶

GeoVista

▲ **Honduras** Ruinas famosas de los mayas en Copán, Honduras

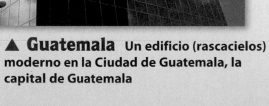

Guatemala La ciudad colonial de Antigua, Guatemala ▶

▲ **Guatemala** Un edificio (rascacielos) moderno en la Ciudad de Guatemala, la capital de Guatemala

Honduras Una iguana en la isla de Roatán ▼

▲ **Guatemala** El lago Atitlán y el volcán San Pedro en Guatemala

MÉXICO

Mar Caribe

BELICE

Tikal
Flores

Islas del Cisne

Islas de la Bahía

Golfo de Honduras

Guatemala Un quetzal—el pájaro nacional de Guatemala ▶

SIERRA DE LOS CUCHUMATANES
GUATEMALA
Cobán
Río Dulce
Puerto Barrios
Puerto Cortés
San Pedro Sula
La Ceiba
SIERRA DE AGALTA
Río Patuca

Huehuetenango
Lago de Izabal
El Progreso
SIERRAS DE MERENDÓN
Río Ulúa
Río Motagua
HONDURAS
Puerto Lempira

Volcán Tajumulco
SIERRA MADRE
Lago de Yojoa
CORDILLERA DE OPALACA
Río Coco

Quetzaltenango
Lago Atitlán
Guatemala
Copán
Juticalpa

Totonicapaque
Mazatenango
Cerro Las Minas
Danlí

Escuintla
Tegucigalpa ★

Puerto Quetzal
EL SALVADOR
Choluteca

NICARAGUA

Golfo de Fonseca

Guatemala El mercado en el pueblo de San Francisco El Alto ▼

▲ **Honduras** Vendedores de vegetales en una plaza de Tegucigalpa, la capital de Honduras

Guatemala Muchachas jóvenes en un traje maya típico ▼

Nicaragua Una vista de Managua, la capital de Nicaragua ▶

▲ **Nicaragua** La ciudad colonial de Granada

▲ **Niacaragua** Un teatro moderno en Managua, la capital de Nicaragua

El Salvador El mono araña, que sigue habitando unas regiones de El Salvador ▼

El Salvador El volcán Chaparrastique ▼

▲ **Nicaragua** Una bahía en San Juan del Sur en la costa del Pacífico

▲ **El Salvador**
La iglesia de Santa Lucía en el pueblo de Suchitoto

Nicaragua Un grupo de amigos en el parque Darío en Matagalpa ▶

Nicaragua Bueyes en un camino rural del Viejo León ▼

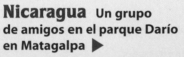

GUATEMALA

HONDURAS

CORDILLERA DE TILARAN

Lago Güija
Cerro El Pital
Santa Ana
Volcán Santa Ana
Embalse Cerrón Grande
San Salvador
Acajulta
La Libertad
Sensuntepeque
El Mozote
Lago Ilopango
Volcán de San Miguel
San Miguel
Puerto El Triunfo
Río Lempa
EL SALVADOR
Golfo de Fonseca
Río Grande de San Miguel

Río Coco
Puerto Cabezas
Pico Mogotón
CORDILLERA ISABELLA
Estelí
Matagalpa
Río Grande de Matagalpa

Mar Caribe

Chinandega
León
Corinto
Lago Managua
NICARAGUA
Río Escondido
Islas del Maíz
Bluefields

Managua
Granada
Lago Nicaragua
Rivas
Isla de Ometepe
San Carlos
Río San Juan

OCÉANO PACÍFICO

COSTA RICA

SH51

GeoVista

Costa Rica ⊛ Panamá

◄ **Costa Rica** Turistas de ecoturismo en el centro Inbioparque en San José, la capital de Costa Rica

▼ **Costa Rica**
Un tucán costarricense

▲ **Panamá** Una vista de la capital de Panamá, la Ciudad de Panamá

▼ **Panamá** El canal de Panamá

▲ **Panamá** El casco antiguo de la Ciudad de Panamá

NICARAGUA

Mar Caribe

COSTA RICA

Lago
Nicaragua

Río San Juan

CORDILLERA DE
GUANACASTE

Liberia

Nicoya

Lago
Arenal

CORDILLERA CENTRAL

Puerto Limón

Alajuela

Puntarenas

Caldera

San
José

Volcán de Irazú

Bocas del Toro

Puerto Quepos

CORDILLERA DE TALAMANCA

San
Isidro

Volcán Barú

Golfito

CORDILLERA CENTRAL

David

PANAMÁ

Santiago

*Río
San Pablo*

Isla de
Coiba

El Porvenir

*Río
Chagres*

Canal de
Panamá

Archipiélago de San Blas

Colón

Ciudad de
Panamá

SERRANÍA DE
SAN BLAS

Lago Gatún

Balboa

Vacamonte

*Río
Chepo*

Lago
Bayano

SERRANÍA DEL
DARIÉN

Penonomé

Isla del
Rey

Archipiélago
de las Perlas

La Palma

*Río
Tuira*

Yaviza

Golfo de
Panamá

COLOMBIA

OCÉANO PACÍFICO

▲ **Panamá** Jóvenes del grupo
indígena emberá de la selva tropical
cerca de la Ciudad de Panamá

Panamá Una estatua
de Vasco Núñez de Balboa
en la avenida Balboa en la
Ciudad de Panamá ▼

Costa Rica El canal Tortuguero a lo
largo de la costa del Caribe en Costa Rica ▼

▲ **Colombia** Jóvenes en un desfile en Cartagena

▲ **Venezuela** El salto de Ángel

Colombia, Venezuela
Un oso autóctono de varias regiones andinas ▼

◀ **Colombia** Un antiguo colgante antropomórfico (en figura de un ser humano) de oro de la región de Tolima

▲ **Venezuela** Una vista de la ciudad moderna de Caracas, la capital de Venezuela

▲ **Venezuela** El teleférico en la ciudad de Caracas

▲ **Colombia** El santuario de Nuestra Señora de las Lajas sobre el río Guaitara en el sur de Colombia

▲ **Venezuela** Una plataforma petrolífera en el lago de Maracaibo

Colombia La bonita ciudad de Cartagena en la costa del Caribe en el norte de Colombia ▼

GeoVista

Perú Las ruinas de la ciudad imperial de los incas, Machu Picchu ▶

Perú La plaza principal de Cuzco ▼

Perú Dos hermanas en trajes tradicionales en el valle del Urubamba ▼

Ecuador Una playa en la ciudad portuaria de Manta ▼

◀ Ecuador
La catedral de Cuenca en el sur de Ecuador

Bolivia
Un joven tocando la zampoña, un tipo de instrumento musical andino, en Potosí ▶

◀ Bolivia, Perú Una vista del lago Titicaca en la frontera entre Bolivia y Perú

▲ Bolivia Vista de la ciudad de Copacabana

◀ Ecuador La Rotonda, un monumento en Guayaquil, que conmemora una famosa reunión entre los dos libertadores de Latinoamérica—San Martín y Simón Bolívar

GeoVista

★ Chile ● Argentina

Argentina Una pareja joven bailando el tango en San Telmo, un barrio de Buenos Aires, la capital de Argentina ▶

▲ **Argentina** Un puente nuevo en el puerto de Buenos Aires que se llama «El Puente de la Mujer»

▲ **Argentina** La Casa Rosada donde tiene su oficina el presidente de la República argentina

Chile Un joven pescador en Puerto Montt, Chile ▶

◀ **Chile** Lo viejo y lo moderno en Santiago, la capital de Chile

Chile Caballos en el Parque Nacional Torres del Paine en la Patagonia chilena ▶

▲ **Chile** Una vista del valle del Elqui en el norte de Chile

PERÚ

BRASIL

BOLIVIA

Arica

Iquique

PARAGUAY

Antofagasta

DESIERTO DE ATACAMA

Salta

San Miguel de Tucumán

Puerto Iguazú

Corrientes

Posadas

Nevado Ojos del Salado

Río Pilcomayo

Río Paraguay

La Serena

Coquimbo

Laguna Mar Chiquita

←Isla de Pascua

CHILE

Córdoba

Santa Fe

San Juan

Río Paraná

Río Uruguay

URUGUAY

Cerro Aconcagua

Viña del Mar

Valparaíso

Santiago

Río Maipo

Rosario

Buenos Aires

La Plata

Río de la Plata

Archipiélago de Juan Fernández

Concepción

ARGENTINA

Mar del Plata

Río Colorado

Bahía Blanca

Temuco

Valdivia

San Carlos de Bariloche

OCÉANO ATLÁNTICO

Puerto Montt

Lago General Carrera

Lago Viedma

Islas Malvinas

Lago Argentino

Río Gallegos

Estrecho de Magallanes

PATAGONIA

Tierra del Fuego

Ushuaia

Canal de Beagle

Cabo de Hornos

ANDES

LOS

Argentina Casas típicas del pintoresco barrio La Boca en Buenos Aires ▶

Torres Paine

G. Perito Moreno

Ushuaia

Cueva Milodón

Argentina Lobos marinos en la Patagonia argentina ▼

GeoVista

Paraguay Uruguay

▲ **Paraguay** Una especie de piña autóctona de Paraguay y Brasil

▲ **Paraguay** Un joven de ascendencia guaraní en Asunción, la capital de Paraguay

Uruguay Una vista de Montevideo, la capital de Uruguay ▼

◀ **Uruguay** Un hotel en las afueras del famoso balneario de Punta del Este

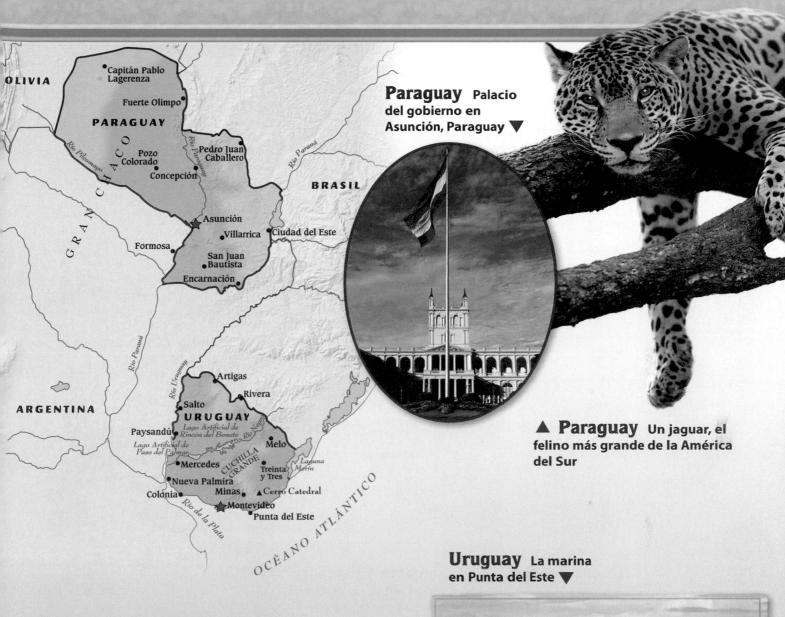

OLIVIA

PARAGUAY

Capitán Pablo
Lagerenza

Fuerte Olimpo

Río Pilcomayo

GRAN CHACO

Pozo
Colorado

Río Paraguay

Pedro Juan
Caballero

Concepción

Río Paraná

BRASIL

Asunción

Villarrica

Ciudad del Este

Formosa

San Juan
Bautista

Encarnación

Río Paraná

ARGENTINA

Río Uruguay

Artigas

Rivera

Salto

URUGUAY

Paysandú

Lago Artificial de
Rincón del Bonete

Río Negro

Lago Artificial de
Paso del Palmar

Melo

Mercedes

CUCHILLA GRANDE

Laguna
Merín

Nueva Palmira

Treinta
y Tres

Minas

▲ Cerro Catedral

Colonia

Río de la Plata

Montevideo

Punta del Este

OCÉANO ATLÁNTICO

Paraguay Palacio
del gobierno en
Asunción, Paraguay ▼

▲ **Paraguay** Un jaguar, el
felino más grande de la América
del Sur

Uruguay La marina
en Punta del Este ▼

◄ **Paraguay** Las cataratas del
Iguazú en la frontera entre Paraguay,
Argentina y Brasil

SH61

GeoVista

◀ **Cuba** El buceo en la costa de Cuba

▲ **República Dominicana** Una plaza en Puerto Plata, un balneario famoso

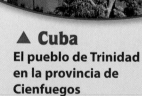

▲ **Cuba**
El pueblo de Trinidad en la provincia de Cienfuegos

Puerto Rico Unos alumnos en su uniforme escolar en Fajardo ▶

Cuba El Vedado, un barrio moderno de la Habana, la capital de Cuba ▼

▲ Puerto Rico El asopao—
un plato típico de Puerto Rico

Puerto Rico El Yunque,
una famosa selva tropical ▼

▲ República Dominicana
La playa de Bayahibe en la República
Dominicana

Puerto Rico
El coquí—una criatura querida
de los puertorriqueños cuyo nombre
se deriva de su canto ▼

GeoVista

Estados Unidos

◀ **Nueva York**
El desfile puertorriqueño en la ciudad de Nueva York

▲ **Nueva York** Un restaurante mexicano en Greenwich Village, un barrio de la Ciudad de Nueva York

◀ **Washington**
Anclas latinos de televisión en Seattle

Florida El fuerte Castillo de San Marcos en San Agustín ▼

▲ **Texas** El famoso paseo del Río en San Antonio

▲ Arizona
César Chávez, el mexicanoamericano que luchó por los derechos de todos los labradores

Florida Un rótulo callejero en Ybor City, un barrio de Tampa ▼

California Una misión española en Santa Bárbara ▼

▲ Florida
El carnaval de la Calle Ocho en la Pequeña Habana en Miami

◄ California Una tienda de música en San Francisco

Estos jóvenes guatemaltecos están sentados en un banco en la Plaza Mayor en la bonita ciudad de Antigua.

Amigos, alumnos y parientes

Objetivos

In this chapter you will review:

- vocabulary associated with friends, family, and home

- the verb **ser**

- the use of nouns, articles, and adjectives

- the verb **tener**

- possessive adjectives

QuickPass

Go to glencoe.com
For: **Online book**
Web code: ASD7837rc

QuickPass

Go to glencoe.com
For: **Vocabulary practice**
Web code: **ASD7837rc**

Vocabulario

¡Hola! Soy Mariana Valdéz. Soy mexicana.

¡Hola! Somos Manuel y Adela.

No somos hermanos. Somos amigos.

¡Hola! Soy Santiago Barros. Soy de Puerto Rico. Tengo dos hermanos.

Mariana es morena y bastante alta.
Ella es de Guanajuato.
Es alumna en el Colegio Rivera.

Manuel y Adela son alumnos en la misma escuela.
Son alumnos buenos. Son muy inteligentes.
Los dos son bastante cómicos.

Santiago tiene dieciséis años.
Su hermano menor tiene catorce.
Y su hermano mayor tiene dieciocho.
Ellos tienen una mascota—Chispa.

La familia Solís tiene una casa privada.
La casa tiene siete cuartos.

el comedor

la cocina

la sala

el cuarto de baño

el cuarto de dormir, la recámara

Práctica

HABLAR • ESCRIBIR

1 Parea y forma frases basado en la información en el vocabulario.

1. Santiago   a. amigos
2. Mariana   b. de Puerto Rico
3. Manuel y Adela   c. dos hermanos
4. Santiago   d. de nacionalidad mexicana

HABLAR

2 Contesta. Presta atención a la palabra interrogativa.

1. ¿De qué nacionalidad es Mariana Valdéz?
2. ¿De dónde es?
3. ¿Cómo es?
4. ¿Dónde es alumna?

LEER • ESCRIBIR

3 Corrige la información falsa.

1. Manuel y Adela son hermanos.
2. Son muy serios.
3. Son alumnos malos.
4. No son muy inteligentes.
5. Son alumnos en escuelas diferentes.

LEER • ESCRIBIR

4 Completa con una palabra apropiada.

1. Santiago Barros es de _____.
2. Tiene dos _____.
3. _____ hermano menor tiene catorce años.
4. Su hermano mayor tiene dieciocho _____.
5. Santiago y sus hermanos tienen una _____.
6. Su perro es _____.

5 **Rompecabezas**

Cambia una letra en cada palabra para formar una palabra nueva.

1. dos
2. hola
3. buen
4. tengo
5. baño

CULTURA

Una joven ecuatoriana mira un lobo marino en las islas Galápagos, Ecuador.

Repaso A

PLANTA BAJA

PLANTA ALTA

6 Describe la casa de los Solís.

Comunicación

7 With a classmate, look at these real estate ads. Describe your family and housing needs to your real estate agent (your partner). He or she will recommend a dwelling and will describe it to you. Take turns.

MILENIUM

PROMOCIONES, FINANCIACION Y VENTAS, S.L.

Teléfono:
956 540 772

Móvil:
679 148 524

VALDELAGRANA
Piso 3 dormitorios, 2 baños,
coc. amueb. 3 arm. empotr.
parking privado.
Ref.- 7151

FUENTEBRAVÍA
Apartamento 1 dormitorio, 1 baño,
coc. amueb. jardines, aparc. cerrado.
A 100 metros de la playa.
Ref.- 7000

VALDELAGRANA
Unifamiliar 160 m2, 3 dormitorios,
2 baños, cocina amueb., aseo,
buhardilla, trastero, piscina.
Ref.- 7083

FUENTEBRAVÍA
Unifamiliar 3 dormitorios, 1 baño,
aseo, cocina amueblada, chimenea,
cerca de la playa.
Ref.- 7009

C/ Almirante Cañas Trujillo, 17 B (Junto Avd. Libertad)
11500 El Puerto de Santa María

Conversación 🎧

¿De dónde son?

Julio	¡Hola!
Rosa	¡Hola! ¿Qué tal?
Julio	Bien, ¿y tú?
Rosa	Bien. Oye, eres un amigo de Teresa Irizarry, ¿no?
Julio	Sí, soy Julio Arenal.
Rosa	¿De dónde eres, Julio?
Julio	¿Yo? Soy de la Ciudad de México. Y tú eres de Puebla como Teresa, ¿no?
Rosa	Sí.
Julio	¿Cuántos años tienes, Rosa?
Rosa	Tengo dieciséis años.
Julio	¿Dieciséis? Tenemos la misma edad.

¿Comprendes?

A Contesta según la información en la conversación.

1. ¿Son mexicanos los dos muchachos?
2. ¿De dónde es Julio?
3. ¿Son amigos los dos muchachos?
4. ¿Quién es amigo de Teresa Irizarry?
5. ¿De dónde es Rosa?
6. ¿Cuántos años tiene ella?
7. Y, ¿cuántos años tiene Julio?
8. ¿Tienen ellos la misma edad?

B **Resumiendo** Cuenta toda la información sobre las tres personas en la conversación en tus propias palabras.

CULTURA

Rascacielos modernos en la Ciudad de México

QuickPass

Go to glencoe.com
For: **Grammar practice**
Web code: **ASD7837rc**

Gramática

Presente del verbo ser

Review the forms of the irregular verb **ser**.

ser	
soy	somos
eres	*sois*
es	son

Los dos jóvenes son alumnos serios.

Práctica

HABLAR

1 Personaliza. Da respuestas personales.

    1. ¿Quién eres?
    2. ¿De qué nacionalidad eres?
    3. ¿Dónde eres alumno(a)?
    4. ¿Cómo es tu escuela?

LEER • ESCRIBIR

2 Completa con las formas apropiadas de **ser.**

    Yo __1__ un amigo de Andrés. Andrés __2__ muy simpático. Y él __3__ gracioso. Andrés y yo __4__ dominicanos. __5__ de la República Dominicana.

    La capital de la República Dominicana __6__ Santo Domingo. Nosotros __7__ alumnos en un colegio en Santo Domingo. Nosotros __8__ alumnos de inglés. La profesora de inglés __9__ la señorita White. Ella __10__ norteamericana. __11__ de Estados Unidos.

CULTURA

¿De qué nacionalidad son los jóvenes? Son dominicanos, ¿no?

Comunicación

3 You are key pals with an exchange student from Peru (your partner). He or she wants to know about your school, your schedule, and your classes. Tell as much as you can about your school and then ask him or her about school life in Peru.

VIDEO Want help with nouns, articles, and adjectives? Watch **Gramática en vivo.**

Sustantivos, artículos y adjetivos

1. Spanish nouns are either masculine or feminine. Most nouns ending in **o** are masculine and most nouns ending in **a** are feminine. The definite articles **el** and **los** accompany masculine nouns; **la** and **las** accompany feminine nouns.

SINGULAR	PLURAL	SINGULAR	PLURAL
el alumno	los alumnos	la amiga	las amigas
el curso	los cursos	la escuela	las escuelas

2. An adjective must agree with the noun it describes or modifies. Adjectives that end in **o** have four forms.

el amigo sincero	los amigos sinceros
la amiga sincera	las amigas sinceras

3. Adjectives that end in **e** or a consonant have only two forms.

el curso interesante	los cursos interesantes
la clase interesante	las clases interesantes
el curso difícil	los cursos difíciles
la clase difícil	las clases difíciles

CULTURA

Julia es una alumna seria, muy estudiosa.

Práctica

HABLAR • ESCRIBIR

4 Describe a Julia. •••••••••••••••••••••••••••••

HABLAR • ESCRIBIR

5 Describe al grupo de amigos. •••••••••••••••••••

HABLAR • ESCRIBIR

6 Describe tu clase favorita.

 Comunicación

7 Work in groups of three or four. In each group, rate your courses as **fácil, difícil, regular, aburrido, fantástico.** Tally the results and report the information to the class.

CULTURA

Los amigos están en el patio de su escuela en Santo Domingo.

El verbo tener

1. Review the forms of the irregular verb **tener**.

tener	
tengo	tenemos
tienes	*tenéis*
tiene	tienen

2. You use **tener** to express age.

¿Cuántos años tienes?

3. Note that the expression **tener que** followed by an infinitive means *to have to.*

Tenemos que estudiar y aprender mucho.

Práctica

Una familia española en una placita en Palma de Mallorca, España

HABLAR

8 Personaliza. Da respuestas personales sobre tu familia.

1. ¿Tienes una familia grande o pequeña?
2. ¿Cuántos hermanos tienes?
3. ¿Cuántos años tienen ellos?
4. ¿Y cuántos años tienes tú?
5. ¿Tienen ustedes un perro o un gato?
6. ¿Tiene tu padre o tu madre un carro?
7. En la escuela, ¿tienes que estudiar mucho?
8. ¿Y tienen que trabajar mucho tus padres?

LEER • ESCRIBIR

9 Completa con las formas apropiadas de **tener.**

La familia Bravo __1__ un piso o apartamento en Madrid. Su piso __2__ seis cuartos. Está en Salamanca, una zona muy bonita de la ciudad. Muchas calles en la zona Salamanca __3__ los nombres de artistas famosos— la calle Goya, la calle Velázquez.

Hay cuatro personas en la familia Bravo. Teresa __4__ diecisiete años y su hermano __5__ quince años. Ellos __6__ un gato adorable.

EXPANSIÓN

Ahora, sin mirar el párrafo, cuenta toda la información sobre la familia Bravo en tus propias palabras. Si no recuerdas algo, un(a) compañero(a) te puede ayudar.

Adjetivos posesivos

1. Review the forms of the possessive adjectives **mi, tu,** and **su.** These adjectives have only two forms.

> **¿Dan una fiesta tu hermana y tus primos?**
> **Sí, mi hermana y mis primos dan una fiesta.**
> **Todos sus amigos van a recibir una invitación a su fiesta.**

2. The possessive adjective **nuestro** has four forms.

> **Nuestro primo, nuestra tía, nuestras sobrinas y nuestros abuelos viven todos en Madrid.**

Práctica

HABLAR

 Personaliza. Da respuestas personales sobre tu familia y casa.

1. ¿Dónde está tu casa o departamento?
2. ¿Cuántas personas hay en tu familia?
3. ¿Cuántos cuartos tiene tu casa o departamento?
4. ¿De dónde son tus abuelos?
5. ¿Tienes muchos primos?
6. ¿Quiénes son los padres de tus primos?

LEER • ESCRIBIR

11 Completa con el adjetivo posesivo apropiado.

—La casa de mi familia está en la calle Independencia. __1__ casa tiene siete cuartos. Detrás de __2__ casa hay un jardín.

—José, ¿tienen __3__ padres un carro?

—Sí, y __4__ carro es bastante nuevo. __5__ carro está en el garaje. Y nosotros tenemos un perro. __6__ perro no está en el garaje. Está en el jardín.

CULTURA

La familia Sánchez tiene una casa privada en Asturias en el norte de España. Delante de su casa hay muchas flores bonitas.

 Comunicación

12 You are spending the summer with a family in Venezuela. Tell your Venezuelan "brother" or "sister" (your partner) all you can about your family. Answer any questions he or she may have. Then reverse roles.

13 Work with a classmate. Be good interviewers. Make up questions with the following question words.

¿Qué?	**¿Quién?**	**¿Quiénes?**	**¿Dónde?**
¿De dónde?	**¿Cómo?**	**¿Cuánto(s)?**	

CULTURA

Un parque en el centro de San Juan, Venezuela

Una banda escolar delante de su colegio en Cartagena, Colombia

En casa y en la escuela

Objetivos

In this chapter you will review:

- vocabulary associated with home and school activities

- the present tense of regular verbs

- the present tense of **ir, dar, estar**

- contractions

QuickPass

Go to glencoe.com
For: **Online book**
Web code: **ASD7837rc**

QuickPass

Go to glencoe.com
For: **Vocabulary practice**
Web code: **ASD7837rc**

Vocabulario 🎧

Los alumnos están en la escuela.
Ellos prestan atención al profesor.
El profesor habla.
Ramón tiene una pregunta y
    levanta la mano.

Después de las clases los alumnos van a casa.
Toman el bus escolar.

La familia de Andrés Salinas vive
    en Nicaragua.
Su familia está en la sala.
La señora Salinas lee un libro.
Su esposo (marido) ve la tele.
Andrés escucha música en su MP3.

La hermana de Andrés está en su cuarto
    (de dormir).
Ella recibe un correo electrónico. Ella
    usa su computadora.
Lee su e-mail.

Práctica

ESCUCHAR

① Escucha las frases. Usa una tabla como la de abajo para indicar si la acción tiene lugar en casa o en la escuela.

casa	escuela

HABLAR • ESCRIBIR

② Contesta.

1. ¿Cómo llegan los alumnos a la escuela? ¿Toman el bus, van en carro o van a pie?
2. ¿Con quién hablan los alumnos cuando entran en la sala de clase?
3. ¿Prestan ellos atención cuando el/la profesor(a) habla?
4. ¿Qué levanta un(a) alumno(a) cuando tiene una pregunta?
5. Los alumnos que estudian mucho, ¿sacan notas buenas o malas?
6. En la escuela, ¿quién da los exámenes y quiénes toman los exámenes?

CULTURA

Los jóvenes usan un ordenador (una computadora) en San Sebastián, España.

LEER • ESCRIBIR

③ Parea para formar expresiones.

1. leer	a. mucho en la escuela
2. escribir	b. al quinto piso
3. vivir	c. una novela
4. aprender	d. un alumno bueno y serio
5. vender	e. la orden
6. comer	f. una limonada
7. ser	g. en una casa particular
8. subir	h. CDs en una tienda
9. beber	i. carne, ensalada y papas

CULTURA

La joven come un bocadillo en una cafetería en Barcelona, España.

HABLAR • ESCRIBIR

④ **Juego** Divide the class into two teams. Your teacher will ask each team to give a word that pertains to a category: **cosas que comemos, bebemos, leemos o escribimos.** Your teacher will keep asking for words until one team is unable to think of a word that pertains to the given category.

QuickPass

Go to glencoe.com
For: **Conversation practice**
Web code: **ASD7837rc**

Conversación

Otro año en la escuela

Paco	Claudia, ¿cómo estás?
Claudia	Muy bien, Paco. ¿Y tú?
Paco	Bien. ¿Qué tal la escuela este año?
Claudia	Muy bien. Pero un poco difícil. Tengo seis cursos.
Paco	¡Seis cursos! Estudias mucho, ¿no?
Claudia	Sí, bastante. Y, a propósito, Paco, ¿dónde están tus primos Enrique y Sara? ¿Dónde viven ahora?
Paco	Pues, viven en la misma casa. ¿Por qué?
Claudia	Pues, no los veo casi nunca.

¿Comprendes?

Contesta según la información en la conversacíon.

1. ¿Quiénes hablan?
2. ¿Cómo está Paco?
3. ¿Y Claudia?
4. ¿Cuántos cursos toma Claudia?
5. ¿Tiene que estudiar mucho?
6. ¿Quiénes son los primos de Paco?
7. ¿Ve Claudia mucho a sus primos?
8. ¿Viven ellos en la misma casa que antes o no?

Gramática

Presente de los verbos regulares

1. Review the present tense forms of regular **-ar, -er,** and **-ir** verbs.

infinitive	mirar	comer	vivir
stem	mir-	com-	viv-
yo	miro	como	vivo
tú	miras	comes	vives
Ud., él, ella	mira	come	vive
nosotros(as)	miramos	comemos	vivimos
vosotros(as)	*miráis*	*coméis*	*vivís*
Uds., ellos, ellas	miran	comen	viven

2. Note that the **-er** and **-ir** verbs have the same endings except nosotros(as) and *vosotros(as).*

comemos	vivimos
coméis	*vivís*

3. Remember, to make a sentence negative, you put **no** before the verb.

No habla francés.
No vivimos en Francia.

4. Remember to use **tú** when talking to a friend, family member, or person your own age. Use **usted** when speaking to an adult, a person you do not know well, or someone to whom you wish to show respect. You use **ustedes** when talking to two or more people.

¿Tú estudias español, Roberto?
¿Y usted, señora? ¿Usted también estudia español?
Ustedes viven aquí, ¿no?

CULTURA

Un puesto de comida en una calle de Oaxaca, México. ¿Qué forma usa la mamá con su hijito? ¿Tú o usted?

Más práctica

☐ Workbook, pp. R9–R10
● StudentWorks™ Plus

Práctica

HABLAR • ESCRIBIR

1 Personaliza. Da respuestas personales.

1. ¿En qué escuela estudias?
2. ¿Cómo llegas a la escuela por la mañana?
3. ¿Cuántos cursos tomas?
4. ¿En qué llevas los materiales escolares?
5. ¿Estudian mucho los alumnos de tu escuela?
6. ¿Sacan ustedes notas buenas?
7. ¿Toman ustedes muchos exámenes?
8. ¿Escuchan ustedes cuando el/la profesor(a) habla?

EXPANSIÓN

Ahora, sin mirar las preguntas, cuenta toda la información en tus propias palabras. Si no recuerdas algo, un(a) compañero(a) te puede ayudar.

LEER • ESCRIBIR

2 Completa con la forma apropiada del verbo.

1. Durante la fiesta todos nosotros _____. (bailar)
2. Felipe _____ el piano. (tocar)
3. Mientras él _____ el piano, Paz y Jaime _____. (tocar, cantar)
4. ¿_____ ustedes refrescos durante la fiesta? (preparar)
5. ¿_____ ustedes fotos durante la fiesta? (tomar)
6. Sí, y todos nosotros _____ las fotografías. (mirar)

HABLAR • ESCRIBIR

3 Personaliza. Da respuestas personales.

1. ¿Qué comes cuando tienes hambre?
2. ¿Qué bebes cuando tienes sed?
3. ¿Qué aprenden tú y tus amigos en la escuela?
4. ¿Qué leen ustedes en la clase de inglés?
5. ¿Qué escriben ustedes?
6. ¿Comprenden los alumnos cuando el/la profesor(a) de español habla?
7. ¿Reciben ustedes notas buenas en todos sus cursos?

CULTURA

Los estudiantes están en la biblioteca de la Universidad de Málaga en España.

VIDEO Want help with the present tense of regular verbs? Watch **Gramática en vivo.**

LEER • ESCRIBIR

4️⃣ Completa sobre una visita a un café.

En el café los clientes __1__ (ver) al mesero. Ellos __2__ (hablar) con el mesero. Los clientes __3__ (leer) el menú y __4__ (decidir) lo que van a tomar. Los meseros __5__ (tomar) la orden y __6__ (escribir) la orden en un cuaderno pequeño. Los meseros no __7__ (leer) el menú. Y los clientes no __8__ (escribir) la orden.

CULTURA

Los clientes toman un refresco en el café al aire libre en Valencia, España.

Comunicación

5️⃣ Tell all the things you do in a typical school day. Present your information to the class. Do you or your classmates do anything different?

CULTURA

Un grupo de estudiantes internacionales en Málaga, España

Los verbos ir, dar, estar

1. Note that the verbs **ir, dar,** and **estar** are the same as regular -ar verbs in all forms except **yo.**

	ir	dar	estar
yo	voy	doy	estoy
tú	vas	das	estás
Ud., él, ella	va	da	está
nosotros(as)	vamos	damos	estamos
vosotros(as)	*vais*	*dais*	*estáis*
Uds., ellos, ellas	van	dan	están

2. The preposition **a** often follows the verb **ir.** Remember that **a** contracts with **el** to form one word—**al.**

Voy al café. No voy a la tienda.

3. Remember you can use **ir a** + infinitive to express a future idea.

Voy a tomar el bus.

Práctica

HABLAR

6 Personaliza. Da respuestas personales.

1. ¿Vas a la escuela?
2. ¿A qué hora vas a la escuela?
3. ¿Con quién vas a la escuela?
4. ¿Están ustedes en la escuela ahora?
5. ¿Cómo van ustedes a la escuela?
6. ¿Da el/la profesor(a) muchos exámenes?
7. ¿Dan los alumnos exámenes también?

CULTURA

El joven va a la escuela en el bus escolar en Barcelona, España.

LEER • ESCRIBIR

7 Completa.

Yo __1__ (ir) a la tienda de ropa. Emilio __2__ (ir) también. Él y yo __3__ (estar) en la tienda. Yo __4__ (comprar) una camiseta y él __5__ (comprar) un blue jean. Nosotros no __6__ (necesitar) mucha ropa porque __7__ (llevar) uniforme a la escuela.

Laura y Tomás __8__ (llevar) uniforme a la escuela también. Ellos __9__ (ir) a una escuela en las afueras de Lima, en Miraflores.

Comunicación

8 Tell some things you're not going to do now because you have to do something else.

9 Work in groups of three or four. You're all friends from Mexico. After school you go to a café where you talk about lots of things—school, teachers, friends, home, family, etc. One of you will be the server. You have to interrupt the conversation once in a while to take the orders and serve. Take turns.

CULTURA

Los jóvenes están delante de un café Internet en Tepoztlán, México.

REPASO C

Personalidad y salud

Objetivos

In this chapter you will review:

- vocabulary related to personality, health, and general well-being

- uses of **ser** and **estar**

- indirect object pronouns

◀ **Estos jóvenes universitarios están caminando por una calle en San Miguel de Allende, México. Lo están pasando bien, ¿no?**

QuickPass

Go to glencoe.com
For: **Online book**
Web code: **ASD7837rc**

QuickPass

Go to glencoe.com
For: **Vocabulary practice**
Web code: **ASD7837rc**

Vocabulario

Alberto no está bien.
Está enfermo.
Tiene fiebre y tiene que
   guardar cama.

El médico está en su consulta
   (consultorio).
Examina al paciente (enfermo).

El médico le da una receta.

contento, alegre

triste, deprimida

energético,
lleno de energía

cansado

Arturo está de mal humor. Algo le molesta (enoja).
Felipe está de buen humor.

Práctica

ESCUCHAR

1 Escucha. Escoge la frase correcta. Usa una tabla como la de abajo para indicar tus respuestas.

a	b

HABLAR • ESCRIBIR

2 Contesta sobre una consulta médica.

1. César está enfermo. Tiene la temperatura alta. ¿Qué tiene?
2. ¿Adónde tiene que ir?
3. ¿Le da un examen físico el médico?
4. ¿Abre la boca César?
5. ¿Le examina la garganta el médico?
6. ¿Está roja la garganta?
7. ¿Tiene César dolor de garganta?
8. ¿Le duele mucho?

(EXPANSIÓN)

Ahora, sin mirar las preguntas, cuenta toda la información en tus propias palabras. Si no recuerdas algo, un(a) compañero(a) te puede ayudar.

LEER

3 Parea.

1. Es bien educado.
2. Es muy terco.
3. Tiene una sonrisa en la cara.
4. Tiene dolor de cabeza.
5. Él es perezoso.

a. Nunca trabaja.
b. Nunca presta atención.
c. Tiene buena conducta.
d. Está contento.
e. Le duele mucho.

HABLAR • ESCRIBIR

4 ¿Cuáles son todas las partes del cuerpo que puedes identificar •········· en español? Usa la foto como guía.

✿ Comunicación

5 Work with a classmate and discuss some traits or characteristics you look for in a good friend.

QuickPass

Go to glencoe.com
For: **Conversation practice**
Web code: **ASD7837rc**

Conversación

¿Qué le pasa a Ana?

Enrique	¿Qué te pasa, Ana? Tienes la cara triste. ¿Estás enferma?
Ana	Sí, me parece que sí. Tengo dolor de garganta y estoy muy cansada.
Enrique	Pues, ¿por qué no vas a ver al médico?
Ana	No, no tengo que ir al médico. Voy a tomar una siesta.
Enrique	Eres muy terca, Ana. Debes ir al médico.

¿Comprendes?

A Contesta según la información en la conversación.

1. ¿Qué le pregunta Enrique a Ana?
2. ¿Cómo tiene la cara?
3. ¿Qué le duele a Ana?
4. ¿Está llena de energía?
5. ¿Debe ir a ver al médico?
6. ¿Va a ir?
7. ¿Qué va a tomar?
8. Según Enrique, ¿cómo es Ana?

B **Resumiendo** Resume toda la información en la conversación en tus propias palabras.

QuickPass

Go to glencoe.com
For: **Grammar practice**
Web code: **ASD7837rc**

Gramática

Ser y estar

1. The verbs **ser** and **estar** both mean *to be.* **Ser** is used to tell where someone or something is from. It is also used to describe an inherent trait or characteristic.

> **Roberto es de Miami.**
> **Él es inteligente y guapo.**

2. Estar is used to tell where someone or something is located. It is also used to describe a temporary state or condition.

> **Roberto es de Miami pero ahora está en Madrid.**
> **Madrid está en España.**
> **Roberto está muy contento en Madrid.**

CULTURA

La Plaza Mayor es una plaza grande. Está en el centro mismo de Madrid y Madrid está en el centro de España.

VIDEO Want help with **ser** and **estar**? Watch **Gramática en vivo.**

Una vista de los rascacielos y montañas en Caracas, la capital de Venezuela

Práctica

HABLAR

1 Personaliza. Da respuestas personales.

1. ¿Estás en la escuela ahora?
2. ¿Dónde está la escuela?
3. ¿En qué clase estás?
4. ¿Está tu profesor(a) en clase también?
5. ¿Cómo es él o ella?
6. Y, ¿cómo es la clase de español?
7. ¿De dónde es el/la profesor(a)?
8. Y tú, ¿de dónde eres?
9. ¿Cómo estás hoy?

LEER • ESCRIBIR

2 Completa con **ser** o **estar.**

Ángel __1__ de Caracas. Él __2__ muy simpático. __3__ gracioso también. Ahora Ángel __4__ en Nueva York. __5__ estudiante en la universidad allí. Ángel __6__ muy contento en Nueva York.

Nueva York __7__ en el nordeste de Estados Unidos. La Ciudad de Nueva York __8__ muy grande y __9__ muy interesante. A Ángel le gusta mucho Nueva York.

HABLAR • ESCRIBIR

3 Forma frases completas con **es** o **está.**

1. contento
2. de buen humor
3. serio
4. inteligente
5. lleno de energía
6. cansado
7. enfermo
8. estudioso
9. ambicioso
10. enojado

El muchacho está contento y tiene una sonrisa agradable. Y es guapo, ¿no?

 Comunicación

4 Tell some things about yourself. Where are you from? What kind of personality do you have? Are you a good student?

Pronombres de complemento indirecto

1. An indirect object is the indirect receiver of the action of a verb.

> **El médico me da la receta.**
> **Yo le doy la receta al farmacéutico.**

2. Review the indirect object pronouns.

me	nos
te	*os*
le	les

3. Since **le** and **les** can refer to different people they are often clarified with a prepositional phrase.

Le hablo { a él. / a ella. / a usted.

Les hablo { a ellos. / a ellas. / a ustedes.

Práctica

HABLAR

5 Personaliza. Da respuestas personales.

1. ¿Te habla en español el/la profesor(a) de español?
2. ¿Les da (a ustedes) muchos exámenes el/la profesor(a)?
3. ¿Te envían correos electrónicos tus amigos?
4. Cuando hablas, ¿te prestan atención tus amigos?

LEER • ESCRIBIR

6 Completa.

1. _____ hablo casi todos los días a mis abuelos.
2. _____ explico la lección a él.
3. Guillermo _____ da un regalo a sus abuelos.
4. La empleada _____ habla a sus clientes.
5. Al pobre José _____ duele mucho la garganta.

La muchacha les lee algo a los otros miembros de su clase de español. El profesor y los otros alumnos le prestan atención.

Comunicación

7 Work with a classmate and describe people who have the following personality traits. Be creative!

Está lleno(a) de energía.	Es dinámico(a) y ambicioso(a).
Tiene mucha paciencia.	Es bien educado(a).
Es bastante perezoso(a).	Siempre les enoja a sus amigos.

◀ Va a empezar un partido de béisbol entre los equipos de la República Dominicana y la República Bolivariana de Venezuela.

Los deportes

Objetivos

In this chapter you will review:

- vocabulary related to sports
- the present tense of stem-changing verbs
- the verbs **aburrir, interesar, gustar**

QuickPass

Go to glencoe.com
For: **Online book**
Web code: ASD7837rc

QuickPass

Go to glencoe.com
For: **Vocabulary practice**
Web code: ASD7837rc

Vocabulario

Los dos equipos quieren ganar.
Pero no pueden.
Un equipo pierde.

Los dos equipos juegan (al) fútbol.
Empieza el segundo tiempo.
Los jugadores vuelven al campo de fútbol.

Es un partido de béisbol.
El jugador batea la pelota.
Luego corre de una base a otra.

Luisa, ¿te gusta el béisbol?

Sí, me gusta mucho. ¿Y a ti?

Sí, me gusta. Pero me gusta más el fútbol.

A mí, no. Me aburre.

Práctica

ESCUCHAR • HABLAR

1 Contesta según se indica.

1. ¿Cuántos tiempos hay en un juego de fútbol? (dos)
2. ¿Cuántos jugadores hay en un equipo de fútbol? (once)
3. ¿Dónde juegan fútbol? (en el campo de fútbol)
4. ¿Quién guarda la portería? (el portero)
5. ¿Qué bloquea? (el balón)
6. ¿Quieren perder los dos equipos? (no, ganar)

LEER

2 **Juego** **Cada uno en su sitio** Determina el deporte que cada frase describe.

1. El jugador lanza el balón con el pie.
2. Hay cinco jugadores en el equipo.
3. La pelota pasa por encima de la red.
4. El jugador corre de una base a otra.
5. Es un deporte de invierno.
6. El portero para o bloquea el balón.
7. El jugador tira el balón y encesta.
8. La jugadora usa una raqueta.

CULTURA

Un juego de fútbol en un parque en Barcelona, España

EL FÚTBOL	EL BÁSQUETBOL	EL BÉISBOL	EL TENIS	EL PATINAJE SOBRE EL HIELO

HABLAR

3 Personaliza. Da respuestas personales.

1. ¿Cuáles son los deportes que a ti te gustan?
2. ¿Cuáles son los comestibles que te gustan?
3. ¿Cuáles son los cursos que te interesan?
4. ¿Cuáles son algunas cosas que no te gustan, que te aburren?

4 **Juego** Work with a classmate. Give him or her some information about a sport. He or she has to guess what sport you're talking about. Take turns.

QuickPass

Go to glencoe.com
For: **Conversation practice**
Web code: **ASD7837rc**

Conversación

Un partido importante

Tadeo	Isabel y Marta, ¿quieren ir al Café Selma?
Isabel	Gracias, Tadeo, pero no podemos. Queremos ver el partido.
Tadeo	¿De qué partido hablas?
Isabel	El Real juega contra el Valencia.
Tadeo	¿Cuál es tu equipo favorito? ¿Cuál te gusta más?
Isabel	Mi equipo favorito es el Real porque soy madrileña.

¿Comprendes?

Contesta según la información en la conversación.

1. ¿Adónde va Tadeo?
2. ¿Quieren ir con él Isabel y Marta?
3. ¿Por qué no pueden ir?
4. ¿Qué equipos juegan?
5. ¿Cuál es el equipo favorito de Isabel?

Gramática
Verbos de cambio radical

1. Review the following forms of the stem-changing verbs. Remember that the **e** changes to **ie** in all forms except **nosotros(as)** and *vosotros(as).*

	empezar	perder
yo	empiezo	pierdo
tú	empiezas	pierdes
Ud., él, ella	empieza	pierde
nosotros(as)	empezamos	perdemos
vosotros(as)	*empezáis*	*perdéis*
Uds., ellos, ellas	empiezan	pierden

Nota

- Other verbs with the **e → ie** stem change like **cerrar** are: **perder, sentarse, comenzar, empezar, pensar.**
- Other **o → ue** verbs like **encontrar** are: **acostarse, recordar, poder, volver.**
- **Sentir** is conjugated like **preferir.**
- Other verbs with the **e → i** stem change like **pedir** are: **repetir, freír, seguir, servir.**

2. The following verbs change the **o** to **ue** in all forms except **nosotros(as)** and *vosotros(as).*

	volver	poder
yo	vuelvo	puedo
tú	vuelves	puedes
Ud., él, ella	vuelve	puede
nosotros(as)	volvemos	podemos
vosotros(as)	*volvéis*	*podéis*
Uds., ellos, ellas	vuelven	pueden

3. The verb **jugar** also has a stem change.

jugar			
yo	juego	nosotros(as)	jugamos
tú	juegas	*vosotros(as)*	*jugáis*
Ud., él, ella	juega	Uds., ellos, ellas	juegan

CULTURA

Los jóvenes juegan fútbol delante de su escuela en la Colonia Renacimiento en la Ciudad de México.

VIDEO Want help with stem-changing verbs? Watch **Gramática en vivo.**

Los amigos tienen una conversación mientras vuelven a casa después de las clases.

Práctica

HABLAR • ESCRIBIR

1 Contesta.

1. ¿Quieres ir a la fiesta?
2. ¿Quieren ustedes bailar durante la fiesta?
3. ¿A qué hora empieza la fiesta?
4. ¿Puedes llegar a tiempo?
5. ¿Pueden ustedes tomar el bus a la fiesta?
6. ¿A qué hora vuelven ustedes a casa?

LEER • ESCRIBIR

2 Completa con la forma apropiada del verbo.

El juego de béisbol ___1___ (empezar) a las tres y media.

Habla Teresa:

—Hoy yo ___2___ (querer) ser la pícher.

La verdad es que Teresa ___3___ (ser) una pícher muy buena. Ella ___4___ (jugar) muy bien. Nosotros ___5___ (tener) un equipo bueno. Todos nosotros ___6___ (jugar) bien. Nuestro equipo no ___7___ (perder) mucho.

HABLAR

3 ¡Te toca a ti!

1. **Puedo...** Tell all that you can do.
2. **Quiero...** Tell all that you want to do.
3. **Quiero pero no puedo...** Tell all that you want to do but for some reason you cannot do.
4. **No quiero porque prefiero...** Tell something you don't want to do because you prefer to do something else.

Comunicación

4 Work with a classmate. Tell him or her what sport you don't want to play because you don't like it. Tell him or her what you prefer to play. Then ask your classmate questions to find out what sports he or she likes.

Una beisbolista que quiere ganar

Verbos como aburrir, interesar y gustar

1. The verbs **interesar** and **aburrir** function the same in Spanish and English.

¿Te aburre el arte?	*Does art bore you?*
¿Te aburren los deportes?	*Do sports bore you?*
No, los deportes me interesan.	*No, sports interest me.*

2. The verb **gustar** functions the same as **interesar** and **aburrir**. **Gustar** conveys the meaning *to like,* but it actually means *to be pleasing to.*

—¿Te gusta el béisbol?   —¿Te gustan los deportes?
—Sí, me gusta mucho.   —Sí, me gustan.

¿Te gustan los camarones?

ESCUCHAR • HABLAR

 Sigue el modelo.

MODELO   ¿A mí? ¿Los tomates? →
          —Me gustan mucho los tomates.
           Y, ¿a ti te gustan también?

1. ¿A mí? ¿El pescado?
2. ¿A mí? ¿Los vegetales?
3. ¿A mí? ¿La carne?
4. ¿A mí? ¿El jamón?
5. ¿A mí? ¿Los mariscos?

¿Te gustan los mejillones?

HABLAR • ESCRIBIR

 Personaliza. Da respuestas personales.

1. ¿Te interesan o te aburren las matemáticas? ¿Te gustan o no?
2. ¿Te interesa o te aburre la historia? ¿Te gusta o no?
3. ¿Te interesan o te aburren las ciencias? ¿Te gustan o no?
4. ¿Te interesa o te aburre la literatura? ¿Te gusta o no?
5. ¿Te interesa o te aburre la geografía? ¿Te gusta o no?

Comunicación

7 Work with a classmate. Tell him or her about your favorite team. Tell all about the sport and tell why you really like this team in particular. Then ask your classmate about his or her favorite team. Do you by chance have the same favorite team?

CULTURA

Los jóvenes celebran la victoria de su equipo. Marchan por una calle de Madrid.

De compras

Una galería en el centro de Lima, Perú. Además de muchas tiendas, hay puestos donde venden todo tipo de mercancías.

Objetivos

In this chapter you will review:

- vocabulary related to shopping for food and clothing
- the verbs **saber** and **conocer**
- comparatives and superlatives

QuickPass

Go to glencoe.com
For: **Online book**
Web code: **ASD7837rc**

QuickPass

Go to glencoe.com
For: **Vocabulary practice**
Web code: **ASD7837rc**

Vocabulario 🎧

Una tienda de ropa

- una camisa de manga larga
- una chaqueta
- una blusa
- una falda
- un pantalón largo

- un par de zapatos
- el número

Un mercado

- las zanahorias
- el maíz
- las judías verdes
- los guisantes
- las papas (patatas)

- los plátanos
- las tomates
- las manzanas
- las naranjas

Hay muchos puestos en el mercado.
La señora conoce a la vendedora.
El el mercado venden frutas y legumbres.
Las frutas y legumbres son más baratas
    en el mercado que en el supermercado.
Cuestan menos.

Para conversar

¿Qué te parece?
¿Me queda bien?

No. Te queda grande.
¿No sabes tu talla?

No.

Práctica

 1 Personaliza. Da respuestas personales.

1. ¿Qué llevas a la escuela?
2. ¿Prefieres una camisa o una blusa de mangas largas o de mangas cortas?
3. ¿Llevas un pantalón corto en verano o en invierno?
4. Cuando compras ropa, ¿cuáles son tus colores favoritos?
5. Si necesitas una camiseta, ¿qué talla usas?
6. Si necesitas zapatos, ¿qué número calzas?
7. ¿Te sale todo más barato o más caro cuando una tienda tiene una liquidación?

Los jóvenes están en una tienda de ropa.

 2 Completa una tabla como la de abajo. ¡A ver cuántas palabras recuerdas o sabes!

ropa	colores	frutas	vegetales

LEER

3 Escoge la palabra apropiada.

1. En un mercado indígena hay muchos (puestos, carritos).
2. Los clientes conocen a los vendedores en el (supermercado, mercado).
3. En el supermercado los clientes llenan (un bote, un carrito) de todas sus compras.
4. —¿Quieres algo más?
   —No, (algo, nada) más gracias.
5. Las sandalias y cerámicas son ejemplos de (utensilios domésticos, artesanía).

HABLAR • ESCRIBIR

4 Parea los antónimos.

1. blanco	a. barato
2. largo	b. aburrir
3. interesar	c. corto
4. algo	d. comprar
5. clientes	e. negro
6. caro	f. invierno
7. verano	g. nada
8. vender	h. empleados

LEER • ESCRIBIR

5 Completa con la palabra apropiada.

1. _____ de atún
2. _____ de agua mineral
3. _____ de zanahorias congeladas
4. _____ de mayonesa
5. _____ de huevos

¡Mira lo que acabo de comprar!

Elena acaba de comprar una camiseta. ¿Qué piensas?
¿A Antonio le gusta la camiseta?

  Comunicación

6 Work with a classmate. Discuss whether or not you like to go shopping for clothes. Also discuss the type of clothing you like and dislike. What's your favorite outfit? Do you know what size you wear?

QuickPass

Go to glencoe.com
For: **Conversation practice**
Web code: **ASD7837rc**

Repaso

Conversación 🎧

En una tienda de ropa

¿Comprendes?

A Contesta según la información en la conversación.

1. ¿Dónde está Jorge?
2. ¿Con quién va de compras?
3. ¿Qué quiere comprar Jorge?
4. ¿Necesita una talla más grande o más pequeña?
5. ¿Qué color prefiere Mariluz?
6. ¿Tienen una chaqueta en la talla que necesita Jorge?
7. ¿Cuánto cuesta?

B **Llegando a conclusiones** ¿Qué piensas? ¿Compra Jorge la chaqueta o no? ¿Por qué?

QuickPass

Go to glencoe.com
For: **Grammar practice**
Web code: **ASD7837rc**

Gramática
Saber y conocer

1. The verbs **saber** and **conocer** both mean *to know.* Like many Spanish verbs, they have an irregular **yo** form in the present tense. All other forms are regular.

saber			
yo	sé	nosotros(as)	sabemos
tú	sabes	*vosotros(as)*	*sabéis*
Ud., él, ella	sabe	Uds., ellos, ellas	saben

conocer			
yo	conozco	nosotros(as)	conocemos
tú	conoces	*vosotros(as)*	*conocéis*
Ud., él, ella	conoce	Uds., ellos, ellas	conocen

2. The verb **saber** means *to know a fact* or *to have information about something.* It also means *to know how to do something.*

> **Yo sé donde está el mercado.**
> **No sabemos a qué hora sale el vuelo.**
> **Ellos saben regatear.**

3. The verb **conocer** means *to know* in the sense of *to be acquainted with.* It is used to talk about people and complex or abstract concepts rather than simple facts.

> **Yo conozco a Luis.**
> **Ella conoce a su hermano.**
> **Los alumnos conocen bien la literatura mexicana.**

CULTURA

Estos alumnos en un instituto en San Miguel de Allende en México saben que tienen que hacer sus tareas.

Práctica

1 Personaliza. Da respuestas personales.

    1. ¿Sabes el número que calzas?
    2. ¿Sabes la talla que usas cuando compras ropa?
    3. ¿Sabes el número del celular de tu mejor amigo(a)?
    4. ¿Sabes su dirección de correo electrónico también?
    5. ¿Conoces a la familia de tu mejor amigo(a)?
    6. ¿Conoces la cultura hispana?

2 Trabajen en grupos de tres. Indiquen todo lo que saben hacer.

3 Completa cada frase con **saber** o **conocer**.

    1. Yo _____ la palabra.
    2. Nosotros _____ a María.
    3. Carlos _____ esquiar.
    4. Ellos _____ la lección.
    5. Yo _____ leer.
    6. ¿_____ tú a Enrique?
    7. Ella _____ el arte de México.
    8. Nosotros _____ que París es la capital de Francia.

4 Escribe frases originales.

    1. yo / saber…
    2. y ellos / saber…
    3. tú / conocer…
    4. y nosotros / conocer…

CULTURA

Los jóvenes saben a quienes ven en las fotos en su móvil.

Comunicación

5 You are now beginning a new year in your study of Spanish. Think about what you have learned so far in Spanish, and tell what you know. Be sure to use **saber** or **conocer** as appropriate.

Comparaciones

El inglés

To form the comparative in English, you add *-er* to short adjectives or adverbs. You put *more* before longer adjectives or adverbs.

He is smarter than the others.

She is more intelligent than the others.

To form the superlative in English, you add *-est* to short adjectives or adverbs and you put *most* before longer ones.

This is the largest size.

This is the most popular color.

Comparativo y superlativo

1. To form the comparative in Spanish you put **más** or **menos** before the adjective or adverb and **que** after it.

> **Ella es más (menos) ambiciosa que su hermana.**
> **Ella es más (menos) ambiciosa que yo también y la verdad es que ella sabe más (menos) que nadie.**

Note that after **que** you use subject pronouns (**yo, tú,** etc.) or **nadie.**

2. You form the superlative by using the appropriate definite article plus **más** or **menos** and the adjective or adverb. The preposition **de** follows the superlative.

> **Es el joven más (menos) inteligente del grupo.**
> **Es el más (menos) inteligente del grupo.**

3. Study the following irregular comparative and superlative forms.

COMPARATIVE		SUPERLATIVE	
bueno	**mejor**	**el/la mejor**	**los/las mejores**
malo	**peor**	**el/la peor**	**los/las peores**
bien	**mejor**		
mal	**peor**		

> **Esta chaqueta te queda mejor que las otras.**
> **Elena es la mejor alumna de la clase.**

4. The adjectives **mayor** and **menor** most often refer to age.

> **Yo soy menor que mi hermana.**
> **Yo soy el/la menor de la familia.**
> **Mi abuelo es el mayor.**

Según Teresa, el libro que ella tiene es más interesante que los libros que tiene Paco.

Práctica

6 Compara.

   1. tu clase de español y tu clase de inglés

   2. el equipo de fútbol y el equipo de béisbol

   3. tu mejor amigo(a) y tu hermano(a)

   4. tu escuela secundaria y tu escuela primaria

7 Forma frases según el modelo.

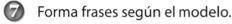

MODELO **inteligente**

       José / Carlos / Diego →

       José es inteligente. Carlos es más inteligente que José y Diego es el más inteligente de los tres.

   1. graciosa

      Julia / Eva / Carla

   2. simpático

      Enrique / Tadeo / Alfonso

   3. interesante

      el curso de biología / el curso de historia / el curso de español

8 Personaliza. Da respuestas personales.

   1. ¿Quiénes en tu familia son mayores que tú?

   2. Y, ¿quiénes son menores?

   3. ¿Quién es el/la menor de tu familia? ¿Quién es el/la mayor?

   4. ¿En qué curso sacas la mejor nota?

   5. ¿En qué curso sacas la peor nota?

9 **Juego** Work in groups of four. Create a sentence that compares two people or things. Have your classmates guess who or what you are comparing. Take turns.

CULTURA

Una familia chilena da un paseo por el parque. Los padres tienen tres hijas. ¿Qué crees? ¿Quién es la menor? ¿Quién es la mayor?

La playa de Pucón en el lago Villarrica en el distrito de los lagos en Chile. El kayaking es un deporte popular en verano. ▼

De vacaciones

Objetivos

In this chapter you will review:

- vocabulary related to summer resorts and activities

- vocabulary related to winter resorts and activities

- the preterite of regular verbs

- the preterite of **ir** and **ser**

- direct and indirect object pronouns

QuickPass

Go to glencoe.com
For: **Online book**
Web code: **ASD7837rc**

QuickPass

Go to glencoe.com
For: **Vocabulary practice**
Web code: **ASD7837rc**

Vocabulario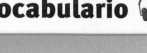

Raúl pasó el verano en la playa.
Nadó en el mar.

Tomó el sol.
Volvió a casa muy bronceado.

Susana pasó una semana en una estación
de esquí.
Tomó el telesilla para subir la montaña.
Subió en el telesilla.

Ella bajó la pista para expertos.
No bajó la pista para principiantes.

Práctica

HABLAR • ESCRIBIR

1 Contesta sobre un día en la playa.

1. ¿Fue Francisco a la playa?
2. ¿Nadó en el mar?
3. ¿Esquió en el agua?
4. ¿Tomó el sol?
5. ¿Volvió a casa muy bronceado?

(EXPANSIÓN)

Ahora, sin mirar las preguntas, cuenta toda la información en tus propias palabras. Si no recuerdas algo, un(a) compañero(a) te puede ayudar.

CULTURA

Esquiadores en Portillo, Chile

HABLAR • ESCRIBIR

2 Contesta sobre una estación de esquí.

1. ¿Fueron a una estación de esquí los amigos?
2. ¿Salieron ellos muy temprano por la mañana?
3. ¿Pasaron el día entero en las pistas?
4. ¿Subieron la montaña en el telesilla?
5. ¿Bajaron la pista para expertos o para principiantes?
6. ¿Volvieron a casa el mismo día?

(EXPANSIÓN)

Ahora, sin mirar las preguntas, cuenta toda la información en tus propias palabras. Si no recuerdas algo, un(a) compañero(a) te puede ayudar.

✿ Comunicación

3 Work with a classmate. Look at these photos. Tell where you prefer to go and why. Take turns.

CULTURA

Snowboarders en un telesilla en una estación de esquí en Granada, España

CULTURA

Un juego de fútbol en una playa de Puerto Vallarta, México

Conversación

¿Adónde fueron los amigos?

Nando	¿Adónde fuiste ayer, Teresa?
Teresa	Fui a casa de Sofi.
Nando	¿Y… ?
Teresa	Jugamos tenis.
Nando	¿Tiene Sofi una cancha de tenis?
Teresa	No. Hay canchas en un parque cerca de su casa. Pero Sofi tiene una piscina.
Nando	¿Sí? ¿Nadaron ustedes?
Teresa	Sí, nadamos después de jugar tenis.

¿Comprendes?

Usa una tabla como la de abajo para indicar si la información
es correcta o no.

	correcta	incorrecta
1. Nando fue con Teresa a casa de Sofi.		
2. La casa de Sofi tiene una cancha de tenis.		
3. Teresa y Sofi jugaron tenis.		
4. Jugaron en una cancha en un parque.		
5. Nadaron también.		
6. Nadaron en una piscina en el parque.		

Gramática

El pretérito

1. Review the forms of the preterite of regular verbs.

	nadar	comer	subir
yo	nadé	comí	subí
tú	nadaste	comiste	subiste
Ud., él, ella	nadó	comió	subió
nosotros(as)	nadamos	comimos	subimos
vosotros(as)	*nadasteis*	*comisteis*	*subisteis*
Uds., ellos, ellas	nadaron	comieron	subieron

Note that **-er** and **-ir** verbs have the same endings in the preterite.

2. The forms of the verbs **ir** and **ser** are the same in the preterite. The meaning is made clear by the context of the sentence.

ir, ser			
yo	fui	nosotros(as)	fuimos
tú	fuiste	*vosotros(as)*	*fuisteis*
Ud., él, ella	fue	Uds., ellos, ellas	fueron

InfoGap For more practice with the preterite, do Activity R on page SR2 at the end of this book.

3. The preterite is used to express an event or action that began and ended at a definite time in the past.

> **Ellos pasaron el verano pasado en México.**
> **Fueron a Acapulco.**

4. Note the forms of the verbs **ver** and **dar**.

VER	vi	viste	vio	vimos	*visteis*	vieron
DAR	di	diste	dio	dimos	*disteis*	dieron

CULTURA

Ellos pasaron el verano pasado en México y fueron a la Ciudad de México.

VIDEO Want help with the preterite? Watch **Gramática en vivo.**

Práctica

Materias	Calificaciones
Sociedad, Cultura y Religión	No Evaluable
Educación Física	7
Lengua Castellana y Literatura	6
Filosofía	7
Inglés	10
Historia Contemporánea	5
Matemáticas	1
Latín	9
Economía	5

Tlf: 917414653

Ministerio de Educación y Cultura

Grupo **B1D**

Alumno: Tomás García

HABLAR • ESCRIBIR

1 Personaliza. Da respuestas personales.

1. ¿Fuiste a la escuela ayer?
2. ¿A qué hora llegaste a la escuela?
3. ¿Hablaste con el/la profesor(a) de español?
4. ¿Tomaste un examen?
5. ¿En qué curso tomaste el examen?
6. ¿Saliste bien en el examen?
7. ¿Comiste en la cafetería de la escuela?
8. ¿A qué hora volviste a casa?

HABLAR • ESCRIBIR

2 Contesta.

1. ¿Fuiste al cine ayer?
   ¿Viste una película?
   ¿Tomaste un refresco en el cine?
2. ¿Salieron ustedes anoche?
   ¿Fueron a una fiesta?
   ¿Bailaron y cantaron durante la fiesta?
3. ¿Esquió Sandra?
   ¿Subió la montaña en el telesilla?
   ¿Bajó la pista para expertos?
4. ¿Pasaron los amigos el fin de semana en la playa?
   ¿Te escribieron una tarjeta postal?
   ¿Nadaron y esquiaron en el agua?

Comunicación

3 Tell what you and your friends did last Friday night.

4 Tell what you did last night.

5 Tell what you or you and your family or friends did during your last vacation.

CULTURA

Una escuela de esquí y snowboard en la estación de esquí en Cerro Catedral en Bariloche, Argentina

Más práctica
■ Workbook, pp. R21–R22
● StudentWorks™ Plus

Los pronombres de complemento

1. The object pronouns **me, te,** and **nos** can be either direct or indirect objects. Note that the object pronoun precedes the conjugated verb.

DIRECT

Él me miró.

¿Te invitó Carlos?

Ella nos vio.

INDIRECT

Él me habló por teléfono.

¿Te dio una invitación?

Mónica nos envió algo.

2. Lo, los, la, and **las** function as direct objects only. They can replace either persons or things.

Pablo compró el boleto.   **Pablo lo compró.**

Pablo compró los boletos.   **Pablo los compró.**

Teresa compró la raqueta.   **Teresa la compró.**

Teresa compró las raquetas.   **Teresa las compró.**

Yo vi a los muchachos.   **Yo los vi.**

3. Le and **les** function as indirect objects only.

Yo le escribí un correo electrónico (a él, a ella, a usted).

Yo les escribí (a ellos, a ellas, a ustedes).

Práctica

HABLAR

6 Contesta.

1. ¿Fuiste al médico?
2. ¿Te habló el médico?
3. ¿Te examinó?
4. ¿Te dio una diagnosis?
5. ¿Te recetó medicina?

ESCUCHAR • HABLAR

7 Sigue el modelo.

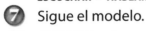

MODELO   **la toalla →**

Aquí la tienes.

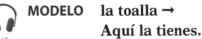

1. el anorak
2. la crema bronceadora
3. el traje de baño
4. los anteojos de sol
5. los boletos para el telesilla
6. las raquetas

CULTURA

Una farmacia en Baños, Ecuador

LEER • ESCRIBIR

8 Completa con **le, lo** o **la.**

Pepe está en el consultorio del médico. Pepe __1__ explica al médico que __2__ duele el estómago. El médico __3__ examina. __4__ da una receta. En la farmacia el farmacéutico __5__ lee y __6__ da los medicamentos a Pepe.

En avión

Aquí y Allí

Vamos a comparar Los medios de transporte más importantes varían de una región del mundo a otra. En España, por ejemplo, el servicio de trenes es excelente. No lo es en Latinoamérica donde mucha gente toma un autobús para ir de un lugar a otro. Pero vas a aprender por qué el avión es el medio de transporte más importante. Donde tú vives, ¿qué medios de transporte públicos hay? ¿Tienen muchos usuarios?

◀ El avión está despegando de la pista del aeropuerto de la Romana en la República Dominicana.

Objetivos

You will:

- talk about packing for a trip and getting to the airport
- tell what you do at the airport
- talk about being on an airplane
- discuss air travel in South America

You will use:

- verbs that have **g** in the **yo** form of the present tense
- the present progressive tense

¡PARE!
BARRERA AUTOMÁTIC
CARROS DE GOLF SOLA
DESDE ESTE PU

QuickPass

Go to glencoe.com
For: **Online book**
Web code: **ASD7837c1**

Introducción al tema
En avión

Look at these photographs to acquaint yourself with the theme of this chapter. Air travel is the most important means of transportation in the world today. As you learn to use your Spanish in an airport and on an airplane, you will also learn why air travel is so extremely important in Latin America.

España ▶
Aquí vemos una terminal nueva en el aeropuerto internacional de Barajas, el aeropuerto que sirve a Madrid.

DEPARTING TO	AIRLINE	FLIGHT	GATE	TIME
CARACAS	American	935	C7	12:30P
HOUSTON-IAH	American	1391	C3	12:07P
SANTO DOMINGO	American	783	C5	1:20P
KEY WEST	American	4987		2:00P
BALTIMORE	American	1060	C7	4:19P
QUITO	American	967	C5	4:30P
INDIANAPOLIS, IN	American	1682	C9	6:21P
SAN JOSE, C.R.	American	2171	C7	6:24P

◄ Estados Unidos
Aquí vemos una pantalla de salidas. ¿Para qué ciudades latinoamericanas hay vuelos?

Chile **El agente de la línea aérea está revisando los documentos de una pasajera que está tomando un vuelo internacional.** ▼

▲ **Perú** El avión está en el aeropuerto de Arequipa en el sur de Perú. En el fondo vemos los Andes.

Argentina ▲
Los pasajeros tienen que esperar en fila delante del mostrador de una línea aérea en el aeropuerto de Ezeiza en Buenos Aires.

▲ **República Dominicana** Es el aeropuerto en Santo Domingo, la República Dominicana. Podemos ver también la torre de control.

México ▶
Los pasajeros están pasando por el control de seguridad en León, México.

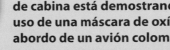

◀ **Colombia** La asistenta de cabina está demostrando el uso de una máscara de oxígeno abordo de un avión colombiano.

Antes de salir para el aeropuerto

¿Te acuerdas?

You will want to be able to discuss packing a suitcase. To review clothing, see Repaso E on page R38.

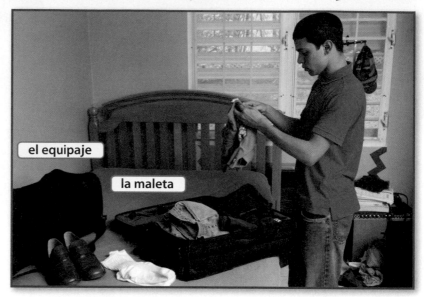

el equipaje

la maleta

Juan va a hacer un viaje.
Antes hace la maleta.
¿Qué pone en la maleta?

Pone la ropa que necesita para el viaje.

Al aeropuerto

el baúl, la maletera

el taxi

Juan sale para el aeropuerto en taxi.
Trae su equipaje.

Pone su equipaje en la maletera del taxi.
El taxista lo ayuda con su equipaje.

En el aeropuerto

Nueva Generación de asientos de clase ejecutiva en el 767

el boleto (billete) electrónico

el agente

el mostrador

¡Así se dice!

When you are in a crowded area and you want to get by someone, you can politely say **¡Con permiso!**

En otras partes

In addition to **la tarjeta de embarque** you will also hear **la tarjeta de abordar** and **el pasabordo.**

la tarjeta de embarque

AEROMEXICO
aeromexico.com

el nombre del pasajero

NOMBRE/NAME
PAYTI/ANDREWMR
ORIGEN/ORIGIN
MEXICO CITY
DESTINO/DESTINATION
OAXACA

el número del vuelo

VUELO/FLIGHT   CLASE   FECHA/DATE
AM 2046   L   04JUNO
SALA/GATE HORA/TIME ASIENTO/SEA
-7A-   1140
NON-SMOKING   5C
CONTROL 28

FTKT 704

la hora de salida

el número del asiento

Su tarjeta de embarque sale de un distribuidor automático.

Juan está en el mostrador de la línea aérea.
Está haciendo un viaje internacional en avión.
Tiene que facturar su equipaje.
Pero no tiene que facturar su equipaje de mano.

ESCUCHAR

1 Escucha las frases. Parea cada frase con el dibujo que describe.

a.

b.

c.

d.

e.

f.

HABLAR • ESCRIBIR

2 Contesta sobre un viaje que Teresa va a hacer a México.

1. ¿Hace Teresa un viaje a México?
2. Antes de hacer su viaje, ¿qué pone en la maleta?
3. ¿Para dónde sale Teresa para empezar su viaje?
4. ¿Cómo va al aeropuerto?
5. ¿Quién la ayuda con su equipaje?
6. ¿Dónde lo pone?

EXPANSIÓN

Ahora, sin mirar las preguntas, relata toda la información en tus propias palabras. Si no recuerdas algo, un(a) compañero(a) te puede ayudar.

LEER • ESCRIBIR

3 Elisa está en el aeropuerto. Va a las Galápagos. Completa con una palabra apropiada.

1. En el aeropuerto Elisa tiene que _____ su equipaje.
2. Va al mostrador de la _____.
3. Elisa tiene un _____ electrónico.
4. El agente le da su _____ para poder abordar el avión.

CULTURA

La señora está en el mostrador de la línea aérea. Va a volar a México.

CULTURA

Una vista de las islas Galápagos, Ecuador

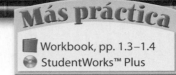
LEER • ESCRIBIR

4 Completa. Escoge del **banco de palabras.**

pone	sale	trae	hace

1. Eduardo _____ un viaje a España.
2. Él _____ su ropa en la maleta.
3. Eduardo no _____ mucho equipaje.
4. _____ solamente una maleta y una mochila.
5. _____ el equipaje en la maletera del taxi.
6. _____ para el aeropuerto.
7. Su vuelo para España _____ a las ocho y media de la tarde.

InfoGap For more practice using your new vocabulary, do Activity 1 on page SR3 at the end of the book.

CULTURA

El famoso acueducto romano de Segovia, España, construido a fines del primer siglo después de Cristo

HABLAR • ESCRIBIR

5 Prepara una pregunta sobre cada frase en la Actividad 4. Usa las siguientes palabras.

¿quién?   ¿cuándo?
¿adónde?   ¿qué?   ¿dónde?

LEER • ESCRIBIR

6 Completa la tarjeta de embarque.

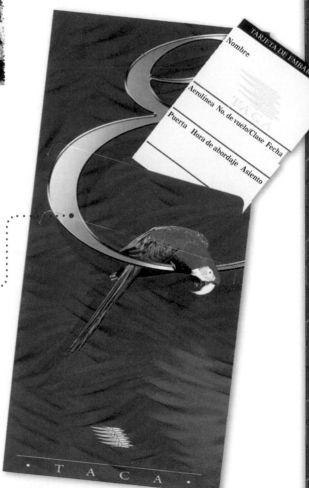

7

Unscramble the letters to reveal words related to airplane travel.

1. a l t a m e
2. n o t i s e a
3. j a q u e p i e
4. r a d o r o m t s
5. s o a r j e p a

En el control de seguridad

hacer cola

el pasaporte

Los pasajeros están pasando por el control de seguridad.
Su equipaje de mano tiene que pasar por el control de seguridad.
Hay que mostrar una forma de identidad con una fotografía.

En la puerta de salida

¡Así se dice!

- **Hay que** is a useful expression that means **Es necesario.**
- **A veces** and **de vez en cuando** are expressions to tell what you do every so often.

La pasajera está en la puerta de salida.
Está esperando la salida de su vuelo.
El avión está saliendo a tiempo. No sale tarde.
No hay un retraso (una demora).
Ella va a embarcar (abordar) dentro de poco.

Abordo del avión

el compartimiento superior

el servicio

la ventanilla

el asistente de vuelo

el pasillo

abrochados

el asiento

el cinturón de seguridad

Los pasajeros tienen que poner su equipaje de mano en el compartimiento superior o debajo del asiento.

Durante el despegue y el aterrizaje, los pasajeros tienen que tener sus cinturones abrochados.

la señal de no fumar

la máscara de oxígeno

el despegue

El avión está despegando.
Está despegando con destino a Madrid.
El avión acaba de despegar de la pista.

el aterrizaje

El avión está aterrizando.
Es un vuelo (procedente) de Lima.

ESCUCHAR • HABLAR • ESCRIBIR

1 Personaliza. Da respuestas personales.

1. ¿Tomas un vuelo de vez en cuando?
2. ¿Te gusta volar?
3. ¿Quieres tomar un vuelo un día?
4. ¿Quieres hacer un viaje nacional o internacional?
5. ¿Adónde quieres ir?
6. ¿Hay un aeropuerto cerca de tu casa? ¿Cuál?
7. ¿Es un aeropuerto nacional o internacional?
8. Si tienes que tomar un vuelo, ¿prefieres un asiento en el pasillo o en la ventanilla?

LEER

2 Escoge la palabra apropiada.

1. Los pasajeros hacen cola en (el asiento, la puerta) de salida.
2. Están (esperando, haciendo) la salida del vuelo.
3. El avión sale con un retraso de cinco minutos. Sale (tarde, a tiempo).
4. Los pasajeros toman su (pasillo, asiento) en el avión.
5. El avión despega de la (cola, pista).
6. Un vuelo (procedente de, con destino a) Panamá llega ahora.

La gente está llegando al aeropuerto de Ixtapa-Zihuatanejo en la costa del Pacífico en México.

LEER

3 Verifica. ¿Sí o no?

1. Los pasajeros tienen que pasar por el control de seguridad abordo del avión.
2. Los pasajeros esperan la salida de su vuelo en la puerta de salida.
3. Los pasajeros embarcan después del aterrizaje.
4. Los pasajeros desembarcan después del aterrizaje.
5. Los pasajeros pueden poner su equipaje en el pasillo.
6. Los pasajeros tienen que tener sus cinturones de seguridad abrochados durante el despegue y el aterrizaje.
7. Un vuelo que sale tarde sale a tiempo.
8. En una cola o fila hay mucha gente.

Comunicación

4 Habla con un(a) compañero(a). Discutan todo lo que necesitan si hacen un viaje internacional.

LEER • ESCRIBIR

5 Pon las actividades en orden.

Llega al aeropuerto.

Toma su asiento.

Pone su ropa en la maleta.

Factura su equipaje y toma su tarjeta de embarque.

Sale de casa para ir al aeropuerto.

Espera el avión en la puerta de salida.

Pone su equipaje en la maletera del taxi.

Pasa por el control de seguridad.

Embarca el avión.

El avión despega.

CULTURA

El mostrador de una línea aérea centroamericana en el aeropuerto de la Ciudad de Guatemala. Es de noche y hay muy poca gente.

Comunicación

6 You are flying to Mexico to visit your key pal. You have never flown before. Once on the plane, you have some questions for the flight attendant (your partner) about the flight and where to put your things. Take turns.

7 **¡Manos a la obra!** Make up a name for a Spanish airline. Create a fun and colorful travel poster advertising the airline and where it flies. See how many new words you can include.

QuickPass

Go to glencoe.com
For: Grammar practice
Web code: ASD7837c1

Presente de **hacer**, **poner**, **traer**, **salir**

Nota

The verbs **oír** and **caer** *(to fall)*
also have a **g** in the **yo** form.
oigo   **caigo**

1. The verbs **hacer** *(to do, to make)*, **poner** *(to put, to place)*,
traer *(to bring)*, and **salir** *(to leave)* have an irregular **yo**
form. The **yo** form has a **g**. All the other forms are regular.

	hacer	poner	traer	salir
yo	hago	pongo	traigo	salgo
tú	haces	pones	traes	sales
Ud., él, ella	hace	pone	trae	sale
nosotros(as)	hacemos	ponemos	traemos	salimos
vosotros(as)	hacéis	ponéis	traéis	salís
Uds., ellos, ellas	hacen	ponen	traen	salen

2. Remember that the verb **tener** has a **g** in the **yo** form. The
verb **venir** *(to come)* follows the same pattern. Note the **g**
and the stem change.

venir			
yo	vengo	nosotros(as)	venimos
tú	vienes	vosotros(as)	venís
Ud., él, ella	viene	Uds., ellos, ellas	vienen

CULTURA

Las señoritas tienen equipaje
porque van a hacer un viaje de
Puerto Rico a Nueva York. Salen
pronto pero antes toman un
refresco en un café en San Juan.

Más práctica

■ Workbook, pp. 1.7–1.8

● StudentWorks™ Plus

Práctica

HABLAR • ESCRIBIR

1 Imagina que vas a hacer un viaje a Ecuador.
Contesta las preguntas.

1. ¿Haces un viaje?
2. ¿Haces un viaje a Ecuador?
3. ¿Haces el viaje con un grupo de tu escuela?
4. ¿Sales para el aeropuerto con tus padres?
5. ¿Traes mucho equipaje?
6. ¿Traes tu cámara digital?
7. ¿Pones tu boleto y tu pasaporte en tu mochila?

EXPANSIÓN

Ahora, sin mirar las preguntas, relata toda la información
en tus propias palabras. Si no recuerdas algo, un(a)
compañero(a) te puede ayudar.

HABLAR • ESCRIBIR

2 Personaliza. Da respuestas personales.

Cuando haces un viaje a la playa donde hace calor,
¿qué pones en la maleta? Y cuando haces un viaje
a una estación de esquí, ¿qué pones en la maleta?

CULTURA

La Plaza de Armas en el casco antiguo
de Quito, Ecuador

ESCUCHAR • HABLAR • ESCRIBIR

3 Sigue el modelo. Presta atención a las terminaciones
-emos, -imos.

MODELO   Ellos hacen un viaje. →
           **Sí, ellos hacen un viaje y nosotros
           también hacemos un viaje.**

1. Ellos hacen un viaje a España.
2. Ellos salen para el aeropuerto.
3. Ellos traen mucho equipaje.
4. Ellos salen en el mismo vuelo.
5. Ellos vienen al aeropuerto en autobús.

CULTURA

Los pasajeros acaban de llegar
al aeropuerto de Barcelona y
toman un taxi para ir al centro
de la ciudad. Hay una fila de taxis
bastante larga, ¿no?

LEER • ESCRIBIR

4 Completa con la forma correcta del presente del verbo. Ahora tienes que usar todas las formas.

    Yo __1__ (hacer) un viaje a Palma. Palma __2__ (estar) en la isla de Mallorca en el Mediterráneo. __3__ (Estar) al este de España no muy lejos de Barcelona. Mi amiga Luisa __4__ (hacer) el viaje también. Nosotros __5__ (hacer) el viaje en avión hasta Barcelona y luego __6__ (ir) en barco, un ferry, desde Barcelona a Palma. Claro que podemos __7__ (hacer) el viaje en avión pero preferimos tomar el barco.

    —¡Ay, Luisa! Pero tú __8__ (traer) mucho equipaje.

    —No, yo no __9__ (traer) mucho. __10__ (Tener) solo dos maletas. Tú exageras. Tú también __11__ (venir) con mucho equipaje.

    —¡Oye! ¿A qué hora __12__ (salir) nuestro vuelo para Barcelona?

    —No __13__ (salir) hasta las seis y media. Nosotros __14__ (tener) mucho tiempo.

    —¡Vamos ya! ¡Con permiso, señora!

CULTURA

Una playa en Palma de Mallorca. Mallorca es una de las islas Baleares en el mar Mediterráneo.

Comunicación

5 Tell a friend all the things you do the day of a flight from packing your suitcase to boarding the plane. Your friend will then ask you questions.

HABLAR

6 **Juego** Play this **Diez preguntas** game with a partner. Think of something related to airline travel for your partner to guess. If your partner guesses in ten questions or less, he or she wins. Take turns.

VIDEO To see a humorous experience at an airport, watch **Diálogo en vivo.**

El presente progresivo

1. You use the present progressive tense in Spanish to express an action in progress, an action that is currently taking place.

2. To form the present progressive you use the verb **estar** and the present participle. Study the forms of the present participle.

INFINITIVE	hablar	comer	vivir	hacer	salir
STEM	habl-	com-	viv-	hac-	sal-
PARTICIPLE	hablando	comiendo	viviendo	haciendo	saliendo

The verbs **leer, traer, oír,** and **caer** have a **y.**

leyendo	trayendo	oyendo	cayendo

3. Study the following examples of the present progressive.

José está haciendo un viaje a México.
Ahora está esperando la salida de su vuelo.
José está mirando su tarjeta de embarque.

Una pantalla de llegadas y salidas en el aeropuerto de la Ciudad de Guatemala. Hace buen tiempo hoy y la mayoría de los vuelos salen a tiempo. ¡Qué suerte para todos!

Práctica

HABLAR

7 Con un(a) compañero(a), practica la conversación en voz alta. Presta atención a todos los verbos en el tiempo progresivo.

Sandra, ¡qué sorpresa! ¿Qué estás haciendo aquí en el aeropuerto?

Estoy esperando a mi padre. Está volviendo de Puerto Rico. ¿Y tú, Julia? ¿Qué estás haciendo aquí?

Pues, estoy viajando a Costa Rica.

¡A Costa Rica! ¡Qué suerte tienes!

Sí, toda mi familia está haciendo el viaje para visitar a nuestros abuelos.

No, no. Son de aquí pero ahora están viviendo en Costa Rica. Les gusta mucho.

Ah, tus abuelos son de Costa Rica.

HABLAR • ESCRIBIR

8 Contesta según la conversación.

1. ¿Por qué está en el aeropuerto Sandra?
2. ¿De dónde está volviendo el padre de Sandra?
3. Y, ¿para dónde está saliendo Julia?
4. ¿Quién está viajando con ella?
5. ¿A quiénes van a visitar?
6. ¿Qué están haciendo sus abuelos en Costa Rica?

EXPANSIÓN

Ahora, sin mirar las preguntas, relata toda la información en tus propias palabras. Si no recuerdas algo, un(a) compañero(a) te puede ayudar.

GeoVistas

To learn more about Costa Rica, take a tour on pages SH52–SH53.

HABLAR • ESCRIBIR

9 Contesta según se indica.

1. ¿Adónde están llegando los pasajeros? (al aeropuerto)
2. ¿Cómo están llegando? (en taxi)
3. ¿Adónde están viajando? (a Argentina en la América del Sur)
4. ¿Cómo están haciendo el viaje? (en avión)
5. ¿Dónde están facturando el equipaje? (en el mostrador de la línea aérea)
6. ¿Qué está mirando el agente? (los boletos y los pasaportes)
7. ¿De qué puerta están saliendo los pasajeros para Buenos Aires? (número siete)
8. ¿Qué están abordando? (el avión)

Comunicación

10 Use the conversation between Julia and Sandra as a guide to role-play a conversation between two friends who run into each other at an airport.

CULTURA

La Casa Rosada en Buenos Aires. Es aquí donde tiene el presidente argentino sus oficinas.

HABLAR • ESCRIBIR

11 Forma frases según el modelo. Escoge palabras del **banco de palabras.**

MODELO   viajar →
Sí, estoy viajando.
No, no estoy viajando.

hablar español	usar mi móvil	hacer una tarea
leer una novela	estudiar	jugar fútbol
aprender mucho	salir ahora	comer

HABLAR

12 **Juego** Form small groups. Take turns pantomiming activities that might take place at an airport or on an airplane. The others will guess what you're doing, using the present progressive.

HABLAR • ESCRIBIR

13 Describe lo que ves en los dibujos. Usa el presente progresivo.

PRONUNCIACIÓN

La consonante r

When a word begins with **r** (initial position), the **r** is trilled in Spanish. Within a word, this trilled **r** sound is spelled **rr**. The Spanish trilled **r** sound does not exist in English. Repeat the following.

ra	re	ri	ro	ru
rápido	receta	Ricardo	Roberto	Rubén
raqueta	red	aterriza	rojo	rubio
párrafo	corre	río	perro	

The sound for a single **r** within a word (medial position) does not exist in English either. It is trilled less than the initial **r** or **rr.** Repeat the following.

ra	re	ri	ro	ru
verano	arena	boletería	número	Perú
maletera	quiere	consultorio	pasajero	Aruba
para		periódico	cinturón	

Dictado

Pronounce the following sentences carefully. Then write them to prepare for a dictation.

> **El perro de Rubén corre en la arena.**
> **El avión para Puerto Rico aterriza con un retraso de una hora.**
> **El pasajero corre rápido por el aeropuerto.**
> **Ricardo pone su raqueta en la maletera del carro.**

Refrán

Can you guess what the following proverb means?

Mal hace quien nada hace.

¡Bravo!

You have now learned all the new vocabulary and grammar in this chapter. Continue to use and practice all that you know while learning more cultural information. ¡Vamos!

CULTURA

El avión está aterrizando en el aeropuerto de Buenos Aires, Argentina.

QuickPass

Go to glencoe.com
For: **Conversation practice**
Web code: ASD7837c1

En el aeropuerto

Susana	¡Oye, Pedro! Está saliendo nuestro vuelo.
Pedro	Sí, ¡vamos ya! Tenemos que pasar por el control de seguridad y siempre hay una cola larga.
Susana	¿Tienes nuestras tarjetas de embarque?
Pedro	Sí, sí. Las tengo. ¿Necesitas ayuda con tu equipaje de mano?
Susana	No, no traigo mucho. Lo puedo llevar. ¿De qué puerta salimos?
Pedro	De la puerta 11. ¿A qué hora empieza el embarque?
Susana	Ahora mismo. ¡Vamos!

¿Comprendes?

A Contesta según la información en la conversación.

1. ¿Dónde están Pedro y Susana?
2. ¿Qué están anunciando?
3. ¿Ya pasaron por el control de seguridad Pedro y Susana?
4. ¿Qué hay siempre en el control de seguridad?
5. ¿Quién tiene las tarjetas de embarque?
6. ¿De qué puerta de salida salen?
7. ¿Está empezando el embarque?

B **Resumiendo** Relata toda la información en la conversación en tus propias palabras.

C **Prediciendo** ¿Piensas que Susana y Pedro van a perder su vuelo? ¿Por qué contestas que sí o que no?

CULTURA

Una vista panorámica de San Juan de Puerto Rico desde el Viejo San Juan hasta el Condado

READING STRATEGY

Identifying the main idea It is important to identify the main idea of a reading. Topic sentences—usually the first sentence in a paragraph—help you determine the main idea of a reading.

Antes de leer

Scan the reading to find the most important idea in each section. Look for topic sentences.

✔ Reading Check

¿Cuál es un medio de transporte muy importante en Sudamérica?

✔ Reading Check

¿Dónde es muy densa la vegetación? ¿En las montañas o en las selvas?

Durante la lectura

Note each topic sentence. Think about the one idea that all the sentences and sections are about.

Después de leer

What was the main idea of the reading and of each section? What do you think was the author's purpose here?

El avión en la América del Sur

El continente sudamericano es vasto. Las distancias entre ciudades son largas. Por eso el avión es un medio de transporte importante. A veces es imposible viajar por tierra[1] de un lugar a otro. ¿Por qué?

Montañas Una gran parte del oeste del continente es montañosa. Los altos picos nevados de los Andes parecen tocar el cielo[2]. Unas ciudades como Bogotá, Quito y La Paz están en los Andes. Y claro que hay también pequeños pueblos aislados en las montañas.

Selvas Al este de los Andes en Colombia, Ecuador, Perú, Bolivia y Brasil hay grandes selvas tropicales del río Amazonas. En las selvas la vegetación es muy densa y una gran parte de la cuenca[3] amazónica es inhóspita e impenetrable.

Desiertos La región a lo largo de la costa desde Perú hasta el centro de Chile es desierto. El Atacama en Chile es el desierto más árido (seco) del mundo—una región de arena y rocas (piedras).

Día y noche los aviones sobrevuelan los picos, selvas y desiertos para enlazar[4] las ciudades y pueblos de Sudamérica.

[1]por tierra   *by land*
[2]cielo   *sky*
[3]cuenca   *basin*
[4]enlazar   *connect*

CULTURA
Un pueblo aislado en los Andes de Venezuela

¿Comprendes?

Más práctica

■ Workbook, pp. 1.10–1.12
◉ StudentWorks™ Plus

A **Recordando hechos** Contesta.

1. ¿Qué montañas corren del norte al sur a lo largo del océano Pacífico en la América del Sur?
2. ¿Qué hay al este de los Andes?
3. ¿Qué región de Sudamérica es desierto?

B **Describiendo** Describe.

1. los picos andinos
2. las selvas tropicales
3. el desierto

C **Analizando** Contesta.

1. ¿Por qué es el avión un medio de transporte muy importante?
2. En muchas regiones de Sudamérica, ¿por qué es difícil viajar por tierra?

CULTURA

Un pico nevado en el desierto de Atacama en Chile

D **Categorizando** Completa la tabla de abajo. Luego, relata la información en la tabla en tus propias palabras.

	a lo largo de la costa peruana y chilena	al este de las montañas	en las montañas
desiertos			
picos cubiertos de nieve			
selvas tropicales			
la cuenca amazónica			
vegetación densa			
tierra árida			
Bogotá, Quito, La Paz			

Un viaje interesante 🎧♻️

Vas a leer sobre un misterio famoso que hay en Perú. ¿Te gustan los misterios? ¿Hay algún misterio donde vives?

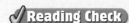

Reading Check

¿Qué son las líneas de Nazca?

Un vuelo interestante Si quieres hacer un viaje interesante en avión tienes que sobrevolar las líneas de Nazca. ¿Qué son las líneas de Nazca? Pues, en el desierto árido del sur de Perú hay una serie de dibujos o figuras misteriosas. Hay figuras geométricas—rectángulos, triángulos y líneas paralelas. Hay también representaciones perfectas de varios animales. A pesar de[1] muchas investigaciones el origen de las líneas o figuras que tienen más de 1.500 años queda[2] un misterio.

Y son tan grandes que la única manera de ver las figuras es tomar un vuelo. Las avionetas salen de Lima o del aeropuerto de la pequeña ciudad de Ica, muy cerca de las figuras.

[1]A pesar de   *In spite of*   [2]queda   *remains*

CULTURA
Las líneas de Nazca

¿Comprendes?

Escoge o completa.

1. Las líneas de Nazca están _____.
   - a. en el pico de una montaña
   - b. en una selva
   - c. en un desierto

2. ¿Qué son las líneas?
   - a. animales
   - b. figuras misteriosas
   - c. solamente figuras geométricas

3. El origen de las líneas de Nazca es _____.

4. ¿Por qué es necesario ver las líneas de un avión?
   - a. porque hay avionetas que salen de Ica y Lima
   - b. porque están en un desierto
   - c. porque son tan inmensas

5. Un avión pequeño es _____.

CULTURA

Recientemente los arqueólogos descubrieron otras figuras delineadas en el costado rocoso no muy lejos de Nazca. Estas figuras son de la civilización de los paracas y son anteriores a las famosas líneas de Nazca.

CULTURA

Una avioneta que sobrevuela las líneas de Nazca

Vocabulario

 1 **Completa.**

1–2. El agente trabaja en el ____ de la línea aérea en el ____.

3. La tarjeta de embarque indica el número del ____ y el número del asiento del pasajero.

4. Antes de ir a la puerta de salida los pasajeros tienen que pasar por el ____ donde inspeccionan su equipaje de mano.

5. El avión no sale a tiempo. Sale ____.

6. Los pasajeros tienen que ____ una forma de identidad.

7. Abordo del avión, hay que poner su equipaje en el ____.

8. Estamos esperando nuestro vuelo en la ____.

9. Antes de facturar mi equipaje, tomo mi tarjeta de embarque del ____.

10. Estás abordo del avión. ¿Sabes el número de tu ____?

To review **Vocabulario 1** and **Vocabulario 2,** turn to pages 4–5 and 8–9.

 2 **Identifica.**

 11.

 12.

 13.

 14.

 15.

Gramática

3 **Contesta.**

16. ¿Haces un viaje?

17. ¿Vienes en junio para mi cumpleaños?

18. ¿Qué pones en tu maleta o mochila?

19. ¿A qué hora sales?

20. ¿Traes mucho equipaje?

To review verbs with a **g** in the **yo** form, turn to page 12.

4 **Completa en el presente.**

21. Ellos _____ mañana. (venir)

22. Nosotros _____ mucho trabajo. (hacer)

23. José _____ su mochila debajo del asiento. (poner)

24. Yo lo _____. (oír)

25. ¿Tú _____ tu equipaje de mano? (traer)

26. Señor, ¿usted _____ esta mañana o esta tarde? (salir)

27. Nosotros _____ al aeropuerto con nuestros padres. (venir)

To review **el presente progresivo,** turn to page 15.

5 **Escribe en el presente progresivo.**

28. El avión despega.

29. Nosotros hacemos cola.

30. Ellos salen a tiempo.

31. Los pasajeros esperan en la puerta de salida.

32. Yo leo mi libro favorito.

33. Juan y Marisol, ¡ustedes nadan en el mar!

34. Tú vives cerca de mi casa ahora.

35. ¿Qué oyen tus primos?

Cultura

CULTURA

La canoa es el medio de transporte más importante de la selva tropical de Latinoamérica. Aquí la madre y su hija van a Iquitos en la selva peruana.

6 **Escoge.**

36. El continente sudamericano es _____.

   a. pequeño   **b.** alto   **c.** inmenso

37. Hay selvas tropicales en _____.

   a. las montañas   **b.** el desierto   **c.** la cuenca amazónica

38. El Amazonas es _____.

   a. un pico andino   **b.** un río   **c.** un desierto

To review this cultural information, turn to pages 22–23.

7 **Contesta.**

39. ¿Por qué es difícil viajar por tierra en muchas partes de la América del Sur?

40. ¿Cuáles son unas características geográficas de la América del Sur?

Prepárate para el examen
Practice for oral proficiency

1 Preparar para un viaje

✓ *Tell about packing for a trip*

You're getting ready to leave on a trip. Tell what you're going to pack. Will you use a suitcase, carry-on, or backpack? Does the weather where you're going influence what you are going to pack?

2 En el mostrador de la línea aérea

✓ *Converse with a ticket agent*

You are at the ticket counter at the airport. You are talking with the ticket agent (your partner). You want to find out details about the flight and check your luggage. The ticket agent asks for confirmation of your e-ticket and passport and answers any questions you have.

3 Un billete para Madrid

✓ *Buy an airplane ticket*

Work with a classmate. You want to fly with your family from somewhere in the United States to Madrid and you will be returning from Barcelona. Call the airline to get a reservation. Your classmate will be the reservation agent. Before you call, think about all the information you will need to provide or get from the airline agent: date of departure, departure time, arrival time in Madrid, flight number, and price.

4 ¿Quién está haciendo qué?

✓ *Tell what people are doing in your classroom*

Who's doing what? Look around you and tell what everyone is doing.

CULTURA

La profesora está enseñando y los alumnos están prestando atención en una clase de matemáticas en San Juan, Puerto Rico.

5 El continente sudamericano

✓ *Tell about travel in South America*

Work in small groups. Your aunt and uncle's family is thinking about traveling around South America. You have already been there. Tell them why it can be difficult to travel from one place to another by land. They will ask you questions.

Prepárate para el examen
✓ Practice for written proficiency

Tarea

Write a letter to a service organization interested in international relations. Your goal is to win an all-expense-paid trip to spend two weeks living with a Spanish-speaking family in a country of your choice.

Writing Strategy

Answering an essay question Many types of applications contain or expect you to answer questions concerning your qualifications or reasons for applying. This requires you to write an essay that convinces that you are the right person.

❶ Prewrite

- Think of your overall goal—to convince all concerned why you are the right person to be sent to a foreign country.

- Look at the list of some types of questions you may have to answer. **¿Qué quieres visitar? ¿Por qué quieres ir allí? ¿Qué esperas hacer, ver o aprender allí? ¿Cómo quieres viajar? ¿Qué tipo de persona eres? ¿Qué estás haciendo ahora?**

- Think of other information the organization may want to know about you.

❷ Write

You really want to go on this trip, so be sure to plan your essay carefully.

- Write an introduction that will make the organization want to find out more about you.

- Start a new paragraph for the answer to each question.

- When you finish writing, check your work. Check spelling, grammar, and verb endings. Make sure your sentences are complete and understandable.

- Read over your work again to make sure all errors are corrected and to make sure that you have effectively communicated your message to the organization.

Evaluate

Don't forget that your teacher will evaluate you on your organization, use of vocabulary and grammar, and on how clear, complete, and convincing your essay is.

Repaso del Capítulo 1

Gramática

- ### Presente de hacer, poner, traer, salir *(page 12)*

  The verbs **hacer, poner, traer, salir,** and **oír** have a **g** in the **yo** form. All other forms are regular. Review the following forms.

  | yo | ha**go** | pon**go** | trai**go** | sal**go** | oi**go** |

  Venir has a **g** in the **yo** form as well as a stem change just like the verb **tener,** which you have already learned.

venir	
ven**go**	venimos
vienes	*venís*
viene	vienen

- ### El presente progresivo *(page 15)*

  The present progressive expresses an action that is taking place at the moment. It is formed with the verb **estar** and the present participle. Review the following forms.

estoy				
estás				
está	viajando	comiendo	saliendo	leyendo
estamos				
estáis				
están				

CULTURA

La señorita está escuchando música en su MP3 mientras regresa a casa después de un viaje.

Vocabulario

Leaving for a trip

el equipaje de mano	el/la taxista	hacer
la maleta	la maletera, el baúl	un viaje
el taxi	poner	la maleta

Describing airport activities

el aeropuerto	el distribuidor	el número del vuelo	pasar por el control
el avión	automático	la hora de salida	de seguridad
el/la agente	la tarjeta de	la hora de embarque	hacer cola
el mostrador	embarque	el número del asiento	mostrar
la línea aérea	el pasaporte	la forma de identidad	esperar
el boleto, el billete	el nombre	la puerta de salida	embarcar, abordar
(electrónico)	el/la pasajero(a)	facturar el equipaje	

Describing a flight

el/la asistente(a)	la máscara de	un retraso, una	internacional
de vuelo	oxígeno	demora	abordo
el asiento	el cinturón de	el despegue	tarde
el pasillo	seguridad	el aterrizaje	a tiempo
la ventanilla	la señal de no fumar	la pista	con destino a
el compartimiento	el servicio	despegar	procedente de
superior		aterrizar	

Other useful words and expressions

hay que	dentro de poco	¡Con permiso!
a veces	debajo de	abrochado(a)
de vez en cuando		

Repaso cumulativo

Repasa lo que ya has aprendido

These activities will help you review and remember what you have learned so far in Spanish.

 Escucha las expresiones. Indica en una tabla como la de abajo si tienes que usar el verbo saber o conocer.

saber	conocer

 Completa con verbos apropiados.

Álvaro Irizarry ___1___ un muchacho alto y guapo. Él ___2___ de San Juan, la capital de Puerto Rico. Puerto Rico ___3___ una isla tropical en el mar Caribe. En la isla siempre ___4___ calor y el tiempo ___5___ muy bueno con mucho sol. A Álvaro y a sus amigos les ___6___ mucho ir a la playa donde ___7___ una tarde agradable. Si ___8___ hambre, ___9___ a uno de los carritos que ___10___ en la playa donde ___11___ una empanada deliciosa.

 Repasa tu vocabulario. Prepara una lista de todos los artículos de ropa que ya aprendiste en español.

CULTURA

Una playa en la isla de Vieques en Puerto Rico

 Contesta.

1. Va a hacer calor. ¿Qué vas a llevar?
2. Va a hacer frío. ¿Qué vas a llevar?
3. ¿Qué te gusta comer cuando tienes hambre?
4. ¿Qué te gusta beber cuando tienes sed?

 Escribe las frases y cambia las palabras indicadas a pronombres.

1. Juan vio *a Ana* después de las clases.
2. Él dio *los boletos* a Ana porque es su amiga buena.
3. Habló también *a Mateo y Gabriela*.
4. Ellos compraron un refresco *para Juan*.

6 Identifica el deporte.

1. El portero quiere bloquear el balón.

2. Es posible bajar una pista fácil para principiantes o una pista difícil para expertos.

3. Los jugadores corren de una base a otra.

4. El balón tiene que pasar por encima de la red.

5. Juegan con una pelota y una raqueta y la pelota tiene que pasar por encima de la red.

7 **Rompecabezas**

 El intruso Choose the word in each group that does not belong and tell why it is **el intruso.**

1. banda   avión   carro   autobús

2. siempre   a veces   nunca   nadie

3. mar   pelota   ola   piscina

4. cama   silla   falda   mesa

5. leer   patinar   escribir   estudiar

8 Contesta.

1. Ellos están jugando voleibol. ¿Tiene que pasar el balón por encima de la red o debajo de la red?

2. Mi padre está trabajando en nuestro jardín. ¿Él está cerca de nuestra casa o lejos de nuestra casa?

3. La agente trabaja en el mostrador de la línea aérea en el aeropuerto. ¿Está delante del mostrador o detrás del mostrador?

4. La pasajera está facturando su equipaje en el aeropuerto. ¿Está delante del mostrador o detrás del mostrador?

5. Abordo del avión, ¿es necesario poner el equipaje de mano debajo del asiento o sobre el asiento?

CULTURA

Los pasajeros están esperando delante del mostrador de una línea aérea en el aeropuerto de Ezeiza en Buenos Aires, Argentina.

¡Una rutina diferente!

Aquí y Allí

Vamos a comparar ¿Qué haces cada día desde el momento que te levantas hasta que te acuestas? Muchas cosas de la rutina diaria pueden ser aburridas, ¿no? Vas a ver si los jóvenes en España y Latinoamérica tienen la misma rutina. Pero vas a observar también que hay maneras de cambiar la rutina—sobre todo si decides viajar con un grupo de jóvenes por un país hispano.

Objetivos

You will:

- identify more parts of the body
- talk about your daily routine
- talk about backpacking and camping

You will use:

- reflexive verbs
- commands with **favor de**

◄ Estos jóvenes están viajando por España con sus mochilas. A muchos jóvenes les gusta ser excursionistas o mochileros. De estas dos parejas, una es escandinava y la otra es norteamericana.

QuickPass

Go to glencoe.com
For: **Online book**
Web code: **ASD7837c2**

¡Una rutina diferente!

Look at these photographs to acquaint yourself with the theme of this chapter. What activities are part of your daily routine? What activities do you enjoy doing occasionally? What do you think **una rutina diferente** refers to? In this chapter you will learn to talk about daily activities, but you will also see that many fun opportunities in Spain and Latin America await anyone with a spirit of adventure.

México La muchacha mexicana se cepilla. Tiene el pelo largo, ¿no? ▶

Perú El cartel que vemos aquí se encuentra delante de un albergue juvenil en Barranco, un barrio de Lima, Perú. ▼

▲ **México** Mochileros en Oaxaca, México

España El joven da una caminata por los picos de Europa en Asturias en el norte de España. ▶

Argentina Un camping rodeado de un paisaje espectacular en el Parque Nacional Los Glaciares en la Patagonia, Argentina ▶

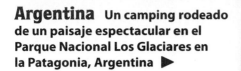

OBELISCO CAMPING

- MOCHILAS
- BOLSAS de DORMIR
- CARPAS
- ART. P/ESCALADA
- ACCESORIOS

Argentina
Una mochila puede llevar muchas cosas—aun un saco de dormir o, como indica el cartel en una tienda de camping en Buenos Aires, una bolsa de dormir. ▶

Chile La muchacha tiene su saco de dormir y su carpa en un camping en una reserva natural en Chile. ▼

Perú Estos jóvenes peruanos están viajando de mochileros por la región andina de su país. Están practicando una rutina importante. Tienen que cepillarse los dientes. ▼

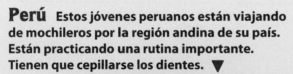

El cuerpo humano

la cabeza

la espalda

el codo

el brazo derecho

el dedo

la pierna

la rodilla

el pie

la mano izquierda

Para mantenerse en forma, Cristina se estira.

La rutina diaria

despertarse

tomar una ducha

lavarse la cara

lavarse el pelo

cepillarse (lavarse) los dientes

peinarse

el espejo

mirarse

sentarse

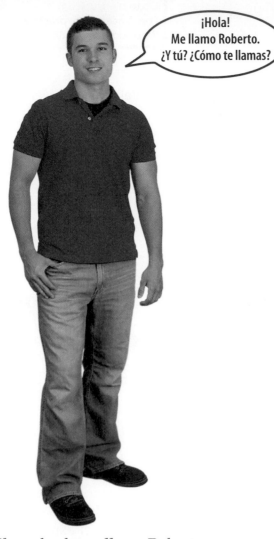

¡Hola!
Me llamo Roberto.
¿Y tú? ¿Cómo te llamas?

El muchacho se llama Roberto.

Ana se levanta temprano.
No se queda en la cama.
Se levanta enseguida. Ella es madrugadora.
Le gusta levantarse temprano.

Roberto se acuesta tarde.
Se acuesta a las once y media de la noche.
Él se duerme enseguida.
Él duerme ocho horas.

Elena tiene frío.
Se pone un suéter.

Elena tiene calor.
Se quita el suéter.

¡UNA RUTINA DIFERENTE!

QuickPass

Go to glencoe.com
For: **Vocabulary practice**
Web code: **ASD7837c2**

ESCUCHAR

1 Escucha las frases. Parea cada frase con el dibujo que describe.

a.

b.

c.

d.

e.

f.

HABLAR • ESCRIBIR

2 Contesta.

1. Cuando Marisol se despierta, ¿se levanta enseguida?
2. Cuando Carlos se despierta, ¿se queda en la cama?
3. Cuando Vicente se peina, ¿se mira en el espejo?
4. Cuando Juanita se lava el pelo, ¿usa agua caliente?
5. Cuando Tomás toma el desayuno, ¿se sienta a la mesa?
6. Cuando Julia se acuesta, ¿se duerme enseguida?
7. ¿Cuándo se levanta un madrugador? ¿Temprano por la mañana o tarde?
8. Cuando Ricardo se levanta, ¿se estira?

3 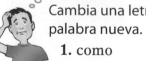 Rompecabezas

 Cambia una letra en cada palabra para formar una palabra nueva.

1. como
2. dolor
3. cada
4. coche

5. tocar
6. peso
7. gano
8. hola

LEER

4 Parea para hacer una frase larga.

1. Él se pone un suéter   a. porque va a comer.
2. Ella se lava las manos   b. porque se peina.
3. Ella se cepilla los dientes   c. porque tiene calor.
4. Él se mira en el espejo   d. porque acaba de comer.
5. Ella se quita el suéter   e. porque tiene frío.

InfoGap For more practice using your new vocabulary, do Activity 2 on page SR4 at the end of this book.

HABLAR • ESCRIBIR

5 **Juego** ¡Corrige todas las frases absurdas!

1. **Cada pierna tiene una mano y la mano tiene un dedo.**
2. **El codo está en la pierna y la rodilla está en el brazo.**
3. **La cara está en la espalda.**
4. Los dientes están en el pelo.
5. **La boca y los ojos están en la rodilla.**

✿ Comunicación

6 ♻ Pick someone in your family and describe his or her weekday routine to the class.

LEER

7 **Juego** Race with a partner to see who can be the first to put José's activities in the correct order.

José se levanta.
José se duerme enseguida.
José se lava la cara y los dientes en el cuarto de baño.
José va al comedor y toma el desayuno.
José se despierta.
José se acuesta.
José se quita la ropa.

CULTURA
La muchacha se mira en el espejo para ver si el pantalón le queda bien.

VIDEO To practice your new words, watch **Vocabulario en vivo.**

El camping

una carpa, una tienda de campaña

un saco (una bolsa) de dormir

Los amigos van de camping.
Lo están pasando bien. Se divierten mucho.
Los jóvenes arman (montan) una carpa.

Para conversar

¡Ya voy!

Alex, favor de venir acá. Favor de ayudarme con la carpa.

¿Qué llevan en su mochila?

En otras partes

- In addition to **una barra** you will also hear **una pastilla.** You will also hear **pasta dentífrica** as well as **crema dental.**
- Una **tienda de campaña** is more common in Spain, **una carpa** in Latin America.

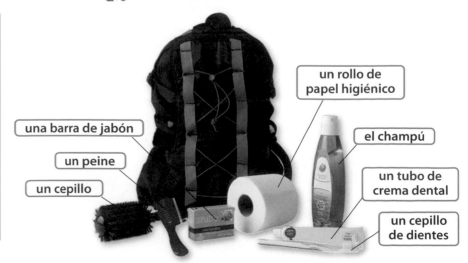

un rollo de papel higiénico

una barra de jabón

el champú

un peine

un tubo de crema dental

un cepillo

un cepillo de dientes

VIDEO To go hiking with new friends, watch **Diálogo en vivo.**

Los mochileros dan una caminata.
Dan una caminata por un parque nacional.

Andrea se acuesta en la carpa.
Duerme en un saco de dormir.

¡Así se dice!

Note that when someone calls and you want to respond *I'm coming* you say: **¡Ya voy!**

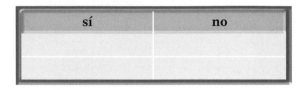
ESCUCHAR

1 Escucha las frases. Indica en una tabla como la de abajo si cada frase es correcta o no.

sí	no

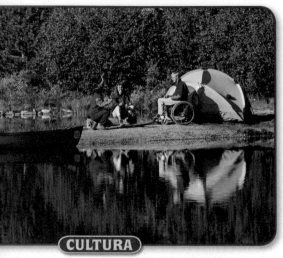

CULTURA

Los amigos están de camping en Chile durante el mes de abril. En Chile es el otoño.

HABLAR • ESCRIBIR

2 Contesta sobre un grupo de amigos que van de camping.

1. ¿Van de camping los amigos?
2. ¿Se divierten en el camping?
3. ¿Qué montan (arman)?
4. ¿En qué duermen?
5. ¿Dónde ponen sus sacos de dormir?
6. ¿Quiere José ayuda para montar la carpa?
7. ¿A ti te gusta el camping?

EXPANSIÓN

Sin mirar las preguntas, da toda la información que recuerdas en tus propias palabras. Si no recuerdas algo, un(a) compañero(a) te puede ayudar.

LEER • HABLAR • ESCRIBIR

3 Completa con una palabra apropiada.

1. María va a cepillarse los dientes. Necesita _____ y _____.
2. Tomás va a tomar una ducha. Necesita _____.
3. Carlos quiere peinarse. Necesita _____.
4. Julia quiere lavarse el pelo. Necesita _____.
5. Claudia va a cepillarse el pelo. Necesita _____.

El joven toma una ducha en agua fría pero no le molesta.

LEER

4 Parea las palabras que significan lo mismo.

1. la carpa
2. armar
3. los que llevan una mochila
4. lo pasa bien
5. el paseo largo

a. los mochileros
b. se divierte
c. la tienda de campaña
d. montar
e. la caminata

Comunicación

5 Estás en una farmacia. Quieres comprar los siguientes objetos. Conversa con el/la empleado(a).

ESCRIBIR

6 Rompecabezas

Join two puzzle pieces to form a word. When you have finished, you should have nine words. Do not use any piece more than once.

jo nata ce pa
espe ro cami
pú pillo ja cham recho
car tes dien dilla bón
de

CULTURA

Los mochileros dan una caminata.

Gramática

QuickPass

Go to glencoe.com
For: **Grammar practice**
Web code: ASD7837c2

Verbos reflexivos

1. Read the following sentences as you look at the illustrations.

Federico lava el carro.
Federico lo lava.

Federico se lava.

Julia cepilla al perro.
Julia lo cepilla.

Julia se cepilla.

Pedro mira a su amigo.
Pedro lo mira.

Pedro se mira en el espejo.

In the sentences to the left, one person performs the action and another person or thing receives the action. In the sentences to the right, the same person performs and receives the action of the verb. For this reason the pronoun **se** must be used. **Se** is called a reflexive pronoun because it refers back to the subject—**Federico, Julia, Pedro.**

2. Study the forms of a reflexive verb. Pay particular attention to the pronoun that goes with each form of the verb. It is called a "reflexive pronoun."

lavarse			
yo	**me** lavo	nosotros(as)	**nos** lavamos
tú	**te** lavas	*vosotros(as)*	**os** *laváis*
Ud., él, ella	**se** lava	Uds., ellos, ellas	**se** lavan

levantarse			
yo	**me** levanto	nosotros(as)	**nos** levantamos
tú	**te** levantas	*vosotros(as)*	**os** *levantáis*
Ud., él, ella	**se** levanta	Uds., ellos, ellas	**se** levantan

3. In the negative form, **no** is placed before the reflexive pronoun.

¿No te lavas las manos?
La familia Martínez no se levanta tarde.

4. In Spanish, when you refer to parts of the body and articles of clothing in a reflexive sentence, you often use the definite article, not the possessive adjective.

Me lavo la cara.
Ella se cepilla los dientes.
Él se pone el suéter.

5. Note that the reflexive pronoun is added to the infinitive.

El niño quiere acostarse.
Voy a lavarme las manos.
¿Quieres quitarte la chaqueta?

CULTURA

Los aficionados van a divertirse mucho durante el concierto que va a dar Enrique Iglesias en la Ciudad de México.

Práctica

ESCUCHAR • HABLAR • ESCRIBIR

1 Contesta.

1. ¿Se levanta tarde o temprano Gregorio?
2. ¿Se lava por la mañana o por la noche?
3. ¿Se lava los dientes antes o después del desayuno?
4. ¿Se pone un suéter cuando hace frío?
5. ¿Se quita el suéter cuando tiene calor?

HABLAR • LEER

2 Completa las conversaciones con un pronombre.

1. ¿A qué hora _____ levantas?
   Soy madrugador(a). _____ levanto temprano,
   a las seis y media.

2. ¿_____ cepillas los dientes con frecuencia?
   Sí, _____ cepillo los dientes unas cuatro veces al día.

3. ¿_____ peinas con frecuencia?
   No, no _____ peino con frecuencia.

4. ¿A qué hora _____ despertaste esta mañana?
   _____ desperté a las siete.

5. Y, ¿a qué hora _____ acostaste anoche?
   Anoche _____ acosté a las diez y media.

HABLAR

3 Trabaja con un(a) compañero(a). Preparen una conversación
según el modelo.

MODELO

—¿Te cepillas?
—Sí, me cepillo.

 1.

 2.

3.

 4.

Conexiones

La salud

Aquí tienes unas
sugerencias importantes
para mantenerte en buena
salud. Debes

- dormir entre siete y ocho
  horas cada noche
- tomar un buen desayuno
- lavarte las manos antes
  de comer
- cepillarte los dientes
  después de comer

HABLAR • ESCRIBIR

4 Personaliza. Da respuestas personales.

    1. ¿Cómo te llamas?
    2. Y tu(s) hermano(s), ¿cómo se llama(n)?
    3. ¿Cómo se llama tu profesor(a) de español?

CULTURA

Es una clase de español en Santa Fe, Nuevo México. La profesora se llama señora Brown. Parece que los alumnos se divierten mucho en clase, ¿no?

LEER • ESCRIBIR

5 Completa con un pronombre reflexivo y la forma correcta del verbo.

    Hola. Yo __1__ llam_2_ Jorge y mi amigo __3__ llam_4_ Felipe. Felipe y yo no __5__ levant_6_ a la misma hora porque él es madrugador y yo no. Él __7__ levant_8_ temprano y yo __9__ levant_10_ tarde. Y tú, ¿__11__ levant_12_ tarde como yo o __13__ levant_14_ temprano como Felipe?

LEER • ESCRIBIR

6 Completa con un pronombre.

    1. Quiero levantar__ temprano.
    2. Niño, tienes que peinar__.
    3. Vamos a lavar__ las manos.
    4. ¿No quieres poner__ un suéter? Está haciendo frío.
    5. Tienen que cepillar__ los dientes después de cada comida.

HABLAR

7 **Juego** Think of an object from this chapter. Your partner will ask **sí/no** questions which you will answer in complete sentences. If your partner guesses it in five questions or less, he or she wins. If you stump your partner, you win. Then reverse roles.

VIDEO Want help with reflexive verbs? Watch **Gramática en vivo.**

Verbos reflexivos de cambio radical

1. The reflexive verbs **acostarse** (o → ue), **dormirse** (o → ue), **sentarse** (e → ie), **despertarse** (e → ie), and **divertirse** (e → ie) are stem-changing verbs.

acostarse			
yo	me acuesto	nosotros(as)	nos acostamos
tú	te acuestas	*vosotros(as)*	*os acostáis*
Ud., él, ella	se acuesta	Uds., ellos, ellas	se acuestan

divertirse			
yo	me divierto	nosotros(as)	nos divertimos
tú	te diviertes	*vosotros(as)*	*os divertís*
Ud., él, ella	se divierte	Uds., ellos, ellas	se divierten

2. Many verbs in Spanish can be used with a reflexive pronoun. Often the reflexive pronoun gives a different meaning to the verb. Study the following examples.

Ana pone su blusa en su mochila.	*Ana puts her blouse in her backpack.*
Ana se pone la blusa.	*Ana puts on her blouse.*
Ana duerme ocho horas.	*Ana sleeps eight hours.*
Ana se duerme enseguida.	*Ana falls asleep immediately.*
Ana llama a Carlos.	*Ana calls Carlos.*
Ella se llama Ana.	*She calls herself Ana. (Her name is Ana.)*
Ana divierte a sus amigos.	*Ana amuses her friends.*
Ana se divierte.	*Ana amuses herself. (Ana has a good time.)*

CULTURA

La joven ciclista se divierte en el Parque de la Ciudadela en Barcelona.

Práctica

Más práctica

Workbook, pp. 2.7–2.9
StudentWorks™ Plus

ESCUCHAR • HABLAR • ESCRIBIR

8 Personaliza. Da respuestas personales.

1. ¿Duermes en una cama o en un saco de dormir?
2. Cuando te acuestas, ¿te duermes enseguida?
3. Por la mañana, ¿te quedas en la cama cuando te despiertas?
4. A veces, ¿despiertas a tus hermanos?
5. ¿Ellos se enfadan cuando los despiertas?
6. ¿Te sientas a la mesa para tomar el desayuno?
7. ¿Te diviertes en la escuela?
8. ¿Diviertes a tus amigos?

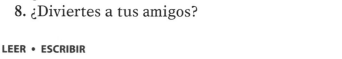

CULTURA

El muchacho acaba de despertarse pero está cansado y no quiere levantarse. Quiere quedarse en la carpa.

LEER • ESCRIBIR

9 Completa sobre un día que María pasa en la playa.

1. María _____ su traje de baño en su mochila. Cuando llega a la playa ella _____ el traje de baño.
2. En la playa María ve a un amigo. Su amigo _____ Luis. Ella _____ a su amigo.
3. María y sus amigos lo pasan muy bien en la playa. Ellos _____ mucho y como María es muy cómica ella también _____ mucho a sus amigos.
4. Después de pasar el día en la playa, María está muy cansada. Cuando ella se acuesta, _____ enseguida y _____ más de ocho horas.

LEER • ESCRIBIR

10 Completa.

Cuando yo __1__ (acostarse), yo __2__ (dormirse) enseguida. Cada noche yo __3__ (dormir) ocho horas. Yo __4__ (acostarse) a las once y __5__ (levantarse) a las siete de la mañana. Cuando yo __6__ (despertarse), __7__ (levantarse) enseguida. Pero cuando mi hermana __8__ (despertarse), ella no __9__ (levantarse) enseguida. Y mi hermano, cuando él __10__ (acostarse), no __11__ (dormirse) enseguida. Él pasa horas escuchando música en la cama. Así él __12__ (dormir) solamente unas seis horas.

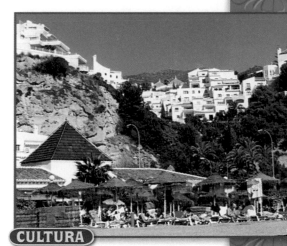

CULTURA

La playa de Nerja en el sur de España

 Comunicación

11 Work with a partner and discuss your typical daily routines. Share your results with your classmates.

Más práctica

■ Workbook, p. 2.9
● StudentWorks™ Plus

Mandatos con favor de

1. The expression **favor de** followed by the infinitive is a very useful way to give a command to tell someone what to do. It is very polite and you can use **favor de** with a friend, an adult, or any group of people.

> **Favor de venir aquí (acá).**
> **Favor de no hablar.**
> **Favor de volver pronto.**

2. Whenever a pronoun is used with the infinitive, the pronoun is attached to it.

> **Favor de ayudarme.**
> **Favor de traerme el menú.**
> **Favor de darme el libro.**
> **Favor de levantarte.** *(to a friend)*
> **Favor de levantarse.** *(to an adult or group of friends)*

Favor de lavarse las manos

Práctica

LEER • HABLAR

12 Escoge.

| un amigo | un adulto o un grupo de personas |

1. Favor de sentarte.
2. Favor de sentarse aquí.
3. Favor de quitarte las botas.
4. Favor de ponerte los zapatos.
5. Favor de quedarse aquí.
6. Favor de lavarte las manos.
7. Favor de levantarse.

 Comunicación

13 You and a friend are planning to do something, for example, take a trip. There are many things you need to do to get ready and you need help. Make a diagram similar to the one below and tell your partner what to do to help. Take turns.

> buscar algo   llamar un taxi
> comprar los boletos   hacer la maleta
> hacer un viaje

FOLDABLES®
Study Organizer

MINIATURE MATCHBOOK
See page SH26 for help with making this foldable. With a partner discuss your daily routines using reflexive verbs. On the front of each matchbook draw something you do every day. On the inside your partner will write a sentence about the picture using the appropriate reflexive verb.

PRONUNCIACIÓN

La h, la y y la ll

H in Spanish is silent. It is never pronounced. Repeat the following.

hijo	**helado**	**higiénico**	**hola**
hace	**hermano**	**huevos**	**hispano**

Y in Spanish can be either a vowel or a consonant. As a vowel, it is pronounced exactly the same as the vowel **i**. Repeat the following.

el hijo y el hermano
el hotel y el hospital

Y is a consonant when it begins a word or a syllable. As a consonant, **y** is pronounced similarly to the **y** in the English word *yo-yo*. This sound has several variations throughout the Spanish-speaking world. Repeat the following.

ya	**desayuno**	**ayuda**	**playa**
yo	**oye**	**leyó**	

Ll is pronounced as a single consonant in Spanish. In many areas of the Spanish-speaking world, it is pronounced the same as the **y**. It too has several variations. Repeat the following.

llama	**botella**	**taquilla**	**toalla**	**lleva**
llega	**pastilla**	**llueve**	**rollo**	**cepillo**

Dictado

Pronounce the following sentences carefully. Then write them to prepare for a dictation.

> La hermana habla hoy con su hermano en el hotel.
> Está lloviendo cuando ella llega a la calle Hidalgo.
> El hombre lleva una botella de agua a la playa bella.
> Él no lo oyó; lo leyó.

Refrán

Can you guess what the following proverb means?

Quien mucho duerme, poco aprende.

¡Bravo!

You have now learned all the vocabulary and grammar in this chapter. Continue to use and practice all that you know while learning more cultural information. ¡Vamos!

De camping

Rafael	A ti te gusta mucho el camping, ¿no?
Pablo	A mí, sí.
Rafael	La verdad es que no me interesa mucho. ¿Dónde duermes? ¿Te acuestas al aire libre?
Pablo	No. Siempre voy con uno o dos amigos y montamos una carpa. Y dormimos en un saco de dormir.
Rafael	¿Qué hacen para comer?
Pablo	Muy fácil. Preparamos hamburguesas y salchichas en una barbacoa.
Rafael	Hay muchos insectos, ¿no?
Pablo	Pues, hay. Pero, ¡qué va! No nos molestan.
Rafael	¿Cómo pasan el día entero? ¿No se aburren?
Pablo	Al contrario, damos caminatas y nadamos en el lago. Nos acostamos temprano porque nos levantamos temprano también.
Rafael	Me parece que tienen que levantarse cuando se levanta el sol.
Pablo	Sí, pero no me molesta porque soy madrugador. Pero hay una cosa que no me gusta.
Rafael	¿Verdad? ¿Qué?
Pablo	Lavarme en agua fría.

¿Comprendes?

A Completa según la información en la conversación.

1. A _____ le gusta el camping.
2. A _____ no le interesa mucho.
3. Cuando Pablo y su(s) amigo(s) van de camping, montan _____.
4. Duermen en _____.
5. Comen _____.
6. Las preparan en _____.
7. _____ no les molestan.
8. Durante el día _____.
9. Se acuestan temprano porque _____.
10. A Pablo no le gusta _____.

B **Resumiendo** Relata la información en la conversación en tus propias palabras.

C **Comparando** Compara y contrasta los gustos de Rafael y Pablo.

D **Dando opiniones** ¿Estás de acuerdo(a) con las opiniones de Rafael o de Pablo sobre el camping?

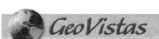

GeoVistas

To learn more about Chile, take a tour on pages SH58–SH59.

CULTURA

Saltos de Petrohue cerca del lago Llanquihue en Chile

Antes de leer

Have you ever done any backpacking? When and where? If not, do you think you would like to? Think about it. Would you rather go camping or stay in a youth hostel? Explain why.

✓ Reading Check

¿Llevan maletas los jóvenes?

Durante la lectura

How would you like to travel and make new friends from around the world? Would it be fun?

✓ Reading Check

¿Por qué van a albergues juveniles?

✓ Reading Check

¿Cuáles son unas inconveniencias?

Después de leer

After reading, are your opinions the same about backpacking around the globe?

Los mochileros

Si decides hacer un viaje por España o Latinoamérica con un grupo de amigos, vas a encontrar a muchos jóvenes de muchas nacionalidades haciendo turismo también. Todos tienen el deseo de ver y conocer el mundo. Pero como no tienen mucho dinero, tienen que viajar de una manera económica. ¿Tú no tienes mucho dinero tampoco? Pues, no hay problema. Como los otros aventureros, puedes poner todo lo que necesitas en una mochila grande y salir a ver el mundo.

Vamos a hablar con un mochilero típico. Se llama Antonio. Es de Tejas.

—Me encanta viajar y ver el mundo y lo hago sin mucho dinero. Como en restaurantes económicos y a veces mis compañeros y yo vamos a un mercado donde compramos comida para un picnic. Por lo general pasamos la noche en un albergue juvenil. Son muy económicos pero sus facilidades son limitadas. No tienes baño privado. Te levantas por la mañana y a veces tienes que lavarte en agua fría porque no hay agua caliente. Pero a mí no me importan estas pequeñas

—¡Hola! Me llamo Antonio y soy de Texas. Me encanta viajar con mi mochila y ver el mundo. Soy un verdadero trotamundos.

inconveniencias. Lo importante es poder hacer nuevos amigos de todas partes del mundo y llegar a apreciar sus costumbres y manera de vivir. ¿Qué te parece? ¿Por qué no nos encontramos un día en México o Chile?

¿Comprendes?

Más práctica
Workbook, p. 2.10
StudentWorks™ Plus

A **Recordando hechos** Contesta.

1. ¿De dónde vienen los mochileros que viajan por España o Latinoamérica?
2. ¿Cuál es una cosa que tienen en común?
3. ¿Dónde comen los mochileros?
4. ¿Dónde se quedan los mochileros?

B **Describiendo** Describe.

1. un albergue juvenil
2. un mochilero
3. a Antonio

C **Analizando** Contesta.

¿Cuáles son las ventajas, o conveniencias, y desventajas, o inconveniencias, de quedarse en un albergue juvenil?

D **Explicando** Antonio piensa que los jóvenes se divierten mucho y al mismo tiempo aprenden a apreciar a gente de muchas culturas. Explica el significado de su opinión.

CULTURA

Un hostal o albergue en Punta Arenas en la Patagonia chilena

CULTURA

Los jóvenes están en un camping en Burgos, España.

57

El camping 🎧♻

Antes de leer

¿Fuiste de camping una vez? Si contestas que sí, ¿te gustó o no? Piensa en tu experiencia. Si contestas que no, que nunca fuiste de camping, ¿qué crees? ¿Te interesa el camping o no? A ver si tienes la misma opinión después de leer esta lectura.

Hoy en día muchos turistas, sobre todo los mochileros jóvenes, llevan equipo para hacer camping. En Latinoamérica hay campings en los parques nacionales y reservas naturales. Pasar unas noches en un camping puede ser una experiencia agradable. Tienes la oportunidad de conocer a otros turistas y también a familias locales porque a muchas familias les gusta hacer camping. Es una manera económica de viajar.

Los campers se levantan temprano—cuando se levanta el sol. Pasan el día dando caminatas por unas regiones de una belleza natural increíble.

CULTURA

Campers al pie del Aconcagua en los Andes de Argentina. El Aconcagua es mucho más alto que el monte McKinley en Alaska.

De noche regresan al camping. Se sientan alrededor de una fogata[1] y preparan comida en la fogata o en una barbacoa. Después de un día de mucha actividad física y una buena comida todos están cansados y van a su carpa. Cada uno desenrolla su saco de dormir y enseguida se duerme. Y, ¿mañana? Otro día de experiencias nuevas.

Con solamente mochila, carpa y saco de dormir es posible disfrutar de[2] unas vacaciones estupendas rodeado de un paisaje espectacular.

[1]fogata   *bonfire*   [2]disfrutar de   *to enjoy*

¿Comprendes?

Escoge.

1. ¿Quiénes hacen camping?
   a. solo los mochileros
   b. solo los turistas de otros países
   c. los mochileros y otros turistas
   d. nadie

2. Los campings en Latinoamérica se encuentran en _____.
   a. las ciudades
   b. los alrededores de una ciudad
   c. zonas rurales
   d. caminatas

3. ¿Cuándo se levantan los campers?
   a. temprano por la mañana
   b. cuando regresan al camping
   c. cuando toman el sol
   d. de noche

4. Las montañas y los lagos ofrecen _____.
   a. una experiencia cultural
   b. un paisaje espectacular
   c. un viaje económico
   d. una comida estupenda

CULTURA Los jóvenes dan una caminata en un valle andino en Chile.

Vocabulario

1 **Escoge la palabra apropiada.**

1. Hay cinco (dedos, pies) en cada mano.
2. Escribo con la (mano, pierna) izquierda.
3. Ana se estira (las piernas, los codos) antes de correr.
4. Cuando tengo dolor de (dientes, cabeza) no puedo leer bien.

2 **Completa.**

5. Los amigos van de camping. Arman una _____.
6. Es mi amiga. ¿Quieres saber su nombre? Ella _____ _____ Susana.
7–8. El joven _____ _____ a las diez y media de la noche. Pero no _____ _____ enseguida porque pasa una hora leyendo en la cama.
9. Necesito _____. Voy a lavarme el pelo.
10. No puedo hacerlo. ¿Me puedes _____?
11. Los mochileros dan una _____ por el parque nacional.

Gramática

3 **Contesta.**

12. ¿Cómo te llamas?
13. ¿A qué hora te levantas?
14. ¿A qué hora te acuestas?

4 **Completa.**

15. Yo _____ a la mesa. (sentarse)
16. ¿Tú _____ a qué hora? (acostarse)
17. Ellos _____ Raúl y Magdalena. (llamarse)
18. Nosotros _____ enseguida. (dormirse)
19. Yo _____ las manos. (lavarse)
20. Ustedes _____ en la sala. (sentarse)
21. Ellos _____ mucho. (divertirse)
22. Ella _____ temprano cada día. (despertarse)

To review **Vocabulario 1,** turn to pages 38–39.

To review **Vocabulario 1** and **Vocabulario 2,** turn to pages 38–39 and 42–43.

To review **los verbos reflexivos,** turn to pages 46–47 and 50.

5 **Forma frases.**

23. tú / sentarse / para comer

24. usted / acostarse / a las diez de la noche

25. mis primos / llamarse / Carlos y Felipe

26. yo / cepillarse / los dientes

27. nosotros / divertirse / durante una fiesta

28. ustedes / ponerse / los guantes

6 **Completa con un pronombre si es necesario.**

29. Ella _____ mira en el espejo cuando se peina.

30. Ella _____ mira a la profesora.

31. Yo _____ lavo a mi perro.

32. Yo _____ lavo antes de ir a la escuela.

7 **Escribe un mandato con favor de. Sigue el modelo.**

MODELO   No como.
              Favor de comer.

33. No salgo.

34. No leo las notas.

35. No escribo la tarea.

36. No paso la sal.

To review **favor de,** turn to page 52.

To review this cultural information, turn to pages 56–57.

Cultura

8 **Contesta.**

37. ¿Cómo viajan muchos jóvenes en España y Latinoamérica?

38. ¿Dónde pasan la noche?

39. ¿Cómo son los albergues?

40. ¿Por qué a los jóvenes les gustan los albergues juveniles?

CULTURA
El camping es muy popular en Asturias, España.

1 **Mi familia**

✓ *Talk about family routines*

Work with a classmate. Discuss your family routines. What things do you and your family typically do and at what times? Do your families have similar routines or are they quite different?

2 **No es siempre igual.**

✓ *Compare your weekday and weekend routines*

Most people like a change of pace on the weekend. Compare the things you do or do not do during the week with the things you do or do not do during the weekend.

CULTURA

Están tomando una siesta en hamacas en un camping en las afueras de Santa Marta, Colombia.

3 **Una excursión de camping**

✓ *Talk about a camping trip*

Work with a classmate. A friend's family invited you both to join them on a camping trip. Discuss the things you will need to take. Also discuss some of the things you'll probably do during the camping trip.

4 **Un día ideal**

✓ *Talk about your ideal day*

Interview a classmate to find out about his or her ideal day. Take turns. See who can come up with the most original ideas. Share the information with the class.

5 **Favor de...**

✓ *Ask someone to do something*

Work with a classmate and tell each other to do things. Act out what you're told to do.

Tarea

For the next week keep **un diario** *(diary)* in Spanish. Write down everything you do in the course of each day.

Writing Strategy

Writing in a journal There are many types of personal writing. One example of personal writing is keeping a journal. One type of journal writing involves writing about what you do each day, along with your thoughts and impressions about these events or activities. It's similar to "thinking out loud."

❶ Prewrite

- Find a notebook or journal in which you will feel comfortable writing.
- Decide what time of day you will write in your journal, preferably before you go to bed.
- Remember that journal writing is informal, but in this case you still want to use correct vocabulary, grammar, and sentence structure. Use as many reflexive verbs as you can. Don't try to write anything you haven't learned yet.

- To help refresh your memory, ask yourself questions such as the following: What did I do when I woke up? Did I go to school? What did I do at school? What did I do after school? Did I eat dinner with my family? What homework did I do? Did I wash my hair? Many activities will be different for the weekend days.
- Read over your diary. Check for correct vocabulary, verb forms, and grammar.

❷ Write

Keeping a diary should be an enjoyable, thoughtful experience.

- Write the date at the top of the page. Write down your activities and thoughts for each day. Remember that your teacher will be reading it!

Evaluate

Don't forget that your teacher will evaluate you on your sequencing of events and activities, use of vocabulary, correctness of grammar and sentence structure, and the completeness of your message.

Repaso del Capítulo ②

Gramática

- ### Verbos reflexivos *(pages 46–47)*
  Review the forms of the reflexive verbs. These verbs have an extra pronoun that refers back to the subject because the subject is both the performer (doer) and receiver of the action of the verb.

lavarse			
yo	**me** lavo	nosotros(as)	**nos** lavamos
tú	**te** lavas	*vosotros(as)*	***os** laváis*
Ud., él, ella	**se** lava	Uds., ellos, ellas	**se** lavan

- ### Verbos reflexivos de cambio radical *(page 50)*
  Some reflexive verbs have a stem change in the present. Review the following verbs.

acostarse			
yo	me ac**ue**sto	nosotros(as)	nos acostamos
tú	te ac**ue**stas	*vosotros(as)*	*os acostáis*
Ud., él, ella	se ac**ue**sta	Uds., ellos, ellas	se ac**ue**stan

divertirse			
yo	me div**ie**rto	nosotros(as)	nos divertimos
tú	te div**ie**rtes	*vosotros(as)*	*os divertís*
Ud., él, ella	se div**ie**rte	Uds., ellos, ellas	se div**ie**rten

- ### Mandatos con favor de *(page 52)*
  You can use the expression **favor de** followed by the infinitive to tell someone what to do. Review the following.

  Favor de empezar ahora.
  Favor de no poner la ropa aquí.

  Remember that when a pronoun is used with the infinitive, the pronoun is attached to it.

  Favor de ayudarme.

CULTURA

Los jóvenes se divierten al aire libre en el Parque Nacional de Cazorla en Andalucía, España.

Vocabulario

Stating daily activities

la rutina diaria	quedarse	peinarse	dormirse
despertarse	tomar una ducha	mirarse	ponerse (la ropa)
estirarse	lavarse	sentarse	quitarse (la ropa)
levantarse	cepillarse	acostarse	llamarse

Identifying articles for grooming and hygiene

el espejo	el peine	el tubo de crema	el rollo de papel
el champú	el cepillo de dientes	dental	higiénico
el cepillo		la barra de jabón	

Identifying more parts of the body

el cuerpo humano	la espalda	el dedo	la pierna
la cabeza	el brazo	la rodilla	el pie
los dientes	el codo		

Describing camping

el parque	el saco (la bolsa)	ir de camping	divertirse,
el camping	de dormir	montar, armar	pasarlo bien
la carpa, la tienda	el/la mochilero(a)	dar una caminata	
de campaña			

Other useful words and expressions

derecho(a)	el/la madrugador(a)	tener frío (calor)	acá
izquierdo(a)	el suéter	Favor de (+ *infinitive*)	¡Ya voy!

Repaso cumulativo

Repasa lo que ya has aprendido

These activities will help you review and remember what you have learned so far in Spanish.

 Escucha las frases. Indica si la frase ocurre en el presente o en el pasado.

en el presente	en el pasado

 Cambia al presente progresivo.

1. Él compra un juego de computadora.
2. Ellos hacen un álbum de fotografías electrónicas.
3. Compro un regalo para mi papá.
4. ¿Qué lees?
5. No comprendemos nada.
6. Ellos viven en Caracas.
7. ¡Vamos! Sale nuestro vuelo.
8. Hacen cola.

 Completa con una palabra apropiada.

1. Tengo que _____ una composición para mi clase de inglés.
2. Mañana voy a _____ a la playa donde voy a _____ en el mar.
3. No tengo hambre porque acabo de _____.
4. Mis amigos acaban de _____ de Colombia donde pasaron sus vacaciones.
5. Yo voy a _____ a la tienda porque tengo que _____ un regalo para el cumpleaños de Teresa.

Una playa en la costa del Caribe en Colombia

 Forma frases en el presente.

1. nosotros / poder
2. nosotros / jugar
3. yo / querer
4. ella / pensar que sí
5. ellos / preferir
6. nosotros / querer
7. nosotros / volver
8. ustedes / volver
9. tú / tener que

Completa con ser o estar.

1. Quiero acostarme. _____ cansado(a).

2. José tiene que prepararse para un examen. _____ un poco nervioso.

3. Teresa no se siente bien. _____ enferma.

4. La muchacha se baña. El jabón que usa _____ muy bueno.

5. Los alumnos se duermen porque el profesor _____ muy aburrido y ellos _____ aburridos.

 Escribe el contrario.

1. El niño tiene algo en la boca.

2. Ellos siempre se acuestan muy temprano.

3. Yo siempre me duermo enseguida.

4. Alguien va a pie y alguien va en bicicleta.

5. Tenemos algo en la mochila.

 Mira los dibujos. Describe todo lo que ves.

En tren

Aquí y Allí

Vamos a comparar Donde tú vives, ¿hay mucho servicio ferroviario—servicio de trenes? ¿Hay solo trenes locales o hay también trenes de larga distancia? En algunas partes de Estados Unidos, el tren es un medio de transporte importante. En otras no hay servicio ferroviario. Existe la misma situación en el mundo hispano. Vamos a ver donde es importante.

Objetivos

You will:

- use vocabulary related to train travel
- discuss interesting train trips in Spain, Peru, and Mexico

You will use:

- the preterite of irregular verbs
- the verb **decir**
- prepositional pronouns

◄ Parece que el tren se para en la acera en Aguas Calientes, Perú.

QuickPass

Go to glencoe.com
For: **Online book**
Web code: **ASD7837c3**

Introducción al tema
En tren

El tema de este capítulo es el viajar en tren. En unas regiones el tren es un medio de transporte muy importante y en otras no es importante. Sin embargo como vas a ver en este capítulo hay unas excursiones espectaculares que puedes hacer en tren en varias partes del mundo hispanohablante.

▲ **Chile** La antigua estación de ferrocarril Arica–La Paz en el norte de Chile es un monumento histórico. Hoy en día la estación sirve de museo ferroviario.

Panamá Estas jóvenes trabajan en el coche cafetería del tren que enlaza la Ciudad de Panamá y Colón. Los pasajeros que tuvieron la experiencia inolvidable de observar la vegetación tropical a lo largo del canal de Panamá desde las ventanillas del tren hacen cola para bajar(se) en Colón. ▶

◀ **Cuba** Qué contraste entre esta locomotora antigua de un tren de turismo en la provincia de Camagüez en Cuba y el AVE.

España El AVE—tren de alta velocidad española—es uno de los trenes más rápidos (veloces) del mundo. Sirve a muchas ciudades españolas y hace el trayecto Madrid–Sevilla en solo dos horas y media. ▼

OJO PARE CRUCE TREN

Perú Durante su recorrido de Cuzco a Machu Picchu, el tren hace parada en Ollantaytambo—un pueblo incaico. Los habitantes esperan la llegada del tren para vender tejidos y comida a los pasajeros. ▶

◀ **México** El tren está cruzando un puente ferroviario en la Sierra Madre cerca de la famosa Barranca del Cobre en el estado de Chihuahua en México.

España Hay muchos jóvenes que viajan por España y se aprovechan del excelente servicio de trenes para ir de una ciudad a otra. ▼

España Si no quieres hacer cola delante de la ventanilla para sacar tu billete (comprar tu boleto) lo puedes sacar de un distribuidor automático como este en la estación de Atocha en Madrid. ▼

Billetes
Venta Automática

71

En la estación de ferrocarril (tren)

el hall

la sala de espera

el horario

Los pasajeros esperan su tren en la sala de espera.
El horario indica las llegadas y salidas de los trenes.

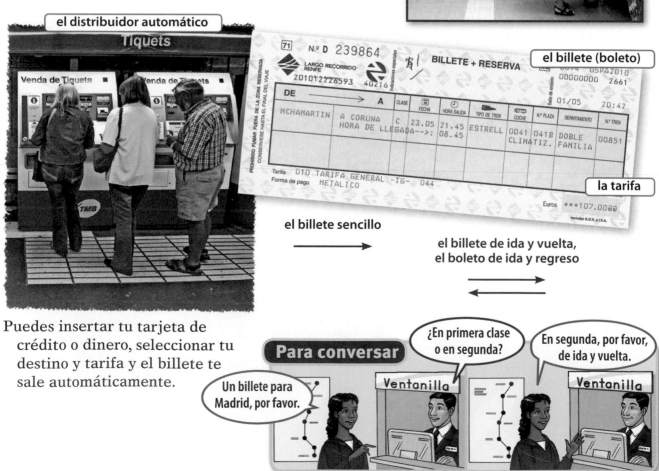

el distribuidor automático

el billete (boleto)

la tarifa

el billete sencillo

el billete de ida y vuelta,
el boleto de ida y regreso

Puedes insertar tu tarjeta de
crédito o dinero, seleccionar tu
destino y tarifa y el billete te
sale automáticamente.

Para conversar

Un billete para
Madrid, por favor.

¿En primera clase
o en segunda?

En segunda, por favor,
de ida y vuelta.

el quiosco

los libros de bolsillo

las revistas

los periódicos

En otras partes

The word **boleto** is used throughout Latin America. **El billete** is used in Spain. **La boletería** is used more frequently in Latin America, while **la ventanilla** is used in Spain. **El boleto de ida y regreso** is common in Latin America for *a round-trip ticket.* In Mexico, however, you will hear **un redondo. El billete de ida y vuelta** is used in Spain. *To buy a ticket* in Latin America is **comprar un boleto;** in Spain it is **sacar un billete.**

el vagón, el coche

el andén

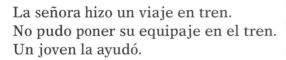

la vía

Los amigos hicieron un viaje en tren.
Tomaron el tren.
No quisieron tomar el autobús.
Los amigos estuvieron en el andén.
Esperaron el tren en el andén.

La señora hizo un viaje en tren.
No pudo poner su equipaje en el tren.
Un joven la ayudó.

QuickPass

Go to glencoe.com
For: **Vocabulary practice**
Web code: ASD7837c3

ESCUCHAR

 Escucha las frases. Parea cada frase con la foto que describe.

a.

b.

HABLAR • ESCRIBIR

 Contesta.

1. La señora no sabe a qué hora sale su tren. ¿Qué consulta?
2. La señora quiere sacar un billete para el tren. ¿Adónde va?
3. La señora piensa volver. ¿Qué tipo de billete (boleto) necesita?
4. Los trenes tienen dos clases. ¿En qué clase es más alta la tarifa? ¿En primera o en segunda?
5. La señora no quiere hacer cola delante de la ventanilla. ¿Dónde puede sacar su billete?
6. ¿Dónde esperan los pasajeros el tren?
7. En el hall de la estación de tren hay un quiosco. ¿Qué venden en el quiosco?

ESCRIBIR

 Da una palabra relacionada.

la ventana   esperar   salir

ir   llegar   volver

CULTURA

En la ventanilla de la estación de ferrocarril en Málaga, España

Vocabulario 1

HABLAR • ESCRIBIR

④ Contesta según la información en el billete. •··········

1. ¿De qué estación en Madrid sale el tren?
2. ¿Cuál es el destino del tren?
3. ¿A qué hora sale?
4. ¿A qué hora llega?
5. ¿Es un billete sencillo o de ida y vuelta?

ESCUCHAR • HABLAR • ESCRIBIR

⑤ Contesta según se indica.

1. ¿Quiso José hacer el viaje en bus? (no)
2. ¿Cómo hizo el viaje? (en tren)
3. ¿Pudo llevar su equipaje? (no)
4. ¿Quién lo ayudó? (su amigo)
5. ¿Dónde esperó el tren? (en el andén)
6. ¿Estuvo mucho tiempo en el andén? (no)

EXPANSIÓN

Ahora, sin mirar las preguntas, cuenta la información en tus propias palabras. Si no recuerdas algo, un(a) compañero(a) te puede ayudar.

LEER • ESCRIBIR

⑥ **Juego** **Cada uno en su sitio** Pon cada palabra en el lugar apropiado.

el vagón	el horario	la vía
la sala de espera	el distribuidor automático	
el tren	el quiosco	la ventanilla

CULTURA

El AVE en un andén de la estación de Atocha, Madrid

EN EL HALL	EN EL ANDÉN
_____	_____
_____	_____
_____	_____

Comunicación

⑦ Trabaja con un(a) compañero(a) de clase. Tu compañero(a) va a ser el/la agente en la ventanilla. Preparen una conversación para comprar un billete.

⑧ Tienes un(a) amigo(a) que está en la estación de Atocha en Madrid. Explícale lo que tiene que hacer para sacar su billete de un distribuidor automático.

VIDEO To practice your new words, watch **Vocabulario en vivo.**

En el tren

subir al tren

el asiento, la plaza

libre

el revisor

ocupado

el pasillo

bajar(se) del tren

El revisor revisó los billetes.
El tren no está completo. Hay asientos libres.

el coche comedor, el coche cafetería, la bufetería

En otras partes

In Spain **el revisor** is a *train conductor.* The term is used in Latin America as well but you will also hear **el cobrador,** particularly on buses or trains where one actually pays the fare on board. **El asiento** is used throughout Latin America, and **la plaza** is used in Spain.

Horarios	
	LLANO
Clase de tren	
Número de tren	9614
Observaciones	(1)(N)(V)
Días de circulación	LMXJV··
MADRID Puerta de Atocha	07:00
CIUDAD REAL	-
PUERTOLLANO	-
CÓRDOBA	08:41
SEVILLA Santa Justa	09:25
Restauración	

El tren salió a tiempo.
No salió tarde.
No salió con retraso (con una demora).

el cañón

el risco

el caballo

una senda

Estos jóvenes estuvieron en México.
Cuando (se) bajaron del tren, alquilaron
(rentaron) unos caballos.
Anduvieron a caballo por los riscos del cañón.

Los pasajeros van a bajar(se) en la
próxima parada (estación).

Tienen que transbordar (cambiar de tren).

Para conversar

¿Este tren va a Barcelona?

No, señor. Tiene que transbordar (cambiar de tren).

Ay, ¿sí? ¿Dónde?

Puede bajar(se) en la próxima parada (estación).

QuickPass

Go to glencoe.com
For: **Vocabulary practice**
Web code: **ASD7837c3**

ESCUCHAR

1 Escucha. Escoge la frase correcta. Usa una tabla como la de abajo para indicar tus respuestas.

a	b

HABLAR

2 Contesta.

1. Cuando el tren sale a tiempo, ¿hay una demora o no?
2. ¿Pasa el revisor por los pasillos del tren?
3. ¿Revisa los boletos de los pasajeros?
4. Cuando el tren está completo, ¿hay asientos libres?
5. Si los pasajeros tienen hambre, ¿pueden ir a la bufetería?

HABLAR • ESCRIBIR

3 Identifica. Luego usa cada palabra en una frase original.

1.

2.

3.

4.

Conexiones

Las matemáticas

Si tienes que leer un anuncio de un evento o el horario en un país hispano, vas a ver que dan la hora usando las veinticuatro horas. La una es la una de la mañana y las doce es el mediodía. Las trece es una hora después del mediodía—es la una de la tarde. Las veinticuatro horas es la medianoche.

HORARIO DE TRENES

JULIO, JULIOL JULY, JULI	AGOSTO, AGOST AUGUST, AUGUST	SEPTIEMBRE, SETEMBRE SEPTEMBER, SEPTEMBER

SÓLLER - PALMA	PALMA - SÓLLER	
8 00	8 00	
9 15	10 40	TREN TURÍSTICO
11 50	13 00	
14 10	15 15	
19 00	20 05	
19 35		

LEER

4 Parea las palabras que tienen el mismo significado.

1. una plaza
2. desocupado
3. el coche cafetería
4. rentar
5. con retraso
6. transbordar

a. la bufetería
b. con una demora
c. cambiar de tren
d. un asiento
e. libre
f. alquilar

HABLAR • ESCRIBIR

5 Contesta las preguntas sobre unos amigos que hicieron un viaje interesante por un cañón famoso.

1. ¿Tomaron los amigos el tren?
2. ¿Pagaron una tarifa estudiantil?
3. Cuando (se) bajaron del tren, ¿dieron una caminata?
4. ¿Rentaron caballos?
5. ¿Por dónde anduvieron?
6. ¿Adónde hicieron una excursión?
7. ¿Fueron solos o tuvieron que ir acompañados de un guía?
8. ¿Vieron todo el cañón?

Unos jóvenes van a cabalgar.

ESCRIBIR

6 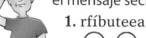 **Rompecabezas**

Forma palabras con las siguientes letras. Luego descubre el mensaje secreto.

1. rfíbuteea

○ ○ ○ ___ ___ ○ ___ ___ ___
  1 2 3   4

2. ilasplo

○ ○ ___ ___ ○ ___
  5 6   7

3. rrsantdabor

○ ___ ___ ___ ○ ___ ___ ○ ___ ___ ___ ○
  8   9   10   11

4. serrivo

___ ___ ○ ○ ___ ___
       12 13

El mensaje secreto

___ ___ ___ ___ ___ ___ ___ ___ ___,
 2 9   1 13 7 7 4 8 4

___ ___ ___ ___ ___ ___ ___ ___
 5 10 11   3 6 12 10 11

InfoGap For more practice using your new vocabulary words, do Activity 3 on page SR5 at the end of this book.

QuickPass

Go to glencoe.com
For: **Vocabulary practice**
Web code: ASD7837c3

GeoVistas

To learn more about Uruguay, take a tour on pages SH60–SH61.

Pretérito de los verbos irregulares

1. The verbs **hacer, querer,** and **venir** are irregular in the preterite. Note that they all have an **i** in the stem. Note too that the endings for **yo** and **usted (él, ella)** are different from the endings of regular verbs.

	hacer	querer	venir
yo	hice	quise	vine
tú	hiciste	quisiste	viniste
Ud., él, ella	hizo	quiso	vino
nosotros(as)	hicimos	quisimos	vinimos
vosotros(as)	*hicisteis*	*quisisteis*	*vinisteis*
Uds., ellos, ellas	hicieron	quisieron	vinieron

2. The verbs **poder, poner,** and **saber** all have a **u** in the stem.

	poder	poner	saber
yo	pude	puse	supe
tú	pudiste	pusiste	supiste
Ud., él, ella	pudo	puso	supo
nosotros(as)	pudimos	pusimos	supimos
vosotros(as)	*pudisteis*	*pusisteis*	*supisteis*
Uds., ellos, ellas	pudieron	pusieron	supieron

3. The verbs **estar, andar,** and **tener** all have a **uv** in the stem.

	estar	andar	tener
yo	estuve	anduve	tuve
tú	estuviste	anduviste	tuviste
Ud., él, ella	estuvo	anduvo	tuvo
nosotros(as)	estuvimos	anduvimos	tuvimos
vosotros(as)	*estuvisteis*	*anduvisteis*	*tuvisteis*
Uds., ellos, ellas	estuvieron	anduvieron	tuvieron

CULTURA

Los peatones anduvieron por la Plaza de la Independencia en Montevideo, Uruguay.

4. Many of these verbs are not used frequently in the preterite. When they are, they take on a special meaning. Observe the following.

Quise ayudar.	*I tried to help.*
No quiso ir en carro.	*He refused to go by car.*
Yo lo supe ayer.	*I found out yesterday.*
No pude terminar.	*(I tried but) I couldn't finish.*
Pude terminar.	*(After much effort) I managed to finish.*

Práctica

HABLAR • ESCRIBIR

1 Imagina que estuviste en una estación de tren. Contesta.

1. ¿Cómo viniste a la estación de tren?
2. ¿Hiciste el viaje en tren?
3. ¿Lo hiciste en tren porque no quisiste ir en carro?
4. ¿Pudiste poner todo tu equipaje en el tren?
5. ¿Tuviste que buscar un asiento libre?
6. ¿Anduviste de un vagón a otro para buscar un asiento?

EXPANSIÓN

Ahora, sin mirar las preguntas, cuenta la información en tus propias palabras. Si no recuerdas algo, un(a) compañero(a) te puede ayudar.

LEER • ESCRIBIR

2 Completa las conversaciones en el pretérito.

1. —Ellos no _____ (querer) hacer el viaje.
   —¿No lo _____ (querer) hacer?
   —No, de ninguna manera.
   —Pues, ¿qué pasó entonces? ¿Lo _____ (hacer) o no lo _____ (hacer)?
   —No lo _____ (hacer).

2. —¿Por qué no _____ (venir) ustedes esta mañana?
   —Nosotros no _____ (venir) porque no _____ (hacer) reservación.
   —¿Ustedes no _____ (tener) reservación?

3. —Carlos no _____ (querer) hacer la cama.
   —Entonces, ¿quién la _____ (hacer)?
   —Pues, la _____ (hacer) yo.
   —¡Qué absurdo! ¿Tú la _____ (hacer) porque él no la _____ (querer) hacer?

Más práctica

📖 Workbook, pp. 3.7–3.8
💻 StudentWorks™ Plus

CATEGORY BOOK

See page SH21 for help with making this foldable. Make a *category book* foldable with ten tabs. On the top tab, write the infinitive of a verb that is irregular in the preterite. On the following tabs, write the subject pronouns: **yo, tú, Ud., él, ella, nosotros(as), Uds., ellos, ellas.** Exchange foldables with your partner. Open each tab and write the correct form of the verb.

LEER • ESCRIBIR

3 Completa con el pretérito del verbo indicado.

El otro día yo ___1___ (estar) en un mercado en Perú. Rafael ___2___ (estar) allí también. Nosotros ___3___ (andar) por el mercado pero no ___4___ (poder) comprar nada. No es que no ___5___ (querer) comprar nada, es que no ___6___ (poder) porque ___7___ (ir) al mercado sin dinero.

Un mercado indígena en un pueblo andino de Perú

ESCUCHAR • HABLAR • ESCRIBIR

4 Sigue el modelo.

MODELO No puedo ahora. →
No puedo ahora y no pude ayer tampoco.

1. No pueden ahora.
2. No tenemos que hacerlo ahora.
3. No lo haces ahora.
4. Ellos no están ahora.
5. Él no viene ahora.

Carlos es un joven peruano. Como los jóvenes en todas partes, Carlos no pudo salir anoche porque tuvo que estudiar.

Comunicación

5 Habla con un(a) compañero(a) de clase. Dile lo que no pudiste o no quisiste hacer porque tuviste que hacer otra cosa. Dile lo que hiciste. Luego tu compañero(a) va a decir lo que no pudo o no quiso hacer porque tuvo que hacer otra cosa.

El verbo decir

The verb **decir** *(to say)* is irregular in the present and preterite tenses. Study the following forms.

PRESENTE		
yo digo	nosotros(as)	decimos
tú dices	*vosotros(as)*	*decís*
Ud., él, ella dice	Uds., ellos, ellas	dicen

PRETÉRITO		
yo dije	nosotros(as)	dijimos
tú dijiste	*vosotros(as)*	*dijisteis*
Ud., él, ella dijo	Uds., ellos, ellas	dijeron

Práctica

Nota

- Note the use of **que** after the verb **decir**.
  Yo digo que sí y ellos dicen que no.
- Note that the verb **traer** follows the same pattern as the verb **decir** in the preterite: **traje.**

HABLAR

6 Personaliza. Da respuestas personales.

1. ¿Qué dices? ¿Quieres dar una caminata? Digo que…
2. ¿Qué dices? ¿Quieres subir hasta las ruinas?
3. ¿Qué dices? ¿Quieres hacer una excursión al cañón?
4. ¿Qué dices? ¿Quieres alquilar un caballo?

LEER • ESCRIBIR

7 Completa con el presente de **decir.**

—Yo __1__ que quiero ir en tren pero Elena me __2__ que prefiere tomar el avión. Ella y Tomás también __3__ que no hay mucha diferencia entre la tarifa del avión y la tarifa del tren. ¿Qué __4__ tú?

—Yo __5__ que es mejor ir en tren.

—Bueno. Tú y yo __6__ la misma cosa. Estamos de acuerdo.

LEER • ESCRIBIR

8 Completa con el presente y el pretérito de **decir.**

1. Yo lo _____ pero ellos no lo _____.
2. Ellos lo _____ pero ellos no lo _____.
3. Él lo _____ pero ustedes no lo _____.
4. Nosotros lo _____ pero ustedes no lo _____.
5. Tú lo _____ pero yo no lo _____.

VIDEO Want help with irregular verbs in the preterite? Watch **Gramática en vivo.**

LEER • ESCRIBIR

9 Completa con el pretérito de **decir.**

1. Tomás me _____ que le gusta mucho la ciudad de Montevideo.
2. Yo le _____ que a mí me gusta también.
3. Nosotros _____ que nos gusta porque es una ciudad bonita.
4. ¿No me _____ (tú) que está cerca del mar?
5. Sí, y (yo) te _____ que en la ciudad misma hay playas.

CULTURA

Montevideo, la capital de Uruguay, es una ciudad cosmopolita. Dentro de la ciudad, hay muchos barrios residenciales.

HABLAR • ESCRIBIR

10 ¿Quién dijo que sí? Contesta usando cada sujeto.

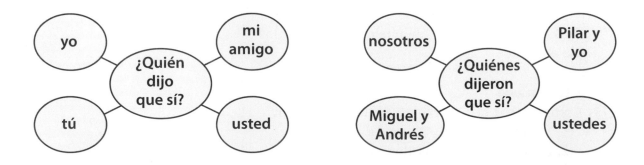

yo · tú · ¿Quién dijo que sí? · mi amigo · usted

nosotros · Miguel y Andrés · ¿Quiénes dijeron que sí? · Pilar y yo · ustedes

Pronombres después de una preposición

1. You already know all the pronouns you use after a preposition. Remember they are the same as the subject pronouns except for **mí** and **ti**. **Mí** takes an accent mark to differentiate it from the possessive adjective **mi—mi casa**.

	mí	
	ti	
	uste	
	él	
Para	ella	está bien, ¿no?
	nosotros(as)	
	ustedes	
	ellos	
	ellas	

2. Note what happens to **mí** and **ti** when used with **con**.

—¿Vienes **conmigo**?
—Sí, voy **contigo**.

—¿Quién hizo el viaje **contigo**?
—Carolina lo hizo **conmigo**.

Refrán

Can you guess what the following proverb means?

Querer y poder, hermanos vienen a ser.

Práctica

HABLAR • ESCRIBIR

11 Contesta.

1. ¿De quién es el boleto? ¿Es de él o de ella?
2. ¿Para quién es la cámara digital? ¿Es para ti?
3. ¿Qué piensas de mí? Puedes ser honesto(a).
4. ¿Quiere Julia hacer una caminata con ustedes?
5. ¿Quieres ir conmigo?
6. ¿Quiénes van a hacer el viaje contigo?
7. ¿A ti te gusta más leer libros de bolsillo o artículos en una revista?

ESCRIBIR

12 Escribe en el singular.

1. No es para *ellos*.
2. Ellos quieren ir con *nosotros*.
3. Es de *ustedes*, ¿no?
4. Estamos pensando en *ellas*.
5. ¿Por qué no lo están discutiendo con *nosotros*?

¡Bravo!

You have now learned all the new vocabulary and grammar in this chapter. Continue to use and practice all that you know while learning more cultural information. **¡Vamos!**

QuickPass

Go to glencoe.com
For: **Conversation practice**
Web code: ASD7837c3

EN LA VENTANILLA

¿Comprendes?

VIDEO To visit a train station, watch **Diálogo en vivo.**

A Completa según la información en la conversación. Indica tus respuestas en una tabla como la de abajo.

el billete				
tipo	clase	destino	tipo de tarifa	precio (tarifa)

B Completa según la información en la conversación. Indica tus respuestas en una tabla como la de abajo.

el viaje		
medio de transporte	hora de salida	andén

C Corrige toda la información falsa.
1. La pasajera compra un billete para Sevilla.
2. Quiere un billete sencillo.
3. Necesita el billete para mañana.
4. Quiere viajar en primera.
5. La pasajera es profesora.
6. El tren sale a las seis y diez de la tarde.

D **Resumiendo** Cuenta todo lo que pasa en la conversación en tus propias palabras.

¿Lo sabes?

Muchos alumnos toman el tren. Hay tarifas escolares (estudiantiles) reducidas.

CULTURA

Córdoba, a orillas del río Guadalquivir, es una ciudad de mucho interés histórico. Aquí vemos el puente romano y la famosa Mezquita.

Antes de leer

Mira y estudia todos los visuales que acompañan la lectura.

Viajes ferroviarios fabulosos

El servicio de trenes El tren es un medio de transporte importante y cómodo en España. Hay trenes que sirven casi todas las ciudades y pueblos del país con salidas frecuentes y muy pocas demoras.

En Latinoamérica el bus y el avión son los medios de transporte más importantes. En muchas regiones el servicio ferroviario no existe. No obstante[1] hay unos recorridos o viajes en tren que son fantásticos. Uno es el viaje de Cuzco a Machu Picchu en los Andes de Perú.

De Cuzco a Machu Picchu Cuzco es una ciudad andina famosa por sus magníficos edificios coloniales. Al borde de un cañón en una región remota no muy lejos de Cuzco está Machu Picchu—una ciudad construida por los incas. Un hecho[2] histórico increíble es que los españoles no descubrieron la ciudad durante su conquista de Perú. Fue el senador estadounidense Hiram Bingham quien la descubrió en 1911.

[1]No obstante *Nevertheless*   [2]hecho *fact*

 **Reading Check**

¿Dónde es más importante el servicio de trenes?

 **Reading Check**

¿Quién descubrió Machu Picchu?

Durante la lectura

Al leer cierto párrafo, estudia el visual específico que clarifica la información en el párrafo.

CULTURA
Plaza de Armas, Cuzco, Perú

¿Quiénes toman el tren de Cuzco a Machu Picchu? La mayoría son turistas, entre ellos muchos mochileros jóvenes, que quieren tener la experiencia de visitar las famosas ruinas incaicas. El tren sale de Cuzco y para llegar a Machu Picchu tiene que bajar unos 1.200 metros. Corre al borde mismo de[3] muchos riscos pendientes[4]. Los pasajeros observan que al bajar el clima y la vegetación cambian mucho. A pesar de[5] su altura, Machu Picchu se encuentra en la región amazónica—una región semitropical de densa vegetación. En Machu Picchu es necesario llevar ropa ligera[6] y un impermeable[7] es imprescindible (obligatorio).

La Barranca del Cobre Otra excursión espectacular es la de la línea de ferrocarril Pacífico-Chihuahua por la Sierra Madre de México. El tren hace parada en Divisadero. De allí los pasajeros pueden contemplar la vista de la Barranca del Cobre—un cañón más profundo que el Gran Cañón de Colorado. Si algún día haces el viaje debes bajar(te) del tren en Divisadero y pasar unos días dando caminatas por esta región espectacular. Si eres más aventurero(a) puedes rentar un caballo y con un guía hacer excursiones por los riscos del cañón.

[3]al borde mismo de   *right on the edge of*   [6]ligera   *light*
[4]pendientes   *steep*   [7]impermeable   *raincoat*
[5]A pesar de   *In spite of*

✓ Reading Check

¿Dónde hace más frío? ¿En Cuzco o en Machu Picchu?

CULTURA
Ruinas en Machu Picchu

CULTURA
La locomotora del tren Pacífico-Chihuahua

✓ Reading Check

¿De dónde pueden ver la Barranca del Cobre los pasajeros del tren?

CULTURA
La Barranca del Cobre

EN TREN

¿Cómo es la vida de los tarahumara?

Después de leer

Explica como los elementos visuales te ayudaron a comprender la lectura.

En la región del cañón viven los tarahumara. Una vez los tarahumara ocuparon todo el estado de Chihuahua pero muchos de ellos murieron[8] por el duro trabajo forzado que tuvieron que hacer en las minas y más tarde en la construcción del ferrocarril. Para sobrevivir fueron a vivir en los lugares más recónditos (aislados) de la Barranca. Hoy son seminómadas y algunos viven en cuevas. En verano vagan (andan) por las mesetas de la Sierra Madre y en invierno bajan al fondo del cañón.

[8]murieron   *died*

CULTURA

Cuevas de los tarahumara en la Sierra Madre Occidental

CULTURA

Los tarahumara vendiendo canastas en la estación de Divisadero

¿Comprendes?

Más práctica

■ Workbook, p. 3.11
● StudentWorks™ Plus

A Confirmando información Indica si la información es correcta o no.

	correcta	incorrecta
1. El tren es un medio de transporte importante en España.		
2. El tren es un medio de transporte importante en todas partes de Latinoamérica.		
3. Hay ruinas de una ciudad azteca en Cuzco.		
4. Cuzco es una ciudad colonial en los Andes peruanos.		
5. Machu Picchu se encuentra al borde de un cañón.		
6. Machu Picchu está a una altura más baja que Cuzco.		
7. Por su altura Machu Picchu está en una zona muy fría.		
8. Nunca llueve en Machu Picchu.		

B Describiendo En tus propias palabras describe el viaje en tren de Cuzco a Machu Picchu.

C Infiriendo La lectura no indica de una manera directa que llueve mucho en Machu Picchu. Pero, ¿qué información en la lectura indica que llueve bastante en Machu Picchu?

D Recordando hechos Contesta.
1. ¿Cuál es una excursión espectacular en México?
2. ¿Qué es posible ver de Divisadero?
3. ¿Qué es la Barranca del Cobre?
4. Hay dos maneras de visitar la Barranca del Cobre. ¿Cuáles son?

E Describiendo Contesta.
1. ¿Cuáles son unas características de los tarahumara?
2. ¿Cómo fue su vida en el pasado y cómo es su vida actual?

CULTURA
Vista de Cuzco, Perú

De Panamá a Colón en tren

Colón es la segunda ciudad más grande de Panamá. La primera es la capital, la Ciudad de Panamá. Colón está en el Atlántico y Panamá está en el Pacífico.

CULTURA

Vista desde la estación de ferrocarril en Colón, Panamá

Si uno quiere ir de la Ciudad de Panamá a Colón, puede tomar el tren. El boleto o el pasaje es bastante barato y el viaje es interesante. El tren corre a lo largo del famoso canal de Panamá y durante el viaje los pasajeros pueden observar los muchos barcos que usan el canal para hacer la travesía desde el Atlántico hasta el Pacífico o viceversa. Es una zona tropical de vegetación densa y paisaje espectacular.

El tren pasa también por la pequeña isla de Barro Colorado. El Instituto Smithsonian mantiene la isla donde hacen investigaciones importantes sobre enfermedades tropicales.

Es muy fácil hacer el viaje de ida y regreso el mismo día porque dura (toma) solamente una hora y media.

Ferrocarril del canal de Panamá en la estación de Colón

CULTURA

¿Comprendes?

Escoge.

1. ¿Cómo sabemos que Colón no es la ciudad más grande de Panamá?
   a. No es la capital.
   b. Está en el Atlántico.
   c. La lectura indica que es la segunda ciudad del país.
   d. Hay solo dos ciudades grandes en Panamá.

2. ¿Cómo puede uno ir de Colón a Panamá?
   a. en el canal
   b. en tren
   c. por la isla de Barro Colorado
   d. observando los barcos

3. ¿Por qué es importante el canal de Panamá?
   a. Los barcos pueden hacer la travesía entre el Atlántico y el Pacífico en muy poco tiempo.
   b. Está en una zona tropical con una vegetación densa.
   c. En una de sus islas hay un instituto que hace investigaciones médicas importantes.
   d. Empalma o enlaza la Ciudad de Panamá con Colón.

4. ¿Cuál es la frase que expresa la misma idea que la siguiente?

   Los pasajeros pueden observar los muchos barcos que usan el canal.

   a. Los pasajeros pueden estudiar los muchos barcos que usan el canal.
   b. Los pasajeros pueden servir los muchos barcos que usan el canal.
   c. Los pasajeros pueden ver los muchos barcos que usan el canal.
   d. Los pasajeros pueden describir los muchos barcos que usan el canal.

5. ¿Cuál es un buen título para esta lectura?
   a. La Ciudad de Panamá
   b. El canal de Panamá
   c. Una región tropical
   d. Un viaje interesante en tren

CULTURA

Vista de unas esclusas del canal de Panamá

Un tren en el desierto de Atacama cerca de Arica, Chile

To review **Vocabulario 1** and **Vocabulario 2,** turn to pages 72–73 and 76–77.

To review **el pretérito de los verbos irregulares,** turn to pages 80–81.

Vocabulario

1 **¿Sí o no?**

1. El revisor trabaja en la ventanilla en la estación de ferrocarril.

2. Un boleto sencillo es para un(a) pasajero(a) que no piensa volver al mismo lugar (sitio).

3. Si no sabes la hora de salida de tu tren tienes que consultar el quiosco.

4. Cuando quieres comer en el tren, vas al coche comedor.

5. Venden los boletos en el andén.

6. Un tren que sale tarde tiene una demora.

2 **Da otra palabra o expresión.**

7. cambiar de tren

8. con retraso

9. de ida y vuelta

10. la bufetería

3 **Completa con palabras apropiadas.**

11–12. Si quieres leer algo puedes comprar _____ y _____ en el quiosco.

13. El tren está completo. No hay _____ libres.

Gramática

4 **Completa con el pretérito.**

14. Yo _____ que salir. (tener)

15. Nosotros no _____ esperar más. (poder)

16–17. Él _____ ir pero no _____. (querer, poder)

18. ¿Cúanto tiempo _____ ustedes allí? (estar)

19. Ellos _____ juntos, ¿no? (venir)

20. ¿Por qué no _____ tú la revista en la mochila? (poner)

21–22. Él no _____ porque no _____ vernos. (estar, querer)

5 Escribe las frases en el pretérito.

23. Hacemos una excursión interesante.
24. Tengo que hacer las maletas.
25. Ustedes ven todo, ¿no?
26. ¿Por qué no quieres ir?

To review **el pretérito de los verbos irregulares,** turn to pages 80–81.

6 Completa con la letra que falta.

27–28. Él lo hi_o pero yo no lo hi_e.

7 Completa con decir.

29–30. Yo lo _____ ahora y lo _____ ayer también.
31–32. Ellos lo _____ ahora y lo _____ ayer también.
33–34. Nosotros lo _____ ahora y lo _____ ayer también.

To review **decir,** turn to page 83.

Cultura

8 Contesta.

35. ¿Dónde es el tren un medio de transporte importante?
36. ¿Qué hay en Machu Picchu?
37. ¿Cómo van muchos turistas de Cuzco a Machu Picchu?
38. ¿Qué es la Barranca del Cobre?
39. ¿Dónde está?
40. ¿Quiénes son los tarahumara?

To review this cultural information, turn to pages 88–90.

CULTURA

El tren entre Cuzco y Machu Picchu hace una parada en el pueblo de Aguas Calientes.

Prepárate para el examen
Practice for oral proficiency

1   **Un viaje en avión o en tren**

   Compare train and plane travel

Trabaja con un(a) compañero(a) de clase. Van a comparar un viaje en tren con un viaje en avión. Cada uno(a) va a dar su preferencia.

2   **En la boletería**

   Talk about buying a train ticket

Prepara una conversación en la boletería de una estación de ferrocarril para comprar el tipo de boleto que necesitas.

3   **Un lugar que conozco**

   Talk about a trip you took

Escoge un lugar que visitaste con unos amigos o parientes. Describe el lugar.

CULTURA
Una calle peatonal en Montenegro, Colombia

4   **El viaje más interesante**

   Discuss train trips in Spanish-speaking countries

De los viajes en tren en las lecturas de este capítulo, ¿cuál te interesa más? ¿Por qué? Habla con un(a) compañero(a) para determinar si ustedes tienen la misma opinión.

Prepárate para el examen
Practice for written proficiency

Tarea

You are going to write about a fabulous trip you took to a place that you love. The place can be real or imaginary.

Writing Strategy

Describing When writing a descriptive essay, use words that enable your reader to visualize the scene you are describing. Choose details and organize them in a way that creates an impression. Use vivid adjectives to make your writing more alive. Think of some adjectives you know in Spanish that you consider "vivid."

CULTURA
Un grupo de jóvenes viajando por España

❶ Prewrite

Use a diagram like the one below to help you organize your writing.

tus actividades— lo que hiciste

la ropa que necesitas allí

cómo fuiste

el lugar

lo que viste allí

el tiempo que hace allí

cómo viajaste

❷ Write

- Read the sentences you wrote in the graphic organizer. Decide the best order for your composition. Each topic could be one paragraph. Give order to the sentences that develop each topic.

- In your description, try to make your readers understand what it is about the place that makes you think it is so great.

Evaluate

Don't forget that your teacher will evaluate you on organization, use of vocabulary, correctness of grammar, and completeness of information.

Repaso del Capítulo ③

Gramática

- ### Pretérito de los verbos irregulares *(pages 80–81)*
  Note the irregular preterite stems of the following verbs.

hacer → hic-	poder → pud-	estar → estuv-
querer → quis-	poner → pus-	andar → anduv-
venir → vin-	saber → sup-	tener → tuv-

venir	poner	tener
vine	puse	tuve
viniste	pusiste	tuviste
vino	puso	tuvo
vinimos	pusimos	tuvimos
vinisteis	*pusisteis*	*tuvisteis*
vinieron	pusieron	tuvieron

  Remember the spelling of **hacer.**

  hice, hizo

- ### El verbo decir *(page 83)*
  Decir is irregular in the present and in the preterite.

presente		pretérito	
digo	decimos	dije	dijimos
dices	*decís*	dijiste	*dijisteis*
dice	dicen	dijo	dijeron

  Traer is conjugated the same as **decir** in the preterite.

- ### Pronombres después de una preposición
  (page 85)
  Except for **mí** and **ti**, prepositional pronouns are the same as subject pronouns.

  mí, ti, usted, él, ella, nosotros(as), ustedes, ellos, ellas

  With **con, mí** and **ti** become **conmigo** and **contigo.**

CULTURA

Los jóvenes consultan las paradas que hacen los trenes de cercanías que sirven Madrid.

There are a number of cognates in this list. See how many you and a partner can find. Who can find the most? Compare your list with those of your classmates.

Vocabulario

Getting around a train station

la estación de
  ferrocarril (tren)
el hall
la sala de espera
el horario
la llegada
la salida
la ventanilla,
  la boletería

el billete, el boleto
  sencillo
  de ida y vuelta
  de ida y regreso
  en primera
    (segunda) clase
la tarifa
  escolar
  (estudiantil)
  reducida

la tarjeta de crédito
el distribuidor
  automático
el tren
el vagón, el coche
el andén
la vía
el destino
subir al tren
bajar(se) del tren

At a kiosk

el quiosco
el periódico

la revista
el libro de bolsillo

On board the train

el pasillo
el asiento, la plaza
el revisor
el coche comedor,
  el coche cafetería,
  la bufetería

la parada
  libre
  ocupado(a)
  completo(a)
  próximo(a)
revisar los billetes

transbordar
  (cambiar de tren)

Describing an excursion

el cañón
el risco

una senda
el caballo

andar a caballo
alquilar, rentar

Other useful words and expressions

a tiempo
tarde

insertar
seleccionar

Literary Reader

You may wish to read the adaptation of the Spanish classic *El Quijote,* found on pages 358–363.

Repaso cumulativo

Repasa lo que ya has aprendido

These activities will help you review
what you have learned so far in Spanish.

 Escucha las palabras. Haz un diagrama como el de
abajo. Indica si cada palabra se relaciona con un
viaje en tren o en avión o los dos.

 Completa en el presente con la forma yo.
1. _____ un viaje en tren. (hacer)
2. _____ a las ocho. (salir)
3. _____ mucho equipaje. (tener)
4. _____ tres maletas. (traer)
5. _____ mucha ropa en mis maletas. (poner)
6. _____ en tren. (venir)
7. _____ que _____ el viaje en tren. (decir, hacer)
8. _____ que me voy a divertir. (saber)
9. _____ a viajar por Argentina. (ir)
10. _____ Argentina. (conocer)

CULTURA

Hay muchos trenes que salen de la
estación General Belgrano para los
suburbios de Buenos Aires.

 Cambia las frases en la Actividad 2 a María.

 Parea los contrarios.

1. el despegue	a. largo
2. la llegada	b. subir
3. bajar	c. temprano
4. sentarse	d. el aterrizaje
5. volver, regresar	e. vender
6. corto	f. la salida
7. comprar	g. salir
8. tarde	h. levantarse

5 Escoge la palabra apropiada del banco de palabras para contestar cada pregunta.

el mostrador de la línea aérea	el cinturón de seguridad
la tarjeta de embarque	el control de seguridad
el boleto electrónico	en el pasillo
la puerta de salida	en la pista

1. ¿Dónde se presenta Felipe para facturar su equipaje en el aeropuerto?
2. ¿De dónde sale el vuelo?
3. ¿Por dónde tienen que pasar los pasajeros antes de ir a la puerta de salida?
4. ¿Qué necesitan los pasajeros para poder abordar el avión?
5. ¿Qué tienen que abrochar los pasajeros abordo del avión?
6. El asiento de José no está en la ventanilla. ¿Dónde está?

6 ¿Qué pone José en su maleta?

7 Personaliza. Da respuestas personales.
1. Cuando estás de vacaciones, ¿a qué hora te despiertas?
2. ¿Te levantas enseguida?
3. Si vas de camping, ¿duermes en una carpa?
4. ¿Te duermes enseguida si tienes que dormir en un saco de dormir?
5. ¿A qué hora te acuestas?
6. ¿Te diviertes cuando estás de vacaciones?

Vamos a comparar ¿Come tu familia a veces en un restaurante? ¿Qué tipo de restaurantes hay donde tú vives? ¿Hay restaurantes elegantes y restaurantes económicos? ¿Hay restaurantes étnicos o no? Vamos a ver los muchos tipos de restaurantes que hay en España y Latinoamérica y lo que uno debe esperar cuando come en un restaurante en un país hispano.

Objetivos

You will:

- order and pay for a meal at a restaurant
- identify more foods
- identify eating utensils and dishes
- discuss restaurants in Spain and Latin America

You will use:

- stem-changing verbs in the present and preterite
- adjectives of nationality
- the passive voice with **se**

◀ Una barra de tapas deliciosas en un local en un pueblo cerca de San Sebastián en Euskadi en el norte de España

QuickPass

Go to glencoe.com
For: **Online book**
Web code: **ASD7837c4**

Introducción al tema
En el restaurante

Mira las fotografías para familiarizarte con el tema del capítulo—experiencias en restaurantes en varias partes del mundo hispano. Consulta los menús y observa unos platos deliciosos regionales para decidir los que te apetecen. Y, ¡buen provecho!

¡RICAS! TORTAS AHOGADAS $17.⁹⁰
LONCHES
JAMON.... $17.⁹⁰
PANELA.... $17.⁹⁰
CARNITAS.... $20.⁰⁰
TOSTADAS
CUERITOS.... $11.⁷⁰
JAMON.... $13.⁹⁰
PANELA.... $13.⁹⁰
CARNITAS.... $16.⁹⁰
TACOS
Vapor 5 × $11.⁰⁰
Dorados 5 × $10.⁰⁰

México ¿Te apetece comer algo? ¿Qué quieres pedir de esta lista delante de una cafetería en Guadalajara, México? ▶

◀ **Ecuador** Es la terraza de un restaurante en Baños, Ecuador. A mucha gente le gusta comer al aire libre.

España La paella es una especialidad de Valencia. Es un plato rico que lleva arroz amarillo y mariscos como langosta, camarones, mejillones y almejas. En el fondo se puede ver Alicante, una ciudad en la comunidad autónoma de Valencia. ▶

◀ **Argentina** El mesero está sirviendo un plato en un restaurante en Necochea. Necochea es un balneario en la costa al sur de Buenos Aires.

Unid. Descripción
recio   Total   P

1 BOC TORTILLA 100G   3.35   3.35
1 AGUA 0.5 L (PC)   1.35   1.35

TOTAL Euro   4.70
  ENTREGADO   20,00
  CAMBIO   15,30

I.V.A Incluido
GRACIAS POR SU VISITA

◄ **Perú** El cocinero acaba de preparar un plato de huevos fritos con pedacitos de jamón para un bufé en un hotel de Lima. Los bufés son populares en muchas partes de Latinoamérica, sobre todo para el desayuno y el almuerzo.

▲ **Costa Rica** El casado es una comida típica de los ticos, o costarricences. Lleva arroz, frijoles, una rodaja de plátano frito y pollo acompañado de una ensalada. El casado puede llevar también yuca y patacones con un filete de carne de res o pescado.

México Este restaurante pintoresco con manteles de varios colores está en Pátzcuaro, México. ▼

▲ **México** El menú es de un restaurante pequeño en Tepoztlán, México. Tepoztlán es un pueblo adonde va mucha gente de la Ciudad de México a pasar un fin de semana placentero en las montañas.

Argentina Aquí vemos la terraza al aire libre de un restaurante en Buenos Aires. Es un restaurante que sirve comida italiana. La cocina italiana es muy apreciada en Argentina donde vive mucha gente de ascendencia italiana. ▶

En el restaurante

el menú

el mesero,
el camarero

¿El biftec?
¿Cómo lo pidió?

casi crudo   bien hecho

a término medio

Carlos y Alicia están en el restaurante.
Alicia pide el menú.

En otras partes

- **El mesero** is used throughout Latin America. **El camarero** is used in Spain.

- **El cerdo** is the general word for *pork* and **chuletas de cerdo** means *pork chops*. Roast suckling pig is a very popular dish—**el cochinillo asado** in Spain, **el lechón asado** in most of Latin America but particularly in the Caribbean. The word **chancho** is also used in several Latin American countries.

Carlos pidió un biftec.
El mesero lo sirvió.

la cuenta

una propina

Alicia pide la cuenta.
Carlos deja una propina.

Más comestibles

La carne

la carne de res

el cordero

la chuleta de cerdo

Los mariscos

la langosta

los mejillones

las almejas

el aceite

la sal

el vinagre

la pimienta

poner la mesa

levantar (quitar) la mesa

¡Así se dice!

When you are really starving you can say **Me muero de hambre,** which literally means *I'm dying of hunger.*

la servilleta

el platillo

la taza

la cucharita

la cuchara

el tenedor

el plato

el cuchillo

el mantel

QuickPass

Go to glencoe.com
For: **Vocabulary practice**
Web code: **ASD7837c4**

ESCUCHAR

1 Escucha. Indica en una tabla como la de abajo si ves en la foto la información que oyes.

sí	no

ESCRIBIR

2 **Juego** **Cada uno en su sitio** Determina en qué categoría pertenece cada palabra.

el jamón   la pimienta   el aceite   el cordero
los mejillones   la sal   los camarones
el biftec   el pollo   la langosta

CARNE	MARISCOS	CONDIMENTOS

HABLAR • ESCRIBIR

3 Contesta sobre un restaurante.
1. ¿Quién sirve la comida en un restaurante?
2. ¿Qué pide el cliente para seleccionar o escoger lo que quiere comer?
3. Después de la comida, ¿qué pide para pagar?
4. ¿Deja una propina a veces?
5. ¿Para quién es la propina?

EXPANSIÓN

Ahora, sin mirar las preguntas, cuenta la información en tus propias palabras. Si no recuerdas algo, un(a) compañero(a) te puede ayudar.

4 **¡Te toca a ti!** Vas a poner la mesa. ¿Qué pones en la mesa?

CULTURA

El mesero sirve los refrescos que pidieron las jóvenes en un restaurante al aire libre en Manta, Ecuador.

Vocabulario

LEER • HABLAR

⑤ Rompecabezas

¡Adivina! ¿Qué es?

1. Se usa para cubrir la mesa.
2. Se usa para tomar agua o leche.
3. Se usa para beber café o té.
4. Se usa para comer sopa.
5. Se usa para cortar la carne.

HABLAR • ESCRIBIR

⑥ Personaliza. Da respuestas personales.

1. ¿Te gusta comer en un restaurante?
2. ¿Te gusta más la carne o el pescado?
3. ¿Te gustan las legumbres?
4. Para tu ensalada, ¿te gusta una salsa de aceite y vinagre?
5. ¿Te gusta la carne bien hecha, a término medio o casi cruda?
6. En tu casa, ¿quién pone la mesa?
7. ¿Quién lava los platos?
8. Y, ¿quién levanta o quita la mesa?

Conexiones

El lenguaje

Ya sabes que en el mundo hispano hay diferencias regionales en cuanto al uso de ciertas palabras. Los nombres de los comestibles tienden a variar de una región a otra. Aquí tenemos unos ejemplos.

- Las judías verdes tienen muchos nombres. Se llaman también «habichuelas tiernas», «chauchas», «vainitas», «ejotes» y «porotos».

- En casi todas partes el maíz es «el maíz» pero en México también se dice «el elote» y en Chile y otros países latinos se dice «el choclo». Un plato chileno delicioso es «el pastel de choclo».

CULTURA

Un restaurante con una terraza al aire libre en Guadalajara, México

QuickPass

Go to glencoe.com
For: **Grammar practice**
Web code: **ASD7837c4**

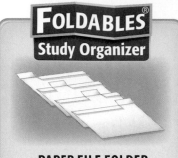

FOLDABLES®
Study Organizer

PAPER FILE FOLDER

See page SH29 for help with making this foldable. Use this foldable to help you review the different tenses of the verbs that you have learned. Make a *paper file folder* for a verb. On separate pieces of paper, write the conjugations of the verb. Continue to file new conjugations in your *paper file folder*.

Presente de los verbos de cambio radical e → i

1. The verbs **pedir, servir, repetir, freír** *(to fry),* **seguir** *(to follow),* and **vestirse** *(to get dressed)* are stem-changing verbs. The **e** of the infinitive stem changes to **i** in all forms of the present tense except **nosotros(as)** and *vosotros(as).* Study the following forms.

pedir			
yo	pido	nosotros(as)	pedimos
tú	pides	vosotros(as)	pedís
Ud., él, ella	pide	Uds., ellos, ellas	piden

servir			
yo	sirvo	nosotros(as)	servimos
tú	sirves	vosotros(as)	servís
Ud., él, ella	sirve	Uds., ellos, ellas	sirven

2. Note the spelling of **seguir.**

sigo, sigues, sigue, seguimos, *seguís,* siguen

3. Note that the present participle of these verbs also has **i.**

No estoy **pidiendo** nada.
El mesero nos está **sirviendo.**

Práctica

HABLAR • ESCRIBIR

1 Personaliza. Da respuestas personales.

1. ¿Qué pides cuando vas a un restaurante?
2. Si te gusta un plato, ¿lo repites?
3. ¿Sigues una dieta o un régimen a veces?
4. ¿Te vistes antes de salir para la escuela?
5. ¿Sigues un horario fijo en la escuela o varía de un día a otro tu horario?

CULTURA

El mesero sirve la comida en un restaurante elegante en la Ciudad de Guatemala.

Gramática

ESCUCHAR • HABLAR

2 Conversa según el modelo.

MODELO —A Juan le gusta la carne de res. ¿Qué pide él?
—Él pide carne de res.

1. A Marta le gustan las legumbres. ¿Qué pide ella?
2. A Andrés le gusta el biftec. ¿Qué pide él?
3. A mis amigos les gustan los mariscos.
¿Qué piden ellos?
4. A mis padres les gusta mucho el postre.
¿Qué piden ellos?
5. Nos gusta la ensalada. ¿Qué pedimos?
6. Nos gustan las tortillas. ¿Qué pedimos?

ESCRIBIR

3 Completa la tabla.

yo	nosotros	usted	tú	ellos
		pide		
sirvo				
	seguimos			
				se visten
			repites	

CULTURA

Un grupo de amigos peruanos comen juntos en un restaurante típico en Lima, Perú.

HABLAR • ESCRIBIR

4 Personaliza. Da respuestas personales.

1. Cuando vas a un restaurante, ¿qué pides?
2. ¿Pides papas? Si no pides papas, ¿pides arroz?
3. ¿Qué más pides con la carne y las papas o el arroz?
4. ¿Quién te sirve en el restaurante?
5. Si te sirve bien, ¿qué le dejas?

LEER • ESCRIBIR

5 Escribe en el plural.

1. Siempre pido postre.
2. No repito nada.
3. Él se viste bien.
4. Sigo un plan definido.
5. ¿Qué repites?
6. Ella fríe las papas.

Comunicación

6 Trabaja con un(a) compañero(a). Lean el menú. Decidan lo que van a pedir y por qué.

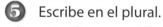

VIDEO Want help with stem-changing verbs in the preterite? Watch **Gramática en vivo.**

Pretérito de los verbos de cambio radical e → i, o → u

1. The verbs **pedir, repetir, freír, servir, seguir,** and **vestirse** have a stem change in the preterite. The **e** of the infinitive stem changes to **i** in the **él** and **ellos** forms.

¡Ojo!

If you pronounce the vowels **e** and **i** correctly, you will never make a spelling error.

repetir			
yo	repetí	nosotros(as)	repetimos
tú	repetiste	vosotros(as)	*repetisteis*
Ud., él, ella	repitió	Uds., ellos, ellas	repitieron

vestirse			
yo	me vestí	nosotros(as)	nos vestimos
tú	te vestiste	vosotros(as)	*os vestisteis*
Ud., él, ella	se vistió	Uds., ellos, ellas	se vistieron

2. The verbs **preferir, divertirse,** and **dormir** also have a stem change in the preterite. The **e** in **preferir** and **divertirse** changes to **i** and the **o** in **dormir** changes to **u** in the **él** and **ellos** forms. The verb **morir** *(to die)* follows the same pattern as **dormir**—**murió, murieron.**

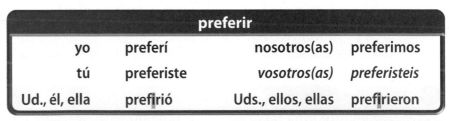

preferir			
yo	preferí	nosotros(as)	preferimos
tú	preferiste	vosotros(as)	*preferisteis*
Ud., él, ella	prefirió	Uds., ellos, ellas	prefirieron

dormir			
yo	dormí	nosotros(as)	dormimos
tú	dormiste	vosotros(as)	*dormisteis*
Ud., él, ella	durmió	Uds., ellos, ellas	durmieron

CULTURA

Los amigos pasaron un rato en un café en Cádiz, España. Alguien pidió un refresco y el mesero lo está sirviendo ahora.

Práctica

HABLAR • ESCRIBIR

7 Contesta según se indica.

1. ¿Te vestiste elegantemente para ir al restaurante? (no)
2. ¿Qué pediste en el restaurante? (una ensalada)
3. ¿Cómo la pediste? (sin aceite y vinagre)
4. ¿Cuántas veces repetiste sin aceite y vinagre? (dos veces)
5. Y, ¿cómo sirvió el mesero la ensalada? (con aceite y vinagre)
6. ¿Qué hiciste? (pedí otra ensalada)
7. ¿Qué pidió tu amigo? (puré de papas)
8. ¿Y qué pasó? (ellos frieron las papas)
9. ¿Qué sirvió el mesero? (papas fritas)
10. ¿Le dieron ustedes una propina al mesero? (no)

EXPANSIÓN

Ahora, sin mirar las preguntas, cuenta la información en tus propias palabras. Si no recuerdas algo, un(a) compañero(a) te puede ayudar.

Después contesta la pregunta, ¿Por qué no le dieron una propina al mesero?

GeoVistas

To learn more about Argentina, take a tour on pages SH58–SH59.

LEER • ESCRIBIR

8 Completa en el pretérito.

Anoche mi amigo Ángel y yo __1__ (ir) a un restaurante. Ángel __2__ (pedir) pescado—más específicamente __3__ (pedir) corvina, un pescado delicioso del Pacífico. Ángel lo __4__ (pedir) frito y el cocinero lo __5__ (freír) muy bien. El mesero __6__ (servir) la corvina en una salsa de mantequilla y limón.

Yo no __7__ (pedir) pescado. Yo __8__ (pedir) mariscos—un plato delicioso de mejillones, almejas y camarones. El mesero __9__ (servir) el plato muy caliente. Luego nosotros __10__ (pedir) un postre rico, delicioso. Nosotros __11__ (divertirse) mucho.

Cuando yo volví a casa __12__ (dormirse) enseguida. No sé si Ángel __13__ (dormirse) enseguida o no.

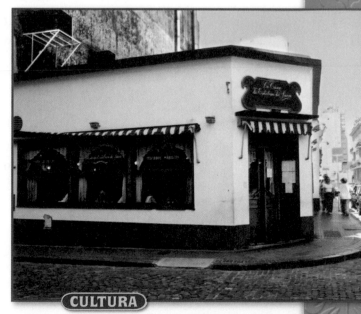

CULTURA

Un restaurante popular en una esquina de San Telmo, un barrio interesante de Buenos Aires, la capital de Argentina

InfoGap For more practice with stem-changing verbs, do Activity 4 on page SR6 at the end of this book.

9 ¡Te toca a ti! Completa la palabra.

1. rep_tió
2. s_rvieron
3. se v_stieron
4. p_dió
5. se div_rtió

6. d_rmieron
7. m_rió
8. pref_rió
9. fr_eron
10. p_dieron

Adjetivos de nacionalidad

1. Adjectives of nationality that end in **o** or **e** follow the same pattern as any other adjective. Those that end in **o** have four forms and those that end in **e** have two forms.

   un restaurante cubano   **una comida cubana**
   unos restaurantes cubanos **unas comidas cubanas**

   un plato nicaragüense   **una comida nicaragüense**
   unos platos nicaragüenses **unas comidas nicaragüenses**

2. Adjectives of nationality that end in a consonant have four forms rather than two.

   un restaurante español   **una comida española**
   unos restaurantes españoles **unas comidas españolas**

3. Adjectives of nationality that end in **s** or **n** have a written accent in the masculine singular. The accent is dropped in all other forms.

francés	francesa	catalán	catalana
franceses	francesas	catalanes	catalanas

   Some other common adjectives of nationality that end in a consonant are: **inglés, portugués, irlandés, japonés, alemán.**

4. Note that with an article the adjective becomes a noun.

   Los portugueses son de Portugal y los brasileños son de Brasil.

Un plato mexicano

CULTURA

Una joven francesa delante de un monumento francés—la famosa Torre Eiffel

Práctica

HABLAR • ESCRIBIR

10 Contesta según el modelo.

MODELO —¿Son de España las muchachas?
—Sí, son españolas.

1. ¿Son de España los muchachos?
2. ¿Es de Colombia el café?
3. ¿Son de Nicaragua las profesoras?
4. ¿Son de Inglaterra los libros?
5. ¿Es de Francia tu amigo?

LEER • ESCRIBIR

11 Completa según se indica.

1. En el restaurante sirven comida _____. (mexicano)
2. La cocina _____ no es como la cocina _____. (catalán, francés)
3. Las rosas _____ son las más bonitas. (ecuatoriano)
4. Los pasajeros _____ comprenden el español. (portugués)
5. Los _____ hablan inglés. (irlandés)
6. Hay muchos restaurantes _____ y _____ en Latinoamérica. En Perú los restaurantes _____ se llaman «chifas». (japonés, chino, chino)

CULTURA

Estos jóvenes venezolanos están comiendo comida japonesa auténtica en un restaurante japonés en Caracas, Venezuela.

La voz pasiva con **se**

1. When you talk about something being done without saying who does it, you use the passive voice in English.

Fish is sold at the fish market.

2. In Spanish, the pronoun **se** is used to express this idea.

Se vende pescado en la pescadería.
Se venden papas en la verdulería.

3. You will often see the **se** construction used to express ideas such as:

They speak Spanish here.
Spanish is spoken here.
One speaks Spanish here.
People speak Spanish here.
} **Aquí se habla español.**

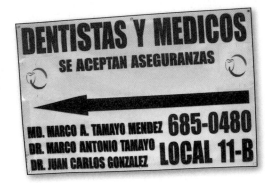

DENTISTAS Y MEDICOS
SE ACEPTAN ASEGURANZAS

MD. MARCO A. TAMAYO MENDEZ 685-0480
DR. MARCO ANTONIO TAMAYO
DR. JUAN CARLOS GONZALEZ LOCAL 11-B

Práctica

ESCUCHAR • HABLAR • ESCRIBIR

12 Contesta. Presta atención a la forma de **vender.**

1. ¿Se vende pan en la panadería?
2. ¿Se venden suéteres en la tienda de ropa?
3. ¿Se vende carne en la carnicería?
4. ¿Se venden guisantes en la verdulería?
5. ¿Se vende fruta en la frutería?
6. ¿Se venden productos congelados en el supermercado?
7. ¿Se vende pescado en la pescadería?
8. ¿Se venden camisas en la tienda de ropa?

CULTURA

Se venden frutas en este puesto en Tepoztlán, México.

HABLAR • ESCRIBIR

 ¿Qué se habla y dónde? Sigue el modelo.

MODELO

—¿Qué lengua se habla en España?
—Se habla español en España.

1.

2.

3.

4.

5.

6.

HABLAR • ESCRIBIR

 Contesta.

1. ¿Se deja una propina (en un restaurante) cuando el servicio está incluido?
2. ¿Se sirve mucha carne en un restaurante argentino?
3. ¿Se usa mucho aceite en España?
4. ¿Se pone el cuchillo a la derecha o a la izquierda del plato?
5. ¿Se pone la taza en un platillo?
6. ¿Se comen muchos mariscos en los restaurantes cerca de la costa?
7. Los tostones son populares en el Caribe. ¿Se sirven tostones con muchas comidas cubanas?
8. ¿Se dice «menú» de la misma manera en inglés y español?

Refrán

Can you guess what the following proverb means?

Con mal vinagre y peor aceite, buen gazpacho no se puede hacer.

¡Bravo!

You have now learned all the new vocabulary and grammar in this chapter. Continue to use and practice all that you know while learning more cultural information. **¡Vamos!**

Una comida muy buena

Adela	Anoche fuimos a un restaurante argentino.
Felipe	Sí, ¿qué pediste?
Adela	Yo pedí un biftec o como dicen en Argentina «bife de lomo».
Felipe	¿Qué tal te gustó?
Adela	Mucho. Lo pedí casi crudo porque yo sé que en Argentina se sirve el bife bien hecho.
Felipe	¿Qué te sirvieron con el bife?
Adela	Papas fritas. Y pedí una ensalada aparte.
Felipe	Se dice que en Argentina se sirven porciones grandes.
Adela	Sí, es verdad. Y después de comer tanto todos pedimos flan.
Felipe	¿Flan? Es un postre español, ¿no?
Adela	Sí, lo es pero es popular en Latinoamérica también.
Felipe	Pues me parece que te divertiste.
Adela	Mucho. Y cuando volví a casa, me dormí enseguida—como se dice «con la panza llena».

¿Comprendes?

VIDEO To visit a restaurant in Argentina, watch **Diálogo en vivo.**

A Contesta según la información en la conversación.

1. ¿Qué pidió Adela en el restaurante argentino?
2. ¿Le gustó?
3. ¿Cómo pidió el bife?
4. ¿Cómo lo sirven en Argentina?
5. ¿Qué más comió Adela?
6. ¿Cómo son las porciones que se sirven en Argentina?
7. ¿Qué pidió Adela de postre?
8. ¿Qué hizo Adela cuando volvió a casa?

B **Resumiendo** Cuenta la información en la conversación en tus propias palabras.

C **Identificando** Indica todo lo que Adela comió en el restaurante argentino.

D **Llegando a conclusiones** Según la información en la conversación, ¿cuáles son unas características típicas de una comida en Argentina?

CULTURA

El cocinero está asando el bife en un restaurante famoso de Buenos Aires.

Antes de leer

Piensa en una visita a un restaurante. ¿Qué comes? ¿Quién te sirve? ¿Dejas una propina?

Restaurantes de España y Latinoamérica 🎧♻️

Algún día vas a tener la oportunidad de visitar un país hispano. Y como tienes que comer unas tres veces al día, debes saber algo sobre los restaurantes.

✓ Reading Check

¿Dónde se puede comer económicamente?

¿Comer dónde? En todas las grandes ciudades hay restaurantes elegantes y económicos. Si quieres solamente una merienda puedes ir a un café. Si quieres una comida es mejor ir a un restaurante o una cafetería. Pero una cafetería no es autoservicio[1]. Es un restaurante generalmente modesto donde se sirve comida en una barra[2] igual que en una mesa. Comer en la barra cuesta menos que en una de las mesas.

[1]autoservicio   *self-service*   [2]barra   *counter*

Durante la lectura

Prepara una lista mental de las cosas que son las mismas en un restaurante aquí en Estados Unidos y las cosas que son diferentes.

CULTURA

Mucha gente pasa un domingo por la tarde en un restaurante como este en Cádiz, España.

CULTURA

A mucha gente le gusta pedir pescado cuando están en la costa como en este restaurante en una playa de Fuerteventura en las islas Canarias.

¿Servir cómo? Por lo general una comida, sobre todo una comida española, consiste en varios platos—primer plato, plato principal y postre. En muchas partes el plato principal se llama «el plato fuerte». En España no se sirve una mezcla[3] de cosas en el mismo plato como aquí en Estados Unidos. Si pides judías verdes o alcachofas salteadas[4], el camarero te va a servir estas legumbres como un primer plato o entrada. Pero como sabemos, siempre hay excepciones. En unos restaurantes modestos o cafeterías se sirve lo que se llama «un plato combinado» que lleva, por ejemplo, carne, papas y una legumbre en el mismo plato.

En Latinoamérica las costumbres varían de país en país. En Puerto Rico y otras islas del Caribe, por ejemplo, la carne o el pescado viene acompañado de arroz blanco o amarillo con frijoles (habichuelas) y tostones o maduros[5]. En México muchos platos llevan arroz y frijoles refritos.

[3]mezcla   *mixture*
[4]alcachofas salteadas   *sautéed artichokes*
[5]maduros   *fried sweet bananas*

Reading Check

¿Cuál es una característica de una comida española?

Reading Check

¿Qué acompaña una comida en los países del Caribe?

¿Tomar el postre? A muchos les gusta terminar una comida con un postre—o una sobremesa. En algunos lugares la palabra «sobremesa» es un sinónimo de postre pero en otros incluye toda la conversación entre los comensales[6] mientras toman el postre. Y en España y Latinoamérica la comida puede durar unas horas—sobre todo una comida en un restaurante o durante una fiesta.

Muchos turistas le preguntan al mesero si el servicio está incluido. La respuesta es casi siempre «sí» y no es necesario dejar una propina.

Reading Check
¿Qué es la sobremesa?

CULTURA
De postre, un dulce y un cafecito

¿Se puede? ¡Un punto muy importante! Si no comes toda la comida no puedes llevar las sobras[7] a casa. La etiqueta no lo permite.
¡Otro punto importante! Después de comer bien en un restaurante, a mucha gente le gusta ir a otro local para tomar su cafecito—un local que se especializa en el café.

¡Buen apetito!

Después de leer

Decide si hay más semejanzas (cosas similares) o diferencias al comer en un restaurante aquí en Estados Unidos y en un restaurante en un país hispano.

[6]comensales   *diners*   [7]sobras   *leftovers*

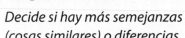
CULTURA
Los cafés al aire libre son muy populares en la Recoleta, un barrio bonito de Buenos Aires.

¿Comprendes?

Más práctica

Workbook, pp. 4.8–4.9
StudentWorks™ Plus

A Confirmando información Indica si la información es correcta o no.

	correcta	incorrecta
1. En las ciudades españolas y latinoamericanas hay solo restaurantes elegantes.		
2. Una cafetería es siempre autoservicio.		
3. En una cafetería cuesta más comer en una mesa que en la barra.		
4. En España siempre ponen muchas cosas diferentes en el mismo plato.		
5. En España una comida típica comprende (consiste en) varios platos.		

B Describiendo Describe.

1. lo que acompaña una típica comida puertorriqueña
2. lo que acompaña una típica comida mexicana
3. lo que es la sobremesa

C Explicando Explica.

1. la diferencia entre un café, un restaurante y una cafetería
2. como se sirve la comida en España
3. lo que es un plato combinado

D Comparando Compara tu experiencia en restaurantes estadounidenses con lo que aprendiste de los restaurantes en los países hispanos.

CULTURA

Es un restaurante-cafetería en Toledo, España. ¿Quién está delante de la cafetería?

Sé lo que pedí 🎧 ♻

Antes de leer

Piensa en unas experiencias personales en un restaurante. ¿Cómo es el servicio? ¿Son corteses los meseros? Una vez, ¿te dio un servicio malo un mesero? Si contestas que sí, recuerda lo que pasó. Si contestas que no, piensa en algunas cosas que pueden pasar.

Anoche Julio y un grupo de sus amigos fueron a cenar en un restaurante. Se divirtieron porque les gusta estar en su grupo pero la verdad es que no comieron bien. Fue un desastre. Nada anduvo bien. Todo salió mal.

Por ejemplo, Julio pidió un biftec a término medio. Y lo repitió dos veces al mesero—a término medio. Pidió también papas fritas y una ensalada de lechuga y tomates. Y, ¿qué le sirvió el mesero? Es verdad que le sirvió un biftec—pero no a término medio. Le sirvió el biftec casi crudo y a Julio no le gusta la carne muy roja. ¿Le sirvió las papas fritas? No. Le puso un plato de arroz y le dio una ensalada pero sin tomates. ¿Qué piensas? ¿Dejó Julio una buena propina para el mesero? Tú puedes decidir. Pero, te digo una cosa. Cuando salió del restaurante Julio dijo: —¡Increíble! Yo le pedí una cosa y él me sirvió otra. No sé si él me comprendió o no.

¿Fuiste una vez a un restaurante cuando tuviste una mala experiencia como la experiencia de Julio y sus amigos? ¿Te enfadaste? ¿Le dijiste algo al mesero o no?

CULTURA

Un restaurante en el mercado del puerto en la capital de Uruguay, Montevideo. Los restaurantes en este barrio de la ciudad son muy populares—sobre todo para el almuerzo.

¿Comprendes?

Escoge o completa.

1. ¿Se divirtieron Julio y sus amigos?
   a. Sí, porque fueron a cenar en un restaurante.
   b. Sí, porque el mesero les dio un servicio bueno.
   c. Sí, porque les gusta pasar tiempo juntos.
   d. Sí, porque fue un desastre.

2. ¿Quién o qué causó el problema?
   a. el mesero
   b. Julio
   c. los amigos de Julio
   d. la propina

3. Los comestibles mencionados en la lectura son _____.

4. ¿Qué no comprendió Julio?
   a. por qué no le dio una buena propina al mesero
   b. por qué él pidió una cosa y el mesero le sirvió otra
   c. por qué el mesero no lo comprendió
   d. por qué decidieron ir al restaurante

5. ¿Cuál es un buen título para la lectura?
   a. Mis amigos
   b. Nos gusta pasar tiempo juntos.
   c. Una comida
   d. Una comida desastrosa

CULTURA

Este restaurante en Antigua, Guatemala tiene el nombre de una famosa artista mexicana. ¿Quién es?

Vocabulario

 Identifica.

To review **Vocabulario,**
turn to pages 106–107.

2 **Completa con una palabra apropiada.**

6. Se puede preparar una salsa para una ensalada con
_____ y vinagre.

7. El cordero no es un pescado. Es _____.

8. Se sirve el café en _____.

9–10. Los clientes en un restaurante piden _____
antes de comer y piden _____ después de comer.

11. La langosta es _____. No es una carne.

3 **¿Sí o no?**

12. Patricia pide el menú porque sabe lo que
quiere comer.

13. Si el servicio no está incluido el cliente deja
una propina para el mesero.

14. El cerdo es un pescado.

15. El flan es un postre.

16. Tomás necesita un tenedor para tomar la sopa.

17. Levantamos la mesa antes de comer.

18. Antonio pide el biftec casi crudo porque no le
gusta la carne muy roja.

Gramática

4 **Completa en el presente.**

19. El mesero les _____ a los clientes en el restaurante. (servir)

20. Yo siempre _____ la misma cosa, un biftec. (pedir)

21. Ellas _____ elegantemente para ir al restaurante. (vestirse)

22. Nosotros no lo _____. (repetir)

23. El cocinero _____ las papas. (freír)

24. El postre _____ el plato principal. (seguir)

To review **el presente de los verbos de cambio radical e → i,** turn to page 110.

5 **Completa en el pretérito.**

25. Ellos se divirtieron. Y yo _____ también.

26. Yo dormí bien. Y él _____ bien también.

27. Tú lo repetiste. Y nosotros lo _____ también.

28. Ellos lo prefirieron. Y su amigo lo _____ también.

29. Nos vestimos. Y ellos _____ también.

30. Abuela les sirvió la comida. Y tú les _____ la comida también.

To review **el pretérito de los verbos de cambio radical e → i, o → u,** turn to page 112.

6 **Completa.**

31. En los restaurantes _____ se sirve comida _____. (japonés)

32. La blusa _____ es preciosa. (guatemalteco)

33. Unos _____ hablan inglés y francés. (canadiense)

To review **adjetivos de nacionalidad,** turn to page 114.

7 **Completa.**

34. _____ sirv_ el postre después del plato principal.

35. _____ com_ muchos mariscos en Chile y en España.

36. _____ habl_ mucho español en Estados Unidos.

To review **la voz pasiva con se,** turn to page 116.

Cultura

8 **Escoge la información correcta.**

37. Se sirven porciones (grandes, pequeñas) de comida en Argentina.

38. En España siempre (ponen, no ponen) muchas cosas en el mismo plato.

39. En España y (Latinoamérica, Estados Unidos) la gente no lleva las sobras a casa.

40. Los tostones o maduros, arroz y frijoles negros acompañan muchas comidas (mexicanas, caribeñas).

To review this cultural information, turn to pages 118 and 120–122.

Prepárate para el examen

Practice for oral proficiency

1 **¡Al restaurante!**

✔ *Order a meal and chat with friends at a restaurant*

Imagínate que tu clase de español está en un restaurante donde se sirve comida española y latinoamericana. Todos los meseros hablan español. Pide lo que quieres en español. Luego prepara una conversación que tiene lugar entre tus compañeros de clase.

2 **Una comida típica**

✔ *Talk about foods*

Ya sabes mucho sobre las comidas latinas. Habla de un plato o de una comida que te gusta o que quieres probar o comer por primera vez.

3 **Preferencias**

✔ *Discuss where you prefer to eat*

Con un(a) compañero(a) indica si prefieres comer en casa o en un restaurante. ¿Por qué? A ver si tu compañero(a) tiene la misma opinión.

4 **En casa**

✔ *Talk about a meal at home*

Describe una comida en casa y todo lo que tienes que hacer cuando comes en casa. Mira el diagrama abajo para ayudarte.

CULTURA

De estas tapas españolas, ¿cuáles te apetecen?

hacer las compras

lavar los platos

preparar la comida

comer en casa

levantar (quitar) la mesa

poner la mesa

servir la comida

5 **Semejanzas y diferencias**

✔ *Compare restaurants where you live with restaurants in Spanish-speaking countries*

Compara y contrasta algunas cosas interesantes sobre restaurantes aquí en Estados Unidos y en los países hispanos.

Prepárate para el examen
Practice for written proficiency

Tarea

You are going to write a letter of complaint to a restaurant you went to where you had a very bad experience. Write a letter to the management. Include the following details.

¿Cuándo fuiste?
¿Con quiénes?
¿Qué pidieron ustedes?
¿Qué tal la comida?
¿Cómo fue el servicio?

CULTURA

Un restaurante pintoresco en Colonia, Uruguay

Writing Strategy

Writing a letter of complaint When you write a letter of complaint your goal is to get a problem corrected. You might be angry when you write the letter; however, to be effective, you must control your emotions and use a businesslike tone. Clearly state the problems you had and suggest what the restaurant should do in order to solve each problem. In addition, it is important that the letter be addressed to the person who has the most authority.

❷ Write

- An appropriate opening to a business letter in Spanish is **Estimado(a) señor(a)** or **Muy distinguido(a) señor(a)**.
- Use the information organized in your prewriting charts to compose your letter.
- An appropriate closing to a business letter is **Atentamente.**

❶ Prewrite

Use a flow chart like the one below to help you organize the sequence of events in your letter.

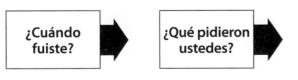

¿Cuándo fuiste? → ¿Qué pidieron ustedes? →

¿Qué tal la comida? → ¿Qué tal el servicio?

Evaluate

Don't forget that your teacher will evaluate you on the businesslike presentation of your letter, your ability to present solutions to the problems you raise, use of vocabulary, and correctness of grammar.

Repaso del Capítulo ④

Gramática

- **Presente de los verbos de cambio radical e → i**
  (page 110)

  The verbs **pedir, servir, repetir, freír, seguir,** and **vestirse** have a stem change in the present tense. Review the following forms.

pedir			
yo	pido	nosotros(as)	pedimos
tú	pides	*vosotros(as)*	*pedís*
Ud., él, ella	pide	Uds., ellos, ellas	piden

- **Pretérito de los verbos de cambio radical e → i, o → u**
  (page 112)

  The verbs **pedir, servir, repetir, seguir, freír, vestirse, preferir, divertirse,** and **dormir** have a stem change in the preterite. Review the following forms.

pedir	preferir	dormir
pedí	preferí	dormí
pediste	preferiste	dormiste
pidió	prefirió	durmió
pedimos	preferimos	dormimos
pedisteis	*preferisteis*	*dormisteis*
pidieron	prefirieron	durmieron

- **Adjetivos de nacionalidad** *(page 114)*

  Unlike other adjectives, adjectives of nationality that end in a consonant have four forms.

  un libro español   una canción española
  unos libros españoles   unas canciones españolas

- **La voz pasiva con se** *(page 116)*

  The passive voice can be expressed in Spanish with the pronoun **se.**

  Se habla español en Chile.
  Se venden calcetines en la tienda de ropa.

CULTURA

¿En qué piso se vende?

There are a number of cognates in this list. See how many you and a partner can find. Who can find the most? Compare your list with those of your classmates.

Vocabulario

Getting along at a restaurant

el restaurante	el/la mesero(a),	el menú	la propina
la mesa	el/la camarero(a)	la cuenta	

Identifying a place setting

la taza	el tenedor	la cuchara
el platillo	el cuchillo	el mantel
el plato	la cucharita	la servilleta

Identifying more foods

los comestibles	los mariscos	el aceite
la carne	los mejillones	el vinagre
la carne de res,	las almejas	casi crudo
el biftec	la langosta	a término medio
la chuleta de cerdo	la sal	bien hecho
el cordero	la pimienta	

Describing some restaurant activities

poner la mesa	pedir	repetir
levantar (quitar)	servir	freír
la mesa	dejar una propina	

Other useful words and expressions

seguir	divertirse	Me muero de hambre.
vestirse	morir	

Repaso cumulativo

Repasa lo que ya has aprendido

These activities will help you review and remember what you have learned so far in Spanish.

 1 Escucha las frases. Indica en una tabla como la de abajo si la persona viaja en tren o en avión.

tren	avión

 2 Parea los contrarios.

1. grande
2. después
3. alto
4. aburrido
5. gordo
6. siempre
7. debajo de
8. triste
9. cerca
10. detrás
11. fácil
12. corto

a. lejos
b. interesante
c. contento
d. nunca
e. pequeño
f. antes
g. difícil
h. encima de
i. largo
j. flaco
k. bajo
l. delante

Una panadería en el patio de comedores en una estación de ferrocarril en Buenos Aires

 3 Personaliza. Da respuestas personales.

1. ¿Qué comes cuando tienes hambre?
2. ¿Qué bebes cuando tienes sed?
3. ¿Qué haces cuando estás cansado(a) o tienes sueño?
4. ¿Qué te pones cuando tienes frío?
5. ¿Qué ropa llevas cuando tienes calor?

4 Escribe una lista de todos los comestibles (alimentos) que puedes decir en español.

legumbres	frutas	carne	pescado y mariscos	postres

5 Cambia al pretérito.

1. Ellos viven en San Francisco.
2. Su hermano asiste a la escuela secundaria en San Francisco.
3. Yo aprendo mucho en la escuela.
4. Nosotros comemos en la cafetería de la escuela.
5. ¿Comprendes lo que lees?

6 Sigue el modelo.

MODELO yo / matemáticas →
   Yo estudié matemáticas y aprendí mucho.

1. tú / biología
2. nosotros / historia
3. Carmen / geografía
4. ellos / álgebra
5. yo / español
6. ustedes / geometría

7 Escribe en la forma negativa.

1. Alguien llama a la puerta.
2. Él siempre hace algo.
3. Ella siempre tiene hambre.
4. Quiero comer algo.
5. Siempre quiere decir algo a alguien.

CULTURA

Son estudiantes del Instituto de Enseñanza Secundaria en Granada, España. Se están preparando para ser profesores en la escuela secundaria.

¿Qué se celebra?

Aquí y Allí

Vamos a comparar El mundo hispano es famoso por sus ferias y fiestas. Hay ferias para celebrar muchas ocasiones. Algunas duran solamente un día y otras una semana entera. ¿Hay ferias y fiestas donde tú vives? ¿Qué celebran o conmemoran? ¿Tienes una fiesta favorita? ¿Cuál es?

Objetivos

You will:

- talk about several Hispanic holidays

- compare holidays that you celebrate with those in some Spanish-speaking countries

You will use:

- regular and irregular forms of the imperfect tense

◄ Las jóvenes están tomado parte en las celebraciones para Carnaval en Puerto Plata en la República Dominicana.

QuickPass

Go to glencoe.com
For: **Online book**
Web code: ASD7837c5

Introducción al tema
¿Qué se celebra?

Mira las fotos para familiarizarte con el tema de este capítulo—un tema de alegría—fiestas, festivales y celebraciones. El mundo hispano es famoso por sus fiestas. A mucha gente le gusta participar en las festividades en la plaza de su ciudad o pueblo o en su propio barrio.

▲ **México** Aquí vemos a una joven chiapaneca vestida en un traje tradicional durante la Fiesta de Enero. Durante todo el mes de enero hay festivales en Chiapas.

Colombia Todo el mundo se divierte durante el Carnaval. Las comparsas desfilan por las calles como aquí en Barranquilla. Los días de alegría y festejo terminan con el Miércoles de Cenizas cuando empieza la Cuaresma—cuarenta días de abstinencia. ▶

Ecuador El festival de la Mamá Negra tiene lugar en Latacunga en septiembre. Hay un desfile de personajes que representan las diferentes herencias étnicas del país—española, indígena, africana. ▼

▲ **Ecuador** Aquí vemos a unos niños en disfraz en Cotacachi durante unas festividades para celebrar la Navidad.

México Estas figuras del Día de los Muertos son de un cuadro de la artista mexicana Dolores Olmedo Patino. ▶

▲ **México** Celebraciones navideñas en una plaza de Oaxaca

▲ **Perú** Unas danzarinas vestidas en trajes tradicionales bailan en una calle de Ollantaytambo durante el festival de Ollantay Raymi en junio.

◀ **Cuba** Unos jóvenes se divierten en La Habana durante el Carnaval. El Carnaval de La Habana es uno de los más famosos del mundo.

España Los fuegos artificiales iluminan el cielo durante las festividades en la plaza de la Cibeles para celebrar el Año Nuevo en Madrid. ▼

España Sevillanas vestidas en los trajes tradicionales para la Feria de Sevilla en el mes de abril ▼

Una feria

una fiesta patronal

la santa patrona

una procesión, un desfile

Había una procesión.
Todo el mundo desfilaba (caminaba) por las calles.
Llevaban una estatua del santo patrón (de la santa patrona).

el camposanto, el cementerio

un mausoleo

una corona de flores

una ofrenda

la tumba

Los difuntos (muertos) están enterrados en el camposanto.
Los parientes ponen coronas de flores en las tumbas.
En el cementerio hay también mausoleos familiares.

El Día de los Muertos

una máscara

un disfraz

¡Ojo!

Note the spelling.
**un disfraz →
dos disfraces**

Para celebrar el Día de los Muertos, algunos
   llevaban disfraz.
Llevaban también una máscara.
La máscara cubría la cara.

una calavera, un cráneo

un esqueleto

un hueso

Confeccionaba (elaboraba) bizcochos.
Los bizcochos tenían la forma
   de las personas muertas.
Los bizcochos son dulces.

¿QUÉ SE CELEBRA?

ciento treinta y nueve **139**

QuickPass

Go to glencoe.com
For: **Vocabulary practice**
Web code: **ASD7837c5**

ESCUCHAR

1 Escucha las frases. Parea cada frase con la foto que describe.

a.

b.

HABLAR • ESCRIBIR

2 Personaliza. Da respuestas personales.

1. ¿Tiene un santo patrón el pueblo o la ciudad donde ustedes viven?
2. ¿Visitas a veces la tumba de un pariente difunto en el cementerio?
3. ¿Es una costumbre o tradición poner una corona de flores en la tumba?
4. ¿Hay una fiesta cuando se llevan disfraces? ¿Cuál es?
5. A veces, ¿tenemos figuras de cráneos o esqueletos? ¿Cuándo?
6. ¿Tenemos bizcochos o dulces en forma de cráneos o esqueletos?

LEER

3 Completa con una palabra del **banco de palabras.**

elaboraba	llevaba	caminaba	tenía	había

1. _____ una procesión en la calle.
2. Mucha gente _____ un disfraz.
3. Todo el mundo _____ detrás del santo patrón.
4. Abuelita _____ bizcochos.
5. Un bizcocho _____ la forma de una calavera.

CULTURA
Bizcochos en forma de calaveras

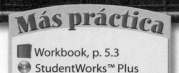

LEER • ESCRIBIR

4 Expresa de otra manera.

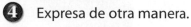

1. Lleva *un disfraz*.
2. Todo el mundo *marchaba* hacia el cementerio.
3. Todo el mundo marchaba hacia *el cementerio*.
4. Todo el mundo *andaba* hacia atrás.
5. La señora *hacía* bizcochos.
6. *Los muertos* están enterrados en el cementerio.
7. Hacía bizcochos en forma de *una calavera*.

ESCRIBIR

5 Completa con la letra que falta.

1. una pro_e_ión
2. un disfra_
3. dos disfra_es
4. un bi_cocho
5. un _ueso

Cultura

Papel picado

Se usa el papel picado para hacer decoraciones para muchas fiestas. Por ejemplo, hay decoraciones de papel picado para los árboles de Navidad. En México usan el papel picado para hacer imágenes de esqueletos para las celebraciones del Día de los Muertos.

Comunicación

6 Habla con un(a) compañero(a) de clase. Describan todo lo que ustedes hacen o no hacen para celebrar *Halloween*. ¿Es una fiesta que les gusta o no?

7 **Rompecabezas**

Escoge la palabra en cada grupo que no pertenece.

1. el hueso · el esqueleto · el dulce · el cráneo

2. el camposanto · el muerto · el santo patrón · la tumba

3. la ofrenda · la corona de flores · el bizcocho · el mausoleo

4. la procesión · enterrar · desfilar · caminar por la calle

VIDEO To practice your new words, watch **Vocabulario en vivo.**

La Navidad, Las Navidades

En otras partes

¡Feliz Navidad! or **¡Felices Navidades!** are the most common ways to say *Merry Christmas,* but you will also hear **¡Felices Pascuas!** In all countries **la Pascua** or **la Pascua Florida** is *Easter.*

el árbol de Navidad

la chimenea

un aguinaldo

La Nochebuena es el 24 de diciembre.
Los niños decoraban el árbol de Navidad.
Había aguinaldos debajo del árbol.

los Reyes Magos

el camello

la paja

Los niños sabían que iban a venir los Reyes Magos.

¡Feliz Hanuka!

la vela

la menora

los fuegos artificiales

La familia siempre celebraba la fiesta de las luces, Hanuka.
La familia encendía una vela de la menora.
Hanuka es una fiesta hebrea (judía).

La fiesta celebraba la llegada del Año Nuevo.
Durante la fiesta había fuegos artificiales.
Los fuegos artificiales iluminaban el cielo.

una banda

un desfile

Todos bailaban mientras tocaba la banda.
Todo el mundo estaba contento.
Lo pasaban bien. Se divertían.

Cultura

La piñata

La piñata es una vasija de cartón o barro. Se llena de dulces y durante muchas fiestas familiares los niños, con los ojos vedados *(blindfolded)* tratan de romper la piñata con un palo o bastón. Si tienen éxito, la piñata se rompe y todos los niños corren a recoger *(gather)* los dulces.

ESCUCHAR

1 Escucha. Escoge la frase correcta. Usa una tabla como la de abajo para indicar tus respuestas.

a	b

HABLAR • ESCRIBIR

2 Contesta.

1. ¿Tienen muchas familias cristianas un árbol de Navidad?
2. ¿Decoran el árbol?
3. ¿Quién les trae aguinaldos a los niños?
4. ¿Dónde los pone?
5. ¿Celebran Hanuka las familias judías?
6. ¿Qué hay en la menora?

CULTURA

Un mercado en Barcelona, España, donde se venden árboles de Navidad

LEER • ESCRIBIR

3 Rompecabezas

¡Adivina! ¿Qué es?

1. un animal del desierto
2. lo que comen ciertos animales
3. un regalo de Navidad
4. lo que hay en una menora
5. lo que hacía la gente mientras tocaba la banda

ESCUCHAR • HABLAR • ESCRIBIR

4 Contesta según se indica.

1. ¿Cuántos Reyes Magos hay? (tres)
2. ¿Cuántas velas hay en una menora? (nueve)
3. ¿Cuándo hay fuegos artificiales? (de noche después del desfile)
4. ¿Cuándo toca la banda municipal? (durante el desfile)
5. ¿Qué decoran los niños? (el árbol de Navidad)
6. ¿Qué reciben los niños para la Navidad? (aguinaldos)

InfoGap For more practice using your new vocabulary, do Activity 5 on page SR7 at the end of this book.

Comunicación

5 Con un grupo de amigos, describe una fiesta típica que se celebra el cuatro de julio en Estados Unidos.

HABLAR • ESCRIBIR

6 Corrige la información falsa.

1. La Navidad es en junio.
2. Un aguinaldo es un regalo que se recibe para el Año Nuevo.
3. Hay cuatro Reyes Magos.
4. Hanuka se llama también la fiesta de los fuegos.

Cultura

El weekend o el fin de semana libre es una costumbre anglosajona. En el mundo hispano mucha gente tiene que trabajar los sábados. No tienen todo el fin de semana libre. Pero tienen muchos días festivos durante el año. Cada país tiene sus propias fiestas o ferias. Y si la fiesta es el martes, el lunes debe ser un día festivo también, ¿no? Incluir un día adicional para tener más días festivos se llama «un puente».

Vocabulario 2

Imperfecto de los verbos en -ar

1. In Spanish there are two simple past tenses—the preterite and the imperfect. You have already learned the preterite. You use the preterite to state an action that began and ended at a definite time in the past.

2. You will now learn the imperfect. The imperfect is used to describe a habitual or repeated past action. The exact time the action began and/or ended is not important.

3. Observe the imperfect forms of regular **-ar** verbs.

infinitive	hablar	mirar
stem	**habl-**	**mir-**
yo	hablaba	miraba
tú	hablabas	mirabas
Ud., él, ella	hablaba	miraba
nosotros(as)	hablábamos	mirábamos
vosotros(as)	*hablabais*	*mirabais*
Uds., ellos, ellas	hablaban	miraban

4. Some common time expressions used with the imperfect are:

siempre	con frecuencia
a veces	a menudo
de vez en cuando	todos los días (años)

Ellos siempre desfilaban detrás de la banda.
A veces bailaban al son de la banda.
De vez en cuando llevaban disfraces.
Lo pasaban bien.

Práctica

HABLAR • ESCRIBIR

1. Contesta.

1. La Nochebuena, ¿se acostaban bastante temprano los niños?
2. ¿Qué esperaban ellos? ¿Esperaban la llegada de Santa Claus?
3. ¿Escuchaban cuando hablaban sus padres?
4. ¿Quiénes decoraban el árbol? ¿Los niños o sus padres?
5. Y en los países hispanos, ¿a quiénes esperaban los niños?

¡Ojo!

There are no verbs with a stem change in the imperfect.

PRESENTE		IMPERFECTO
juego	→	**jugaba**
empiezo	→	**empezaba**

CULTURA

Esta muchacha guatemalteca regresaba a casa cada día después de sus clases. Siempre llevaba sus materiales escolares en su mochila.

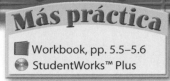
HABLAR • ESCRIBIR

2 Personaliza. Da respuestas personales.

1. Cuándo estabas en la escuela primaria, ¿cómo llegabas a la escuela? ¿Llegabas a pie o tomabas el bus escolar?
2. ¿Estaba tu casa lejos o cerca de tu escuela?
3. ¿Con quiénes jugabas?
4. ¿Qué jugaban ustedes?
5. ¿Tomabas el almuerzo con tus amigos en la cafetería de la escuela?

HABLAR • ESCRIBIR

3 Da la frase con el nuevo sujeto.

Ellas jugaban fútbol.

1. él
2. nosotros
3. yo

4. ustedes
5. tú
6. Javier

LEER • ESCRIBIR

4 Completa en el imperfecto sobre unos veranos en la playa.

Cada año cuando __1__ (llegar) el verano, yo __2__ (estar) contento(a). Mi familia siempre __3__ (pasar) el mes de julio en la playa. Por la mañana mi hermano y yo __4__ (levantarse) y __5__ (tomar) el desayuno. Pero después de tomar el desayuno, no __6__ (caminar) a la escuela. Nosotros __7__ (pasar) el día en la playa.

Yo siempre __8__ (nadar) en el mar. Me __9__ (gustar) las olas altas. De vez en cuando mi hermano __10__ (alquilar) un barquito y nosotros __11__ (esquiar) en el agua.

Cada tarde a eso de las tres __12__ (llegar) algunos amigos y (nosotros) __13__ (formar) un equipo de voleibol. Si digo la verdad (nosotros) __14__ (jugar) muy bien.

El mismo equipo no __15__ (ganar) siempre pero lo importante es que (nosotros) lo __16__ (pasar) bien.

—Y tú, ¿__17__ (pasar) los veranos en la playa o __18__ (quedarse) en casa?

La muchacha norteamericana jugaba «soccer» con el equipo de su escuela. Su equipo ganaba casi siempre.

Comunicación

5 Trabajen en grupos de cuatro o cinco. Un miembro del grupo es el/la entrevistador(a) que va a preguntar a los otros dónde pasaban los veranos. Presenten las respuestas a la clase.

¡Ojo!

There are no verbs with a stem change in the imperfect.

PRESENTE		IMPERFECTO
quiero	→	quería
vuelvo	→	volvía

Imperfecto de los verbos en -er, -ir

1. Regular **-er** and **-ir** verbs have the same endings in the imperfect tense.

infinitive	leer	escribir
stem	le-	escrib-
yo	leía	escribía
tú	leías	escribías
Ud., él, ella	leía	escribía
nosotros(as)	leíamos	escribíamos
vosotros(as)	*leíais*	*escribíais*
Uds., ellos, ellas	leían	escribían

2. The imperfect of **hay** is **había**. Note that either a singular or plural noun follows **había**.

> **Había un concierto durante la fiesta.**
> **Había fuegos artificiales durante la fiesta.**

Práctica

HABLAR • ESCRIBIR

 Personaliza. Da respuestas personales.

1. ¿Vivías en la misma casa cuando tenías doce años?
2. ¿A qué escuela asistías?
3. ¿Recibías buenas o malas notas?
4. ¿Tenías muchos amigos donde vivías?
5. ¿Leías muchos libros de bolsillo?
6. ¿Aprendías mucho?
7. ¿Sabías usar la computadora?
8. ¿Escribías muchos correos electrónicos?
9. ¿Recibías muchos también?

EXPANSIÓN

Ahora, sin mirar las preguntas, cuenta la información en tus propias palabras. Si no recuerdas algo, un(a) compañero(a) te puede ayudar.

CULTURA

Los fuegos artificiales iluminaban las torres de la Sagrada Familia en Barcelona, España.

Más práctica

■ Workbook, pp. 5.7–5.8
● StudentWorks™ Plus

LEER • ESCRIBIR

7 Completa en el imperfecto.

Yo recuerdo que durante la fiesta __1__ (haber) fuegos artificiales que __2__ (iluminar) el cielo. Todo el mundo __3__ (divertirse). Todos nosotros __4__ (beber) y __5__ (comer). __6__ (Haber) muchos puestos de comida donde se __7__ (vender) perros calientes, hamburguesas, pizza y papas fritas.

__8__ (Haber) un desfile. Durante el desfile algunos __9__ (ponerse) máscaras. Yo no __10__ (poder) reconocer a varios amigos porque __11__ (llevar) disfraces.

Nosotros __12__ (tener) mucha suerte. Durante la fiesta __13__ (hacer) buen tiempo y no __14__ (llover).

Yo tengo muy buenos recuerdos (memorias) de esta fiesta.

CULTURA

Había celebraciones para conmemorar el Día de la Independencia en Puebla, México.

HABLAR • ESCRIBIR

8 Forma frases en el imperfecto con los siguientes verbos.

| comer | beber | aprender | conocer | saber | volver |
| vivir | subir | recibir | salir | escribir | tener |

Comunicación

9 Dile a un(a) compañero(a) las cosas que hacías a menudo cuando eras alumno(a) en la escuela primaria.

GeoVistas

To learn more about Mexico, take a tour on pages SH46–SH47.

FOLDABLES®
Study Organizer

MINIBOOK

See page SH28 for help with making this foldable. Use this foldable to illustrate and tell about things you did frequently. On each page, draw a picture of an activity you enjoyed. Below each picture, write a sentence in Spanish describing what was happening. Remember to use the imperfect tense and to stick to the words that you already know in Spanish.

VIDEO Want more practice with the imperfect? Watch **Gramática en vivo.**

Imperfecto de los verbos irregulares

The verbs **ser, ir,** and **ver** are the only verbs that are irregular in the imperfect tense.

	ser	ir	ver
yo	era	iba	veía
tú	eras	ibas	veías
Ud., él, ella	era	iba	veía
nosotros(as)	éramos	íbamos	veíamos
vosotros(as)	*erais*	*ibais*	*veíais*
Uds., ellos, ellas	eran	iban	veían

CULTURA

Los niños se divertían en el patio de su escuela primaria en Antigua, Guatemala.

Práctica

HABLAR • ESCRIBIR

10 Personaliza. Da respuestas personales.

1. Cuando eras alumno(a) en la escuela primaria, ¿eran tus amiguitos tus vecinos que vivían cerca de tu casa?
2. A veces, ¿ibas al parque con tus amigos?
3. ¿Adónde iban ustedes los sábados?
4. ¿Quién era tu maestro(a) en el tercer grado?
5. ¿Cómo ibas a la escuela?
6. Cuando volvías a casa, ¿veías la televisión?

ESCUCHAR • LEER • ESCRIBIR

11 Cambia al imperfecto.

1. Ellos son de la República Dominicana.
2. Veo a mis parientes con frecuencia.
3. Vamos muy a menudo a la República Dominicana.
4. La casa de mis parientes es bonita.
5. Cuando estás allí, ¿vas a la playa?
6. ¿Quién va a la playa contigo?
7. ¿Ven ustedes a otros amigos en la playa?

CULTURA

Los niños de la primaria hacían una excursión escolar al Parque Güell en Barcelona, España. Sus maestros los acompañaban.

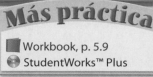
Gramática

Usos del imperfecto

In addition to expressing repeated, habitual actions or events in the past, the imperfect is used to describe persons, places, objects, events, weather, dates, and time in the past.

APPEARANCE	Eloísa era alta y bonita.
AGE	Tenía trece años.
PHYSICAL CONDITION	Siempre estaba llena de energía.
EMOTIONAL STATE	Y estaba muy contenta.
ATTITUDES AND DESIRES	Le gustaban las fiestas.
LOCATION	Estaba en una fiesta en casa de Lucio.
DATE	Era el ocho de octubre.
TIME	Eran las diez de la noche.
WEATHER	Hacía bastante frío.

Práctica

ESCUCHAR • HABLAR • ESCRIBIR

12 Contesta según se indica.

1. ¿Quién era alto? (don Quijote)
2. ¿Quién era bajo? (Sancho Panza)
3. ¿Quién tenía un asno? (Sancho Panza)
4. ¿Quién tenía un caballo? (don Quijote)
5. ¿Quién era idealista? (don Quijote)
6. ¿Quién era realista? (Sancho Panza)
7. ¿Quién quería viajar? (don Quijote)
8. ¿Quién quería volver a casa? (Sancho Panza)
9. ¿Quién quería conquistar los males del mundo? (don Quijote)
10. ¿Quién estaba loco? (don Quijote)

HABLAR • ESCRIBIR

13 Personaliza. Da respuestas personales.

1. ¿Quién era tu mejor amigo(a) en la escuela elemental?
2. ¿Cómo era?
3. ¿Cuántos años tenían cuando eran amigos?
4. ¿Qué tipo de personalidad tenía él o ella?
5. ¿Son ustedes amigos ahora?

Comunicación

14 Describe el tiempo que hacía ayer.

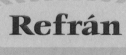

Refrán

Can you guess what the following proverb means?

Con sus libros,
los muertos
abren los ojos
a los vivos.

El Día de San Juan

Patricia José, eres de Puerto Rico, ¿no?

José Sí, ¿por qué?

Patricia Pues, ¿me puedes decir lo que es una fiesta patronal?

José ¡Cómo no! Es una fiesta en honor del santo patrón de un lugar. El santo patrón de Puerto Rico, por ejemplo, es San Juan Bautista.

Patricia ¿Hay una fiesta en su honor?

José Sí, el 24 de junio. Durante toda una semana hay fiestas.

Patricia ¿Qué hacen para celebrar la fiesta?

José Pues, hay una tradición interesante. El Día de San Juan todos vamos a la playa y entramos en el mar.

Patricia ¿Siempre nadan el Día de San Juan?

José No dije que nadamos. Dije que entramos en el mar. ¿Sabes cómo? Caminamos hacia atrás hasta llegar al mar.

Patricia Y, ¿por qué andan hacia atrás?

José Entrar en el mar así nos trae buena suerte durante el año.

¿Comprendes?

VIDEO To learn about another celebration in the Hispanic world, the **Quinceañera,** watch **Diálogo en vivo.**

A Completa según la información en la conversación.

1. José es de _____.
2. Una fiesta patronal rinde honor a _____.
3. El santo patrón de Puerto Rico es _____.
4. Su fiesta patronal es _____.
5. Todo el mundo va _____.
6. _____ para entrar en el mar.
7. Si entran en el mar así, van a tener _____.

B Resumiendo Cuenta la información en la conversación en tus propias palabras.

CULTURA

Maite preparaba a su amigo del continente para las celebraciones del Día de San Juan. Le enseñaba como andar hacia atrás.

C Analizando Los sanjuaneros tienen una costumbre interesante. ¿Qué hacen? ¿Por qué lo hacen?

Conversación

Antes de leer

Visualiza unas fiestas o ferias que tienen lugar donde tú vives—la Navidad, el Año Nuevo, el cuatro de julio, etc.

ESTRATEGIA DE LECTURA

Visualizando Es importante visualizar lo que estás leyendo. Al leer, pinta un cuadro mental de la información. Este cuadro mental te permite apreciar más la información y recordar mejor lo que estás leyendo.

✓ **Reading Check**

¿Por qué celebraba la familia de Carmencita el Día de los Muertos?

Durante la lectura

Pinta un cuadro mental de lo que está haciendo la gente—lo que todos están llevando, lo que preparan, adónde van.

Unas fiestas hispanas

El Día de los Muertos Carmencita Dávila es alumna en nuestra clase de español. Cuando ella era niña, vivía en México y asistía a la primaria en Guadalajara. Ella nos quiere hablar de los recuerdos que tiene de una fiesta mexicana que le gustaba mucho.

—Cuando yo era niña en México me encantaban todas las festividades que tenían lugar[1] para celebrar el Día de los Muertos, el primero y el dos de noviembre. Celebrábamos para rendirles honor a todos nuestros parientes difuntos.

Mi mamá y abuelita siempre tenían que hacer muchos preparativos. Confeccionaban calaveras, un tipo de bizcocho dulce en forma de caras de muertos. Elaboraban también el delicioso pan de los muertos, un pan dulce en forma de huesos y cráneos. Unos días antes de la fiesta íbamos al cementerio o camposanto donde limpiábamos[2] y decorábamos con coronas de flores las tumbas de nuestros parientes difuntos. Durante las fiestas las tumbas servían de altar.

[1]tenían lugar   *took place*   [2]limpiábamos   *we cleaned*

CULTURA

Día de los Muertos, la Ciudad de México

CULTURA

Una familia celebraba el Día de los Muertos en el cementerio de Tzintzuntzan en Pátzcuaro, México.

Mamá y abuelita preparaban también lo que eran las comidas favoritas de los difuntos. El primero de noviembre la familia entera se reunía e íbamos juntos al cementerio. Colocábamos las calaveras, las coronas de flores, unas velas y la comida en las tumbas como una ofrenda. Algunos parientes llevaban calacas, disfraces de madera[3] en forma de esqueletos. En el cementerio teníamos un gran picnic. Comíamos con los difuntos.

CULTURA

Una familia está celebrando el Día de los Muertos en el cementerio de Tzintzuntzan en Pátzcuaro. En este momento están comiendo con sus parientes difuntos como parte de la celebración.

Roberto Jones levanta la mano y le hace una pregunta a Carmencita.

—Carmencita, me parece que la fiesta que nos describes es una ocasión mórbida, bastante triste.

Contesta Carmencita: —No, Roberto. La verdad es que es una ocasión festiva. Tiene sus orígenes entre los indígenas en la época precolombina. Los indígenas no consideran la muerte el final de la vida[4] sino la continuación de la vida. Creen también que las almas[5] de los muertos vuelven cada año para visitar a sus parientes vivos. Luego, ¿por qué no reunirnos con ellos para tener una fiesta?

[3]de madera *wooden*   [5]almas *souls*
[4]vida *life*

✓ Reading Check

¿Cómo reciben los niños sus aguinaldos en los países hispanos?

CULTURA

Los Reyes Magos en un desfile durante una fiesta para el Día de los Reyes en la isla de Fuerteventura en las islas Canarias

✓ Reading Check

¿Qué reciben los niños durante Hanuka? ¿Cuántas veces?

Después de leer

De las tres fiestas ¿cuáles podías visualizar mejor? ¿Por qué?

La Navidad Y ahora la señora Salas, nuestra profesora de español, nos describe otra fiesta—una fiesta celebrada en todos los países hispanos.

Dice la señora Salas: —La mayoría de los niños en los países hispanos no reciben sus regalos de Navidad, sus aguinaldos, el 25 de diciembre. Los reciben el 6 de enero, el Día de los Reyes. La fiesta conmemora la llegada de los tres Reyes Magos al establo en Belén.

Los niños hispanos escriben sus cartas a los Reyes, no a Santa Claus, porque saben que son los Reyes quienes les traen los aguinaldos. Así, en sus cartas ponen una lista de los regalos que quieren recibir. La noche del cinco de enero, antes de acostarse, los niños dejan sus zapatos a la puerta de la casa, delante de la chimenea o debajo de su cama. Llenan sus zapatos de heno, paja o hierba porque saben que los animales de los Reyes van a querer comer. Y saben que los Reyes van a dejar los regalos que quieren en sus zapatos. Pero saben algo más. Si no se comportan bien durante el año los Reyes van a llenar sus zapatos de carbón[6].

Hanuka Isaac del Olmo tiene familia que vive en Panamá.

Dice la señora Salas: —Isaac, ¿sabes cómo celebra tu familia Hanuka en Panamá?

—Sí. Ellos celebran Hanuka de la misma manera que nosotros aquí en Estados Unidos. Es una fiesta alegre que empieza el 25 del mes hebreo de *Kislev* y dura ocho días. La primera noche un miembro de la familia enciende dos velas en la menora. Cada noche después se enciende una vela más. Cada noche los niños reciben regalos y bombones[7]. Y a todos les gusta comer *latkes,* panqueques de papas.

[6]carbón   *coal*   [7]bombones   *candies*

¿Comprendes?

Más práctica

📕 Workbook, pp. 5.10–5.12
💿 StudentWorks™ Plus

A Recordando hechos Contesta.

1. ¿Dónde vivía Carmencita Dávila cuando era niña?
2. ¿Qué día de fiesta le encantaba?
3. ¿Quiénes hacían muchos preparativos?
4. ¿Adónde iban todos durante la fiesta?

B Describiendo Describe.

1. una calavera
2. una calaca

C Categorizando Completa la tabla.

lo que hacía la familia de Carmencita en casa	lo que hacía la familia de Carmencita en el cementerio

D Analizando Contesta.

¿Por qué no se considera el Día de los Muertos una ocasión mórbida?

E Recordando hechos Contesta.

1. ¿Cuándo reciben la mayoría de los niños hispanos sus aguinaldos?
2. ¿Qué conmemora el Día de los Reyes?
3. ¿De quiénes reciben sus aguinaldos los niños hispanos?
4. ¿Qué ponen en sus zapatos?
5. ¿Dónde dejan sus zapatos la noche del 5 de enero?
6. ¿Qué les dan los Reyes a los niños que no se comportan bien durante el año?

F Buscando información Completa.

1. Hanuka es _____.
2. Hanuka dura _____.
3. _____ enciende una vela en la menora.
4. Cada una de las ocho noches de Hanuka los niños reciben _____.
5. Los *latkes* son _____.

CULTURA

Una celebración para la fiesta de las luces

La Nochevieja en España

Antes de leer

Piensa en unas cosas que haces el 31 de diciembre para celebrar la llegada del Año Nuevo. En la Ciudad de Nueva York, por ejemplo, miles y miles de personas van a Times Square para ver caer un gran balón a la medianoche. Al leer esta lectura, compara las actividades en Madrid con las de Nueva York. Compáralas también con tus actividades tradicionales.

En España el día final del año es «la Nochevieja» y en los otros países hispanos es «la víspera del Año Nuevo». Fernando Orjales nació en Madrid, la capital de España, y ahora está viviendo con su familia en Nueva York. Es la noche del 31 de diciembre y Fernando va con su familia a *Times Square* para celebrar la llegada del Año Nuevo. Mientras está en *Times Square,* Fernando piensa en lo que él hacía para celebrar la Nochevieja cuando estaba en Madrid.

Dice: —Recuerdo que nosotros, como casi todos los madrileños, íbamos a la Puerta del Sol, una gran plaza en el centro mismo de la ciudad. Nos reuníamos frente a una campana[1]. Recuerdo que casi siempre hacía

La Nochevieja (la víspera del Año Nuevo) en la Puerta del Sol en Madrid

frío y soplaba[2] un viento bastante fuerte de la Sierra de Guadarrama. Todo el mundo estaba bien abrigado[3] para protegerse del frío.

Pero a pesar del[4] frío todos tenían la mirada fija en la campana. Y en la mano cada uno tenía su racimo de doce uvas. Estábamos listos para recibir el Año Nuevo. Esperábamos las doce campanadas que anunciaban la llegada del Año Nuevo.

Fernando dice que recuerda bien que él comía una uva con cada una de las campanadas. Y por cada uva pedía un deseo. Por eso se llaman «las doce uvas de la felicidad».

[1]campana   *bell tower*
[2]soplaba   *blew*

[3]abrigado   *wrapped up*
[4]a pesar del   *in spite of the*

¡Así se dice!

If you want to wish someone a happy New Year, you say **¡Próspero Año Nuevo!**

¿Comprendes?

VIDEO To learn about **La Romería** in Spain, watch **Cultura en vivo.**

Escoge.

1. ¿De dónde es Fernando?
   a. de Nueva York
   b. de Madrid
   c. de la Nochevieja

2. ¿Adónde va Fernando ahora para celebrar la llegada del Año Nuevo?
   a. a *Times Square*
   b. a la Puerta del Sol
   c. a la Sierra de Guadarrama

3. ¿Qué hay en la Puerta del Sol?
   a. el sol
   b. una plaza
   c. una campana

4. ¿Por qué estaban todos bien abrigados?
   a. Siempre llevaban un abrigo nuevo.
   b. Hacía mucho frío.
   c. Estaban en la Sierra de Guadarrama.

5. ¿Cómo comía Fernando las uvas?
   a. todo un racimo
   b. doce a la vez
   c. una a una

6. ¿Cuándo las comía?
   a. al llegar a la Puerta del Sol
   b. al oír cada campanada
   c. al anunciar la llegada del Año Nuevo

CULTURA

Los madrileños celebraban la Nochevieja en la Puerta del Sol en el centro de la capital. Estaban bien abrigados, ¿no? ¿Hacía frío?

Vocabulario

1 Identifica.

1.

2.

3.

4.

5.

To review **Vocabulario 1** and **Vocabulario 2,** turn to pages 138–139 and 142–143.

2 Da otra palabra.

6. el muerto

7. un tipo de desfile

8. confeccionar

9. el cementerio

10. un disfraz

11. un regalo de Navidad

12. pasarlo bien

3 Completa.

13. Todo el mundo _____ hacia el cementerio.

14. Abuelita _____ bizcochos.

15. La familia pone _____ de flores en la tumba.

16. La noche de la fiesta había _____ que iluminaban el cielo.

17. _____ es la fiesta de las luces.

Gramática

4 **Completa con el imperfecto.**

18. La banda _____. (tocar)

19. Todos nosotros _____. (bailar)

20. _____ muy buen tiempo. (hacer)

21. Ellos _____. (celebrar)

22. Y tú, ¿qué _____? (hacer)

23–24. Yo _____ y _____. (comer, beber)

25. ¿Qué hora _____? (ser)

26–27. Yo _____ quedarme pero ellos _____ salir. (querer, preferir)

28. La gente _____. (divertirse)

To review **el imperfecto**, turn to pages 146, 148, 150, and 151.

5 **Escribe en el imperfecto.**

29. Yo sé hacerlo.

30. Ellos pueden ir.

31. Es alumno en la primaria.

32. ¿Qué va a decir?

33. Tienes quince años.

34. Antonia ve el desfile.

To review this cultural information, turn to pages 154–156.

Cultura

6 **Contesta.**

35. Cuando Carmencita vivía en México, ¿qué ponían los miembros de la familia en las tumbas de sus parientes difuntos?

36. El Día de los Muertos no es una ocasión triste ni mórbida. ¿Por qué?

37. ¿Cuándo reciben la mayoría de los niños hispanos sus regalos de Navidad?

38. ¿Quiénes traen los regalos a los niños y dónde los dejan?

39. ¿Por qué ponen los niños paja en los zapatos?

40. ¿Durante qué fiesta se comen *latkes*?

CULTURA

La tumba de Eva Perón y su familia en el cementerio de la Recoleta, Buenos Aires, Argentina

Prepárate para el examen
Practice for oral proficiency

1 **Una fiesta latina**

✓ *Describe a Hispanic holiday*

Escoge una de las siguientes fiestas. Describe la fiesta
a un(a) amigo(a).

el Día de los Muertos	el Día de los Reyes
el Día de San Juan	la Nochevieja

2 **Mi fiesta favorita**

✓ *Talk about your favorite holiday*

De todas las fiestas en la lectura, ¿cuál es tu predilecta (favorita)?
Explica por qué.

3 **Comparaciones**

✓ *Compare holidays in the United States with Hispanic holidays*

Compara el Día de los Muertos con *Halloween*. También compara
el día de Navidad con el Día de los Reyes.

4 **Recuerdos**

✓ *Talk about your childhood*

Relata unos recuerdos placenteros (agradables) que tienes de los
años de tu niñez. Empieza con «Cuando yo era niño(a)… ».

CULTURA

Estas niñas de Cotacachi,
Ecuador, llevan trajes para
celebrar las Navidades.

Tarea

Write a journal entry in which you reminisce about a holiday you enjoyed as a youngster. Describe the general characteristics of that holiday, such as when you would celebrate it, how it was celebrated, what would often happen, who would always be there, and why you always enjoyed it.

Writing Strategy

Reminiscing One technique frequently used in journal writing is reminiscing. When you reminisce, you use your memory to recall how things were in the past. The primary source of information will be the thoughts and images that your mind produces of "the way things were back then." Use what you have learned about the imperfect and the vocabulary from this chapter to make your journal entry as descriptive and lively as possible.

❶ Prewrite

Make a list of the thoughts and images that come to mind when you reminisce about your favorite holiday. Think about when it would take place, who would be there, what the scene would be like, what would often happen, why it was always fun, etc.

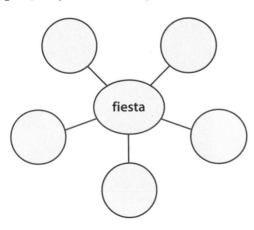

fiesta

❷ Write

- Be sure to stick to vocabulary that you already know.
- Remember to incorporate time expressions often used to indicate habitual or repeated actions in the past, such as **siempre, cada, a menudo, con mucha frecuencia, a veces,** etc.
- Use descriptive adjectives and include as many details as possible to make the memory of your favorite holiday come alive.

It is important to keep in mind that you are not writing about specific events that took place one time during your favorite holiday. Your goal is to capture the overall essence of this habitual or repeated event from your childhood as you remember it.

Evaluate

Don't forget that your teacher will evaluate you on use of vocabulary, correctness of grammar, and the vivid description of details.

Repaso del Capítulo 5

Gramática

- ### Imperfecto de los verbos regulares *(pages 146 and 148)*
  The imperfect is used to describe a habitual or repeated action in the past. Some words commonly used with the imperfect are **siempre, con frecuencia, a menudo,** and **todos los días.** Review the imperfect forms of regular verbs.

bailar	beber	vivir
bailaba	bebía	vivía
bailabas	bebías	vivías
bailaba	bebía	vivía
bailábamos	bebíamos	vivíamos
bailabais	*bebíais*	*vivíais*
bailaban	bebían	vivían

- ### Imperfecto de los verbos irregulares *(page 150)*
  Ser, ir, and **ver** are irregular in the imperfect. Review the following forms.

ser	ir	ver
era	iba	veía
eras	ibas	veías
era	iba	veía
éramos	íbamos	veíamos
erais	*ibais*	*veíais*
eran	iban	veían

- ### Usos del imperfecto *(page 151)*
  The imperfect is used to express continuous action in the past and to describe persons, places, objects, events, weather, and time in the past.

  Ellos siempre hacían mucho.
  Dolores estaba muy contenta.
  Llovía mucho en la primavera.
  Era el seis de enero y nevaba.

CULTURA

Un desfile pasaba por el Zócalo en la Ciudad de México.

Juego   There are a number of cognates in this list. See how many you and a partner can find. Who can find the most? Compare your list with those of your classmates.

Vocabulario

Talking about a patron saint's day

una feria	la santa patrona	patronal
una fiesta	una procesión,	desfilar
el santo patrón	un desfile	caminar

Talking about the Day of the Dead

los muertos, los difuntos	la tumba	una calavera, un cráneo	un disfraz
el camposanto, el cementerio	una ofrenda	un esqueleto	una máscara
el mausoleo	una corona de flores	un hueso	enterrado(a)

Talking about Christmas and Three Kings Day

la Navidad, las Navidades	la chimenea	el camello	decorar
la Nochebuena	un aguinaldo	la paja	
	los Reyes Magos	el árbol de Navidad	

Talking about Hanukkah

Hanuka	la fiesta de las luces	la vela	hebreo(a)
¡Feliz Hanuka!	la menora	judío(a)	encender

Talking about Independence Day

un desfile	los fuegos artificiales	el cielo	iluminar
una banda municipal		bailar	

Other useful words and expressions

el bizcocho	celebrar	elaborar
todo el mundo	confeccionar	mientras
dulce		

Repaso cumulativo

Repasa lo que ya has aprendido

These activities will help you review and remember
what you have learned so far in Spanish.

1 Escucha las frases. Indica en una tabla como la de abajo
si la frase describe una acción en el presente o el pasado.

presente	pasado

2 Personaliza. Da respuestas personales.

1. ¿A qué escuela fuiste el año pasado?
2. ¿Cuántos cursos tomaste?
3. ¿En qué curso recibiste la nota más alta?
4. ¿Qué curso te gustó más?
5. El año pasado, ¿trabajaste después de las clases?
6. Y este año, ¿a qué escuela vas?
7. ¿Cuántos cursos tienes?
8. ¿En qué curso recibes la nota más alta?
9. ¿Qué curso te gusta más?
10. ¿Trabajas después de las clases?

CULTURA

El corredor de un
colegio en Rawson en
la Patagonia argentina

3 Describe todo lo que ves en la tienda de ropa. ¿Qué está haciendo la gente?

4 Completa con el pronombre reflexivo.

1. Yo _____ levanto a las seis y media.
2. Mi hermano _____ viste enseguida.
3. Yo no. Yo _____ lavo la cara y _____ cepillo los dientes.
4. Nosotros _____ sentamos a la mesa para tomar el desayuno.
5. Luego yo _____ visto y salimos para la escuela.
6. Ellos _____ divierten durante la fiesta.
7. Y tú, ¿a qué hora _____ acuestas?
8. ¿_____ bañas por la mañana o por la noche?

5 Completa con **peinarse.**

1. Yo quiero _____.
2. Él quiere _____.
3. Ellos quieren _____.
4. Nosotros queremos _____.
5. ¿Tú quieres _____?

6 **Juego** Mira los dibujos. Son similares pero hay unas pequeñas diferencias. ¿Cuáles son?

Tecnomundo

Vamos a comparar ¿Puedes imaginar el mundo sin computadoras? ¿Usas tu computadora con frecuencia? ¿Para qué la usas? ¿Qué piensas? ¿Tienen computadora los jóvenes de España y Latinoamérica? Vamos a ver la influencia de la tecnología en su vida diaria.

Objetivos

You will:

- talk about computers, the Internet, and e-mail
- talk about a digital camera and an MP3 player
- make and receive phone calls
- discuss technology in Hispanic countries

You will use:

- the preterite and imperfect tenses

◄ Estos estudiantes de varios países latinos se sirven de la tecnología al hacer sus estudios en California.

QuickPass

Go to glencoe.com
For: **Online book**
Web code: **ASD7837c6**

Introducción al tema
Tecnomundo

Mira estas fotos para familiarizarte con el tema de este capítulo—la tecnología hoy en día. No hay duda que los avances tecnológicos en el campo de la informática cambian rápidamente y siguen influyendo la vida de muchos en todos los rincones del mundo.

▲ **México** Los amigos de esta joven en Baja California tienen mucho interés en su nuevo móvil.

TARJETA CHIP, TU OTRO MÓVIL

Siempre es bueno tener un teléfono a mano

Telefónica

◀ **España**
El teléfono público sigue siendo un medio de comunicación corriente en muchas partes del mundo hispano. Aquí vemos unos teléfonos públicos en Arrecife, Lanzarote, en las islas Canarias.

◀ **Estados Unidos**
Esta joven de ascendencia mexicana se divertía escuchando música en su MP3 después de las clases.

▲ **España** Un joven en Madrid pasa unos momentos libres jugando un videojuego.

Costa Rica Este joven está navegando la red en su casa en Puntarenas, Costa Rica. Puntarenas es un puerto en el océano Pacífico. ▼

▲ **España** Esta joven española quería una foto de la bahía de la Concha en San Sebastián en el País Vasco (Euskadi) y la sacó con su móvil.

Argentina ▶
Una muchacha argentina usa su computadora portátil en un parque de Buenos Aires.

◀ **Nicaragua** Los alumnos aprenden a usar la computadora en una clase de informática en la isla de Mancarrón en el lago Nicaragua.

La computadora, El ordenador

la página de inicio (inicial, frontal)

la pantalla de escritorio

la alfombrilla

el ratón

el teclado

el botón regresar (retroceder)

Atrás

Cristina navegaba la red (el Internet). Quería regresar a un sitio Web anterior. Hizo clic en el botón regresar.

Cristina estaba sentada delante de su computadora.
Prendió la computadora.
Quería entrar en línea.
Por eso, hizo clic con el ratón.
Cuando terminó, apagó la computadora.

En otras partes

La computadora is used in all of Latin America. **El ordenador** is used in Spain.

la carpeta

oprimir, pulsar

José no quería guardar cierto archivo.
Ya no lo necesitó y lo borró.
Oprimió (Pulsó) el botón borrador.

el correo electrónico, el e-mail

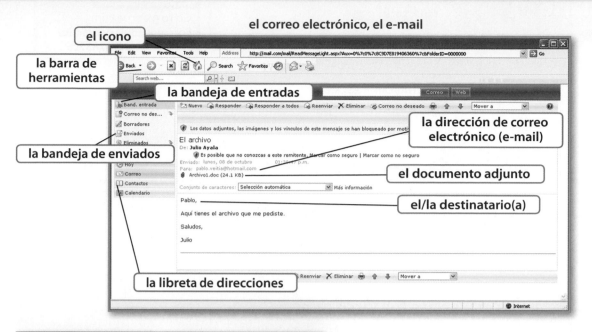

la barra de herramientas

el icono

la bandeja de entradas

la bandeja de enviados

la libreta de direcciones

la dirección de correo electrónico (e-mail)

el documento adjunto

el/la destinatario(a)

Hoy Paco recibió muchos correos electrónicos.
Los leyó todos pero no contestó todos.
Había tres que no le interesaron y los borró.
Enviaba un correo cuando sonó su móvil (celular).

la impresora

El padre de José Luis recibió un boleto aéreo electrónico por correo electrónico.
Quería una copia dura de su boleto y lo imprimió.
La sacó de la impresora.

QuickPass

Go to glencoe.com
For: **Vocabulary practice**
Web code: **ASD7837c6**

HABLAR • ESCRIBIR

1 Identifica las partes de la computadora.

LEER

2 Verifica. ¿Sí o no?

	sí	no
1. Cada sitio Web tiene su página inicial.		
2. Si quieres volver a un sitio, haz clic en el botón retroceder.		
3. Dentro de (En) un archivo hay varias carpetas.		
4. Si quieres guardar un documento lo tienes que borrar.		
5. Cada correo electrónico tiene un documento adjunto.		
6. Para hacer una copia dura de un documento necesitas una impresora.		
7. Si quieres leer de nuevo (una vez más) un correo electrónico que enviaste ayer tienes que abrir tu bandeja de entradas.		

CULTURA

Las alumnas van a la escuela a pie en San Pedro La Laguna, Guatemala. Cada una lleva una computadora portátil.

HABLAR • ESCRIBIR

3 Personaliza. Da respuestas personales.
1. ¿Tienes una computadora portátil?
2. ¿Eres muy aficionado(a) a la computadora?
3. ¿Usas la computadora para hacer tus tareas escolares? ¿Cómo?
4. ¿Para qué navegas el Internet (la red)?
5. ¿Recibes y envías muchos correos electrónicos?
6. ¿Cuál es tu dirección de e-mail?
7. ¿Recibes muchos correos electrónicos que borras enseguida?
8. ¿Cuándo tienes que consultar tu libreta de direcciones?
9. ¿Apagas la computadora cuando no la usas?

EXPANSIÓN

Ahora, sin mirar las preguntas, cuenta la información en tus propias palabras. Si no recuerdas algo, un(a) compañero(a) te puede ayudar.

LEER

 ¡Te toca a ti! Parea cada verbo con una palabra o expresión apropiada.

1. sonar   **a.** en línea
2. imprimir   **b.** el correo electrónico
3. enviar   **c.** el botón
4. borrar   **d.** una copia
5. entrar   **e.** el archivo
6. oprimir   **f.** el móvil

HABLAR • ESCRIBIR

❺ Usa cada expresión de la Actividad 4 en una frase original.

LEER • ESCRIBIR

❻ Completa con una palabra apropiada.

1. César quería abrir su bandeja de entradas e hizo clic con el _____.
2. Había muchos _____ nuevos en su bandeja de entradas. Los recibió hoy.
3. Él los leyó. Había tres que no le interesaron y los _____.
4. Recibió uno de un buen amigo. Él lo contestó enseguida y guardó la respuesta en su _____.
5. César _____ la computadora cuando empezó a trabajar y la _____ cuando terminó.

LEER • ESCRIBIR

❼ Expresa de otra manera.

1. Ella siempre está sentada delante de su *ordenador.*
2. El sitio tiene una página *de inicio* interesante.
3. Ella navegaba *el Internet.*
4. Tienes que *pulsar* el botón borrador.
5. ¿Cuál es tu dirección de *e-mail?*

✿ **Comunicación**

❽ Trabaja con un(a) compañero(a) de clase. Discutan lo que hacen con su computadora. ¿Quién la usa más?

Fotos y música

una cámara digital

A Cristina le encanta la fotografía.
Siempre descarga (baja) las fotos que
toma con su cámara digital o su móvil
a su computadora.

A Anita le encanta la música.
Siempre baja sus canciones favoritas
a su MP3.

Llamadas telefónicas

¡Ah!
Es mi amigo Paco.

el timbre (sonoro)

un móvil,
un (teléfono) celular

Sonó el móvil de Patricia.
Sabía quien la llamaba por el timbre.
Es el timbre que asignó a su mejor amigo.

Para conversar

¡Hola! Pepe, ¿eres
tú? No te oigo bien. Estás
cortando. ¿Me escuchas?

¡Hola!

Ah, se nos cortó la
línea. Una llamada
perdida (caída).

la tarjeta telefónica

el teléfono público

la guía telefónica

el número de teléfono

la clave de área

Juan y Teresa estaban en España.
Usaron un teléfono público para llamar a casa.
Para llamar a Estados Unidos, tenían que
    marcar el prefijo del país.

Descolgó (el
auricular).

Introdujo su tarjeta
en la ranura.

Esperó el tono.

Marcó el número
que deseaba.

Como contestar el teléfono

¡Hola!

Sí, está. ¿De parte de quién, por favor?

Un momento, por favor.

¿Está Teresa, por favor?

De Rafael. Rafael Lugones.

¡Hola!

Lo siento, pero no está.

Cómo no, Señor.

¿Está Teresa, por favor?

¿Le puedo dejar un mensaje?

FOLDABLES®
Study Organizer

ENVELOPE FOLD
See page SH30 for help with making this foldable. Use this study organizer with a partner to help you practice your new words. Draw a picture of a word on the top of each flap. Then pass the foldable to your partner who will write the word that corresponds with each picture on the reverse side of each flap. Take turns.

ESCUCHAR

1 Escucha y decide. Escucha cada frase y decide si la información es correcta o no. Usa una tabla como la de abajo para indicar tus respuestas.

correcta	incorrecta

HABLAR

2 Personaliza. Da respuestas personales.

1. ¿Tienes una cámara digital?
2. A veces, ¿bajas (descargas) las fotos que tomas en tu computadora?
3. ¿Qué bajas más en tu computadora? ¿Fotografías o canciones?
4. ¿Te gusta jugar videojuegos? ¿Cuál es tu favorito?
5. ¿Tienes un móvil?
6. ¿Cuál es el número de tu móvil?
7. ¿Tiene tu móvil un solo timbre o varios timbres?
8. ¿Tienes a veces llamadas perdidas cuando usas tu móvil?
9. ¿Hay muchos teléfonos públicos donde vives?
10. ¿Tiene tu familia un teléfono en casa? ¿Cuál es el número de su teléfono?

LEER • ESCRIBIR

3 Parea los sinónimos.

1. un celular
2. un ordenador
3. le gusta mucho
4. bajar
5. el código de área
6. una llamada perdida
7. ¡Bueno! (al contestar el teléfono)

a. descargar
b. una llamada caída
c. un móvil
d. le encanta
e. ¡Dígame!
f. la clave de área
g. una computadora

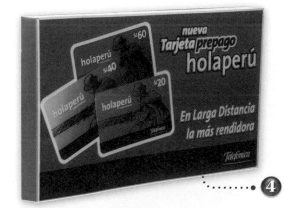

LEER • HABLAR

4 Contesta.

¿De qué país es la tarjeta telefónica? ¿Qué significa **prepago**?

HABLAR • ESCRIBIR

5 Estás hablando por teléfono. ¿Qué vas a decir?

1. Quieres saber si alguien está.
2. Quieres saber quién está llamando.
3. Quieres saber si la persona con quien hablas (tu interlocutor) te puede oír.
4. Quieres decirle que la conexión es mala.
5. Quieres decirle a la persona con quien hablas que alguien no está.
6. Quieres dejarle un mensaje a una persona que no está.
7. Quieres decirle a otra persona que tuviste una llamada perdida.

LEER • ESCRIBIR

6 Completa.

Para hacer una llamada de un teléfono público en España o Latinoamérica debes comprar una __1__. Primero tienes que __2__ el auricular y luego __3__ la tarjeta en la ranura. Es necesario esperar __4__ antes de __5__ el número que deseas. Si haces una llamada de larga distancia tienes que marcar primero __6__ y si haces una llamada internacional tienes que marcar __7__ también. Si no sabes un número de teléfono lo puedes buscar en __8__.

Comunicación

7 Trabaja con un(a) compañero(a) de clase. Uno(a) de ustedes hace una llamada telefónica y el/la otro(a) contesta. Conversen.

CULTURA

Mamá está haciendo una llamada telefónica en Miraflores, Perú. ¿Está introduciendo el niño una tarjeta en la ranura o está jugando?

InfoGap For more practice using your new vocabulary, do Activity 6 on page SR8 at the end of this book.

Una joven hablaba en su móvil mientras la otra leía un mensaje de texto.

Verbos como querer, creer en el pasado

Since most mental processes involve duration or continuance, verbs that deal with mental activities or conditions are most often expressed in the imperfect tense in the past. The most common of these verbs are:

creer	**pensar**
desear	**preferir**
querer	**poder**
tener ganas de *(to feel like)*	**saber**
sentir	**gustar**

Él sabía lo que preferíamos.
Yo tenía ganas de salir.

Práctica

CULTURA

Esta señorita guatemalteca siempre tenía ganas de ser artista y ahora tiene su propio taller en Antigua, Guatemala.

HABLAR • ESCRIBIR

1 Personaliza. Da respuestas personales.

1. ¿Te gustaba jugar videojuegos cuando eras joven?
2. ¿Sabías usar la computadora cuando eras muy joven?
3. ¿Siempre querías salir o preferías quedarte en casa?
4. ¿Siempre sabías lo que preferías hacer?
5. ¿Creías que siempre tenías razón o no?

LEER • ESCRIBIR

2 Completa en el pasado con el imperfecto del verbo indicado.

1. Yo _____ que sí pero no sé por qué, pero ellos _____ que no. (creer, creer)
2. Yo _____ que a ellos les _____ mucho hablar en su móvil. (saber, gustar)
3. Ella _____ lo mismo. (pensar)
4. Nosotros _____ ganas de hacer el viaje. (tener)
5. Nosotros _____ que ellos _____ salir. (saber, preferir)

 Comunicación

3 Cuenta algunas cosas que tú siempre querías hacer pero que tu hermano(a) o mejor amigo(a) casi nunca quería hacer. Casi siempre prefería hacer otra cosa. ¿Qué prefería hacer él o ella?

Gramática

El pretérito y el imperfecto

1. The choice of whether to use the preterite or imperfect depends upon whether the speaker is describing an action completed in the past or a continuous, recurring action in the past.

2. You use the preterite to express actions or events that began and ended at a specific time in the past.

> **Anoche volví a casa y envié unos correos electrónicos.**
> **Luego pasé un rato navegando la red.**
> **Y a eso de las nueve fui a ver la tele.**

3. You use the imperfect to talk about a continuous, habitual, or repeated action in the past. The moment when the action began or ended is unimportant.

> **Cada noche volvía a casa y enviaba unos correos**
>   **electrónicos.**
> **Luego pasaba un rato navegando la red.**
> **Y después iba a la sala donde veía la tele.**

4. Compare the following sentences.

REPEATED, HABITUAL ACTION	COMPLETED ACTION
Él hablaba con sus abuelos cada semana.	**Él habló con sus abuelos la semana pasada.**
Ella siempre navegaba la red.	**Ella navegó la red anoche.**
Yo siempre me acostaba tarde.	**Pero anoche me acosté temprano.**

Práctica

ESCUCHAR

4 Escucha. Usa una tabla como la de abajo para indicar si es una acción repetida o terminada.

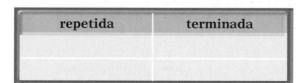

repetida	terminada

La joven usaba su computadora portátil y tenía su móvil muy cerca. ¿Esperaba una llamada?

ESCUCHAR • HABLAR

5 Contesta. Presta atención a la expresión de tiempo.

1. ¿Jugaron los niños un videojuego anoche?
   ¿Cuándo jugaron un videojuego?
   ¿Jugaban los niños videojuegos todos los días?
   ¿Cuándo jugaban videojuegos?
2. ¿Compraste algo en línea ayer? ¿Qué compraste?
   ¿Cuándo lo/la compraste?
   ¿Siempre hacías compras en línea?
   ¿Cuándo hacías compras en línea?
3. ¿Fue José a España el año pasado?
   ¿Cuándo fue a España?
   ¿Iba José a España cada año?
   ¿Cuándo iba a España?

Cada vez que José iba a España visitaba Sevilla. Sevilla es una típica ciudad andaluza en el sur de España.

LEER • ESCRIBIR

6 Cambia **todos los sábados** a **el sábado pasado** y haz los cambios necesarios.

Todos los sábados Juan Antonio se levantaba muy temprano. Bajaba a la cocina y él mismo preparaba el desayuno. Después de comer, subía a su cuarto y prendía su computadora. Cuando hacía la conexión a Internet mandaba un correo electrónico a un buen amigo en España. En pocos segundos se comunicaba con su amigo. Los dos escribían de muchas cosas durante horas.

HABLAR • ESCRIBIR

7 Contesta.

1. Por lo general, ¿guardabas la mayoría de los correos electrónicos que recibías o los borrabas?
2. ¿Guardaste el correo que recibiste anoche o lo borraste?
3. ¿Abría Teresa su bandeja de entradas con frecuencia?
4. ¿La abrió ayer o no?
5. ¿Enviabas mensajes de texto a tus amigos muy a menudo?
6. ¿A quién le enviaste un mensaje de texto ayer?
7. ¿Usabas el Internet muy a menudo?
8. ¿Usaste el Internet anoche?

8 Mira la fotografía y contesta las preguntas.

1. ¿Andaba mucha gente por la placita?
2. ¿Había una fuente en el centro?
3. ¿De qué color eran las casas?
4. ¿Qué tiempo hacía?
5. ¿Había un muchacho en su bici?
6. ¿Decidió andar en solo una rueda?
7. ¿Lo miraban sus amigos mientras hacía esta tontería?
8. ¿Había una señora que caminaba con sus perros?
9. ¿Le hizo caso al muchacho? ¿Lo miró o lo ignoró?
10. Y los perros de la señora, ¿le prestaban atención al muchacho?

EXPANSIÓN

 Se dice que un muchacho como este es fanfarrón.
¿Qué significa «fanfarrón»?

9 Personaliza. Da respuestas personales.

¿Conocías a un niño fanfarrón cuando eras más joven? ¿Qué hacía? ¿Veías lo que hacías? ¿Qué hacías tú mientras él cometía sus tonterías? Una vez, ¿hizo algo que le causó un problema? ¿Qué hizo y qué pasó? Y ¿qué hiciste (tú)?

 Comunicación

10 Di algunas cosas que hacías con frecuencia cuando eras niño(a) y que hiciste ayer también.

Dos acciones pasadas en la misma frase

1. Often a sentence may have two or more verbs in the past. The verbs may be in the same tense or in different tenses. In the sentence below, both verbs are in the preterite. Both describe simple actions that began and ended at a specific time in the past.

> **Laura llegó ayer y Pepe la vio.**

2. In the sentence below, the two verbs are in the imperfect because they both describe habitual or continuous actions. The moment when the actions began or ended is unimportant.

> **Durante el invierno, Adela iba a las montañas a esquiar, pero yo trabajaba.**

3. In the sentence below, the verb **estudiaba** is in the imperfect; it describes the background—what was going on. The verb in the preterite, **entró,** expresses the action or event that interrupted the ongoing action.

> **Yo estudiaba cuando Julia entró.**

El joven estudiaba mientras su hermana hablaba por teléfono.

Práctica

HABLAR • ESCRIBIR

 11 Contesta.

1. ¿Enviaba José un correo electrónico cuando sonó su móvil? ¿Contestó el móvil?
2. Mientras ellos hablaban, ¿estaba cortando la línea?
3. Mientras ellos hablaban, ¿se les cortó la línea?
4. ¿Estaba Teresa en casa cuando Rafael la llamó?
5. ¿Navegaba Anita el Internet cuando su hermanito apagó la computadora?
6. ¿Se puso furiosa Anita cuando él la apagó?

LEER • ESCRIBIR

12 Completa con la forma apropiada del pretérito o imperfecto.

1. Él ____ cuando yo le ____. (enfadarse, hablar)
2. Yo ____ su e-mail cuando él me ____ en mi móvil. (leer, llamar)
3. La conexión no ____ muy buena. ____ cortando y por fin se nos ____ la línea. (ser, estar, cortar)
4. Mi hermanita no ____ que yo ____ la red y cuando (yo) ____ de mi cuarto ella ____ la computadora. (saber, usar, salir, apagar)

HABLAR • ESCRIBIR

13 Di lo que hacías cuando algo te interrumpió. Forma frases según el modelo.

MODELO leer →
Yo leía cuando sonó el teléfono.

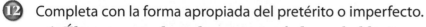

| leer | correr | ver | jugar | beber | hablar | sonar |
| llamar | bailar | comer | subir | servir | llover | pagar |

Comunicación

14 Trabaja con un(a) compañero(a) de clase. Dile lo que hacía cada miembro de tu familia anoche mientras tú hacías otra cosa. Di también lo que tú hacías. Luego comparen sus actividades.

15 Habla con un(a) compañero(a) de clase. Dile algo que hacías ayer. Tu compañero(a) te va a decir algo que ocurrió e interrumpió lo que hacías. Luego en una sola frase, describe lo que hacías y lo que pasó (ocurrió).

Refrán

Can you guess what the following proverb means?

No me importa nada. No están maduras.

Así dijo la zorra a las uvas: que no estaban maduras.

¡Bravo!

You have now learned all the new vocabulary and grammar in this chapter. Continue to use and practice all that you know while learning more cultural information. **¡Vamos!**

Conversación

Se cortó la línea.

Perdón, José. Es el timbre de Alejandra y le quiero hablar. ¿Alejandra?

Sí, ¿qué tal, Andrés?

Mira, ¿qué hacías anoche? Te llamé dos veces y no contestaste.

¡Qué barbaridad! Tenía mi móvil y no sonó. ¿Dejaste un mensaje? Andrés, ¿me escuchas? ¿Andrés?

Sí, sí. Pero estás cortando.

¿Ahora?

No. Estás cortando más. ¡Alejandra! Ah, se nos cortó la línea.

¿Comprendes?

A Contesta según la información en la conversación.

1. ¿Cómo sabe Andrés que es Alejandra quien lo llama cuando suena su móvil?
2. ¿Qué pasó anoche?
3. ¿Por qué no contestó ella?
4. ¿Sabemos si Andrés dejó un mensaje?
5. ¿Qué problema están teniendo?
6. ¿Cómo terminó la llamada?

B **Analizando** ¿Por qué es conveniente dar un timbre diferente a cada uno de tus amigos o miembros de la familia que te llaman con frecuencia?

C **Personalizando** ¿Tienes a veces unos problemas con tu móvil como los que tenían (experimentaban) Andrés y Alejandra en la conversación? Describe los problemas. Luego habla con tus compañeros para ver si ellos tienen las mismas dificultades.

Antes de leer

Piensa en todo lo que tú haces con tu computadora y otros aparatos electrónicos.

ESTRATEGIA DE LECTURA

Personalizando Una buena estrategia de lectura es personalizar la información que estás leyendo. Determina cuáles son cosas que tú también haces o cosas que no haces. Cuando personalizas puedes identificarte más con la información.

Durante la lectura

Relata las actividades de los jóvenes hispanos en la lectura con tus propias actividades.

✓ Reading Check

¿Qué información buscaba Manuel?

En un mundo tecnológico 🎧 ♻

Vamos a hablar con unos amigos hispanohablantes.

—¡Hola! Me llamo Manuel Ramos. Tengo dieciséis años y vivo en la Ciudad de México. Anoche navegaba el Internet para buscar información sobre Simón Bolívar para mi clase de historia. Yo no sabía que Bolívar era de una familia acomodada, una familia que tenía mucho dinero, y que desde su niñez le interesaban mucho las condiciones en que vivían los pobres.

Creo que esta información es correcta pero antes de incluirla en mi composición tengo que verificar su confiabilidad[1]. Todos sabemos que hay sitios que no son confiables.

✓ Reading Check

¿Cuál es un pasatiempo favorito de Julia?

—¡Hola! Me llamo Julia González y soy de Ponce, Puerto Rico. A mí me encanta la música. Anoche bajé (descargué) unas ocho canciones más en mi computadora y en mi MP3. Me encanta escuchar mis canciones favoritas en cualquier[2] momento del día. ¡Una cosa importante! Siempre verifico si es legal bajar las canciones.

✓ Reading Check

¿Por qué es interesante la información que envió el hermano de Raúl?

Después de leer

¿Con qué actividades podías identificar más? ¿Usan estos jóvenes sus computadoras y otros aparatos de la misma manera que tú?

— ¡Hola! Soy Raúl Torres. Soy de Málaga, España. Anoche recibí una noticia interesante. Mi hermano mayor está estudiando en la Universidad de Salamanca. Me envió un correo electrónico y me dijo que algunos de sus profesores ponen sus conferencias en el Internet. Si un(a) estudiante no puede asistir a clase puede escuchar la conferencia en su MP3. ¿Qué piensas de tal idea? Vale, ¿no?

¹confiabilidad *reliability*   ²cualquier *any*

¿Comprendes?

Más práctica

Workbook, pp. 6.10–6.12
StudentWorks™ Plus

A **Hojeando** Hojea la lectura para determinar quién hace las siguientes actividades.

	Manuel Ramos	Julia González	Raúl Torres
1. descarga su música favorita			
2. navega el Internet buscando datos para una tarea escolar			
3. lee un correo electrónico que acaba de recibir			

B **Buscando información** Da la información para cada persona—Manuel, Julia, Raúl—usando frases completas.
    1. de donde es
    2. lo que tiene
    3. detalles sobre sus actividades

C **Recordando hechos** Contesta.
    1. ¿Qué aprendió Manuel Ramos mientras navegaba el Internet?
    2. ¿Qué tiene que verificar Manuel? ¿Por qué?
    3. Y Julia, ¿qué tiene ella que verificar?
    4. ¿Qué noticia interesante recibió Raúl Torres de su hermano?

D **Pronosticando** Contesta.
    1. ¿Cuáles son unos avances tecnológicos no mencionados en esta lectura?
    2. ¿Cuáles son otros avances que piensas que van a ocurrir en el futuro?

La tecnología de hoy y ayer

Antes de leer

Piensa en como la tecnología moderna te afecta casi a diario (todos los días). ¿Cuáles son unos aparatos que usas tanto que los consideras indispensables? ¿Cómo te ayudan estos aparatos? En tu opinión, ¿cómo era la vida de tus abuelos sin la tecnología que tienes a tu disposición?

Tomás Navarro vive en Martínez, un suburbio de Buenos Aires, la capital de Argentina. Nos va a hablar de su nuevo juguete[1] que le gusta mucho.

—Ayer me compré un móvil. Es increíble la cantidad de opciones que tiene. Claro que puedo hacer y recibir llamadas y para saber quién me está llamando puedo personalizar los timbres asignando canciones u otros sonidos a mis amigos y familiares. Además mi móvil me permite enviar mensajes de texto, acceder mi correo electrónico y bajar música y videojuegos. Tiene otra opción que se llama fotomensajería. Puedo tomar fotografías digitales con mi móvil y enviarlas instantáneamente a mis amigos. Y puedo grabar y enviar un videomensaje con sonido. Las opciones no tienen límite.

Tú tienes un móvil, ¿no? ¿Te ofrece otras opciones que no me ofrece el mío? ¿Cuáles?

Sí, la tecnología está cambiando el mundo de una manera rápida y radical. Si no lo crees, debes hablar con tus abuelos. Cuando ellos eran niños, ¿tenían computadora y móvil? De ninguna manera. Si querían escuchar música ponían la radio o ponían un disco[2] en un tocadiscos. Cuando querían comunicarse con alguien escribían una carta o usaban el teléfono. Hoy día, en Estados Unidos, España y Latinoamérica la gente se comunica por medio de la comunicación electrónica. Pero en España y Latinoamérica, además de los móviles, sigue siendo popular y conveniente el teléfono público. Para usarlo compras una tarjeta telefónica que contiene una cantidad de unidades. La tarjeta que se introduce en la ranura del teléfono te permite hacer llamadas locales, interurbanas, de larga distancia y hasta[3] internacionales. Mientras hablas, se deduce automáticamente el número apropiado de unidades. ¡Otro ejemplo de la tecnología!

CULTURA

Aquí hay un quiosco de teléfonos públicos en el centro del pueblo de San Juan en Venezuela. Los teléfonos públicos tienen muchos usuarios.

[1]juguete *toy*
[2]disco *record*
[3]hasta *even*

¿Comprendes?

VIDEO To visit an internet café, watch **Diálogo en vivo.**

Escoge.

1. ¿Qué compró Tomás?
   a. un juguete
   b. un móvil
   c. una cámara

2. Tomás asigna timbres personales para _____.
   a. poder hacer y recibir llamadas
   b. poder oír sus canciones favoritas
   c. poder identificar quien lo está llamando

3. ¿Qué no puede hacer Tomás con su móvil?
   a. escuchar la radio
   b. tomar fotos
   c. enviar mensajes de texto

4. ¿Cómo se comunicaban nuestros abuelos cuando eran jóvenes?
   a. Usaban la radio.
   b. Usaban su tocadiscos.
   c. Usaban el teléfono.

5. ¿Qué contiene una tarjeta telefónica?
   a. números de teléfono
   b. unidades que te permiten hacer una llamada de un teléfono público
   c. un teléfono público

6. Una llamada interurbana es una llamada _____.
   a. local, dentro de la misma ciudad
   b. de una ciudad a otra en la misma región
   c. de larga distancia

Use monedas o tarjetas.

CULTURA

Es un teléfono público en una calle de Buenos Aires, la capital de Argentina. ¿Qué se puede usar para hacer una llamada de este teléfono?

Prepárate para el examen

Self-check for achievement

Vocabulario

 To review **Vocabulario 1,** turn to pages 172–173.

 To review **Vocabulario 1** and **Vocabulario 2,** turn to pages 172–173 and 176–177.

1 **Identifica.**

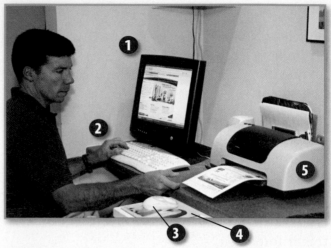

2 **Completa.**

6. La muchacha quiere entrar en línea y _____ con su ratón.

7–8. Si estás navegando y quieres regresar a un sitio anterior tienes que _____ en el _____ regresar.

9. Una _____ contiene varios archivos.

10. Si quieres saber si tienes correos electrónicos tienes que abrir tu _____.

11. No quiero guardar el correo. Lo voy a _____.

12. Si necesitas una copia dura de un correo o de una página del Internet, tienes que tener _____.

13. Puedes tener diferentes _____ en tu móvil para identificar quienes te llaman.

A esta pareja les gusta usar su móvil pero no tenían móvil cuando eran jóvenes.

3 **Parea.**

14. un móvil
15. la computadora
16. descargar
17. llamada perdida
18. @
19. regresar
20. oprimir

a. bajar
b. punto
c. guardar
d. un celular
e. pulsar
f. llamada caída
g. el ordenador
h. arroba
i. retroceder

Gramática

4 **Escribe en el pasado.**

21. Quiero comprarme un nuevo móvil.

22. A mis abuelos les gusta usar un teléfono fijo.

23. Él está contento cuando recibe la buena noticia.

To review **verbos como querer, creer en el pasado,** turn to page 180.

5 **Completa con el imperfecto o el pretérito.**

24–25. Él _____ muy a menudo y _____ ayer también. (ir, ir)

26–27. Ellos me _____ correos casi todos los días pero ayer yo no _____ ninguno. (enviar, recibir)

28–29. Cuando yo _____ niño(a) mis abuelos siempre me _____ en español. (ser, hablar)

To review **el pretérito y el imperfecto,** turn to page 181.

6 **Completa con el imperfecto o el pretérito.**

30–31. Teresa _____ en el supermercado cuando _____ su móvil. (estar, sonar)

32–33. Yo _____ en mi móvil cuando el empleado me _____ una pregunta. (hablar, hacer)

34–35. Él _____ canciones en su MP3 mientras yo _____ fotografías en el mío. (bajar, bajar)

36–37. Mientras ellos _____ nosotros _____. (divertirse, trabajar)

To review **dos acciones pasadas en la misma frase,** turn to page 184.

Cultura

7 **Corrige las frases falsas.**

38. En algunas universidades si un(a) estudiante no puede ir a clase, puede mirar las conferencias de sus profesores en la televisión.

39. Siempre sabemos que la información que leemos en el Internet es correcta.

40. Se puede bajar canciones sin permiso.

To review this cultural information, turn to page 188.

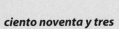

1 **La tecnología**

Talk about your opinion of technology

¿A ti te gusta la tecnología? Explica por qué dices que sí o que no.

2 **Mi móvil**

Discuss your new cell phone

Imagínate que acabas de comprar un nuevo móvil con todas las opciones más avanzadas. Dile a un(a) compañero(a) todo lo que puedes hacer con tu móvil. Luego discutan las opciones que les gustan más o que consideran las más interesantes.

3 **El uso de los celulares**

Debate the use of cell phones

Trabajen en grupos y debatan sus ideas sobre el uso de los celulares. ¿Deben permitir el uso de celulares en la escuela, abordo de un avión, mientras uno maneja (conduce) un carro, en el teatro o cine, etc.? Defiendan sus opiniones.

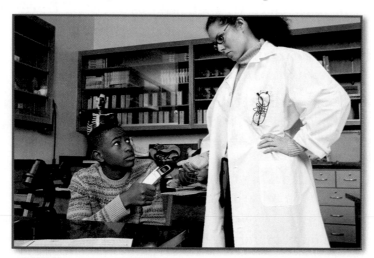

4 **Cuando mis abuelos eran jóvenes**

Tell about what your grandparents had and didn't have

Habla con tus abuelos. Ellos te van a decir las muchas cosas que tú tienes que ellos no tenían cuando eran niños. Te van a decir lo que tenían. Comparte los resultados de tus conversaciones con unos(as) compañeros(as) de clase y decidan si sus abuelos dicen más o menos la misma cosa.

5 **Interrupciones**

Talk about one activity interrupting another in the past

Trabaja con un(a) compañero(a) de clase. Ayer ustedes hacían muchas cosas. Pero siempre había interrupciones. Hablen de todo lo que hacían y todo lo que interrumpió lo que hacían.

Tarea

You have just received an e-mail message from a Spanish-speaking friend who hasn't heard from you in awhile and wants to know what's up. Write a reply informing him or her of how you are doing and what you did today. Use this opportunity to impress your friend with some of the grammar and vocabulary that you have learned recently, and don't forget to follow the rules of *netiquette.*

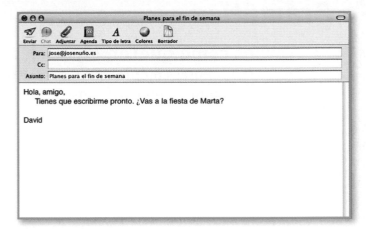

Writing Strategy

Netiquette E-mail is a quick and fun way to communicate with friends all over the world. Still, it is important to ensure that your message is not carelessly written. Tone of voice can easily be misunderstood, especially when sarcasm is used, and misspelled words or incorrect grammar can lead to confusion. To avoid hurt feelings and misunderstandings, it is important to adhere to net etiquette, or *netiquette,* and to always check your message for errors before sending it.

❶ Prewrite

Although e-mail between friends is an informal means of expression, your message should still follow a logical structure so that it is both easy to understand and fun to read. As you think about what you want your message to contain, categorize the information in terms of whether it belongs in the introduction, in the body or main part of the text, or in the conclusion.

❷ Write

Be sure to adhere to the following rules of *netiquette.*

- Be certain that you have typed the correct e-mail address. Sending a personal message to the wrong person can be embarrassing!
- Make sure that your subject line reflects the content of your e-mail.
- Use the correct spelling of words and proper grammar.
- Be cautious when using sarcasm as it can easily be misunderstood.
- Use capital letters appropriately. Words with all capital letters are read as SHOUTING and can be interpreted as rude.
- Remember that good manners are just as important in cyberspace as they are in real life.
- Always re-read your message carefully before sending it.

Evaluate

Don't forget that your teacher will evaluate you on correct use of vocabulary, proper spelling and grammar, logical structure, and good *netiquette.*

Repaso del Capítulo 6

Gramática

- **Verbos como querer, creer en el pasado** *(page 180)*

  Verbs that express mental processes or conditions in the past are usually expressed in the imperfect tense.

  Tenía ganas de ver a mis amigos.
  Mi abuela sabía lo que preferíamos comer.

- **El pretérito y el imperfecto** *(page 181)*

  The choice of whether to use the preterite or imperfect depends upon whether the action began and ended at a specific time in the past or if it was a continuous, habitual, or repeated action in the past. Compare the following sentences.

PRETERITE	IMPERFECT
Ella habló con su madre anoche.	**Ella hablaba con su madre cada día.**
El sábado fuiste al cine.	**Siempre ibas al cine.**
Comieron en el restaurante una vez.	**Comían en el restaurante a menudo.**

- **Dos acciones pasadas en la misma frase** *(page 184)*

  A sentence may have two or more verbs in the past. In the sentence below, both verbs are in the preterite because they both tell of events that began and ended at a specific point in the past.

  Pablo escribió el e-mail y lo envió.

  In the following sentence, both verbs are in the imperfect because they describe continuous actions in the past.

  En el verano Tito siempre iba a la playa y yo me quedaba en casa.

  Some sentences contain both the preterite and the imperfect. In this case, the preterite expresses an action that interrupted an ongoing action in the past.

  Mamá y papá hablaban cuando sonó el teléfono.

CULTURA

Los jóvenes se divertían mientras una amiga les leía un textomensaje que alguien le envió en su móvil. ¿Qué crees? ¿Es gracioso o serio el mensaje que recibió?

There are a number of cognates in this list. See how many you and a partner can find. Who can find the most? Compare your list with those of your classmates.

Vocabulario

Describing a computer

la computadora, el ordenador
la pantalla de escritorio
la alfombrilla

el ratón
el teclado
el icono
la barra de herramientas

un sitio Web
la página de inicio, (inicial, frontal)
el botón regresar (retroceder)

el botón borrador
el archivo
la carpeta
la impresora
una copia dura

Discussing e-mail

el correo electrónico, el e-mail
el/la destinatario(a)

la dirección de correo electrónico (de e-mail)
arroba
punto

la libreta de direcciones
la bandeja de entradas

la bandeja de enviados
el documento adjunto

Describing computer activities

prender
apagar
entrar en línea

hacer clic
oprimir, pulsar
guardar

borrar
navegar la red (el Internet)

bajar, descargar
imprimir

Discussing cell phones and other technology

el móvil, el celular
el timbre (sonoro)

una llamada perdida (caída)

la cámara digital
el MP3

sonar
asignar

Making a phone call

el teléfono público
la ranura
un mensaje

llamar
descolgar (el auricular)

introducir la tarjeta telefónica
esperar el tono

marcar el número
¿Está…?
¿De parte de quién?

Discussing telephone numbers

la guía telefónica

el número de teléfono

el prefijo del país

la clave de área

Other useful words and expressions

Estás cortando.
¿Me escuchas?

Se nos cortó la línea.
anterior

cierto(a)
encantar

 **Literary Reader**

You may wish to read the excerpts from the famous poem *Versos sencillos,* found on pages 364–367.

Repaso cumulativo

Repasa lo que ya has aprendido

These activities will help you review
what you have learned so far in Spanish.

GeoVistas

To learn more about Puerto
Rico, take a tour on pages
SH62–SH63.

 1 Escucha las frases. Parea cada frase con
el dibujo que describe.

a.      b.

 2 Completa con el imperfecto.
1. _____ una fiesta. (haber)
2. Todo el mundo _____ durante la fiesta. (bailar)
3. Una banda _____. (tocar)
4. Nosotros _____. (divertirse)
5. Yo no _____ ir a casa. (querer)
6. Me _____ los fuegos artificiales. (gustar)
7. Mucha gente _____ mientras _____ los fuegos
   artificiales. (comer, mirar)

 3 Completa con cada verbo que falta.
1. Él lo hizo y tú lo _____ pero ellos no lo _____.
2. Ellos vinieron y nosotros _____ pero tú no _____.
3. Yo estuve y él _____ pero tú no _____.
4. Tú lo supiste y yo lo _____ pero los otros no lo _____.

 4 Sigue el modelo.

MODELO   Lo pido. →
              Lo pedí.

1. Juan lo pide.
2. Tú lo sirves.
3. Nosotros lo repetimos.
4. Ella lo prefiere así.
5. El cocinero fríe las papas.
6. Usted lo sigue.

CULTURA

El mesero dio un servicio excelente
en un restaurante en las afueras de
San Juan, Puerto Rico.

5 **Identifica.** Usa un diagrama como el de abajo para escribir palabras relacionadas con una estación de tren.

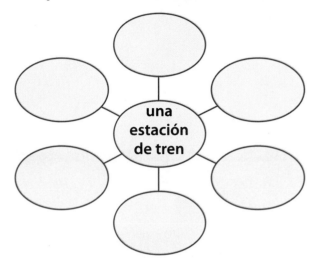

una estación de tren

6 Escribe una frase original con cada una de las palabras de la Actividad 5.

7 Escribe una pregunta.

1. *Juan* fue al restaurante.
2. Juan fue *al restaurante.*
3. El mesero trabajaba *en el restaurante.*
4. Juan pidió *un menú.*
5. El mesero era *de México.*
6. El mesero era *muy simpático.*
7. *Todos* comieron muy bien.
8. Todos comieron *mucho.*
9. Juan volvió a casa *en bus.*
10. Juan volvió *tarde.*

CULTURA
Los pasajeros están en el andén en una estación de metro en Medellín, Colombia. El metro acaba de llegar a la estación y van a subir abordo.

8   **Rompecabezas**

Cambia una letra en cada palabra para formar una nueva palabra.

1. base
2. peso
3. jamón
4. piso

5. llenar
6. fue
7. hay
8. cada

En el hotel

Aquí y Allí

Vamos a comparar ¿Has pasado una noche en un hotel aquí en Estados Unidos? ¿Cuándo? Y, ¿cómo era el hotel? ¿Hay muchas categorías de hoteles en Estados Unidos? En este capítulo vas a aprender algo sobre los muchos tipos de hoteles que hay en los países hispanos. Algunos son muy interesantes.

◄ **Los mochileros están saliendo de un hostal en San Cristóbal de las Casas en Chiapas, México.**

Objetivos

You will:

- check into a hotel or hostel
- ask for things you may need while at a hotel or hostel
- discuss hotel stays in Latin America and Spain

You will use:

- the present perfect tense
- double object pronouns

QuickPass

Go to glencoe.com
For: **Online book**
Web code: **ASD7837c7**

Introducción al tema
En el hotel

¿Te has alojado una vez en un hotel? ¿Por cuántas noches? Mira estas fotos para familiarizarte con el tema de este capítulo—una estadía en un hotel en un país hispano. Como vas a observar hay muchos tipos de hoteles—de los más económicos a los más elegantes.

España Muchos hoteles tienen llaves magnéticas pero algunos siguen usando una llave grande que los huéspedes tienen que dejar en la recepción cada vez que salen. ▼

▲ **España** Este hostal en Navarra fue un lugar favorito del autor Ernest Hemingway.

◄ **España** Un típico desayuno continental con croissants, pan dulce, pan tostado, jugo de naranja y café

Favor de Arreglar la Habitación

Please Make Up room
Prière De Faire La Chambre

Hoteles Calinda
Hoteles, Suites, Resorts
Mexico

Argentina Los recepcionistas en un hotel comercial de Buenos Aires ▶

Nicaragua ▶
El hall de entrada de un
hotel bonito en Granada

▲ **Puerto Rico** Es un hotel bonito
en la isla de Vieques.

▲ **México** Un hotel elegante en Tepotzlán
adonde va mucha gente de la Ciudad de
México a pasar el fin de semana

◀ **Chile** Un hotel
moderno con piscina
en el centro mismo de
Santiago de Chile

◀ **Perú** Es el patio de
una hacienda colonial en
el altiplano peruano en
Yucay, cerca de Cuzco. Hoy
la hacienda es un hotel.

203

VIDEO To practice your new words, watch **Vocabulario en vivo.**

Una estadía en un hotel

la recepcionista

la recepción

la llave (magnética)

el cliente, el huésped

un hotel

un albergue juvenil, un hostal

José está en la recepción.
Él ha hecho una reservación en línea.
Ha reservado un cuarto sencillo, no doble.
El huésped va a hospedarse en el hotel.

Un desayuno continental

la mermelada

la mantequilla

el pan dulce

el panecillo

el café

el ascensor

el mozo

El mozo ha subido el equipaje en el ascensor.

Un desayuno americano

el pan tostado

el tocino, el bacón, el lacón

el jugo de naranja

huevos revueltos

El cuarto, La habitación

la percha, el colgador

el armario

la manta, la frazada

la almohada

la sábana

la cama

La camarera ha limpiado el cuarto.
Ha hecho la cama.

Para conversar

Necesitamos toallas limpias. ¿Nos las ha cambiado la camarera?

No, no nos las ha cambiado.

El cuarto de baño

la ducha

una toalla limpia

el jabón

la bañera

el lavabo

el inodoro, el váter

una toalla sucia

En otras partes

In addition to **la camarera,** you will also hear **la mucama,** especially in Mexico.

el aire condicionado

El huésped va a salir.
Ha abandonado el cuarto.

QuickPass

Go to glencoe.com
For: **Vocabulary practice**
Web code: **ASD7837c7**

ESCUCHAR

Escucha las frases. Parea cada frase con la foto que describe.

a.

b.

c.

HABLAR • ESCRIBIR

Contesta sobre la llegada a un hotel.

1. ¿Ha reservado el señor un cuarto?
2. ¿Adónde va el cliente cuando llega al hotel?
3. ¿Quién lo saluda en la recepción?
4. ¿Quién lo va a ayudar con sus maletas?
5. ¿Qué le da el recepcionista para abrir la puerta de su cuarto?

EXPANSIÓN

Ahora, sin mirar las preguntas, cuenta la información en tus propias palabras. Si no recuerdas algo, un(a) compañero(a) te puede ayudar.

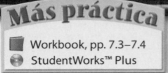

LEER

3 Escoge la palabra apropiada.

1. (Una manta, Una almohada) cubre la cama.
2. Hay (perchas, sábanas) en el armario.
3. (El mozo, La camarera) ha hecho la cama.
4. Me gusta dormir con dos (camas, almohadas).
5. Es necesario cambiar las toallas (limpias, sucias).
6. El desayuno (continental, americano) incluye huevos.
7. La huéspeda ha (abandonado, reservado) el cuarto porque va a salir.
8. Necesito (jabón, champú) para lavarme la cara.

CULTURA

Es una habitación en un hotel en Madrid, España. Identifica todo lo que ves en la habitación.

ESCRIBIR

4 Rompecabezas

Usa las letras en la tabla para formar palabras de este capítulo. Puedes usar unas letras más de una vez. Luego, escribe frases originales con tus palabras.

a	r	e
p	i	s
t	d	v
l	n	c
o	b	m

HABLAR • ESCRIBIR

5 Describe.

1. el cuarto de un hotel
2. un desayuno continental
3. un desayuno americano
4. las actividades en la recepción de un hotel

Carreras

Si conoces el español y lo sabes hablar por lo menos un poquito, hay muchas oportunidades para trabajar en la industria hotelera. Además de los muchos hispanohablantes que viven aquí, hay miles de turistas de España y Latinoamérica que visitan Estados Unidos cada año.

Vocabulario

Go to glencoe.com
For: **Grammar practice**
Web code: ASD7837c7

El presente perfecto

1. The present perfect tense is called a compound tense because it consists of two parts—the present tense of the verb **haber** and the past participle.

2. The past participle is formed by adding **-ado** to the stem of **-ar** verbs and **-ido** to the stem of **-er** and **-ir** verbs.

llegar → llegado	comer → comido	subir → subido
cambiar → cambiado	tener → tenido	vivir → vivido

3. Study the forms of regular present perfect verbs.

	llegar	comer	salir
yo	he llegado	he comido	he salido
tú	has llegado	has comido	has salido
Ud., él, ella	ha llegado	ha comido	ha salido
nosotros(as)	hemos llegado	hemos comido	hemos salido
vosotros(as)	habéis llegado	habéis comido	habéis salido
Uds., ellos, ellas	han llegado	han comido	han salido

4. The present perfect tense is used when speaking of a past event without reference to any particular time. It brings the action right up to the present. Some time expressions frequently used with the present perfect are:

ya	*already, yet*
todavía no	*not yet*
hasta ahora	*until now, so far*
jamás	*ever, never*
nunca	*never*

—**En tu vida, ¿has viajado a México?**
—**No. No he ido nunca a México.**
—**Yo sí. Hasta ahora he estado tres veces.**

5. The verb **haber** and the past participle are never separated.

Ella ha llegado pero sus amigos no han llegado.
Y ella no les ha hablado.

CULTURA

Es una calle peatonal en Guadalajara, México. ¿Jamás has viajado a México?

Práctica

ESCUCHAR • HABLAR • ESCRIBIR

1 Contesta sobre la visita de Sofía a un hotel.

1. ¿Ha llegado Sofía al hotel?
2. ¿Ha ido a la recepción?
3. ¿Ha hablado con la recepcionista?
4. ¿Le ha dado su llave la recepcionista?
5. ¿Ha subido a su cuarto?
6. ¿Ha subido la escalera o ha tomado el ascensor?
7. ¿La ha ayudado el mozo?

EXPANSIÓN

Ahora, sin mirar las preguntas, cuenta la información en tus propias palabras. Si no recuerdas algo, un(a) compañero(a) te puede ayudar.

HABLAR

2 Personaliza. Da respuestas personales.

1. ¿Has viajado por Ecuador?
2. ¿Te has hospedado en un albergue juvenil?
3. ¿Jamás has comido tacos o enchiladas?
4. ¿Has asistido a un concierto de rock?
5. Tú y tus amigos, ¿han ido a un museo?
6. ¿Han viajado ustedes en avión?

LEER • ESCRIBIR

3 Completa con el presente perfecto.

Los huéspedes ___1___ (llegar) al hotel y ___2___ (presentarse) en la recepción. El recepcionista les ___3___ (dar) su llave pero (ellos) no ___4___ (subir) a su cuarto todavía. ¿Tú ___5___ (ir) a un hotel recientemente?

CULTURA

Si quieres estar cerca del mercado en Otavalo, Ecuador, puedes hospedarte en este hostal.

Comunicación

4 Tus tíos y primos están visitando tu ciudad. Están hospedándose en un hotel. Llama al hotel por teléfono y habla con el/la recepcionista (tu compañero[a]). Quieres saber si ya han llegado tus parientes y si ya han subido a su cuarto. Después cambien de rol.

InfoGap For more practice using the present perfect, do Activity 7 on page SR9 at the end of this book.

Conexiones

El inglés

There are very few verbs that have an irregular past participle in Spanish. Such is not the case in English. There are many verbs with irregular past participles and many people learning English, as well as native speakers, have trouble with them. Can you give the past participle of the following verbs? *be, begin, bite, break, bring, buy, catch, come, eat, fall, find, fly, go, hear, hide, leave, make, meet, ride, run, see, sing, sit, speak, stand, swim, throw, write*

Participios irregulares

The following verbs have irregular past participles.

decir → dicho	volver → vuelto
hacer → hecho	devolver → devuelto
ver → visto	morir → muerto
escribir → escrito	abrir → abierto
poner → puesto	cubrir → cubierto *(covered)*
romper → roto *(broken)*	freír → frito

Práctica

HABLAR

5 Conversa según el modelo.

MODELO —¿Van a verlo?
—Pero, ya lo hemos visto.

1. ¿Van a abrirlo?
2. ¿Van a ponerlo?
3. ¿Van a devolverlo?

4. ¿Van a escribirlo?
5. ¿Van a decirlo?
6. ¿Van a cubrirlo?

HABLAR

6 Contesta según el modelo.

MODELO ¿Hacer tal cosa? →
¿Hacer tal cosa? ¡Vaya, hombre! ¿Yo?
En mi vida he hecho tal cosa.

1. ¿Ver tal cosa?
2. ¿Decir tal cosa?

3. ¿Leer tal cosa?
4. ¿Escribir tal cosa?

HABLAR • ESCRIBIR

7 Contesta según se indica.

1. ¿Ustedes se han ayudado? (sí)
2. ¿Quién ha hecho la cama? (yo)
3. ¿Quién ha frito los huevos? (Elena y Tomás)
4. ¿Quién ha abierto la lata? (yo)
5. ¿Quién ha puesto la mesa? (yo)
6. ¿Quién no ha hecho nada? (tú)

Comunicación

8 Hay muchas cosas que queremos hacer algún día que hasta ahora no hemos hecho. Con un(a) compañero(a) de clase, hablen de las cosas que quieren hacer pero que todavía no han hecho. Cuando posible, expliquen por qué no las han hecho o no las han podido hacer.

CULTURA

¿Quién ha puesto esta mesa en un restaurante en Guatemala?

Dos complementos me lo, te lo, nos lo

1. Many sentences have both a direct and an indirect object pronoun. In Spanish the indirect object pronoun always precedes the direct object pronoun. Both pronouns precede the conjugated form of the verb.

2. Study the following sentences.

Ella nos sirvió **el helado**.　　　Ella nos **lo** sirvió.

El mozo me dio **la llave**.　　　El mozo me **la** dio.

Él me vendió **los libros**.　　　Él me **los** vendió.

Papá te hizo **las reservaciones**.　　Papá te **las** hizo.

Foldables Study Organizer

LARGE SENTENCE STRIPS
See page SH31 for help with making this foldable. Use this study organizer to help you practice object pronouns. Write a sentence with a direct and indirect object on the front of each flap. Then pass the foldable to your partner who will open each flap and rewrite the sentences using pronouns. When you're finished, switch roles.

Práctica

HABLAR

9 Conversa según el modelo.

MODELO　　los videos →
　　　　　　—¿Quién te dio los videos?
　　　　　　—Mi tío Julio me los dio.

1. la raqueta
2. los esquís
3. las botas
4. el boleto
5. las gafas para el sol
6. la computadora

HABLAR • ESCRIBIR

10 Contesta con **la camarera** o **el mozo** y los pronombres apropiados.

1. ¿Quién te ha traído las perchas?
2. ¿Quién te ha cambiado las toallas?
3. ¿Quién te ha limpiado el baño?
4. ¿Quién te ha subido el equipaje?
5. ¿Quién te ha abierto la puerta?
6. ¿Quién te ha servido el desayuno?

CULTURA

Es un cuarto con dos camas en un hotel bonito en Cotacachi, Ecuador. La camarera ha limpiado el cuarto y ha puesto las batas en la cama para los huéspedes.

HABLAR

11 Conversa según el modelo.

MODELO cámara nueva →

    —¿Quieres ver mi cámara nueva?

    —¿Quién te la compró?

    —Me la compró mi tía Adela.

1. zapatos nuevos
2. casco nuevo

3. mochila nueva
4. botas nuevas

ESCUCHAR • HABLAR • ESCRIBIR

12 Contesta con **nuestra profesora** y los pronombres apropiados.

MODELO —¿Quién les dio (a ustedes) el examen?

    —Nuestra profesora nos lo dio.

1. ¿Quién les explicó (a ustedes) la regla?
2. ¿Quién les enseñó la gramática?
3. ¿Quién les explicó las diferencias?
4. ¿Quién les presentó el vocabulario?
5. ¿Quién les leyó los poemas?

Refrán

Can you guess what the following proverb means?

Sobre gustos no hay nada escrito.

Comunicación

13 Habla con un(a) compañero(a) de clase. Tu compañero(a) está llevando unas cosas que te gustan y quieres saber quién se las dio. Sigue el modelo.

MODELO —_____, me gusta mucho tu camisa. ¿Quién te la dio?

    —_____ me la dio. *or* No me la dio nadie. Me la compré.

CULTURA
La alberca de un hotel a orillas del lago Atitlán, Guatemala

Gramática

Dos complementos con se

1. The indirect object pronouns **le** and **les** change to **se** when used with **lo, la, los,** or **las.** Note that the indirect object **se** always precedes the direct object.

El mozo les subió el equipaje.   El mozo se lo subió.

El recepcionista le dio las llaves a José.   El recepcionista se las dio.

2. Because the pronoun **se** can refer to many different people, it is often clarified with a prepositional phrase.

Yo se lo di
{
a él.
a ella.
a usted.

Yo se lo di
{
a ellos.
a ellas.
a ustedes.

Práctica

ESCUCHAR • HABLAR

 14 Conversa según el modelo.

  MODELO —¿Quién le compró el regalito?
        —Su abuela se lo compró.

1. ¿Quién le compró la bicicleta?
2. ¿Quién le compró las entradas?
3. ¿Quién le compró la tabla hawaiana?
4. ¿Quién le compró los esquís acuáticos?
5. ¿Quién le compró el balón?

LEER • ESCRIBIR

 15 Contesta con los pronombres apropiados.

1. ¿Les abrió la puerta a los huéspedes el mozo?
2. ¿Les subió las maletas el mozo?
3. ¿Le dio la llave a la cliente el recepcionista?
4. ¿Le dieron su nombre al recepcionista los huéspedes?
5. ¿Les ha cambiado las toallas sucias la camarera?

 ## Comunicación

 16 Alguien que conoces acaba de recibir algo nuevo. Decide lo que es. Con un(a) compañero(a) de clase, prepara una conversación como la siguiente.

     MODELO —¿Viste el carro nuevo de Isabel?
            —Sí, lo vi. ¿Quién se lo dio?
            —No sé si alguien se lo dio o si
                se lo compró.

CULTURA

La recepcionista en este hotel en Buenos Aires, Argentina, ha recibido un mensaje para un cliente. Se lo va a dar.

¡Bravo!

You have now learned all the new vocabulary and grammar in this chapter. Continue to use and practice all that you know while learning more cultural information. **¡Vamos!**

QuickPass

Go to glencoe.com
For: **Conversation practice**
Web code: ASD7837c7

EN LA RECEPCIÓN

¿Comprendes?

VIDEO To visit a hotel of an unusual sort, watch **Diálogo en vivo.**

A Contesta según la información en la conversación.

1. ¿Con quién están hablando las muchachas? ¿Dónde?
2. ¿Han hecho una reservación las dos muchachas?
3. ¿Hay una habitación disponible?
4. ¿Cuál es la tarifa?
5. ¿Cuánto tiempo piensan estar en el hotel las muchachas?
6. ¿Por qué están cansadas?
7. ¿Han abandonado la habitación los otros clientes?
8. ¿Qué está incluido en la tarifa?

B **Resumiendo** Cuenta la información en la conversación en tus propias palabras.

C **Llegando a conclusiones** ¿Qué piensas? ¿Van a tomar un desayuno continental o un desayuno americano las muchachas? ¿Por qué has llegado a esta conclusión?

D **Investigando** En línea o en el periódico busca el tipo de cambio del dólar al euro. Luego, calcula el precio de la habitación en dólares.

Comparaciones

Los hoteles

En España y Latinoamérica todavía hay hoteles económicos que no tienen baño privado pero menos que en el pasado. Hasta recientemente había muchos que no lo tenían y un cuarto con baño privado costaba mucho. Cuando vas a un hotel, ¿prefieres un baño privado?

CULTURA

La recepción en un hotel en Palma de Mallorca

Antes de leer

Imagina que tienes unos amigos que están disfrutando de un viaje en un país hispano pero no tienen mucho dinero. ¿Cuáles son unas cosas que pueden hacer para economizar?

Durante la lectura

Identifícate con lo que tus amigos están haciendo. ¿Encuentras unas cosas bastante graciosas? ¿Cuáles?

✔ **Reading Check**

¿Por qué se hospedan los viajeros en un albergue juvenil?

✔ **Reading Check**

¿Cómo han botado la casa por la ventana los amigos? Y, ¿por qué?

Un hostal y un parador 🎧♻

De: Verónica Valverde
A: maripaz.contador@estrella.com
Asunto: Viaje a Latinoamérica

Queridos amigos,

Ya hemos viajado bastante y no pueden imaginar todo lo que hemos visto y hecho. ¡El Perú! ¡Una maravilla! Y aquí estamos en Bariloche—después de un vuelo de cinco horas de Lima a Buenos Aires y dos más a Bariloche. Son largos, ¿no? Como siempre, hemos decidido hospedarnos en un albergue juvenil porque cuestan mucho menos que en un hotel. La mayoría de los albergues son bastante cómodos pero en algunos hasta ocho personas duermen en un solo cuarto. A veces no hay agua caliente pero nos hemos acostumbrado a tomar una ducha en agua fría. Todos han estado limpios—y baratos. Además hemos conocido a estudiantes de todas partes del mundo.

Besitos,
Verónica

De: Agustín Echevarría
A: maripaz.contador@estrella.com
Asunto: Viaje por España

Queridos amigos,

Saludos de Galicia en el norte de España. Ya hemos visitado a lo menos diez ciudades españolas y después de muchas noches en albergues juveniles hemos decidido botar la casa por la ventana. Estamos pasando una noche en el parador de los Reyes Católicos en Santiago de Compostela. En España, los paradores son del gobierno. Casi todos son antiguos castillos o monasterios. Son elegantes y NO baratos. Somos los únicos clientes del hotel con mochilas. Pero, ¡qué va!

Hemos elegido a Phil rey del castillo. Como él es rey él va a pagar la cuenta. ¡Ja, ja! Dice Phil que si él es el rey es también el dueño del castillo y no tiene que pagar nada. Ustedes conocen a Phil, ¿no?

Agustín

¿Comprendes?

Más práctica

Workbook, pp. 7.9–7.10
StudentWorks™ Plus

A **Buscando información** Da la siguiente información.

Verónica y sus amigos	
por donde viajan	
donde están ahora	
donde se hospedan	
por qué les gustan los albergues	
como son los albergues	

Agustín, Phil y sus amigos	
por donde viajan	
donde están ahora	
donde se hospedan en este momento	
cuantas noches van a estar	
como son los paradores	

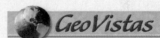

GeoVistas

To learn more about Spain, take a tour on pages SH44–SH45.

B **Explicando** Explica lo que es un parador nacional en España.

C **Comparando** Compara un albergue juvenil con un parador nacional.

D **Resumiendo** En tus propias palabras, cuenta el episodio entre Phil y sus compañeros de viaje en el parador de los Reyes Católicos.

E **Llegando a conclusiones** Basado en el episodio entre Phil y sus compañeros, ¿qué concluyes sobre la personalidad de Phil? ¿Qué tipo de persona es?

CULTURA

Es una habitación en el parador de los Reyes Católicos. Es elegante y lujosa, ¿no? Ahora sabes que es verdad que los amigos botaron la casa por la ventana o, como dicen en España, «tiraron la casa por la ventana».

El Camino de Santiago 🎧♻️

Antes de leer

¿Te interesa hacer un viaje si tienes que caminar muchos kilómetros cada día por una semana entera o más? ¿Por qué contestas que sí o que no? Luego decide si el viaje en la lectura es para ti o no.

Durante la Edad Media[1] había unas peregrinaciones[2] importantes. Una era la peregrinación a Santiago de Compostela.

Santiago de Compostela está en Galicia, una región en el noroeste de España que se parece mucho a Irlanda. Llueve mucho en Galicia y todo es muy verde. Además hay mucha influencia de los celtas—como en Irlanda. Muchos gallegos son rubios o pelirrojos y tienen ojos azules o verdes.

Los peregrinos de la Edad Media iban a Santiago porque creían que allá estaba enterrado el apóstol Santiago. El Camino empezaba en Francia. Cruzaba los Pirineos y todo el norte de España—una región de altos picos montañosos. Los peregrinos viajaban a pie de un pueblo a otro. Cada día cubrían un trecho[3] fijo. Al final de cada trecho había un hostal donde los peregrinos podían comer y pasar la noche. Aun[4] en el siglo XI había industria hotelera.

Hoy en día el Camino de Santiago es una vez más muy popular. A muchos turistas les gusta seguir el mismo camino que los peregrinos de la Edad Media. Muchos de ellos son mochileros jóvenes. Unos siguen andando a pie pero hay también quienes van en bicicleta o aun en carro.

[1]Edad Media   *Middle Ages*
[2]peregrinaciones   *pilgrimages*
[3]trecho   *stretch*
[4]Aun   *Even*

CULTURA

Los mochileros siguen el Camino de Santiago en Navarra.

CULTURA

Estos jóvenes lo están pasando bien en un café en Santiago de Compostela. ¿Qué piensas? ¿Son peregrinos?

¿Comprendes?

Escoge.

1. ¿Qué es una peregrinación?
   a. un viaje al extranjero
   b. un viaje de motivo religioso
   c. un viaje por las montañas

2. ¿Por qué son rubios y pelirrojos muchos gallegos?
   a. Son de ascendencia celta.
   b. Son irlandeses.
   c. Tienen ojos azules.

3. ¿Por qué hacían los peregrinos el viaje?
   a. Querían ver la catedral de Santiago de Compostela.
   b. Querían ver la tumba del apóstol Santiago.
   c. Querían cruzar el norte de España.

4. ¿Qué hay hoy en día?
   a. un interés nuevo en el camino de Santiago
   b. un nuevo camino de Santiago
   c. hostales del siglo XI

5. ¿Cuál es una diferencia entre la peregrinación durante la Edad Media y hoy?
   a. Hoy no hay hostales.
   b. Hoy todos los peregrinos no van a pie.
   c. La ruta ha cambiado.

CULTURA

La catedral en Santiago de Compostela en la famosa plaza del Obradoiro

Vocabulario

 1 Identifica siete cosas que están en una habitación y en un cuarto de baño de un hotel.

 To review **Vocabulario,** turn to pages 204–205.

 2 **Completa.**

8. Cecilia y Gloria han llegado al hotel. Han reservado un cuarto doble con _____.

9. Necesito _____ para abrir la puerta.

10. _____ te puede ayudar con tu equipaje en un hotel.

11. La camarera tiene que cambiar las toallas porque están _____.

12. Los clientes del hotel tienen que _____ su cuarto al mediodía.

13. Es más caro pasar una noche en un hotel que en un _____.

14. Para subir al piso doce de un hotel, los clientes usan _____.

3 **Describe.**

15–16. un desayuno continental

17–18. un desayuno americano

Gramática

4 **Completa con el presente perfecto.**

19. Ellos _____ al hotel. (llegar)

20. ¿Todavía no _____ (tú) el desayuno? (tomar)

21. ¿_____ ustedes en el hotel? (comer)

22. No, (nosotros) no _____ todavía. (salir)

23. Yo _____ en tres estados. (vivir)

24. Mónica ya _____ con este libro. (terminar)

To review **el presente perfecto,** turn to page 208.

5 **Sigue el modelo.**

MODELO ¿Hacerlo? →
        Ya lo he hecho.

25. ¿Decirlo?

26. ¿Verlo?

27. ¿Escribirlo?

28. ¿Abrirlo?

29. ¿Devolverlo?

To review **participios irregulares,** turn to page 210.

6 **Contesta con pronombres.**

30. ¿Te ha devuelto el dinero Tomás?

31. ¿Te ha dado las llaves la recepcionista?

32. ¿Le has enviado el correo electrónico a Tomás?

33. ¿Les has escrito la carta a tus padres?

34. ¿Les has dicho la información a tus tíos?

To review **los complementos,** turn to pages 211 and 213.

7 **Completa con pronombres.**

35. El profesor les explicó la gramática a los alumnos. El profesor _____ explicó _____.

36. Yo le di los boletos a Teresa. Yo _____ di _____.

37. ¿Te ha cambiado las toallas la camarera? Sí, _____ ha cambiado.

38. ¿Les ha abierto la puerta el mozo a ustedes? Sí, el mozo _____ ha abierto.

Cultura

8 **Contesta.**

39. ¿Por qué a muchos viajeros jóvenes les gustan los albergues juveniles?

40. ¿Qué es un parador nacional en España?

CULTURA

Es un hostal en Barcelona, España. Muchos hostales ocupan un piso o parte de un edificio, no el edificio entero.

To review this cultural information, turn to page 216.

EN EL HOTEL

doscientos veintiuno **221**

1 **Una extravagancia**

✓ *Discuss a time when you splurged on something*

En tu vida, ¿has botado la casa por la ventana? ¿Qué has hecho?

2 **Experiencias interesantes**

✓ *Talk about interesting experiences you have had*

Habla con un(a) compañero(a). Dile a tu compañero(a) las cosas que tú has hecho en la vida que consideras interesantes. Tu compañero(a) te va a decir lo que ha hecho él/ella. Van a llegar a una conclusión. ¿Quién ha tenido las experiencias más interesantes?

3 **Ya no lo he hecho**

✓ *Talk about things you have not done yet*

Habla con un(a) compañero(a). Los dos van a hablar de algunas cosas que todavía no han hecho pero que quieren hacer un día.

4 **Una estadía personal**

✓ *Describe a stay at a hotel*

¿Te has hospedado o pasado unas vacaciones en un hotel? ¿En qué hotel? Describe tu experiencia. Si nunca has estado en un hotel, da una descripción ficticia.

5 **Una habitación, por favor.**

✓ *Make a hotel reservation*

Tú has llegado a Burgos, España. Necesitas una habitación en un hotel. Llama a un hotel y habla con el/la recepcionista (tu compañero[a]). Quieres saber si tienen una habitación disponible, la tarifa, lo que está incluido en la tarifa, etc.

6 **Las preferencias de un(a) viajero(a) joven**

✓ *Compare and contrast travel preferences*

Por lo general un viaje fabuloso para una persona joven no es un viaje fabuloso para una persona mayor y viceversa. Describe lo que para ti es un viaje ideal. ¿Cuáles son las necesidades que tú consideras importantes y las que no son importantes? ¿Qué buscas en un hotel? ¿Qué piensas? ¿Tienen tus abuelos las mismas opiniones que tú? ¿Tienen ellos los mismos deseos o las mismas necesidades que tú?

Tarea

You and your classmates are on an educational tour of a Spanish-speaking country and your teacher has given everyone the assignment of keeping a travel journal in Spanish. Write about everything you have done since you arrived there. You will need to use the library and/or the Internet to find out more about the country you have chosen to visit.

Writing Strategy

Transition Words To make your writing flow more smoothly, it is a good idea to use a variety of transition words, because they help connect different ideas. Some useful transition words in Spanish are listed below:

antes (de)	luego
después (de)	por último
primero	también
segundo	sobre todo
tercero	por eso

As you research, answer the questions with information you want to include in your travel narrative. You should consult multiple sources to ensure that your information is accurate.

❶ Prewrite

Create a rough outline using the following questions.

❷ Write

- Use the present perfect tense and vocabulary from the textbook to describe what you and your classmates have done on the trip.
- Use your outline as a guide to help keep your information organized.
- Incorporate transition words so that your writing flows smoothly.

Evaluate

Your teacher will evaluate you on correct use of vocabulary and grammar, organization, accuracy and completeness of information, and effective use of transition words.

Repaso del Capítulo 7

Gramática

- ### El presente perfecto *(page 208)*
  The present perfect tense is used to speak about a past event without reference to any particular time. It is formed with the present tense of the verb **haber** and a past participle. The past participle of an **-ar** verb is formed by adding **-ado** to the stem, and the past participle of an **-er** or **-ir** verb is formed by adding **-ido** to the stem. Review the following forms.

hablar	beber	asistir
he hablado	he bebido	he asistido
has hablado	has bebido	has asistido
ha hablado	ha bebido	ha asistido
hemos hablado	hemos bebido	hemos asistido
habéis hablado	*habéis bebido*	*habéis asistido*
han hablado	han bebido	han asistido

Los huéspedes han pasado unos días agradables en la piscina de este hotel en Manta, Ecuador.

- ### Participios irregulares *(page 210)*
  Review the verbs that have irregular past participles.

decir → dicho	poner → puesto
hacer → hecho	volver → vuelto
romper → roto	devolver → devuelto
escribir → escrito	morir → muerto
freír → frito	abrir → abierto
ver → visto	cubrir → cubierto

- ### Dos complementos en la misma frase *(pages 211, 213)*
  When a sentence has two object pronouns, the indirect object always precedes the direct object. The indirect object pronouns **le, les** change to **se** when used with **lo, la, los** or **las**.

Teodoro me vendió el carro.	Teodoro me lo vendió.
Tu padre te dio los regalos.	Tu padre te los dio.
El cliente le devolvió las llaves a la recepcionista.	El cliente se las devolvió.

Vocabulario

Making a hotel reservation

una reservación	un cuarto, una habitación	un cuarto sencillo un cuarto doble	reservar

Arriving at/leaving a hotel

el hotel	la recepción	la llave (magnética)	hospedarse
el albergue juvenil, el hostal	el/la recepcionista el/la cliente, el/la huésped(a)	el mozo el ascensor	abandonar el cuarto

Having breakfast in a hotel

el desayuno continental	la mermelada la mantequilla	el desayuno americano	el tocino, el bacón, el lacón
el panecillo el pan dulce	el café	los huevos revueltos el pan tostado	el jugo de naranja

Talking about a hotel room

la cama la sábana la manta, la frazada	la almohada el armario	la percha, el colgador	el aire acondicionado

Talking about a bathroom

el cuarto de baño la bañera la ducha	el inodoro, el váter el lavabo el jabón	una toalla sucio(a) limpio(a)

Talking about cleaning a hotel room

la camarera	limpiar	hacer la cama	cambiar

Repaso cumulativo

Repasa lo que ya has aprendido

These activities will help you review and remember what you have learned so far in Spanish.

1 Escucha las frases. Indica si la frase describe el dibujo o no.

2 Imagina que vas de camping por una noche. ¿Qué vas a poner en tu mochila?

3 Completa con el pronombre reflexivo.

1. Cuando voy de camping, _____ acuesto en una carpa.
2. Marcos _____ duerme enseguida en su saco de dormir.
3. Nosotros _____ lavamos con agua fría.
4. Ellos _____ divierten mucho cuando van de camping.
5. ¿Por qué no _____ peinas? Tienes el pelo desarreglado.

4 Completa con el pronombre apropiado.

1. Él tiene que levantar___.
2. Voy a cepillar___ los dientes.
3. Y yo voy a vestir___.
4. ¿A qué hora tenemos que reunir___?
5. Ellos quieren acostar___ temprano porque tienen que levantar___ mañana a las cinco y media.
6. ¿Quieres sentar___ aquí?

Unos campers con sus caravanas y carpas en una playa cerca de Arica, Chile

5 Escoge.

1. _____ llave que tengo no es para mi puerta.

   a. Esta   **b.** Esa   **c.** Aquella

2. _____ muchacho que ves allá es el primo de Esteban.

   a. Este   **b.** Ese   **c.** Aquel

3. Carlos, _____ novela que estás leyendo, ¿te gusta?

   a. esta   **b.** esa   **c.** aquella

6 Cambia al plural.

1. ¿De quién es *este libro de bolsillo*?

2. ¿Quiénes han dejado *aquella mochila* allí?

3. Me gusta mucho *ese juego* que tiene José.

4. ¿Es caro *aquel carro*?

7 ¿Sí o no?

1. Hay muchas tiendas en un centro comercial.

2. Los precios son más bajos cuando hay un saldo.

3. Si una camisa no te queda bien necesitas otra talla.

4. Venden objetos de artesanía en una tienda de ropa.

5. Mucha gente regatea en una tienda elegante.

6. En un mercado municipal hay muchos puestos diferentes.

CULTURA

En este mercado en Chiapas, México, se puede comprar muchos artículos de artesanía.

8 **Tienes que comprar mucho. Decide en qué tienda vas a comprar las siguientes cosas. Puedes comprar algunas cosas en más de una tienda.**

lo que necesitas	la tienda de ropa	la frutería	la verdulería	el supermercado	el mercado indígena
1. el papel higiénico					
2. la artesanía					
3. el maíz					
4. un vestido					
5. un paquete de judías verdes congeladas					
6. un racimo de uvas					

Ciudad y campo

Vamos a comparar La vida en el campo es muy diferente que la vida en una ciudad. Los problemas que existen en el campo y en la ciudad son diferentes también. Piensa en las zonas urbanas y rurales donde tú vives. Vas a observar si en Latinoamérica hay muchas diferencias entre la vida en una ciudad y la vida en el campo. Y aprenderás también si hay diferencias entre Latinoamérica y Estados Unidos.

Objetivos

You will:

- describe life in the city
- describe life in the country
- discuss the differences between the city and the country in Latin America

You will use:

- the future tense
- object pronouns with infinitives and gerunds

◄ Los jóvenes andan por la Plaza de Armas en Santiago de Chile, la capital del país.

QuickPass

Go to glencoe.com
For: Online book
Web code: ASD7837c8

Introducción al tema
Ciudad y campo

Mira estas fotos para familiarizarte con el tema de este capítulo—ciudad y campo. Vas a observar que hay unas diferencias interesantes entre la vida urbana y la vida rural en las muchas regiones del mundo hispanohablante.

Chile Es un campo de girasoles cerca de Santiago de Chile. Se usa la semilla del girasol para hacer aceite de girasol. ▲

▼ **Perú** El Jirón de la Unión en el centro de Lima es una calle peatonal comercial.

▲ **Venezuela**
Santo Domingo es un pueblo idílico en los Andes venezolanos. Las casas se parecen a los chalets en los Alpes suizos.

◄ **Perú** Estas jóvenes indígenas viven en una zona rural de los Andes peruanos no muy lejos de Cuzco.

◄ México Muchas ciudades latinoamericanas son muy modernas con edificios altos de muchos pisos—rascacielos—como este edificio bancario en la Ciudad de México.

Argentina La famosa Avenida 9 de Julio en Buenos Aires tiene fama de ser la avenida más ancha del mundo. ►

▲ México El pueblo de Taxco es conocido por sus calles estrechas adoquinadas, sus edificios coloniales y sus joyerías de plata.

▲ España Es una parada de autobuses en Valencia. Muchas ciudades tienen un sistema metropolitano de transporte—autobuses, tranvías y metros. Nota que este bus tiene una puerta delantera para subir y una puerta trasera y central para bajar.

Costa Rica No, no es un burro. Es una raza de ganado bovino en Costa Rica. Es una vaca. ▼

▲ Argentina Un vaquero argentino cepilla al caballo en una estancia en Salta.

231

En el centro de la ciudad

un rascacielos

una oficina

la plaza

una avenida ancha, un paseo

el casco (el barrio) antiguo

la esquina

una calle angosta (estrecha)

Para conversar

¿Vas al centro mañana? Es viernes y habrá mucho tráfico. Si tomas el carro, no podrás aparcar en la calle. Tendrás que buscar un parking.

un parking, un parqueo

En otras partes

- In Spain you will hear both **estacionar** and **aparcar.** These terms are also used in Latin America as well as **parquear.** A parking spot or lot can be **el parking, el parqueo, el aparcamiento** or **el estacionamiento.**
- There are many words used for **autobús.** It is not necessary for you to learn them all. In general **el autobús** is used in Spain, **el camión** in Mexico, and **la guagua** in the Caribbean and in the Canary Islands. You will also frequently hear **el bus.**

un semáforo

los peatones

la acera

el cruce

una calle

Medios de transporte urbanos

la estación de metro

la boca del metro

la escalera mecánica

el autobús, el camión, la guagua

Los pasajeros esperan el autobús
en la parada de autobús.

El señor no subirá la escalera.
Tomará la escalera mecánica.

El parque de atracciones

el mimo

la montaña
rusa

la noria

el zoológico

el tiovivo

El sábado los jóvenes irán al parque de atracciones.

QuickPass

Go to glencoe.com
For: **Vocabulary practice**
Web code: **ASD7837c8**

ESCUCHAR

 Escucha cada frase y decide si la información es correcta o no. Usa una tabla como la de abajo para indicar tus respuestas.

correcta	incorrecta

HABLAR

 Contesta sobre unos jóvenes en un parque en Latinoamérica.

1. ¿Está en la ciudad el parque?
2. ¿Irán los jóvenes al parque el sábado?
3. ¿Caminarán por las sendas del parque?
4. ¿Irán al parque de atracciones?
5. ¿Subirán a la montaña rusa?
6. ¿Visitarán el zoológico?
7. ¿Verán los animales?
8. ¿Les darán de comer a los animales?

Conexiones

La ecología

El término «ecología» significa el equilibrio entre los seres humanos y la naturaleza. Hoy en día hay grandes problemas ecológicos en todas partes del mundo. Muchos consideran la contaminación del aire el número uno. En las zonas urbanas el aire que se respira está contaminado principalmente por las emisiones de gases que escapan de los automóviles, los camiones y las chimeneas de las fábricas.

CULTURA

Las jóvenes están mirando a sus perros en un parque de Buenos Aires, Argentina.

Más práctica

📖 Workbook, p. 8.3
💿 StudentWorks™ Plus

LEER • ESCRIBIR

3 Expresa de otra manera.

1. una avenida ancha
2. el casco antiguo
3. parquear
4. un parking
5. el autobús
6. una calle estrecha

LEER • ESCRIBIR

4 Completa con una palabra del banco de palabras.

la esquina	mimos	peatones	el parque de
un rascacielos	estrechas	la escalera	atracciones
el zoológico	la parada	la boca	

1. Hay un semáforo en ____ de la calle para controlar la circulación del tráfico.
2. Una calle peatonal es solo para ____.
3. La entrada al metro en la calle se llama ____.
4. Él bajó ____ para ir a la estación de metro.
5. Un edificio muy alto de muchos pisos es ____.
6. Hay calles ____ en el casco antiguo de la ciudad.
7. Mucha gente está esperando el bus en ____.
8. Muchas veces los ____ tienen la cara pintada.
9. Hay una montaña rusa y una noria en ____.
10. Hay elefantes, tigres, leones y cocodrilos en ____ en el parque.

ESCRIBIR

5 **Rompecabezas**

 Join two puzzle pieces to form a word. When you have finished you should have six words. Do not use any piece more than once.

ción rada es bús

quina esta rasca pa

auto pea cielos tones

CULTURA

Un edificio interesante con una torre alta en la Plaza de la Independencia en el centro de Montevideo, la capital de Uruguay

Comunicación

6 Describe la ciudad en que vives. Si no vives en una ciudad describe una que está cerca de donde tú vives.

En el campo

una finca, una granja, una chacra

una casa de campo

el campesino, el peón

la cosecha

el trigo

Los peones cultivan (labran, trabajan) la tierra.
Están cultivando trigo.
Siembran el trigo en la primavera.
¿Cuándo será la cosecha?
Cosecharán el trigo en el otoño.

la huerta

la vaca

la hierba

la gallina

el cordero

el cerdo

En una huerta cultivan legumbres o frutas.

Los caballos están en el corral.
Las muchachas montarán (andarán) a caballo.
Les gusta mucho la equitación.

El ganado pace en el campo.
El verano que viene Enrique y su hermana
   visitarán a sus primos en el campo.
Pasarán un mes con ellos.

QuickPass

Go to glencoe.com
For: **Vocabulary practice**
Web code: ASD7837c8

FOLDABLES®
Study Organizer

FORWARD-BACKWARD BOOK
See page SH22 for help with making this foldable. On the front cover, write **la ciudad.** Open your book. On the right-hand page list words that you have learned that pertain to the city. On the next right-hand page, draw a picture illustrating the words on your list. Close your book and flip it over. On the back cover, write **el campo** and do the same.

ESCUCHAR

 1 Escucha cada frase y decide si la información es correcta o no. Usa una tabla como la de abajo para indicar tus respuestas.

correcta	incorrecta

LEER

2 Parea los sinónimos.

1. cultivar la tierra
2. persona del campo
3. practicar la equitación
4. una finca grande
5. recoger o recolectar el trigo
6. el rancho

   a. cosechar
   b. una estancia
   c. trabajar, labrar la tierra
   d. la hacienda
   e. montar a caballo
   f. un(a) campesino(a)

HABLAR • ESCRIBIR

3 Contesta.

1. ¿Dónde trabajan los campesinos?
2. ¿Qué hay en una finca?
3. ¿Qué hay en una huerta?
4. ¿Cuáles son algunos animales que producen carne?
5. Ella es aficionada a la equitación. ¿Qué hace ella?

LEER • ESCRIBIR

4 Completa con una palabra apropiada.

1. La _____ es verde y el trigo es amarillo.
2. El ganado _____ en el campo.
3. Las _____ ponen huevos.
4. Las _____ dan leche.
5. Cuando los caballos no están en el establo, están en _____.
6. Guardan el trigo y el heno en _____.
7. Los _____ trabajan la tierra.
8. Una _____ produce vegetales y frutas.

CULTURA

Unos niños andan con su rebaño de ovejas. Están al lado de una carretera en un pueblo en las afueras de Riobamba, Ecuador.

Más práctica
Workbook, pp. 8.4–8.5
StudentWorks™ Plus

ESCRIBIR

5 Usa diagramas como los de abajo para categorizar las palabras que ya sabes en español.

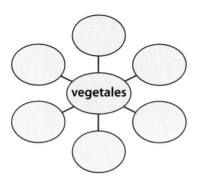

vegetales

animales

frutas

HABLAR • ESCRIBIR

6 Utiliza cada palabra en una frase original.

la finca   una estancia   el ganado   la huerta

cosechar   una casa de campo   el corral

Comunicación

7 Con unos compañeros de clase, preparen una encuesta *(survey)* para determinar si la mayoría de los alumnos en su clase aprecian más o conocen mejor la vida urbana o la vida rural. Basado en los resultados de su encuesta, analicen y expliquen el por qué.

LEER

8 Rompecabezas

Choose the word in each group that does not belong. Then switch the wrong words to make each group correct.

1. la vaca   la gallina   la hacienda

2. el trigo   una granja   el heno

3. el rancho   el cordero   la estancia

4. una finca   una chacra   sembrar

5. la hierba   cosechar   labrar

InfoGap For more practice using your new vocabulary, do Activity 8 on page SR10 at the end of this book.

QuickPass

Go to glencoe.com
For: **Grammar practice**
Web code: ASD7837c8

Futuro de los verbos regulares

1. The future tense is used to tell what will take place in the future. The endings for the future tense come from the verb **haber**.

he	has	ha	hemos	habéis	han

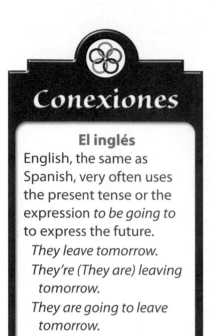

Conexiones

El inglés

English, the same as Spanish, very often uses the present tense or the expression *to be going to* to express the future.

They leave tomorrow.

They're (They are) leaving tomorrow.

They are going to leave tomorrow.

They'll (They will) leave tomorrow.

2. You add these endings to the entire infinitive to form the future tense of regular verbs.

infinitive	estudiar	leer	escribir
stem	estudiar-	leer-	escribir-
yo	estudiaré	leeré	escribiré
tú	estudiarás	leerás	escribirás
Ud., él, ella	estudiará	leerá	escribirá
nosotros(as)	estudiaremos	leeremos	escribiremos
vosotros(as)	*estudiaréis*	*leeréis*	*escribiréis*
Uds., ellos, ellas	estudiarán	leerán	escribirán

Algún día él irá a la América del Sur.
Visitará Perú y otros países.
Yo estaré en Bogotá en el mes de julio.

3. The future tense is not used a great deal in Spanish. It is more common to use **ir a** + the infinitive or the present tense.

Voy a salir mañana.	**Salgo mañana.**
Ellos van a volver en	**Ellos vuelven en**
dos meses.	**dos meses.**

4. The future tense can be used to express what is called the future of probability.

¿Cuántos años tendrá él?	*How old can he be?*
No sé.	*I don't know.*
¿Qué hora será?	*What time can it be?*
Serán las once.	*It must be about eleven o'clock.*

CULTURA

Los peatones cruzan la calle en Buenos Aires, Argentina. ¿Adónde irán?

Práctica

Más práctica

📘 Workbook, pp. 8.6–8.7
💿 StudentWorks™ Plus

HABLAR

1 Contesta sobre un viaje futuro de Mónica.

1. ¿Irá Mónica a Quito el año que viene?
2. ¿Pasará unos días en Quito?
3. ¿Visitará el casco antiguo?
4. ¿Irá al Museo de Arte Moderno?
5. ¿Caminará por el parque el Ejido?
6. ¿Verá una exposición de arte en el parque?
7. ¿Comerá ceviche?
8. ¿Asistirá a un concierto?

CULTURA

¿Caminarás un día por una de estas pintorescas calles en el barrio de Panecillo en Quito, Ecuador?

ESCUCHAR • HABLAR • ESCRIBIR

2 Sigue el modelo.

MODELO Tomaré el carro. →
         Voy a tomar el carro.

1. Aparcaré el carro en un parking.
2. Tomaremos el metro para llegar al centro.
3. ¿Visitarán ustedes el barrio viejo?
4. ¿Andarás por las calles estrechas del barrio viejo?
5. ¿Tú irás al parque de atracciones?
6. Pasaré unas horas en el zoológico.

ESCUCHAR • HABLAR • ESCRIBIR

3 Sigue el modelo.

MODELO Voy a ir al campo. →
         Iré al campo.

1. Van a cultivar trigo.
2. Vamos a comer vegetales de la huerta.
3. ¿Vas a montar a caballo?
4. ¿Quién va a limpiar el establo?
5. Voy a visitar una estancia.

CULTURA

Una joven a caballo en la Cordillera Oriental en Guasca, Colombia

LEER • ESCRIBIR

4 Completa con el futuro.

1. Ellos _____ dentro de poco. (volver)
2. Yo los _____. (ver)
3. Nosotros _____ de muchas cosas. (hablar)
4. ¿Tú los _____ a tu casa? (invitar)
5. Sí, (yo) _____ una comida y (nosotros) _____ juntos. (preparar, comer)
6. El postre _____ el plato principal. (seguir)

Gramática

Futuro de los verbos irregulares

1. Study the following forms of verbs that have an irregular stem in the future tense. Note that the endings for all irregular verbs are the same as those for the regular verbs.

infinitive	tener	salir	venir
stem	tendr-	saldr-	vendr-
yo	tendré	saldré	vendré
tú	tendrás	saldrás	vendrás
Ud., él, ella	tendrá	saldrá	vendrá
nosotros(as)	tendremos	saldremos	vendremos
vosotros(as)	tendréis	saldréis	vendréis
Uds., ellos, ellas	tendrán	saldrán	vendrán

2. Other verbs that follow the same pattern are **poner, saber,** and **poder.**

poner → pondré   saber → sabré   poder → podré

3. The verbs **decir, hacer,** and **querer** also have an irregular future stem.

infinitive	decir	hacer	querer
stem	dir-	har-	querr-
yo	diré	haré	querré
tú	dirás	harás	querrás
Ud., él, ella	dirá	hará	querrá
nosotros(as)	diremos	haremos	querremos
vosotros(as)	diréis	haréis	querréis
Uds., ellos, ellas	dirán	harán	querrán

4. Note that the future of **hay (haber)** is **habrá.**

¿Cuántos habrá?
Habrá más de uno.
Habrá por lo menos cuatro.

¿Harás un viaje a Ecuador algún día para conocer mejor el país?

Práctica

HABLAR

 5 Personaliza. Da respuestas personales.

1. Algún día, ¿tendrás la oportunidad de viajar a Latinoamérica?
2. ¿Podrás visitar varias ciudades?
3. ¿Harás el viaje en avión?
4. ¿Podrás tomar fotos digitales?
5. ¿Las podrás descargar a tu computadora?
6. ¿Las imprimirás y las pondrás en un álbum?

ESCUCHAR • HABLAR

 6 Conversa según el modelo.

 MODELO —Beatriz no vino hoy.

—No, pero vendrá mañana.

 1. Ella no salió de casa a tiempo.
2. Él no me lo dijo.
3. No lo hice.
4. No tuvimos tiempo.
5. Antonio no sabía hacerlo.
6. Ellos no podían decirlo.

CULTURA

Un paseo en el casco histórico de la Ciudad de Panamá

LEER • ESCRIBIR

 7 Completa sobre Ricardo en Panamá.

El invierno que viene Ricardo Rojas __1__ (tener) dos semanas de vacaciones. Él y su familia __2__ (hacer) un viaje a Panamá. Allí ellos __3__ (poder) pasar unos días con sus parientes. El padre de Ricardo __4__ (llamar) a Panamá y les __5__ (decir) a sus parientes la hora de su llegada. Todos los parientes de Ricardo __6__ (querer) ir al aeropuerto a recibirlos. Ricardo y sus padres __7__ (salir) en el vuelo de las once. El vuelo __8__ (hacer) escala en Miami antes de llegar a Panamá.

 ## Comunicación

 8 Tu familia va a hacer un viaje a un país latinoamericano. Di a un(a) compañero(a) todas las cosas que ustedes harán y verán durante el viaje. Después, cambien de rol.

VIDEO To learn more about the Argentine countryside, watch **Cultura en vivo.**

Los pronombres con el infinitivo y el gerundio

1. You have already learned that the pronoun is attached to the infinitive in the expression **favor de** and with the reflexive verbs.

Favor de darme el menú.	**¿Quieres levantarte?**
Favor de pasarle el pan.	**¿Puedo sentarme aquí?**
Favor de decírmelo.	**Vamos a divertirnos.**

2. When the object pronouns are used with the infinitive and a helping verb, the object pronouns can either be placed before the helping verb or attached to the infinitive.

Voy a tomar el metro.	**Quiero mostrar la finca a mi primo.**
Lo voy a tomar.	**Se la quiero mostrar a él.**
Voy a tomarlo.	**Quiero mostrársela a él.**

3. When the object pronouns are used with the present participle, they may also precede the helping verb or they may be attached to the present participle.

Está visitando el parque de atracciones.
Lo está visitando.
Está visitándolo.

4. To maintain the same stress, a participle carries a written accent with either one or two attached pronouns. The infinitive carries a written accent only when two pronouns are attached to it.

PARTICIPLE	INFINITIVE
Está sirviéndolo.	**Quiero darle el plano.**
Está sirviéndomelo.	**Quiero dárselo.**

El mesero está sirviéndoles a sus clientes en un café en la famosa Plaza Dorrego en el barrio de San Telmo en Buenos Aires, Argentina.

Práctica

ESCUCHAR • HABLAR • ESCRIBIR

9 Sigue el modelo.

MODELO la fecha →
No la puedo recordar.
No puedo recordarla.

1. el día
2. la hora
3. el número de teléfono

4. las direcciones
5. los nombres

ESCUCHAR • HABLAR • ESCRIBIR

10 Contesta con pronombres.

1. ¿Acabas de comprar el periódico?
2. ¿Acabas de leer el periódico?
3. ¿Acabas de dar el periódico a Pedro?
4. ¿Acabas de hacer tus planes finales?
5. ¿Acabas de comunicarlos a tus padres?

LEER • ESCRIBIR

11 Sigue el modelo.

MODELO Los campesinos están labrando la tierra. →
Los campesinos están labrándola.
Los campesinos la están labrando.

1. Están cultivando el trigo.
2. Están cosechando las legumbres.
3. Están limpiando el corral.
4. Los corderos están comiendo la hierba.
5. Los caballos están comiendo el heno.

LEER • ESCRIBIR

12 Escribe las frases con pronombres.

1. En la clase de español los alumnos están aprendiendo *la gramática.*
2. Ahora algunos están escuchando *los CDs.*
3. Todos están prestando atención *a la profesora.*
4. Carlos está revisando *su composición.*
5. León está enviando *el correo electrónico a un amigo.*
6. El profesor está devolviendo *los exámenes a los alumnos.*

ESCUCHAR • HABLAR • ESCRIBIR

13 Contesta con **sí** usando pronombres.

1. ¿Quiere ver la película Marisol?
2. ¿Va a ver la película?
3. ¿Está comprando las entradas ahora?
4. ¿Está comprando las entradas en la taquilla del cine?
5. ¿Quiere Marisol ver la película desde la primera fila o está demasiado cerca de la pantalla?
6. Desde la primera fila, ¿puede ver bien la película?

Refrán

Can you guess what the following proverb means?

Alegría ten, y vivirás bien.

¡Bravo!

You have now learned all the new vocabulary and grammar in this chapter. Continue to use and practice all that you know while learning more cultural information. ¡Vamos!

Un verano en el campo

Clara ¿Vas a pasar el verano en la casa de campo de tus primos?

Julio Sí, estaré dos meses en su estancia.

Clara ¡Dos meses en el campo! ¿Qué harás? ¿No te pondrás aburrido?

Julio ¡Aburrido! ¿Estás loca? Hay un montón de cosas que hacer. Montamos a caballo, limpiamos los establos, recogemos verduras y frutas frescas, damos caminatas, nadamos en un lago o río…

Clara Eso no es para mí. Me quedaré en la ciudad.

Julio Sí, con el calor, el tráfico, el ruido de las sirenas, la contaminación…

Clara Eso no me molesta nada. Iré a un concierto, visitaré un museo y a veces iré a la piscina en el parque municipal. Habrá mucho que hacer.

Julio Pues, cada uno a su gusto.

¿Comprendes?

VIDEO To meet some friends who live in the city and in the country, watch **Diálogo en vivo.**

A Contesta según la información en la conversación.

1. ¿Quién va a pasar el verano en el campo?
2. ¿A quiénes visitará?
3. ¿Qué tienen sus primos en el campo?
4. ¿Por qué a Julio no le gusta la ciudad en el verano?
5. ¿Se aburrirá Clara en el campo?

B Completa la tabla según la conversación.

actividades en el campo	actividades en la ciudad

C **Explicando** Contesta.

1. ¿Cuál es la diferencia de opinión entre Clara y Julio?
2. ¿Qué significa «Cada uno a su gusto»?

CULTURA

Los alumnos están esperando un bus en una parada en una esquina de Quito, Ecuador. ¿Qué piensas? ¿Tomarán el bus que está pasando ahora?

Antes de leer

Reflexiona sobre lo que ya sabes de la vida urbana y rural según tus experiencias personales.

La ciudad y el campo

La ciudad Si vas algún día a una ciudad latinoamericana, observarás que en el centro mismo de casi todas hay un casco antiguo. En el centro del casco antiguo se encuentra una gran plaza que muchas veces se llama «la Plaza de Armas». En la plaza verás la catedral y algunos edificios gubernamentales que datan de la época colonial. De la plaza salen callecitas pintorescas.

Cada ciudad tiene también barrios modernos con grandes rascacielos que tienen oficinas y condominios donde vive la gente de las clases media y alta. En los barrios modernos hay avenidas anchas y paseos bonitos. Hay también calles peatonales donde no se permite entrar el tráfico vehicular.

CULTURA

Plaza de Armas, Quito

Reading Check

¿Cuáles son características del casco viejo y del barrio moderno?

CULTURA

Es una vista de Bogotá, Colombia. Observarás que la ciudad tiene muchas avenidas anchas y rascacielos modernos.

Cada ciudad tiene uno o más parques donde los habitantes disfrutan del aire libre y espacio abierto. Los fines de semana dan un paseo por el parque y se divierten mirando a los mimos. En muchos parques hay un parque de atracciones y a veces un zoológico.

Las afueras Desafortunadamente en las afueras de casi todas las ciudades verás los barrios bajos. Sus nombres varían de país en país—ranchos, villas miseria, pueblos jóvenes, etc. No importa el nombre. En todos viven los pobres en chozas o casuchas[1] sin luz (electricidad), gas ni agua corriente[2]. Para saber una de las razones que tanta gente vive en tales condiciones iremos al campo.

[1]chozas, casuchas *shacks*   [2]agua corriente *running water*

Durante la lectura

Al leer, toma notas o apuntes sobre los detalles que consideras importantes y que crees que debes recordar.

 **Reading Check**

¿Qué hay en las afueras de las ciudades?

CULTURA

Mucha gente va al Bosque de Chapultepec los domingos. Es un parque muy grande en la Ciudad de México.

CULTURA

Un barrio pobre con ranchos en las afueras de Caracas, Venezuela

CIUDAD Y CAMPO

El campo La vida de muchos campesinos es difícil. Los problemas rurales tienen una larga historia. Desde la época de los españoles había grandes extensiones de tierras llamadas latifundios. Sus dueños o propietarios eran grandes terratenientes[3] ricos y más tarde grandes compañías de Estados Unidos y Europa. Debido a reformas agrarias estos latifundios han sido divididos en parcelas pequeñas y distribuidas entre los campesinos pobres que antes las tenían que trabajar para los terratenientes. Pero los campesinos no tienen suficiente dinero para comprar lo que necesitan para labrar la tierra de una manera productiva. Así toman la decisión de salir para la ciudad en busca de una vida mejor y añaden al problema de la sobrepoblación[4] que ya existe en las ciudades latinoamericanas.

Sí, hay problemas pero hay que señalar[5] que al viajar por Latinoamérica verás paisajes de una belleza increíble—montañas, volcanes, jardines, estancias o ranchos—todo.

[3]terratenientes *landowners*   [5]señalar *point out*
[4]sobrepoblación *overpopulation*

CULTURA

El cultivo de flores, como estas orquídeas, es una industria importante en Ecuador.

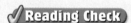
Reading Check

¿Siguen existiendo problemas económicos en las zonas rurales?

Después de leer

Los detalles pueden ser interesantes o aburridos. De los detalles en esta lectura, ¿cuáles consideras interesantes? ¿Cuáles te interesan menos?

CULTURA

Una estancia en la Patagonia argentina

¿Comprendes?

Más práctica

Workbook, pp. 8.10–8.12
StudentWorks™ Plus

A **Confirmando información** Corrige la información falsa.

1. Muy pocas ciudades latinoamericanas tienen un casco antiguo.
2. La gran plaza que se encuentra en el centro de muchas ciudades latinoamericanas se llama la Catedral.
3. Casi todos los edificios en el casco viejo datan de la época de las civilizaciones indígenas o precolombinas.
4. Los barrios bajos donde viven los pobres se encuentran en el centro de las ciudades.

B **Describiendo y analizando** Describe un parque de una ciudad latinoamericana y explica por qué los parques son importantes y populares.

C **Recordando hechos** Contesta.

1. ¿Cómo es la vida de muchos campesinos?
2. ¿Qué es un latifundio?
3. ¿Quiénes eran sus dueños o propietarios?
4. ¿Cuál es el resultado de muchas reformas agrarias?
5. ¿Por qué no pueden labrar bien la tierra?
6. ¿Adónde van?
7. ¿Cuál es un problema que ya existe en muchas ciudades latinoamericanas?

CULTURA

Es la entrada a un rancho en Cozumel, México.

D **Describiendo y categorizando** Completa las tablas.

la ciudad en Latinoamérica		
el barrio antiguo	**el barrio moderno**	**problemas en las afueras**

el campo en Latinoamérica		
distribución de la tierra en el pasado	**distribución de la tierra actualmente**	**problemas en las zonas rurales**

E **Explicando** Completa.

Visitar el campo en Latinoamérica puede ser una experiencia fabulosa porque…

Una ciudad interesante 🎧♻

Antes de leer

Durante toda la historia de Estados Unidos ha habido ciudades con grandes poblaciones de gente de otros países. ¿Conoces tal ciudad?

La ciudad de Miami en la Florida empezó a desarrollarse[1] en 1895 cuando Henry Flagler tomó la decisión de extender el ferrocarril hacia el sur. Hoy la aglomeración de Miami tiene casi dos millones quinientos mil de habitantes y está aumentándose cada día. Es uno de los grandes focos latinos de Estados Unidos. Empezó una gran migración de cubanos a fines de los años cincuenta cuando Fidel Castro derrocó[2] la dictadura de Fulgencio Batista. Hoy en día sigue llegando y estableciéndose en Miami gente de casi todas partes de Centroamérica, Sudamérica y del Caribe.

Una zona típicamente cubana de Miami se llama «la Pequeña Habana». Aquí se oye más español que inglés. El corazón[3] de la Pequeña Habana es la calle Ocho. Aquí hay muchos cafés, restaurantes y tiendas cubanas tradicionales. Si quieres comprarte una guayabera no hay problema. Hay una cantidad de tiendas de ropa. Si tienes sed, puedes sentarte en un café para tomar un guarapo, un café con leche o un típico cafecito cubano—un expreso muy fuerte con mucho azúcar. A los cubanos les gusta su cafecito muy dulce.

En una calle llamada *Cuban Memorial Boulevard,* hay una serie de monumentos dedicados a patriotas cubanos que lucharon[4] por la libertad de su país. Hay también un mapa de relieve de Cuba. Es imposible pasar un día en Miami sin observar la influencia y las contribuciones de los cubanos y otros hispanos o latinos a la vitalidad y personalidad de esta gran ciudad cosmopolita.

[1]desarrollarse *develop*
[2]derrocó *brought down*
[3]corazón *heart*
[4]lucharon *fought*

CULTURA

El parque de Máximo Gómez se conoce como el Parque Dominó porque a muchos cubanos de mayor edad les gusta reunirse allí para jugar dominó.

CULTURA

Plaza de la Cubanidad en Miami

¿Comprendes?

Escoge o completa.

1. ¿Cuál es el mejor título para esta lectura?
   a. El establecimiento de Miami
   b. Un parque interesante
   c. La Pequeña Habana
   d. Miami, ayer y hoy

2. ¿Qué tuvo mucha importancia en el desarrollo de Miami?
   a. el Parque Dominó
   b. el ferrocarril
   c. la calle Ocho
   d. Cuba

3. ¿Por qué es Miami uno de los grandes focos hispanos o latinos de Estados Unidos?
   a. Hay muchos inmigrantes de Cuba y de todo Latinoamérica.
   b. Castro derrocó la dictadura de Fulgencio Batista.
   c. Está en el mar Caribe.
   d. Ya había muchos hispanos en Miami cuando llegó Henry Flagler.

4. ¿Cuál es una característica de la Pequeña Habana?
   a. Está en el corazón de la ciudad.
   b. Es la única zona donde hay restaurantes y cafés.
   c. Allí se oye más español que inglés.
   d. Nadie habla inglés.

5. Sabemos que podemos llevar una guayabera porque la lectura dice _____.

6. ¿Cuál de los siguientes es una bebida?
   a. un dominó
   b. un guarapo
   c. el azúcar
   d. una guayabera

GeoVistas

To learn more about the United States, take a tour on pages SH64–SH65.

CULTURA

Un café popular en la Pequeña Habana donde se sirve comida cubana incluyendo los típicos sándwiches cubanos

Vocabulario

1 **Completa con una palabra apropiada.**

1. Puedes aparcar en la calle o en un _____.
2. Los peatones deben cruzar la calle en _____.
3. Hay _____ para bajar a la estación del metro.
4. Un _____ es un edificio alto que tiene muchos pisos.
5–6. _____ y _____ son dos atracciones en el parque de atracciones.
7. Hay animales exóticos en el _____.

To review **Vocabulario 1,** turn to pages 232–233.

CULTURA

Llamas en una hacienda cerca de Puerto Montt, Chile

To review **Vocabulario 1** and **Vocabulario 2,** turn to pages 232–233 and 236–237.

2 **Corrige.**

8. El semáforo está en la boca del metro.
9. Un paseo es una calle angosta.
10. Tienes que aparcar el carro en la parada de autobús.
11. El ganado cosecha en el campo.
12. Los caballos están en el granero.
13. Los campesinos cultivan trigo en la huerta.

To review **Vocabulario 2,** turn to pages 236–237.

3 **Identifica.**

14. contrario de «sembrar»
15. los que cultivan o trabajan la tierra
16–17. dos cosas que comen unos animales

Gramática

4 **Escribe en el futuro.**

18. Visitamos Lima.
19. Él va a la Plaza de Armas.
20. Ellos comen en el Café Haití.
21. ¿Tú nos reservas un cuarto en el hotel?
22. No vivo en Lima.
23. Ellos no rentan un departamento.

To review **el futuro de los verbos regulares,** turn to page 240.

5 **Completa con el futuro.**

24. Yo ____ mañana. (salir)
25. Ellos ____ todo en orden. (poner)
26. ¿Tú me ____ ayudar? (poder)
27. Él me lo ____. (decir)
28. Nosotros ____ el viaje juntos. (hacer)
29. Yo ____ que recordar los billetes. (tener)

To review **el futuro de los verbos irregulares,** turn to page 242.

6 **Escribe con pronombres.**

30. Acabo de comprar el plano de la ciudad.
31. ¡Bueno! Ahora puedes consultar el plano.
32. Estoy mirando el plano ahora.
33. Voy a darte las direcciones.
34. Estoy escribiendo las direcciones.
35. Tenemos que llamar a nuestros amigos.
36. Quiero darles la hora de nuestra llegada.

To review **los pronombres con el infinitivo y el gerundio,** turn to page 244.

Cultura

7 **Describe.**

37. el casco antiguo de una ciudad latinoamericana
38. un parque típico en una ciudad latinoamericana
39. un barrio bajo
40. el problema agrario en el campo

To review this cultural information, turn to pages 248–250.

CULTURA

Una calle típica del Casco Viejo en la Ciudad de Panamá

CIUDAD Y CAMPO

1 **La ciudad**

Describe a city that you know

Describe una ciudad que has visitado y que te gusta. Explica por qué volverás a esta ciudad.

2 **Una ciudad hispana**

Describe a Latin American city

Describe una típica ciudad latinoamericana. Luego mira las fotos que salen en el libro o en el Internet y escoge la ciudad que a ti te gusta más. Explica por qué te gusta.

3 **Transporte público**

Talk about modes of transportation

Describe los medios de transporte que existen en muchas ciudades.

CULTURA

El bus local de León a Managua, Nicaragua

4 **El campo**

Describe what you like about the country

Describe algunos aspectos del campo que a ti te gustan.

5 **¿El campo o la ciudad?**

Compare and contrast the city and the country

Trabajen en grupos. Van a preparar una encuesta *(survey)* contestando las siguientes preguntas:

¿Prefieres vivir en la ciudad o en el campo? ¿Por qué?

¿Cuáles son las ventajas y desventajas de cada lugar?

Después de terminar las entrevistas para la encuesta, presentarán los resultados a la clase.

6 **En el futuro**

Talk about what you will do in the future

Habla de todo lo que harás en el futuro. Luego habla con un(a) compañero(a) y comparen sus deseos o planes.

CULTURA

La campesina está cosechando heno a mano en la isla Taquile en el lago Titicaca en Perú.

Prepárate para el examen
Practice for written proficiency

Tarea

Think about all you have learned so far about the countryside and the city in parts of Latin America. Using vocabulary and information contained in the textbook, write a short essay comparing and contrasting life in the countryside with life in the city. Conclude your essay with a paragraph in which you predict what the city and the countryside will be like in fifty years. In what ways do you think they will change and why?

Writing Strategy

Comparing and contrasting When you write an essay that compares and contrasts, you write about similarities and differences between two things. To start organizing the main ideas of your essay, ask yourself a few questions. How does life in the countryside differ from life in the city? What similarities are there? What aspects of city and country life do I want to focus on and do I have enough information to compare and contrast them?

❶ Prewrite

Create a Venn diagram like the one below to help you illustrate the similarities and differences between the city and the countryside. List the similarities in the area where the two circles intersect. List the differences in the main body of each circle.

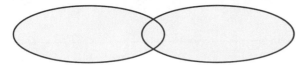

Try to maintain a balance of the details that you would like to include in your essay. In other words, for each detail that you provide for life in the city, you should also provide a detail about the countryside.

❷ Write

- Be sure to include a topic sentence that presents the purpose of your essay to the reader.
- Use the information from your Venn diagram to present similarities in an organized way.
- Use the future tense in your concluding paragraph to predict what you think the city and the countryside will be like in fifty years.

Evaluate

Your teacher will evaluate you on correct use of vocabulary and grammar, organization, completeness of information, and presence of comparable and contrastable details.

Repaso del Capítulo 8

Gramática

- ### Futuro de los verbos regulares *(page 240)*
  Review the forms of regular **-ar, -er,** and **-ir** verbs in the future tense.

bailar	comer	vivir
bailaré	comeré	viviré
bailarás	comerás	vivirás
bailará	comerá	vivirá
bailaremos	comeremos	viviremos
bailaréis	*comeréis*	*viviréis*
bailarán	comerán	vivirán

- ### Futuro de los verbos irregulares *(page 242)*
  The following verbs have irregular stems in the future.

tener → tendr-	poner → pondr-	decir → dir-
salir → saldr-	saber → sabr-	hacer → har-
venir → vendr-	poder → podr-	querer → querr-

- ### Los pronombres con el infinitivo y el gerundio *(page 244)*
  Note that object pronouns can be added to an infinitive or present participle, or they can precede the helping verb.

  Voy a comer la manzana.
  Voy a comerla.
  La voy a comer.

  Estoy preparando la comida.
  Estoy preparándola.
  La estoy preparando.

Vocabulario

Talking about the city

la ciudad	la avenida,	el/la peatón(ona)	el parking, el
el centro	el paseo	el cruce	parqueo
el casco (el barrio)	la calle	el rascacielos	ancho(a)
antiguo	el semáforo	la oficina	angosto, estrecho(a)
la plaza	la esquina	el tráfico	urbano(a)
		la acera	aparcar, estacionar

Talking about public transportation

el medio de	la boca del metro	el autobús, el
transporte	la escalera	camión, la guagua
la estación de metro	la escalera mecánica	la parada de autobús

Talking about an amusement park and a zoo

el parque de	el tiovivo	la montaña rusa	el zoológico
atracciones	la noria	el mimo	

Talking about the country

el campo	el/la campesino(a),	el granero	la hacienda, el
la finca, la granja, la	el peón	el heno	rancho, la estancia
chacra	el establo	la hierba	montar (andar)
la casa de campo	el corral	la equitación	a caballo

Talking about farming

la tierra	la huerta	cosechar	cultivar, labrar
el trigo	la cosecha	sembrar	

Talking about some farm animals

el cerdo	la gallina	el ganado	pacer
el cordero	la vaca		

Repaso cumulativo

Repasa lo que ya has aprendido

These activities will help you review and remember what you have learned so far in Spanish.

1 Escucha las frases. Indica en una tabla como la de abajo si la acción ocurrió en el pasado o si va a ocurrir en el futuro.

pasado	futuro

2 Parea los antónimos.

1. derecho	**a.** delante
2. sencillo	**b.** viejo
3. guardar	**c.** izquierdo
4. detrás	**d.** encima, sobre
5. bajar	**e.** de ida y vuelta
6. ancho	**f.** estrecho
7. largo	**g.** borrar
8. joven	**h.** subir
9. debajo	**i.** corto

Pastoras con sus ovejas en la isla Taquile en el lago Titicaca en Perú

3 Completa con el imperfecto o el pretérito.

1. Yo _____ ayer pero él _____ todos los días. (ir, ir)

2. Él lo _____ ayer pero nosotros lo _____ todos los días. (ver, ver)

3. Tú le _____ ayer pero yo le _____ todos los días. (hablar, hablar)

4. Ellas lo _____ con frecuencia y tú lo _____ solamente una vez. (hacer, hacer)

5. Yo _____ el verano pasado en el campo y él _____ todos los veranos allí. (pasar, pasar)

6. Mi abuelita _____ todo lo que _____ cada día. (comprar, necesitar)

7. Yo _____ hablar con José y lo _____ ayer pero él no _____. (querer, llamar, contestar)

8. ¿_____ tú hacer lo que _____ el profesor? (poder, querer)

Cambia al pasado.

1. Hace buen tiempo.
2. Hay sol.
3. La niña es adorable.
4. Tiene solo quince meses.
5. Está muy contenta.
6. Tiene una sonrisa grande.
7. Su papá la adora.
8. Él sabe que yo los conozco.

Usa cada palabra en una frase original.

1. el cine
2. el museo
3. un concierto

Describe el dibujo.

¿Vas en carro?

Aquí y Allí

Vamos a comparar Piensa en la importancia del carro como medio de transporte donde tú vives. ¿Qué problemas crean los carros? Ahora vas a aprender algo sobre el tráfico vehicular en Latinoamérica. Leerás también sobre una carretera famosa de Latinoamérica—la carretera más larga del mundo.

◄ Es aquí donde los que usan la autopista tienen que pagar la cuota en la Ciudad de Panamá.

Objetivos

You will:

- talk about cars and driving
- give directions
- discuss the Pan American Highway

You will use:

- **tú** affirmative commands
- the conditional

QuickPass

Go to glencoe.com
For: **Online book**
Web code: **ASD7837c9**

Introducción al tema
¿Vas en carro?

Mira las fotos para familiarizarte con el tema del capítulo—el carro y la carretera. Como observarás hay mucho tráfico vehicular en todas partes del mundo hispanohablante. Hay autopistas modernas y pintorescos caminos rurales.

▲ **España** Un camino rural en la Mancha, en España

PUERTO RICO
DYA 525
Isla Del Encanto

3A **A7177**
HONDURAS, C.A.

Panamá El puente de las Américas se encuentra en la desembocadura del canal de Panamá y forma parte de la carretera panamericana. Es el puente que une las dos Américas—la América norteña y la América sureña. ▶

◀ **Argentina** Estos dos turistas jóvenes (se) bajan de un taxi en Buenos Aires.

▲ **España** Unos semáforos en la ciudad de Barcelona

▲ **Venezuela** La avenida Bolívar en Caracas es una avenida ancha con varios carriles en cada sentido. Como en todas las ciudades hay mucho tráfico.

▲ **España** Esta gasolinera en Estepona ofrece un servicio excelente a los dueños de mascotas—un lugar donde pueden lavar su perro mientras llenan de gasolina el tanque de su coche.

PARE

Ecuador Si uno no tiene carro y no quiere tomar el bus, puede tomar un taxi. ▼

En la carretera

la garita (la cabina) de peaje

el rótulo

la autopista, la autovía

una línea continua

el carril

km 68

la velocidad máxima

el arcén, el acotamiento

En la carretera nacional hay solo un carril en cada sentido.

Está prohibido pasar (adelantar, rebasar) otro carro cuando hay una línea continua.

Hay que quedarse en su carril.

Para conversar

Carolina, paga el peaje. Después de pagar el peaje, sal de la autopista en la próxima salida.

PEAJE

Para conversar

Yo tomaría la autopista porque llegaríamos en menos tiempo.

Yo la tomaría también, pero José no. Él no pagaría el peaje. Es muy tacaño.

En la ciudad

una calle de sentido único

la luz roja

Al llegar a una bocacalle (donde se cruzan dos calles) debes reducir la velocidad. Debes ir más despacio.

¡Mira! Hay una luz roja. Párate.

el parabrisas

el parquímetro

una moneda

—Mete una moneda en el parquímetro. Te saldrá un tiquete. Pon el tiquete en el parabrisas. ¡Ten cuidado! Si no metes el tiquete, te clavarán con (darán) una multa.

Pidiendo direcciones

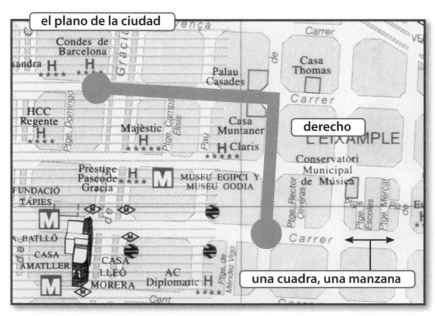

el plano de la ciudad

derecho

una cuadra, una manzana

Para llegar al Hotel Condes de Barcelona:
Da la vuelta.
Sigue derecho dos cuadras.
En el segundo cruce (la segunda bocacalle), dobla a la izquierda.
A cien metros, verás el Hotel Condes de Barcelona.

QuickPass

Go to glencoe.com
For: **Vocabulary practice**
Web code: **ASD7837c9**

Conexiones

La ecología

La contaminación del aire es un problema serio en casi todas las áreas urbanas del mundo. España y Latinoamérica no son ninguna excepción. El aire de muchas de sus ciudades está contaminado. Los gases que salen de los tubos de escape de los automóviles, camiones y buses son una causa principal de la contaminación. ¿Está contaminado el aire donde tú vives? Si contestas que sí, ¿cuál es la causa de la contaminación?

ESCUCHAR

1 Escucha cada frase y decide si la información es correcta o no. Usa una tabla como la de abajo para indicar tus respuestas.

correcta	incorrecta

HABLAR • ESCRIBIR

2 Contesta.

1. ¿Tiene varios carriles en cada sentido una autopista?
2. Por lo general, ¿hay que pagar un peaje para tomar la autopista?
3. ¿Dónde se paga el peaje?
4. Si hay una línea continua en el medio de una carretera de solo dos carriles, ¿es posible adelantar un carro que anda despacio?
5. En las autopistas, ¿hay rótulos que indican la velocidad máxima?

LEER • ESCRIBIR

3 Completa con una palabra apropiada.

1. Hay _____ en muchas esquinas de una ciudad.
2. Donde se cruzan dos calles es _____.
3. Para aparcar el carro, debes tomar el tiquete que sale del _____ y ponerlo en el _____ del carro.
4. Si excedes la velocidad máxima o si no pagas para aparcar el carro, el policía te dará _____.
5. No puedes entrar porque es una calle de _____ único.
6. Si buscas una calle en la ciudad debes consultar _____.
7. José no tomaría la autopista porque tendría que pagar _____.
8. No lo (la) pagaría porque es muy _____. No le gusta gastar dinero.

CULTURA

Aquí ves un rótulo en una esquina de Quito, Ecuador. ¿Cómo se dice «sentido único» en Ecuador?

LEER

4 Parea las expresiones que tienen el mismo significado.

1. ir en el sentido contrario   **a.** derecho
2. ni a la izquierda ni a la derecha   **b.** rebasar
3. una cuadra   **c.** una manzana
4. un cruce   **d.** la dirección
5. el arcén   **e.** dar la vuelta
6. adelantar   **f.** el acotamiento
7. el sentido   **g.** una bocacalle

LEER • ESCRIBIR

5 Escribe de otra manera.

1. Tienes que pagar *el peaje* en *la cabina.*
2. *El rótulo* indica que estamos llegando a la entrada de *la autovía.*
3. *El arcén* está a cada lado de la carretera.
4. No se puede *rebasar* cuando hay una línea continua entre los carriles.
5. Debes reducir la velocidad al llegar a *un cruce.*
6. Debes *reducir la velocidad.*
7. Tienes que seguir *unas* cinco *manzanas* más.
8. Te *darán* una multa.

Comunicación

6 Conversa con un(a) compañero(a) sobre las reglas de la autopista—lo que uno puede y no puede hacer.

El coche, El carro

el permiso de conducir, la licencia, el carnet

el conductor

la maletera, el baúl

las direccionales, las intermitentes

la guantera

la puerta

el capó

los frenos

el volante

las luces

un descapotable, un convertible

un coche deportivo

un sedán a cuatro puertas

un SUV

un camión

Para conversar

¡Cuánto me gustaría tener un coche deportivo! Me compraría uno pero no puedo.

¿Por qué no?

Porque no tengo bastante dinero.

En la estación de servicio (la gasolinera)

El tanque está casi vacío.
La señorita llena el tanque.

¡Ay! Tengo un pinchazo. Tengo que cambiar la llanta. Tengo una rueda de repuesto y un(a) gato(a) en la maletera.

la llanta, la goma, el neumático

el/la gato(a)

una rueda (llanta) de repuesto (recambio)

QuickPass

Go to glencoe.com
For: **Vocabulary practice**
Web code: ASD7837c9

HABLAR • ESCRIBIR

1 Identifica.

Conexiones

Las finanzas

Muchas veces cuando uno quiere comprar un carro no tiene suficiente dinero para pagar el precio total. Así tiene que pedir un préstamo. Pero hay que tener cuidado porque la tasa de interés de un préstamo a corto plazo (por poco tiempo) es más alta que la tasa de interés de un préstamo a largo plazo. Un(a) consumidor(a) inteligente siempre tiene que verificar la tasa de interés que tiene que pagar.

Calculadora de Pagos Mensuales

Ingresa el precio del vehículo que estás considerando y otras variables para calcular una estimación del pago mensual. Este cálculo refleja montos en dólares aproximados al valor entero más cercano. Esta estimación de pagos mensuales no incluye licencia, documentación, cobros por emisiones u otros posibles pagos extra.

Precio	25000
Pago adelantado	5000
Tasa de interés	6.0 %

[Calcular]

LEER

2 Indica si la información es correcta o no.

	correcta	incorrecta
1. Para conducir (manejar) un carro es necesario tener un permiso de conducir.		
2. Un descapotable es más bien un coche deportivo.		
3. Antes de doblar el conductor debe poner las direccionales.		
4. Si por a caso tienes un pinchazo, siempre debes tener una gata y una rueda de repuesto en la guantera.		
5. Para parar el carro tienes que poner los frenos.		
6. El motor del carro está en la maletera.		
7. Tienes que llenar el tanque de gasolina cuando está lleno.		

HABLAR • ESCRIBIR

3 Personaliza. Da respuestas personales.
   1. ¿Tienes un carro?
   2. ¿Tienes tu permiso de conducir?
   3. En tu estado, ¿a qué edad puedes conseguir (tener) un permiso de conducir?
   4. En tu estado, ¿son de autoservicio las gasolineras?

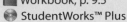
 Conexiones

4 **El lenguaje** Como el mundo hispano es tan grande, hay muchas maneras de decir la misma cosa. Puedes familiarizarte con los siguientes términos relacionados con un carro o una carretera pero no tienes que aprenderlos todos. En esta lista debes saber por lo menos la primera palabra.

- el carril, la pista, la vía, la banda, el canal
- el arcén, el acotamiento, la banquina, la berma, el hombrillo
- adelantar, pasar, rebasar
- el tráfico, el tránsito
- estacionar, aparcar, parquear
- el permiso de conducir, la licencia, el carnet
- la llanta, el neumático, la goma, el caucho
- el pinchazo, la llanta desinflada, la llanta pinchada
- de repuesto, de recambio, de refacción
- la gasolina, la nafta, la benzina

Si hay unos alumnos latinos en tu clase, pregúntales cuáles son las palabras que ellos usan. Pregúntales también si usan otra palabra para expresar la misma idea.

LEER

5 Parea para crear una historia.

1. A Alejandra le gustaría tener
2. Lo compraría pero
3. No puede porque
4. Para comprarlo
5. Para ganar bastante dinero

a. necesitaría mucho dinero.
b. no tiene bastante dinero.
c. un carro nuevo.
d. tendría que trabajar mucho.
e. no puede.

EXPANSIÓN

Ahora, sin mirar las frases, cuenta la historia en tus propias palabras. Si no recuerdas algo, tu compañero(a) te puede ayudar.

HABLAR

6 **Juego** Trabaja con un(a) compañero(a). Piensa en una palabra relacionada con los carros. Tu compañero(a) te va a hacer unas preguntas para adivinar la palabra en que estás pensando. Después, cambien de rol. ¡A ver quién hace menos preguntas antes de adivinar la palabra!

CULTURA

Entrada a un servicio para autos en la Ciudad de México.

QuickPass

Go to glencoe.com
For: **Grammar practice**
Web code: **ASD7837c9**

Imperativo familiar—formas regulares

1. Just as in English, you use the imperative in Spanish to give a command. You use the **tú** command when speaking to a friend, a family member, someone you know well, or a child. The regular **tú** form of the command is the same as the **usted** form of the present tense of the verb.

PRESENT (UD.)	IMPERATIVE (TÚ)
Usted habla.	¡Habla!
Usted conduce.	¡Conduce!
Usted escribe.	¡Escribe!
Usted comienza.	¡Comienza!
Usted vuelve.	¡Vuelve!
Usted sigue.	¡Sigue!

2. The object pronouns are added to this command form and the verb takes a written accent.

Quédate en el carril izquierdo.
El plano, por favor. Dámelo.

Nuestra responsabilidad es conservar y proteger el Bosque.

- Evita encender fogatas, hornillas, explosivos o cohetes.
- Está prohibido introducir armas.
- Se prohíbe consumir bebidas alcohólicas.
- No alimentes a los animales del Bosque.
- Deposita la basura en su lugar.
- Respeta las señales.
- Evita traer mascotas.

Práctica

ESCUCHAR • HABLAR

① Conversa según el modelo.

MODELO —¿Debo hablar?
—Sí, Pepe. ¡Habla!

1. ¿Debo parar?
2. ¿Debo doblar?
3. ¿Debo dar la vuelta?
4. ¿Debo doblar a la derecha?
5. ¿Debo leer el rótulo?
6. ¿Debo seguir derecho?
7. ¿Debo volver?
8. ¿Debo pedir direcciones?

¿Qué es el programa Hoy No Circula?

Si visitas la Ciudad de México o el Área Metropolitana, tienes que cumplir con el Programa Hoy No Circula, el cual prohíbe la circulación de vehículos algunos días de la semana. Opera de lunes a viernes de las 05:00 a las 22:00 horas, de acuerdo con el último número de placa de tu vehículo. Revisa qué día no circula tu auto:

Lunes 5 y 6
Martes 7 y 8
Miércoles 3 y 4
Jueves 1 y 2
Viernes 9 y 0, así como permisos y placas personalizadas que no cuenten con números.

LEER • ESCRIBIR

2 Completa con el imperativo familiar del verbo indicado.

1. Oye, Magda, _____ a la derecha. (doblar)
2. _____ derecho. (seguir)
3. _____ derecho hasta el tercer cruce. (seguir)
4. _____ a la izquierda. (mirar)
5. A mano izquierda, verás la tienda. _____. (entrar)
6. _____ el ascensor. (tomar)
7. _____ al sexto piso. (subir)
8. _____ allí. (esperar)

HABLAR

3 Mira las ilustraciones. Usa el imperativo para decirle a tu compañero(a) lo que debe hacer.

1.   2.   3.   4.

HABLAR

4 **Juego** Escoge a un(a) compañero(a) para jugar «Simón dice».

ESCUCHAR • HABLAR • ESCRIBIR

5 Sigue el modelo.

MODELO la mantequilla →
　　　　Pásame la mantequilla, por favor.

1. el pan   4. la botella
2. el vaso   5. los panecillos
3. la taza

ESCUCHAR • HABLAR • ESCRIBIR

6 Sigue el modelo.

MODELO la toalla →
　　　　Ramón, dámela, por favor.

1. la cámara   4. los boletos
2. el jabón   5. las entradas
3. el peine

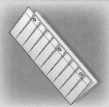

FOLDABLES®
Study Organizer

VOCABULARY BOOK
See page SH24 for help with making this foldable. Use this study organizer to practice your informal commands. On the front of each flap, write the infinitive form of a verb. Then open each flap and write the informal (tú) command of the verb. For extra practice, exchange *vocabulary book* foldables with a partner.

InfoGap For more practice with affirmative commands, do Activity 9 on page SR11 at the end of this book.

Imperativo familiar—formas irregulares

The following verbs are irregular in the **tú** form of the command.

INFINITIVE	IMPERATIVE (TÚ)
decir	di
ir	ve
ser	sé
salir	sal
hacer	haz
tener	ten
venir	ven
poner	pon

Práctica

ESCUCHAR • HABLAR • ESCRIBIR

 7 Contesta con **sí** y el imperativo.

1. ¿Debo venir mañana?
2. ¿Debo salir temprano?
3. ¿Debo hacer el viaje en carro?
4. ¿Debo poner aire en las llantas?
5. ¿Debo decir «adiós» a mi hermano?
6. ¿Debo ir por la carretera vieja?
7. ¿Debo tener cuidado?

HABLAR

 8 Tu compañero(a) no sabe lo que debe hacer. Conversa según el modelo.

MODELO   ir →
—No sé si debo ir.
—Sí, ve.

1. hacer el viaje
2. salir de la ciudad
3. manejar
4. ir por la autopista
5. pedir un día libre
6. volver tarde

 CULTURA

El monumento de la Independencia en el Paseo de la Reforma en la Ciudad de México

Comunicación

9 Escríbele las direcciones a un(a) amigo(a) diciéndole como llegar a tu casa del aeropuerto.

10 Habla con un(a) compañero(a) de clase. Dale direcciones para ir de la escuela a tu casa. Luego tu compañero(a) te dirá como ir a su casa.

El condicional

1. As with the future, the infinitive serves as the stem for the conditional of regular verbs. The endings added to the infinitive to form the conditional are the same endings you use for the imperfect of **-er** and **-ir** verbs.

	llegar	**ver**	**ir**
yo	llegaría	vería	iría
tú	llegarías	verías	irías
Ud., él, ella	llegaría	vería	iría
nosotros(as)	llegaríamos	veríamos	iríamos
vosotros(as)	*llegaríais*	*veríais*	*iríais*
Uds., ellos, ellas	llegarían	verían	irían

CULTURA

¿Te gustaría nadar en esta alberca en Tepoztlán, México?

2. Verbs that have an irregular stem in the future have the same irregular stem in the conditional.

INFINITIVE	FUTURE STEM	CONDITIONAL
tener	tendr-	tendría
poner	pondr-	pondría
salir	saldr-	saldría
venir	vendr-	vendría
poder	podr-	podría
saber	sabr-	sabría
hacer	har-	haría
decir	dir-	diría
querer	querr-	querría

3. You use the conditional in Spanish the same as you do in English. The conditional expresses what would take place under certain conditions.

> **Ellos podrían llegar en menos tiempo, pero no quieren tomar la autopista.**
> **Él adelantaría el otro carro, pero no quiere exceder el límite de velocidad.**
> **No excederíamos el límite porque no queremos tener una multa.**

4. You can also use the conditional to soften requests.

> **¿Me pasaría usted la sal, por favor?**
> **¿Me dirías cómo llegar a la Plaza de Armas?**

CULTURA

—Perdón, ¿me diría, por favor, cómo llegar a la avenida General O'Higgins de la avenida Santa Rosa?
La señora habla de una manera cortés al agente de policía en Santiago de Chile.

Práctica

ESCUCHAR

11 Escucha. Indica el tiempo del verbo.

futuro	condicional

HABLAR • ESCRIBIR

12 Personaliza. Da respuestas personales.

1. ¿Te gustaría ser millonario(a) o no?
2. ¿Vivirías en el campo o en la ciudad?
3. ¿Tendrías una casa de verano?
4. ¿Viajarías mucho?
5. ¿Adónde irías?
6. ¿Con quién harías tus viajes?

CULTURA

¿Podrías ayudar a este joven a reparar su moto en Guasca, Colombia?

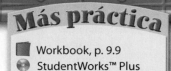
Gramática

LEER • ESCRIBIR

13 Completa con el condicional.

1. Yo sé que él no lo hará, pero yo lo _____.
2. Yo sé que a ellos les gustará la idea, pero a mí no me _____ nada.
3. Yo sé que ellos no lo dirán, pero tú se lo _____ a todos.
4. Yo sé que ella irá, pero ustedes no _____.
5. Yo sé que tú contestarás, pero ella no _____.
6. Nosotros sabemos que él comerá el pescado pero nosotros no lo _____.

ESCUCHAR • HABLAR

14 Conversa según el modelo.

MODELO —¿Se quedará tu hermano?
—Dijo que se quedaría.

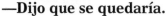

1. ¿Estará tu hermano?
2. ¿Hará el viaje?
3. ¿Vendrá mañana?
4. ¿Saldrá con Elena?
5. ¿Tendrá mucho tiempo?

ESCUCHAR • HABLAR • ESCRIBIR

15 Sigue el modelo para ser más cortés.

MODELO Pásame la sal, por favor. →
Me pasarías la sal, por favor.

1. Pásame el pan, por favor.
2. Ayúdame, por favor.
3. Llámame mañana, por favor.
4. Repítelo, por favor.

Refrán

Can you guess what the following proverb means?

Si ves las estrellas brillar, sal, marinero, a la mar.

🏵 Comunicación

16 ¿Hay muchas cosas que te gustaría hacer pero que no puedes porque tienes otras obligaciones? Ten una conversación con un(a) compañero(a). Discutan todo lo que les gustaría hacer pero que no pueden. Expliquen por qué no pueden.

¡Bravo!

You have now learned all the new vocabulary and grammar in this chapter. Continue to use and practice all that you know while learning more cultural information. ¡Vamos!

QuickPass

Go to glencoe.com
For: **Conversation practice**
Web code: **ASD7837c9**

UN SITIO PARA APARCAR

¿Comprendes?

VIDEO To take a road trip with some friends, watch **Diálogo en vivo.**

A Contesta según la información en la conversación.

1. ¿Por qué no puede Gregorio aparcar el carro donde lo quiere aparcar?
2. ¿Qué hay en la esquina donde tiene que doblar a la derecha?
3. ¿Hasta dónde debe seguir derecho?
4. ¿Qué hay en la plaza?
5. ¿Qué indica su entrada?

B Busca todas las direcciones que Carmen le da a Gregorio para llegar a la plaza.

C **Resumiendo** Cuenta la información en la conversación en tus propias palabras.

CULTURA

Es la caja de un parking en Tenerife en las islas Canarias de España.

Antes de leer

Piensa en las carreteras donde vives. ¿Son anchas con muchos carriles en cada sentido o son más bien caminos estrechos con solo un carril en cada sentido?

✓ Reading Check

¿Entre qué países se extiende la carretera panamericana?

✓ Reading Check

¿Por qué es muy importante la carretera panamericana?

Durante la lectura

Escribe a lo menos dos frases sobre cada párrafo. Al terminar cada párrafo lee todos tus apuntes.

La panamericana

¿Te gustaría rentar un carro y explorar a lo menos una o más regiones de Latinoamérica? Sería una experiencia que no olvidarías nunca. Pues, ¡al volante! ¡Empieza tu aventura! Tendrías que tomar, sin duda, una parte de la carretera panamericana—pero solo una parte pequeña porque la panamericana es la carretera más larga del mundo—cubre 47.516 kilómetros.

La panamericana es una red o sistema de carreteras y caminos que se extiende desde la frontera de Estados Unidos y México hasta la ciudad de Puerto Montt en la Patagonia chilena. En unos lugares la carretera enlaza también la costa occidental con la costa oriental de la América del Sur. La carretera es una ruta importante para el transporte de todo tipo de mercancías y productos agrícolas. Muchos camiones están tan cargados que parecen[1] que van a volcar[2]. Cuando llegan a una pendiente[3] su peso[4] no les permite agarrar velocidad[5] y los sigue una larga cola (fila) de vehículos que querrían adelantarlos.

[1]parecen *seem as if*
[2]volcar *flip over*
[3]pendiente *incline*
[4]peso *weight*
[5]agarrar velocidad *to pick up speed*

CULTURA

Una garita de peaje en la carretera panamericana en Perú

Unas partes de la panamericana son modernas con dos o más carriles en cada sentido. La mayor parte de la carretera está pavimentada—a veces en buenas condiciones y otras veces no. Por eso tendrías que manejar con mucho cuidado sobre todo de noche. En las áreas remotas no hay luces pero hay baches[6] que frecuentemente no puedes ver. De repente puede terminar el pavimento y la carretera se convierte en un camino de rocas, piedras[7] y lodo[8].

[6]baches   *ruts*   [8]lodo   *mud*
[7]piedras   *stones*

✓ **Reading Check**

¿Cómo cambia la carretera de una región a otra?

Este rótulo en el centro de Cotacachi indica como ir a Quito vía la panamericana.

CULTURA

Es un trecho de la panamericana al borde de una pendiente de los Andes en Ecuador. ¿Tiene acotamiento? ¿Hay luces?

¡Ten cuidado! Hay otro peligro[9] posible. Una gran parte de la carretera no tiene acotamiento. Por consiguiente, cuando un carro, camión o bus tiene una avería[10], el conductor pone unas ramas de árboles o plantas unos metros detrás del vehículo. Estas ramas les advierten[11] a los otros conductores que hay cerca un vehículo averiado que está bloqueando el camino. Y después de cambiar una llanta o reparar el vehículo, ¿qué hace el conductor? Pues, sale y deja en su lugar las ramas. Y de noche es difícil verlas.

Como te he dicho, en muchas áreas la panamericana es una carretera moderna y conveniente. Pero en unas zonas remotas, tomar la panamericana es una verdadera aventura.

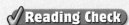

Reading Check

¿Qué pone el conductor en la carretera cuando hay una avería?

[9]peligro *danger*
[10]avería *breakdown*

[11]advierten *warn*

CULTURA

Es un rótulo en el sur de Perú. Hay que ir derecho (recto) si quieres ir a Pisco. Pero si quieres seguir la panamericana tienes que doblar a la derecha en el siguiente cruce.

Después de leer

Lee todos tus apuntes. Añade algunos detalles o descripciones que quieres recordar. Puedes consultar tus apuntes antes de tomar un examen.

¿Comprendes?

Más práctica

Workbook, p. 9.10
StudentWorks™ Plus

A Recordando hechos Contesta.

1. ¿Cuál es la carretera más larga del mundo?
2. ¿Qué es la panamericana?
3. ¿Dónde empieza (nace) y dónde termina (muere) la panamericana?
4. ¿Cómo es la carretera en algunas partes?
5. ¿Cómo es en otras partes?

B Confirmando información Verifica. ¿Sí o no?

1. Toda la carretera panamericana es una carretera moderna con muchos carriles en cada sentido.
2. De noche la carretera está bien iluminada.
3. Una gran parte de la panamericana no tiene acotamiento.
4. No se puede usar la panamericana en ninguna parte para viajar de la costa occidental a la costa oriental de la América del Sur.
5. La panamericana es una ruta usada exclusivamente por razones turísticas.

CULTURA

Es una parte de la panamericana en la Ciudad de Guatemala. Hay mucha distancia entre este trecho de la carretera y el otro cerca de Pisco, Perú, ¿no?

C Describiendo Describe.

1. unas características de la panamericana
2. los posibles peligros en la panamericana

GeoVistas

To learn more about Guatemala, take a tour on pages SH48–SH49.

D Analizando Contesta.

¿Por qué es muy importante la carretera panamericana?

E Describiendo y categorizando Completa la tabla.

la panamericana		
por donde pasa	**su condición**	**unos peligros**

Tráfico y más tráfico 🎧♻

Antes de leer

Piensa en el tráfico donde tú vives. ¿Hay mucho o no? ¿Es un problema o no? ¿Tiene la mayoría de las familias carros que usan casi siempre o hay un buen sistema de transporte público?

Hay muchos que dicen que hay más tráfico en Caracas, Buenos Aires o México que en Chicago, Jacksonville o Dallas, y puede ser verdad. En estas ciudades el tráfico es denso y hay muchos embotellamientos o tapones[1]. Se observará también que muchos carros son bastante viejos. Son viejos pero en su mayoría están en buenas condiciones. En Latinoamérica los carros suelen ser muy caros. Los gobiernos les imponen impuestos[2] altos a los automóviles. Un carro de ocasión, es decir un carro usado, que ya tiene más de diez años puede costar unos quince mil dólares o más. ¿Cuánto cuesta un carro nuevo? Depende, pero puede costar casi el doble de lo que cuesta en Estados Unidos. Por eso, los dueños de los carros los cuidan bien y los reparan frecuentemente para mantenerlos en excelentes condiciones.

CULTURA

El bus es un medio de transporte importante en Latinoamérica. El bus que vemos aquí está en la Ciudad de Panamá.

No hay duda que los vehículos viejos contaminan el aire. Por eso, la contaminación del aire es un problema serio en muchas ciudades latinoamericanas. Tan grave es el problema que en algunas ciudades el gobierno no permite circular todos los vehículos todos los días. Algunos pueden circular los días pares[3] y otros los días impares[4].

Como los carros cuestan tanto, los autobuses son el medio de transporte más popular en los países latinoamericanos. Viajar en bus, sea en bus municipal o el de una compañía privada, resulta muy barato. Y es interesante notar que la palabra «autobús» no es universal en el mundo hispanohablante. Otros términos son el autocar, el bus, el camión, la guagua, el ómnibus, la camioneta, el micro y el colectivo.

CULTURA

Hay mucho tráfico en Caracas, Venezuela, ¿no? Los embotellamientos o tapones son frecuentes.

[1]tapones   *traffic jams*
[2]impuestos   *taxes*

[3]pares   *even*
[4]impares   *odd*

VIDEO To learn more about transportation in Peru, watch **Cultura en vivo.**

¿Comprendes?

Escoge o completa.

1. ¿Por qué hay muchos carros viejos en Latinoamérica?
   a. Nadie tiene el dinero para comprarse un carro nuevo.
   b. Los carros son muy caros.
   c. La gente prefiere carros de ocasión.
   d. A mucha gente le gusta repararlos.

2. ¿Por qué cuestan tanto dinero los carros en Latinoamérica?
   a. Los gobiernos les imponen impuestos altos.
   b. La mayoría de la gente es muy rica.
   c. Pueden costar hasta el doble de lo que cuestan en Estados Unidos.
   d. Los dueños los cuidan bien.

3. Los carros viejos causan mucha _____.

4. ¿Qué hacen algunos gobiernos para tratar de eliminar la contaminación del aire?
   a. Imponen impuestos altos cada vez que el dueño usa su vehículo.
   b. No permiten circular todos los vehículos todos los días.
   c. Imponen impuestos altos para los carros viejos.
   d. No permiten circular los carros en malas condiciones.

5. En inglés se dice *bottleneck* al hablar de un problema de mucho tráfico. Hay dos palabras en español que también tienen que ver con una botella y que expresan la misma idea. Estas dos palabras son _____.

CULTURA

Muchos carros y taxis pasan delante del monumento a la Revolución en la Ciudad de México.

Vocabulario

1 **Completa.**

1–2. En una autopista hay varios _____ en cada _____.

3. El _____ indica donde está la salida.

4. Quiero _____ el carro delante de mí porque va muy despacio.

5. En muchas autopistas hay que pagar _____.

6. Hay _____ en el cruce que indica que tienes que pararte.

7. El museo está a tres _____ de aquí.

8. Para llegar al hotel tienes que _____ a la derecha en el segundo cruce.

To review **Vocabulario 1,** turn to pages 266–267.

2 **Identifica.**

9. donde se ponen las maletas en el carro

10. lo que se usa en el carro de noche

11. se usan para indicar a otros conductores que vas a doblar

12. un vehículo que transporta muchas cosas

13. adonde vas cuando necesitas llenar el tanque de gasolina

14. lo que se usa para levantar el carro cuando hay un pinchazo

15. cada carro tiene cuatro y uno de recambio

16. lo necesitas para conducir un carro; tiene una foto del/de la conductor(a)

To review **Vocabulario 2,** turn to pages 270–271.

Gramática

3 **Completa con el imperativo familiar.**

17. José, _____ la vuelta. (dar)

18. _____ dos cuadras. (seguir)

19. Luego _____ a la izquierda. (doblar)

20. Si te pierdes, _____ el plano de la ciudad. (consultar)

21. _____ una moneda en el parquímetro. (introducir)

22. _____ si necesitas gasolina. (verificar)

23. _____ antes de las seis de la tarde. (volver)

24. _____ con el agente de policía. (hablar)

To review **las formas regulares del imperativo familiar,** turn to page 274.

4 Completa con el imperativo familiar.

25. _____ cuidado. (tener)

26. _____ las direccionales para indicar que vas a doblar. (poner)

27. _____ de la autopista en la próxima salida. (salir)

28. _____ el viaje en carro. (hacer)

29. _____ la verdad. (decir)

To review **las formas irregulares del imperativo familiar,** turn to page 276.

5 Completa con el condicional.

30. Yo tomaré la autovía, pero Lupe no la _____ porque no quiere pagar el peaje.

31. Estaremos muy cansados, pero Nando y Eduardo no _____ cansados porque siempre se acuestan temprano.

32. Aunque no debes exceder la velocidad máxima, yo sé que ella la _____.

33. Mis padres no asistirán al concierto, pero yo sí _____.

34. Luis no lo hará, pero tú lo _____.

35. El niño le tendrá miedo al perro, pero nosotros no _____ miedo.

36. Yo iré pero sé que tú no _____.

To review **el condicional,** turn to pages 277–278.

Cultura

6 Contesta.

37. ¿Qué es la panamericana?

38. ¿Cómo es la panamericana en algunas áreas remotas?

39–40. ¿Por qué tienes que tener cuidado cuando conduces en la carretera panamericana? Puedes dar más de una respuesta.

To review this cultural information, turn to pages 282–284.

CULTURA

La panamericana pasa por la provincia de Buenos Aires en Argentina. ¿Cuántos carriles hay en cada sentido aquí?

1 **Leyendo el mapa**

Create and describe a travel route through Spain

Con un(a) compañero(a), mira un mapa de España. Han alquilado un coche y quieren ir de Madrid a otra ciudad que ustedes dos han escogido. Discutan como van a ir y las carreteras que van a tomar. ¡A ver si pueden adivinar cuánto tiempo tardará *(will take)* el viaje!

2 **Las carreteras de tu estado**

Describe highways in your state

Describe las carreteras de tu estado. ¿Cómo son? ¿Adónde van? ¿Hay mucho tráfico?

3 **¿Qué piensas de la panamericana?**

Explain your opinion

Algún día, ¿quieres tener la experiencia de tomar la panamericana? Explica por qué dices que sí o que no.

CULTURA

Hay mucho tráfico en las calles en el centro de Caracas, Venezuela.

4 **Uno de tus padres te habla**

Tell what needs to be done

Imagínate que eres tu madre o padre. Imita como habla él o ella. Dile a un(a) compañero(a) las tareas que te da con frecuencia. Usa el imperativo familiar.

5 **¿Yo? ¿Millonario(a)?**

Talk about what you would do with a million dollars

Tú y un(a) compañero(a) acaban de recibir un millón de dólares. Cada uno de ustedes hará una lista de todo lo que haría con tal cantidad de dinero. Comparen sus listas y decidan quién haría las cosas más interesantes.

6 **Una encuesta**

Prepare a survey and present the results

Trabaja con un(a) compañero(a). Van a hacer una encuesta. Esta es la situación. Hay un billete de cien dólares en la calle. Cada uno(a) de ustedes preguntará a cinco compañeros lo que harían al encontrar los cien dólares. Luego organicen las respuestas para informar a la clase sobre los resultados.

Tarea

A Spanish-speaking friend who is always getting lost calls to tell you he or she is coming to visit but doesn't remember how to get to your house. Write a dialogue of a phone conversation between you and your friend in which you are trying to give directions but he or she keeps getting mixed up.

Writing Strategy

Dialogue Composing a dialogue between two or more people is a good way to practice the way language is naturally spoken. Although a conversation between friends involves informal speech, when writing dialogue, it is important to use correct spelling and punctuation, appropriate vocabulary, and proper grammar. This is especially true in the context of giving directions, because you don't want misunderstandings or confusion to cause your friend to get lost!

① Prewrite

Give your Spanish-speaking friend an identity and decide where he or she will be coming from. Then use the vocabulary from this chapter to make a list of the information you will need to know in order to give accurate directions. Break the information down in steps.

② Write

- Be sure to review the information in Chapter 6 on how to make and receive phone calls.
- Use the affirmative **tú** commands when giving directions.
- Make sure your phone conversation flows smoothly and sounds natural.
- Remember that your friend keeps getting mixed up. Be creative!

Evaluate

Your teacher will evaluate you on correct spelling and punctuation, proper vocabulary and grammar, organization, and completeness of information.

Repaso del Capítulo 9

Gramática

- ### Imperativo familiar—formas regulares (page 274)
  You use the **tú** command when speaking to a friend, family member, a child, or someone you know well. The **tú** form of the command is the same as the **usted** form of the present tense.

PRESENT (UD.)	IMPERATIVE (TÚ)
Usted habla.	¡Habla!
Usted come.	¡Come!
Usted sigue.	¡Sigue!

  Object pronouns are added to the imperative.

  Dame la mano.   **Devuélvemelo.**

- ### Imperativo familiar—formas irregulares (page 276)
  Review the following irregular forms of the **tú** command.

decir → di	venir → ven	salir → sal
ir → ve	tener → ten	hacer → haz
ser → sé	poner → pon	

- ### El condicional (pages 277–278)
  To form the conditional of regular verbs, you add the endings of the imperfect tense of **-er** and **-ir** verbs to the infinitive.

pagar	comer	seguir
pagaría	comería	seguiría
pagarías	comerías	seguirías
pagaría	comería	seguiría
pagaríamos	comeríamos	seguiríamos
pagaríais	*comeríais*	*seguiríais*
pagarían	comerían	seguirían

  Verbs that have an irregular stem in the future tense have the same irregular stem in the conditional. Review the following forms.

tener → tendría	poner → pondría	hacer → haría
salir → saldría	venir → vendría	decir → diría
poder → podría	saber → sabría	querer → querría

  The conditional is used the same in Spanish as in English.

Vocabulario

Talking about driving on the highway

la carretera	el sentido	la salida	el arcén, el
la autopista, la	el peaje	el rótulo	acotamiento
autovía	la garita (la cabina)	la velocidad máxima	una línea continua
el carril	de peaje		

Giving directions

el plano de la ciudad	quedarse en el carril	adelantar, rebasar,	estar prohibido
dar la vuelta	doblar	pasar	
seguir derecho		parar(se)	

Talking about the city

la cuadra, la	el parquímetro	una calle de sentido	reducir la velocidad
manzana	una moneda	único	cruzar
el cruce, la bocacalle	el tiquete	despacio	
la luz roja	una multa	clavar	

Talking about cars

el coche, el carro	el SUV	la estación de	llenar
el descapotable, el	el camión	servicio, la	cambiar la llanta
convertible	el/la conductor(a)	gasolinera	vacío(a)
el coche deportivo	el permiso de	el/la gato(a)	
el sedán a cuatro	conducir, la	el tanque	
puertas	licencia, el carnet	un pinchazo	

Identifying parts of a car

el capó	las luces	la guantera	la llanta (la rueda)
la puerta	los frenos	el volante	de repuesto (de
la maletera, el baúl	las direccionales,	la llanta, la goma,	recambio)
el parabrisas	las intermitentes	el neumático	

Other useful words and expressions

tacaño(a)	tener cuidado

 **Literary Reader**

You may wish to read the adapted version of *Marianela,* found on pages 368–379.

Repaso cumulativo

Repasa lo que ya has aprendido

These activities will help you review and remember
what you have learned so far in Spanish.

1 Escucha las frases. Indica si la frase describe el dibujo o no.

2 Personaliza. Da respuestas personales.

1. ¿Cuántos años tienes?
2. ¿Haces mucho trabajo cada día?
3. ¿Te pones un suéter cuando hace frío?
4. ¿A qué hora sales de casa por la mañana?
5. ¿Conoces a muchos compañeros de clase?
6. ¿Conduces un carro?

3 Da la forma de yo en el presente.

1. hacer   6. decir
2. poner   7. venir
3. traer   8. conocer
4. salir   9. conducir
5. tener   10. oír

4 Categoriza las siguientes palabras.

	legumbres	frutas	carnes	productos lácteos	pescado o mariscos
1. el jamón					
2. el queso					
3. la lechuga					
4. el helado					
5. la naranja					
6. el pollo					
7. los camarones					
8. las judías verdes					
9. la piña					
10. las almejas					

5 Personaliza. Da respuestas personales.

1. ¿A qué escuela ibas cuando tenías siete años?

2. ¿Quiénes eran algunos de tus maestros en la escuela primaria?

3. ¿Te gustaba ir a un parque de atracciones cuando eras niño(a)?

4. ¿Había un parque de atracciones cerca de donde vivías?

5. ¿Qué atracciones te gustaban más?

6. ¿Ibas de vez en cuando a un zoológico?

7. ¿Qué animales veías?

8. ¿Podías darles de comer a los animales o estaba prohibido?

6 Completa con el adjetivo posesivo.

1. La hermana de mi padre es _____ tía y _____ hermano es _____ tío.

2. Los hijos de mis tíos son _____ primos y _____ hijos son los sobrinos de mis padres.

3. Mi hermano y yo queremos mucho a los abuelos. Los adoramos. _____ abuelos son los padres de _____ padres.

4. Dime algo de _____ familia. ¿Tienes hermanos? ¿Cuántos años tienen _____ hermanos?

Cocina hispana

Aquí y Allí

Vamos a comparar Ya has aprendido que las sobras son la comida que queda después de comer. Has aprendido también que las sobras de una comida en un restaurante de Latinoamérica o España no se llevan a casa «para el perrito». Ahora vamos a ver si las familias hispanas elaboran unos platos sirviéndose de las sobras en vez de botarlas. Y en tu casa, ¿hay unos platos que llevan sobras?

◄ Estas señoras están elaborando una deliciosa comida mexicana en Guadalajara, México.

Objetivos

You will:

- talk about foods and food preparation
- talk about a Spanish recipe

You will use:

- the subjunctive
- formal commands
- negative informal commands

QuickPass

Go to glencoe.com
For: **Online book**
Web code: **ASD7837c10**

Introducción al tema
Cocina hispana

Mira estas fotos para familiarizarte con el tema de este capítulo—la cocina hispana. Al mirar las fotos, ¿qué piensas? Hay una gran variedad de platos. ¿Hay algunos que quieres probar?

México La señora está preparando unas tortillas con salsa y frijoles refritos en Mérida. ▶

◀ **España** En unos restaurantes antiguos de España hay hornos de barro en que asan el cordero y el cochinillo, o como dicen en Latinoamérica «el lechón».

▲ **México** Un plato de chiles rellenos acompañado de arroz y aguacate en un restaurante en Tepoztlán

Los pimientos se usan en la cocina de muchos países hispanos. Hay muchos tipos de pimientos—unos picantes y otros dulces—que llevan muchos nombres diferentes: pimientos, ajíes, chiles, chipotles, etc. ▼

▲ **España** El cocinero está asando pollos en una parrilla a la entrada de un restaurante en Barcelona.

LA PAELLA

INGREDIENTES

3 tomates
2 cebollas grandes
2 pimientos (uno verde y uno rojo)
4 dientes de ajo
1/2 kilo de camarones

4 calamares
12 almejas
12 mejillones
langosta (opcional)
1 pollo en partes
3 chorizos

1 paquete de guisantes congelados
1 bote de pimientos morrones
1 1/2 tazas de arroz
3 tazas de consomé de pollo
4 pizcas de azafrán
1/4 taza de aceite de oliva

PREPARACIÓN

1. Pique los tomates, los pimientos, las cebollas y el ajo.
2. Lave las almejas y los mejillones en agua fría.
3. Limpie y pele los camarones.
4. Limpie y corte en rebanadas los calamares.
5. Corte en rebanadas los chorizos.
6. Fría o ase el pollo aparte.

▲ **España** Una receta para la paella en un libro de cocina española

▲ **Estados Unidos** El señor prepara pinchos y maíz en una parrilla durante el festival cubano de la Calle Ocho en la Pequeña Habana de Miami.

◄ **Argentina** El cocinero asa el famoso bife argentino en un restaurante de Buenos Aires.

Puerto Rico La señora vende empanadas, piononos, alcapurrias y pescado frito en su restaurante en San Juan. ▼

299

La cocina

el congelador

el refrigerador, la nevera

el horno

el horno de microondas

la estufa, la cocina

el lavaplatos

freír las papas

el/la sartén

hervir el agua

la tapa

la olla, la cacerola

asar la carne

la parrilla

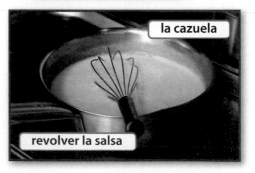

la cazuela

revolver la salsa

Para conversar

¿Quiere usted que yo ase el pollo o que lo fría?

Fríalo, por favor. Me gusta el pollo frito.

SOPA DE POLLO

una receta

INGREDIENTES
1 taza de cebolla picada
1 taza de apio
1 taza de zanahorias
cortadas en rebanadas
3 dientes de ajo machacados

½ cucharadita de
pimienta negra
10 tazas de caldo de pollo
1½ tazas de pollo cortado
en cubitos (¾ de una libra)

RECETA
Poner la cebolla, el apio, las zanahorias, el ajo y el caldo de pollo en un horno holandés. Poner a hervir; remover una o dos veces. Baje el fuego y déjelo cocer a fuego lento sin tapar por 15 minutos. Añadir el pollo; dejar cocer a fuego lento de 5 a 10 minutos.

los pimientos · la cebolla · el aguacate · el pepino · el ajo · las zanahorias

 **cortar en pedacitos**

 **cortar en rebanadas**

 **picar**

Pique usted el ajo.

 **pelar**

Pele usted las zanahorias.

 **la chuleta de cerdo**

el escalope de ternera

 **el muslo de pollo**

las alitas

la pechuga de pollo

Para conversar

¿Quiere usted que yo ponga la cacerola al fuego?

Sí, póngala, por favor. Pero, cocínela (cuézala) a fuego lento. No quiero que se queme.

Cuando el cocinero cocina algo tiene que añadir condimentos.
Los condimentos le dan sabor a la comida.

En otras partes

- **El aguacate** is **la palta** in Chile.
- There are many terms that mean *slice*. Some general guidelines are:
  rebanada (de pan, pastel)
  tajada (de carne)
  lonja, loncha (de jamón)
  rodaja (de limón, pepino)
  raja (de melón)
- **Pedazos** and **trozos (trocitos)** refer to pieces.

Conexiones

Las matemáticas

Si lees una receta en español tienes que comprender los pesos métricos. La onza, la libra y la tonelada no existen en el sistema métrico que es un sistema decimal. Las medidas para el peso se basan en el kilogramo o kilo. Hay mil gramos en un kilo. El kilo es igual a 2,2 libras. Una libra inglesa o estadounidense es un poco menos de medio kilo.

ESCUCHAR

1 Escucha cada frase y decide si la información es correcta o no. Usa una tabla como la de abajo para indicar tus respuestas.

correcta	incorrecta

LEER

2 Escoge.

1. Antes de hervirlas, debes (freír, pelar) las zanahorias.
2. Puedes freír las pechugas de pollo en (una cacerola, una sartén).
3. Tienes que (revolver, asar) la salsa.
4. Favor de poner los vasos sucios en (la nevera, el lavaplatos).
5. Si lo quieres cocinar rápido lo debes poner en (el horno, el horno de microondas).
6. ¿Quiere usted que yo ponga la olla (al agua, al fuego)?
7. ¿Quiere usted que yo pele (las zanahorias, los pimientos)?
8. Voy a cortar el pan en (rebanadas, pedacitos).

ESCRIBIR

3 **¡Manos a la obra!** Good nutrition is an important part of staying healthy. Working in groups, use a piece of poster board and markers to make a food pyramid. Label the pyramid with each of the food groups: grains, vegetables, fruits, oils, milk, and meat/beans. Within each food group, write the names of foods that you know. Then present your pyramid to the class and suggest a healthy meal based on the foods you listed in each group.

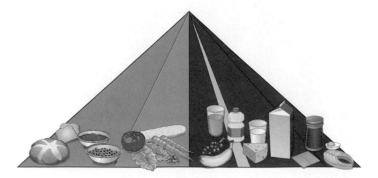

HABLAR • ESCRIBIR

4 Personaliza. Da respuestas personales.

1. Cuando comes pollo, ¿prefieres el muslo o la pechuga?
2. ¿Te gusta más una chuleta de cerdo o un escalope de ternera?
3. ¿Prefieres el pescado asado o frito?
4. ¿Prefieres tus legumbres muy cocidas o casi crudas?
5. ¿Te gusta la carne con una salsa o sin salsa?
6. ¿Te gusta la comida salada o no? ¿Añades mucha sal?

LEER

5 Usa una tabla como la de abajo para indicar si se puede poner los siguientes ingredientes en una ensalada.

CULTURA

El señor está asando carne en un puesto de comida en una calle de la Ciudad de Panamá.

sí	no

1. la lechuga
2. el ajo
3. la carne cruda
4. el aguacate
5. las zanahorias
6. el aceite
7. el café
8. una cebolla

HABLAR • ESCRIBIR

6 Describe.

1. tu comida favorita
2. las legumbres que te gustan
3. los ingredientes de una buena ensalada
4. algunos alimentos que pones en el refrigerador
5. unas cosas que se preparan a la parrilla
6. una cocina moderna

▲ Unos platos populares ▼

 Comunicación

7 Trabajen en grupos de cuatro y discutan sus platos o comidas favoritas. ¿Tienen ustedes los mismos gustos o no?

QuickPass

Go to glencoe.com
For: Grammar practice
Web code: ASD7837c10

El subjuntivo

1. All verbs you have learned so far are in the indicative mood. The indicative mood is used to express actions that actually do, did, or will take place. The indicative is used to express real events.

> **Juan es un alumno bueno.**
> **Estudia mucho.**
> **Recibe buenas notas.**

All the preceding information is factual.

> *John is a good student, he studies a lot, and he gets good grades.*

2. You are now going to learn the subjunctive mood. The subjunctive is used to express something that is not necessarily factual or real. It expresses things that might happen. Compare the following.

> **Juan estudia mucho y recibe buenas notas.**
> **Los padres de Juan quieren que él estudie mucho y que reciba buenas notas.**

The first sentence tells you that Juan studies a lot and gets good grades. The information is factual, and for this reason you use the indicative. The second sentence states that Juan's parents want him to study a lot and get good grades, but that doesn't mean that Juan will actually do it even though his parents want him to. The second sentence tells what may happen. It does not present facts, and for this reason you must use the subjunctive in the clause that depends upon **quieren.** Such a clause is called a dependent clause.

3. To form the present tense of the subjunctive of regular verbs, you drop the **o** ending of the **yo** form of the present indicative. This is also true for verbs that have an irregular form in the present tense of the indicative. Add **e** endings to all **-ar** verbs and **a** endings to all **-er** and **-ir** verbs.

La profesora ayuda a una alumna porque quiere que salga bien en su examen y que tenga éxito.

¿Te acuerdas?

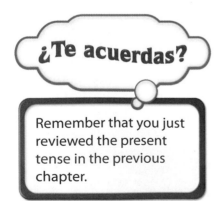

Remember that you just reviewed the present tense in the previous chapter.

INFINITIVE	PRESENT (YO)	STEM	PRESENT SUBJUNCTIVE (YO)
mirar	miro	mir-	mire
comer	como	com-	coma
vivir	vivo	viv-	viva
salir	salgo	salg-	salga
hacer	hago	hag-	haga
decir	digo	dig-	diga
conducir	conduzco	conduzc-	conduzca

4. Study the forms for the present tense of the subjunctive.

	mirar	comer	vivir	salir
yo	mire	coma	viva	salga
tú	mires	comas	vivas	salgas
Ud., él, ella	mire	coma	viva	salga
nosotros(as)	miremos	comamos	vivamos	salgamos
vosotros(as)	*miréis*	*comáis*	*viváis*	*salgáis*
Uds., ellos, ellas	miren	coman	vivan	salgan

5. The following are the only verbs that do not follow the regular pattern for the formation of the present subjunctive.

	dar	estar	ir	saber	ser
yo	dé	esté	vaya	sepa	sea
tú	des	estés	vayas	sepas	seas
Ud., él, ella	dé	esté	vaya	sepa	sea
nosotros(as)	demos	estemos	vayamos	sepamos	seamos
vosotros(as)	*deis*	*estéis*	*vayáis*	*sepáis*	*seáis*
Uds., ellos, ellas	den	estén	vayan	sepan	sean

Práctica

ESCUCHAR • HABLAR • ESCRIBIR

① Sigue el modelo.

MODELO   estudiar mucho →
　　　　　Los padres de Mateo quieren que
　　　　　　　él estudie mucho.

1. trabajar
2. leer mucho
3. comer bien
4. aprender mucho
5. asistir a la universidad
6. recibir buenas notas
7. hacer el trabajo
8. poner todo en orden
9. salir bien en todo
10. ir a clase
11. estar aquí
12. ser bueno

CULTURA

Los señores están preparando una paella grande en Tenerife, España. Quieren que salga deliciosa y que a todos les guste.

CULTURA

La señora está haciendo pupusas en un restaurante en San Salvador, El Salvador.

LEER • ESCRIBIR

2 Forma una frase completa usando el subjuntivo.

Yo quiero que Luis…

1. preparar la comida
2. cortar las cebollas
3. asar la carne
4. leer la receta
5. pelar los tomates
6. picar el ajo
7. poner la mesa
8. hacer una ensalada

HABLAR • ESCRIBIR

3 Completa la frase con tus propias ideas usando los siguientes nombres y pronombres.

Yo quiero que…

1. tú
2. Justina y Roberto
3. todos ustedes
4. ella
5. todos nosotros
6. mi profesor

LEER • ESCRIBIR

4 Completa con la forma apropiada del verbo.

1. Yo quiero que tú le _____ y ellos quieren que nosotros le _____. (hablar)
2. Yo quiero que él _____ el postre y él quiere que yo lo _____. (comer)
3. Ellos quieren que yo _____ el paquete y yo quiero que ellos lo _____. (abrir)
4. Tú quieres que yo lo _____ y yo quiero que tú lo _____. (hacer)
5. Ellos quieren que nosotros _____ la mesa y nosotros queremos que ellos la _____. (poner)
6. Él quiere que yo lo _____ pero no quiere que tú lo _____. (saber)
7. Ellos quieren que tú _____ pero no quieren que yo _____. (ir)
8. Yo quiero que ustedes se lo _____ y ellos quieren que nosotros se lo _____. (dar)

GeoVistas

To learn more about El Salvador, take a tour on pages SH50–SH51.

InfoGap For more practice with the subjunctive, do Activity 10 on page SR12 at the end of this book.

Comunicación

5 Trabajen en grupos y discutan todo lo que tu profesor(a) de español quiere que ustedes hagan.

El imperativo formal

1. The formal commands (**usted, ustedes**), both affirmative and negative, use the subjunctive form of the verb.

(no) prepare usted	(no) preparen ustedes
(no) lea usted	(no) lean ustedes
(no) sirva usted	(no) sirvan ustedes
(no) haga usted	(no) hagan ustedes
(no) salga usted	(no) salgan ustedes
(no) conduzca usted	(no) conduzcan ustedes
(no) vaya usted	(no) vayan ustedes
(no) sea usted	(no) sean ustedes

2. You have already learned that object pronouns can be attached to an infinitive or gerund or come before the helping verb. In the case of commands, the object pronouns must be added to the affirmative command, as you already know from the **tú** commands. They must come before the negative command.

AFFIRMATIVE	NEGATIVE
Háblele.	**No le hable usted.**
Démelo.	**No me lo dé usted.**
Levántense.	**No se levanten ustedes.**

CULTURA

En un parque en San Pablo, Ecuador

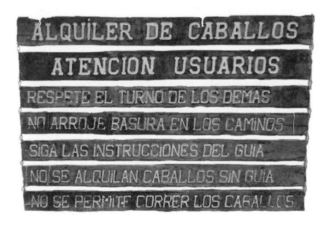

Práctica

ESCUCHAR • HABLAR • ESCRIBIR

6 Contesta según el modelo.

 MODELO —¿Preparo la comida?

—Sí, prepare usted la comida.

1. ¿Preparo el postre?
2. ¿Aso la carne?
3. ¿Pelo los tomates?
4. ¿Pico el ajo?
5. ¿Frío el pollo?
6. ¿Pongo la mesa?
7. ¿Hago la ensalada?
8. ¿Pongo la cacerola al fuego?

El señor está asando carne en Tikal, Guatemala. ¿Quieres que él te prepare la carne bien hecha o a término medio?

ESCUCHAR • HABLAR • ESCRIBIR

7 Contesta según el modelo.

MODELO —¿Preparamos la comida?
—No, no preparen ustedes la comida.
Yo la voy a preparar.

1. ¿Preparamos el postre?
2. ¿Lavamos la lechuga?
3. ¿Pelamos las papas?
4. ¿Cortamos el pepino?
5. ¿Hacemos la ensalada?
6. ¿Ponemos la mesa?

ESCUCHAR • HABLAR • ESCRIBIR

8 Contesta según el modelo.

MODELO —¿Quiere usted que yo ase la chuleta?
—No, no la ase usted. Fríala.

1. ¿Quiere usted que yo ase el pollo?
2. ¿Quiere usted que yo ase las papas?
3. ¿Quiere usted que yo ase las chuletas de cordero?
4. ¿Quiere usted que yo ase los pimientos?
5. ¿Quiere usted que yo ase el pescado?
6. ¿Quiere usted que yo ase los camarones?

ESCUCHAR • HABLAR • ESCRIBIR

9 Sigue el modelo.

MODELO Páseme la sal, por favor. →
Pásemela, por favor.

1. Páseme la pimienta, por favor.
2. Páseme el pan, por favor.
3. Páseme la ensalada, por favor.
4. Páseme los platos, por favor.
5. Páseme el tenedor, por favor.
6. Páseme las zanahorias, por favor.

LEER • ESCRIBIR

10 Completa la tabla.

¿Te acuerdas?

Remember other polite ways you learned to express a command.

Favor de pasarme la sal.

¿Me pasaría usted la sal, por favor?

sí	no
Démelo.	
	No me lo diga usted.
Cocínelo a fuego lento.	
	No la revuelva usted.
Léamela.	

El imperativo familiar—formas negativas

1. The negative **tú** or informal command uses the **tú** form of the verb in the subjunctive.

No hables más.	**No salgas.**
No comas más.	**No vayas.**
No sirvas más.	**No conduzcas.**

2. As with the formal commands, object pronouns are added to the affirmative command and come before the negative command.

Háblame.	**No me hables.**
Dímelo.	**No me lo digas.**

Práctica

ESCUCHAR • HABLAR • ESCRIBIR

⑪ Contesta según el modelo.

MODELO —¿Miro ahora o no?
　　　　　 —No, no mires ahora.

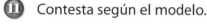

1. ¿Hablo ahora o no?
2. ¿Como ahora o no?
3. ¿Subo ahora o no?

4. ¿Sirvo ahora o no?
5. ¿Salgo ahora o no?
6. ¿Voy ahora o no?

LEER • ESCRIBIR

⑫ Completa la tabla.

sí	no
Ponlo allí.	
Dámelo.	
Dímelo.	
	No me hables.
	No lo hagas.
Llámala.	

 Comunicación

⑬ Acabas de recibir un gatito para tu cumpleaños. Como todos los gatitos, es muy curioso. Dale un nombre al gatito y dile que no haga cosas peligrosas o destructivas.

Refrán

Can you guess what the following proverb means?

Espinacas, cómelas a sacas.

¡Bravo!

You have now learned all the new vocabulary and grammar in this chapter. Continue to use and practice all that you know while learning more cultural information. ¡Vamos!

¿Yo? ¿En la cocina?

¿Comprendes?

VIDEO To prepare an Argentine meal, watch **Diálogo en vivo.**

A Contesta según la informacíon en la conversación.

1. ¿A quién le gusta cocinar?
2. ¿Quién es un desastre en la cocina?
3. Algún día, ¿qué quiere ser Jorge?
4. ¿Cuál es el plato que más le gusta preparar?
5. ¿De qué región de España es la paella una especialidad?
6. ¿A Alicia le va a gustar una paella?
7. ¿Son caros los mariscos?

B Identifica quien lo dice.

	Jorge	Alicia
1. Le gusta cocinar y sabe cocinar.		
2. No sabe si le gustan los mariscos.		
3. Es un desastre en la cocina.		
4. Come mariscos.		

C Analizando Contesta.

1. ¿De qué país es Jorge? ¿Cómo lo sabes?
2. ¿Es Alicia de España?

D Personalizando ¿Qué piensas? ¿A ti te gustaría la paella o no? ¿Por qué?

CULTURA

En esta tienda en Valencia, España, se venden utensilios para elaborar una buena paella.

Antes de leer

Dale una ojeada a la receta para familiarizarte con los ingredientes y la preparación.

ESTRATEGIA DE LECTURA

Leyendo información detallada A veces cuando lees algo como una receta es necesario prestar atención a muchos detalles. Para hacerlo debes leer o consultar la selección más de una vez siempre concentrando y prestando mucha atención.

Durante la lectura

Al leer asegúrate que comprendes el orden de cada procedimiento durante la elaboración del plato.

✓ **Reading Check**

¿Por qué es amarillo el arroz?

Una receta latina 🎧♻

Otro plato delicioso y muy apreciado en España y otros países hispanohablantes es el arroz con pollo. Hay muchas variaciones en las recetas para elaborar un buen arroz con pollo pero aquí tiene usted una receta bastante sencilla. Decida si a usted le gustaría comer este plato delicioso.

Antes de leer la receta hay que saber algo más. El arroz en el arroz con pollo igual que el arroz en una paella es amarillo. Es el azafrán, una hierba de origen árabe, que le da al arroz el color amarillo. Pero el azafrán es muy caro y como colorante se puede usar bujol. El bujol se vende en muchos supermercados.

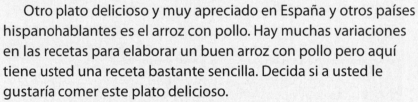

CULTURA

Los ingredientes para hacer arroz con pollo

Arroz con pollo

Ingredientes
- 3 tomates
- 2 cebollas grandes
- 2 pimientos (uno verde y uno rojo)
- 4 dientes[1] de ajo
- 1 pollo en partes
- 3 chorizos[2]
- 1 paquete de guisantes congelados
- 1 frasco de (pimientos) morrones (rojos)
- 1 ½ tazas de arroz
- 3 tazas de consomé de pollo
- unas pizcas[3] de azafrán o bujol
- ¼ (una cuarta) taza de aceite de oliva
- una pizca de sal y pimienta

Preparación
1. Pique los tomates, pimientos, cebollas y ajo.
2. Corte en rodajas los chorizos.
3. Fría o ase el pollo aparte (se puede preparar el pollo en partes [muslos, media pechuga, piernas] o se puede cortarlo en pedazos deshuesados[4]).

Elaboración
Se usa una sartén o una olla grande.
1. Fría ligeramente[5] en el aceite los pimientos y las cebollas picadas.
2. Agregue (Añada) a la misma sartén el ajo y los tomates y fría ligeramente a fuego lento unos dos o tres minutos.
3. Agregue el arroz.
4. Revuelva el arroz con los tomates, cebollas, morrones y ajo.
5. Añada el pollo.
6. Agregue el consomé de pollo y llévelo a la ebullición[6].
7. Agregue el azafrán o bujol.
8. Ponga sal y pimienta a su gusto.
9. Tape[7] la sartén o la olla y cocine a fuego lento encima de la estufa unos treinta minutos.
10. Al final agregue los guisantes y pimientos morrones.

Después de leer

Trata de contar la receta de la manera más detallada posible a un(a) compañero(a) de clase.

[1]dientes   *cloves*
[2]chorizos   *Spanish sausage*
[3]pizcas   *pinches*
[4]deshuesados   *deboned*

[5]ligeramente   *lightly*
[6]a la ebullición   *to a boil*
[7]tape   *cover*

¿Comprendes?

Más práctica

■ Workbook, pp. 10.9–10.10

◉ StudentWorks™ Plus

A **Buscando palabras específicas** ¿Cuál es la palabra?
Completa según la receta.

1. una _____ para hacer (elaborar) arroz con pollo
2. un _____ de guisantes congelados
3. cuatro _____ de ajo
4. una _____ de sal
5. tres _____ de consomé de pollo

B **Recordando detalles importantes** Lee la receta una vez más.
Luego, sin consultar la receta, escribe una lista de todos los
ingredientes necesarios. Luego consulta la receta para verificar
si has omitido algo.

C **Confirmando información** Verifica. ¿Sí o no?

	sí	no
1. Se puede cocinar el arroz con pollo encima de la estufa.		
2. El arroz con pollo lleva muchas papas.		
3. Hay muchos mariscos en un arroz con pollo.		
4. El arroz se pone amarillo.		
5. El chorizo es un tipo de salchicha española.		

Una receta para «la ropa vieja»

Antes de leer

A veces no podemos comer todo lo que está en nuestro plato. Lo que no comemos y dejamos en el plato son «las sobras». Piensa en unas recetas que tiene tu familia en que se usan las sobras.

Aquí tienes otra receta para un plato que es popular en muchas partes de Latinoamérica—sobre todo en Cuba. Se llama «ropa vieja»—un nombre divertido, ¿no? Se llama «ropa vieja» porque se puede elaborar con muchas sobras. Este plato tan conocido se originó en las islas Canarias.

Ropa vieja

Ingredientes
½ kg de carne (de ternera, bife) picada
1 cebolla
1 pimiento verde y un pimiento rojo
3 dientes de ajo
1 cucharadita de orégano
una pizca de pimienta
½ taza de tomate cocido (o enlatado)
3 cucharadas de aceite de oliva
½ taza de caldo (consomé de pollo)

Preparación o cocción
Corte los pimientos, las cebollas y los ajos en trocitos. Fría los pimientos, las cebollas y los ajos en el aceite de oliva con una pizca de pimienta y el orégano. Añada la carne picada y revuelva todos los ingredientes (unos dos minutos). Añada el caldo y cueza (cocine) a fuego mediano hasta que se evapore el caldo. Sirva con arroz blanco.

¿Comprendes?

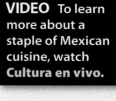

VIDEO To learn more about a staple of Mexican cuisine, watch **Cultura en vivo.**

Escoge o completa.

1. La ropa vieja viene de _____.
   a. Latinoamérica
   b. Cuba
   c. las islas Canarias

2. Se llama «ropa vieja» porque se puede elaborar (hacer) con _____.
   a. ropa
   b. comida que queda
   c. ingredientes divertidos

3. _____ es una cantidad muy pequeña.

4. Hay que _____ los pimientos verdes y rojos, la cebolla y los dientes de ajo en trocitos.
   a. cortar
   b. picar
   c. freír

5. Dos especias que lleva el plato son _____ y _____.

6. Cueza los ingredientes hasta que se evapore _____.
   a. el aceite
   b. el tomate
   c. el caldo

7. La ropa vieja se sirve acompañada de
   a. caldo
   b. azafrán
   c. arroz blanco

8. Un amigo vegetariano comerá la ropa vieja si no pones _____.

Vocabulario

1 **Parea.**

1. hervir   a. la salsa
2. freír   b. el pan
3. revolver   c. las zanahorias
4. pelar   d. el agua
5. cortar en rebanadas   e. sal y pimienta
6. añadir   f. el pollo

To review **Vocabulario,** turn to pages 300–301.

2 **Identifica.**

7.

8.

9.

10.

11.

12.

Gramática

3 **Completa.**

13–14. Él quiere que yo _____ y yo quiero que él _____. (hablar)

15–16. Tú quieres que nosotros lo _____ y nosotros queremos que tú lo _____. (leer)

17–18. Yo quiero que tú lo _____ y tú quieres que yo lo _____. (escribir)

19–20. Tú quieres que yo lo _____ y él quiere que tú lo _____. (hacer)

21–22. Nosotros queremos que ellos _____ y ellos quieren que nosotros _____. (ir)

To review **el subjuntivo,** turn to pages 304–305.

4 **Completa con el imperativo formal.**

23. _____ usted la comida. (preparar)

24. _____ usted la receta. (leer)

25. _____ usted la lata. (abrir)

26. _____ usted ahora. (salir)

27. Y _____ usted mañana. (regresar)

28. No me lo _____ usted. (decir)

29. No _____ usted más. (añadir)

To review **el imperativo formal,** turn to page 307.

5 **Escribe con el pronombre.**

30. Prepare usted *la ensalada*.

31. No prepare usted *el postre*.

32. Déme *las direcciones*.

6 **Escribe en la forma negativa.**

33. Luis, habla.

34. Jacinta, come más.

35. Carlos, levántate.

36. Teresa, ven.

To review **las formas negativas del imperativo familiar,** turn to page 309.

Cultura

7 **Contesta.**

37–40. ¿Cuáles son algunos ingredientes que lleva el arroz con pollo?

To review this cultural information, turn to page 312.

1 Yo en la cocina
✅ *Talk about cooking*
Habla con un(a) compañero(a) de clase. Dile si te gusta cocinar o no. Explícale por qué. Luego verifica si tu compañero(a) tiene las mismas opiniones que tú.

2 Comidas étnicas
✅ *Discuss and describe a restaurant and the food it serves*
¿Hay restaurantes étnicos, restaurantes que sirven comida de otras partes del mundo, en tu comunidad? Si hay, con un(a) compañero(a) preparen una lista de estos restaurantes y el tipo de comida que sirven. Luego describan un plato típico de uno de los restaurantes que les gusta.

3 ¡Qué comida más deliciosa!
✅ *Describe a delicious meal*
Estás viajando por México. Anoche fuiste a cenar en un restaurante y pediste algo que salió delicioso, muy rico. Te gustó mucho. Llama a tus padres y descríbeles el restaurante y el plato que te gustó tanto. Si puedes, explícales como crees que el cocinero preparó el plato.

CULTURA

La gente está sentada en la terraza de un café en Puebla, México.

4 Simón dice
✅ *Give and receive commands*
Trabajen ustedes en grupos de cinco. Van a jugar «Simón dice». Cada líder dará cinco órdenes a todos los miembros del grupo y luego escogerá a otro líder.

5 Mis padres
✅ *Discuss what your parents want you to do*
Tus padres quieren que hagas muchas cosas, ¿no? Dile a un(a) compañero(a) todo lo que quieren tus padres que hagas. Tu compañero(a) te dirá si sus padres quieren que él o ella haga las mismas cosas.

Tarea

Your teacher wants to know the recipe for the warm quesadillas and chilled fresh tomato salsa that you brought to the last Spanish Club meeting. Use the ingredients listed below and additional vocabulary from the chapter to give your teacher instructions on how to make this delicious, easy-to-prepare Mexican snack.

Quesadillas	Salsa de tomate
unas tortillas de harina	tomates
queso triturado	pimientos verdes
(shredded cheese)	cebolla
aceite de oliva	chiles jalapeños
	ajo
	cilantro
	jugo de lima

Writing Strategy

Giving Instructions When giving instructions, it is important to present the details accurately, clearly, and in logical order. This is especially true when writing a recipe because directions that are incorrect, unclear, or out of order could cause the dish to taste bad or be ruined altogether.

❶ Prewrite

Make a list of the steps for completing the recipe and put them in chronological order. Also think about what utensils and/or appliances will be used, and remember that timing and presentation are very important. What should be prepared first? What should be prepared last? How will the dish be served?

❷ Write

- Use formal commands since this is a recipe for your teacher.
- Make sure all of the steps follow a logical order.
- Use transition words to help you present your information in an organized way.
- Remember to stick to vocabulary you already know and don't attempt to translate from English to Spanish.

Evaluate

Your teacher will evaluate you on accurate and logical presentation of details, correct use of vocabulary and grammar, and completeness of information.

Repaso del Capítulo 10

Gramática

- **El subjuntivo** *(pages 304–305)*

  The subjunctive expresses that which is not necessarily factual or real.
  It expresses things that might happen.

  > **El profesor quiere que los alumnos lean el libro.**

  Review the following forms of the present subjunctive.

hablar	beber	escribir	poner
hable	beba	escriba	ponga
hables	bebas	escribas	pongas
hable	beba	escriba	ponga
hablemos	bebamos	escribamos	pongamos
habléis	*bebáis*	*escribáis*	*pongáis*
hablen	beban	escriban	pongan

  Review the following irregular forms of the present subjunctive.

dar	estar	ir	saber	ser
dé	esté	vaya	sepa	sea
des	estés	vayas	sepas	seas
dé	esté	vaya	sepa	sea
demos	estemos	vayamos	sepamos	seamos
deis	*estéis*	*vayáis*	*sepáis*	*seáis*
den	estén	vayan	sepan	sean

- **El imperativo** *(pages 307 and 309)*

  The affirmative and negative formal commands and the negative
  familiar commands use the subjunctive form of the verb.

(no) mire usted	(no) miren ustedes	no mires
(no) coma usted	(no) coman ustedes	no comas
(no) asista usted	(no) asistan ustedes	no asistas
(no) salga usted	(no) salgan ustedes	no salgas
(no) vaya usted	(no) vayan ustedes	no vayas

  Object pronouns are attached to affirmative commands but must
  come before negative commands. Review the following sentences.

Mírelo.	**No lo mire usted.**	**No lo mires.**
Démelas.	**No me las dé usted.**	**No me las des.**
Levántenlas.	**No las levanten ustedes.**	**No las levantes.**

¿Te acuerdas?

You learned the affirmative **tú** command in the previous chapter.

Juego There are a number of cognates in this list. See how many you and a partner can find. Who can find the most? Compare your list with those of your classmates.

Vocabulario

Talking about some kitchen appliances and utensils

la cocina	el horno	la olla, la cacerola
el refrigerador, la nevera	el horno de microondas	la tapa
el congelador	el lavaplatos	la cazuela
la estufa, la cocina	el/la sartén	la parrilla

Talking about food preparation

la receta	cortar	quemarse
el/la cocinero(a)	en pedacitos	hervir
el sabor	en rebanadas	freír
pelar	añadir	asar
picar	poner al fuego	revolver
	cocinar, cocer a fuego lento	

Identifying more foods

la chuleta de cerdo	la pechuga de pollo	el aguacate
el escalope de ternera	la cebolla	el ajo
el muslo de pollo	la zanahoria	el condimento
las alitas de pollo	el pepino	
	el pimiento	

Repaso cumulativo

Repasa lo que ya has aprendido

These activities will help you review and remember what you have learned so far in Spanish.

 Escucha las frases. Indica en una tabla como la de abajo si la información en cada frase es correcta o no.

sí	no

 Identifica.

1. todas las legumbres que ya conoces en español
2. todas las carnes que ya conoces en español
3. todo lo que necesitas para poner la mesa
4. la diferencia entre un desayuno continental y un desayuno americano

 Completa en el presente.

1. Yo _____ bife y Anita _____ pescado y nosotros dos _____ flan. (pedir)
2. Nosotros no nos _____. El mesero nos _____. (servir)
3. Yo _____ esto y él _____ el otro. Nosotros nunca _____ la misma cosa. (preferir)

 Describe las siguientes fiestas.

1. el Día de los Muertos
2. el Día de los Reyes
3. el Cuatro de Julio en Estados Unidos

 Completa con el imperativo.

1. José, _____ más. (comer)
2. Rosario, _____ el correo electrónico. (leer)
3. Manuel, _____ tu regalo. (abrir)
4. Adela, _____ acá. (venir)
5. Alberto, _____ pronto. (volver)
6. Federico, _____ la mesa. (poner)
7. Magda, _____ la verdad. (decir)
8. Gabriel, _____ la comida. (servir)

CULTURA

Una barbacoa para celebrar el Cuatro de Julio en Estados Unidos

6 Categoriza según el deporte.

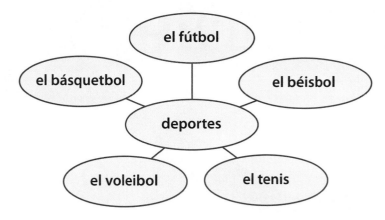

1. Un jugador lanza el balón y quiere que entre en la portería.
2. El portero no pudo bloquear el balón y el balón entró en la portería.
3. Un jugador corre de una base a otra.
4. Para marcar un tanto hay que meter el balón en el cesto.
5. El jugador corre y dribla con el balón.
6. La jugadora atrapa la pelota con el guante.
7. El balón o la pelota tiene que pasar por encima de la red.
8. Podemos jugar dobles o individuales.
9. Los jugadores juegan con un balón.
10. Los jugadores juegan con una pelota.

7 Usa las siguientes palabras en frases originales.

el campo   la cancha   el balón
   la pelota   el segundo tiempo   marcar
el tanto   lanzar   devolver

8 Prepara una lista de lo que tienes que comprar para preparar un plato favorito. Da las cantidades también.

¡Cuídate bien!

Aquí y Allí

Vamos a comparar Hoy en día todos quieren cuidarse bien y mantenerse en forma. No importa que sea aquí en Estados Unidos o en España o Latinoamérica—todos van a un parque o gimnasio para hacer ejercicios. Pero, a veces, ¿qué tenemos? ¡Un accidente pequeño!

Esta joven se mantiene en forma corriendo delante del museo de Artes y Ciencias en Valencia, España.

Objetivos

You will:

- identify more parts of the body
- talk about exercise
- talk about having a little accident and a trip to the emergency room
- discuss physical fitness

You will use:

- the subjunctive with impersonal expressions
- ojalá, quizás, tal vez
- the subjunctive of stem-changing verbs
- the comparison of like things

QuickPass

Go to glencoe.com
For: **Online book**
Web code: ASD7837c11

Introducción al tema

¡Cuídate bien!

Mira estas fotos para familiarizarte con el tema de este capítulo—cuídate bien. ¿Qué haces para cuidarte? ¿Hay algunas actividades que ves aquí que tú también practicas o que te gustan? Y, ¿puedes simpatizar con el joven ecuatoriano que ha tenido un accidente?

▲ **Chile** El joven anda en bici por las montañas. Nota que él también lleva casco. La seguridad siempre es importante, ¿no?

Ecuador Estos jóvenes van a jugar fútbol en un parque en Quito. ▼

▲ **Argentina** Mucha gente toma agua mineral porque la consideran buena para la salud.

◄ **México** La muchacha hace ejercicios en un gimnasio en la Ciudad de México.

▲ España El joven está practicando el monopatín en Barcelona. ¿Qué piensas? ¿Debe llevar casco?

▲ Guatemala Una ambulancia en Antigua, Guatemala

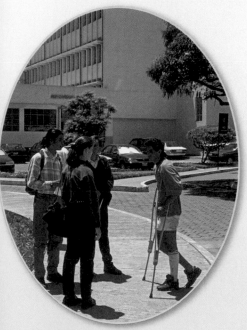

◄ Ecuador Uno de estos estudiantes de la Universidad Católica en Quito ha tenido un accidente y tiene que andar con muletas. Pero no es nada serio. No se ha hecho mucho daño.

▲ México Un hospital privado en Oaxaca, México

◄ España Esta familia en Barcelona patina en línea. Es un ejercicio bastante duro. Y nota que llevan casco para protegerse en caso de un accidente.

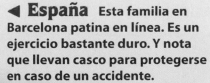

Más partes del cuerpo

la frente

el cuello

el pecho

el hombro

la muñeca

el dedo del pie

el tobillo

Los amigos están practicando yoga.
Hacen ejercicios de respiración.
Hacen movimientos lentos.
Liberan su espíritu de tensiones.

En el gimnasio

estirarse los brazos

hacer planchas

levantar pesas

La muchacha está haciendo
   ejercicios.
El señor anda en bicicleta.
El muchacho levanta pesas.
Es necesario que él tenga
   cuidado.
Es importante que todos
   hagamos ejercicios.

el casco

las rodilleras

el monopatín

un buzo

descansar

hacer jogging

Las jóvenes están patinando
en línea.
Es importante que lleven
casco y rodilleras.

Los corredores participan en un maratón.

Están corriendo una carrera de relevos.
Cada corredora corre una vuelta.

Es una carrera a campo traviesa.
Una carrera a campo traviesa es de larga distancia.

ESCUCHAR

 Escucha las frases. Parea cada frase con la foto que describe.

a.   b.   c.

ESCUCHAR • HABLAR

 Personaliza. Da respuestas personales.

1. ¿Haces muchos ejercicios?
2. ¿Haces ejercicios aeróbicos o abdominales?
3. ¿Te estiras los brazos y las piernas?
4. ¿Levantas pesas?
5. ¿Andas en bicicleta?
6. ¿Haces jogging?
7. ¿Participas en carreras?
8. ¿Corres vueltas?
9. ¿Practicas yoga?
10. ¿Has participado en un maratón?

LEER • ESCRIBIR

 Completa con una palabra apropiada.

1. Uno se pone _____ cuando va al gimnasio o cuando hace jogging.
2. Es importante ponerse _____ para proteger el cráneo al andar en bicicleta.
3. Es importante llevar _____ al patinar en línea.
4. ¿Cuántas _____ puedes correr sin descansar?
5. El yoga ayuda a liberar el espíritu de _____.
6. Muchas ciudades y organizaciones tienen _____ que son carreras de muy larga distancia.
7. Dos tipos de carreras son _____ y _____.

LEER • ESCRIBIR

 Pon las siguientes partes del cuerpo en orden desde la parte más alta del cuerpo hasta la más baja.

el pecho   la mano   el dedo del pie
la frente
el tobillo   el cuello   el hombro   la rodilla

Conexiones

La anatomía

La anatomía es el estudio de la estructura del cuerpo de un ser viviente y de sus órganos. Ya sabemos las partes del cuerpo humano pero son aun más importantes los órganos vitales—el corazón, los pulmones, los riñones, el hígado y el páncreas.

Más práctica

📖 Workbook, pp. 11.3–11.4
🌐 StudentWorks™ Plus

HABLAR

5 Dramatiza. Trabajen en grupos. Escojan a un líder. El líder va a dramatizar un ejercicio o un deporte. Los otros miembros del grupo adivinarán la actividad. Cambien de líder.

HABLAR • ESCRIBIR

6 Usa las siguientes expresiones en frases originales.

hacer ejercicios	**patinar en línea**	**hacer jogging**
practicar yoga	**correr vueltas**	**hacer planchas**

CULTURA

Equipo para hacer ejercicios en un gimnasio en un hotel en Montelimar, Nicaragua

ESCRIBIR

7 Completa con lo que falta.

1. el cue_o
2. las rodi_eras
3. el tobi_o
4. el _imnasio
5. los _óvenes
6. un bu_o
7. el bra_o

Comunicación

8 Trabajen en grupos y discutan las actividades que practican en su clase de educación física. Indiquen las actividades que les gustan y que no les gustan. Expliquen por qué.

Vocabulario 2

presentación

VIDEO To practice your new words, watch **Vocabulario en vivo**.

Unos accidentes

una herida

Pilar se cortó el dedo.
Tiene una herida.
Pero no es seria. No se ha hecho mucho daño.

José corría y se torció el tobillo.
El tobillo está hinchado.
Le duele mucho.

El joven se cayó.
¿Se rompió (Se quebró) la pierna?

la camilla

los socorristas

la ambulancia

En la sala de emergencia

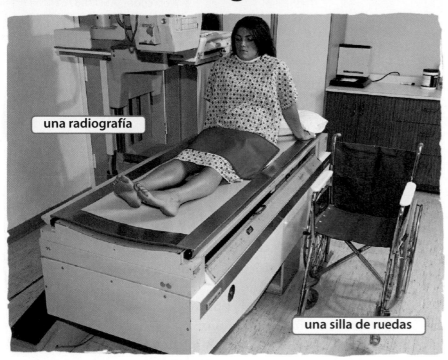

una radiografía

una silla de ruedas

Nota

- In addition to **hacerse daño,** you will hear **lastimarse.** Another term for **radiografía** is **rayos equis.**

Le toman (hacen) una radiografía.

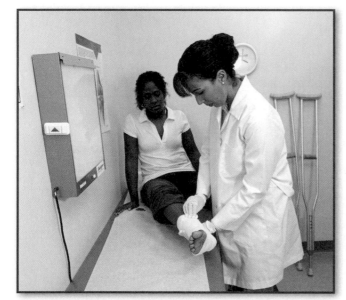

La cirujana ortopédica le ha reducido (acomodado) el hueso.
Le ha puesto la pierna en un yeso.
Paula tendrá que andar con muletas.

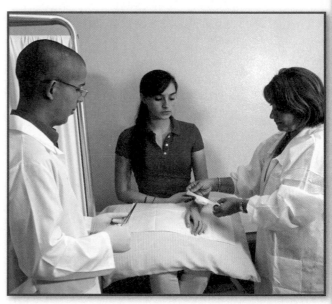

Es necesario que el médico cierre la herida.
El médico pone unos puntos (unas suturas).
La enfermera le va a poner una venda.

QuickPass

Go to glencoe.com
For: **Vocabulary practice**
Web code: **ASD7837c11**

ESCUCHAR

1 Escucha cada frase y decide si la información es correcta o no. Usa una tabla como la de abajo para indicar tus respuestas.

correcta	incorrecta

HABLAR • ESCRIBIR

2 Contesta sobre un accidente que tuvo Mariana.

1. Mariana ha tenido un accidente. ¿Se cayó ella?
2. ¿Se torció el tobillo?
3. ¿Le duele mucho el tobillo?
4. ¿Está hinchado el tobillo?
5. ¿Le duele mucho cuando anda a pie?
6. ¿Tendrá que andar con muletas?
7. ¿Se ha hecho mucho daño o no?

EXPANSIÓN

Ahora, sin mirar las preguntas, cuenta la información en tus propias palabras. Si no recuerdas algo, un(a) compañero(a) te puede ayudar.

ESCUCHAR • HABLAR • ESCRIBIR

3 Contesta según se indica.

1. ¿Qué tuvo Tomás? (un accidente serio)
2. ¿Qué le pasó? (se quebró la pierna)
3. ¿Qué le causó la pierna quebrada? (mucho dolor)
4. ¿Adónde fue? (a la sala de emergencia)
5. ¿Cómo fue? (en ambulancia)
6. ¿Quiénes lo ayudaron? (los socorristas)
7. ¿En qué lo pusieron? (una camilla)
8. ¿Qué le tomaron en el hospital? (radiografías)
9. ¿A qué médico llamaron? (al cirujano ortopédico)
10. Al salir del hospital, ¿qué necesitará Tomás? (una silla de ruedas)

EXPANSIÓN

Ahora, sin mirar las preguntas, cuenta la información en tus propias palabras. Si no recuerdas algo, un(a) compañero(a) te puede ayudar.

CULTURA

Un hospital grande y moderno en Barcelona, España

HABLAR • ESCRIBIR

4 Trabajen en grupos. Describan unas actividades que tienen lugar en esta sala de emergencia.

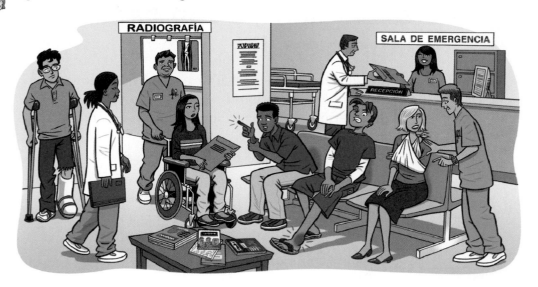

ESCRIBIR

5 Completa con lo que falta.

1. una _erida
2. un tobi_o _inchado
3. el _ospital
4. la cami_a y la si_a de ruedas
5. se ca_ó
6. el _eso
7. el _ueso
8. una _enda

ESCRIBIR

6 Rompecabezas

Pon las palabras en orden para formar frases. Luego, pon las frases en orden para crear una historia.

1. dijo no que le la necesitaba enfermera suturas
2. corrió la de cerca bicicleta perro muy un
3. calle la andaba por en Catalina bicicleta
4. de sala fue la a emergencia
5. rodilla enfermera venda la le en la puso una
6. ella perro a le cayó el se sorprendió y Catalina
7. rodilla cayó cortó se se la cuando

CULTURA

Los socorristas ayudan a un herido en una ambulancia en Madrid.

InfoGap For more practice with your new vocabulary, do Activity 11 on page SR13 at the end of this book.

QuickPass

Go to glencoe.com
For: Grammar practice
Web code: ASD7837c11

El subjuntivo con expresiones impersonales

The subjunctive is used after each of the following impersonal expressions because it is not known if the information in the clause that follows will actually take place. It may or may not.

es importante	es fácil
es necesario	es difícil
es imposible	es bueno
es posible	es probable
es mejor	es improbable

Es probable que él esté bien.
Pero es necesario que vea al médico.
Es importante que sepa lo que tiene.

Práctica

ESCUCHAR • HABLAR • ESCRIBIR

1 Sigue el modelo.

MODELO Tú haces ejercicios. →
Es necesario que tú hagas ejercicios.

1. Hablas con el entrenador.
2. Vas al gimnasio.
3. Haces jogging.
4. Corres por lo menos cinco vueltas.
5. Participas en el maratón.

HABLAR • ESCRIBIR

2 Prepara una lista de cosas que es probable que tú hagas con frecuencia porque es fácil hacerlas. Prepara otra lista que indica lo que es difícil que tú hagas. Luego compara tus listas con las listas que ha preparado un(a) compañero(a).

LEER • ESCRIBIR

3 Sigue el modelo.

MODELO es necesario / saber la receta →
Es necesario que el cocinero sepa la receta.

1. es importante / lavar las ollas
2. es fácil / pelar las papas
3. es probable / freír el pescado
4. es mejor / asar el cordero
5. es posible / servir la comida

CULTURA

Papi corre en un maratón con sus dos niños en Tenerife en las islas Canarias. Es posible que ganen, ¿no?

CULTURA

¿Es posible que el cocinero esté aprendiendo a cocinar algo en esta escuela culinaria en España?

HABLAR

4 Contesta.

1. ¿Es importante que los jóvenes de Estados Unidos estudien una lengua?
2. ¿Es necesario que ellos sepan hablar otra lengua?
3. ¿Es bueno que ellos hablen otra lengua?
4. ¿Es necesario que ellos conozcan otra cultura?
5. ¿Es posible que algún día ellos tengan la oportunidad de visitar otros países?
6. ¿Es probable que ellos vayan a otros países?

EXPANSIÓN

Ahora, sin mirar las preguntas, cuenta la información en tus propias palabras. Si no recuerdas algo, un(a) compañero(a) te puede ayudar.

LEER • ESCRIBIR

5 Completa.

Abuelito está un poco nervioso. Es posible que sus nietos ___1___ (llegar) mañana por la mañana. Es importante que abuelito ___2___ (saber) cuándo van a llegar. Pero es difícil que abuelita le ___3___ (decir) la hora precisa de la llegada de los nietos. Es posible que mañana ___4___ (hacer) mal tiempo. Como los nietos vienen en carro será necesario que ___5___ (conducir) despacio y con mucho cuidado si hay nieve. Es mejor que ellos ___6___ (llegar) un poco tarde. Abuelito no quiere que ellos ___7___ (tener) un accidente. Es mejor que ___8___ (llegar) tarde pero sanos y salvos.

FOLDABLES®
Study Organizer

TAB BOOK
See page SH25 for help with making this foldable. Use this study organizer to help you practice the subjunctive. On the top of each tab, write an expression that requires the subjunctive, for example **Es imposible que...** Then open each tab and write a sentence using that expression with the subjunctive.

Comunicación

6 Trabaja con un(a) compañero(a) de clase. Dile cosas que haces. Tu compañero(a) te dará su opinión sobre las cosas que haces usando las siguientes expresiones: **es importante, es bueno, es necesario, es mejor.**

¡Ojalá! ¡Quizás! ¡Tal vez!

The expression **¡Ojalá!** or **¡Ojalá que!** comes from Arabic and it means *Would that . . .* Since the information that follows **ojalá** may or may not happen, it is followed by the subjunctive. The expressions **¡Quizás!** and **¡Tal vez!** mean *perhaps* or *maybe* and can also be followed by the subjunctive.

> **¡Ojalá que vengan!**
> **¡Quizás lleguen mañana!**
> **¡Tal vez estén aquí!**

Práctica

ESCUCHAR • HABLAR

7 Contesta con **quizás** según el modelo.

MODELO ¿Carla lo va a saber? →
        ¡Quizás lo sepa!

1. ¿Carla va a estar aquí?
2. ¿Va a ir al parque?
3. ¿Va a participar en la carrera?
4. ¿Va a salir primero?
5. ¿Va a romper un récord?
6. ¿Va a ganar un trofeo?

LEER • ESCRIBIR

8 Sigue el modelo.

MODELO tener cuidado →
        ¡Ojalá que tengan cuidado!

1. prestar atención
2. no tomar una decisión ridícula
3. ponerse el casco
4. llevar rodilleras
5. no tener ningún accidente
6. no ir al hospital

CULTURA

Esta joven que anda con muletas acaba de salir de un centro médico en Trelew, Argentina. ¡Ojalá que se mejore pronto!

Comunicación

9 Work with a partner. Share some things that you hope will take place in your lifetime. Introduce your wishes with **¡ojalá!**

El subjuntivo de los verbos de cambio radical

1. Verbs that have a stem change in the present indicative also have a stem change in the present subjunctive.

E → IE			
cerrar			
yo	cierre	nosotros(as)	cerremos
tú	cierres	*vosotros(as)*	*cerréis*
Ud., él, ella	cierre	Uds., ellos, ellas	cierren

O → UE			
encontrar			
yo	encuentre	nosotros(as)	encontremos
tú	encuentres	*vosotros(as)*	*encontréis*
Ud., él, ella	encuentre	Uds., ellos, ellas	encuentren

2. The verbs **preferir** (e → ie), **dormir** (o → ue), and **pedir** (e → i) have a stem change in every person of the present subjunctive.

	E → IE, I	O → UE, U	E → I
	preferir	**dormir**	**pedir**
yo	prefiera	duerma	pida
tú	prefieras	duermas	pidas
Ud., él, ella	prefiera	duerma	pida
nosotros(as)	prefiramos	durmamos	pidamos
vosotros(as)	*prefiráis*	*durmáis*	*pidáis*
Uds., ellos, ellas	prefieran	duerman	pidan

Nota

- Other verbs with the **e → ie** stem change like **cerrar** are: **perder, sentarse, comenzar, empezar, pensar.**
- Other **o → ue** verbs like **encontrar** are: **acostarse, recordar, poder, volver.**
- **Sentir** is conjugated like **preferir.**
- Other verbs with the **e → i** stem change like **pedir** are: **repetir, freír, seguir, servir.**

HABLAR • ESCRIBIR

10 Contesta.

1. ¿Dónde quieres que yo me siente?
2. ¿Es importante que yo no pierda el juego?
3. ¿Quieres que yo vuelva temprano?
4. ¿Es posible que yo duerma aquí?
5. ¿Es necesario que yo se lo repita?

Según los jóvenes, es importante que todos sigamos una dieta sana.

VIDEO Want help with the subjunctive? Watch **Gramática en vivo.**

Práctica

LEER • ESCRIBIR

11 Sigue el modelo.

MODELO Quiere que tú lo cierres. →
Quiere que nosotros lo cerremos.

1. Quiere que te sientes aquí.
2. Quiere que tú pierdas.
3. Quiere que tú lo encuentres.
4. Quiere que tú vuelvas pronto.
5. Quiere que duermas aquí.
6. Quiere que lo pidas.
7. Quiere que lo sigas.
8. Quiere que tú no lo repitas.

HABLAR • LEER • ESCRIBIR

12 Cambia el segundo verbo al verbo indicado.

1. Yo quiero que ellos lo cierren. (empezar, perder, encontrar, recordar, devolver, preferir, pedir, repetir)
2. Es posible que yo lo encuentre. (cerrar, perder, recordar, devolver, servir, pedir, repetir)
3. Es necesario que nosotros volvamos. (comenzar, sentarnos, recordar, dormir, seguir)

Comparación de igualdad

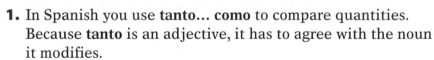

1. In Spanish you use **tanto… como** to compare quantities. Because **tanto** is an adjective, it has to agree with the noun it modifies.

   Elena tiene tanta energía como yo.
   Pero ella no tiene tantos accidentes como yo.

2. In Spanish you use **tan… como** to compare qualitites with either an adjective or adverb.

   Él está tan enfermo como su amiga.
   Él se va a curar tan rápido como ella.

3. The subject pronoun always follows the comparison of equality.

   Él es tan bueno como tú.
   Y tiene tanto dinero como yo.

Conexiones

El inglés

To compare equal quantities in English you use:
as much money as I
as many problems as I
To compare equal qualities you use:
as smart as she
as tall as he

Práctica

Más práctica

📘 Workbook, pp. 11.11–11.12
💻 StudentWorks™ Plus

HABLAR

 13 Personaliza. Da respuestas personales.

1. ¿Eres tan inteligente como tus amigos?
2. ¿Eres tan cómico(a) como tus amigos?
3. ¿Eres tan ambicioso(a) como tus amigos?
4. ¿Eres tan aficionado(a) a los deportes como tus amigos?
5. ¿Tienes tanta paciencia como tus amigos?
6. ¿Tienes tanto éxito como tus amigos?
7. ¿Tienes tanto trabajo como tus amigos?
8. ¿Tienes tantas ambiciones como tus amigos?

LEER • ESCRIBIR

 14 Completa con **tan** o **tanto como**.

1. Ella corre en _____ carreras _____ yo.
2. Y ella va _____ rápido _____ yo.
3. Él puede levantar _____ pesas _____ yo.
4. Pero él no es _____ fuerte _____ yo.
5. Yo no hago _____ ejercicios _____ tú.
6. Yo no soy _____ aficionado(a) a los ejercicios físicos _____ tú.

Refrán

Can you guess what the following proverb means?

La mejor almohada es la conciencia sana.

CULTURA

Un grupo de gente mayor (de la tercera edad) está jugando voleibol en un gimnasio en Oaxaca, México.

Comunicación

 15 Trabaja con un(a) compañero(a). Piensen en algunas personas que ustedes conocen que, en su opinión, tienen mucho en común o que tienen las mismas características físicas. Comparen a estas personas.

¡Bravo!

You have now learned all the new vocabulary and grammar in this chapter. Continue to use and practice all that you know while learning more cultural information. ¡Vamos!

QuickPass

Go to glencoe.com
For: **Conversation practice**
Web code: ASD7837c11

¿Comprendes?

A Contesta según la información en la conversación.

1. ¿Qué hacía Enrique cuando se cayó?
2. ¿Qué le duele?
3. ¿Cómo está el tobillo?
4. ¿Qué crees? ¿Quiere Enrique que Catalina lo lleve a la sala de emergencia? ¿Le gusta la idea?
5. Según Catalina, ¿por qué debe ir Enrique a la sala de emergencia?
6. ¿Es posible que no tenga el tobillo quebrado?

B **Resumiendo** Cuenta todo lo que pasó en la conversación en tus propias palabras.

C **Prediciendo** Predice lo que va a pasar a Enrique y Catalina en la sala de emergencia. Prepara una conversación que tiene lugar en el hospital. Debes incluir a otros en la conversación como el médico o el enfermero. ¡Usa tanta imaginación posible!

VIDEO To see how one friend helps another after a skateboarding accident, watch **Diálogo en vivo.**

GeoVistas

To learn more about Panama, take a tour on pages SH52–SH53.

Entrada a la sala de emergencias en un hospital en la Ciudad de Panamá

CULTURA

EMERGENCIAS

HOSPITAL PUNTA PACIFICA
Afiliado a Johns Hopkins Medicine International

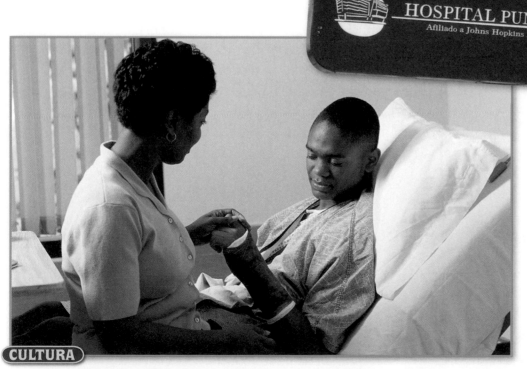

CULTURA

Es necesario que él se cuide bien.
Es posible que le duela mucho el brazo, ¿no?

Antes de leer

Dale una ojeada a la lectura y busca palabras que consideres desconocidas. No habrá muchas.

CULTURA

Están haciendo ejercicios aeróbicos en un gimnasio en Buenos Aires, Argentina.

✓ **Reading Check**

¿Qué hacen todos en el gimnasio?

Durante la lectura

Busca clarificaciones—si hay una palabra que no sabes, tal vez haya un sinónimo en la frase.

✓ **Reading Check**

¿Cuál es la ventaja de los parques?

Vida activa y buena salud

Hoy en día el interés que tenemos en nuestra salud y forma física es fenomenal. Y este interés existe en España y Latinoamérica igual que en Estados Unidos.

Como es importante que uno haga ejercicios a lo menos tres veces a la semana, hay una gran proliferación de gimnasios. Estos gimnasios tienen muchos socios[1]. En el gimnasio hacen ejercicios aeróbicos y abdominales. Se estiran los brazos y las piernas. Hacen planchas. Algunos levantan pesas. ¡Todo para mantenerse en forma!

Además de los gimnasios los parques son inmensamente populares, y para ir a un parque no hay que ser socio o miembro. Un parque es un buen lugar para hacer jogging o correr unas vueltas. A muchos les gusta dar un paseo por el parque en bicicleta. Andar en bicicleta es una forma excelente de ejercicio. Otros se sientan en un lugar aislado del parque donde disfrutan del silencio y de la tranquilidad. Se relajan practicando yoga y meditando.

[1]socios *members*

CULTURA

El ciclista está haciendo ejercicios en un parque en Viña del Mar, Chile.

Muchas ciudades tienen un maratón a lo menos una vez al año. Muchos maratones tienen un propósito benévolo[2] y atraen a muchos participantes. Además atraen a muchos espectadores que animan a los corredores que tienen que correr largas distancias.

Entre los jóvenes el patinaje en línea y el monopatín son muy apreciados. Tienen muchos aficionados. Pero, una advertencia[3]—al practicar estas formas de patinaje hay que tener mucho cuidado porque puedes lastimarte fácilmente. Siempre tienes que llevar casco y rodilleras. Nadie quiere que te hagas daño y que te encuentres en una sala de emergencia.

[2]propósito benévolo   *charitable purpose*   [3]advertencia   *warning*

Más práctica

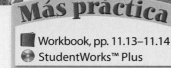

■ Workbook, pp. 11.13–11.14
● StudentWorks™ Plus

✓ **Reading Check**
¿Quiénes animan a los corredores en el maratón?

✓ **Reading Check**
¿Qué hay que tener al practicar el patinaje o el monopatín? ¿Por qué?

¿Comprendes?

A **Categorizando** Completa la tabla según la información en la lectura.

actividades en un gimnasio	actividades en el parque	actividades durante un maratón	actividades populares entre los jóvenes

B **Personalizando** Contesta.
¿En qué actividades de la Actividad A participas? Explica por qué te gustan.

C **Analizando** Contesta.
¿Por qué son populares los gimnasios y los parques?

Después de leer

Prepara una lista de palabras aparentadas que encontraste en la lectura.

CULTURA
Los jóvenes están patinando en línea en Barcelona, España.

Médicos Sin Fronteras 🎧♻️

Antes de leer

Piensa en unas organizaciones benévolas o caritativas donde vives. ¿Qué tipo de trabajo hacen? ¿Has oído de *Médicos Sin Fronteras,* una famosa organización internacional?

Hay gente que se cuida bien y también hay gente que cuida de otros como los Médicos Sin Fronteras. La organización Médicos Sin Fronteras tuvo su origen en Francia en 1971. Un grupo de médicos y periodistas franceses fueron a África con la Cruz Roja donde vieron morir a millones de biafranos[1] de guerra[2] y de hambre. Su situación fue tan desesperada que a su regreso a Francia este grupo de médicos creó una organización pequeña, *Médecins Sans Frontières.* Hoy es una organización internacional independiente con más de dos mil quinientos benévolos (voluntarios) presentes en más de setenta países, incluyendo unos en Latinoamérica. La organización tiene proyectos en zonas de guerra, campos de refugiados y en regiones devastadas por desastres naturales o epidemias de enfermedades como el sida[3].

Entre los benévolos hay médicos, cirujanos, enfermeros y técnicos. Hay también personas que se responsabilizan por los materiales que necesitan y la administración de los proyectos. Todos reciben muy poco dinero por el trabajo maravilloso que hacen.

En 1999 Médicos Sin Fronteras ganó el prestigioso Premio Nobel de la Paz.

[1]biafranos   *people from Biafra*   [3]sida   *AIDS*
[2]guerra   *war*

¿Comprendes?

Escoge.

1. Los Médicos Sin Fronteras _____.
   a. se cuidan bien
   b. cuidan de otros
   c. no tienen país
   d. son todos franceses

2. La organización Médicos Sin Fronteras tuvo su origen en _____.
   a. Francia
   b. Biafra, África
   c. la Cruz Roja
   d. una situación desesperada

3. ¿Quiénes establecieron la organización?
   a. miembros de la Cruz Roja
   b. un grupo internacional independiente
   c. un grupo de médicos y periodistas franceses
   d. un grupo de benévolos

4. Los biafranos morían _____.
   a. de un desastre natural
   b. de una epidemia
   c. de malnutrición y guerra
   d. a causa del calor

5. Por lo general, ¿quiénes toman refugio en los campos de refugiados?
   a. las víctimas de guerra
   b. los benévolos
   c. los enfermos
   d. los soldados

6. Los benévolos que trabajan con la organización _____.
   a. son todos personal médico
   b. tienen un salario
   c. reciben muy poco dinero
   d. viven de proyectos

CULTURA

Un médico de la organización Médicos Sin Fronteras da atención médica a una familia hondureña después de un huracán.

Vocabulario

1 **Identifica.**

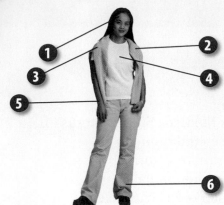

To review **Vocabulario 1,** turn to pages 328–329.

2 **Corrige.**

7. Es importante que uno lleve casco y rodilleras si levanta pesas.

8. A mucha gente le gusta andar en monopatín en el hospital.

9. Un maratón es una carrera de corta distancia.

10. Antes de correr, los corredores se estiran los dedos y los pies.

11. Cuando practicas yoga, haces muchas planchas.

3 **Identifica.**

12.  13.

14.  15.

To review **Vocabulario 2,** turn to pages 332–333.

4 **Completa.**

16. El niño se _____ el tobillo y lo tiene muy hinchado.

17. Se _____ la pierna y el cirujano ortopédico la tiene que poner en un yeso.

18. Los socorristas pusieron a la víctima en una camilla y la llevaron al hospital en _____.

19. José necesita ayuda para andar. Anda con _____.

Gramática

5 **Completa.**

20. Es importante que nosotros _____ ejercicios. (hacer)
21. Es necesario que ellos nos _____. (acompañar)
22. Es posible que ella _____. (estar)
23. Es probable que yo _____. (ir)
24. Es imposible que tú lo _____. (saber)

To review **el subjuntivo con expresiones impersonales,** turn to page 336.

6 **Completa formando una frase.**

25. Es necesario que…
26. Es posible que…
27. Es difícil que…

7 **Completa.**

28. ¡Ojalá _____ su equipo! (ganar)
29. ¡Quizás _____ ellos! (venir)
30. ¡Tal vez _____ (ellos) en el gimnasio! (estar)
31. ¡Ojalá _____ (tú) los resultados mañana! (tener)

To review **ojalá, quizás, tal vez,** turn to page 338.

8 **Completa las frases con nosotros.**

32. Ellos quieren que tú se lo pidas a Javier.
    Ellos quieren que nosotros…
33. Ella quiere que yo me siente aquí.
    Ella quiere que nosotros…

To review **el subjuntivo de los verbos de cambio radical,** turn to page 339.

9 **Completa con tan… como o tanto… como.**

34. A veces los hospitales en las zonas rurales no son _____ buenos _____ los de las grandes ciudades.
35. Esta clínica es _____ moderna _____ la otra.
36. Ella tiene _____ paciencia _____ yo.
37. Yo hago _____ ejercicios _____ tú.

To review **la comparación de igualdad,** turn to page 340.

Cultura

10 **Contesta.**

38. ¿Por qué hay gimnasios que tienen muchos socios?
39. ¿Cuáles son algunas actividades atléticas que practica la gente en un parque?
40. ¿Qué propósito tienen muchos maratones?

To review this cultural information, turn to pages 344–345.

1 Actividades atléticas

✓ *Discuss which sports you play*

Trabajen en grupos de tres o cuatro. Discutan todas las actividades atléticas en que participan ustedes. Determinen si tienen los mismos intereses o no.

2 Peligros

✓ *Talk about avoiding danger*

Las actividades atléticas pueden ser buenas para la salud pero cuando practicas ciertas actividades hay que tener cuidado de no lastimarte. ¿Cuáles son algunas cosas que debes hacer para evitar (no tener) accidentes?

3 Un accidente

✓ *Describe an accident you had when you were young*

Explica si tú eres propenso(a) a accidentes o si lo eras de niño(a). ¿Has tenido unos accidentes? Descríbelos. Si nunca has tenido un accidente explica como es posible que tengas tanta suerte.

4 Importante y necesario

✓ *Talk about what is important for you to do and what is necessary for you to do*

Completa una tabla como la de abajo y presenta la información a tu clase.

Es importante que yo	Y es necesario que yo
porque	

5 En la sala de emergencia

✓ *Helping someone out after an accident*

Estás en la sala de espera de la sala de emergencia en un hospital. Entran los padres con su hijo que ha tenido un accidente y se ha hecho daño. Los padres están nerviosos y solo hablan español. Ayúdalos.

Prepárate para el examen
Practice for written proficiency

Tarea

You have learned about many sports in Spanish. You have also learned about the parts of the body and physical fitness. Now you are going to write a research paper that discusses the physical benefits of some sports. Use the library and the Internet to find out more about how your body stays fit by doing each sport. Be sure to cite your sources.

Writing Strategy

Researching As you prepare to write your research paper, you will be consulting many sources for information. It is important that your sources be reliable, especially when they are found on the Internet. It is advisable to consult more than one source for any fact you present. If your two sources disagree, consult a third.

1 Prewrite

- Before you begin your research, create a rough outline of your paper. This will help you identify the topics you need to research.

Título
A. El fútbol
1. ¿Cómo se mantiene uno en forma jugando fútbol?
a.
b.
2. ¿Cuáles son algunas desventajas o peligros del fútbol?
a.
b.
B. El jogging
1. ¿Cómo se mantiene uno en forma haciendo jogging?

- As you research, fill the holes in your outline.

CULTURA

El andinista venezolano tiene todo el equipo necesario para escaladar montañas.

2 Write

- Use your outline as a guide while you write. It will ensure your information is organized and that nothing is omitted.
- It is very important to cite the sources you used to obtain information. This will add validity to your paper and it will also ensure that you do not plagiarize.

Evaluate

Your teacher will evaluate you on organization of information, correctness of grammar, and proper citation.

Repaso del Capítulo 11

Gramática

- ### El subjuntivo con expresiones impersonales *(page 336)*
  The subjunctive is used after many impersonal expressions when it is not known if the information that follows will or will not take place.

  Es importante que tengas cuidado cuando levantas pesas.
  Es necesario que la niña lleve casco cuando anda en bicicleta.
  Es probable que ellos lleguen a tiempo.

- ### ¡Ojalá! ¡Quizás! ¡Tal vez! *(page 338)*
  The expressions **¡Ojalá!**, **¡Quizás!**, and **¡Tal vez!** are also followed by the subjunctive. Review the following sentences.

  ¡Ojalá no te hagas daño!
  Quizás vengan mañana.

- ### El subjuntivo de los verbos de cambio radical *(page 339)*
  Verbs that have a stem change in the present indicative also have a stem change in the present subjunctive.

cerrar		encontrar	
cierre	cerremos	encuentre	encontremos
cierres	*cerréis*	encuentres	*encontréis*
cierre	cierren	encuentre	encuentren

  Preferir and **sentir** (e → ie, i), **dormir** (o → ue, u), and **pedir, repetir, freír, seguir,** and **servir** (e → i, i) have a stem change in every person of the subjunctive. Review the following forms.

preferir		dormir		pedir	
prefiera	prefiramos	duerma	durmamos	pida	pidamos
prefieras	*prefiráis*	duermas	*durmáis*	pidas	*pidáis*
prefiera	prefieran	duerma	duerman	pida	pidan

- ### Comparación de igualdad *(page 340)*
  You use **tanto… como** to compare like quantities and **tan… como** to compare like qualities.

  Yo tengo tanta paciencia como mi padre.
  Anita hace tantos ejercicios como yo.

  La señora Mayo es tan simpática como la señora Hernández.
  Manolo corre tan rápido como tú.

CULTURA

Los jóvenes están haciendo jogging en Barcelona, España.

Vocabulario

Identifying more parts of the body

la frente	el hombro	la muñeca	el dedo del pie
el cuello	el pecho	el tobillo	

Talking about physical fitness

el gimnasio	las pesas	una carrera	estirarse
el buzo	el movimiento	de relevos	patinar
el casco	la respiración	a campo traviesa	en línea
las rodilleras	el monopatín	de larga distancia	practicar yoga
los ejercicios	el jogging	una vuelta	descansar
las planchas	el/la corredor(a)	un maratón	liberar

Talking about an accident

una herida	cortarse	caerse	doler
hinchado(a)	torcerse	romperse, quebrarse	hacerse daño

Talking about medical emergencies and a hospital

la ambulancia	la sala de	la silla de ruedas
el/la socorrista	emergencia	andar con muletas
la camilla		

Talking about medical care

el/la cirujano(a) ortopédico(a)	una radiografía	los puntos, las suturas	reducir, acomodar
el/la enfermero(a)	un yeso	una venda	
	un hueso		

Other useful words and expressions

el espíritu	lento(a)
la tensión	

Repaso cumulativo

Repasa lo que ya has aprendido

These activities will help you review and remember
what you have learned so far in Spanish.

 1 Escucha las frases. Indica en una tabla como la de
abajo a quien habla el joven en cada frase.

a un(a) amigo(a)	a su profesor(a)	a sus padres

 2 Sigue el modelo.

MODELO —Son mis zapatos nuevos.
—¿Quién te los compró?

1. Es mi cámara nueva.
2. Es mi casco nuevo.
3. Son mis gafas nuevas.
4. Son mis esquís nuevos.
5. Son mis botas nuevas.

 3 Completa con los pronombres.

1. Yo le di los CDs a Anita.

   Yo _____ di a ella.
2. Carlos le devolvió el dinero a Juan.

   Carlos _____ devolvió a él.
3. Sara le dio las direcciones a usted.

   Sara _____ dio.
4. Yo leí la receta a Susana.

   Yo _____ leí a ella.
5. Yo no le preparé la comida.

   Yo no _____ preparé.

Completa cada serie de frases en el presente, el pretérito y el imperfecto.

hablar

1. a. Yo _____ con Juan todos los días.

   b. Yo _____ con Juan ayer.

   c. Yo _____ mucho con Juan cuando éramos niños.

vender

2. a. Mi padre _____ carros.

   b. Ayer él _____ dos.

   c. Pero cuando yo era niño él no _____ carros.

escribir

3. a. Ahora nosotros le _____ un correo electrónico todos los días.

   b. Nosotros le _____ un correo electrónico el otro día.

   c. Nosotros le _____ correos electrónicos casi a diario cuando estaba en España.

hacer

4. a. No lo _____ yo.

   b. No lo _____ yo ayer.

   c. Yo no lo _____ nunca.

poner

5. a. ¿Por qué no _____ (tú) las maletas en la maletera?

   b. ¿Por qué no _____ (tú) las maletas en la maletera cuando fuiste al aeropuerto?

   c. Cada vez que hacías un viaje _____ las maletas en la maletera.

decir

6. a. Yo siempre _____ la verdad.

   b. Yo no te _____ una mentira. Fue la verdad.

   c. Yo nunca _____ mentiras—siempre la verdad.

poder

7. a. Ellos _____ hacerlo ahora.

   b. Ellos intentaron pero no _____ hacerlo.

   c. Ellos _____ hacerlo cuando eran más jóvenes.

CULTURA

El señor compraba el periódico cada día en el mismo quiosco en Buenos Aires, Argentina.

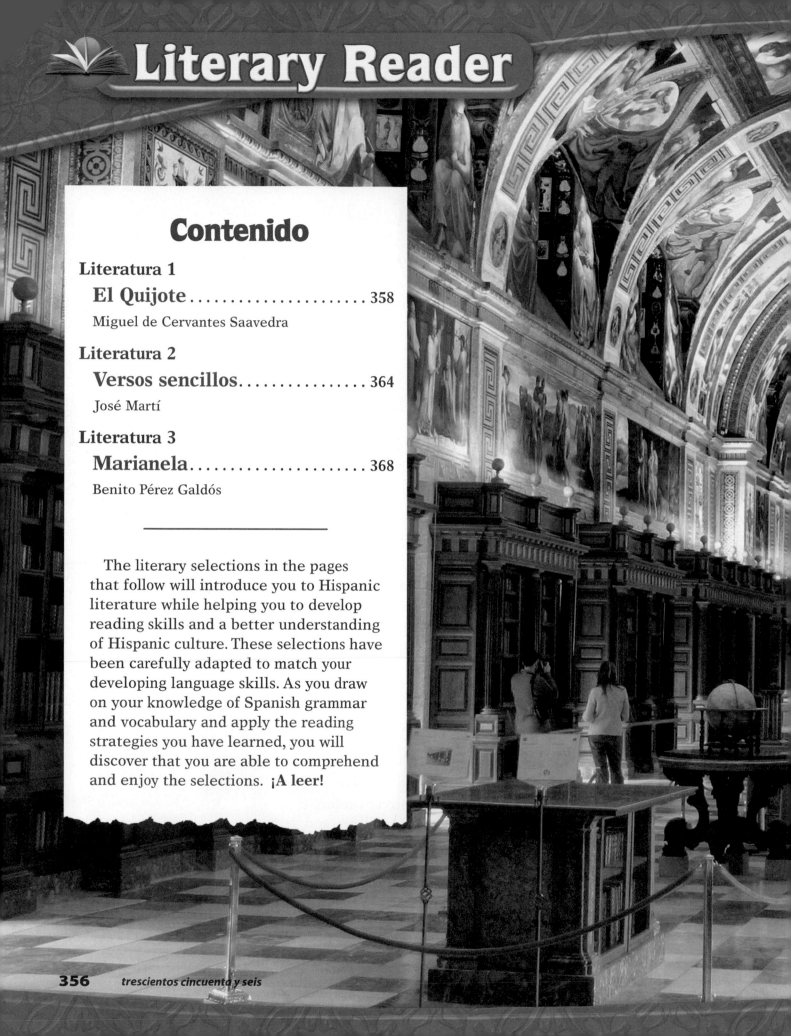

Literary Reader

Contenido

The literary selections in the pages that follow will introduce you to Hispanic literature while helping you to develop reading skills and a better understanding of Hispanic culture. These selections have been carefully adapted to match your developing language skills. As you draw on your knowledge of Spanish grammar and vocabulary and apply the reading strategies you have learned, you will discover that you are able to comprehend and enjoy the selections. **¡A leer!**

El Quijote

de Miguel de Cervantes Saavedra

flaco

la lanza

el caballo

gordo

CULTURA

Don Quijote es un caballero andante. Sancho Panza es su escudero. Don Quijote tiene una lanza.

Vocabulario

Estudia las siguientes palabras y sus definiciones.

el mal   lo contrario de «bien»; una desgracia, un daño
una tontería   una cosa absurda
la guerra   una larga serie de batallas
espantable   horrible
sabio(a)   muy inteligente
desviar   disuadir, apartar o alejar a alguien de su camino
hacerle caso a alguien   prestarle atención
a toda prisa   rápido

Práctica

A Contesta.

1. ¿Tiene escudero don Quijote? ¿Quién es su escudero?
2. ¿Monta don Quijote a caballo o en un asno?
3. ¿Existen males en el mundo o es todo bueno?
4. ¿Hay una guerra en este momento?
5. ¿Son espantables las guerras?

B Expresa de otra manera.

1. Él siempre está haciendo *cosas ridículas*.
2. No hay duda. Es un señor *muy inteligente*.
3. Ellos tenían miedo y salieron *rápido*.
4. Él nunca quiere *prestarle atención* a nadie.
5. Cuando quiere hacer algo es díficil *disuadirlo*.

C Da la palabra cuya definición sigue.

1. a toda velocidad
2. de mucha inteligencia
3. una estupidez
4. espantoso, asqueroso
5. vicio, imperfección

INTRODUCCIÓN

La obra más famosa de todas las letras hispanas es la novela *El ingenioso hidalgo don Quijote de la Mancha* de Miguel de Cervantes Saavedra.

Los dos personajes principales de la novela son don Quijote y Sancho Panza. Don Quijote, un hombre alto y delgado, es un caballero andante. Es un idealista que quiere conquistar todos los males del mundo. Su escudero, Sancho Panza, es un hombre bajo y gordo. Él es un realista puro. Siempre trata de° desviar a don Quijote de sus ilusiones y aventuras.

trata de *he tries*

El Quijote
⁓ 1 ⁓

Un día, don Quijote salió de su pueblo en la región de la Mancha. Un idealista sin par°, don Quijote salió en busca de aventuras para conquistar los males del mundo. Es el trabajo de un verdadero caballero andante. Pero después de unos pocos días, don Quijote volvió a casa porque hizo su primera expedición sin escudero. No hay caballero andante sin escudero—sobre todo un caballero andante de la categoría de don Quijote.

sin par *without equal*

Cuando volvió a su pueblo, empezó a buscar un escudero. Por fin encontró a un vecino, Sancho Panza, un hombre bajo y gordo. Salió por segunda vez, esta vez acompañado de su escudero. Don Quijote montó a su caballo, Rocinante, y Sancho lo siguió montado en su asno.

CULTURA

Don Quijote anda a caballo y Sancho anda en su asno.

⤬2⤬

Los dos hicieron muchas expediciones por la región de la Mancha. El idealista don Quijote hizo muchas cosas que no quiso hacer el realista Sancho Panza. Más de una vez Sancho le dijo: —Pero, don Quijote, noble caballero y fiel compañero, Vuestra Merced° está loco°. ¿Por qué no dejamos con° estas tonterías? ¿Por qué no volvemos a casa? Yo quiero comer. Y quiero dormir en mi cama.

Don Quijote no les hizo mucho caso a los consejos° de Sancho. Uno de los episodios más famosos de nuestro estimado caballero es el episodio de los molinos de viento.

Vuestra Merced *Your Highness*
loco *crazy*
dejamos con *we put an end to*

consejos *advice*

⤬3⤬

Del buen suceso que el valeroso don Quijote tuvo en la espantable y jamás imaginada aventura de los molinos de viento.

En esto descubrieron treinta o cuarenta molinos de viento que hay en aquel campo; y así como° don Quijote los vio, dijo a su escudero: —¡Sancho! ¡Mira! ¿Tú ves lo que veo yo?

—No, Vuestra Merced. No veo nada.

—Amigo Sancho, ¿no ves allí unos treinta o más gigantes que vienen hacia nosotros a hacer batalla?

—¿Qué gigantes?

—Aquellos que allí ves, de los brazos largos.

—Don Quijote. No son gigantes. Son simples molinos de viento. Y lo que en ellos parecen° brazos son aspas.

—Bien parece, Sancho, que tú no sabes nada de aventuras. Ellos son gigantes. Y si tienes miedo...

—¡Don Quijote! ¿Adónde va Vuestra Merced?

así como *as soon as*

parecen *appear to be*

CULTURA

Los molinos de viento tienen aspas.

¿Adónde fue don Quijote? Él fue a hacer batalla con los terribles gigantes. Gigantes como estos no deben ni pueden existir en el mundo. En nombre de Dulcinea, la dama de sus pensamientos°, don Quijote los atacó. Puso su lanza en el aspa de uno de los molinos. En el mismo instante vino un viento fuerte. El viento movió las aspas. El viento las revolvió con tanta furia que hizo pedazos° de la lanza de don Quijote y levantó a don Quijote en el aire.

A toda prisa el pobre Sancho fue a socorrer° a su caballero andante. Lo encontró en el suelo muy mal herido°.

—Don Quijote, le dije a Vuestra Merced que no vio gigantes. Vio simples molinos de viento. No puedo comprender por qué los atacó.

—Sancho, tú no sabes lo que dices. Son cosas de guerra que tú no comprendes. Tú sabes que tengo un enemigo. Mi enemigo es el horrible pero sabio monstruo Frestón. Te dije las cosas malas que él hace. Y ahora convirtió a los gigantes en molinos de viento.

—Yo no sé lo que hizo vuestro enemigo, Frestón. Pero yo sé lo que le hizo el molino de viento.

Sancho levantó a don Quijote del suelo. Don Quijote subió de nuevo sobre Rocinante. Habló más de la pasada aventura pero Sancho no le hizo caso. Siguieron el camino hacia Puerto Lápice en busca de otras aventuras jamás imaginadas.

dama de sus pensamientos *lady of his dreams*

pedazos *pieces*

socorrer *help*
herido *injured*

¿Comprendes?

A **Recordando hechos** Escoge.

1. Don Quijote es _____.
   a. un realista
   b. un idealista
   c. un escudero

2. Don Quijote salió de su pueblo _____.
   a. en busca de la Mancha
   b. en busca de un escudero
   c. en busca de aventuras

3. Don Quijote volvió a casa para _____.
   a. comenzar su primera expedición
   b. buscar un escudero
   c. ver a Dulcinea

4. Sancho Panza es _____.
   a. un caballero andante también
   b. un idealista sin par
   c. un vecino de don Quijote

5. Sancho Panza tiene _____.
   a. un asno
   b. un caballo
   c. una lanza

B **Confirmando información** Usa una tabla como la de abajo para indicar si la información es correcta o no.

	correcta	incorrecta
1. Don Quijote y Sancho Panza hicieron solo dos expediciones.		
2. Sancho le dice a don Quijote que está loco.		
3. Don Quijote siempre quiere volver a casa.		
4. Un episodio famoso del *Quijote* es el episodio de los molinos de viento.		

C **Buscando información** Busca la información en la lectura para completar cada frase.

    1. Hay unos _____ molinos de viento en el campo.

    2. Don Quijote le dice a Sancho que ve unos _____.

    3. Estos vienen hacia don Quijote y Sancho para _____.

    4. Don Quijote dice que tienen _____.

    5. Pero Sancho no ve _____, solamente _____.

                 4

D **Recordando hechos** Contesta.

    1. ¿Contra quiénes fue don Quijote a hacer batalla?

    2. ¿En dónde puso su lanza?

    3. ¿Qué hizo mover el aspa?

    4. ¿Revolvió rápidamente el aspa?

    5. ¿Adónde levantó a don Quijote?

    6. ¿Dónde encontró Sancho a don Quijote?

    7. ¿Quién convirtió a los gigantes en molinos de viento?

    8. Cuando Sancho levantó a don Quijote del suelo, ¿volvieron a casa?

    9. Después de este episodio, ¿admite don Quijote que los gigantes son molinos de viento?

E **Causa y efecto** When an event or action causes other things to happen it is called a *cause-and-effect relationship*. In English, explain the cause and effect of don Quijote's actions.

F **Comparando y contrastando** When you describe how two or more things are similar, you are *comparing* them. When you describe how they are different, you are *contrasting* them. Compare and contrast Sancho Panza's reasoning with that of Don Quijote.

CULTURA

Una librería en León, Nicaragua, que lleva el nombre de don Quijote

Versos sencillos

de José Martí

Estatua de José Martí en La Habana

Esta pulsera de diamantes es una joya preciosa.

Vocabulario

Estudia las siguientes palabras y sus definiciones.

el monte   elevación natural de terreno, montaña
las joyas   adornos de oro, plata, diamantes, esmeraldas, etc.
el joyero   el que vende joyas
el corazón   órgano vital muscular que impulsa la sangre
arrancar   sacar o quitar con violencia

Práctica

Completa con la palabra apropiada.

1. Me causó tanto dolor y tristeza que me _____ el corazón.
2. El _____ y los pulmones son órganos vitales.
3. Un anillo de oro con diamantes es una _____.
4. El _____ vende anillos, brazaletes (pulseras) y pendientes (aretes) en su joyería.
5. No hay muchos _____ en un estado como Kansas o Nebraska.

INTRODUCCIÓN

José Martí (1853–1895) nació en Cuba de padres españoles. Dedicó su vida a la causa de la independencia de su país. Fue deportado dos veces a España por sus actividades políticas. Martí vivió también en México, Guatemala, Honduras y Venezuela. Dice que en cada país se encontró en casa—lo que le hizo proclamar «De América soy hijo». Pasó catorce años en Estados Unidos donde organizó un grupo revolucionario. Martí murió en el campo de batalla en Cuba en 1895. Murió sin realizar su sueño de ver a su Cuba libre e independiente.

Además de ser político y revolucionario, la gran pasión de Martí durante toda su vida era la poesía. Escribió sus famosos *Versos sencillos* durante su estadía en Nueva York.

CULTURA

Las palmas crecen en regiones tropicales.

Versos sencillos

I

Yo soy un hombre sincero

de donde crece la palma;

y antes de morirme, quiero

echar mis versos del alma°.

alma *soul*

Yo vengo de todas partes

y hacia todas partes voy:

arte soy entre las artes;

en los montes, monte soy.

Si dicen que del joyero

tome la joya mejor,

tomo a un amigo sincero

y pongo a un lado el amor°.

amor *love*

La rosa es una flor bonita, pero la planta tiene cardos.

XXXIX

Cultivo una rosa blanca

en julio como en enero,

para el amigo sincero

que me da su mano franca.

Y para el cruel que me arranca

del corazón con que vivo

cardo ni ortiga° cultivo

cultivo la rosa blanca.

ortiga *nettle*

¿Comprendes?

A **Interpretando** ¿Cómo lo dice José Martí?

1. Soy de un país tropical.
2. Quiero ser poeta.
3. Me siento o me encuentro en casa en muchos lugares diferentes.
4. Quiero ver el mundo.
5. Puedo adaptarme a muchas situaciones.

B **Buscando hechos** Contesta.

1. ¿Cuál es la mejor joya para Martí?
2. ¿Cuál prefiere? ¿A un amigo sincero o el amor?
3. ¿Qué cultiva para un amigo?
4. ¿Cómo trata a una persona que no lo trata bien?

C **Personalizando** En estos versos aprendemos mucho sobre la personalidad y las aspiraciones del poeta José Martí. Compara tres ideas y opiniones tuyas con las de José Martí.

CULTURA

El Morro, La Habana, Cuba

Marianela
de Benito Pérez Galdós

Vocabulario

Estudia las siguientes palabras y sus definiciones.

una colina   elevación de terreno menor que un monte o una montaña

un buen mozo   un joven guapo

la estrella   lo que brilla en el cielo de noche

una tontería   una cosa absurda

bello(a)   bonito, hermoso

desconocido(a)   no conocido

feliz   contento, alegre

acercarse a   ir cerca de algo

despedirse de   salir y decirles «adiós» a todos

huir   escapar

ladrar   lo que hace el perro

ponerse a   empezar

a lo lejos   en la distancia

a menudo   con frecuencia

a solas   solo, sin nadie, no acompañado

lentamente   despacio, no rápido

Práctica

A Contesta.

    1. ¿Es el hermano de Teresa un buen mozo?

    2. ¿Comete una persona inteligente y sabio muchas tonterías?

    3. ¿Te sientes feliz cuando te ocurre algo agradable?

    4. ¿Tienes miedo cuando te acerca una persona desconocida?

    5. ¿Brillan las estrellas en el cielo de día o de noche?

    6. ¿Te despides de tus amigos cuando tienes que salir?

    7. ¿Ladra el perro si quiere atención?

B Expresa de otra manera.

    1. Ella es una persona *alegre*.

    2. Ellos lo hacen *con frecuencia*.

    3. Yo sé que van a *escapar*.

    4. ¡Qué *cosa más ridícula*!

    5. Vi las colinas *en la distancia*.

    6. Andaba *despacio*.

    7. Él lo hizo *solo*.

    8. Tiene paisajes *hermosos*.

C Da el contrario.

    1. feo   **4.** rápido

    2. triste   **5.** de cerca

    3. famoso   **6.** alejarse de

CULTURA

Las Palmas de Gran Canaria, ciudad natal de Benito Pérez Galdós

INTRODUCCIÓN

Benito Pérez Galdós es uno de los mejores novelistas de España. Nació en Las Palmas de Gran Canaria en 1843 pero pasó casi toda su vida en Madrid donde murió en 1920. Un escritor fecundo, Galdós escribió setenta y siete novelas y veintidós obras teatrales. Dijo Galdós en un discurso «la novela es la imagen de la vida y su arte consiste en reproducir sus caracteres humanos; pasiones, debilidades, grandezas y bajezas».

Una de sus novelas más populares es *Marianela*. En esta novela Galdós trata el problema social de la miseria y del trabajo en las minas del norte de España. De todas sus novelas *Marianela* es la más sentimental como observarás al conocer a los dos protagonistas—Pablo Penáguilas y Marianela.

Marianela
⁓ 1 ⁓

Un día se acercó cierto Teodoro Golfín al pueblo de Socartes. En el camino él se perdió. Andaban por la región un joven, Pablo Penáguilas, y su perro Choto. Pablo era un muchacho guapo. Tenía unos veinte años. Pablo y Choto oyeron al señor y lo ayudaron a encontrar su camino. Como el pueblo de Socartes está situado en la región de las minas es fácil desorientarse. Para llegar a Socartes hay que bajar y subir muchas colinas y pasar por una cueva misteriosa.

Cuando Pablo y el señor Golfín salieron de la cueva oscura el señor observó algo en el muchacho que le hizo preguntar a Pablo:

—Chico, ¿eres ciego?

—Sí, señor. No tengo vista. No puedo ver. Soy ciego desde mi nacimiento° —contestó Pablo.

—¡Qué pena!—pensó el señor Golfín—un buen mozo como este y no tiene el don de ver.

Los dos seguían el camino de Socartes cuando a lo lejos oyeron una voz muy bella. Era la voz de Marianela. Pablo le explicó al señor Golfín que Marianela era una muchacha muy buena que siempre lo acompañaba por las minas.

nacimiento *birth*

Cuando el señor Golfín vio a Marianela observó enseguida que la pobre muchacha era muy fea. Era muy pequeña de estatura. Sus ojos negros le daban una expresión de mujer pero tenía el cuerpo de una niña. Marianela tenía dieciséis años pero parecía° menor.

El señor Golfín le habló a Pablo. Le dijo que era el hermano de Carlos Golfín, el ingeniero de las minas.

—Ah, don Carlos es muy amigo de mi padre y sé que le espera a usted desde ayer—dijo Pablo.

Por fin el joven tuvo que despedirse del grupo para volver a casa. Sabía que su padre le esperaba. El señor Golfín, guiado por Marianela, continuó su viaje hacia la casa de su hermano. Mientras caminaban hacia la casa, Marianela le hablaba al señor Golfín de su vida.

—Soy una muchacha pobre. No tengo ni padre ni madre. Soy huérfana. Mi padre fue el primero que encendía y limpiaba faroles en este pueblo. Cada día él me ponía en un cesto y yo lo acompañaba en su trabajo. Un día tenía que subir a un farol que había en un puente. Puso el cesto sobre el antepecho del puente. Yo me salí fuera° y me caí° al río. Me caí sobre unas piedras. Antes del accidente yo era bonita pero ahora soy fea. Poco después del accidente mi padre se puso enfermo y fue al hospital donde se murió. Mi madre fue a trabajar en las minas y un día ella se cayó en una cueva y no ha vuelto a salir. Y ahora yo vivo con los Centeno. Ellos tienen una casa aquí en las minas.

Después de caminar un rato más, los dos llegaron a la casa del hermano de Teodoro Golfín.

Marianela le dice «adiós» al señor Golfín y vuelve a la casa de los Centeno. Antes de salir el señor le da una moneda.

parecía *she seemed*

CULTURA

Un farol

me salí fuera *fell out*
me caí *I fell*

CULTURA

Un cesto

CULTURA

Puente sobre el río Duero en el Parque Nacional de los Picos de Europa en Asturias

⟨2⟩

Cuando salió el señor Golfín, Marianela, que se llama también la Nela, fue a la casa de los Centeno.

La casa de los Centeno es bastante humilde. Viven en la casa el señor Centeno, la señora Centeno, sus cuatro hijos y la pobre Marianela. La señora Centeno es una persona cruel. Le encanta contar su dinero pero no se lo da a nadie. Trata a la Nela peor que a un animal. La hace dormir en una cesta en un rincón° de la cocina. A pesar de° toda la miseria en que vive la Nela, ella es muy generosa. En cuanto° vuelve a casa, ella le da la moneda del señor Golfín a Celipín.

Celipín es el hijo menor de los Centeno. Él no quiere seguir viviendo como está viviendo ahora. Quiere salir de Socartes para ir a estudiar en Madrid para hacer algo de su vida. Quiere ser un hombre importante. Marianela le dice que siempre tiene que ser bueno para con sus padres y que les debe escribir a menudo.

Al día siguiente, igual que todos los días, Marianela sale de casa y va a buscar a su amigo Pablo Penáguilas. Como el joven no tiene vista hay muchas cosas que le son desconocidas. La pobre Marianela no tiene educación alguna pero siempre quiere explicarle a Pablo como son las cosas del mundo. Mientras andan a diario por los campos discuten muchas tonterías. La Nela le dice que las estrellas en el cielo son las sonrisas de los muertos que están en el cielo.

Durante sus muchas conversaciones Pablo promete a Marianela que un día va a casarse con° ella. Una muchacha tan buena como ella tiene que ser bonita. Cada vez que Pablo le dice a Marianela que es bonita, ella se mira en el agua de un arroyo° y una vez más ve que es fea.

un rincón *corner*
A pesar de *In spite of*
En cuanto *As soon as*

Biblioteca Nacional, Madrid

casarse con *marry*

arroyo *brook*

Casas típicas en el País Vasco, Euskadi, en el norte de España

Teodoro Golfín es médico y después de observar mucho a Pablo, toma la decisión de operarle de los ojos. No sabe si la operación tendrá éxito o no pero quiere intentar de darle vista al hijo del mejor amigo de su hermano. Pablo le dice a Marianela que después de la operación él se casará con ella.

Todos se preparan para la operación. Llega a Socartes Florentina, la prima de Pablo. Florentina es una muchacha muy bonita y es además una persona buena y generosa. Cuando ve por primera vez a Marianela se pone triste. No puede comprender como algunas personas como ella y su familia tienen mucho y otras no tienen nada. La pobre Marianela no tiene zapatos. Florentina le dice a Marianela que le comprará un vestido y un par de zapatos. Promete que se cuidará° de Marianela para siempre. La Nela cree que Florentina es una santa. Una persona tan buena tiene que ser santa.

⟨**3**⟩

Ha llegado el día de la operación. Todo el mundo está muy ansioso para saber los resultados. ¿Pablo tendrá vista o no? ¡Es la cuestión! Pasan unos días y el médico decide que ha llegado la hora de quitarle° las vendas a Pablo. ¿Puede ver o no? Sí, puede ver. Todos se alegran° con una sola excepción. La única persona que no es feliz es la Nela. Está contenta porque sabe que Pablo tiene vista pero está triste porque sabe que Pablo querrá casarse con Florentina y no con ella.

La pobre Marianela no sabe qué hacer. No quiere estar con nadie. Quiere estar a solas con sus pensamientos°. Decide vagar por los campos.

A lo lejos, Marianela oye un ruido°. ¿Quién puede ser? Es Florentina.

Habla Florentina:

—Pero, Nela, ¿dónde has estado? ¿No sabes que Pablo tiene vista? La operación ha sido un éxito.

—Sí, lo sé—contesta la Nela.

—Pablo te quiere ver. Siempre pregunta dónde está la Nela. Tú sabes que él te quiere mucho.

La pobre Nela se cayó al suelo.

—Florentina, usted ha sido muy buena conmigo. La quiero mucho y no quiero ser ingrata. Y adoro a Pablo. Pero no puedo, no puedo.

—¿No puedes qué?—preguntó Florentina. De repente° la Nela se levantó y empezó a correr.

Gritó—No, no puedo, Florentina. Perdóneme, pero no puedo hablar más con usted. ¡Adiós! ¡Adiós!

se cuidará *she will take care*

quitarle *to take off*
se alegran *rejoices*

pensamientos *thoughts*

ruido *noise*

De repente *Suddenly*

Con estas palabras la Nela desapareció entre los árboles. Tomó la decisión de huir. No quiso pasar más tiempo en Socartes.

Durante la noche la Nela oyó otro ruido. Oyó a Celipín, el hijo de los Centeno.

—¿Adónde vas, Celipín?—preguntó Marianela.

—Nela, por fin voy a Madrid. Pero me tienes que hacer una promesa. No vas a decir nada a mis padres.

—De acuerdo, Celipín. No les voy a decir nada. Pero les escribirás, ¿no? Tienes que ser bueno para con tus padres.

—Sí, les escribiré. Te lo prometo. Pero, Nela, ¿por qué no vienes conmigo a Madrid? No tienes que quedarte aquí en Socartes. Podemos salir juntos.

—¡Buena idea! Te acompaño—contestó la Nela.

Luego se puso a° pensar. La Nela pensó en su madre enterrada en una cueva de Socartes. Por fin le dijo a Celipín:

—Celipín. Lo siento pero no puedo ir contigo. No puedo salir de Socartes. Tengo mis razones. Tú tienes que ir solo. Y, ¡escribe mucho! Adiós, Celipín y ¡buena suerte!

—No me olvidaré° de mis padres ni de ti que me has ayudado tanto… Adiós, Nelilla. Siento pasos°… Me voy—dijo Celipín.

se puso a *she began*

No me olvidaré *I will not forget*
Siento pasos *I hear steps*

CULTURA
Picos de Europa, Asturias

≈4≈

Celipín desapareció entre las sombras° de la noche. Los pasos que había sentido eran de Choto, el perro de Pablo. Al ver a Marianela, Choto saltó alrededor de ella acariciándola con sus patas°. Luego empezó a correr hacia la casa de los Penáguilas.

A la misma hora que Choto llegaba a la casa, Teodoro Golfín salía de la casa. Cuando el perro lo vio dio unas cuarenta vueltas en torno de él y no dejó de ladrar. El señor Golfín sabía que el perro trataba de decirle algo. Choto empezó a correr y el doctor Golfín decidió seguirlo. Lo siguió y el perro lo llevó hasta donde estaba la Nela delante de la cueva donde está enterrada su madre.

El doctor gritó:

—Nela, ¿qué haces allí? Te quiero hablar.

—No puedo—contestó la Nela.

—Sí—insistió el doctor.

Marianela subió de la cueva. Le dijo al doctor que quería estar con su madre. No quería ver a Pablo porque él creía que era bonita y ella sabía que no lo era.

Por fin el doctor levantó a la Nela, la puso en sus hombros y la llevó a la casa de Pablo.—¡Ay! Marianela, ¡qué enferma estás!—pensó el médico.

Cuando llegaron a la casa, el doctor puso a la Nela en el sofá. Todos se cuidaron de ella—Florentina, el padre de Pablo, el doctor Golfín.

sombras *shadows*

acariciándola con sus patas *caressing her with its paws*

Al día siguiente Pablo salió de su cuarto para hablar con Florentina. Consideró a Florentina la muchacha más bonita del mundo. Cuando vio a Florentina le dijo:

—Florentina, no te vi esta mañana. ¿Por qué no viniste a hablar conmigo?

Pablo vio solo a Florentina—a nadie más. Luego miró hacia el sofá y vio la cara de una pobre muchacha fea con los ojos cerrados y la boca abierta.

—¡Ah!—dijo Pablo. Florentina ha encontrado a una pobre fea y la quiere ayudar. ¡Qué buena es Florentina!

Pablo se acercó al sofá. Extendió una mano hasta tocar aquella cabeza en la cual veía una expresión de dolor y tristeza. Entonces la Nela movió los ojos y los fijó en Pablo. Sacó de entre las mantas una mano flaca y tomó la mano de Pablo. Al sentir° su contacto Pablo se estremeció° de pies a cabeza y gritó.

Con voz temblorosa°, Marianela le dijo:

—Sí, señorito mío, yo soy la Nela.

Lentamente ella llevó a sus secos labios la mano de Pablo y le dio un beso°... después un segundo beso... y al darle el tercero, sus labios se quedaron inertes.

El primero que dijo algo fue Pablo.

—Eres tú... , eres tú.

Pablo la llamó repetidas veces.

—No responde—dijo con terror.

Pablo se inclinó sobre ella y acercando sus labios al oído de Marianela, gritó:

—Nela, Nela, amiga querida°, que tanto me has ayudado y ahora estás muerta. Adiós, Nelilla. Adiós.

sentir *to feel*
se estremeció *shook*
temblorosa *trembling*

beso *kiss*

querida *dear, beloved*

CULTURA
Paisaje del norte de España

¿Comprendes?

~1~

A **Identificando** Identifica quien es.

	Pablo Penáguilas	Teodoro Golfín	don Carlos	los Centeno	Marianela
1. un señor que se perdió un día en el camino de Socartes					
2. un muchacho ciego que vive en Socartes y que le ayudó al señor que se perdió					
3. una muchacha fea que siempre le ayuda al joven ciego y que guió al señor que se perdió					
4. el ingeniero de las minas a quien iba a visitar el señor que se perdió					
5. la familia con quien vive la muchacha					

B **Describiendo** Escoge las frases que describen a Marianela.
1. Es una muchacha muy buena.
2. Es ciega.
3. Su madre y su padre trabajan en las minas de Socartes.
4. Es muy fea.
5. Tiene ojos azules.
6. Es muy alta.
7. Tiene una estatura baja.
8. Ayuda mucho al muchacho ciego.
9. Sufrió un accidente horrible cuando era niña.

C **Describiendo** Describe a los siguientes personajes.
1. Pablo Penáguilas
2. Marianela
3. Teodoro Golfín

D **Analizando** Contesta.
1. El camino de Socartes es un camino difícil y es fácil perderse en el camino. ¿Por qué?
2. ¿Qué indica que el señor Golfín es un hombre generoso?

E Aumentando tu vocabulario Parea.

1. se perdió
2. andaba
3. está situado
4. oscura
5. ser ciego
6. buen mozo
7. bello
8. huérfano
9. un rato

a. se encuentra
b. guapo
c. sin padres
d. bonito
e. se desorientó
f. caminaba, iba
g. sin luz
h. poco tiempo
i. no tener vista

F Identificando Usa una tabla como la de abajo para indicar quien es.

1. un señor que es médico y que le puede operar a Pablo de los ojos
2. un joven de unos veinte años que es guapo
3. el hijo menor de la familia Centeno que no quiere seguir viviendo como está viviendo ahora
4. una muchacha generosa que no tiene nada pero que siempre quiere ayudar a los otros
5. una muchacha bonita y generosa que viene a Socartes antes de la operación de Pablo
6. una señora cruel que nunca le da nada a nadie

Marianela	Pablo Penáguilas	Celipín	Teodoro Golfín	la Sra. Centeno	Florentina	don Carlos

G Recordando hechos Contesta.

1. ¿Con quién vive Marianela?
2. ¿Cómo la trata la señora?
3. ¿En qué cuarto de la casa duerme Marianela?
4. ¿En qué duerme ella?
5. ¿A quién le da Marianela la moneda del señor Golfín?
6. ¿Quién es Celipín?
7. ¿Por qué quiere él ir a Madrid?
8. ¿Qué le dice siempre Marianela?

H Analizando Contesta.

1. El autor dice que Marianela le dice muchas tonterías a Pablo. ¿Por qué son tonterías la información que Marianela le da?
2. Pablo siempre le dice a Marianela que va a casarse con ella. ¿Por qué quiere Pablo casarse con ella?
3. Marianela dice que Florentina es una santa. ¿Por qué?

I Describiendo Describe.

Describe a Florentina. En tu descripción indica por qué se le considera una persona generosa y compasiva.

CULTURA

Paisaje cerca de Santillana del Mar en el norte de España

≈3≈

J **Analizando** Contesta.

1. Unos días después de la operación, el médico le quita las vendas a Pablo y todos se alegran. ¿Por qué?
2. La única persona que no es feliz es la Nela. ¿Por qué?
3. Florentina le dice a Marianela que Pablo la quiere ver. ¿Por qué quiere verla?
4. La pobre Marianela no puede hablar más con Florentina. ¿Por qué?
5. Cuando Celipín invita a Marianela a acompañarlo a Madrid, Marianela cree que es una buena idea. Luego dice que no, que ella no puede ir con él. ¿Por qué?
6. Marianela le dice a Florentina que no quiere ser ingrata. ¿Por qué le dice tal cosa a Florentina?

K **Confirmando información** Usa una tabla como la de abajo para indicar si la información es correcta o no.

	correcta	incorrecta
1. Marianela no quiere ir a la casa de Pablo porque sabe que todos son muy felices.		
2. Marianela está triste porque Pablo tiene vista.		
3. Marianela quiere estar sola con sus pensamientos porque está muy triste.		
4. Está muy triste porque sabe que Pablo va a casarse con Florentina.		

L **Creando un diálogo** El diálogo, una conversación entre dos personas, es un elemento importante en muchas novelas. Prepara una conversación que tiene lugar entre Celipín y Marianela cuando él se despide de ella.

M **Llegando a conclusiones** ¿Qué opinión tienes? ¿Se casará Pablo con Florentina o no?

N Recordando hechos Contesta.

1. ¿De quién eran los pasos que oyó Celipín?
2. ¿Hacia dónde corrió el perro?
3. ¿Qué hizo el perro cuando llegó a la casa de Pablo?
4. ¿Quién siguió al perro?
5. ¿Adónde lo llevó el perro?
6. ¿Quería Marianela hablar con el doctor?
7. ¿Qué hizo el doctor?
8. ¿Adónde la llevó?
9. ¿Dónde la puso?
10. Al día siguiente, ¿quién salió de su cuarto?
11. ¿Con quién habló?

O Confirmando información Usa una tabla como la de abajo para indicar si la información es correcta o no.

	correcta	incorrecta
1. Cuando Pablo mira hacia el sofá, sabe que la muchacha en el sofá es Marianela. La reconoce enseguida.		
2. Pablo cree que la muchacha en el sofá es otra pobre a quien ayudaba Florentina.		
3. Pablo reconoció a Marianela cuando le tocó la cabeza y vio la expresión en su cara.		
4. Pablo no reconoció a Marianela hasta que ella le tomó la mano.		

P Interpretando Explica el significado de la siguiente frase.

«Al sentir su contacto Pablo se estremeció de pies a cabeza y gritó».

Q Interpretando y analizando En la novela *Marianela,* el doctor Teodoro Golfín representa la ciencia. Él da nueva vida a Pablo al darle vista. Pero, ¿qué le pasa a Marianela? Lee el siguiente párrafo. ¿Qué opinión tienes? ¿Han triunfado la ciencia y el progreso? Defiende tu opinión.

Después de la muerte de Marianela el doctor Teodoro Golfín dice:
—La realidad ha sido para él nueva vida; para ella ha sido dolor y asfixia, la humillación, la tristeza, el dolor… ¡la muerte!

En realidad, ¿qué nos está diciendo el doctor? ¿Es posible que sea también la opinión del autor Galdós?

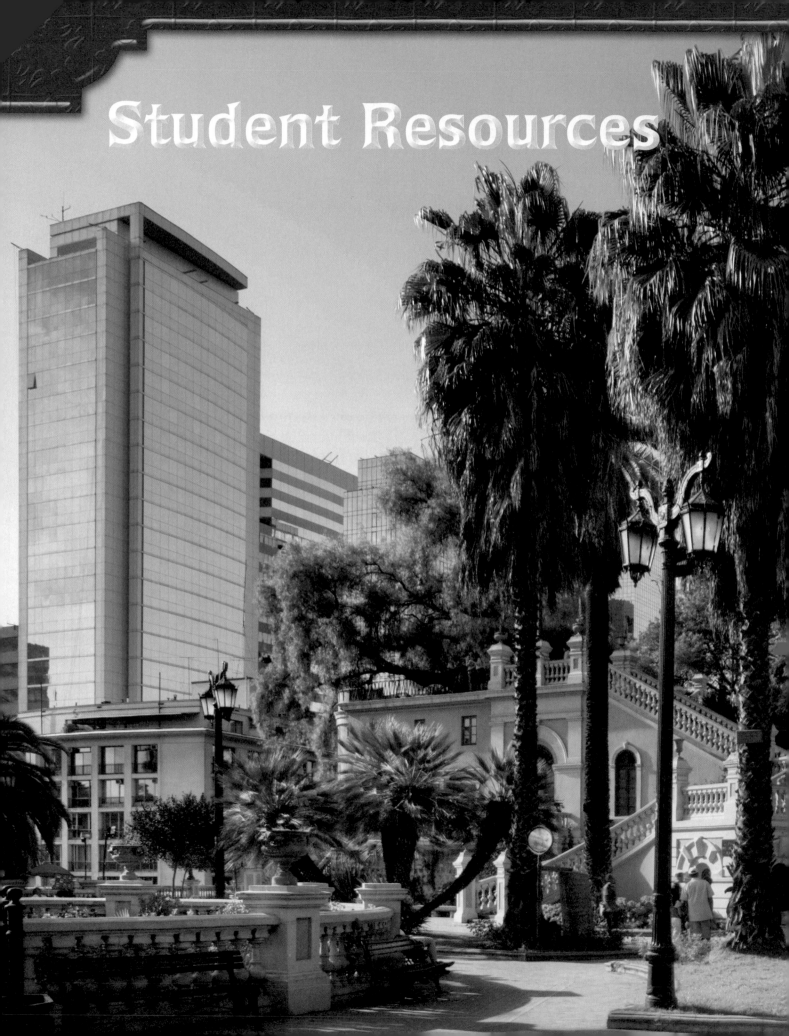

Student Resources

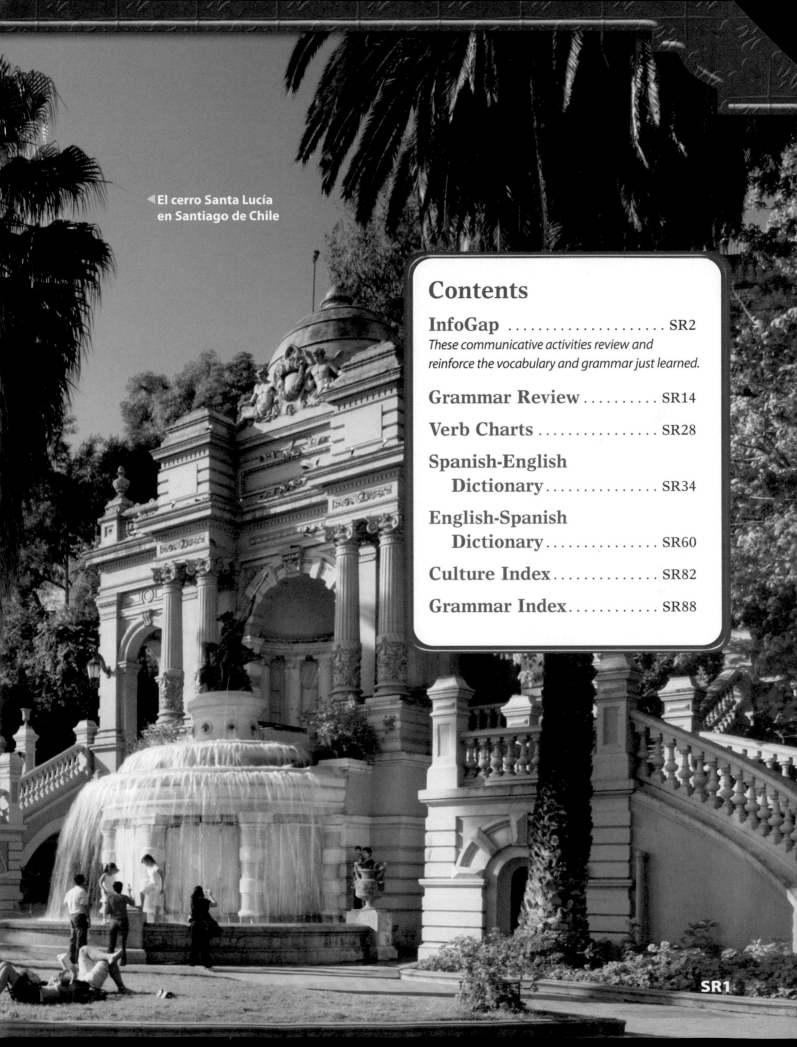

El cerro Santa Lucía
en Santiago de Chile

Contents

InfoGap

Activity R

REPASO F, Gramática, page R51

Alumno A Ask your partner the following questions. Correct answers are in parentheses.

1. ¿Dónde nadaste? *(Nadé en el mar.)*
2. ¿Adónde fueron ustedes? *(Fuimos al mercado.)*
3. ¿Qué viste? *(Vi una película.)*
4. ¿Qué comieron ustedes? *(Comimos una tortilla a la española.)*
5. ¿Dónde viviste? *(Viví en El Salvador.)*

Alumno A Use the clues below to answer your partner's questions.

1. el telesilla
2. una camisa roja
3. una exposición de arte colombiano
4. yo
5. no

Alumno B Use the clues below to answer your partner's questions.

1. el mar
2. al mercado
3. una película
4. una tortilla a la española
5. El Salvador

Alumno B Ask your partner the following questions. Correct answers are in parentheses.

1. ¿Cómo subieron la montaña ustedes? *(Subimos la montaña en el telesilla.)*
2. ¿Qué le compraste a Sofi? *(Le compré una camisa roja.)*
3. ¿Qué vieron ustedes? *(Vimos una exposición de arte colombiano.)*
4. ¿Quién fue el/la ganador(a)? *(Yo fui el/la ganador[a].)*
5. ¿Tomaron mucho sol ustedes? *(No, no tomamos mucho sol.)*

Activity 1

Alumno A Ask your partner the following questions. Correct answers are in parentheses.

1. ¿Es una tarjeta de embarque o un carnet de identidad? *(Es una tarjeta de embarque.)*

2. ¿Qué hace Julia? *(Julia factura su equipaje.)*

3. ¿Quiénes esperan a los pasajeros? *(Los taxistas esperan a los pasajeros.)*

4. ¿Dónde están la madre y su hija? *(La madre y su hija están en el aeropuerto.)*

Alumno A Answer your partner's questions based on the photos below.

1.

2.

3.

4.

Alumno B Answer your partner's questions based on the photos below.

1.

2.

3.

4.

Alumno B Ask your partner the following questions. Correct answers are in parentheses.

1. ¿Dónde pone el padre el equipaje? *(El padre pone el equipaje en la maletera [el baúl].)*

2. ¿Dónde está la pasajera? *(La pasajera está en el mostrador de la línea aérea.)*

3. ¿El avión acaba de despegar o de aterrizar? *(El avión acaba de aterrizar.)*

4. ¿Cuál es el número del asiento del pasajero? *(El número del asiento del pasajero es 8A.)*

InfoGap

Activity 2

InfoGap

los muchachos

Federico

Rolando

Elisa

Alumno A Answer your partner's questions based on the photos below.

Alumno A Ask your partner the following questions. Correct answers are in parentheses.

1. ¿Qué hace Catalina? *(Catalina se cepilla los dientes.)* or *(Catalina se lava los dientes.)*

2. ¿Se acuesta Omar o se estira? *(Omar se acuesta.)*

3. ¿Qué hace Ernesto? *(Ernesto se pone un suéter.)*

4. ¿Se sienta la joven a la mesa o se cepilla el pelo? *(La joven se sienta a la mesa.)*

Alumno B Answer your partner's questions based on the photos below.

la joven

Ernesto

Omar

Catalina

Alumno B Ask your partner the following questions. Correct answers are in parentheses.

1. ¿Qué hace Elisa? *(Elisa se despierta.)* or *(Elisa se estira.)*

2. ¿Qué hace Rolando? *(Rolando se lava la cara.)*

3. ¿Qué hacen los muchachos? *(Los muchachos se peinan.)* or *(Los muchachos se miran en el espejo.)*

4. ¿Se mira en el espejo Federico o se lava el pelo? *(Federico se lava el pelo.)*

Alumno A Ask your partner the following questions. Correct answers are in parentheses.

Alumno A Answer your partner's questions based on the photos below.

1. ¿Dónde compra Clarisa su billete? (*Clarisa compra su billete en la ventanilla [la boletería].*)

2. ¿Dónde comen Marcos y Mariana? (*Marcos y Mariana comen en el coche comedor [el coche cafetería].*)

3. ¿Dónde están los pasajeros? (*Los pasajeros están en el vagón [el coche].*) or (*Los pasajeros están en el tren.*)

4. ¿Qué lee la señora? (*La señora lee una revista.*)

2–3.

1.

4.

Alumno B Answer your partner's questions based on the photos below.

1.

2.

3–4.

Alumno B Ask your partner the following questions. Correct answers are in parentheses.

1. ¿Dónde compras tu billete? (*Compro mi billete en el distribuidor automático.*)

2. ¿A quién le dan sus billetes los amigos? (*Los amigos le dan sus billetes al revisor.*)

3. ¿Está el revisor en la plaza o en el pasillo? (*El revisor está en el pasillo.*)

4. ¿Van a bajar del tren Marcos y Mariana o van a subir al tren? (*Marcos y Mariana van a bajar[se] del tren.*)

InfoGap

Activity 4

Alumno A Ask your partner the following questions. Correct answers are in parentheses.

1. ¿Qué piden ustedes? (*Nosotros pedimos los mariscos.*)

2. ¿Quién repitió la orden? (*El mesero repitió la orden.*)

3. ¿Cuántas horas durmieron los muchachos? (*Los muchachos durmieron cinco horas.*)

4. ¿Qué prefieres tomar? (*Prefiero tomar jugo.*)

5. ¿Cuántas veces repetí yo «el postre»? (*Tú repetiste «el postre» tres veces.*)

Alumno A Use the clues below to answer your partner's questions.

1. José Luis

2. los tostones

3. el arroz con frijoles

4. sí

5. el cocinero

Alumno B Use the clues below to answer your partner's questions.

1. los mariscos

2. el mesero

3. cinco horas

4. jugo

5. tres veces

Alumno B Ask your partner the following questions. Correct answers are in parentheses.

1. ¿Quién se viste?
(*José Luis se viste.*)

2. ¿Qué prefirieron comer tus amigos?
(*Mis amigos prefirieron comer los tostones.*)

3. ¿Qué pediste tú? (*Pedí el arroz con frijoles.*)

4. ¿Se divierten ustedes?
(*Sí, nosotros nos divertimos.*)

5. ¿Quién frió las papas?
(*El cocinero frió las papas.*)

Alumno A Answer your partner's questions based on the pictures below.

Alumno A Ask your partner the following questions. Correct answers are in parentheses.

1. ¿Qué celebraba la familia? (*La familia celebraba Hanuka [la fiesta de las luces].*)

2. ¿Qué había enfrente de la puerta? (*Había un esqueleto enfrente de la puerta.*)

3. ¿Qué hay en los zapatos? (*Hay paja en los zapatos.*)

4. ¿Qué llevaba la muchacha? (*La muchacha llevaba una máscara.*)

Alumno B Answer your partner's questions based on the pictures below.

1.
3.

2.
4.

Alumno B Ask your partner the following questions. Correct answers are in parentheses.

1. ¿Qué hay en la sala? (*Hay un árbol de Navidad en la sala.*) or (*Hay muchos aguinaldos en la sala.*)

2. ¿Qué enciende el joven? (*El joven enciende una vela de la menora.*)

3. ¿Quiénes son ellos? (*Ellos son los Reyes Magos.*)

4. ¿Es un desfile o una tumba? (*Es un desfile.*)

InfoGap

InfoGap

Alumno A Ask your partner the following questions. Correct answers are in parentheses.

1. ¿Las amigas navegan el Internet o envían correos electrónicos? *(Las amigas navegan el Internet.)*

2. ¿Qué compraste ayer? *(Compré un móvil [un teléfono] celular].)*

3. ¿Cuál es el prefijo del país? *(El prefijo del país es 34.)*

4. ¿Cuál es la clave de área? *(La clave de área es 952.)*

Alumno A Answer your partner's questions based on the photos below.

1.

2-3.

Alumno B Answer your partner's questions based on the pictures below.

1.

2.

3-4.
(034) 952 822-5364

Alumno B Ask your partner the following questions. Correct answers are in parentheses.

1. ¿Qué va a enviar José? *(José va a enviar un correo electrónico.)*

2. ¿Qué usa Maripaz? *(Maripaz usa el teléfono público.)*

3. ¿Usa una tarjeta telefónica o unas monedas para hacer la llamada? *(Usa una tarjeta telefónica.)*

4. ¿Qué va a comprar Felipe para su computadora? *(Felipe va a comprar un ratón para su computadora.)*

Activity 7

CAPÍTULO 7, Gramática, page 208

Alumno A Ask your partner the following questions. Correct answers are in parentheses.

1. ¿Adónde no has ido todavía? *(Todavía no he ido al museo.)*
2. ¿Quién ya ha llegado? *(El mozo ya ha llegado.)*
3. ¿Quién te ha ayudado? *(Mi padre me ha ayudado.)*
4. ¿Qué ha comido Sara? *(Sara ha comido el desayuno continental.)*
5. ¿Qué han bebido ustedes? *(Hemos bebido un café.)*

Alumno A Use the clues below to answer your partner's questions.

1. el huésped
2. Colombia
3. Francisco
4. en el restaurante nuevo
5. Fernando

Alumno B Use the clues below to answer your partner's questions.

1. al museo
2. el mozo
3. mi padre
4. el desayuno continental
5. un café

Alumno B Ask your partner the following questions. Correct answers are in parentheses.

1. ¿Quién ha abandonado el cuarto? *(El huésped ha abandonado el cuarto.)*
2. ¿Adónde ya han viajado ustedes? *(Ya hemos viajado a Colombia.)*
3. ¿Con quién has hablado? *(He hablado con Francisco.)*
4. ¿Dónde hemos comido ya? *(Ya hemos comido en el restaurante nuevo.)*
5. ¿Quién te ha dado un regalo? *(Fernando me ha dado un regalo.)*

InfoGap

Alumno A   Ask your partner the following questions. Correct answers are in parentheses.

1. ¿Dónde entra la joven?
   (La joven entra en la boca del metro.)

2. ¿Qué cosecha el campesino?
   (El campesino cosecha el trigo.)

3. ¿Es un cordero o es un cerdo?
   (Es un cerdo.)

4. ¿Cruza el señor una avenida ancha o una calle estrecha?
   (El señor cruza una avenida ancha.)

Alumno A   Answer your partner's questions based on the pictures below.

1.

2.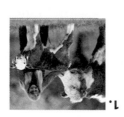

3.

4.

Alumno B   Answer your partner's questions based on the photos below.

1.

2.

3.

4.

Alumno B   Ask your partner the following questions. Correct answers are in parentheses.

1. ¿Es una vaca o es una gallina? *(Es una vaca.)*

2. ¿Dónde están los caballos? *(Los caballos están en el corral.)*

3. ¿Adónde van los jóvenes este fin de semana? *(Los jóvenes van al parque de atracciones este fin de semana.)*

4. ¿Dónde vive la familia, en la ciudad o en el campo? *(La familia vive en el campo.)*

Alumno A Ask your partner the following questions. Correct answers are in parentheses.

1. ¿Debo tomar el ascensor o las escaleras? (*Toma el ascensor.*)

2. ¿Quieres el vaso?
   (*Sí, pásame el vaso, por favor.*) or
   (*Sí, pásamelo, por favor.*)

3. ¿Quieres saber el secreto? (*Sí, dime el secreto.*) or (*Sí, dímelo.*)

4. ¿Qué hago con los libros?
   (*Pon los libros en la mesa.*) or
   (*Ponlos en la mesa.*)

5. ¿Adónde debo ir el viernes?
   (*Ve a la fiesta.*)

Alumno A Answer your partner's questions with an affirmative command based on the cues and the verbs given below.

1. llevar / a la playa

2. venir / aquí

3. sí / pasarme

4. estudiar / todos los días

5. salir / conmigo

Alumno B Answer your partner's questions with an affirmative command based on the cues and the verbs given below.

1. tomar / el ascensor

2. sí / pasarme

3. sí / decirme

4. poner / en la mesa

5. ir / a la fiesta

Alumno B Ask your partner the following questions. Correct answers are in parentheses.

1. ¿Qué hago con la cámara digital? (*Lleva la cámara digital a la playa.*) or (*Llévala a la playa.*)

2. ¿Adónde debo ir? (*Ven aquí.*)

3. ¿Quieres el pan? (*Sí, pásame el pan, por favor.*) or (*Sí, pásamelo, por favor.*)

4. ¿Qué debo hacer para sacar notas buenas?
   (*Estudia todos los días.*)

5. ¿Con quién debo salir?
   (*Sal conmigo.*)

Activity 10

Alumno A Ask your partner the following questions. Correct answers are in parentheses.

1. ¿Qué quiere Marisa que su primo haga? *(Marisa quiere que su primo se acueste.)*

2. ¿Qué quieren sus amigos que Marta haga? *(Sus amigos quieren que Marta salga este fin de semana.)*

3. ¿Qué quieres que hagamos esta noche? *(Quiero que miremos la tele esta noche.)*

4. ¿Qué quiere la madre de Diego que él haga? *(La madre de Diego quiere que él limpie la casa.)*

Alumno A Answer your partner's questions based on the clues below.

1. jugar tenis

2. preparar la comida

3. conducir con cuidado

4. decir la verdad

Alumno B Answer your partner's questions based on the clues below.

1. acostarse

2. salir este fin de semana

3. mirar la tele

4. limpiar la casa

Alumno B Ask your partner the following questions. Correct answers are in parentheses.

1. ¿Qué quieren los padres que sus hijos hagan? *(Los padres quieren que sus hijos jueguen tenis.)*

2. ¿Qué quieres que yo haga? *(Quiero que tú prepares la comida.)*

3. ¿Qué quiere Olivia que su hermana haga? *(Olivia quiere que su hermana conduzca con cuidado.)*

4. ¿Qué quiere el profesor que sus alumnos hagan? *(El profesor quiere que sus alumnos digan la verdad.)*

Alumno A Ask your partner the following questions. Correct answers are in parentheses.

1. ¿Qué se ha cortado la joven? *(La joven se ha cortado el dedo.)*

2. ¿Ella está en la ambulancia? *(No, ella no está en la ambulancia.)*

3. ¿Ella se ha hecho mucho daño? *(No, ella no se ha hecho mucho daño.)*

4. ¿Qué le pone la enfermera? *(La enfermera le pone una venda.)*

Alumno A Answer your partner's questions based on the photo below.

Alumno B Answer your partner's questions based on the photos below.

Alumno B Ask your partner the following questions. Correct answers are in parentheses.

1. ¿Qué se ha torcido el joven? *(El joven se ha torcido el tobillo.)*

2. ¿Habla el joven con los socorristas? *(No, el joven no habla con los socorristas.)*

3. ¿Con quién habla el joven? *(El joven habla con la médica.)*

4. ¿Está en una silla de ruedas? *(Sí, está en una silla de ruedas.)*

InfoGap

Grammar Review

Nouns and articles

Nouns and definite articles

A noun is the name of a person, place, or thing. Unlike English, all nouns in Spanish have a gender—either masculine or feminine. Almost all nouns that end in **-o** are masculine and almost all nouns that end in **-a** are feminine. Note that the definite article **el** is used with masculine nouns. The definite article **la** is used with feminine nouns.

MASCULINE	FEMININE
el muchacho	la muchacha
el libro	la escuela
el curso	la sala

Nouns that end in **-e** can either be masculine or feminine. It is necessary for you to learn the gender.

MASCULINE	FEMININE
el padre	la madre
el restaurante	la carne
el nombre	la leche
el norte	la gente
el billete	la nube

Many nouns that end in **-e** and refer to a person can be either masculine or feminine.

el cliente	la cliente
el paciente	la paciente

It is also necessary to learn the gender of nouns that end in a consonant.

el comedor	la flor
el animal	la capital
el jamón	la mujer

Note, however, that nouns that end in **-ción, -dad, -tad** are always feminine.

la habitación	la universidad	la dificultad

Grammar Review

Irregular nouns

There are not very many irregular nouns in Spanish. The ones you have learned so far are:

la mano **el problema** **la foto** (from **la fotografía**)

Plural of nouns

To form the plural of nouns you add **-s** to nouns that end in a vowel. You add **-es** to nouns that end in a consonant. Note, too, that the definite articles **el** and **la** become **los** and **las** in the plural.

MASCULINE PLURAL	FEMININE PLURAL
los libros	**las novelas**
los cuartos	**las casas**
los coches	**las carnes**
los comedores	**las flores**

Nouns that end in **-z** change the **-z** to **-c** and add **-es**.

el lápiz **los lápices**

Nouns that end in **-ción** drop the accent in the plural.

la estación **las estaciones**
la conversación **las conversaciones**

Indefinite articles

The indefinite articles are *a, an,* and *some* in English. They are **un, una, unos, unas** in Spanish. Note that the indefinite article, like the definite article, must agree with the noun it modifies in both gender (masculine or feminine) and number (singular or plural).

SINGULAR		PLURAL	
un alumno	**una alumna**	**unos alumnos**	**unas alumnas**
un café	**una clase**	**unos cafés**	**unas clases**
un árbol	**una flor**	**unos árboles**	**unas flores**

Contractions

The prepositions **a** *(to, at)* and **de** *(of, from)* contract (combine) with the definite article **el** to form one word, **al** or **del**. There is no contraction with **la, los,** or **las.**

> **Voy al mercado; no vuelvo del mercado.**
> **Es el dinero del empleado, no del cliente.**

A personal

Remember that whenever a person is the direct object of the verb, it must be preceded by **a.** This **a personal** also contracts with **el.**

> **Conozco a Juan.**
> **Pero no conozco al hermano de Juan.**

Nouns and adjectives

Agreement of nouns and adjectives

An adjective is a word that describes a noun. An adjective must agree in gender (masculine or feminine) and number (singular or plural) with the noun it describes or modifies.

Adjectives that end in **-o** have four forms, the same as nouns that end in **-o.**

	SINGULAR	PLURAL
MASCULINE	**el muchacho simpático**	**los muchachos simpáticos**
FEMININE	**la muchacha simpática**	**las muchachas simpáticas**

Adjectives that end in **-e** have only two forms—singular and plural.

	SINGULAR	PLURAL
MASCULINE	**el alumno inteligente**	**los alumnos inteligentes**
FEMININE	**la alumna inteligente**	**las alumnas inteligentes**

Adjectives that end in a consonant have only two forms—singular and plural. Note that the plural ends in **-es.**

	SINGULAR	PLURAL
MASCULINE	**un curso fácil**	**dos cursos fáciles**
FEMININE	**una tarea fácil**	**dos tareas fáciles**

Adjectives of nationality

Adjectives of nationality that end in a consonant have four forms. Observe the following.

> **un joven francés**   **unos jóvenes franceses**
> **una joven francesa**   **unas jóvenes francesas**

Note that adjectives of nationality that end in **-s, -n** (**inglés, japonés, tailandés, alemán, catalán**) drop the written accent in all forms except the masculine singular.

Possessive adjectives

A possessive adjective tells who owns or possesses something—*my* book and *your* pencil. Like other adjectives in Spanish, possessive adjectives agree with the noun they modify. Note that only **nuestro** and *vuestro* have four forms.

MASCULINE SINGULAR	FEMININE SINGULAR	MASCULINE PLURAL	FEMININE PLURAL
mi tío	**mi tía**	**mis tíos**	**mis tías**
tu tío	**tu tía**	**tus tíos**	**tus tías**
su tío	**su tía**	**sus tíos**	**sus tías**
nuestro tío	**nuestra tía**	**nuestros tíos**	**nuestras tías**
vuestro tío	*vuestra tía*	*vuestros tíos*	*vuestras tías*

Since **su** can refer to many different people, it is often accompanied by a phrase that gives clarification.

su familia

la familia de Juan	la familia de él
la familia de María	la familia de ella
la familia de Juan y María	la familia de ellos

la familia de usted

la familia de ustedes

Demonstrative adjectives

Until recently the demonstrative pronoun (*this one, that one, these, those*) had to carry a written accent to differentiate it from a demonstrative adjective. That is no longer the case and the pronouns are the same as the adjectives.

In Spanish there are three demonstrative adjectives (pronouns): **este** (*this*), **ese** (*that*), and **aquel** (*that, farther away*). Each of the demonstratives has four forms and must agree in gender and number with the nouns they modify or replace.

MASCULINE SINGULAR	FEMININE SINGULAR	MASCULINE PLURAL	FEMININE PLURAL
este libro	**esta chaqueta**	**estos libros**	**estas chaquetas**
ese libro	**esa chaqueta**	**esos libros**	**esas chaquetas**
aquel libro	**aquella chaqueta**	**aquellos libros**	**aquellas chaquetas**

Comparative and superlative

Regular forms

You use the comparative *(more, -er)* and the superlative *(most, -est)* to compare people or things.

To form the comparative in Spanish you use **más** (or **menos**) before the adjective. The comparative is followed by **que: más… que.**

> **Él es más inteligente que los otros.**
> **Ella es más ambiciosa que los otros.**

To form the superlative you use the definite article with **más.** Note that **de** follows the superlative: **el (la) más… de.**

> **Él es el más ambicioso de todos.**
> **Ella es la alumna más inteligente de todos.**

Irregular forms

The adjectives **bueno** and **malo** as well as the adverbs **bien** and **mal** have irregular comparative and superlative forms.

	COMPARATIVE	SUPERLATIVE
bueno	mejor	el/la mejor
malo	peor	el/la peor
bien	mejor	el/la mejor
mal	peor	el/la peor

> **Él es mejor jugador que su hermano.**
> **Pero su hermana Teresa es la mejor jugadora de los tres.**
> **La verdad es que ella juega mejor que nadie.**
> **Ella juega mejor que yo.**

Note that the comparative is followed by the subject pronoun or a negative word.

> **más alto que yo (tú, él, nosotros)**
> **más alto que nadie**

(El) mayor and **(el) menor** are also comparative and superlative forms. They most often refer to age and sometimes size.

> **Mi hermano menor tiene trece años.**
> **Y mi hermana mayor tiene diecisiete.**
> **La Ciudad de México tiene el mayor número de habitantes.**

Comparison of equality

To compare things that have equal qualities *as . . . as* you use **tan... como** in Spanish. Note that **tan** can precede an adjective or an adverb.

> **Ella es tan inteligente como sus hermanos.**
>
> **Sus hermanos son tan inteligentes como ella.**
>
> **Ella habla tan rápido como los otros.**

To compare equal quantities *as much . . . as, as many . . . as* you use **tanto... como.** Since **tanto** is an adjective it must agree with the noun it modifies.

> **Él tiene tanta paciencia como su hermana.**
>
> **Susana no tiene tantos primos como yo.**

Note that the subject pronouns follow **como.**

Pronouns

Grammar Review

A pronoun is a word that replaces a noun. Review the forms of the pronouns that you have learned so far.

SUBJECT PRONOUNS	DIRECT OBJECT PRONOUNS	INDIRECT OBJECT PRONOUNS	REFLEXIVE PRONOUNS	PREPOSITIONAL PRONOUNS
yo	me	me	me	mí
tú	te	te	te	ti
Ud., él, ella	lo, la	le	se	Ud., él, ella
nosotros(as)	nos	nos	nos	nosotros(as)
vosotros(as)	*os*	*os*	*os*	*vosotros(as)*
Uds., ellos, ellas	los, las	les	se	Uds., ellos, ellas

Remember that an object pronoun comes right before the conjugated form of the verb.

> **Ella me ve.** **Ella nos habla.** **Ella lo ha escrito.**

The direct object pronoun is the direct receiver of the action of the verb. The indirect object is the indirect receiver of the action of the verb.

The direct object pronouns **lo, la, los, las** can refer to a person or a thing.

> **Ellos tiraron la pelota.** **Ellos la tiraron.**
>
> **Ellos vieron a sus amigos.** **Ellos los vieron.**

The indirect object pronouns **le, les** refer to people only. They are often accompanied by a prepositional phrase for clarification.

> **Ella le habló** { **a él** / **a ella.** / **a usted.** } **Yo les hablé** { **a ellos.** / **a ellas.** / **a ustedes.** }

Note that the prepositional pronouns **mí** and **ti** form one word with **con.**

> **Yo voy contigo y tú vas conmigo.**

Double object pronouns

When there are two object pronouns in the same sentence, the indirect object pronoun always precedes the direct object pronoun.

> Él me **lo** dijo.
>
> Nuestros padres nos **los** da.
>
> ¿Quién te **lo** dio?

The indirect object pronouns **le** and **les** change to **se** when used with a direct object pronoun (**lo, la, los, las**).

> El profesor se **lo** explica muy bien.
>
> ¿Quién se **las** compró?

Se is often accompanied by a prepositional phrase to clarify its meaning.

Yo se **lo** di
- a usted.
- a él.
- a ella.
- a ustedes.
- a ellos.
- a ellas.

Position of object pronouns

The object pronouns always precede the conjugated form of the verb.

> José me vio.
>
> El profesor se lo explicó a ustedes.
>
> Ellos no lo han hecho.

With the progressive tenses or the infinitive the pronouns can either come before the helping verb or can be added to the present participle or the infinitive.

> Ellos nos están ayudando.   Ella te lo va a explicar.
>
> Ellos están ayudándonos.   Ella va a explicártelo.
>
> Ella se la está vendiendo a ellos.   Ellos nos quieren ayudar.
>
> Ella está vendiéndosela a ellos.   Ellos quieren ayudarnos.

Note that in order to maintain the same stress you add a written accent mark to the present participle with either one or two pronouns. You add an accent to the infinitive with two pronouns only.

The object pronouns are added to an affirmative command. They precede the negative command.

AFFIRMATIVE	NEGATIVE
Háblame.	**No me hables.**
Dáselo.	**No se lo des.**
Invítelos usted.	**No los invite.**
Díganmelo.	**No me lo digan.**

Note that in order to maintain the same stress, you add a written accent to the command with a pronoun.

Negative expressions

To make a sentence negative, you merely put **no** before the verb or before the object pronoun that precedes the verb.

El gato no está en el jardín.

No lo veo.

Review the following affirmative and negative expressions.

AFFIRMATIVE	NEGATIVE
algo	**nada**
algien	**nadie**
siempre	**nunca**

Nadie está aquí.

Note that in Spanish, unlike in English, more than one negative word can be used in the same sentence.

No ves a nadie.

Ellos nunca hablan a nadie de nada.

The negative of **también** is **tampoco**.

A Juan le gusta. A mí también.

A Juan no le gusta. Ni a mí tampoco.

Verbs such as interesar, aburrir, gustar

Note the construction with verbs such as **interesar** and **aburrir**.

La historia me interesa.
Me interesa la historia. } *History interests me.*

Los deportes no les aburren.
No les aburren los deportes. } *Sports don't bore them.*

Gustar functions the same as **interesar** and **aburrir**. It conveys the meaning *to like*, but it literally means *to please*.

Me
Te
Le } gusta el helado.
Nos
Les

Me
Te
Le } gustan los vegetales.
Nos
Les

Expressions with the infinitive

The infinitive is the form of the verb that ends in **-ar, -er,** or **-ir.** The infinitive often follows another verb.

Ellos quieren salir.
Yo debo estudiar más.
Me gusta leer.

Three very common expressions that are followed by the infinitive are **tener que** *(to have to)*, **ir a** *(to be going to)*, and **acabar de** *(to have just)*.

Tengo que trabajar y estudiar más.

Y voy a trabajar y estudiar más.

Acabo de recibir una nota mala.

You can use the expression **favor de** followed by an infinitive to ask someone in a polite way to do something.

Favor de escribir tu nombre.

Favor de ayudarme.

Note that the object pronoun is added to the infinitive.

Ser and estar

Spanish has two verbs that mean *to be*. They are **ser** and **estar** and each one has distinct uses.

Ser

You use **ser** to express a characteristic, where someone or something is from, or what something is made of.

> **Él es guapo. Es inteligente también.**
> **Ellos son de Nuevo México.**
> **Su casa es de adobe.**

Estar

You use **estar** to express a condition or location.

> **Él está muy cansado y está triste también.**
> **Madrid está en España.**
> **Sus amigos están en Madrid.**

Saber and conocer

Both **saber** and **conocer** mean *to know*.

Saber means to know a fact or to have information about something. With an infinitive it expresses how to do something.

> **Yo sé su número de teléfono.**
> **Sabemos que ella va a viajar.**
> **Todos saben usar el Internet.**

Conocer means *to know* in the sense *to be familiar with*. It is used with people or complex, abstract concepts.

> **Yo conozco a su amigo, Tadeo.**
> **Ellos conocen bien la historia de España.**

Reflexive verbs

When the subject is both the doer and receiver of the action of the verb, you have to use a reflexive pronoun with the verb. Study the following examples of the reflexive construction.

REFLEXIVE	NONREFLEXIVE
Ella se levanta.	**Ella levanta al niño.**
Él se divierte.	**Él divierte a sus amigos.**
Me cepillo.	**Cepillo a mi perro.**

When the reflexive is followed by an article of clothing or a part of the body, you use a definite article in Spanish. (In English the possessive adjective is used.)

> **Me lavo la cara y las manos.**
> **Ella tiene frío y se pone el suéter.**

Verbs tenses

See the charts on pages SR28–SR33 for the verb forms you have learned.

Verb tense usage

Present

You use the present tense to state what is taking place now or what always takes place.

> **Hablamos español.**
> **Juegan fútbol en el otoño.**
> **Siempre hacen la misma cosa.**

You can also use the present tense to express a future action.

> **Salen mañana.**
> **Vamos a México en julio.**

Preterite

You use the preterite to express an action that began and ended at a specific time in the past.

> **Ellos salieron la semana pasada.**
> **Nosotros llegamos ayer.**
> **Los árabes invadieron España en 711.**

Imperfect

You use the imperfect to describe a continuous, habitual action in the past. The time at which the action began or ended is not important.

> **Ellos siempre hacían la misma cosa.**
> **Yo los veía de vez en cuando.**
> **Ellos iban a España con frecuencia porque tenían una casa allí.**

Grammar Review

You use the imperfect to describe things in the past.

Él era joven.

Tenía solo dos años.

Hacía buen tiempo.

Su hermana era muy simpática.

You use the imperfect to reminisce about past events.

Cuando yo era niño vivíamos en Puerto Rico y siempre celebrábamos el Día de los Reyes. Yo recuerdo bien que recibíamos nuestros regalos el seis de enero.

You use the imperfect with verbs to express mental activities or emotions in the past.

Él lo creía.

Querían hacerlo.

Estaban contentos.

Future

The true future *will* is used less frequently in Spanish than in English.

Le hablaré a él mañana.

Volverán la semana que viene.

The present tense and the **ir a** + infinitive construction are often used to convey the future.

Le hablo a él mañana.	**Le voy a hablar mañana.**
Vuelven la semana que viene.	**Van a volver la semana que viene.**

Conditional

You use the conditional in Spanish the same as in English. It tells what would or could happen.

¿Iría él?	**Sí, él iría.**
¿Lo sabrían ellos?	**Sí, ellos lo sabrían.**
¿Estarías contento?	**Sí, yo estaría contento.**

Present perfect

The present perfect is used to describe an action without reference to a specific past time. It is accompanied by time expressions such as **ya, todavía no, jamás, nunca.**

> **Nunca hemos hecho tal cosa.**
> **En mi vida he tenido un accidente.**
> **Todavía no han llegado.**

Progressive tense

The progressive tense is formed by using the verb **estar** (or **ir, seguir**) and the present participle. You use the progressive to indicate that the action is actually taking place.

> **Estamos pasando tiempo en la playa.**
> **Estoy mirando a los niños.**
> **Están nadando en el mar.**

Subjunctive

You use the subjunctive in a dependent clause. As the word *subjunctive* implies, it is used to express a subjective action that is not necessarily a fact. It may or may not take place. So far you have learned the following uses of the subjunctive.

You use the subjunctive in a clause introduced by **querer.**

> **Quiero que ellos salgan ahora.**
> **Ellos quieren que estudiemos y que tengamos éxito.**

You use the subjunctive following many impersonal expressions.

> **Es importante que lleguemos a tiempo.**
> **Es necesario que ellos lo sepan.**
> **Es mejor que tú lo hagas.**

The subjunctive follows the expressions **ojalá, quizás,** and **tal vez.**

> **¡Ojalá vengan a la fiesta!**
> **¡Quizá(s) vayan!**
> **¡Tal vez lo sepan!**

Passive voice with se

The pronoun **se** is used to express something being done without saying by whom.

Se habla español en México.
> *Spanish is spoken in Mexico.*
> *One speaks Spanish in Mexico.*
> *They speak Spanish in Mexico.*

> **¿A qué hora se abre el restaurante?**
> **Se sirven comidas mexicanas y peruanas.**

Imperative (commands)

You use the subjunctive form of the verb for all formal (**usted, ustedes**) commands and the negative familiar (**tú**) command.

Hable Ud.	**No hable Ud.**	**Hablen Uds.**	**No hablen Uds.**	**No hables.**
Coma Ud.	**No coma Ud.**	**Coman Uds.**	**No coman Uds.**	**No comas.**

You use the **usted** form of the present indicative for the familiar (**tú**) command.

Habla.

Come.

Note that you add the object pronouns to affirmative commands. The pronouns come before the negative command.

AFFIRMATIVE	NEGATIVE
Prepárelo.	**No lo prepare.**
Escríbanlo Uds.	**No lo escriban Uds.**
Háblame.	**No me hables.**

There are no irregular formal commands. You will find any irregular familiar (**tú**) commands in the following verb charts.

Verb Charts

	Regular verbs		
INFINITIVO	hablar *to speak*	comer *to eat*	vivir *to live*
PARTICIPIO PRESENTE	hablando	comiendo	viviendo
PARTICIPIO PASADO	hablado	comido	vivido
PRESENTE	hablo hablas habla hablamos *habláis* hablan	como comes come comemos *coméis* comen	vivo vives vive vivimos *vivís* viven
PRETÉRITO	hablé hablaste habló hablamos *hablasteis* hablaron	comí comiste comió comimos *comisteis* comieron	viví viviste vivió vivimos *vivisteis* vivieron
IMPERFECTO	hablaba hablabas hablaba hablábamos *hablabais* hablaban	comía comías comía comíamos *comíais* comían	vivía vivías vivía vivíamos *vivíais* vivían
FUTURO	hablaré hablarás hablará hablaremos *hablaréis* hablarán	comeré comerás comerá comeremos *comeréis* comerán	viviré vivirás vivirá viviremos *viviréis* vivirán
CONDICIONAL	hablaría hablarías hablaría hablaríamos *hablaríais* hablarían	comería comerías comería comeríamos *comeríais* comerían	viviría vivirías viviría viviríamos *viviríais* vivirían
PRESENTE PERFECTO	he hablado has hablado ha hablado hemos hablado *habéis hablado* han hablado	he comido has comido ha comido hemos comido *habéis comido* han comido	he vivido has vivido ha vivido hemos vivido *habéis vivido* han vivido

Verb Charts

Regular verbs *(continued)*

SUBJUNTIVO: PRESENTE	hable hables hable hablemos *habléis* hablen	coma comas coma comamos *comáis* coman	viva vivas viva vivamos *viváis* vivan

Stem-changing verbs (-ar and -er verbs)

INFINITIVO	empezar (e→ie) *to begin*	perder (e→ie) *to lose*	recordar (o→ue) *to remember*	volver (o→ue) *to return*
PRESENTE	empiezo empiezas empieza empezamos *empezáis* empiezan	pierdo pierdes pierde perdemos *perdéis* pierden	recuerdo recuerdas recuerda recordamos *recordáis* recuerdan	vuelvo vuelves vuelve volvemos *volvéis* vuelven
SUBJUNTIVO: PRESENTE	empiece empieces empiece empecemos *empecéis* empiecen	pierda pierdas pierda perdamos *perdáis* pierdan	recuerde recuerdes recuerde recordemos *recordéis* recuerden	vuelva vuelvas vuelva volvamos *volváis* vuelvan

e→ie

Other verbs conjugated like **empezar** and **perder** are: **cerrar, comenzar, despertar, pensar, defender, entender, querer.**

o→ue

Other verbs conjugated like **recordar** and **volver** are: **acordar, almorzar, contar, costar, probar, acostar(se), jugar (u→ue), devolver, mover, poder.**

Stem-changing verbs (-ir verbs)

INFINITIVO	preferir (e→ie, i) *to prefer*	dormir (o→ue, u) *to sleep*	pedir (e→i, i) *to ask for*
PARTICIPIO PRESENTE	prefiriendo	durmiendo	pidiendo
PRESENTE	prefiero prefieres prefiere preferimos *preferís* prefieren	duermo duermes duerme dormimos *dormís* duermen	pido pides pide pedimos *pedís* piden

Stem-changing verbs (-ir verbs) (continued)

PRETÉRITO	preferí preferiste prefirió preferimos *preferisteis* prefirieron	dormí dormiste durmió dormimos *dormisteis* durmieron	pedí pediste pidió pedimos *pedisteis* pidieron
SUBJUNTIVO: PRESENTE	prefiera prefieras prefiera prefiramos *prefiráis* prefieran	duerma duermas duerma durmamos *durmáis* duerman	pida pidas pida pidamos *pidáis* pidan

e→ie, i
Other verbs conjugated like **preferir** are: **sentir, sugerir.**

o→ue
Another verb conjugated like **dormir** is **morir.**

e→i, i
Other verbs conjugated like **pedir** are: **repetir, servir, seguir, vestirse.**

Irregular verbs

PARTICIPIO PASADO	**abrir** *to open* **abierto**					
PRETÉRITO	**andar** *to walk* anduve	anduviste	anduvo	anduvimos	*anduvisteis*	anduvieron
PRESENTE	**conocer** *to know, to be familiar with* conozco	conoces	conoce	conocemos	*conocéis*	conocen
PARTICIPIO PASADO	**cubrir** *to cover* **cubierto**					
PRESENTE PRETÉRITO SUBJUNTIVO	**dar** *to give* doy di dé	das diste des	da dio dé	damos dimos demos	*dais* *disteis* *deis*	dan dieron den

Irregular verbs *(continued)*

decir *to say*

PARTICIPIO PRESENTE	diciendo				
PARTICIPIO PASADO	dicho				
PRESENTE	digo	dices	dice	decimos	*decís*	dicen
PRETÉRITO	dije	dijiste	dijo	dijimos	*dijisteis*	dijeron
FUTURO	diré	dirás	dirá	diremos	*diréis*	dirán
CONDICIONAL	diría	dirías	diría	diríamos	*diríais*	dirían
IMPERATIVO FAMILIAR	di					

devolver *to return (bring back)*

PARTICIPIO PASADO	devuelto

escribir *to write*

PARTICIPIO PASADO	escrito

estar *to be*

PRESENTE	estoy	estás	está	estamos	*estáis*	están
PRETÉRITO	estuve	estuviste	estuvo	estuvimos	*estuvisteis*	estuvieron
SUBJUNTIVO	esté	estés	esté	estemos	*estéis*	estén

freír *to fry*

PARTICIPIO PASADO	frito

haber *to have (in compound tenses)*

PRESENTE	he	has	ha	hemos	*habéis*	han

hacer *to do, to make*

PARTICIPIO PASADO	hecho				
PRESENTE	hago	haces	hace	hacemos	*hacéis*	hacen
PRETÉRITO	hice	hiciste	hizo	hicimos	*hicisteis*	hicieron
FUTURO	haré	harás	hará	haremos	*haréis*	harán
CONDICIONAL	haría	harías	haría	haríamos	*haríais*	harían
IMPERATIVO FAMILIAR	haz					

ir *to go*

PARTICIPIO PRESENTE	yendo				
PRESENTE	voy	vas	va	vamos	*vais*	van
PRETÉRITO	fui	fuiste	fue	fuimos	*fuisteis*	fueron
IMPERFECTO	iba	ibas	iba	íbamos	*ibais*	iban
SUBJUNTIVO	vaya	vayas	vaya	vayamos	*vayáis*	vayan
IMPERATIVO FAMILIAR	ve					

morir *to die*

PARTICIPIO PASADO	muerto

Verb Charts

oír to hear

PRESENTE	oigo	oyes	oye	oímos	*oís*	oyen

poder to be able to

PARTICIPIO PRESENTE	pudiendo					
PRETÉRITO	pude	pudiste	pudo	pudimos	*pudisteis*	pudieron
FUTURO	podré	podrás	podrá	podremos	*podréis*	podrán
CONDICIONAL	podría	podrías	podría	podríamos	*podríais*	podrían

poner to put

PARTICIPIO PASADO	puesto					
PRESENTE	pongo	pones	pone	ponemos	*ponéis*	ponen
PRETÉRITO	puse	pusiste	puso	pusimos	*pusisteis*	pusieron
FUTURO	pondré	pondrás	pondrá	pondremos	*pondréis*	pondrán
CONDICIONAL	pondría	pondrías	pondría	pondríamos	*pondríais*	pondrían
IMPERATIVO FAMILIAR	pon					

querer to want

PRETÉRITO	quise	quisiste	quiso	quisimos	*quisisteis*	quisieron
FUTURO	querré	querrás	querrá	querremos	*querréis*	querrán
CONDICIONAL	querría	querrías	querría	querríamos	*querríais*	querrían

romper to break

PARTICIPIO PASADO	roto					

saber to know (how)

PRESENTE	sé	sabes	sabe	sabemos	*sabéis*	saben
PRETÉRITO	supe	supiste	supo	supimos	*supisteis*	supieron
FUTURO	sabré	sabrás	sabrá	sabremos	*sabréis*	sabrán
CONDICIONAL	sabría	sabrías	sabría	sabríamos	*sabríais*	sabrían
SUBJUNTIVO	sepa	sepas	sepa	sepamos	*sepáis*	sepan

salir to leave, to go out

PRESENTE	salgo	sales	sale	salimos	*salís*	salen
FUTURO	saldré	saldrás	saldrá	saldremos	*saldréis*	saldrán
CONDICIONAL	saldría	saldrías	saldría	saldríamos	*saldríais*	saldrían
IMPERATIVO FAMILIAR	sal					

ser to be

PRESENTE	soy	eres	es	somos	*sois*	son
PRETÉRITO	fui	fuiste	fue	fuimos	*fuisteis*	fueron
IMPERFECTO	era	eras	era	éramos	*erais*	eran
SUBJUNTIVO	sea	seas	sea	seamos	*seáis*	sean
IMPERATIVO FAMILIAR	sé					

Irregular verbs *(continued)*

tener *to have*

PRESENTE	tengo	tienes	tiene	tenemos	*tenéis*	tienen
PRETÉRITO	tuve	tuviste	tuvo	tuvimos	*tuvisteis*	tuvieron
FUTURO	tendré	tendrás	tendrá	tendremos	*tendréis*	tendrán
CONDICIONAL	tendría	tendrías	tendría	tendríamos	*tendríais*	tendrían
IMPERATIVO FAMILIAR	ten					

traer *to bring*

PRESENTE	traigo	traes	trae	traemos	*traéis*	traen
PRETÉRITO	traje	trajiste	trajo	trajimos	*trajisteis*	trajeron

venir *to come*

PARTICIPIO PRESENTE	viniendo					
PRETÉRITO	vine	viniste	vino	vinimos	*vinisteis*	vinieron
FUTURO	vendré	vendrás	vendrá	vendremos	*vendréis*	vendrán
CONDICIONAL	vendría	vendrías	vendría	vendríamos	*vendríais*	vendrían
IMPERATIVO FAMILIAR	ven					

ver *to see*

PARTICIPIO PASADO	visto					
PRESENTE	veo	ves	ve	vemos	*veis*	ven
PRETÉRITO	vi	viste	vio	vimos	*visteis*	vieron
IMPERFECTO	veía	veías	veía	veíamos	*veíais*	veían

volver *to return*

PARTICIPIO PASADO	vuelto

Spanish-English Dictionary

The Spanish-English Dictionary contains all productive and receptive vocabulary from Levels 1 and 2. The numbers following each productive entry indicate the chapter and vocabulary section in which the word is introduced. For example, **3.2** in dark print means that the word was first taught in **Capítulo 3, Vocabulario 2.** A light print number means that the word was introduced in **¡Así se dice!** Level 1. LP refers to the **Lecciones preliminares** in Level 1. If there is no number following an entry, this means that the word or expression is there for receptive purposes only.

a at; to
  a eso de las tres (cuatro, diez, etc.) at around three (four, ten, etc.) o'clock
  a fines de at the end of
  a la una (a las dos, a las tres…) at one o'clock (two o'clock, three o'clock), LP
  a lo lejos in the distance
  a lo menos at least
  a menudo often
  a pesar de in spite of
  a pie on foot, 3.2
  ¡A propósito! By the way!, 8.2
  ¿a qué hora? at what time?, LP
  a solas alone
  a tiempo on time, 10.2; **1.2**
  a veces at times, sometimes, 6.1; **1.2**
  a ver let's see
abajo down; below
  de abajo below
  (ir) para abajo (to go) down
abandonar el cuarto to check out *(hotel)*, 7
el **abono** fertilizer
abordar to board, 10.2; **1.2**
abordo aboard, on board, 10.2; **1.2**
abreviado(a) abbreviated, shortened
abrigado(a) wrapped up
el **abrigo** coat
abril April, LP
abrir to open, 4.2
abrochado(a) fastened, 10.2; **1.2**
la **abuela** grandmother, 2.1
el **abuelo** grandfather, 2.1

los **abuelos** grandparents, 2.1
abundoso(a) abundant
aburrido(a) boring, 1.2
aburrir to bore, 5.2
acá here, 11.2; **2.2**
acabar de to have just (done something), 4.2
la **academia** school
acaso: por si acaso just in case
acceder to access
el **accidente** accident, **11.2**
el **aceite** oil, 4
la **aceituna** olive, 4.2
el **acento** accent
la **acera** sidewalk, **8.1**
acercarse to approach
acomodado(a) wealthy, well-off
acomodar to set *(bone)*, **11.2**
acordarse (ue) to remember
  ¿Te acuerdas? Do you remember?
acostarse (ue) to go to bed, 11.1; **2.1**
acostumbrarse to get used to
el **acotamiento** shoulder *(road)*, **9.1**
la **actividad** activity
actual present-day, current
actuar to act, to take action
acudir to go to
acuerdo: estar de acuerdo con to agree with
adelantar(se) to pass *(car)*, **9.1**
adelante ahead
  ir hacia adelante to move forward, ahead
además furthermore, what's more; besides
además de in addition to, besides
¡Adiós! Good-bye., LP
adivinar to guess
adjunto: el documento

adjunto attached file, **6.1**
admitir to admit
¿adónde? (to) where?, 3.2
la **advertencia** warning
advertir (ie) to warn
aérea: la línea aérea airline, 10.1; **1.1**
aeróbico(a) aerobic
el **aeropuerto** airport, 10.1; **1.1**
aficionado(a): ser aficionado(a) a to like, to be a fan of
el/la **aficionado(a)** fan, 5.1
afine: la palabra afine cognate
las **afueras** suburbs, 2.2; outskirts
agarrar velocidad to pick up speed
el/la **agente** agent, 10.1; **1.1**
la **aglomeración** big city
agosto August, LP
agradable pleasant, friendly, agreeable
agrario(a) agrarian
agresivo(a) aggressive
agrícola agricultural
el **agua** *(f.)* water, 4.1
  el agua mineral (con gas) (sparkling) mineral water, 4.2
  el agua corriente running water
el **aguacate** avocado, **10**
el **aguinaldo** Christmas gift, **5.2**
ahora now
el **aire** air
  al aire libre open-air, outdoor
el **aire acondicionado** air conditioning, 7
aislado(a) isolated
el **ají** chili pepper
el **ajo** garlic, **10**
al to the, on the, in the
  al aire libre open-air, outdoor

al borde mismo de right on the edge of

al contrario on the contrary

al lado de beside, next to, 2.2

las **alitas** wings, **10**

la **alberca** swimming pool, 7.1

el **albergue juvenil** youth hostel, **7**

la **albóndiga** meatball, 4.2

el **álbum** album

la **alcachofa** artichoke

    las **alcachofas salteadas** sautéed artichokes

    alcanzar to reach

la **alcoba** bedroom

la **aldea** small village

    alegrarse to rejoice

    alegre happy, 6.1

la **alegría** happiness, joy

    alemán(ana) German

los **alemanes** Germans

la **alfombrilla** mouse pad, **6.1**

el **álgebra** algebra

    algo something, 4.1; anything, 9.2

        ¿Algo más? Anything else?, 9.2

    alguien someone, somebody, 8.2

    algunos(as) some

el **alimento** food

    allá over there, 9.1

    allí there

el **alma** (f.) soul

las **almejas** clams, **4**

la **almohada** pillow, **7**

el **almuerzo** lunch, 4.1

    tomar el almuerzo to have lunch, 4.1

    ¡Aló! Hello! (on the phone)

    alpino: el esquí alpino downhill skiing, 7.2

    alquilar to rent, 7.1; **3.2**

    alrededor de around, 2.2

los **alrededores** outskirts, surroundings

    altivo(a) arrogant

    alto(a) tall, 1.1; high, 3.1; upper

        la clase alta upper class

        la nota alta high grade, 3.1

la **altura** altitude

el/la **alumno(a)** student, 1.2

    amarillo(a) yellow, 5.1

la **ambición** ambition

    ambicioso(a) hard-working, 1.2

el **ambiente** atmosphere, environment

la **ambulancia** ambulance, **11.2**

la **América del Sur** South America

    americano(a) American

el/la **amigo(a)** friend, 1.1

el **amor** love

    amurallado(a) walled

    anaranjado(a) orange (color), 5.1

    ancho(a) wide, broad, **8.1**

    andar to go, to walk; to ride, **3.2**

        andar a caballo to ride a horse, **3.2**

        andar en bicicleta to ride a bike, **11.1**

el **andén** (railway) platform, **3.1**

    andino(a) Andean, of the Andes

    angosto(a) narrow, **8.1**

la **angustia** distress, anguish

    animado(a) lively

el **animal** animal

    animar to cheer (somebody, something) on

    anoche last night, 7.1

    anónimo(a) anonymous

el **anorak** anorak, ski jacket, 7.2

los **anteojos de sol** sunglasses, 7.1

el **antepecho** parapet

    anterior previous, **6.1**

    antes de before, 10.1; **1.1**

los **antibióticos** antibiotics

    antiguo(a) ancient, old, **8.1**; former

        el casco (barrio) antiguo the old city, **8.1**

    antipático(a) unpleasant, not nice 1.1

los **antojitos** snacks, nibbles, 4.2

    anunciar to announce

el **anuncio** announcement

    añadir to add, **10**

el **año** year, LP

        el Año Nuevo New Year

        el año pasado last year, 7.1

        ¿Cuántos años tiene? How old is he (she)?, 2.1

        cumplir... años to be (turn) . . . years old

    apagar to turn off, **6.1**

el **aparato** device

    aparcar to park, **8.1**

    aparentado(a) related

la **apariencia** appearance, looks

    ¿Qué apariencia tiene? What does he (she) look like?

el **apartamento** apartment, 2.2

    la casa de apartamentos apartment house

el **apartamiento** apartment, 2.2

    aparte apart, on the side

    apetecer to feel like, to crave

    apetito: ¡Buen apetito! Bon appétit! Enjoy your meal!

    aplaudir to applaud, to clap, 5.1

el **aplauso** applause, 5.1

        recibir aplausos to be applauded, 5.1

    apreciado(a) appreciated, liked

    aprender to learn, 4.2

    apropiado(a) appropriate

    aproximadamente approximately

    aquel(la) that, 9.1

    aquí here, 9.1

        Aquí (lo, la, etc.) tienes. Here it (they) is (are).

el/la **árabe** Arab

    aragonés(esa) from Aragon (Spain)

el **árbol** tree, 2.2

        el árbol de Navidad Christmas tree, **5.2**

el **arcén** shoulder (road), **9.1**

el **archivo** file, **6.1**

la **arena** sand, 7.1

    argentino(a) Argentine

    árido(a) dry, arid

la **aritmética** arithmetic

    armar to put up (tent), 11.2; **2.2**

el **armario** closet, **7**

la **arqueología** archeology

el **arroyo** brook

la **arroba** the @ sign, **6.1**

el **arroz** rice, 4.1

el **arte** art, 1.2

    arterial: la tensión arterial blood pressure, 6.2

la **artesanía** crafts, 9.2

el/la **artista** artist

    asar to grill, to roast, **10**

la **ascendencia** heritage, background

el **ascensor** elevator, **7**

    asegurarse to make sure

    así thus, so, in this way

el **asiento** seat, 10.1; **1.1**

        el número del asiento seat number, 10.1; **1.1**

    asignar to assign, **6.2**

la **asistencia médica** medical care

el/la **asistente de vuelo** flight attendant, 10.2; **1.2**

asistir a to attend, 8.1

el **asno** donkey

el **aspa** sail *(windmill)*

astuto(a) astute, smart

atacar to attack

la **atención** attention

¡Atención! Careful!

prestar atención to pay attention, 3.1

el **aterrizaje** landing, 10.2; **1.2**

aterrizar to land, 10.2; **1.2**

el/la **atleta** athlete

las **atracciones** rides *(amusement park)*, **8.1**

el **parque de atracciones** amusement park, **8.1**

atraer to attract

atrapar to catch, 5.2

atrás: hacia atrás backwards

el **atributo** attribute, positive feature

el **atún** tuna, 9.2

aumentar to grow, to increase, to enlarge

aun even

aún still

aunque although, even though

ausente absent

auténtico(a) authentic, real

el **autobús** bus, 8.1; **8.1**

perder el autobús to miss the bus, 8.1

automático(a) automatic, 10.2; **1.2**

el **distribuidor automático** boarding pass kiosk, 10.2; **1.2;** automatic dispenser, **3.1**

la **autopista** highway, **9.1**

el/la **autor(a)** author

autoservicio self-serve

la **autovía** highway, **9.1**

avanzado(a) difficult, 7.2; advanced

la **avenida** avenue, **8.1**

la **aventura** adventure

la **avería** breakdown

averiado(a) broken down

el **avión** airplane, 10.1; **1.1**

la **avioneta** small plane, light aircraft

ayer yesterday, 7.1

ayer por la tarde yesterday afternoon, 7.1

la **ayuda** help, assistance

ayudar to help, 10.1; **1.1**

el **azafrán** saffron

el **azúcar** sugar

azul blue, 2.1

el **azulejo** glazed tile, floor tile

B

el **bache** pothole

el **bacón** bacon, 4.1; **7**

el/la **bailador(a)** dancer

bailar to dance, **5.2**

bajar to go down, 7.2; to download, **6.2**

bajar(se) to get off *(train)*, **3.2**

la **bajeza** baseness

bajo(a) short, 1.1; low, 3.1; poor, lower-class

la nota baja low grade, 3.1

el **balcón** balcony

el **balneario** seaside resort, beach resort, 7.1

el **balón** ball, 5.1

el **baloncesto** basketball, 5.2

la **banda** band, 8.1; **5.2;** lane *(highway)*

la banda municipal municipal band, **5.2**

la **bandeja de entradas** inbox *(e-mail)*, **6.1**

la **bandeja de enviados** sent mailbox *(e-mail)*, **6.1**

la **bandera** flag

el **bañador** swimsuit, 7.1

bañarse to take a bath, to bathe oneself

la **bañera** bathtub, **7**

el **baño** bath; bathroom

el cuarto de baño bathroom, 2.2; **7**

barato(a) inexpensive, cheap, 9.1

Todo te sale más barato. It's all a lot cheaper., 9.1

la **barbacoa** barbecue

barbaridad: ¡Qué barbaridad! That's awful!

¡Bárbaro! Great!, Awesome!, **5.2**

el **barco** boat

el **barquito** small boat, 7.1

la **barra** bar *(soap)*, 11.2; **2.2;** counter, bar *(restaurant)*

la barra de jabón bar of soap, 11.2; **2.2**

la **barra de herramientas** toolbar, **6.1**

el **barrio** neighborhood, area, quarter, district, **8.1**

la **base** base, 5.2

el **básquetbol** basketball, 5.2

la cancha de básquetbol basketball court, 5.2

bastante rather, quite, 1.2; enough

el **bastón** ski pole, 7.2

la **batalla** battle

el **bate** bat, 5.2

el/la **bateador(a)** batter, 5.2

batear to hit, to bat, 5.2

batear un jonrón to hit a home run, 5.2

el **batido** shake, smoothie, 4.2

el **baúl** trunk *(car)*, 10.1; **1.1**

beber to drink, 4.1

la **bebida** beverage, drink, 4.1

el **béisbol** baseball, 5.2

el/la beisbolista baseball player, 5.2

el campo de béisbol baseball field, 5.2

el/la jugador(a) de béisbol baseball player, 5.2

la **belleza** beauty

bello(a) beautiful

la **benzina** gas(oline)

el **beso** kiss

los **biafranos** people from Biafra

la **biblioteca** library

la **bicicleta** bicycle, 2.2

andar en bicicleta to ride a bike, **11.1**

bien well, fine, LP

bien educado(a) polite, well-mannered, 6.1

bien hecho(a) well-done *(meat)*, **4**

estar bien to be (feel) well, fine, 6.2

Muy bien. Very well., LP

la **bienvenida: dar la bienvenida** to greet, to welcome

bienvenido(a) welcome

el **bife** beef

el **biftec** steak, **4**

el **billete** ticket, 10.1; **1.1**

el billete electrónico e-ticket, 10.1; **1.1**

el billete de ida y vuelta round-trip ticket, **3.1**

el billete sencillo one-way ticket, **3.1**

la **biología** biology

el/la **biólogo(a)** biologist

el **bizcocho** cake, **5.1**
blanco(a) white, **5.1**
blando(a) soft
bloquear to block, **5.1**
el **blue jean** jeans, 9.1
la **blusa** blouse, 3.1
la **boca** mouth, 6.2
la **boca del metro** subway entrance, **8.1**
la **bocacalle** intersection, 9.1
el **bocadillo** sandwich, 4.1
los **bocaditos** snacks
la **boda** wedding
la **bodega** grocery store
la **boletería** ticket window, 7.2; **3.1**
el **boleto** ticket, 7.2; **3.1**
    el **boleto electrónico** e-ticket, 10.1; **1.1**
    el **boleto de ida y regreso** round-trip ticket, **3.1**
    el **boleto sencillo** one-way ticket, **3.1**
el **bolígrafo** pen, 3.1
el **bolívar** bolivar (*currency of Venezuela*)
la **bolsa de dormir** sleeping bag, 11.2; **2.2**
bolsillo: el libro de bolsillo paperback, **3.1**
la **bombilla** (*drinking*) container
los **bombones** candy
bonito(a) pretty, 1.1
el **borde** side (*of a street, sidewalk*)
    al borde mismo de right on the edge of
borrador: el botón borrador delete key, **6.1**
borrar to delete, **6.1**
el **bosque** woods
la **bota** boot, 7.2
botar to throw out
    botar la casa por la ventana to splurge
el **bote** can, 9.2
la **botella** bottle, 9.2
el **botón** button, key (*computer*), **6.1**
    el **botón regresar (retroceder)** back button, **6.1**
    el **botón borrador** delete key, **6.1**
Brasil Brazil
brasileño(a) Brazilian
bravo(a) rough, stormy
el **brazo** arm, 11.1; **2.1**
brillar to shine
bronce: de bronce bronze (*adj.*), 8.2

bronceador(a): la loción bronceadora suntan lotion, 7.1
bucear to go snorkeling, 7.1; to scuba dive
el **buceo** snorkeling, 7.1; scuba diving
buen good, LP
    estar de buen humor to be in a good mood, 6.1
    Hace buen tiempo. The weather is nice., LP
    tener un buen sentido de humor to have a good sense of humor, 6.1
bueno(a) good, 1.1; Hello! (*on the phone*)
    Buenas noches. Good evening., LP
    Buenas tardes. Good afternoon., LP
    Buenos días. Good morning., Hello., LP
    sacar notas buenas to get good grades, 3.1
la **bufetería** dining car, **3.2**
el **burrito** burrito
el **bus** bus
    el bus escolar school bus, 3.2
    perder el autobús to miss the bus, 8.1
    tomar el autobús to take the bus
busca: en busca de seeking, in search of
buscar to look for, to seek, 3.2
el **buzo** sweat suit, warm-ups, **11.1**

el **caballero** gentleman
    el caballero andante knight errant
el **caballo** horse, 3.2
    andar a caballo to ride a horse, 3.2
    montar a caballo to go horseback riding, 8.2
la **cabeza** head, 6.2; **2.1**
    tener dolor de cabeza to have a headache, 6.2
la **cabina de mando** cockpit (*airplane*)
la **cabina de peaje** tollbooth, 9.1
el **cacahuate** peanut, 8.1
el **cacahuete** peanut
la **cacerola** saucepan, **10**
el **cacique** leader, chief
cada each, every, 2.2

caer to fall
caerse to fall, **11.2**
el **café** café, 3.1; coffee, 4.1; **7**
la **cafetería** cafeteria, 4.1
    el coche cafetería dining car, **3.2**
la **caída** drop
    la llamada caída dropped call (*cell phone*), **6.2**
la **caja** cash register, 3.2
la **calavera** skull, **5.1;** sweet cake made for the Day of the Dead
los **calcetines** socks, 5.1
la **calculadora** calculator, 3.1
el **caldo** broth
caliente hot, 4.1
    el chocolate caliente hot chocolate, 4.1
la **calle** street, 8.1
    la calle de sentido único one-way street, 9.1
calmo(a) calm, 6.1
el **calor** heat
    Hace calor. It's hot., LP
    tener calor to be hot, 11.1; **2.1**
calzar to wear, to take (*shoe size*), 9.1
    ¿Qué número calzas? What size shoe do you wear (take)?, 9.1
la **cama** bed, 2.2; **7**
    guardar cama to stay in bed (*illness*), 6.2
    hacer la cama to make the bed, **7**
    quedarse en la cama to stay in bed, 11.1; **2.1**
la **cámara digital** digital camera, 7.1; **6.2**
el/la **camarero(a)** server, waiter (waitress), **4;** (*hotel*) housekeeper, **7**
los **camarones** shrimp, 4.2
cambiar to change, 3.2
el **camello** camel, 5.2
la **camilla** stretcher, **11.2**
caminar to walk, 5.1
la **caminata: dar una caminata** to take a hike, 11.2; **2.2**
el **camino** road
    tomar el camino to set out for
el **camión** bus (*Mexico*), 8.1; truck, 9.2
la **camisa** shirt, 3.1
    la camisa de manga corta (larga) short- (long-) sleeved shirt, 9.1

Spanish-English Dictionary

la **camiseta** T-shirt, 5.1
la **campana** bell tower
la **campanada** peal of the bell
el/la **campeón(ona)** champion
el/la **campesino(a)** farmer, peasant, **8.2**
el **camping** camping, 11.2; **2.2**; campsite
   ir de camping to go camping, 11.2; **2.2**
el **campo** field, 5.1; **8.2**; country, countryside, **8.2**
   el campo de béisbol baseball field, 5.2
   el campo de fútbol soccer field, 5.1
   la carrera a campo traviesa cross-country race, **11.1**
   la casa de campo country house, **8.2**
el **camposanto** cemetery, **5.1**
   canadiense Canadian
el **canal** lane *(highway)*
la **canasta** basket, 5.2
la **cancha** court, 5.2
   la cancha de básquetbol (tenis) basketball *(tennis)* court, 5.2
   la cancha de voleibol volleyball court, 7.1
la **candela** candle
el **cangrejo de río** crayfish
el **cañón** canyon, **3.2**
   cansado(a) tired, 6.1
el/la **cantante** singer, 8.1
   cantar to sing, 8.1
la **cantidad** quantity, amount, number of
la **cantina** cafeteria
la **capital** capital
el **capítulo** chapter
el **capó** hood *(car)*, **9.2**
la **cara** face, 6.1
la **característica** feature, trait
el **carbón** coal
el **cardo** thorn
   cargado(a) thrown (over one's shoulders); loaded
el **Caribe** Caribbean
   el mar Caribe Caribbean Sea
   cariñoso(a) adorable, affectionate, 2.1
   caritativo(a) charitable
la **carne** meat, 4.1; **4**
la **carne de res** beef, **4**
el **carnet** driver's license, **9.2**

el **carnet de identidad** ID card, 10.2; **1.2**
la **carnicería** butcher shop
   caro(a) expensive, 9.1
la **carpa** tent, 11.2; **2.2**
   armar (montar) una carpa to put up a tent, 11.2; **2.2**
la **carpeta** folder, 3.2; **6.1**
la **carrera** race, **11.1**; career
   la carrera a campo traviesa cross-country race, **11.1**
   la carrera de larga distancia long-distance race, **11.1**
   la carrera de relevos relay race, **11.1**
la **carretera** highway, 9.1
el **carril** lane *(highway)*, 9.1
el **carrito** shopping cart, 9.2
el **carro** car, 2.2; **9.2**
   en carro by car
la **carta** letter
la **casa** house, 2.2
   la casa de apartamentos apartment building, 2.2
   la casa de campo country house, **8.2**
   en casa at home
   regresar a casa to go home, 3.2
   casarse to get married
el **casco** helmet, 7.2; **11.1**
el **casco antiguo** the old city, **8.1**
   casi almost, practically, 8.2; **4**
   casi crudo rare *(meat)*, **4**
el **caso** case
   hacer caso pay attention
   castaño(a) brown, chestnut *(eyes, hair)*, 2.1
el **castillo** castle
la **casucha** shack
   catarro: tener catarro to have a cold, 6.2
el/la **cátcher** catcher, 5.2
la **catedral** cathedral
la **categoría** category
   catorce fourteen, LP
el **caucho** tire
   cautivar to captivate, to charm
la **cazuela** saucepan, pot, **10**
el **CD** CD
la **cebolla** onion, 9.2; **10**
   celebrar to celebrate, 5.2
el **celular** cell phone, 3.2; **6.1**
el **cementerio** cemetery, **5.1**

la **cena** dinner, 4.1
   cenar to have dinner, 4.1
el **cenote** natural water well
el **centro** downtown, **8.1**; center
el **centro comercial** shopping center, mall, 9.1
   cepillarse to brush, 11.1; **2.1**
   cepillarse los dientes to brush one's teeth, 11.1; **2.1**
el **cepillo** brush, 11.2; **2.2**
   el cepillo de dientes toothbrush, 11.2; **2.2**
las **cerámicas** ceramics, 9.2
   cerca (de) near, 3.2
el **cerdo** pig, **8.2**
   la chuleta de cerdo pork chop; **4**
el **cereal** cereal, 4.1
   cero zero, LP
   cerrar (ie) to close, 11.2; **2.2**
la **cesta** basket
el **cesto** basket, 5.2
la **chacra** farm, **8.2**
el **champú** shampoo, 11.2; **2.2**
   ¡Chao! Good-bye!, Bye!, LP
la **chaqueta** jacket, 9.1
   la chaqueta de esquí ski jacket, anorak, 7.2
las **chauchas** green beans
el **chico** boy
   chileno(a) Chilean
la **chimenea** fireplace, 5.2
el **chipotle** jalapeño pepper
el **chiringuito** refreshment stand
el **chisme** rumor, gossip
el **choclo** corn
el **chocolate** chocolate, 4.1
   el chocolate caliente hot chocolate, 4.1
el **chorizo** Spanish sausage
la **choza** shack
la **chuleta de cerdo** pork chop, **4**
el **churro** (type of) doughnut
   ciego(a) blind
el/la **ciego(a)** blind man (woman)
el **cielo** sky, **5.2**
   cien(to) one hundred, LP
la **ciencia** science, 1.2
   cierto(a) true, certain, **6.1**
   cinco five, LP
   cincuenta fifty, LP
el **cine** movie theater, movies, 8.2
   ir al cine to go to the movies, 8.2

el **cinturón de seguridad** seat belt, 10.2; **1.2**

el/la **cirujano(a) ortopédico(a)** orthopedic surgeon, **11.2**

la **ciudad** city, 2.2; **8.1**

la **civilización** civilization

claro(a) clear

claro que of course

la **clase** class *(school)*, 1.2; class *(ticket)*, **3.1**

en primera (secunda) clase first-class (second-class), **3.1**

la sala de clase classroom, 3.1

clavar con una multa to give (someone) a ticket, **9.1**

la **clave de área** area code, **6.2**

clic: hacer clic to click *(computer)*, **6.1**

el/la **cliente** customer, 9.2; **7**

el **clima** climate

la **clínica** clinic

la **cocción** cooking

cocer (ue) to cook, **10**

el **coche** car, 9.2; train car, 3.1

el coche deportivo sports car, **9.2**

el **coche comedor (cafetería)** dining car, **3.2**

el **cochinillo asado** roast suckling pig

la **cocina** kitchen, 2.2; **10**; stove, **10**; cooking, cuisine

cocinar to cook, **10**

el/la **cocinero(a)** cook, **10**

el **cocodrilo** crocodile

el **codo** elbow, 11.1; **2.1**

la **cola** cola (soda) 4.1; line *(of people)*, 10.2; **1.2**

hacer cola to wait in line, 10.2; **1.2**

el **colegio** secondary school, high school

el **colgador** hanger, **7**

colgar (ue) to hang up

la **colina** hill

la **colocación** placement

colocar to place, to put

colombiano(a) Colombian

colonial colonial

el **color** color, 5.1

de color marrón brown, 5.1

¿De qué color es? What color is it?

el **comando** command

combinado: el plato combinado combination plate

el **comedor** dining room, 2.2

el **coche comedor** dining car, 3.2

el/la **comensal** diner

comenzar (ie) to begin

comer to eat, 4.1

dar de comer a to feed

los **comestibles** food, **4**

cómico(a) funny, comical, 1.1

la **comida** meal, 4.1; food

como like, as; since

¿cómo? How?; What?, 1.1

¿Cómo es él? What's he like? What does he look like?, 1.1

¿Cómo está…? How is…?

¡Cómo no! Sure! Of course!

cómodo(a) comfortable

el/la **compañero(a)** companion

comparar to compare

el **compartimiento superior** overhead bin, 10.2; **1.2**

compartir to share

completar to complete, to fill in

completo(a) full, **3.2**

el **comportamiento** behavior, conduct, 6.1

comportarse to behave

la **composición** composition

la **compra** purchase, 9.2

el/la **comprador(a)** shopper, customer

comprar to buy, 3.2

compras: ir de compras to shop, to go shopping, 9.1

comprender to understand, 4.2; to include

la **computadora** computer, 3.2; **6.1**

comunicarse to communicate with each other

con with

con frecuencia often

con retraso (una demora) late, delayed, 10.2; **1.2**

el **concierto** concert, 8.1

el **condimento** condiment, **10**

el **condominio** condominium

conducir to drive, **9.2**

la **conducta** conduct, behavior, 6.1

tener buena conducta to be well-behaved, 6.1

el/la **conductor(a)** driver, **9.2**

conectado(a) on-line, connected

conectar to connect

la **conexión** connection

confeccionar to make, to prepare, **5.1**

la **conferencia** lecture

confiabilidad reliability

confiable reliable, trustworthy

conforme: estar conforme to agree, to be in agreement

confortar to soothe

congelado(a) frozen, 9.2

los productos congelados frozen food, 9.2

el **congelador** freezer, **10**

el **conjunto** band, musical group, 8.1

conocer to know, to be familiar with, 9.1; to meet

conocido(a) known

el **conquistador** conqueror

conquistar to conquer

consecuencia: por consecuencia as a result, consequently

el/la **consejero(a)** counselor

el **consejo** advice

considerar to consider

consiguiente: por consiguiente consequently

el **consomé** bouillon, consommé

la **consonante** consonant

constar (de) to consist of, to be made up of

la **consulta** doctor's office, 6.2

consultar to consult

el **consultorio** doctor's office, 6.2

el/la **consumidor(a)** consumer

contagioso(a) contagious

la **contaminación del aire** air pollution

contaminar to pollute

contar (ue) to tell, to count

contemporáneo(a) contemporary

el **contenido** contents

contento(a) happy, 6.1

contestar to answer, 3.1

continental: el desayuno continental Continental breakfast, **7**

el **continente** continent

continua: la línea continua solid line *(road)*, **9.1**

continuar to continue

contra against

contrario(a) opposite; opposing

al contrario on the contrary

contrastar to contrast

Spanish-English Dictionary

contribuir to contribute

el **control de seguridad** security (checkpoint), 10.2; **1.2**

pasar por el control de seguridad to go through security, 10.2; **1.2**

la **conversación** conversation

conversar to converse

el **convertible** convertible, **9.2**

convertir to convert, to transform

la **copa: la Copa Mundial** World Cup

la **copia** copy, **6.1**

la copia dura hard copy, **6.1**

el **corazón** heart

la **corbata** tie, 9.1

el **cordero** lamb, **4**

la **corona** wreath, **5.1**

el **corral** corral, **8.2**

el/la **corredor(a)** runner

el **correo electrónico** e-mail, 3.2; **6.1**

correr to run, 5.2

cortar to cut off, **6.2**; to cut, to chop, **10**

cortar en pedacitos to cut in small pieces, to dice, **10**

cortar en rebanadas to slice, **10**

Estás cortando. You're breaking up. *(telephone)*, **6.2**

Se nos cortó la línea. We've been cut off. *(telephone)*, **6.2**

cortarse to cut oneself, **11.2**

la **cortesía** courtesy

corto(a) short, 9.1

de manga corta short-sleeved, 9.1

el pantalón corto shorts, 5.1

la **corvina** corbina, drumfish

la **cosa** thing, 3.1

la **cosecha** harvest, **8.2**

cosechar to harvest, **8.2**

cosmopolito(a) cosmopolitan

la **costa** coast

costar (ue) to cost, 9.1

¿Cuánto cuesta? How much does it cost?, 3.2

costarricense Costa Rican

la **costumbre** custom

el **cráneo** skull, **5.1**

crear to create

crecer to grow

creer to believe, to think

creo que sí (que no) I (don't) think so, 4.2

la **crema dental** toothpaste, 11.2; **2.2**

la **crema solar** suntan lotion, 7.1

el/la **criado(a)** housekeeper

cristiano(a) Christian

criticar to criticize

el **cruce** crosswalk, pedestrian crossing, **8.1**; intersection, **9.1**

crudo(a) raw, 8.1

casi crudo rare *(meat)*, **4**

los vegetales crudos raw vegetables, crudités, 8.1

cruzar to cross; to intersect, **9.1**

el **cuaderno** notebook, 3.1

la **cuadra** *(city)* block, **9.1**

el **cuadro** painting, 8.2

¿cuál? which? what?, LP

¿Cuál es la fecha de hoy? What is today's date?, LP

¿cuáles? which ones? what?

cualquier(a) any

cualquier otro(a) any other

cuando when, 3.1

¿cuándo? when?, 3.2

cuanto: en cuanto as soon as

cuanto: en cuanto a in terms of, as far as . . . is concerned

¿cuánto? how much?

¿A cuánto está(n)... ? How much is (are) . . . ?, 9.2

¿Cuánto es? How much is it (does it cost)?, LP

¿cuántos(as)? how many?, 2.1

¿Cuántos años tiene? How old is he (she)?, 2.1

cuarenta forty, LP

el **cuarto** room, 2.2; **7**; quarter

el cuarto de baño bathroom, 2.2; **7**

el cuarto de dormir bedroom, 2.2

el cuarto sencillo (doble) single (double) room, **7**

y cuarto a quarter-past (the hour), LP

cuatro four, LP

cuatrocientos(as) four hundred, 9.2

el/la **cubano(a)** Cuban

el/la **cubanoamericano(a)** Cuban American

cubierto(a) covered; indoor

cubrir to cover

la **cuchara** tablespoon, **4**

la **cucharada** tablespoonful

la **cucharadita** teaspoonful

la **cucharita** teaspoon, **4**

el **cuchillo** knife, **4**

el **cuello** neck, **11.1**

la **cuenca** basin *(river)*

la **cuenta** check *(restaurant)*, 4.2; **4**; account

darse cuenta to realize

por su cuenta on its own

tomar en cuenta to take into account

el **cuento** story

el **cuerdo** string

el **cuerpo** body, 11.1; **2.1**

la **cueva** cave

cuidado: con (mucho) cuidado (very) carefully

tener cuidado to be careful, **9.1**

cuidar to take care of, to care for

¡Cuídate! Take care of yourself!

la **culpa** blame, guilt

cultivar to work *(land)*; to grow, **8.2**

la **cultura** culture

el **cumpleaños** birthday, 8.1

cumplir... años to be (turn) . . . years old

cumplir un sueño to fulfill a wish, to make a wish come true

la **cuota** toll

curarse to get better, to recover

el **curso** class, course, 1.2

cuyos(as) whose

daño: hacerse daño to harm oneself, to get hurt, **11.2**

dar to give, 3.1

dar de comer a to feed

dar la vuelta to turn around, **9.1**

dar un examen (una prueba) to give a test, 3.1

dar una caminata to take a hike, 11.2; **2.2**

dar una fiesta to throw a party, **8.1**

darse cuenta to realize

datar to date *(time)*

los **datos** data, facts

de of, from, LP

¿de dónde? from where?, **1.1**

De nada. You're welcome., LP

¿De parte de quién, por favor? Who's calling, please?, **6.2**

¿de qué nacionalidad? what nationality?, **1.1**

de vez en cuando from time to time, 10.2; **1.2**

No hay de qué. You're welcome., LP

debajo de below, underneath, 10.2; **1.2**

deber should, **4.2**

debido a owing to

la **debilidad** weakness

decidir to decide

decir to say, to tell

la **decisión** decision

tomar una decisión to make a decision

decorar to decorate, **5.2**

dedicado(a) devoted

el **dedo** finger, 11.1; **2.1**

el **dedo del pie** toe, **11.1**

deducirse to deduct

el **defecto** defect

defender (ie) to defend

definido(a) definite

dejar to leave (something), **4**; to let, to allow

dejar con to put an end to

dejar un mensaje to leave a message, **6.2**

dejar una propina to leave a tip, **4**

del of the, from the

delante de in front of, **2.2**

delantero(a) front *(adj.)*, **8.1**

delgado(a) thin

demás (the) rest

demasiado too *(adv.)*, too much

la **demora** delay, 10.2; **1.2**

con una demora late, 10.2; **1.2**

dental: el tubo de crema dental tube of toothpaste, 11.2; **2.2**

dentífrica: la pasta dentífrica toothpaste

dentro de within

dentro de poco soon, shortly thereafter, 10.2; **1.2**

el **departamento** apartment, **2.2**

el **departamento de orientación** guidance office

el/la **dependiente** salesperson, employee, **9.1**

el **deporte** sport, **5.1**

el **deporte de equipo** team sport

el **deporte individual** individual sport

deportivo(a) *(related to)* sports

el **coche deportivo** sports car, **9.2**

deprimido(a) sad, depressed, **6.1**

derecho(a) right, 11.1; **2.1**

a la derecha on the right, **9.1**

derecho straight (ahead), **9.1**

derrocar to bring down

desafortunadamente unfortunately

desagradable unpleasant, not nice

desaparecer to disappear

desarrollarse to develop

el **desastre** disaster

desastroso(a) disastrous, catastrophic

el **desayuno** breakfast, 4.1; **7**

el **desayuno americano** American breakfast, **7**

el **desayuno continental** Continental breakfast, **7**

tomar el desayuno to have breakfast, **4.1**

descansar to rest, **11.1**

el **descapotable** convertible, **9.2**

descargar to download, **6.2**

descolgar (el auricular) to unhook (the telephone receiver), **6.2**

desconocido(a) unknown

desconsolado(a) very sad

describir to describe

la **descripción** description

el **descuento** discount

desde since; from

desear to want, to wish, **4.2**

¿Qué desean tomar? What would you like *(to eat, drink)?*, **4.2**

desembarcar to deplane, disembark, 10.2; **1.2**

desembocar to lead, to go (from one street into another), to come out onto

el **deseo** wish, desire

desesperado(a) desperate

desfilar to walk (in a parade or procession), **5.1**

el **desfile** parade, **5.2**

desgraciadamente unfortunately

deshuesado(a) deboned

el **desierto** desert

desinflada: la llanta desinflada flat tire, **9.2**

despacio slow, slowly, **9.1**

despedirse (i, i) to take leave

despegar to take off *(plane)*, 10.2; **1.2**

el **despegue** takeoff, 10.2; **1.2**

despertarse (ie) to wake up, 11.1; **2.1**

después (de) after, 3.1; later

el/la **destinatario(a)** addressee, recipient, **6.1**

el **destino** destination, **3.1**

destino: con destino a (going) to; for, 10.2; **1.2**

las **desventajas** disadvantages

el **detalle** detail

detrás de in back of, behind, **2.2**

devolver (ue) to return (something), **5.2**

el **día** day

Buenos días. Good morning., LP

el Día de los Muertos Day of the Dead, **5.1**

el Día de los Reyes Epiphany (January 6), **5.1**

hoy en día nowadays

¿Qué día es hoy? What day is it today?, LP

el **diablo** devil

el **diagnóstico** diagnosis

el **diálogo** dialogue

diaria: la rutina diaria daily routine, 11.1; **2.1**

el **dibujo** drawing, illustration

diciembre December, LP

el **dictado** dictation

diecinueve nineteen, LP

dieciocho eighteen, LP

dieciséis sixteen, LP

diecisiete seventeen, LP

el **diente** clove (of garlic)

los **dientes** teeth, 11.1; **2.1**

cepillarse (lavarse) los dientes to brush one's teeth, 11.1; **2.1**

la **dieta** diet

Spanish-English Dictionary

diez ten, LP

  de diez en diez by tens

la **diferencia** difference

diferente different

difícil difficult, 1.2

la **dificultad** difficulty

  sin dificultad easily

difunto(a) dead, deceased, **5.1**

el/la **difunto(a)** deceased, dead person, **5.1**

  ¡Diga! Hello! *(on the phone)*

  ¡Dígame! Hello! *(on the phone)*

dinámico(a) dynamic, 6.1

el **dinero** money, 3.2

la **dirección** address, **6.1;** direction

  la dirección de correo electrónico (e-mail) e-mail address, **6.1**

las **direccionales** turn signals, **9.2**

el **disco** record

el **disfraz** disguise, costume, **5.1**

disfrutar (de) to enjoy

disponible available

distancia: de larga distancia long-distance *(race)*, **11.1**

distinto(a) different

el **distribuidor automático** boarding pass kiosk, 10.1; **1.1;** ticket dispenser, **3.1**

el **distrito** district, area, section

divertido(a) fun, funny, amusing

divertir (ie) to amuse, 11.2; **2.2**

divertirse (ie) to have a good time, to have fun, 11.2; **2.2**

divino(a) divine, heavenly

doblar to turn, **9.1**

doble: el cuarto doble double *(hotel room)*, **7**

dobles doubles *(tennis)*, 5.1

doce twelve, LP

la **docena** dozen

el **documento adjunto** attached file, **6.1**

el **dólar** dollar

doler (ue) to ache, to hurt, 6.2; **11.2**

  Le (me, etc.) duele mucho. It hurts him (me, etc.) a lot., **11.2**

  Me duele(n)… My . . . ache(s)., 6.2

el **dolor** pain, ache, 6.2

  tener dolor de cabeza to have a headache, 6.2

  tener dolor de estómago to have a stomachache, 6.2

  tener dolor de garganta to have a sore throat, 6.2

domesticado(a) domesticated

el **domingo** Sunday, LP

dominicano(a) Dominican

  la República Dominicana Dominican Republic

el **dominó** dominos

donde where

¿dónde? Where?, 1.1

  ¿de dónde? from where?, 1.1

dormir (ue, u) to sleep, 5.2

  el cuarto de dormir bedroom, 2.2

  el saco de dormir sleeping bag, 11.2; **2.2**

  la bolsa de dormir sleeping bag, 11.2; **2.2**

dormirse (ue, u) to fall asleep, 11.1; **2.1**

el **dormitorio** bedroom, 2.2

dos two

doscientos(as) two hundred, 9.2

driblar to dribble, 5.2

la **ducha** shower, 11.1; **2.1**

  tomar una ducha to take a shower, 11.1; **2.1**

la **duda** doubt

el/la **dueño(a)** owner

dulce sweet, **5.1**

  el pan dulce pastry, 7

el **dulce** sweet

durante during, 3.2

durar to last

duro(a) hard, difficult, 1.2

  la copia dura hard copy, **6.1**

el **DVD** DVD, 3.2

la **ebullición** boiling

echar to throw, to expel

económico(a) inexpensive

ecuatoriano(a) Ecuadoran, 1.1

la **edad** age

  la Edad Media Middle Ages

el **edificio** building, 2.2

la **educación** education

  la educación física physical education, 1.2

educado(a) mannered

  estar bien (mal) educado(a) to be polite (rude), 6.1

egoísta selfish, egotistical

el **ejemplo** example

  por ejemplo for example

los **ejercicios** exercises, **11.1**

  ejercicios de respiración breathing exercises, **11.1**

  hacer ejercicios to exercise, **11.1**

los **ejotes** green beans

el **the** *(m. sing.)*, 1.1

él he, 1.1

elaborar to make, to produce, **5.1**

electrónico electronic, 10.1; **1.1**

  el boleto (billete) electrónico e-ticket, 10.1; **1.1**

  el correo electrónico e-mail, 3.2; **6.1**

el **elefante** elephant

elegante elegant, fancy

elegir (i, i) to elect

elemental elementary

ella she, 1.1

ellos(as) they, 1.2

el **elote** corn

el **e-mail** e-mail, **6.1**

embarcar to board, 10.2; **1.2**

el **embarque** boarding, 10.1; **1.1**

  la hora de embarque boarding time, 10.1; **1.1**

el **embotellamiento** traffic jam

emergencia: la sala de emergencia emergency room, **11.2**

emocionante moving; exciting

la **empanada** meat pie, 4.2

empezar (ie) to begin, 5.1

el/la **empleado(a)** salesperson, employee, 3.2

empujar to push

en in; on; at

  en casa at home

el/la **enamorado(a)** sweetheart

  enamorado(a) de in love with

encantar to love, to adore, 6.2

encender (ie) to light, 5.2

SR42

STUDENT RESOURCES

encerrar (ie) to enclose

encestar to make a basket *(basketball)*, 5.2

la **enchilada** enchilada

encima: por encima de above, over, 5.2

encontrar (ue) to find, to encounter

encontrarse (ue) to be found; to meet

la **encuesta** survey

el/la **enemigo(a)** enemy

energético(a) energetic, 6.1

la **energía** energy, 6.1

enero January, LP

el primero de enero January 1, LP

enfadado(a) angry, mad, 6.1

enfadar to make angry, 6.1

la **enfermedad** sickness, disease

el/la **enfermero(a)** nurse, 6.2; **11.2**

enfermo(a) ill, sick, 6.2

el/la **enfermo(a)** patient, sick person

enfrente de in front of

enlatado(a) canned

enlazar to connect

enojado(a) angry, mad, annoyed, 6.1

enojar to make angry, to annoy, 6.1

enorme enormous

la **ensalada** salad, 4.1

enseguida right away, 4.2

enseñar to teach, 3.1

entender (ie) to understand, 8.2

entero(a) entire, whole

enterrado(a) buried, **5.1**

enterrar (ie) to bury

la **entrada** ticket, 8.1; entrée *(meal)*; entrance

entradas: la bandeja de entradas e-mail inbox, **6.1**

entrar to enter, to go into, 5.1

entrar en línea to go online, **6.1**

entre between, among

el/la **entrenador(a)** coach, manager

el/la **entrevistador(a)** interviewer

entusiasmado(a) enthusiastic

el **entusiasmo** enthusiasm, 6.1

enviados: la bandeja de enviados sent mailbox, **6.1**

enviar to send, 3.2

el **episodio** episode

la **época** times, period

el **equilibrio** balance

el **equipaje** luggage, baggage, 10.1; **1.1**

el equipaje de mano hand luggage, carry-on bags, 10.2; **1.2**

el **equipo** team, 5.1; equipment

el deporte de equipo team sport

la **equitación** horseback riding, **8.2**

escala: hacer escala to stop over, to make a stop

la **escalera** stairs, staircase, **8.1**

la escalera mecánica escalator, **8.1**

el **escalope de ternera** veal cutlet, **10**

el **escaparate** store window, 9.1

la **escena** scene

escoger to choose

escolar *(related to)* school

el bus escolar school bus, 3.2

los materiales escolares school supplies, 3.1

la tarifa escolar student fare

escribir to write, 4.2

escrito(a) written

el **escrito** document, paper

escritorio: la pantalla de escritorio *(computer)* screen, 6.1

escuchar to listen (to), 3.2

¿Me escuchas? Can you hear me? *(telephone)*, **6.2**

el **escudero** squire

la **escuela** school, 1.2

la escuela primaria elementary school

la escuela secundaria secondary school, high school, 1.2

el/la **escultor(a)** sculptor

la **escultura** sculpture

ese(a) that, that one

eso: a eso de at about *(time)*

por eso for this reason, that is why

esos(as) those

la **espalda** back, 11.1; **2.1**

espantable horrendous

España Spain

español(a) Spanish *(adj.)*

el **español** Spanish *(language)*; person, 1.2

la **especia** spice

la **especialidad** specialty

especialmente especially

específico(a) specific

espectacular spectacular

el **espectáculo** show, spectacle

el/la **espectador(a)** spectator

el **espejo** mirror, 11.1; **2.1**

espera: la sala de espera waiting room, **3.1**

esperar to wait (for), 10.2; **1.2;** to hope; to expect

el **espíritu** mind, spirit, **11.1**

la **esplendidez** splendor

espontáneo(a) spontaneous

la **esposa** wife, 2.1

el **esposo** husband, 2.1

el **esqueleto** skeleton, **5.1**

el **esquí** ski; skiing, 7.2

el esquí acuático waterskiing, 7.1

el esquí alpino downhill skiing

el esquí nórdico cross-country skiing

el/la **esquiador(a)** skier, 7.2

esquiar to ski, 7.2

esquiar en el agua to water-ski, 7.1

la **esquina** corner, 8.1

¿Está... , por favor? Is . . . there, please?, **6.2**

establecer(se) to establish; to settle

el **establecimiento** establish, settling

el **establo** stable, **8.2;** manger

la **estación** season, LP; resort, 7.1; station, **3.1**

la estación de esquí ski resort, 7.2

la estación de ferrocarril (tren) railroad (train) station, **3.1**

la estación de metro subway (metro) station, **8.1**

la estación de servicio gas station, 9.2

¿Qué estación es? What season is it?, LP

estacionar to park

la **estadía** stay

el **estadio** stadium

Estados Unidos United States

estadounidense from the United States

la **estancia** ranch, **8.2**

estar to be, 3.1

¿Está...? Is . . . there?, **6.2**

estar bien to feel fine, 6.2

estar cansado(a) to be tired, 6.1

estar contento(a) (triste, nervioso[a], etc.) to be happy (sad, nervous, etc.), 6.1

Spanish-English Dictionary

estar de buen (mal) humor to be in a good (bad) mood, 6.1

estar enfermo(a) to be sick, 6.2

la **estatua** statue, 8.2

la **estatura** stature, height

este(a) this, this one, 9.1

el **este** east

estereofónico(a) stereo

el **estilo** style

estimado(a) esteemed

estirarse to stretch, 11.1; **2.1**

el **estómago** stomach, 6.2

el dolor de estómago stomachache, 6.2

estos(as) these

la **estrategia** strategy

estrecho(a) narrow, **8.1**

la **estrella** star

estremecerse to shake

el **estrés** stress, 6.2

la **estructura** structure

el/la **estudiante** student

estudiantil: la tarifa estudiantil student fare

estudiar to study, 3.1

el **estudio** study

los estudios sociales social studies, 1.2

la **estufa** stove, **10**

estupendo(a) terrific, stupendous

la **etnia** ethnicity, ethnic group

étnico(a) ethnic

el **euro** euro (currency of most of the countries of the European Union)

Europa Europe

el **evento** event

evitar to avoid

el **examen** test, exam, 3.1

el examen físico physical, 6.2

examinar to examine, 6.2

exceder to go over (speed limit)

excelente excellent

la **excepción** exception

la **excursión** excursion, outing

el/la **excursionista** hiker

existir exist

el **éxito** success, 6.1

tener éxito to succeed, to be successful, 6.1

exótico(a) exotic

experimentar to try, to try out

el/la **experto(a)** expert

explicar to explain

el/la **explorador(a)** explorer

la **exposición de arte** art show, exhibition, 8.2

la **expresión** expression

extenderse (ie) to extend

extranjero(a) foreign

al extranjero abroad

extraordinario(a) extraordinary

la **fábrica** factory

fabuloso(a) fabulous

fácil easy, 1.2

la **factura** bill

facturar el equipaje to check luggage, 10.1; **1.1**

la **falda** skirt, 3.1

falso(a) false

faltar to lack, not to have, 6.1

Le falta paciencia. He (She) has no patience., 6.1

la **familia** family, 2.1

familiar (related to) family

los **familiares** family members

famoso(a) famous

la **fantasía** fantasy

fantástico(a) fantastic

el/la **farmacéutico(a)** druggist, pharmacist

la **farmacia** pharmacy, drugstore, 6.2

el **favor** favor

Favor de (+ infinitive). Please (do something)., 11.2; **2.2**

por favor please, LP

favorito(a) favorite

febrero February, LP

la **fecha** date, LP

¿Cuál es la fecha de hoy? What is today's date?, LP

fecundo(a) prolific

la **felicidad** happiness

feliz happy, **5.2**

¡Feliz Hanuka! Happy Hanukkah!, **5.2**

¡Feliz Navidad! Merry Christmas!, **5.2**

¡Felices Pascuas! Happy Easter!

feo(a) unattractive, ugly, 1.1

la **feria** festival, fair, **5.1**

ferrocarril: la estación de ferrocarril train station, railroad station, **3.1**

festivo: el día festivo holiday

la **fiebre** fever, 6.2

tener fiebre to have a fever, 6.2

fiel loyal, faithful

la **fiesta** party, 8.1; holiday, **5.1**

dar una fiesta to throw a party, 8.1

la fiesta de las luces festival of lights (Hanukkah), **5.2**

fijo(a) fixed, unchanging

la **fila** line (of people); row (of seats)

estar en fila to wait in line

el **film** film, movie

el **filme** film, movie, 8.2

el **fin** end

el fin de semana weekend, 7.1

por fin finally

final: al final de at the end of

la **finca** farm, **8.2**

fines: a fines de at the end of

fingir to pretend

físico(a) physical

la apariencia física physical appearance, looks

la educación física physical education, 1.2

flaco(a) thin

el **flan** flan, custard, 4.1

la **flauta** flute

la **flecha** arrow

flexible open-minded, flexible, 6.1

la **flor** flower, 2.2

el **foco** center, focal point

la **fogata** bonfire, campfire

fondo: al fondo to the bottom

los **fondos** funds, money

la **forma** form, piece, 10.2; **1.2**; shape

la forma de identidad piece of ID, 10.2; **1.2**

formar to form, to make up; to put together

el **formulario** form

forzado(a) forced

la **foto(grafía)** photo, 7.1

la **fractura** fracture

el **francés** French, 1.2

el **franciscano** Franciscan

franco(a) frank, sincere, candid

el **frasco** jar, 9.2

la **frase** sentence

la **frazada** blanket, **7**

frecuencia: con frecuencia often, frequently

freír (i, i) to fry, **4**

los **frenos** brakes, **9.2**

la **frente** forehead, **11.1**

frente a in front of

fresco(a) cool, LP

   Hace fresco. It's cool (weather)., LP

los **frijoles** beans, 4.1

frío(a) cold, 4.2

   Hace frío. It's cold (weather)., LP

   tener frío to be cold, 11.1; **2.1**

el **frío** cold

frito(a) fried

   las patatas (papas) fritas french fries, 4.1

frontal: la página frontal home page, **6.1**

la **frontera** border

la **fruta** fruit, 9.2

   el puesto de frutas fruit stand, 9.2

la **frutería** fruit stand, 9.2

el **fuego** flame, heat, **10**

   a fuego lento on low heat, **10**

los **fuegos artificiales** fireworks, **5.2**

la **fuente** fountain

fuera de outside

fuerte strong; substantial

las **fuerzas** (armed) forces

fumar: la señal de no fumar no-smoking sign, 10.2; **1.2**

el **fútbol** soccer, 5.1

   el campo de fútbol soccer field, 5.1

   el fútbol americano football

el/la **futbolista** soccer player

el **futuro** future

G

las **gafas para el sol** sunglasses, 7.1

el **galán** elegant man, heartthrob

gallardo(a) brave, dashing

las **galletas** crackers, 8.1

la **gallina** hen, **8.2**

la **gamba** shrimp, prawn

---

el **ganado** cattle, livestock, **8.2**

ganar to win, 5.1; to earn

ganas: tener ganas de to feel like

el **garaje** garage, 2.2

la **garganta** throat, 6.2

   el dolor de garganta sore throat, 6.2

la **garita de peaje** tollbooth, **9.1**

el **gas: el agua mineral con gas** carbonated (sparkling) mineral water, 4.2

la **gaseosa** soda, carbonated drink, 4.2

la **gasolina** gas

la **gasolinera** gas station, **9.2**

gastar to spend; to waste

el/la **gato(a)** cat, 2.1; jack (car), **9.2**

el/la **gemelo(a)** twin, 2.1

general general

   en general in general

   por lo general usually, as a rule

generalmente usually, generally

generoso(a) generous

la **gente** people, 9.1

la **geografía** geography

la **geometría** geometry

el **gigante** giant

el **gimnasio** gym(nasium), **11.1**

la **gitanilla** little gypsy

el **gobierno** government

el **gol** goal, 5.1

   meter un gol to score a goal, 5.1

golpear to hit (ball), 5.2

la **goma** tire, **9.2**

gordo(a) fat

el **gorro** ski hat, 7.2

gozar de to enjoy

grabar to record

Gracias. Thank you., LP

   dar gracias a to thank

gracioso(a) funny, 1.1

la **gramática** grammar

gran, grande big, large, 1.2

la **grandeza** greatness, grandeur

el **granero** barn, **8.2**

la **granja** farm, **8.2**

gratis for free

gratuito(a) free

grave serious

gris gray, 5.1

gritar to yell, to shout

el **grupo** group, 8.1

la **guagua** bus (Puerto Rico, Cuba), 8.1

el **guante** glove, 5.2

---

la **guantera** glove compartment, **9.2**

guapo(a) attractive, good-looking, 1.1

guardar to guard, 5.1; to save, to keep, **6.1**

   guardar cama to stay in bed (illness), 6.2

la **guardería** shelter

guatemalteco(a) Guatemalan

la **guerra** war

el **guerrero** warrior

la **guía** guidebook

   la guía telefónica phone book, **6.2**

guiar to guide

el **guisante** pea, 9.2

la **guitarra** guitar

gustar to like, to be pleasing to, 5.1

el **gusto** pleasure; like; taste

   Mucho gusto. Nice (It's a pleasure) to meet you.

H

haber to have (in compound tenses)

las **habichuelas** beans

   las habichuelas tiernas green beans, string beans

la **habitación** bedroom; hotel room, **7**

el/la **habitante** inhabitant

hablar to speak, to talk, 3.1

   hablar en el móvil to talk on the cell phone

   hablar por teléfono to talk on the phone

   ¿Hablas en serio? Are you serious?

hace: Hace... años ... years ago

   Hace buen tiempo. The weather is nice., LP

   Hace (mucho) calor. It's (very) hot (weather)., LP

   Hace fresco. It's cool (weather)., LP

   Hace frío. It's cold (weather)., LP

   Hace mal tiempo. The weather is bad., LP

   Hace sol. It's sunny., LP

   Hace viento. It's windy., LP

hacer to do, to make, 10.2; **1.2**

   hacer clic to click (computer), **6.1**

   hacer cola to stand (wait) in line, 10.2; **1.2**

Spanish-English Dictionary

hacer ejercicios to exercise, **11.1**

hacer jogging to go jogging, **11.1**

hacer la cama to make the bed, **7**

hacer la maleta to pack, 10.1; **1.1**

hacer planchas to do push-ups, **11.1**

hacer un viaje to take a trip, 10.1; **1.1**

hacerse daño to hurt oneself, **11.2**

hacia toward

hacia atrás backwards

la **hacienda** ranch, **8.2**

el **hall** concourse *(train station)*, **3.1**

el **hambre** *(f.)* hunger

  Me muero de hambre. I'm starving., **4**

  tener hambre to be hungry, **4.1**

la **hamburguesa** hamburger, **4.1**

el **Hanuka** Hanukkah, **5.2**

  ¡Feliz Hanuka! Happy Hanukkah!, **5.2**

la **harina** flour

hasta until; up to; as far as; even

  ¡Hasta luego! See you later!, LP

  ¡Hasta mañana! See you tomorrow!, LP

  ¡Hasta pronto! See you soon!, LP

hay there is, there are, **2.2**

  hay que it's necessary to (do something), one must, 10.2; **1.2**

  Hay sol. It's sunny., LP

  No hay de qué. You're welcome., LP

  ¿Qué hay? What's new (up)?

la **hazaña** achievement

hebreo(a) Jewish, Hebrew, **5.2**

el **hecho** fact

hecho(a): bien hecho(a) well-done *(meat)*, **4**

el **helado** ice cream, **4.1**

el **heno** hay, **8.2**

la **herida** wound, injury, **11.2**

el/la **herido(a)** injured person

la **hermana** sister, **2.1**

la **hermanastra** stepsister, **2.1**

el **hermanastro** stepbrother, **2.1**

el **hermano** brother, **2.1**

hermoso(a) beautiful

el **héroe** hero

la **heroína** heroine

herramientas: la barra de herramientas toolbar, **6.1**

hervir (ie, i) to boil, **10**

el **hielo** ice, **7.2**

  el patinaje sobre el hielo ice-skating, **7.2**

la **hierba** grass, **8.2**

las **hierbas** herbs

el **hígado** liver

higiénico: el rollo de papel higiénico roll of toilet paper, 11.2; **2.2**

la **hija** daughter, **2.1**

el **hijo** son, child, **2.1**

  el hijo único only child, **2.1**

los **hijos** children, **2.1**

hinchado(a) swollen, **11.2**

hincharse to get swollen, to swell

hispano(a) Hispanic

hispanohablante Spanish-speaking

el/la **hispanohablante** Spanish speaker

la **historia** history, **1.2**

el/la **historiador(a)** historian

la **hoja de papel** sheet of paper, **3.1**

hojear to skim, to scan

¡Hola! Hello!, LP

el **hombre** man

el **hombro** shoulder, **11.1**

honesto(a) honest

la **hora** hour; time, 10.1; **1.1**

  ¿a qué hora? at what time?, LP

  la hora de embarque boarding time, 10.1; **1.1**

  la hora de salida departure time, 10.1; **1.1**

  ¿Qué hora es? What time is it?, LP

el **horario** *(train)* schedule, timetable, **3.1**

el **horno** oven, **10**

el **horno de microondas** microwave oven, **10**

hospedarse to stay in a hotel, **7**

el **hospital** hospital

el **hostal** hostel, small (inexpensive) hotel, **7**

el **hotel** hotel, **7**

hoy today, LP

  ¿Cuál es la fecha de hoy? What's today's date?, LP

  hoy en día nowadays

  ¿Qué día es hoy? What day is it today?, LP

la **huerta** orchard, **8.2**

el **hueso** bone, **5.1**

el/la **huésped(a)** guest, **7**

el **huevo** egg, 4.1; **7**

  los huevos pasados por agua soft-boiled eggs

  los huevos revueltos scrambled eggs, **7**

huir to flee

humanitario(a) humanitarian

humano(a) human, 11.1; **2.1**

  el ser humano human being

humilde humble

el **humor** mood; humor

  estar de buen (mal) humor to be in a good (bad) mood, **6.1**

  tener un buen sentido de humor to have a good sense of humor, **6.1**

el **huso horario** time zone

el **icono** icon, **6.1**

ida y vuelta (regreso): un boleto (billete) de ida y vuelta (regreso) round-trip ticket, **3.1**

la **idea** idea

la **identidad** identification, 10.2; **1.2**

  el carnet de identidad ID card, 10.2; **1.2**

identificar to identify

la **iglesia** church

igual que as well as; like; just as

iluminar to light up, to illuminate, **5.2**

la **imagen** picture, image

impaciente impatient, **6.1**

impares odd *(numeric)*

impermeable raincoat

importa: No importa. It doesn't matter.

la **importancia** importance

importante important

imposible impossible
la impresora printer, **6.1**
imprimir to print, **6.1**
el impuesto tax
incluir to include
¿Está incluido el servicio?
Is the tip included?, 4.2
increíble incredible
indicar to indicate
indígena native, indigenous,
9.2
el/la indígena indigenous person
**individual: el deporte
individual** individual sport
individuales singles *(tennis)*,
5.2
industrializado(a)
industrialized
la infinidad infinity
la influencia influence
la información information, 3.2
el inglés English, 1.2
el ingrediente ingredient
inhóspito(a) inhospitable,
desolate
inicial: la página inicial
home page, **6.1**
inicio: la página de inicio
home page, **6.1**
inmenso(a) immense
el inodoro toilet, 7
insertar to insert, **3.1**
inteligente intelligent, 1.2
el interés interest
interesante interesting, 1.2
interesar to interest, 5.1
internacional
international, 10.1; **1.1**
el Internet Internet, 3.2; **6.1**
navegar el Internet to surf
the Net, 3.2; **6.1**
interurbano(a) city-to-city
intervenir (ie) to intervene
la introducción introduction
introducir to insert, **6.2**
el invierno winter, LP
la invitación invitation
el/la invitado(a) guest, 8.1
invitar to invite
ir to go, 3.2
ir a (+ infinitive) to be going
to (do something), 4.2
ir a casa to go home, 3.2
ir a pie to go on foot, 3.2
ir al cine to go to the
movies, 8.2
ir de camping to go
camping, 11.2; **2.2**
ir de compras to go
shopping, 9.1

irlandés(esa) Irish
la isla island
el istmo isthmus
italiano(a) Italian
izquierdo(a) left, 11.1; **2.1**
a la izquierda to the left,
9.1

el jabón soap, 11.2; **2.2**
la barra (pastilla) de jabón
bar of soap, 11.2; **2.2**
jamás never
el jamón ham, 4.1
**el sándwich de jamón y
queso** ham and cheese
sandwich, 4.1
el jardín garden, 2.2
el/la jardinero(a) outfielder, 5.2
jogging: hacer jogging to go
jogging, **11.1**
el jonrón home run
batear un jonrón to hit a
home run
joven young
el/la joven young person, 1.1
la joya jewel, piece of jewelry
judío(a) Jewish, **5.2**
las judías verdes green beans, 9.2
el juego game, 5.1
el jueves Thursday, LP
el/la jugador(a) player, 5.1
jugar (ue) to play, 5.1
**jugar (al) fútbol (béisbol,
básquetbol)** to play
soccer (baseball,
basketball), 5.1
el jugo juice, 4.1
el jugo de naranja orange
juice, 4.1; **7**
el juguete toy
julio July, LP
junio June, LP
juntos(as) together

el kilo kilogram *(2.2 lbs.)*, **9.2**
el kilómetro kilometer

la the *(f. sing.)*, 1.1; it, her
(pron.)
el labio lip
el laboratorio laboratory
laborioso(a) hardworking

labrar to work *(land)*, **8.2**
el lacón bacon, 7
**lácteo(a): productos
lácteos** dairy products
el lado side
al lado de beside, next to,
2.2
ladrar to bark
el lago lake
la lámpara lamp, 2.2
la langosta lobster, **4**
la lanza lance
el/la lanzador(a) pitcher, 5.2
lanzar to kick, to throw, 5.1
el lapicero ballpoint pen
el lápiz pencil, 3.1
largo(a) long, 5.1
a lo largo de along
las the *(f. pl.)*; them *(pron.)*
lastimarse to harm oneself, to
get hurt
la lata can, 9.2
latino(a) Latino
Latinoamérica Latin America
el/la latinoamericano(a) Latin
American
el lavabo washbasin, sink, 7
el lavaplatos dishwasher, 10
lavar to wash, 11.2; **2.2**
lavarse to wash oneself,
11.1; **2.1**
**lavarse el pelo (la cara, las
manos)** to wash one's hair
(face, hands), 11.1; **2.1**
lavarse los dientes to clean
(brush) one's teeth, 11.1;
2.1
le to him, to her; to you
(formal) (pron.)
la lección lesson
la leche milk, 4.1
el café con leche coffee
with milk, café au lait
el lechón asado roast suckling
pig
la lechuga lettuce, 4.1
la lectura reading
leer to read, 4.2
la legumbre vegetable, 4.1
lejos (de) far *(from)*, 3.2
a lo lejos in the distance
la lengua language
lentamente slowly
lento(a) slow, **11.1**; low
(heat), **10**
a fuego lento on low heat,
10
el león lion
les to them; to you *(formal)*
(pron.)

Spanish-English Dictionary

la **letra** letter (of alphabet)

las **letras** literature

levantar to raise, 3.1; to clear, 4; to lift, **11.1**

  levantar la mano to raise one's hand, 3.1

  levantar la mesa to clear the table, 4

  levantar pesas to lift weights, **11.1**

levantarse to get up, 11.1; **2.1**

la **leyenda** legend

liberar to free, to rid, **11.1**

la **libertad** freedom

la **libra** pound (weight)

libre free, unoccupied, 4.2; **3.2**

  al aire libre outdoor, open-air

  el tiempo libre spare time, 8.1

la **libreta de direcciones** (e-mail) address book, **6.1**

el **libro** book, 3.1

  el libro de bolsillo paperback, **3.1**

la **licencia** driver's license, **9.2**

el **líder** leader

la **liga** league

  las Grandes Ligas Major Leagues

ligeramente lightly

ligero(a) light

el **límite de velocidad** speed limit

el **limón** lemon

la **limonada** lemonade

limpiar to clean, 7

limpio(a) clean, 7

lindo(a) beautiful

la **línea** (telephone) line, **6.2**; (road) line, **9.1**

  línea continua solid line, **9.1**

  Se nos cortó la línea. We've been cut off. (phone), **6.2**

línea: en línea online, **6.1**

  entrar en línea to go online, **6.1**

la **línea aérea** airline, 10.1; **1.1**

la **liquidación** sale, 9.1

listo(a) ready

la **litera** bunk

la **literatura** literature

la **llama** llama

la **llamada** (telephone) call, **6.2**

la **llamada perdida (caída)** dropped call (cell phone), **6.2**

llamar to call, 11.2; **2.2**

llamarse to call oneself, to be called, named, 11.1; **2.1**

  Me llamo… My name is . . . , 11.1; **2.1**

la **llanta** tire, **9.2**

  la llanta de repuesto (recambio) spare tire, **9.2**

la **llave** key, 7

  la llave magnética magnetic key, 7

la **llegada** arrival, **3.1**

llegar to arrive, 4.1

llenar to fill, **9.2**

lleno(a) de full of, 6.1

llevar to carry; to wear, 3.1; to take; to bear; to have

llorar to cry

llover (ue) to rain

  Llueve. It's raining., LP

lluvioso(a) rainy

lo it, him, you (formal) (pron.)

lo que what

la **loción bronceadora** suntan lotion, sunblock, 7.1

loco(a) crazy

el **lodo** mud

lógico(a) logical

la **loncha** slice (ham)

la **lonja** slice (ham)

el **loro** parrot

los them (m. pl.) (pron.)

el **lote** lot

las **luces** lights, 5.2; headlights, **9.2**

  la fiesta de las luces festival of lights (Hanukkah), **5.2**

luchar to fight

luego later, LP; then, 3.2

  ¡Hasta luego! See you later!, LP

el **lugar** place

  tener lugar to take place

lujoso(a) luxurious

el **lunes** Monday, LP

la **luz** light, **5.2**

  la luz roja red light, **9.1**

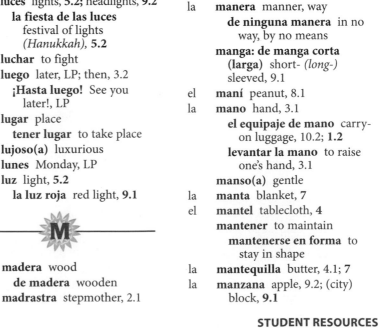

M

la **madera** wood

  de madera wooden

la **madrastra** stepmother, 2.1

la **madre** mother, 2.1

los **madrileños** citizens of Madrid

el/la **madrugador(a)** early riser, 11.1; **2.1**

los **maduros** ripe bananas

magnético(a) magnetic, 7

magnífico(a) magnificent, splendid

Magos: los Reyes Magos the Three Wise Men, **5.2**

el **maíz** corn, 9.2

mal bad

  estar de mal humor to be in a bad mood, 6.1

  Hace mal tiempo. The weather is bad., LP

  mal educado(a) ill-mannered, rude, 6.1

el **malécon** boardwalk (seafront)

los **males** the evil (things), the ills

la **maleta** suitcase, 10.1; **1.1**

  hacer la maleta to pack, 10.1; **1.1**

la **maletera** trunk (car), 10.1; **1.1**

malicioso(a) malicious

malo(a) bad, 1.2

  sacar notas malas to get bad grades, 3.1

mamá mom, mommy

mandar to send

el **mandato** command

mando: la cabina de mando cockpit

manejar to drive

la **manera** manner, way

  de ninguna manera in no way, by no means

manga: de manga corta (larga) short- (long-) sleeved, 9.1

el **maní** peanut, 8.1

la **mano** hand, 3.1

  el equipaje de mano carry-on luggage, 10.2; **1.2**

  levantar la mano to raise one's hand, 3.1

manso(a) gentle

la **manta** blanket, 7

el **mantel** tablecloth, 4

mantener to maintain

  mantenerse en forma to stay in shape

la **mantequilla** butter, 4.1; 7

la **manzana** apple, 9.2; (city) block, **9.1**

mañana tomorrow, LP

¡Hasta mañana! See you tomorrow!, LP

la mañana morning

de la mañana A.M.

por la mañana in the morning

el mapa map

la máquina machine

la maquinaría machinery, equipment

el mar sea, ocean, 7.1

el mar Caribe Caribbean Sea

el maratón marathon, 11.1

marcar to score, 5.1; to dial, 6.2

marcar el número to dial the number, 6.2

marcar un tanto to score a point, 5.1

la marcha march

en marcha working

marchar to march

el marido husband, 2.1

el marinero sailor

los mariscos shellfish, seafood, 4

marrón: de color marrón brown, 5.1

el martes Tuesday, LP

marzo March, LP

más more, 9.1

¡Qué... más...! What a . . . !

la máscara mask, 5.1

la máscara de oxígeno oxygen mask, 10.2; 1.2

la mascota pet, 2.1

las matemáticas mathematics, math, 1.2

los materiales escolares school supplies, 3.1

el mausoleo mausoleum, 5.1

máximo(a) highest, top

la velocidad máxima speed limit, top speed

mayo May, LP

la mayonesa mayonnaise, 9.2

mayor older

el/la mayor the oldest; the greatest

la mayoría majority

mayoritario(a) (related to) majority

me me (pron.)

mediano(a) medium, medium-size

la medianoche midnight

el medicamento medicine, 6.2

la medicina medicine, 6.2

el/la médico(a) doctor, 6.2

la medida measurement

las medidas measures

el medio means; middle

a término medio medium (meat), 4

el medio de transporte means of transport, 8.1

medio(a) half; middle

la clase media middle class

y media half-past (the hour), LP

el mediodía noon

los mejillones mussels, 4

mejor better

el/la mejor the best

menor younger; lesser

el/la menor the youngest; the least

la menora menorah, 5.2

menos less, 9.1

a lo menos at least

menos cuarto a quarter to (the hour)

el mensaje message, 6.2

el menú menu, 4.2; 4

menudo: a menudo often

el mercado market, 9.2

la mercancía merchandise

la merienda snack, 4.2

la mermelada jam, marmalade, 7

el mes month, LP

la mesa table, 2.2; 4

levantar la mesa to clear the table, 4

poner la mesa to set the table, 4

quitar la mesa to clear the table, 4

el/la mesero(a) waiter (waitress), server, 4.2; 4

la meseta meseta, plateau

la mesita table, 2.2; 4

meter to put, to place

meter un gol to score a goal, 5.1

el metro subway, metro, 8.1; meter

la boca del metro subway station entrance, 8.1

la estación de metro subway station, 8.1

el metrópoli metropolis, big city

mexicano(a) Mexican, 1.2

la mezcla mixture

mi my

mí me

el miedo fear

tener miedo to be afraid, 7.2

el/la miembro(a) member, 2.1

mientras while, 5.2

el miércoles Wednesday, LP

mil (one) thousand, 9.2

el millón million, 9.2

el/la millonario(a) millionaire

mimado(a) spoiled (person)

el mimo mime, 8.1

la mina mine

el minuto minute

¡Mira! Look! 3.1

la mirada gaze, look

tener la mirada fijada to keep one's eyes fixed on

mirar to look at, 3.2

mirarse to look at oneself, 11.1; 2.1

la miseria poverty

mismo(a) same, 1.2; own; very

misterioso(a) mysterious

mixto(a) co-ed

la mochila backpack, knapsack, 3.1

el/la mochilero(a) backpacker, hiker, 11.2; 2.2

viajar de mochilero to go backpacking, hiking

los modales manners, 6.1

tener buenos (malos) modales to have good (bad) manners, to be well-behaved (rude), 6.1

moderno(a) modern

modesto(a) inexpensive

molestar to bother, to annoy, 6.1

el molino de viento windmill

el monasterio monastery

la moneda coin, 9.1

el mono monkey

el monopatín skateboard, 11.1

el monstruo monster

la montaña mountain, 7.2

la montaña rusa roller coaster, 8.1

montañoso(a) mountainous

montar to put up (tent), 11.2; 2.2; to ride, 8.2

montar a caballo to go horseback riding, 8.2

el montón bunch, heap

el monumento monument

mórbido(a) morbid

morder (ue) to bite

moreno(a) dark-haired, brunette, 1.1

morir (ue, u) to die, 4

el morrón sweet red pepper

el mostrador (ticket) counter, 10.1; 1.1

mostrar (ue) to show, 10.2; 1.2

Spanish-English Dictionary

Spanish-English Dictionary

el **móvil** cell phone, 3.2; **6.1**

el **movimiento** movement, **11.1**

el **mozo** bellhop, 7

el **MP3** MP3 player, **6.2**

la **muchacha** girl, 1.1

el **muchacho** boy, 1.1

mucho a lot, many, much, 2.2; very, LP

Hace mucho calor (frío). It's very hot (cold)., LP

Mucho gusto. Nice to meet you.

los **muebles** furniture, 2.2

la **muerte** death

muerto(a) dead

el/la **muerto(a)** dead person, deceased, **5.1**

el Día de los Muertos the Day of the Dead, **5.1**

la **mujer** wife, 2.1

la **mula** mule

las **muletas** crutches, **11.2**

andar con muletas to walk on crutches, **11.2**

la **multa** fine, **9.1**

mundial: la Copa Mundial World Cup

el **mundo** world

todo el mundo everyone

la **muñeca** wrist, **11.1**

el **mural** mural

el/la **muralista** muralist

el **muro** wall

el **museo** museum, 8.2

la **música** music, 1.2

el/la **músico(a)** musician, 8.1

el **muslo** thigh, **10**

muy very, LP

muy bien very well, LP

nacer to be born

el **nacimiento** birth

nacional national

la **nacionalidad** nationality 1.1

¿de qué nacionalidad? what nationality?, 1.1

nada nothing, not anything, 8.2

De nada. You're welcome., LP

Nada más. Nothing else., 9.2

Por nada. You're welcome., LP; for no reason

nadar to swim, 7.1

nadie nobody, not anybody, 8.2

la **nafta** gasoline

la **naranja** orange *(fruit),* 4.1

natal pertaining to where someone was born

la **naturaleza** nature

navegar la red (el Internet) to surf the Web (the Internet), 3.2; **6.1**

la **Navidad** Christmas, **5.2**

el árbol de Navidad Christmas tree, **5.2**

¡Feliz Navidad! Merry Christmas!

necesario: Es necesario. It's necessary., **11.2**

necesitar to need, 3.2

negativo(a) negative

negro(a) black, 2.1

nervioso(a) nervous, 6.1

el **neumático** tire, **9.2**

nevado(a) snowy, snow-covered

nevar (ie) to snow

Nieva. It's snowing., LP

la **nevera** refrigerator, **10**

ni neither, nor

Ni idea. No idea.

nicaragüense Nicaraguan

la **nieta** granddaughter, 2.1

el **nieto** grandson, 2.1

la **nieve** snow, 7.2

ninguno(a) none, not any

de ninguna manera in no way, by no means

la **niñez** childhood

el/la **niño(a)** boy, girl, child, 6.2

el **nivel** level

no no

No hay de qué. You're welcome., LP

no obstante nevertheless

la **noche** night, evening

Buenas noches. Good evening., LP

esta noche tonight, 4.1

por la noche in the evening

la **Nochebuena** Christmas Eve, **5.2**

la **Nochevieja** New Year's Eve

nombrar to name

el **nombre** name, 2.1; **10.1**

la **noria** Ferris wheel, **8.1**

la **normal** normal, 6.2

el **norte** north

norteamericano(a) American, North American

nos us *(pron.)*

nosotros(as) we

la **nota** grade, mark, 3.1

sacar notas buenas (malas) to get good (bad) grades, 3.1

la(s) **noticia(s)** news, piece of news

novecientos(as) nine hundred, 9.2

la **novela** novel

noventa ninety, LP

noviembre November, LP

la **nube** cloud, 7.1

nublado(a) cloudy, 7.1

nuestro(a) our

nueve nine, LP

nuevo(a) new, 1.1

de nuevo again

el **número** shoe size, 9.1; number, 10.1; **1.1**

el número del asiento seat number, 10.1; **1.1**

el número de teléfono telephone number, **6.2**

el número del vuelo flight number, 10.1; **1.1**

¿Qué número calzas? What size shoe do you wear (take)?, 9.1

nunca never, not ever, 8.2

o or

objetivo objective

obligatorio(a) required, obligatory

la **obra** work; work of art

observar to observe, to notice

el **obstáculo** obstacle

obstinado(a) obstinate, stubborn, 6.1

occidental western

el **océano** ocean

ochenta eighty, LP

ocho eight, LP

ochocientos(as) eight hundred, 9.2

octubre October, LP

ocupado(a) occupied, 4.2; **3.2**
el **oeste** west
la **oficina** office, **8.1**
ofrecer to offer
la **ofrenda** offering, **5.1**
el **oído** ear
oír to hear, 8.1
Ojalá que… Would that . . . , I hope . . . , **11.2**
ojeada: dar una ojeada to take a look at
¡Ojo! Watch out! Be careful!
el **ojo** eye, 2.1
   tener mucho ojo to be very careful
   tener ojos azules (castaños, verdes) to have blue (brown, green) eyes, 2.1
la **ola** wave, 7.1
oliva: el aceite de oliva olive oil
la **olla** pot, **10**
olvidar to forget
once eleven, LP
la **onza** ounce
la **opinión** opinion
la **oportunidad** opportunity
el/la **opresor(a)** oppressor
oprimir to press, to push (*button, key*), **6.1**
opuesto(a) opposite
la **oración** sentence
la **orden** order (*restaurant*), 4.2
el **orden** order
el **ordenador** computer, 3.2; **6.1**
la **orfebrería** craftsmanship in precious metals
organizar to organize, to set up
el **órgano** organ
oriental eastern
el **origen** origin, background
originarse to come from
las **orillas** banks, shores
   a orillas de on the shores of
el **oro** gold
la **orquesta** orchestra, band
la **orquídea** orchid
ortopédico(a): el/la cirujano(a) ortopédico(a) orthopedic surgeon, **11.2**
oscuro(a) dark
el **otoño** autumn, fall, LP
otro(a) other, another
otros(as) others
el **oxígeno: la máscara de oxígeno** oxygen mask, 10.2; **1.2**
¡Oye! Listen!, 1.2

P

---

pacer to graze, **8.2**
la **paciencia** patience
paciente patient (*adj.*), 6.1
el/la **paciente** patient, 6.2
el **padrastro** stepfather, 2.1
el **padre** father, 2.1
los **padres** parents, 2.1
pagar to pay, 3.2
la **página** page
   la página de inicio (inicial, frontal) home page, **6.1**
el **país** country
el **paisaje** landscape
la **paja** straw, **5.2**
el **pájaro** bird
la **palabra** word
   la palabra afine cognate
el **palacio** palace
la **palma** palm tree
la **paloma** pigeon
la **palta** avocado
el **pan** bread
   el pan dulce pastry, **7**
   el pan tostado toast, 4.1; **7**
la **panadería** bakery
el **panecillo** roll, 4.1; **7**
el **panqueque** pancake
la **pantalla de escritorio** (computer) screen, monitor, **6.1**
el **pantalón** pants, 3.1
   el pantalón corto shorts, 5.1
   el pantalón largo long pants, 9.1
la **panza** belly
la **papa** potato, 4.1
   las papas fritas french fries, 4.1
el **papel** paper, 3.1; role
   la hoja de papel sheet of paper, 3.1
   el rollo de papel higiénico roll of toilet paper, 11.2; **2.2**
el **paquete** package, 9.2
el **par** pair, 9.1
   el par de zapatos pair of shoes, 9.1
para for; in order to
el **parabrisas** windshield, **9.1**
la **parada** stop, station, 3.2
   la parada de autobús bus stop, **8.1**
el **parador** inn
el **paraíso** paradise

parar(se) to stop, **9.1**
parear to match
parecer to seem, to look like
   a mi (tu, su) parecer in my (*your, his*) opinion
   ¿Qué te parece? What do you think?
pares even (*numeric*)
el/la **pariente** relative, 2.1
el **parking** parking lot, **8.1**
el **parque** park, 11.2; **2.2**
   el parque de atracciones amusement park, **8.1**
parquear to park
el **parqueo** parking lot, **8.1**
el **parquímetro** parking meter, **9.1**
el **párrafo** paragraph
la **parrilla** grill, **10**
la **parte** part; place
   ¿De parte de quién, por favor? Who's calling, please?, **6.2**
   en muchas partes in many places
   la mayor parte the greatest part, the most
participar to participate, to take part in
el **partido** game, 5.1
el **pasabordo** boarding pass
pasado(a) last, 7.1
   el año pasado last year, 7.1
   la semana pasada last week, 7.1
el/la **pasajero(a)** passenger, 10.1; **1.1**
el **pasaporte** passport, 10.2; **1.2**
pasar to pass, to go, 5.2; to spend (*time*), 7.1; to pass (*car*), **9.1**
   pasarlo bien to have a good time, to have fun, 11.2; **2.2**
   pasar por el control de seguridad to go through security, 10.2; **1.2**
   ¿Qué pasa? What's going on? What's happening?
   ¿Qué te pasa? What's the matter (with you)?
la **Pascua (Florida)** Easter
el **paseo** broad street, avenue, **8.1**
   dar un paseo to take a walk
   dar un paseo en bicicleta to take a (bike) ride
el **pasillo** aisle, 10.2; **1.2**
la **pasta dentífrica** toothpaste
el **pastel** cake

Spanish-English Dictionary

la **pastilla** bar (soap)

los **patacones** slices of fried plantain

la **patata** potato, 4.1

    las patatas fritas french fries, 4.1

el **patín** ice skate, 7.2

el/la **patinador(a)** ice-skater, 7.2

el **patinaje** skating, 7.2; **11.1**

    el patinaje en línea in-line skating, **11.1**

    el patinaje sobre hielo ice-skating, 7.2

    patinar to skate, to go skating, 7.2; **11.1**

    patinar en línea to go in-line skating, **11.1**

    patinar sobre el hielo to ice-skate, 7.2

    patrón patron, **5.1**

    el/la santo patrón(ona) patron saint, **5.1**

    patronal pertaining to a patron saint, **5.1**

    pausado(a) slow, deliberate

    pavimentado(a) paved

el **pavimento** pavement

el **peaje** toll, **9.1**

    la cabina (garita) de peaje tollbooth, **9.1**

el/la **peatón(ona)** pedestrian, **8.1**

    peatonal (related to) pedestrians, **8.1**

el **pecho** chest, **11.1**

la **pechuga (de pollo)** (chicken) breast, **10**

el **pedacito** little piece, **10**

el **pedazo** piece

    pedir (i, i) to ask for, to request, **4**

    peinarse to comb one's hair, 11.1; **2.1**

el **peine** comb, 11.2; **2.2**

    pelar to peel, **10**

la **película** movie, film, 8.2

el **peligro** danger

    peligroso(a) dangerous

    pelirrojo(a) redheaded, 1.1

el **pelo** hair, 2.1

    tener el pelo rubio (castaño, negro) to have blond (brown, black) hair, 2.1

la **pelota** ball (baseball, tennis), 5.2

    la pelota vasca jai alai

la **pena** pain, sorrow

    ¡Qué pena! What a shame!, 5.1

el **pendiente** incline

    pendiente steep

el **pensamiento** thought

    pensar (ie) to think, 5.1

    pensar en to think about

    ¿Qué piensas? What do you think?, 5.1

el **peón** peasant, farm laborer, **8.2**

    peor worse

el/la **peor** worst

el **pepino** cucumber, **10**

    pequeño(a) small, little, 1.2

la **percha** hanger, **7**

    perder (ie) to lose, 5.1; to miss, 8.1

    perdida: la llamada perdida dropped call (cell phone), **6.2**

    perdón pardon me, excuse me

la **peregrinación** pilgrimage

    perezoso(a) lazy, 1.2

el **periódico** newspaper, **3.1**

    permiso: Con permiso. Excuse me., 10.1; **1.1**

el **permiso de conducir** driver's license, **9.2**

    permitir to permit

    pero but

el/la **perro(a)** dog, 2.1

la **persona** person

el **personaje** character (in a novel, play)

la **personalidad** personality, 6.1

    pertenecer to belong

    peruano(a) Peruvian

la **pesa** weight, **11.1**

    levantar pesas to lift weights, **11.1**

    pesar: a pesar de in spite of

la **pescadería** fish market

el **pescado** fish, 4.1

el **peso** peso (monetary unit of several Latin American countries); weight

    picar to nibble on; to chop; to mince, **10**

    picaresco(a) picaresque

el/la **pícher** pitcher, 5.2

el **pico** mountain top, peak, 7.2

el **pie** foot, 5.1; **2.1**

    a pie on foot, 3.2

    de pie standing

la **piedra** stone

la **pierna** leg, 11.1; **2.1**

la **pieza** bedroom; piece

la **pila** swimming pool

el **pimentón** pepper (vegetable)

la **pimienta** pepper (spice), **4**

el **pimiento** bell pepper, 9.2; **10**

el **pinchazo** flat tire, **9.2**

los **pinchitos** kebabs, 4.2

    pintado(a) painted

    pintar to paint

el/la **pintor(a)** painter, artist, 8.2

    pintoresco(a) picturesque

la **piña** pineapple, 9.2

la **piscina** swimming pool, 7.1

el **piso** floor, 2.2; apartment (Spain)

la **pista** ski slope, 7.2; runway, 10.2; **1.2**; lane (highway)

    la pista de patinaje ice-skating rink, 7.2

la **pizca** pinch

la **pizza** pizza, 4.1

    placentero(a) pleasant

la **plancha de vela** windsurfing; sailboard, 7.1

    practicar la plancha de vela to windsurf, to go windsurfing, 7.1

    planchas: hacer planchas to do push-ups, **11.1**

el **plano** map, **9.1**

la **planta** plant, 2.2

la **plata** silver

el **plátano** banana, 9.2

el **platillo** home plate, 5.2; saucer, **4**

el **plato** dish (food); plate, **4**; course (meal)

la **playa** beach, 7.1

la **plaza** square, plaza, **8.1**; seat (train), **3.2**

la **pluma** (fountain) pen

la **población** population

    pobre poor

el/la **pobre** poor boy (girl)

    poco(a) a little; few, 2.2

    dentro de poco soon; shortly thereafter

    un poco más a little more

    poder (ue) to be able, 5.1

el **poema** poem

el/la **policía** police officer

el **pollo** chicken, 4.1; **10**

    poner to put, to place, to set, 10.2; **1.2**

poner al fuego to heat, **10**

poner la mesa to set the table, **4**

poner unos puntos (unas suturas) to give (someone) stitches, **11.2**

ponerse to put on *(clothes)*, 11.1; **2.1**; to become

popular popular

por for, by

por ejemplo for example

por encima de over, 5.2

por eso that's why, for this reason

por favor please, LP

por fin finally

por la mañana in the morning

por la noche at night, in the evening

por la tarde in the afternoon

por lo general in general

Por nada. You're welcome., LP; for no reason

¿por qué? why?, 3.2

los **porotos** green beans

porque because, 3.2

el/la **porrista** cheerleader

portátil: la computadora portátil laptop computer

el/la **porteño(a)** person from Buenos Aires

la **portería** goal line, 5.1

el/la **portero(a)** goalie, 5.1

portugués(esa) Portuguese

poseer to possess

posible possible

positivo(a) positive

el **postre** dessert, 4.1

practicar to practice *(sport)*

practicar la plancha de vela (la tabla hawaiana) to go windsurfing *(surfing)*, 7.1

practicar yoga to do yoga, **11.1**

el **precio** price, 9.1

precolombino(a) pre-Columbian

la **preferencia** preference

preferir (ie, i) to prefer, 5.2; **4**

el **prefijo del país** country code, **6.2**

la **pregunta** question, 3.1

preguntar to ask (a question)

el **premio** prize, award

prender to turn on, **6.1**

preparar to prepare; to get ready

la **prepa(ratoria)** high school

presentar to introduce

el **préstamo** loan

el préstamo a corto (largo) plaza short- (long-) term loan

prestar: prestar atención to pay attention, 3.1

el **pretendiente** suitor

el **primario(a): la escuela primaria** elementary school

la **primavera** spring, LP

primero(a) first, LP

el primero de enero (febrero, etc.) January (February, etc.) 1, LP

en primera clase first-class, **3.2**

el/la **primo(a)** cousin, 2.1

la **princesa** princess

principal main

el/la **principiante** beginner, 7.2

prisa: de prisa fast, hurriedly

a toda prisa with full speed

privado(a) private, 2.2

probable probable, likely

el **problema** problem

No hay problema. No problem.

procedente de coming, arriving from, 10.2; **1.2**

el **procedimiento** step *(recipe)*

la **procesión** procession, parade, **5.1**

producir to produce

el **producto** product; food, 9.2

los productos congelados frozen food, 9.2

la **profesión** profession, occupation

profesional professional

el/la **profesor(a)** teacher, 1.2

profundo(a) deep

prohibido(a) forbidden, **9.1**

prometer to promise

el **pronombre** pronoun

pronto: ¡Hasta pronto! See you soon!, LP

propenso(a) prone to

la **propina** tip *(restaurant)*, 4

propio(a) own, 5.1

propósito: ¡A propósito! By the way . . . , 8.2

propósito benévolo charitable purpose

protectora: la loción bronceadora suntan lotion, sunblock, 7.1

próximo(a) next, **3.2**

la **prueba** test, exam, 3.1

el **pueblo** town

el **puente** bridge

la **puerta** gate *(airport)*, 10.2; **1.2**; door, **9.2**

la puerta delantera (trasera) front (back) door (bus)

la puerta de salida gate *(airport)*, 10.2; **1.2**

el **puerto** port

puertorriqueño(a) Puerto Rican

pues well

el **puesto** market stall, 9.2

los **pulmones** lungs

pulsar to press *(button, key)*, **6.1**

la **pulsera** bracelet

el **pulso: tomar el pulso** to take (someone's) pulse, 6.2

el **punto** point; dot *(Internet)*, **6.1**; stitch, **11.2**

poner puntos (a alguien) to give (somebody) stitches, **11.2**

el **pupitre** desk, 3.1

Q

que that; who

¿qué? what? how?, LP

¿a qué hora? at what time?, LP

¿de qué nacionalidad? what nationality?

No hay de qué. You're welcome., LP

¿Qué desean tomar? What would you like (to eat)?, 4.2

¿Qué día es hoy? What day is it today?, LP

¿Qué hay? What's new (up)?

¿Qué hora es? What time is it?, LP

¿Qué... más... ! What a . . . !

¿Qué pasa? What's going on? What's happening?

¡Qué pena! What a shame!, 5.1

¿Qué tal? How are things? How are you?, LP

¿Qué tal le gustó? How did you like it? *(formal)*

¿Qué tiempo hace? What's the weather like?, LP

quebrarse to break, **11.2**

quedar (bien) to fit, to look good on, 9.1

Esta chaqueta no te queda

Spanish-English Dictionary

bien. This jacket doesn't fit you., 9.1

quedar(se) to remain, to stay, 11.1; **2.1**

quemarse to burn, **10**

querer (ie) to want, to wish, 5.1; to love

querido(a) dear, beloved

el **queso** cheese, 4.1

    el sándwich de jamón y queso ham and cheese sandwich, 4.1

el **quetzal** quetzal *(currency of Guatemala)*

¿quién? who?, 1.1

    ¿De parte de quién, por favor? Who's calling, please?, **6.2**

¿quiénes? who? *(pl.)*, 1.2

quince fifteen, LP

la **quinceañera** fifteen-year-old girl

quinientos(as) five hundred, 9.2

el **quiosco** kiosk, newsstand, **3.1**

quitar la mesa to clear the table, **4**

quitarse to take off *(clothes)*, 11.1; **2.1**

quizá(s) maybe, perhaps, 7.2

R

la **racimo** bunch *(grapes)*

la **radiografía** X ray, 11.2

    Le toman (hacen) una radiografía. They're taking an X ray of him (her)., **11.2**

la **raja** slice *(melon)*

la **rama** branch

el **rancho** ranch, **8.2**

la **ranura** slot, **6.2**

rápidamente quickly

rápido(a) fast

la **raqueta** *(tennis)* racket, 5.2

raro(a) rare

el **rascacielos** skyscraper, **8.1**

el **rato** time, while

el **ratón** mouse, **6.1**

la **raza** breed

la **razón** reason

    tener razón to be right

el/la **realista** realist

rebajar to lower *(prices)*, 9.1

la **rebanada** slice *(bread)*, **10**

    cortar en rebanadas to

slice, **10**

rebasar to pass *(car)*, **9.1**

la **recámara** bedroom, 2.2

recambio: la rueda (llanta) de recambio spare tire, 9.2

la **recepción** front desk *(hotel)*, **7**

el/la **recepcionista** hotel clerk, **7**

el/la **receptor(a)** catcher, 5.2

la **receta** prescription, 6.2; recipe, **10**

recetar to prescribe, 6.2

recibir to receive, 4.2; to catch

    recibir aplausos to be applauded, 5.1

reclamar to claim

recoger to collect, to gather

reconocer to recognize

recordar (ue) to remember

el **recorrido** trip, route

los **recuerdos** memories

recuperar to claim, to get back

la **red** the Web, 3.2; **6.1**; net, 5.2

    navegar la red to surf the Web, 3.2; **6.1**

    pasar por encima de la red to go over the net, 5.2

reducido(a) reduced

reducir to reduce; to set *(bone)*, **11.2**

    reducir la velocidad to reduce speed, **9.1**

refacción: la rueda (llanta) de refacción spare tire

el **refresco** soft drink, 4.2

el **refrigerador** refrigerator, **10**

refrito(a) refried

el **refugio** refuge

el **regalo** gift, present, 8.1

regatear to bargain, 9.2

el **régimen** diet

la **región** region

la **regla** rule

regresar to go back, to return, 3.2

    el botón regresar back button, back key, **6.1**

    regresar a casa to go home, 3.2

regreso: el boleto de ida y regreso round-trip ticket, **3.1**

regular regular, average

la **reina** queen

reinar to rule, reign

relacionado(a) related

relevos: la carrera de

relevos relay race, **11.1**

religioso(a) religious

rendir (i, i) honor to honor

renombrado(a) famous

rentar to rent, 7.1; **3.2**

repartido(a) distributed, split up among

repasar to review

el **repaso** review

repente: de repente suddenly, all of a sudden

repetir (i, i) to repeat, to have seconds *(meal)*, **4**

la **república** republic

    la República Dominicana Dominican Republic

repuesto: la rueda (llanta) de repuesto spare tire, 9.2

la **reserva** reservation

la **reservación** reservation, 7

reservar to reserve, 7

respetado(a) respected

respetar to respect

la **respiración** breathing, **11.1**

respirar to breathe

responsable responsible

la **respuesta** answer

el **restaurante** restaurant, **4**

resultar to turn out to be, to wind up being

el **retraso** delay, 10.2; **1.2**

    con retraso late, 10.2; **1.2**

el **retrato** portrait

retroceder: el botón retrodecer back button, back key, 6.1

la **reunión** meeting, get-together

reunirse to meet, to get together

revisar to check *(ticket)*, **3.2**

el/la **revisor(a)** conductor, **3.2**

la **revista** magazine, **3.1**

revolver (ue) to stir, **10**

revueltos: los huevos revueltos scrambled eggs, 7

el **rey** king

    el Día de los Reyes Epiphany (January 6), **5.2**

    los Reyes Magos the Three Wise Men, **5.2**

rico(a) rich; delicious

    ¡Qué rico! How delicious!

el **rincón** corner

los **riñones** kidneys

el **río** river

SR54

STUDENT RESOURCES

Spanish-English Dictionary

el **risco** cliff, **3.2**

el **ritmo** rhythm

robar to steal

la **roca** rock, stone

la **rodaja** slice (lemon, cucumber)

rodeado(a) surrounded

la **rodilla** knee, 11.1; **2.1**

la **rodillera** kneepad, **11.1**

rojo(a) red, 5.1

   la luz roja red light, **9.1**

el **rol** role

el **rollo de papel higiénico** roll of toilet paper, 11.2; **2.2**

el **rompecabezas** puzzle

romper(se) to break, **11.2**

   Se rompió la pierna. He (She) broke his (her) leg., **11.2**

la **ropa** clothing, 9.1

la **rosa** rose

rosado(a) pink, 5.1

roto(a) broken

el **rótulo** sign, **9.1**

rubio(a) blonde, 1.1

la **rueda** tire, 9.2

   la rueda de repuesto (recambio) spare tire, **9.2**

   la silla de ruedas wheelchair, **11.2**

el **ruido** noise

las **ruinas** ruins

la **ruta** route

la **rutina diaria** daily routine, 11.1; **2.1**

S

el **sábado** Saturday, LP

la **sábana** sheet, 7

saber to know, 9.1

sabio(a) wise

el **sabor** flavor, **10**

sacar to get, 3.1; to take, 7.1

   sacar fotos to take pictures, 7.1

   sacar notas buenas (malas) to get good (bad) grades, 3.1

el **saco de dormir** sleeping bag, 11.2; **2.2**

el **sacrificio** sacrifice

la **sal** salt, **4**

la **sala** living room, 2.2

   la sala de clase classroom, 3.1

   la sala de emergencia emergency room, **11.2**

la **sala de espera** waiting room, **3.1**

salado(a) salty

el **saldo** sale, 9.1

la **salida** departure, 10.1; **1.1**; exit, **9.1**

   la hora de salida time of departure, 10.1; **1.1**

   la puerta de salida gate (airport), 10.2; **1.2**

salir to leave; to go out, 8.1; to turn out, to result

   Todo te sale más barato. Everything costs a lot less.; It's all a lot less expensive., 9.1

la **salsa** sauce, gravy, **10**; dressing

saltar to jump (over)

salteado(a) sautéed

la **salud** health, 6.1

saludar to greet

el **saludo** greeting

salvar to save

la **sandalia** sandal, 9.2

el **sándwich** sandwich, 4.1

   el sándwich de jamón y queso ham and cheese sandwich, 4.1

sano(a) healthy

el/la **santo(a)** saint

   el/la santo patrón(ona) patron saint, **5.1**

el **sarape** blanket

el/la **sartén** skillet, frying pan, **10**

satisfacer to satisfy

el **sato** a type of dog from Puerto Rico

seco(a) dry

secundario(a): la escuela secundaria high school, 1.2

la **sed** thirst, 4.1

   tener sed to be thirsty, 4.1

el **sedán** sedan, 9.2

seguir (i, i) to follow, **4**; to continue, **9.1**

según according to

segundo(a) second

   el segundo tiempo second half (soccer), 5.1

   en segunda clase second-class (ticket), **3.1**

seguramente surely, certainly

la **seguridad: el control de seguridad** security (airport), 10.2; **1.2**

   el cinturón de seguridad seat belt, 10.2; **1.2**

seguro(a) sure; safe

seguro que certainly

seis six, LP

seiscientos(as) six hundred, 9.2

seleccionar to choose, **3.1**

la **selva** jungle, forest

el **semáforo** traffic light, **8.1**

la **semana** week, LP

   el fin de semana weekend, 7.1

   la semana pasada last week, 7.1

sembrar (ie) to plant, to sow, **8.2**

seminómada seminomad

sencillo one-way, **3.1**; single (hotel room), **7**; simple

   el billete (boleto) sencillo one-way ticket, **3.1**

   el cuarto sencillo single room, **7**

la **senda** path, **3.2**

sentado(a) seated

sentarse (ie) to sit down, 11.1; **2.1**

el **sentido** direction, **9.1**; sense, 6.1

   la calle de sentido único one-way street, **9.1**

sentir (ie, i) to be sorry; to feel

   Lo siento mucho. I'm very sorry.

sentirse (ie, i) to feel

la **señal** sign, 10.2; **1.2**

   la señal de no fumar no-smoking sign, 10.2; **1.2**

señalar to point out

el **señor** sir, Mr., gentleman, LP

la **señora** Ms., Mrs., madam, LP

los **señores** Mr. and Mrs.

la **señorita** Miss, Ms., LP

septiembre September, LP

ser to be

el **ser** being

   los seres humanos human beings

   los seres vivientes living beings

serio(a) serious, 1.1

   ¿Hablas en serio? Are you serious?

el **servicio** tip, 4.2; restroom, 10.2; **1.2**; service, 9.2

   ¿Está incluido el servicio? Is the tip included?, 4.2

   la estación de servicio gas station, 9.2

la **servilleta** napkin, **4**

servir to serve, **4**

   servir de to serve as

sesenta sixty, LP

Spanish-English Dictionary

setecientos(as) seven hundred, 9.2

setenta seventy, LP

severo(a) harsh, strict

si if

sí yes, LP

siempre always, 8.2

siento: Lo siento mucho. I'm sorry. (That's too bad.), 5.1

la **siesta** nap

siete seven, LP

el **siglo** century

significar to mean

siguiente following

la **silla** chair, 2.2

    la silla de ruedas wheelchair, **11.2**

similar similar

simpático(a) nice, 1.1

sin without

sincero(a) sincere

sino but rather

el **síntoma** symptom

el **sistema** system

el **sitio** space (parking)

el **sitio Web** Web site, **6.1**

el/la **snowboarder** snowboarder, 7.2

las **sobras** leftovers

sobre on, on top of; about

    sobre todo above all, especially

la **sobremesa** dessert; after-dinner conversation

la **sobrepoblación** overpopulation

sobrevivir to survive

sobrevolar (ue) to fly over

la **sobrina** niece, 2.1

el **sobrino** nephew, 2.1

social social

    los estudios sociales social studies, 1.2

la **sociedad** society

el/la **socio(a)** member

socorrer to help

el/la **socorrista** paramedic, **11.2**

el **sofá** sofa, 2.2

el **sol** sun

    Hace (Hay) sol. It's sunny., LP

    tomar el sol to sunbathe, 7.1

solamente only

solar: la crema solar suntan lotion, 7.1

solas: a solas alone

el **soldado** soldier

soler (ue) to be used to, to do something usually

solo(a) single; alone

solo only

el/la **soltero(a)** single, unmarried person

el **sombrero** hat

sonar (ue) to ring, **6.1**

el **sonido** sound

la **sonrisa** smile, 6.1

la **sopa** soup

soplar to blow (wind)

la **sorpresa** surprise, 4.1

su his, her, their, your (formal)

subir to go up, 7.2; to get on (train, etc.), **3.1**

subterráneo(a) underground

los **suburbios** suburbs, 2.2

sucio(a) dirty, 7

Sudamérica South America

sudamericano(a) South American

el **suegro** father-in-law

el **suelo** ground, floor

el **sueño** dream

    tener sueño to be sleepy

la **suerte** luck

    ¡Buena suerte! Good luck!

    ¡Qué suerte tengo! How lucky I am!, 9.1

el **suéter** sweater, 11.1; **2.1**

sufrir to suffer

superior upper, top

    el compartimiento superior overhead bin (airplane), 10.2; **1.2**

el **supermercado** supermarket, 9.2

el **sur** south

    la América del Sur South America

el **surtido** assortment

sus their, your (pl.)

el **susto** fear

la **sutura** stitch, **11.2**

suturar to give (someone) stitches

el **SUV** SUV, **9.2**

T

la **tabla** chart, table

la **tabla hawaiana** surfboard, 7.1

    practicar la tabla hawaiana to surf, to go surfing, 7.1

tacaño(a) stingy, cheap, **9.1**

el **taco** taco

la **tajada** slice (ham, meat), 9.2

tal such

    ¿Qué tal? How are things? How are you?, LP

    ¿Qué tal tu clase de español? How's your Spanish class?

tal vez maybe, perhaps, 7.2

la **talla** size, 9.1

    ¿Qué talla usas? What size do you take?, 9.1

el **tamaño** size

también also, too, 1.2

el **tambor** drum

el **tamborín** small drum

tampoco either, neither

tan so

tan... como as . . . as

el **tanque** gas tank, **9.2**

el **tanto** score, point, 5.1

    marcar un tanto to score a point, 5.1

tanto(a) so much

    tanto(a)... como as much . . . as

    tantos(as)... como as many . . . as

la **tapa** lid, **10**

tapar to cover (pot)

las **tapas** snacks, nibbles, 4.2

el **tapón** traffic jam

la **taquilla** box office, ticket window, 8.2

tarde late, 10.2; **1.2**

la **tarde** afternoon

    ayer por la tarde yesterday afternoon, 7.1

    Buenas tardes. Good afternoon., LP

la **tarea** homework; task

la **tarifa** fare, **3.1**; price

la **tarjeta** card; pass

    la tarjeta de abordar boarding pass

    la tarjeta de crédito credit card, **3.1**

    la tarjeta de embarque boarding pass, 10.1; **1.1**

    la tarjeta telefónica telephone card, **6.2**

la **tarta** cake, 8.1

la **tasa de interés** interest rate

el **taxi** taxi, 10.1; **1.1**

el/la **taxista** taxi driver, 10.1; **1.1**

la **taza** cup, 4.1; **4**

te you (*fam. pron.*)

el **té** tea

el **teclado** keyboard, **6.1**

el/la **técnico(a)** technician

la **tecnología** technology

tejano(a) Texan

los **tejidos** fabrics, 9.2

la **tele** TV

telefónico(a) (*related to*) phone, **6.2**

   la guía telefónica phone book, **6.2**

   la tarjeta telefónica phone card, **6.2**

el **teléfono** telephone

   el número de teléfono phone number, **6.2**

   el teléfono celular cell phone, **6.1**

   el teléfono público pay phone, **6.2**

   hablar por teléfono to speak on the phone

la **telenovela** serial, soap opera

el **telesilla** chairlift, ski lift, 7.2

el **telesquí** ski lift, 7.2

la **televisión** television

el **tema** theme

tembloroso(a) trembling

la **temperatura** temperature, 7.2

temprano(a) early, 11.1; **1.2**

el **tenderete** market stall, 9.2

el **tenedor** fork, **4**

tener (ie) to have, 2.1

   tener… años to be . . . years old, 2.1

   tener calor (frío) to be hot (cold), 11.1; **2.1**

   tener catarro to have a cold, 6.2

   tener cuidado to be careful, **9.1**

   tener dolor de… to have a(n) . . . -ache, 6.2

   tener el pelo rubio (castaño, negro) to have blond (brown, black) hair, 2.1

   tener éxito to be successful, 6.1

   tener fiebre to have a fever, 6.2

   tener ganas de to feel like

   tener hambre to be hungry, 4.1

   tener lugar to take place

   tener miedo to be afraid, 7.2

   tener ojos azules (castaños, verdes) to have blue (brown, green) eyes, 2.1

   tener que to have to (*do something*), 4.2

   tener sed to be thirsty, 4.1

el **tenis** tennis

   la cancha de tenis tennis court, 5.2

   jugar (al) tenis to play tennis, 5.2

los **tenis** sneakers, tennis shoes, 9.1

el/la **tenista** tennis player

la **tensión** tension, stress, **11.1**

   la tensión arterial blood pressure, 6.2

tercer(o)(a) third

terco(a) stubborn, 6.1

terminar to end, finish

término: a término medio medium (*meat*), **4**

el **término** term

la **ternera** veal, **10**

   el escalope de ternera veal cutlet, **10**

el/la **terrateniente** landowner

la **terraza** terrace, balcony

el **terremoto** earthquake

el **tesoro** treasure

ti you

la **tía** aunt, 2.1

el **ticket** ticket, 7.2

el **tiempo** weather, LP; half (*soccer*), 5.1

   a tiempo on time, 10.2; **1.2**

   a tiempo completo (parcial) full- (part-) time

   el segundo tiempo second half (*soccer*), 5.1

   Hace buen (mal) tiempo. The weather is nice (bad)., LP

   ¿Qué tiempo hace? What's the weather like?, LP

la **tienda** store, 3.2

   la tienda de ropa clothing store, 9.1

la **tienda de campaña** tent, 11.2; **2.2**

la **tierra** land, **8.2**

el **tigre** tiger

los **timbales** small drums, kettledrums

el **timbre (sonoro)** ringtone, **6.2**

tímido(a) shy

el **tío** uncle, 2.1

los **tíos** aunt and uncle, 2.1

el **tiovivo** merry-go-round, **8.1**

típico(a) typical

el **tipo** type, 6.1

el **tiquete** ticket, **9.1**

tirar to throw, 5.2

el **título** title

la **toalla** towel, 7.1; **7**

el **tobillo** ankle, **11.1**

el **tocadiscos** record player

tocar to touch, 5.1; to play (*musical instrument*), 8.1; **5.2**

   ¡Te toca a ti! It's your turn!

el **tocino** bacon, 4.1; **7**

todavía still; yet

todo(a) everything; all

   sobre todo above all, especially

   todo el mundo everyone, **5.2**

todos(as) everyone, 8.1; everything; all

   en todas partes everywhere

tomar to take, 3.1; to have (*meal*), 4.1

   tomar el almuerzo (el desayuno) to have lunch (breakfast), 4.1

   tomar el bus to take the bus

   tomar el pulso to take someone's pulse, 6.2

   tomar el sol to sunbathe, 7.1

   tomar fotos to take pictures, 7.1

   tomar la tensión arterial to take someone's blood pressure, 6.2

   tomar un examen to take a test, 3.1

   tomar una ducha to take a shower, 11.1; **2.1**

   tomar una radiografía to take an X ray of someone, **11.2**

el **tomate** tomato, 4.1

la **tonelada** ton

el **tono** dial tone, **6.2**

las **tonterías** foolish things

tonto(a) foolish, crazy

torcerse (ue) to sprain, to twist, **11.2**

   Se torció el tobillo. He (She) sprained his (her) ankle., **11.2**

torcido(a) sprained, twisted

la **torta** cake, 4.1; sandwich

la **tortilla** tortilla

la **tos** cough, 6.2

   tener tos to have a cough, 6.2

toser to cough, 6.2

la **tostada** tostada

Spanish-English Dictionary

las **tostadas** toast, 4.1
tostado(a) toasted
  el pan tostado toast, 4.1; **7**
los **tostones** slices of fried plantain, 4.2
trabajar to work, 3.2; **8.2**
el **trabajo** work
tradicional traditional
traer to carry, to bring, to take, 10.1; **1.1**
el **tráfico** traffic, **8.1**
el **traje** suit
el **traje de baño** swimsuit, 7.1
tranquilo(a) calm, 6.1
transbordar to transfer (trains), **3.2**
el **tránsito** traffic
transporte: los medios de transporte means of transportation, **8.2**
trasero(a) back
el **tratamiento** treatment
tratar to treat
tratar de to try to (do something)
  tratar de desviar to try to dissuade
la **travesía** crossing
traviesa: a campo traviesa cross-country (race), **11.1**
el **trayecto** stretch (of road)
trece thirteen, LP
el **trecho** stretch (distance)
treinta thirty, LP
treinta y uno thirty-one, LP
el **tren** train, 3.1
tres three, LP
trescientos(as) three hundred, 9.2
el **trigo** wheat, **8.2**
triste sad, 6.1
el **trocito** little piece
la **trompeta** trumpet
las **tropas** troops
tropical tropical
el **trotamundos** globe-trotter
el **trozo** piece
el **T-shirt** T-shirt
tu your (sing. fam.)
tú you (sing. fam.)
el **tubo de crema dental** tube of toothpaste, 11.2; **2.2**
la **tumba** grave, tomb, **5.1**
el **turismo** tourism
el/la **turista** tourist

U

u or (used instead of **o** before words beginning with **o** or **ho**)
Ud., usted you (sing.) (formal)
Uds., ustedes you (pl.) (formal)
último(a) last; final
un(a) a, an, 1.1
la **una** one o'clock, LP
único(a) only, 2.1; one-way, **9.1**
  la calle de sentido único one-way street, **9.1**
  el/la hijo(a) único(a) only child, 2.1
la **unidad** unit
el **uniforme** uniform, 3.1
la **universidad** university
uno one, LP
unos(as) some
urbano(a) urban, **8.1**
usar to use, 3.2; to wear (size), 9.2
  ¿Qué talla usas? What size do you wear (take)?, 9.1
el **uso** use
el/la **usuario(a)** user
la **uva** grape, 9.2

V

la **vaca** cow, **8.2**
las **vacaciones** vacation, 7.1
  estar de vacaciones to be on vacation
vacante vacant
vacío(a) empty, **9.2**
vagar to wander, to roam
el **vagón** train car, **3.1**
la **vainilla** vanilla
las **vainitas** green beans
Vale. It's a good idea.
  No vale. It's not worth it., 7.1
valeroso(a) brave
el **valle** valley
¡Vamos! Let's go!
varios(as) several
el **varón** man, boy
vasco(a) Basque
  la pelota vasca jai-alai

el **vaso** glass, 4.1
el **váter** toilet, **7**
veces: a veces at times, sometimes, 6.1
el/la **vecino(a)** neighbor
el **vegetal** vegetable, 4.1
  los vegetales crudos raw vegetables, crudités, 8.1
vegetariano(a) vegetarian, 4.1
veinte twenty, LP
veinticinco twenty-five, LP
veinticuatro twenty-four, LP
veintidós twenty-two, LP
veintinueve twenty-nine, LP
veintiocho twenty-eight, LP
veintiséis twenty-six, LP
veintisiete twenty-seven, LP
veintitrés twenty-three, LP
veintiuno twenty-one, LP
la **vela** candle, 8.1; **5.2**
vela: la plancha de vela windsurfing; sailboard, 7.1
la **velocidad** speed, **9.1**
  la velocidad máxima speed limit, **9.1**
la **venda** bandage, **11.2**
el/la **vendedor(a)** merchant, 9.2
vender to sell, 6.2
venezolano(a) Venezuelan
venir (ie) to come, 10.2; **1.2**
  el verano (año, mes) que viene next summer (year, month), **8.2**
la **venta** small hotel
las **ventajas** advantages
la **ventanilla** ticket window, 7.2, **3.1**; window (plane), 10.2; **1.2**
ver to see, 4.2
el **verano** summer, LP
el **verbo** verb
la **verdad** truth
  Es verdad. That's true (right)., 9.1
  ¿Verdad? Right?
verdadero(a) real, true
verde green, 2.1
  las judías verdes green beans, 9.2
la **verdulería** greengrocer (vegetable) store, 9.2
la **verdura** vegetable, 4.1
verificar to check
el **vestido** dress, 9.1
  el vestido de novia wedding dress

la   **vestirse (i, i)** to get dressed, to dress, **4**

la   **vez** time

     a veces at times, sometimes, 6.1; **1.2**

     cada vez each time, every time

     de vez en cuando from time to time, occasionally, 10.2; **1.2**

     en vez de instead of

     una vez más (once) again, one more time

la   **vía** track, **3.1;** lane *(highway)*

     viajar to travel

     viajar en avión (tren) to travel by plane (train)

el   **viaje** trip, voyage 10.1; **1.1**

     hacer un viaje to take a trip, 10.1; **1.1**

la   **víctima** victim

la   **vida** life

el   **video** video

     viejo(a) old, 2.2

el   **viento** wind, LP

     Hace viento. It's windy., LP

el   **viernes** Friday, LP

el   **vinagre** vinegar, **4**

el   **vino** wine

el   **violín** violin

     visitar to visit, 8.2

la   **víspera de Año Nuevo** New Year's Eve

la   **vista** view; sight

la   **viuda** widow

     vivir to live, 4.2

     vivo(a) lively

los **vivos** the living

la   **vocal** vowel

el   **volante** steering wheel, **9.2**

     volar (ue) to fly

el   **volcán** volcano

     volcar to flip over

el   **voleibol** volleyball, 7.1

     la cancha de voleibol volleyball court, 7.1

     volver (ue) to return, 5.1

     volver a casa to go back (return) home, 8.1

     vosotros(as) you *(pl.)*

la   **voz** voice

el   **vuelo** flight, 10.1; **1.1**

     el número del vuelo flight number, 10.1; **1.1**

     vuelta: un boleto (billete) de ida y vuelta round-trip ticket, **3.1**

la   **vuelta** lap, **11.1**

     Vuestra Merced Your Highness

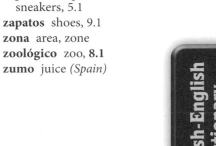

     y and, LP

     y cuarto a quarter past (the hour), LP

     y media half past (the hour), LP

     ya already

     ¡Ya voy! I'm coming!, 11.2; **2.2**

el   **yeso** cast, **11.2**

     yo I; me

el   **yoga** yoga, **11.1**

Z

la   **zanahoria** carrot, 9.2; **10**

las **zapatillas** (sports) shoes, sneakers, 5.1

los **zapatos** shoes, 9.1

la   **zona** area, zone

el   **zoológico** zoo, **8.1**

el   **zumo** juice *(Spain)*

Spanish-English Dictionary

English-Spanish Dictionary

*This English-Spanish Dictionary contains all productive and some receptive vocabulary from Levels 1 and 2. The numbers following each productive entry indicate the chapter and vocabulary section in which the word is introduced. For example, **3.2** in dark print means that the word was first taught in **Capítulo 3, Vocabulario 2**. A light print number means that the word was introduced in **¡Asi Se Dice!**, Level 1. LP refers to the **Lecciones preliminares** in Level 1. If there is no number following an entry, this means that the word or expression is there for receptive purposes only.*

A

@ la arroba, **6.1**
a, an un(a), 1.1
able: to be able poder (ue), 5.1
aboard abordo (de), 10.2; **1.2**
about sobre; *(time)* a eso de
above por encima de, 5.2
　above all sobre todo
abroad al extranjero
accident el accidente, **11.2**
accompanied by acompañado(a) de, **3.2**
according to según
ache el dolor, 6.2
to **ache** doler, 6.2; **11.2**
　My . . . ache(s). Me duele(n)... , 6.2
activity la actividad
to **add** añadir, **10**
addition: in addition to además de
address la dirección, **6.1**
　address book la libreta de direcciones, **6.1**
　e-mail address la dirección de correo electrónico (e-mail), **6.1**
addressee el/la destinatario(a), **6.1**
adorable cariñoso(a), 2.1; adorable
advanced avanzado(a), 7.2
advantage la ventaja
afraid: to be afraid tener miedo, 7.2
after después (de), 3.1; *(time)* y
　It's ten after one. Es la una y diez., LP
afternoon la tarde
　Good afternoon. Buenas tardes., LP
　this afternoon esta tarde, 7.1
　yesterday afternoon ayer por la tarde, 7.1
again de nuevo

against contra
age la edad
agent el/la agente, 10.1; **1.1**
agricultural agrícola
air el aire
　open-air (outdoor) café (market) el café (mercado) al aire libre
air conditioning el aire acondicionado, **7**
airline la línea aérea, 10.1; **1.1**
airplane el avión, 10.1; **1.1**
airport el aeropuerto, 10.1; **1.1**
aisle el pasillo, 10.2; **1.2**
album el álbum
algebra el álgebra
all todo(a), 6.2; todos(as), 8.1
　above all sobre todo
to **allow** dejar
almost casi, 8.2; **4**
alone solo(a); a solas
already ya
also también, 1.2
although aunque
always siempre, 8.2
A.M. de la mañana
ambulance la ambulancia, **11.2**
American americano(a)
among entre
to **amuse** divertir (ie), 10.2; **1.2**
amusement park el parque de atracciones, **8.1**
　amusement park ride la atracción, **8.1**
amusing divertido(a)
ancient antiguo(a), **8.1**
and y, LP
Andean andino(a)
angry enfadado(a), enojado(a), 6.1
　to make angry enfadar, 6.1
animal el animal
ankle el tobillo, **11.1**
to **annoy** molestar, enojar, 6.1
another otro(a)
answer la respuesta
　to answer contestar, 3.1

any cualquier
　any other cualquier otro(a)
anybody nadie, 8.2
anything algo, 9.2
　Anything else? ¿Algo más?, 9.2
apartment el apartamento, el apartamiento, el departamento, 2.2; el piso
　apartment building la casa de apartamentos, 2.2
appearance la apariencia
to **applaud** aplaudir, 5.1
　to be applauded recibir aplausos, 5.1
applause el aplauso, 5.1
apple la manzana, 9.2
appreciated apreciado(a)
to **approach** acercarse de
April abril, LP
archeology la arqueología
area la zona
area code la clave de área, **6.2**
Argentine argentino(a)
arithmetic la aritmética
arm el brazo, 11.1; **2.1**
around alrededor de, 2.2; *(time)* a eso de
arrival la llegada, **3.1**
to **arrive** llegar, 4.1
arriving from procedente de, 10.2; **1.2**
art el arte, 1.2
　art show (exhibition) la exposición de arte, 8.2
artichoke (sautéed) alcachofa salteada
artist el/la artista; el/la pintor(a), 8.2
as como
　as . . . as tan... como
　as many . . . as tantos(as)... como
　as much . . . as tanto(a)... como
to **ask (a question)** preguntar
to **ask for** pedir (i, i), **4**

assign asignar, **6.2**
assistance la ayuda
at a, en
    at (@) sign la arroba, **6.1**
    at around *(time)* a eso de
    at home en casa, 2.2
    at night por la noche; de noche
    at one o'clock (two o'clock, three o'clock . . .) a la una (a las dos, a las tres…), LP
    at times a veces, 6.1; **1.2**
    at what time? ¿a qué hora?, LP
athlete el/la atleta
attached file el documento adjunto, **6.1**
to **attend** asistir a, 8.1
attention: to pay attention prestar atención, 3.1
attractive guapo(a), 1.1
August agosto, LP
aunt la tía, 2.1
aunt and uncle los tíos, 2.1
author el/la autor(a)
automatic automático(a), 10.2; **1.2**
    automatic dispenser el distribuidor automático, **3.1**
autumn el otoño, LP
available disponible
avenue la avenida, **8.1**
average regular
avocado el aguacate, 10; la palta
Awesome! ¡Bárbaro!, 5.2

B

back la espalda, 11.1; **2.1**
back *(adj.)* trasero(a)
    back button *(key)* el botón regresar (retroceder), **6.1**
    back door la puerta trasera, **8.1**
back: in back of detrás de, 2.2
background la ascendencia
backpack la mochila, 3.1
backpacker el/la mochilero(a), 11.2; **2.2**
backwards hacia atrás
bacon el tocino, el bacón, 4.1; **7;** el lacón, 7
bad malo(a), 1.2; mal, LP
    The weather is bad. Hace mal tiempo., LP
    to be in a bad mood estar de mal humor, 6.1
    to get bad grades sacar notas malas, 3.1

baggage el equipaje, 10.1; **1.1**
    carry-on baggage el equipaje de mano, 10.1; **1.1**
bakery la panadería
balcony el balcón
ball *(soccer, basketball)* el balón, 5.1; *(volleyball)* el voleibol, 7.1; *(baseball, tennis)* la pelota, 5.2
    to hit the ball batear, 5.2; golpear, 5.2
    to kick (throw) the ball lanzar el balón, 5.1
    to hit the ball batear, 5.2; golpear, 5.2
ballpoint pen el bolígrafo, 3.1; el lapicero, la pluma
banana el plátano, 9.2
    ripe bananas los maduros
band *(music)* la banda, 8.1; **5.2;** el conjunto, 8.1
    city band la banda municipal, **5.2**
bandage la venda, **11.2**
bar: bar of soap la barra de jabón, 11.2; **2.2;** la pastilla de jabón
to **bargain** regatear, 9.2
barn el granero, **8.2**
base *(baseball)* la base, 5.2
baseball el béisbol, 5.2
    baseball field el campo de béisbol, 5.2
    baseball game el juego (partido) de béisbol, 5.2
    baseball player el/la jugador(a) de béisbol, el/la beisbolista, 5.2
basket *(basketball)* el cesto, la canasta, 5.2
    to make a basket encestar, meter el balón en la cesta, 5.2
basketball el básquetbol, el baloncesto, 5.2
    basketball court la cancha de básquetbol, 5.2
bat el bate, 5.2
to **bat** batear, 5.2
bath el baño, 2.2; **7**
bathing suit el bañador, el traje de baño, 7.1
bathroom el cuarto de baño, 2.2; **7**
bathtub la bañera, 7
batter el/la bateador(a), 5.2
to **be** ser, 1.1; estar, 3.1
    to be able (to) poder (ue), 5.1
    to be afraid tener miedo, 7.2
    to be applauded recibir aplausos, 8.1

    to be born nacer
    to be called (named) llamarse, 11.1; **2.1**
    to be careful tener cuidado, **9.1**
    to be cold (hot) tener frío (calor), 11.1; **2.1**
    to be cut off cortar la linea (a alguien), **6.2**
    to be familiar with conocer, 9.1
    to be fine (well) estar bien, 6.2
    to be going to (do something) ir a + *infinitive*, 4.2
    to be happy estar contento(a), alegre, 6.1
    to be hungry tener hambre, 4.1
    to be in a good (bad) mood estar de buen (mal) humor, 6.1
    to be pleasing (to someone) gustar, 5.1
    to be sad estar triste, deprimido(a), 6.1
    to be sick estar enfermo(a), 6.2
    to be sorry sentir (ie, i)
    to be successful tener éxito, 6.1
    to be thirsty tener sed, 4.1
    to be tired estar cansado(a), 6.1
    to be . . . years old tener… años, 2.1
beach la playa, 7.1
beach resort el balneario, 7.1
beans los frijoles, 4.1
    green beans (string beans) las judías verdes, 9.2
beautiful bello(a), hermoso(a)
because porque, 3.2
bed la cama, 2.2; **7**
    to go to bed acostarse (ue), 11.1; **2.1**
    to make the bed hacer la cama, 7
    to stay in bed guardar cama, 6.2; quedarse en la cama, 11.1; **2.1**
bedroom el cuarto de dormir, la recámara, 2.2; la habitación, **7;** el dormitorio, la alcoba, la pieza
beef la carne de res, **4;** el bife
before antes de, 3.2
beforehand antes, 10.1; **1.1**
to **begin** empezar (ie), 5.1; comenzar (ie)

English-Spanish Dictionary

beginner el/la principiante, 7.2
behaved: to be well-behaved tener buena conducta, 6.1
behavior la conducta, el comportamiento, 6.1
behind detrás de, 2.2
to **believe** creer
bell pepper el pimiento, 9.2
bell tower la campana
bellhop el mozo, 7
to **belong** pertenecer
below debajo de, 10.2; **1.2**
beside al lado de, 2.2
besides además
best el/la mejor
better mejor
between entre
beverage la bebida, el refresco, 4.1
bicycle la bicicleta, 2.2
to ride a bicycle andar en bicicleta, **11.1**
big gran, grande, 1.2
bike ride: to go for a bike ride dar un paseo en bicicleta
bike riding: to go bike riding andar en bicicleta, **11.1**
bill la factura
biologist el/la biólogo(a)
biology la biología
bird el pájaro
birthday el cumpleaños, 8.1
black negro(a), 2.1
blanket la manta, la frazada, 7
block (city) la cuadra, la manzana, **9.1**
to **block** bloquear, 5.1
blond(e) rubio(a), 1.1
to have blond hair tener el pelo rubio, 2.1
blood pressure la tensión arterial, 6.2
blouse la blusa, 3.1
to **blow (wind)** soplar
blue azul, 2.1
blue jeans el blue jean, 9.1
board: on board abordo (de), 10.2; **1.2**
to **board** embarcar, abordar, 10.2; **1.2**
boarding el embarque, 10.1; **1.1**
boarding pass la tarjeta de embarque, 10.1; **1.1;** el pasabordo, la tarjeta de abordar
boarding pass kiosk el distribuidor automático, 10.1; **1.1**

boarding time la hora de embarque, 10.1; **1.1**
boat el barquito, 7.1
body (human) el cuerpo (humano), 11.1; **2.1**
to **boil** hervir (ie, i), **10**
boiling la ebullición
bone el hueso, **5.1**
to set the bone reducir, acomodar el hueso, **11.2**
book el libro, 3.1
boot la bota, 7.2
border la frontera
to **bore** aburrir, 5.2
boring aburrido(a), 1.2
born: to be born nacer
to **bother** molestar, enfadar, enojar, 6.1
bottle la botella, 9.2
box office la taquilla, 8.2
boy el muchacho, 1.1; el niño, 6.2
brakes los frenos, **9.2**
to put on (apply) the brakes poner los frenos
brave valeroso(a)
Brazilian brasileño(a)
bread el pan
to **break** romper; romperse, quebrarse, **11.2**
He (She) broke his (her) leg. Se rompió (se quebró) la pierna., **11.2**
breakdown la avería
breakfast el desayuno, 4.1; **7**
Continental breakfast el desayuno continental, **7**
to have breakfast tomar el desayuno, 4.1; desayunarse
breaking: You're breaking up. (telephone) Estás cortando., **6.2**
breast (chicken) la pechuga, **10**
breathing la respiración, **11.1**
breed la raza
to **bring** traer, 10.1; **1.1**
to **bring down** derrocar
broad ancho(a), **8.1**
broken roto(a); quebrado(a)
bronze (adj.) de bronce, 8.2
brother el hermano, 2.1
brown castaño(a), 2.1; de color marrón, 5.1
to have brown eyes tener ojos castaños, 2.1
to have brown hair tener el pelo castaño, 2.1

brunette moreno(a), 1.1
brush el cepillo, 11.2; **2.2**
toothbrush el cepillo de dientes, 11.2; **2.2**
to **brush** cepillar, 11.1; **2.1**
to brush one's hair cepillarse, 11.1; **2.1**
to brush one's teeth cepillarse (lavarse) los dientes, 11.1; **2.1**
building el edificio, 2.2
bunk la litera
buried enterrado(a), **5.1**
to **burn** quemarse, **10**
burrito el burrito
to **bury** enterrar (ie)
bus el autobús, el camión, la guagua, **8.1;** el bus
bus stop la parada de autobús (de camiones, de guaguas), **8.1**
school bus el bus escolar, 3.2
to miss the bus perder el autobús, 8.1
but pero
butcher shop la carnicería
butter la mantequilla, 4.1; 7
button el botón, 6.1
back button el botón regresar (retroceder), **6.1**
delete button el botón borrador, **6.1**
to **buy** comprar, 3.2
by por; en
by plane (car, bus) en avión (carro, autobús)
by tens de diez en diez
By the way! ¡A propósito!, 8.2
Bye! ¡Chao!, LP

C

café el café, 3.1
outdoor café el café al aire libre
cafeteria la cafetería, 4.1
cake la torta, 4.1; el bizcocho, **5.1;** el pastel, la tarta, 8.1
calculator la calculadora, 3.1
call (phone) la llamada, 6.2
dropped call la llamada perdida (caída), **6.2**
to **call** llamar, 11.2; **2.2**
Who's calling, please? ¿De parte de quién, por favor?, **6.2**
calm calmo(a), tranquilo(a), 6.1

camel el camello, **5.2**

camera la cámara, 7.1; **6.2**

    digital camera la cámara digital, 7.1; **6.2**

camping el camping, 11.2; **2.2**

    to go camping ir de camping, 11.2; **2.2**

can el bote, la lata, 9.2

Canadian canadiense

candle la vela, 8.1; **5.2**

canned enlatado(a)

canyon el cañón, 3.2

cap el gorro, 7.2

capital la capital

car el carro, 2.2; **9.2**; el coche, **9.2**; *(train)* el coche, el vagón, **3.1**

    dining car el coche comedor (cafetería), la bufetería, **3.1**

    sports car el coche deportivo, **9.2**

carbonated drink la gaseosa, 4.1

card la tarjeta, 3.1; **6.2**; el carnet, 10.2; **1.2**

    credit card la tarjeta de crédito, 3.1

    ID card el carnet de identidad, 10.2; **1.2**

    phone card la tarjeta telefónica, **6.2**

careful: to be careful tener cuidado, **9.1**

carefully con cuidado

Caribbean Sea el mar Caribe

carrot la zanahoria, 9.2; **10**

to carry llevar, 3.1; traer, 10.1; **1.1**

carry-on luggage el equipaje de mano, 10.2; **1.2**

cart el carrito, 9.2; **3.1**

case: in case en caso de; por si acaso

cash register la caja, 3.2

cashier el/la cajero(a)

cast el yeso, **11.2**

castle el castillo

cat el/la gato(a), 2.1

to catch atrapar, 5.2

catcher el/la cátcher, el/la receptor(a), 5.2

Catholic católico(a)

cattle el ganado, **8.2**

to cause causar

to celebrate celebrar, **5.2**

celebration la celebración

cell phone el móvil, el celular, 3.2; **6.1**

cemetery el cementerio, el camposanto, **5.1**

century el siglo

ceramics las cerámicas, 9.2

cereal el cereal, 4.1

certain cierto(a), **6.1**

chair la silla, 2.2

chairlift el telesilla, el telesquí, 7.2

to change cambiar, **3.2**

    to change trains (transfer) transbordar, **3.2**

chapter el capítulo

character el personaje

charitable purpose el propósito benévolo

cheap barato(a), 9.1

    It's all a lot cheaper. Todo te sale más barato., 9.1

check *(restaurant)* la cuenta, 4.2; **4**

to check *(ticket)* revisar, **3.2**; *(facts)* verificar

to check luggage facturar el equipaje, 10.1; **1.1**

to check out *(hotel room)* abandonar el cuarto, 7

cheese el queso, 4.1

    ham and cheese sandwich el sándwich de jamón y queso, 4.1

chemistry la química

chest el pecho, **11.1**

chicken el pollo, 4.1; **10**

    chicken breast la pechuga de pollo, **10**

    chicken thigh el muslo de pollo, **10**

    chicken wings las alitas de pollo, **10**

child el/la niño(a), 6.2

children los hijos, 2.1

Chilean chileno(a)

chili pepper el ají

chocolate el chocolate, 4.1

    hot chocolate el chocolate caliente, 4.1

to choose escoger; seleccionar, **3.1**

chop: pork chop la chuleta de cerdo, **10**

to chop picar, **10**

Christian cristiano(a)

Christmas la Navidad, las Navidades, **5.2**

    Christmas Eve la Nochebuena, **5.2**

    Christmas gift el aguinaldo, **5.2**

    Christmas tree el árbol de Navidad, **5.2**

    Merry Christmas! ¡Feliz Navidad!

church la iglesia

city la ciudad, 2.2; **8.1**

civilization la civilización

clams las almejas, 4

to clap aplaudir, 5.1

clarinet el clarinete

class *(school)* la clase; el curso, 1.2; *(ticket)* la clase, **3.1**

    first (second) class en primera (secunda) clase, **3.1**

classroom la sala de clase, 3.1

clean limpio(a), **7**

to clean limpiar, **7**

to clear the table levantar, quitar la mesa, **4**

clerk el/la empleado(a), 3.1; el/la dependiente, 9.1

to click *(computer)* hacer clic, **6.1**

cliff el risco, 3.2

climate el clima

close (to) cerca de

to close cerrar (ie), 11.2; **2.2**

closet el armario, **7**

clothes la ropa, 9.1

clothes hanger la percha, el colgador, **7**

clothing la ropa, 9.1

    clothing store la tienda de ropa, 9.1

cloud la nube, 7.1

cloudy nublado(a), 7.1

clove (of garlic) el diente

coach el/la entrenador(a)

coast la costa

code: area code la clave de área, **6.2**

    country code el prefijo del país, **6.2**

co-ed mixto(a)

coffee el café, 4.1; **7**

cognate la palabra afine

coin la moneda, **9.1**

cola la cola, 4.1

cold el frío; frío(a), 4.2; *(illness)* el catarro, 6.2

    It's cold (weather). Hace frío., LP

    to be cold tener frío, 11.1; **2.1**

    to have a cold tener catarro, 6.2

Colombian el/la colombiano(a)

color el color, 5.1

comb el peine, 11.2; **2.2**

to comb one's hair peinarse, 11.1; **2.1**

to come venir (ie), 10.2; **1.2**

    I'm coming! ¡Ya voy!, 11.2; **2.2**

to come out onto desembocar

coming from procedente de, 10.2; **1.2**

English-Spanish Dictionary

comical cómico(a), gracioso(a), **1.1**

companion el/la compañero(a)

to **complete** completar

completely totalmente

composition la composición

computer la computadora, el ordenador, 3.2; **6.1**

concert el concierto, 8.1

concourse *(train station)* el hall, **3.1**

condiment el condimento, 10

condo(minium) el condominio

conduct la conducta, el comportamiento, 6.1

conductor *(train)* el revisor, **3.2**

connected conectado(a)

connection la conexión

consonant la consonante

to **consult** consultar

to **contain** contener (ie)

continent el continente

Continental breakfast el desayuno continental, 7

to **continue** continuar; seguir, **9.1**

contrary: on the contrary al contrario

conversation la conversación

convertible el descapotable, el convertible, **9.2**

to **convince** convencer

cook el/la cocinero(a), 10

to **cook** cocinar, cocer (ue), 10

cooking la cocción

cool fresco(a), LP

It's cool (weather). Hace fresco., LP

copy la copia, **6.1**

hard copy la copia dura, **6.1**

corn el maíz, 9.2; el elote, el choclo

corner la esquina, **8.1**

corral el corral, **8.2**

to **cost** costar (ue), 9.1

How much does it cost? ¿Cuánto cuesta?, 3.2

Costa Rican costarricense

costume el disfraz, **5.1**

cough la tos, 6.2

to have a cough tener tos, 6.2

to **cough** toser, 6.2

counter *(airline)* el mostrador, 10.1; **1.1**

country el país; el campo, **8.2**

country code el prefijo del país, **6.2**

country house la casa de campo, **8.2**

Spanish-speaking countries los países hispanohablantes

countryside el campo, **8.2**

course el curso, 1.2

court la cancha, 5.2

basketball (tennis) court la cancha de básquetbol (tenis), 5.2

volleyball court la cancha de voleibol, 7.1

courtesy la cortesía

cousin el/la primo(a), 2.1

to **cover** cubrir, tapar

cow la vaca, **8.2**

crackers las galletas, 8.1

crafts la artesanía, 9.2

crazy loco(a)

credit card la tarjeta de crédito, **3.1**

to **cross** cruzar, **9.1**

cross-country *(skiing)* el esquí nórdico, 7.2; *(race)* la carrera a campo traviesa, **11.1**

crosswalk el cruce, **8.1**

crutches las muletas, **11.2**

to walk on crutches andar con muletas, **11.2**

Cuban el/la cubano(a)

Cuban American el/la cubanoamericano(a)

cucumber el pepino, 10

cuisine la cocina

culture la cultura

cup la taza, 4.1; **4**

custard el flan, 4.1

custom la costumbre

customer el/la cliente, 9.2; **7**

to **cut** cortar, 10

to cut (up) in small pieces cortar en pedacitos, 10

to **cut off: We've been cut off.** *(telephone)* Se nos cortó la línea., **6.2**

to **cut oneself** cortarse, **11.2**

cutlet: veal cutlet el escalope de ternera, 10

daily diario(a)

daily routine la rutina diaria, 11.1; **2.1**

dairy products los productos lácteos

to **dance** bailar, 5.2

danger el peligro

dangerous peligroso(a)

dark-haired moreno(a), 1.1

data los datos

date la fecha, LP

What's today's date? ¿Cuál es la fecha de hoy?, LP

daughter la hija, 2.1

day el día, LP; fiesta, 5.1

the Day of the Dead el Día de los Muertos, **5.1**

patron saint's day la fiesta patronal, **5.1**

What day is it (today)? ¿Qué día es hoy?, LP

dead muerto(a), difunto(a), **5.1**

dead person, deceased person el/la muerto(a), el/la disfunto(a), **5.1**

dear querido(a)

death la muerte

deboned deshuesado(a)

December diciembre, LP

to **decide** decidir

to **decorate** decorar, **5.2**

deep profundo(a)

definition la definición

delay el retraso, la demora, 10.2; **1.2**

to **delete** borrar, **6.1**

delete key *(computer)* el botón borrador, **6.1**

delicious delicioso(a); rico(a)

to **demand** exigir

departure la salida, 10.1; **1.1**

departure gate la puerta de salida, 10.2; **1.2**

departure time la hora de salida, 10.1; **1.1**

to **depend** depender (ie) (de)

to **deplane** desembarcar, 10.2; **1.2**

to **describe** describir

description descripción

desert el desierto

desk el pupitre, 3.1

desolate inhóspito(a)

dessert el postre, 4.1

destination el destino, **3.1**

to **develop** desarrollarse

device el aparato

diagnosis el diagnóstico

to dial marcar el número, **6.2**

dial tone el tono, **6.2**

to dice cortar en pedacitos, **10**

dictation el dictado

to die morir (ue, u), **4**

diet la dieta

difference la diferencia

different diferente, **9.2**

difficult difícil; duro(a), **1.2**; avanzado(a), **7.2**

difficulty la dificultad

digital camera la cámara digital, **7.1**; **6.2**

diner el/la comensal

dining car el coche comedor (cafetería), la bufetería, **3.2**

dining room el comedor, **2.2**

dinner la cena, **4.1**

to have dinner cenar, **4.1**

direction (road) sentido, **9.1**

in each direction en cada sentido, **9.1**

directions las direcciones

dirty sucio(a), **7**

disadvantage la desventaja

disagreeable desagradable

to disappear desaparecer

to discover descubrir

to disembark desembarcar, **1.2**

disguise el disfraz, **5.1**

dish el plato, **4**

dishwasher el lavaplatos, **10**

dispenser: automatic boarding pass dispenser el distribuidor automático, **10.1**; **1.1**

distance: long distance de larga distancia

district el casco, el barrio, **8.1**

to dive bucear, **7.1**

divine divino(a)

to do hacer, **10.2**; **1.2**

to do homework hacer las tareas

to do push-ups hacer planchas, **11.1**

to do yoga practicar yoga, **11.1**

doctor el/la médico(a), **6.2**

doctor's office el consultorio, la consulta, **6.2**

document el documento

attached document el documento adjunto, **6.1**

dog el/la perro(a), **2.1**

dollar el dólar

Dominican dominicano(a)

Dominican Republic la República Dominicana

door la puerta, **9.2**

front (back) door la puerta delantera (trasera)

dot (Internet) el punto, **6.1**

double (room) un cuarto doble, **7**

doubles (tennis) dobles, **5.2**

doubt la duda

to doubt dudar

doughnut (type of) el churro

down: to go down bajar, **7.2**

downhill skiing el esquí alpino, **7.2**

to download bajar, descargar, **6.2**

downtown el centro, **8.1**

dozen la docena

drawing el dibujo

dream el sueño

dress el vestido, **9.1**

to dress vestirse (i, i), **4**

to dribble driblar (con el balón), **5.2**

drink (beverage) el refresco, **4.2**; la bebida, **4.1**

to drink beber, **4.1**

to drive conducir, manejar, **9.2**

driver el/la conductor(a), **9.2**

driver's license el permiso de conducir, la licencia, el carnet, **9.2**

dropped call una llamada caída (perdida), **6.2**

drugstore la farmacia, **6.2**

dry seco(a)

during durante, **3.2**

DVD el DVD, **3.2**

dynamic dinámico(a), **6.1**

E

e-mail el correo electrónico, **3.2**; **6.1**; el e-mail

e-mail address la dirección de correo electrónico (e-mail), **6.1**

e-mail inbox la bandeja de entradas, **6.1**

e-ticket el boleto (billete) electrónico, **10.1**; **1.1**

each cada, **2.2**

early temprano, **11.1**; **2.1**

early riser el/la madrugador(a), **11.1**; **2.1**

to earn ganar

easily sin dificultad, **7.2**

east el este

easy fácil, **1.2**

to eat comer, **4.1**

to eat breakfast (lunch) tomar el desayuno (el almuerzo), **4.1**

to eat dinner cenar, **4.1**

Ecuadoran ecuatoriano(a), **1.1**

education la educación

physical education la educación física, **1.2**

egg el huevo, **4.1**; **7**

scrambled eggs los huevos revueltos, **7**

eight ocho, LP

eight hundred ochocientos(as), **9.2**

eighteen dieciocho, LP

eighty ochenta, LP

either tampoco

elbow el codo, **11.1**; **2.1**

electronic electrónico(a), **10.1**; **1.1**

elementary school la escuela primaria

elevator el ascensor, **7**

eleven once, LP

else: Anything else? ¿Algo más?, **9.2**

Nothing else. Nada más., **9.2**

emergency room la sala de emergencia, **11.2**

employee el/la empleado(a), **3.2**; el/la dependiente, **9.1**

empty vacío(a), **9.2**

enchilada la enchilada

end el fin

at the end (of) al final (de); a fines de

to end terminar

energetic energético(a), **6.1**

energy la energía, **6.1**

engine el motor

English (language) el inglés, **1.2**

to enjoy disfrutar; gozar

to enjoy oneself divertirse (ie, i), **11.2**; **2.2**

enormous enorme

enough bastante; suficiente

to enter entrar, **5.1**

enthusiasm el entusiasmo, **6.1**

enthusiastic lleno(a) de entusiasmo, **6.1**; entusiasmado(a)

entire entero(a)

entrance la entrada; (subway) la boca del metro, **8.1**

Epiphany el Día de los Reyes, **5.2**

equal igual

English-Spanish Dictionary

escalator la escalera mecánica, **8.1**

especially especialmente; sobre todo

ethnic étnico(a)

euro el euro

European europeo(a)

even aun; hasta

even *(numeric)* par

evening la noche

  Good evening. Buenas noches., LP

  in the evening por la noche

  yesterday evening anoche, 7.1

every cada, 2.2; todos(as)

  every day (year) todos los días (años)

everybody todo el mundo, todos(as), 8.1

everyone todo el mundo, 5.1 todos(as), 8.1

everything todo, 6.2

everywhere en todas partes

exactly exactamente

exam el examen, la prueba, 3.1

  physical exam el examen físico, 6.2

  to take an exam tomar un examen, 3.1

to **examine** examinar, 6.2

example: for example por ejemplo

to **exceed** exceder

excellent excelente

exception la excepción

Excuse me. Con permiso., 10.1; **1.1**

exercise los ejercicios, **11.1**

to **exercise** hacer ejercicios, **11.1**

exhibition la exposición (de arte), 8.2

to **exist** existir

exit la salida, 9.1

exotic exótico(a)

expensive caro(a), 9.1

  less expensive más barato, 9.1

expert el/la experto(a), 7.2

to **explain** explicar

expressway la autopista, la autovía, **9.1**

extraordinary extraordinario(a)

eye el ojo, 2.1

  to have blue (green, brown) eyes tener ojos azules (verdes, castaños), 2.1

F

fabrics los tejidos, 9.2

fabulous fabuloso(a)

face la cara, 6.1

fact el hecho

fair la feria, **5.1**

fall el otoño, LP

to **fall** caerse, **11.2**

to **fall asleep** dormirse (ue), 11.1; **2.1**

false falso(a)

family la familia, 2.1

family *(related to)* familiar

famous famoso(a)

fan el/la aficionado(a), 5.1

fantastic fantástico(a)

far lejos (de), 3.2

fare la tarifa, **3.1**

farm la finca, la granja, la chacra, **8.2**

farmer el/la campesino(a), el peón, **8.2**

farmhand el peón, **8.2**

to **fascinate** fascinar

fast rápido(a)

fastened abrochado(a), 10.2; **1.2**

fat gordo(a)

father el padre, 2.1

favor el favor

favorite favorito(a)

fear el miedo

feature la característica

February febrero, LP

to **feel** sentirse (ie, i)

to **feel like (doing something)** tener ganas de + *infinitive*

Ferris wheel la noria, **8.1**

fertilizer el abono

festival la feria, **5.1**

  festival of lights (Hanukkah) la fiesta de las luces, **5.2**

fever la fiebre, 6.2

  to have a fever tener fiebre, 6.2

few poco(a), pocos(as), 2.2

  a few unos(as)

fewer menos

field el campo, 5.1; **8.2**

  baseball field el campo de béisbol, 5.2

  soccer field el campo de fútbol, 5.1

fifteen quince, LP

fifteen-year-old girl la quinceañera

fifty cincuenta, LP

to **fight** luchar

file el archivo, **6.1;** el documento

  attached file el documento adjunto, **6.1**

to **fill up** *(gas tank)* llenar el tanque, **9.2**

film el filme, la película, 8.2; el film

finally por fin

to **find** encontrar (ue)

fine la multa, **9.1**

fine *(adj.)* bien, LP

  to be fine estar bien, 6.2

finger el dedo, 11.1; **2.1**

to **finish** terminar

fire el fuego, **10**

fireplace la chimenea, **5.2**

fireworks los fuegos artificiales, **5.2**

first primero(a), LP

  first-class primera clase, **3.1**

  first of January el primero de enero, LP

fish el pescado, 4.1

fish market la pescadería

to **fit** quedar, **9.1**

  This jacket doesn't fit you. Esta chaqueta no te queda bien., **9.1**

five cinco, LP

five hundred quinientos(as), **9.2**

flame el fuego, **10**

  on a low flame (heat) a fuego lento, **10**

flan el flan, 4.1

flat *(tire)* el pinchazo, **9.2**

flavor el sabor, **10**

flight el vuelo, 10.1; **1.1**

  flight number el número del vuelo, 10.1; **1.1**

  flight attendant el/la asistente(a) de vuelo, 10.2; **1.2**

to **flip over** volcar

floor el piso, 2.2

flower la flor, 2.2

flute la flauta

to **fly** volar (ue)

folder la carpeta, 3.2; **6.1**

to **follow** seguir (i, i), **4**

following siguiente

food la comida, 4.1; los comestibles, **4**; el alimento

  frozen food los productos congelados, 9.2

foot el pie, 5.1; **2.1**

  on foot a pie, 3.2

football el fútbol americano

for por, para; con destino a, 10.2; **1.2**

  for example por ejemplo

forbidden prohibido(a), **9.1**

forehead la frente, **11.1**

foreign extranjero(a)

to **forget** olvidar

fork el tenedor, **4**

form una forma, 10.2; **1.2**

former antiguo(a)

forty cuarenta, LP

fountain pen la pluma, 5.1

four cuatro, LP

four hundred cuatrocientos(as), 9.2

fourteen catorce, LP

fracture la fractura

free libre, 4.2; **3.2**

to **free** liberar, **11.1**

freezer el congelador, 10

French el francés, 1.2; *(adj.)* francés(esa), **4**

french fries las papas (patatas) fritas, 4.1

frequently con frecuencia, frecuentemente

fresh fresco(a)

Friday el viernes, LP

fried frito(a)

friend el/la amigo(a), 1.1; el/la compañero(a)

friendly agradable

from de, LP; desde

  from time to time de vez en cuando

  from where? ¿de dónde?, 1.1

front *(adj.)* delantero(a), **8.1**

  in front of delante de, 2.2

front desk *(hotel)* la recepción, **7**

front door *(car, bus)* la puerta delantera, **8.1**

frozen congelado(a), 9.2

  frozen food los productos congelados, 9.2

fruit la fruta, 9.2

fruit stand la frutería, el puesto de frutas, 9.2

to **fry** freír (i, i), **4**

frying pan el/la sartén, 10

full completo(a), **3.2**

full of lleno(a) de, 6.1

fun: to have fun divertirse (ie, i), pasarlo bien, 11.2; **2.2**

funny cómico(a); gracioso(a), 1.1; divertido(a)

furious furioso(a)

furniture los muebles, 2.2

future el futuro

game el juego; *(match)* el partido, 5.1

garage el garaje, 2.2

garden el jardín, 2.2

garlic el ajo, 10

gasoline la gasolina, la nafta, la benzina

gas station la estación de servicio, la gasolinera, **9.2**

gas tank el tanque, 9.2

gate *(airport)* la puerta de salida, 10.2; **1.2**

general general

  generally, in general en general, por lo general

generous generoso(a)

gentle manso(a)

gentleman el señor, LP

geography la geografía

geometry la geometría

German alemán(ana)

to **get** sacar, 3.1

  to get good (bad) grades sacar notas buenas (malas), 3.1

to **get dressed** ponerse la ropa, 11.1; **2.1**; vestirse (i, i), **4**

to **get off** *(train, bus)* bajar(se), **3.2**

to **get on** *(train, bus)* subir, 3.1; *(plane)* abordar, 10.2; **1.2**

to **get together** reunirse

to **get up** levantarse, 11.1; **2.1**

gift el regalo, 8.1; **Christmas gift** el aguinaldo, **5.2**

girl la muchacha, 1.1; la niña, 6.2

to **give** dar, 3.1

  to give an exam dar un examen (una prueba), 3.1

  to give (throw) a party dar una fiesta, 8.1

  to give back devolver (ue)

  to give (someone) stitches poner unos puntos (unas suturas) (a alguien)

  to give up renunciar

glass (drinking) el vaso, 4.1; **4**

glove el guante, 5.2

glove compartment la guantera, 9.2

to **go** ir, 3.2; pasar, 5.2; andar, 3.2

  Let's go! ¡Vamos!

  to be going (to do something) ir a + *infinitive*, 4.2

  to go back regresar, 3.2; volver (ue), 5.1

  to go bike riding andar en bicicleta, **11.1**

  to go camping ir de camping, 11.2; **2.2**

  to go down bajar, 7.2

  to go for a hike dar una caminata, 11.2; **2.2**

  to go home regresar a casa, ir a casa, 3.2; volver (ue) a casa, 8.1

  to go horseback riding andar a caballo, **3.2**; montar a caballo, **8.2**

  to go ice-skating patinar sobre el hielo, 7.2

  to go jogging hacer jogging, **11.1**

  to go on a trip hacer un viaje

  to go online entrar en línea, **6.1**

  to go out salir, 8.1

  to go over the net pasar por encima de la red, 5.2

  to go rollerblading (inline skating) patinar en línea, **11.1**

  to go scuba diving bucear

  to go shopping ir de compras, 9.1

  to go skiing esquiar, 7.2

  to go snorkeling bucear, 7.1

  to go surfing practicar la tabla hawaiana, 7.1

  to go swimming nadar, 7.1

  to go to bed acostarse (ue), 11.1; **2.1**

  to go to the movies ir al cine, 8.2

  to go through pasar por, 10.2; **1.2**

  to go up subir, 7.2

  to go waterskiing esquiar en el agua, 7.1

  to go windsurfing practicar la plancha de vela, 7.1

goal el gol, 5.1

  to score a goal meter un gol, 5.1

goal line la portería, 5.1

goalie el/la portero(a), 5.1

English-Spanish Dictionary

going to con destino a, 10.2; **1.2**
gold el oro
good buen, LP; bueno(a), 1.1
  to be in a good mood estar de buen humor, 6.1
  to get good grades sacar notas buenas, 3.1
  Good afternoon. Buenas tardes., LP
  Good evening. Buenas noches., LP
  Good morning. Buenos días., LP
  Good-bye. Adiós!; ¡Chao!, LP
good-looking guapo(a), bonito(a), 1.1
government el gobierno
grade la nota, 3.1
  high grade la nota alta, 3.1
  low grade la nota baja, 3.1
  to get good (bad) grades sacar notas buenas (malas), 3.1
grandchildren los nietos, 2.1
granddaughter la nieta, 2.1
grandfather el abuelo, 2.1
grandmother la abuela, 2.1
grandparents los abuelos, 2.1
grandson el nieto, 2.1
grape la uva, 9.2
grass la hierba, **8.2**
grave la tumba, **5.1**
gravy la salsa, **10**
gray gris, 5.1
to **graze** pacer, **8.2**
great gran, grande
Great! ¡Bárbaro!, 5.2
greater (greatest) part (la) mayor parte
green verde, 2.1
green beans las judías verdes, 9.2
green pepper el pimiento, 9.2; **10**
greengrocer (vegetable) store la verdulería, 9.2
greeting el saludo, LP
grill la parrilla, **10**
to **grill** asar, **10**
ground el suelo
group *(musical)* el grupo, el conjunto, 8.1
to **grow** *(agriculture)* cultivar, **8.2**
to **guard** guardar, 5.1
Guatemalan guatemalteco(a)
to **guess** adivinar

guest el/la invitado(a), 8.1; *(hotel)* el/la cliente, el/la huésped(a), **7**
guitar la guitarra, 8.1
guy el tipo, 6.1
gymnasium el gimnasio, **11.1**

H

hair el pelo, 2.1
  to brush one's hair cepillarse, 11.1; **2.1**
  to comb one's hair peinarse, 11.1; **2.1**
  to have blond (brown, black) hair tener el pelo rubio (castaño, negro), 2.1
half *(soccer)* el tiempo, 5.1
  second half *(soccer)* el segundo tiempo, 5.1
half past *(hour)* y media, LP
ham el jamón, 4.1
  ham and cheese sandwich el sándwich de jamón y queso, 4.1
hamburger la hamburguesa, 4.1
hand la mano, 3.1
  to raise one's hand levantar la mano, 3.1
handsome guapo(a), 1.1
hanger la percha, el colgador, **7**
Hanukkah el Hanuka, **5.2**
to **happen** pasar; ocurrir
  What's happening? ¿Qué pasa?
happiness la alegría, la felicidad
happy alegre, contento(a), 6.1; feliz, **5.2**
  Happy Hanukkah! ¡Feliz Hanuka!, **5.2**
hard difícil, duro(a), 1.2
hard copy la copia dura, **6.1**
hard-working ambicioso(a), 1.2
harvest la cosecha, **8.2**
to **harvest** cosechar, **8.2**
hat el sombrero; *(ski)* el gorro, 7.2
to **have** tener (ie), 2.1; haber *(in compound tenses)*
  to have a cold tener catarro, 6.2
  to have a cough tener tos, 6.2
  to have a fever tener fiebre, 6.2
  to have fun pasarlo bien, divertirse (ie, i), 11.2; **2.2**

  to have a good time pasarlo bien, divertirse (ie, i), 11.2; **2.2**
  to have a headache tener dolor de cabeza, 6.2
  to have a party dar una fiesta, 8.1
  to have a snack tomar una merienda, 4.2
  to have a sore throat tener dolor de garganta, 6.2
  to have a stomachache tener dolor de estómago, 6.2
  to have blond (brown, black) hair tener el pelo rubio (castaño, negro), 2.1
  to have blue (brown, green) eyes tener ojos azules (castaños, verdes), 2.1
  to have breakfast (lunch) tomar el desayuno (el almuerzo); 4.1
  to have dinner cenar, 4.1
  to have fun pasárselo bien, divertirse (ie, i), 11.2; **2.2**
  to have just (done something) acabar de + *infinitive,* 4.2
  to have to (do something) tener que, 4.2
hay el heno, **8.2**
he él, 1.1
head la cabeza, 6.2; **2.1**
headache: to have a headache tener dolor de cabeza, 6.2
headlights las luces, 9.2
health la salud, 6.1
to **hear** oír, 8.1
  ¿Can you hear me? *(telephone)* ¿Me escuchas?, 6.2
heart el corazón
heat el calor; el fuego, **10**
  on low heat a fuego lento, **10**
to **heat** poner en el fuego, **10**
heavy pesado(a)
height la altura
Hello! ¡Hola!, LP; **6.2;** *(on the phone)* ¡Diga!, ¡Dígame!, ¡Alo!, ¡Bueno!
helmet el casco, 7.2; **11.1**
help la ayuda
to **help** ayudar, 10.1; **1.1**
hen la gallina, **8.2**
her *(f. sing.) (pron.)* la
  to her *(pron.)* le
her su(s)

here aquí, 9.1; acá, 11.2; **2.2**

  Here it (they) is (are) . . .
Aquí lo (la, los, etc.) tienes.

hero el heroe

heroine la heroína

Hi! ¡Hola!, LP

high alto(a), 3.1

high school la escuela
secundaria, 1.2; el colegio

highway la autopista, la
autovía, la carretera, **9.1**

hike: to take (go for) a hike
dar una caminata, 11.2; **2.2**

hiker el/la mochilero(a), 11.2;
2.2

him *(m. sing.) (pron.)* lo

  to him *(pron.)* le

his su(s)

Hispanic hispano(a)

history la historia, 1.2

to **hit** *(baseball)* batear; *(tennis,
volleyball)* golpear, 5.2

  to hit a home run batear
un jonrón, 5.2

holiday la fiesta, **5.1**

home la casa, 2.2; a casa; 3.2

at home en casa

to go home regresar a casa,
3.2; volver a casa, 8.1

home page la página de inicio
(inicial, frontal), **6.1**

home plate el platillo, 5.2

home run el jonrón, 5.2

  to hit a home run batear
un jonrón, 5.2

homework las tareas

honest honesto(a)

hood *(car)* el capó, **9.2**

to **hope** esperar

  I hope . . . Ojalá… , **11.2**

horse el caballo, 3.2

horseback riding la
equitación, **8.2**

  to go horseback riding
andar a caballo, **3.2;**
montar a caballo, **8.2**

hospital el hospital

hostel: youth hostel el albergue
juvenil, el hostal, **7**

hot: to be hot tener calor,
11.1; **2.1**

  It's (very) hot (weather).
Hace (mucho) calor., LP

hot caliente, 4.1

hotel el hotel, 7

  small (inexpensive) hotel
el hostal, 7

hotel clerk el/la recepcionista, 7

hour la hora

house la casa, 2.2

apartment house la casa de
apartamentos

private house la casa
privada, 2.2

housekeeper la camarera, 7

how? ¿cómo?, 1.1; ¿qué?, LP

  How are things going?
¿Qué tal?, LP

  How are you? ¿Qué tal?,
LP; ¿Cómo estás?

  How much does it cost?
¿Cuánto cuesta?, 3.2

  How much is (are) . . . ?
¿A cuánto está(n)… ?, 9.2

  How much is it? ¿Cuánto
es?, LP

  How old is he (she)?
¿Cuántos años tiene?, 2.1

how many? ¿cuántos(as)?, 2.1

how much? ¿cuánto?, 3.1

human humano(a), 11.1; **2.1**

human being el ser humano

humble humilde

**humor: to have a good sense
of humor** tener un buen
sentido de humor, 6.1

hundred cien(to, ta), LP

hunger el hambre *(f.)*

hungry: to be hungry tener
hambre, 4.1

to **hurt** doler, 6.2; **11.2**

  It hurts him (me, etc.) a lot.
Le (Me, etc.) duele mucho.,
11.2

  **My head (stomach, etc.)
hurts.** Me duele la cabeza
(el estómago, etc.), **11.2**

to **hurt (oneself)** hacerse daño,
11.2

husband el esposo, el marido,
2.1

I yo

ice el hielo, 7.2

ice cream el helado, 4.1

ice skate el patín, 7.2

to **ice-skate** patinar sobre el hielo,
7.2

ice-skater el/la patinador(a), 7.2

ice-skating el patinaje sobre
(el) hielo, 7.2

  ice-skating rink la pista
de patinaje, 7.2

icon el icono, **6.1**

ID card el carnet
de identidad, 10.2; **1.2**

idea la idea

idealist el/la idealista

identification
la identidad, 10.2; **1.2**

  piece of identification
la forma de identidad,
10.2; **1.2**

to **identify** identificar

if si

ill enfermo(a), 6.2

ill-mannered
mal educado(a), 6.1

illness la enfermedad

to **imagine** imaginar

immediately enseguida, 4.2;
inmediatamente

immense inmenso

impatient impaciente, 6.1

important importante

impossible imposible

in en

  in back of detrás de, 2.2

  in front of delante de, 2.2

  in general por lo general

inbox *(e-mail)* la bandeja
de entradas, **6.1**

incline pendiente

to **include** incluir

  Is the tip included?
¿Está incluido el servicio?,
4.2

to **increase** aumentar

incredible increíble

to **indicate** indicar

indigenous indigeno(a), 9.2

individual: individual sport
el deporte individual

inexpensive barato(a), 9.1

influence la influencia

to **inform** informar

information la información,
3.2

ingredient el ingrediente

inhabitant el/la habitante

inhospitable inhóspito(a)

injured herido(a)

injury la herida, 11.2

inline skating el patinaje en
línea, 11.1

  to go inline skating patinar
en línea, 11.1

inn el parador

to **insert** insertar, **3.1;** introducir,
6.2

instead of en vez de

instrument el instrumento

intelligent inteligente, 1.2

interest el interés

to **interest** interesar, 5.1

interesting interesante, 1.2

international internacional,
10.1; **1.1**

English-Spanish Dictionary

Internet el Internet, 3.2; **6.1**
  to surf the Net navegar el
    Internet, 3.2; **6.1**
to **interrupt** interrumpir
to **intersect** cruzarse
intersection la bocacalle,
  el cruce, **9.1**
interview la entrevista
to **interview** entrevistar
interviewer el/la
  entrevistador(a)
to **invite** invitar
Irish irlandés(esa)
Is ... there, please? ¿Está... ,
  por favor?, **6.2**
island la isla
it lo, la
Italian italiano(a)

jack *(car)* el/la gato(a), **9.2**
jacket la chaqueta, 9.1
  ski jacket la chaqueta de
    esquí, el anorak, 7.2
jam la mermelada, 7
January enero, LP
Japonese japonés(esa)
jar el frasco, 9.2
jeans el blue jean, 9.1
Jewish judío(a), hebreo(a), **5.2**
jogging: to go jogging hacer
  jogging, **11.1**
juice el jugo, el zumo, 4.1
  orange juice el jugo de
    naranja, 4.1; 7
July julio, LP
June junio, LP
just: to have just (done
  something) acabar de +
  infinitive, 4.2
just as (like) igual que

kebabs los pinchitos, 4.2
to **keep** guardar, **6.1**
key la llave, 7; *(computer)* el
  botón, **6.1**
  back key el botón de regresar
    (retroceder), **6.1**
  delete key el boton
    borrador, **6.1**
  magnetic key la llave
    magnética, 7

keyboard el teclado, **6.1**
to **kick** lanzar, 5.1
kilogram el kilo, 9.2
kilometer el kilómetro
king el rey
  the Three Kings (Wise Men)
    los Reyes Magos, **5.2**
kiosk *(newsstand)* el quiosco,
  3.1; *(ticket dispenser)* el
  distribuidor automático, **3.1**
kitchen la cocina, 2.2, **10**
knapsack la mochila, 3.1
knee la rodilla, 11.1; **2.1**
kneepad la rodillera, **11.1**
knife el cuchillo, 4
to **know** saber; conocer, 9.1
  to know how (to do
    something) saber, 9.1

to **lack** faltar, 6.1
  He/She lacks ... Le falta... ,
    6.1
lamb el cordero, 4
lamp la lámpara, 2.2
land la tierra, 8.2
to **land** aterrizar, 10.2; **1.2**
landing el aterrizaje, 10.2; **1.2**
landowner el/la terrateniente
landscape el paisaje
lane *(highway)* el carril, **9.1;** la
  pista, la vía, la banda, el canal
language la lengua
lap *(track)* la vuelta, **11.1**
laptop computer la
  computadora portátil
large gran, grande, 1.2
last pasado(a) 7.1; último(a)
  last night anoche, 7.1
  last week la semana pasada,
    7.1
  last year el año pasado, 7.1
to **last** durar
late tarde; con retraso
  (una demora), 10.2; **1.2**
later luego, LP; más tarde;
  después
  See you later! ¡Hasta
    luego!, LP
Latin America Latinoamérica
Latin American
  latinoamericano(a)
Latino latino(a)
to **laugh** reír
lazy perezoso(a), 1.2

to **lead (from one street into**
  another) desembocar
league la liga
to **learn** aprender, 4.2
least: at least a lo menos
to **leave** salir, 8.1
to **leave (something)** dejar, 4
  to leave a message dejar un
    mensaje, **6.2**
  to leave a tip dejar una
    propina, 4
left izquierdo(a), 11.1; **2.1**
  to the left a la izquierda, **9.1**
leftovers las sobras
leg la pierna, 11.1; **2.1**
lemon el limón
lemonade la limonada
less menos, 9.1
lesson la lección
to **let** dejar; permitir
letter la carta
letter (of alphabet) la letra
lettuce la lechuga, 4.1
lid la tapa, **10**
life la vida
to **lift** levantar
  to lift weights levantar
    pesas, **11.1**
light la luz, **5.2**
  red light la luz roja, **9.1**
  traffic light el semáforo, 8.1
to **light** encender, 5.2
to **light up** iluminar, 5.2
lightly ligeramente
lights las luces, 5.2;
  (headlights) las luces, **9.2**
  festival of lights
    (Hanukkah) la fiesta
    de las luces, **5.2**
like como
to **like** gustar, 5.1; encantar, **6.2**
  What would you like *(to eat)?*
    ¿Qué desean tomar?, 4.2
line *(of people)* la cola, 10.2;
  1.2; la fila
  to wait in line hacer cola,
    10.2; **1.2;** estar en fila
line la línea, **6.2**
  solid line *(road)* la línea
    continua, **9.1**
to **line up** hacer cola, 10.2; **1.2**
lion el león
lip el labio
to **listen to** escuchar, 3.2
  Listen! ¡Oye!, 1.2
literature la literatura, las letras

little pequeño(a), 1.2
  a little poco(a), 2.2
to **live** vivir, 4.2
livestock el ganado, **8.2**
living room la sala, 2.2
lobster la langosta, **4**
logical lógico(a)
long largo(a), 5.1
long-distance *(race)* de larga distancia, **11.1**
long-sleeved de manga larga, 9.1
Look! ¡Mira!, 3.1
to **look at** mirar, 3.2
to **look at oneself** mirarse, 11.1; **2.1**
to **look for** buscar, 3.2
to **lose** perder (ie), 5.1
lot: a lot mucho(a), LP; muchos(as), 2.1
lotion: suntan lotion la crema solar, la loción bronceadora, 7.1
low bajo(a), 3.1
  low (heat), a fuego lento, **10**
to **lower** *(price)* rebajar, 9.1
love el amor
  in love with enamorado(a) de
  loved one el/la amado(a)
to **love** encantar, **6.2;** querer (ie)
  Le encanta la música. She loves the music.
luck: How lucky I am! ¡Qué suerte tengo!, 9.1
luggage el equipaje, 10.1; **1.1**
  carry-on luggage el equipaje de mano, 10.1; **1.1**
  luggage cart carrito, **3.1**
  to check luggage facturar el equipaje, 10.1; **1.1**
lunch el almuerzo, 4.1
  to have lunch tomar el almuerzo, 4.1
luxurious lujoso(a)

M

mad enojado(a), enfadado(a), 6.1
Madam la señora, LP
made hecho(a)
magazine la revista, **3.1**
magnetic magnético(a), **7**
magnificent magnífico(a)
maid la camerera, **7**
mail el correo
  e-mail el correo electrónico, **6.1**

main principal
majority la mayoría; mayoritario(a) *(adj.)*
to **make** hacer, 10.2; **1.2;** confeccionar, elaborar, 5.1
  to make a basket *(basketball)* encestar, 5.2
  to make the bed hacer la cama, 7
mall el centro comercial, 9.1
man el hombre
manners los modales, 6.1
  to have good *(bad)* **manners** tener buenos (malos) modales, 6.1
many muchos(as), 2.2
  as many . . . as tantos(as)… como
  how many? ¿cuántos(as)?, 2.1
map el plano, **9.1;** el mapa
marathon el maratón, **11.1**
March marzo, LP
mark la nota, 3.1
  bad (low) mark la nota mala (baja), 3.1
  good (high) mark la nota buena (alta), 3.1
  to get good (bad) marks sacar notas buenas (malas), 3.1
market el mercado, 9.2
  native market el mercado indígena, 9.2
market stall el puesto, el tenderete, 9.2
marmalade la mermelada, 7
mask la máscara, **5.1**
to **match** parear
mathematics las matemáticas, 1.2
mausoleum el mausoleo, **5.1**
maximum máximo(a)
May mayo, LP
maybe quizá, quizás, tal vez, 7.2
mayonnaise la mayonesa, 9.2
me *(pron.)* me
  to *(for)* **me** a (para) mí
meal la comida, 4.1
to **mean** significar
means of transport el medio de transporte, 8.1
meat la carne, 4.1; **4**
meatball la albóndiga, 4.2
meat pie la empanada, 4.2
medicine el medicamento, la medicina, 6.2
medium *(meat)* a término medio, **4**
medium-sized mediano(a)

to **meet** encontrarse (ue); conocer
member el miembro, 2.1; socio(a)
menorah la menora, **5.2**
menu el menú, 4.2; **4**
merchant el/la vendedor(a), 9.2
Merry Christmas! ¡Feliz Navidad!
merry-go-round el tiovivo, **8.1**
message el mensaje, **6.2**
meter el metro
Mexican mexicano(a)
Mexican American mexicanoamericano(a), 1.2
microwave oven el horno de microondas, **10**
Middle Ages la Edad Media
midnight la medianoche
mile la milla
milk la leche, 4.1
million el millón, 9.2
  million dollars un millón de dólares, 9.2
mime el mimo, **8.1**
to **mince** picar, **10**
mind el espíritu, **11.1**
mineral water el agua mineral, 4.2
mirror el espejo, 11.1; **2.1**
Miss señorita, LP
to **miss the bus** perder (ie) el autobús, 8.1
mobil phone el móvil, 3.2; el célular, **6.2**
modern moderno(a)
mom mamá
moment el momento
monastery el monasterio
Monday el lunes, LP
money el dinero, 3.2
monitor *(computer)* la pantalla de escritorio, **6.1**
month el mes, LP
monument el monumento
mood el humor, 6.1
  to be in a good (bad) mood estar de buen (mal) humor, 6.1
moon la luna
more más, 9.1
morning la mañana
  Good morning. Buenos días., LP
  in the morning por la mañana; de la mañana
mother la madre, 2.1
motive el motivo

English-Spanish Dictionary

mountain la montaña, 7.2
mountaintop el pico, 7.2
mouse el ratón, **6.1**
mousepad la alfombrilla, **6.1**
mouth la boca, 6.2
to **move** mover (ue)
movement el movimiento, **11.1**
movie la película, el filme, 8.2; el film
movie theater el cine, 8.2
movies: to go to the movies ir al cine, 8.2
MP3 player el MP3, **6.2**
Mr. el señor, LP
Mr. and Mrs. los señores
Mrs. la señora, LP
Ms. la señorita, la señora, LP
much mucho(a), LP
  as much . . . as tan… como, **11.2**
  How much is it (does it cost)? ¿Cuánto es?, LP; ¿Cuánto cuesta?, 3.2
mud el lodo
museum el museo, 8.2
music la música, 1.2
musician el/la músico(a), 8.1
mussels los mejillones, **4**
my mi
mysterious misterioso(a)

name el nombre, 2.1
My name is . . . Me llamo… , 11.1; **2.1**
What is your name? ¿Cómo te llamas?, 11.1; **2.1**; ¿Cuál es su nombre?
napkin la servilleta, **4**
narrow angosto(a), estrecho(a), **8.1**
national nacional
nationality la nacionalidad, 1.1
  what nationality? ¿de qué nacionalidad?, 1.1
native indígena, 9.2
native person el/la indígena
nature la naturaleza
near cerca de, 3.2
necessary necesario(a)
  It's necessary. Es necesario., **11.2**
  it's necesssary to (do something) hay que, 10.2; **1.2**

neck el cuello, **11.1**
necktie la corbata, 9.1
to **need** necesitar, 3.2
negative negativo(a)
neighbor el/la vecino(a)
neighborhood el casco, el barrio, **8.1**
neither tampoco
nephew el sobrino, 2.1
nervous nervioso(a), 6.1
net *(World Wide Web)* la red, 3.2; **6.1**; *(tennis),* 5.2
  to surf the Net navegar el Internet, 3.2; **6.1**
never nunca, 8.2; jamás
new nuevo(a), 1.1
  New Year el Año Nuevo
  New Year's Eve la Nochevieja, la víspera del Año Nuevo
news la(s) noticia(s)
newspaper el periódico, 3.1
newsstand el quiosco, 3.1
next próximo(a), 3.2; que viene, **8.2**
  next stop la próxima parada, **3.2**
  next summer (year, etc.) el verano (año, etc.) que viene, **8.2**
next to al lado de, 2.2
Nicaraguan nicaragüense
nice simpático(a), 1.1; *(weather)* buen (tiempo)
  Nice to meet you. Mucho gusto., 1.2
  The weather is nice. Hace buen tiempo., LP
niece la sobrina, 2.1
night la noche
  at night por la noche
  Good night. Buenas noches., LP
  last night anoche, 7.1
nine nueve, LP
nine hundred novecientos(as), 9.2
nineteen diecinueve, LP
ninety noventa, LP
no no, LP; ninguno(a)
  by no means de ninguna manera
no one nadie, 8.2
nobody nadie, 8.2
none ninguno(a)
noon el mediodía

no-smoking sign la señal de no fumar, 10.2; **1.2**
normal normal, 6.2
north el norte
North American norteamericano(a), 1
not no, 1.2
notebook el cuaderno, 3.1
nothing nada, 8.2
  Nothing else. Nada más., 9.2
novel la novela
November noviembre, LP
now ahora
nowadays hoy en día
number el número, 10.1; **1.1**
  flight number el número del vuelo, 10.1; **1.1**
  seat number el número del asiento, 10.1; **1.1**
  telephone number el número de teléfono, **6.2**
nurse el/la enfermero(a), 6.2; **11.2**

object el objeto
objective el objetivo
obligatory obligatorio(a)
to **observe** observar
obstinate obstinado(a), 6.1
occasionally de vez en cuando
occupied ocupado(a), 4.2; **3.2**
ocean el océano
o'clock: It's two o'clock. Son las dos., LP
October octubre, LP
odd *(numeric)* impar
of de LP
  Of course! ¡Cómo no!; ¡Claro!
  of the del, de la
to **offer** ofrecer
offering la ofrenda, **5.1**
office la oficina, **8.1**
  doctor's office la consulta del médico, 6.2
often con frecuencia, a menudo
oil el aceite, **4**
  olive oil el aceite de oliva
OK de acuerdo
old viejo(a), 2.2; antiguo(a), **8.1**
  How old is he (she)? ¿Cuántos años tiene?, 2.1
  old city el casco (barrio) antiguo, **8.1**

older mayor

oldest el/la mayor

olive la aceituna, 4.2

on sobre; en

  on board abordo, 10.2; **1.2**

  on foot a pie, 3.2

  on the edge of al borde mismo de

  on time a tiempo, 10.2; **1.2**

  on top of sobre

online: to go online entrar en línea, **6.1**

one uno; uno(a), LP

one hundred cien(to), LP

one thousand mil, 9.2

one-way (ticket) el boleto (billete) sencillo, **3.1;** **(street)** la calle de sentido único, **9.1**

onion la cebolla, 9.2; **10**

only único(a), 2.1; solo; solamente

to **open** abrir, 4.2

open-air al aire libre

open-minded flexible, 6.1

opinion la opinión

opponents el equipo contrario, 5.2

opposite el contrario

or o, u *(used instead of o in front of words beginning with o or ho)*

orange *(color)* anaranjado(a), 5.1

orange *(fruit)* la naranja, 4.1

  orange juice el jugo (zumo) de naranja, 4.1; **7**

orchard la huerta, **8.2**

order *(restaurant)* la orden, 4.2

to **order** *(restaurant)* pedir (i, i)

to **organize** organizar

origin el origen

orthopedic surgeon el/la cirujano(a) ortopédico(a), **11.2**

other otro(a)

  any other cualquier otro(a)

our nuestro(a), nuestros(as)

outdoor *(adj.)* al aire libre

outfielder el/la jardinero(a), 5.2

outskirts los alrededores, las afueras

oven el horno, **10**

over por encima de, 5.2

overhead bin el compartimiento superior, 10.2; **1.2**

overpopulation la sobrepoblación

own: propio(a), 5.1

oxygen mask la máscara de oxígeno, 10.2; **1.2**

to **pack** hacer la maleta, 10.1; **1.1**

package el paquete, 9.2

page la página

  home page la página de inicio (inicial, frontal), **6.1**

pain el dolor, 6.2

to **paint** pintar

painter el/la pintor(a), 8.2

painting el cuadro, 8.2; la pintura

pair el par, 9.1

  pair of shoes el par de zapatos, 9.1

pants el pantalón, 3.1

  long pants el pantalón largo, 9.1

paper el papel, 3.1

  sheet of paper la hoja de papel, 3.1

  toilet paper el papel higiénico, 11.2; **2.2**

paperback (book) el libro de bolsillo, 3.1

parade el desfile, 5.2

  to walk in a parade desfilar, **5.1**

paramedic el/la socorrista, **11.2**

parents los padres, 2.1

park el parque, 11.2; **2.2**

to **park** aparcar, **8.1;** estacionar, parquear

parka el anorak, 7.2

parking lot un parking, un parqueo, **8.1**

parking meter el parquímetro, **9.1**

part la parte

  la mayor parte the greatest part, the majority

party la fiesta, 8.1

  to (have) throw a party dar una fiesta, 8.1

to **pass** pasar, 5.2; *(car)* adelantar(se), rebasar, pasar, **9.1**

passenger el/la pasajero(a), 10.1; **1.1**

passport el pasaporte, 10.2; **1.2**

past el pasado

pastry el pan dulce, 7

path la senda, **3.2**

patience la paciencia, 6.1

patient el/la paciente, 6.2

patient *(adj.)* paciente, 6.1

patron saint el santo patrón, **5.1**

  patron saint's day la fiesta patronal, **5.1**

pavement el pavimento

to **pay** pagar, 3.2

  to pay attention prestar atención, 3.1; hacer caso

pay phone el teléfono público, **6.2**

pea el guisante, 9.2

peaceful tranquilo(a), 6.1

peak el pico, 7.2

peanut el cacahuate, el maní, 8.1; el cacahuete

peasant el campesino, el peón, 8.2

pedestrian el/la peatón(ona), **8.1**

  pedestrian crossing el cruce peatonal, **8.1**

to **peel** pelar, **10**

pen el bolígrafo, 3.1; el lapicero, la pluma

pencil el lápiz, 3.1

people la gente, 9.1

pepper *(spice)* la pimienta, 4; *(bell pepper)* el pimiento, 9.2; **10;** el pimentón; el ají; el chipotle; el morron

perhaps quizá, quizás, tal vez, 7.2

to **permit** permitir

person la persona

personality la personalidad, 6.1

Peruvian el/la peruano(a)

peso el peso

pet la mascota, 2.1

pharmacist el/la farmacéutico(a)

pharmacy la farmacia, 6.2

phone el teléfono

  cell phone el móvil, 3.2; el (teléfono) celular, **6.1**

  pay phone el teléfono público, **6.2**

  phone book la guía telefónica, **6.2**

  phone call la llamada telefónica, **6.2**

  phone card la tarjeta telefónica, **6.2**

  phone number el número de teléfono, **6.2**

  phone receiver el auricular, **6.2**

English-Spanish Dictionary

public phone el teléfono público, **6.2**

to pick up the phone descolgar (ue) el auricular, **6.2**

to speak on the phone hablar por teléfono

photo(graph) la foto(grafía), 7.1

to take photos sacar (tomar) fotos, 7.1

physical (exam) el examen físico, 6.2

physical education la educación física, 1.2

physics la física

piano el piano

to **pick up (phone)** descolgar (ue) el auricular, **6.2**

to **pick up (speed)** agarrar velocidad

picture la foto(grafía); la imagen

to take pictures sacar (tomar) fotos, 7.1

picturesque pintoresco(a)

piece el pedazo, el trozo (trocito)

little piece el pedacito, **10**

pig el cerdo, **8.2;** el cochinillo, el lechón, el chancho

pillow la almohada, 7

pinch la pizca

pineapple la piña, 9.2

pink rosado(a), 5.1

pitcher (baseball) el/la pícher, el/la lanzador(a), 5.2

pizza la pizza, 4.1

place el lugar; el sitio

to **plan** planear

plane el avión, 10.1; **1.1**

plant la planta, 2.2

to **plant** sembrar (ie), **8.2**

plantain: slices of fried plantain los tostones, 4.2; los patacones

plate el plato, **4**

platform (railway) el andén, **3.1**

to **play (sport)** jugar (ue), 5.1; **(musical instrument)** tocar, 8.1; **5.2**

to play soccer (baseball, etc.) jugar (al) fútbol (béisbol, etc.), 5.1

player el/la jugador(a), 5.1

baseball player el/la jugador(a) de béisbol, el/la beisbolista, 5.2

plaza la plaza, **8.1**

pleasant agradable, placentero(a)

please por favor, LP; favor de (+ *infinitive*), 11.2; **2.2**

pleasure: It's a pleasure to meet you. Mucho gusto.

P.M. de la tarde, de la noche

poem el poema

point el tanto, 5.1; el punto

to score a point marcar un tanto, 5.1

to **point out** señalar

polite bien educado(a), 6.1

polluted contaminado(a)

pollution la contaminación

pool la piscina, la alberca, 7.1; la pila

poor pobre

popular popular

population la población

pork chop la chuleta de cerdo, **4**

portrait el retrato

Portuguese portugués(esa)

to **possess** poseer

possibility la posibilidad

possible posible

pot la olla, la cacerola, **10**

potato la papa, la patata, 4.1

french fried potatoes las papas (patatas) fritas, 4.1

pothole el bache

practically casi, 8.2

to **practice** practicar

to **prefer** preferir (ie, i), 5.2; **4**

to **prepare** preparar; confeccionar, **5.1**

to **prescribe** recetar, 6.2

prescription la receta, 6.2

present el regalo, 8.1

Christmas present el aguinaldo, **5.2**

to **present** presentar

president el/la presidente

to **press (button)** oprimir, pulsar, **6.1**

pretty bonito(a), 1.1; hermoso(a)

previous anterior, **6.1**

price el precio, 9.1

primary primario(a)

to **print** imprimir, **6.1**

printer la impresora, **6.1**

private privado(a), 2.2

probable probable

problem el problema

procession la procesión, 5.1

product el producto, 9.2

public público(a)

Puerto Rican puertorriqueño(a)

pulse el pulso, 6.2

purchase la compra, 9.2

to **push (button)** oprimir, pulsar, **6.1**

push-ups: to do push-ups hacer planchas, 11.1

to **put** poner, 10.2; **1.2;** meter, 5.2

to **put on (clothes)** ponerse, 11.1; **2.1 (brakes)** poner los frenos

to **put up (tent)** armar, montar, 11.2; **2.2**

puzzle el rompecabezas

quarter (city) el casco, el barrio, **8.1;** *(time)* el cuarto, LP

a quarter past (the hour) y cuarto, LP

question la pregunta, 3.1

to ask a question preguntar, 3.1

quickly rápidamente

quiet tranquilo(a), calmo(a), 6.1

quite bastante, 1.2

race la carrera, **11.1**

cross-country race la carrera a campo traviesa, **11.1**

long-distance race la carrera de larga distancia, **11.1**

relay race la carrera de relevos, **11.1**

racket la raqueta, 5.2

railroad el ferrocarril, **3.1**

railroad platform el andén, **3.1**

railroad station la estación de ferrocarril, **3.1**

to **rain** llover (ue)

It's raining. Llueve., LP

raincoat impermeable

to **raise** levantar, 3.1
to raise one's hand levantar
la mano, 3.1
ranch la hacienda, la estancia,
el rancho, **8.2**
rare *(meat)* casi crudo, 4
rate la tarifa; la tasa
rather bastante, 1.2
raw crudo(a), 8.1
raw vegetables los vegetales
crudos, 8.1
reaction la reacción
to **read** leer, 4.2
reading la lectura
ready listo(a)
really realmente
reason la razón, el motivo
to **receive** recibir, 4.2
receiver *(telephone)*
el auricular, **6.2**
recipe la receta, **10**
recipient el/la destinatario(a),
6.1
to **recognize** reconocer
record el disco
red rojo(a), 5.1
red light la luz roja, **9.1**
redheaded pelirrojo(a), 1.1
to **reduce** *(price)* rebajar, 9.1
to **reduce** *(speed)* reducir la
velocidad, **9.1**
reduced reducido(a)
refrigerator el refrigerador, la
nevera, **10**
region la región
relative el/la pariente, 2.1
relay: relay race la carrera
de relevos, **11.1**
reliability la confiabilidad
religious religioso(a)
to **remain** quedarse, 11.1; **2.1**
to **remember** recordar (ue)
to **rent** alquilar, rentar, 7.1; **3.2**
to **repeat** *(take second helping)*
repetir (i, i), **4**
to **represent** representar
republic la república
Dominican Republic
la República Dominicana
to **request** pedir (i, i), **4**
required obligatorio(a)
reservation la reservación, **7;**
la reserva
to **reserve** reservar, **7**
resort: seaside resort
el balneario, 7.1
ski resort la estación
de esquí, 7.2
rest lo demás
to **rest** descansar, **11.1**

restaurant el restaurante, **4**
restroom el servicio, 10.2; **1.2**
result el resultado
to **return** regresar, 3.2; volver
(ue), 5.1
to return *(something)*
devolver (ue), 5.2
review el repaso
to **review** repasar
rice el arroz, 4.1
rich rico(a)
to **rid** liberar, 11.1
ride: to go for a (bike) ride
dar un paseo en bicicleta
to **ride** *(horse)* andar a caballo,
3.2; montar a caballo, **8.2;**
(bicycle) andar en bicicleta,
11.1
rides *(amusement park)*
las atracciones, **8.1**
right derecho(a), 11.1; **2.1**
right on the edge of
al borde mismo de
to the right a la derecha, **9.1**
right: That's right! ¡Verdad!
right away enseguida, 4.2
to **ring** sonar (ue), **6.1**
ringtone el timbre (sonoro), **6.2**
rink *(ice-skating)*
la pista de patinaje, 7.2
river el río
roast asado(a)
roast suckling pig
el cochinillo asado, el
lechón asado, el chancho
asado
to **roast** asar, **10**
roll *(bread)* el panecillo, 4.1; **7**
roll of toilet paper el rollo de
papel higiénico, 11.2; **2.2**
rollerblading el patinaje en
línea, **11.1**
rollerblading: to go
rollerblading patinar
en línea, **11.1**
roller coaster la montaña
rusa, **8.1**
romantic romántico(a)
room el cuarto, 2.2; **7**
bathroom el cuarto
de baño, 2.2; **7**
bedroom el cuarto de
dormir, la recámara, 2.2;
el dormitorio, la habitación,
la alcoba, la pieza
classroom la sala de clase, 3.1
dining room el comedor, 2.2
emergency room la sala
de emergencia, **11.2**
living room la sala, 2.2
restroom el servicio, 10.2; **1.2**

single (double)
room el cuarto
sencillo (doble), **7**
waiting room la sala
de espera, **3.1**
round-trip (ticket) el boleto
(billete) de ida y vuelta
(regreso), **3.1**
routine la rutina, 11.1; **2.1**
daily routine la rutina
diaria, 11.1; **2.1**
rude mal educado(a), 6.1
ruins las ruinas
rule la regla
to **run** correr, 5.2
running water el agua
corriente
runway la pista, 10.2; **1.2**
rural rural

sad triste, deprimido(a), 6.1
saffron el azafrán
sailboard la plancha de vela, 7.1
saint el santo, 5.1
patron saint el santo
patronal, **5.1**
salad la ensalada, 4.1
sale el saldo, la liquidación, 9.1
salesperson el/la empleado(a),
3.2; el/la dependiente, 9.1
salt la sal, **4**
salty salado(a)
same mismo(a), 1.2
sand la arena, 7.1
sandal la sandalia, 9.2
sandwich el sándwich, el
bocadillo, 4.1; la torta
ham and cheese sandwich
el sándwich de jamón
y queso, 4.1
satisfied satisfecho(a)
to **satisfy** satisfacer
Saturday el sábado, LP
sauce la salsa, 10
saucepan la cacerola, la olla, 10
saucer el platillo, 4
sausage el chorizo
to **save** guardar, 6.1
saxophone el saxófono
to **say** decir, 3.2
scenery el paisaje
schedule *(train)* el horario, 3.1
school la escuela, 1.2;
el colegio; la academia
elementary school
la escuela primaria
high school la escuela
secundaria, 1.2; el colegio

English-Spanish Dictionary

school *(related to)* escolar
   school bus el bus escolar, 3.2
   school supplies
      los materiales escolares, 3.1
science la ciencia, 1.2
score el tanto, 5.1
   to score a goal meter un
      gol, 5.1
   to score a point marcar un
      tanto, 5.1
scrambled: scrambled eggs
   los huevos revueltos, 7
screen *(computer)* la pantalla
   de escritorio, **6.1**
scuba diving el buceo
   to go scuba diving bucear
sculptor el/la escultor(a)
sculpture la escultura, 8.2
sea el mar, 7.1
   Caribbean Sea el mar Caribe
seafood los mariscos, 4
seaside resort el balneario, 7.1
search: in search of en busca de
to **search** buscar, 3.2
season la estación, LP
   ¿Qué estación es? What
      season is it?, LP
seat el asiento, 10.1; **1.1;**
   la plaza, **3.2**
   seat number el número
      del asiento, 10.1; **1.1**
   seat belt el cinturón de
      seguridad, 10.2; **1.2**
second segundo(a), 5.1
   second-class segunda clase,
      3.1
   second half *(soccer)*
      el segundo tiempo, 5.1
secondary secundario(a), 1.2
security *(checkpoint)* el control
   de seguridad, 10.2; **1.2**
   to go through security
      pasar por el control de
      seguridad, 10.2; **1.2**
sedan el sedán, 9.2
   four-door sedan el sedán
      a cuatro puertas, **9.2**
to **see** ver, 4.2
   let's see a ver
   See you later. ¡Hasta luego!,
      LP
   See you soon! ¡Hasta
      pronto!, LP
   See you tomorrow! ¡Hasta
      mañana!, LP
to **seem** parecer

   It seems to me . . . Me
      parece…
to **select** seleccionar, **3.1**
self-serve autoservicio
to **sell** vender, 6.2
to **send** enviar, 3.2; mandar
sense: sense of humor
   el sentido de humor, 6.1
   to have a good sense of
      humor tener un buen
      sentido de humor, 6.1
sent mailbox la bandeja
   de enviados, **6.1**
sentence la frase, la oración
September septiembre, LP
serious serio(a), 1.1
to **serve** servir (i, i), **4**
   to serve as servir (i, i) de
server el/la mesero(a), 4.2, **4;**
   el/la camarero(a), **4**
service el servicio, 9.2
to **set** *(table)* poner la mesa, **4;**
   (bone) reducir, acomodar
   el hueso, **11.2**
seven siete, LP
seven hundred
   setecientos(as), 9.2
seventeen diecisiete, LP
seventy setenta, LP
several varios(as)
shack la choza, la casucha
shake *(drink)* el batido, 4.2
shame: What a shame!
   ¡Qué pena!, 5.1
shampoo el champú, 11.2; **2.2**
shape la forma
she ella, 1.1
sheet la sábana, **7**
sheet of paper la hoja de papel,
   3.1
shellfish los mariscos, **4**
shirt la camisa, 3.1
   short- (long-) sleeved shirt
      la camisa de manga corta
      (larga), 9.1
shoe size el número, 9.1
   What size shoe do you wear
      (take)? ¿Qué número
      calzas (usas)?, 9.1
shoes las zapatillas, 5.1; los
   zapatos, 9.1
to **shop** ir de compras, 9.1
shopping cart el carrito, 9.2
shopping center el centro
   comercial, 9.1
short *(person)* bajo(a), 1.1;
   (length) corto(a), 9.1

short-sleeved de manga corta,
   9.1
shorts el pantalón corto, 5.1
should deber, 4.2
shoulder *(road)*
   el acotamiento, el arcén, **9.1;**
   (body) el hombro, **11.1**
to **show** mostrar (ue), 10.2; **1.2**
shower la ducha, 11.1; **2.1**
   to take a shower tomar una
      ducha, 11.1; **2.1**
shrimp los camarones, 4.2
shy tímido(a)
sick enfermo(a), 6.2
sick person el/la enfermo(a)
side el lado
sidewalk la acera, **8.1**
sign la señal, 10.2; **1.2;** *(road)*
   el rótulo, **9.1**
   no-smoking sign la señal
      de no fumar, 10.2; **1.2**
similar similar
since desde; como
sincere sincero(a); franco(a)
to **sing** cantar, 8.1
singer el/la cantante, 8.1
single solo(a); **(room)** un
   cuarto sencillo, **7**
singles *(tennis)* individuales, 5.2
sink el lavabo, **7**
sir señor, LP
sister la hermana, 2.1
to **sit down** sentarse (ie), 11.1; **2.1**
site (Web site) el sitio, **6.1**
six seis, LP
six hundred seiscientos(as), 9.2
sixteen dieciséis, LP
sixty sesenta, LP
size *(clothing)* la talla; *(shoes)*
   el número, 9.1
   What size (clothing) do
      you wear (take)? ¿Qué
      talla usas?, 9.1
   What size (shoe) do you
      wear (take)? ¿Qué
      número calzas?, 9.1
to **skate** patinar, 7.2; **11.1**
   to ice-skate patinar sobre
      el hielo, 7.2
   to inline skate (rollerblade)
      patinar en línea, **11.1**
skateboard el monopatín, **11.1**
skeleton el esqueleto, **5.1**
ski el esquí, 7.2
   ski hat el gorro, 7.2
   ski jacket la chaqueta de
      esquí, el anorak, 7.2

ski lift el telesilla, el telesquí, 7.2

ski pole el bastón, 7.2

ski resort la estación de esquí, 7.2

ski slope la pista, 7.2

to **ski** esquiar, 7.2

    to water-ski esquiar en el agua, 7.1

skier el/la esquiador(a), 7.2

skiing el esquí, 7.2

    cross-country skiing el esquí nórdico

    downhill skiing el esquí alpino, 7.2

    waterskiing el esquí acuático (náutico), 7.1

skillet el/la sartén, 10

skirt la falda, 3.1

skull el cráneo, la calavera, 5.1

sky el cielo, 5.2

skyscraper el rascacielos, 8.1

to **sleep** dormir (ue, u), 5.2

sleeping bag el saco (una bolsa) de dormir, 11.2; **2.2**

sleeved: short- (long-) sleeved de manga corta (larga), 9.1

slice la tajada, 9.2; la rebanada, 10; *(ham)* la lonja, la loncha; *(lemon, cucumber)* la rodaja; *(melon)* la raja

to **slice** cortar en rebanadas, 10

slope la pista, 7.2

slot la ranura, **6.2**

slow lento(a), **11.1**

slowly despacio, 9.1

small pequeño(a), 1.2

smile la sonrisa, 6.1

smoking: no-smoking sign la señal de no fumar, 10.2; **1.2**

smoothie el batido, 4.2

snack la merienda; las tapas, los antojitos, 4.2; los bocaditos

sneakers las zapatillas, 5.1; los tenis, 5.2

to **snorkel** bucear, 7.1

    snorkeling el buceo 7.1

snow la nieve, 7.2

to **snow** nevar (ie), 7.2

    It's snowing. Nieva., LP

snowboarder el/la snowboarder, 7.2

so tan; **(thus)** así

soap el jabón, 11.2; **2.2**

    bar of soap la barra de jabón, 11.2; **2.2**; la pastilla de jabón

soap opera la telenovela

soccer el fútbol, 5.1

soccer field el campo de fútbol, 5.1

social studies los estudios sociales, 1.2

socks los calcetines, 5.1

soda la cola, la gaseosa, 4.1

sofa el sofá, 2.2

soft blando(a)

soft drink el refresco, 4.2

solid line *(road)* la línea continua, **9.1**

some algunos(as); unos(as)

someone alguien, 8.2

something algo, 4.1

sometimes a veces, 6.1; **1.2**; de vez en cuando

son el hijo, 2.1

soon pronto, LP; dentro de poco, 10.2; **1.2**

    See you soon! ¡Hasta pronto!, LP

sore throat: to have a sore throat tener dolor de garganta, 6.2

sorry: to be sorry sentir (ie, i)

    I'm sorry. Lo siento mucho., 5.1

soul el alma *(f.)*

soup la sopa

south el sur

South America la América del Sur, la Sudamérica

to **sow** sembrar (ie), 8.2

space el espacio; *(parking)* el sitio (para estacionar)

Spain España

Spanish *(language)* el español, 1.2; *(person)* el/la español(a)

Spanish *(adj.)* español(a)

Spanish speaker el/la hispanohablante

Spanish-speaking hispanohablante

spare time el tiempo libre, 8.1

spare tire la rueda (llanta) de repuesto (recambio), **9.2**; de refacción

to **speak** hablar, 3.1

    to speak on the phone hablar por teléfono

special especial

specialty la especialidad

spectator el/la espectador(a)

speed la velocidad, 9.1

speed limit la velocidad máxima, **9.1**; el límite de velocidad

to **spend** *(time)* pasar, 7.1; *(money)* gastar

spice la especia

spirit el espíritu, **11.1**

to **splurge** botar la casa por la ventana

spoon (tablespoon) la cuchara, 4; *(teaspoon)* la cucharita, 4

sport el deporte, 5.1

    individual sport el deporte individual

    team sport el deporte de equipo

sports *(related to)* deportivo(a)

sports car el coche deportivo, **9.2**

to **sprain** torcerse, **11.2**

    He (She) sprained his (her) ankle. Se torció el tobillo., **11.2**

spring la primavera, LP

square *(town)* la plaza, **8.1**

stable el establo, **8.2**

stadium el estadio

stairs la escalera, **8.1**

stall *(market)* el puesto, el tenderete, 9.2

to **stand in line** hacer cola, 10.2; **1.2**; estar en fila

standing de pie

star la estrella

starving: I'm starving. Me muero de hambre, 4

state el estado

station *(train)* la estación de ferrocarril (tren), **3.1**; *(subway)* la estación de metro, **8.1**; *(gas)* la estación de servicio, la gasolinera, 9.2

statue la estatua, 8.2

stay la estadía

to **stay** quedarse, 11.1; **2.1**

    to stay in bed *(illness)* guardar cama, 6.2; *(idleness)* quedarse en la cama, 11.1; **2.1**

to **stay in a hotel** hospedarse, 7

steak el biftec, 4

steep pendiente

steering wheel el volante, 9.2

stepbrother el hermanastro, 2.1

stepfather el padrastro, 2.1

stepmother la madrastra, 2.1

stepsister la hermanastra, 2.1

still todavía

stingy tacaño(a), 9.1

to **stir** revolver (ue), 10

stitch el punto, la sutura, 11.2

    to give (someone) stitches poner unos puntos (unas suturas) (a alguien), 11.2

English-Spanish Dictionary

stomach el estómago, 6.2

  to have a stomachache tener dolor de estómago, 6.2

stone la piedra

stop la parada, **3.2**

  next stop la próxima parada, **3.1**

to **stop** parar(se), **9.1**

store la tienda, 3.2

story el cuento, la historia

stove la cocina, la estufa, **10**

straight (ahead) derecho, **9.1**

  to go straight (ahead) seguir derecho, **9.1**

straw la paja, **5.2**

street la calle, **8.1**

  one-way street la calle de sentido único, 9.1

stress el estrés, 6.2; las tensiones, **11.1**

stretch (distance) trecho

to **stretch** estirarse, 11.1; **2.1**

stretcher la camilla, **11.2**

string beans las judías verdes, 9.2

strong fuerte

stubborn obstinado(a), terco(a), 6.1

student el/la alumno(a), 1.2; estudiante; *(adj.)* estudiantil, escolar, **3.1**

study el estudio

  social studies los estudios sociales, 1.2

to **study** estudiar, 3.1

stupendous estupendo(a)

style el estilo

suburbs las afueras, los suburbios, 2.2

subway el metro, **8.1**

  subway entrance la boca del metro, **8.1**

  subway station la estación de metro, **8.1**

to **succeed** tener éxito, 6.1

success el éxito, 6.1

successful: to be successful tener éxito, 6.1

such tal

suddenly de repente

to **suffer** sufrir

sugar el azúcar

suitcase la maleta, 10.1; **1.1**

  to pack one's suitcase hacer la maleta, 10.1; **1.1**

summer el verano, LP

sun el sol

to **sunbathe** tomar el sol, 7.1

Sunday el domingo, LP

sunglasses los anteojos de sol, las gafas para el sol, 7.1

sunny: It's sunny. Hace (Hay) sol., LP

suntan lotion la crema solar, la loción bronceadora, 7.1

supermarket el supermercado, 9.2

supplies: school supplies los materiales escolares, 3.1

sure seguro(a)

to **surf** practicar la tabla hawaiana, 7.1

to **surf the Web (the Net)** navegar la red (el Internet), 3.2; **6.1**

surfboard la tabla hawaiana, 7.1

surfing la tabla hawaiana, el surfing, 7.1

  to go surfing practicar la tabla hawaiana, el surfing, 7.1

surgeon: orthopedic surgeon el/la cirujano(a) ortopédico(a), **11.2**

surprise la sorpresa, 4.1

survey la encuesta

SUV el SUV, **9.2**

sweat suit el buzo, **11.1**

sweater el suéter, 11.1; **2.1**

sweet dulce, **5.1**

to **swim** nadar, 7.1

swimming pool la piscina, la alberca, 7.1; la pila

swimsuit el bañador, el traje de baño, 7.1

swollen hinchado(a), **11.2**

symptom el síntoma

T

T-shirt la camiseta, 5.1; el T-shirt

table la mesa, la mesita, 2.2; **4**

  to clear the table levantar, quitar la mesa, **4**

  to set the table poner la mesa, **4**

tablecloth el mantel, 4

tablespoon la cuchara, **4**; *(in recipe)* la cucharada

taco el taco

to **take** tomar, 3.1; traer, 10.1; **1.1**; sacar, 7.1

  to take (size) usar, calzar, 9.1

  to take a bath bañarse

  to take a flight tomar un vuelo

  to take a hike dar una caminata, 11.2; **2.2**

  to take a shower tomar una ducha, 11.1; **2.1**

  to take a test tomar un examen, 3.1

  to take a trip hacer un viaje, 10.1; **1.1**

  to take an X ray of someone tomar una radiografía, **11.2**

  to take pictures (photos) sacar (tomar) fotos, 7.1

  to take place tener lugar

  to take someone's blood pressure tomar la tensión arterial, 6.2

  to take someone's pulse tomar el pulso, 6.2

  to take the (school) bus tomar el bus (escolar), 3.2

to **take off (airplane)** despegar, 10.2; **1.2**; *(clothes)* quitarse, 11.1; **2.1**

to **take out** sacar

taken ocupado(a), 4.2; **3.2**

takeoff el despegue, 10.2; **1.2**

to **talk** hablar, 3.1

  to talk on a cell phone hablar en el móvil

  to talk on the phone hablar por teléfono

tall alto(a), 1.1

tank (car) el tanque, **9.2**

taste el gusto

tax el impuesto

taxi el taxi, 10.1; **1.1**

taxi driver el/la taxista, 10.1; **1.1**

tea el té

to **teach** enseñar, 3.1

teacher el/la profesor(a), 1.2

team el equipo, 5.1

  team sport el deporte de equipo

teaspoon la cucharita, **4**; *(in recipe)* la cucharadita

teeth los dientes, 11.1; **2.1**

  to brush one's teeth cepillarse (lavarse) los dientes, 11.1; **2.1**

telephone el teléfono

  pay telephone el teléfono público, **6.2**

  (related to) **telephone** telefónico(a), **6.2**

  telephone book la guía telefónica, **6.2**

  telephone call la llamada telefónica, **6.2**

  telephone card la tarjeta telefónica, **6.2**

  telephone line la línea, **6.2**

  telephone number el número de teléfono, **6.2**

  telephone receiver el auricular, **6.2**

  to pick up the telephone descolgar (ue) el auricular, 6.2

  to speak on the telephone hablar por teléfono

television la televisión, la tele

temperature la temperatura, 7.2

ten diez, LP

tennis el tenis

  to play tennis jugar (al) tenis, 5.2

  tennis court la cancha de tenis, 5.2

  tennis player el/la tenista, 5

  tennis racket la raqueta, 5.2

  tennis shoes los tenis, 9.1

tension la tensión, **11.1**

tent la carpa, la tienda de campaña, 11.2; **2.2**

to put up a tent armar, montar la carpa (la tienda de campaña), 11.2; **2.2**

terrace la terraza

terrible terrible

test el examen, la prueba, 3.1

  to give a test dar un examen (una prueba), 3.1

  to take a test tomar un examen, 3.1

Texan tejano(a)

text message el mensaje de texto

Thank you. Gracias., LP

that aquel, aquella, 9.1; ese(a)

that *(one)* eso

the el, la, 1.1

their su(s)

them las, los

  to them *(form. pl.) (pron.)* les

then luego, 3.2

there allí, allá, 9.1

  Is . . . there? ¿Está… ?, **6.2**

there is, there are hay, 2.2

therefore por eso

these estos(as)

they ellos(as), 1.2

thigh el muslo, **10**

thin flaco(a); delgado(a)

thing la cosa, 3.1

to **think** pensar (ie), 5.1

  What do you think? ¿Qué piensas?, 5.1

thirsty: to be thirsty tener sed, 4.1

thirteen trece, LP

thirty treinta, LP

thirty-one treinta y uno, LP

this este(a), 9.1

those aquellos(as), esos(as)

thousand mil, 9.2

three tres, LP

  the Three Wise Men los Reyes Magos, **5.2**

three hundred trescientos(as), 9.2

throat la garganta, 6.2

  to have a sore throat tener dolor de garganta, 6.2

to **throw** tirar, 5.2

  to throw (give) a party dar una fiesta, 8.1

Thursday el jueves, LP

thus así

ticket el boleto, el ticket, 7.2; **3.1;** la entrada, 8.1; el billete, 10.1; **1.1;** el tiquet(e); *(car)* la multa, **9.1**

  e-ticket el boleto (billete) electrónico, 10.1; **1.1**

  one-way ticket el boleto (billete) sencillo, **3.1**

  round-trip ticket el boleto (billete) de ida y vuelta (regreso), **3.1**

  to give (someone) a ticket clavar con una multa, **9.1**

ticket counter *(airport)* el mostrador, 10.1; **1.1**

ticket dispenser el distribuidor automático, **3.1**

ticket window la ventanilla, la boletería, 7.2, **3.1;** la taquilla, 8.2

tie la corbata, 9.1

tiger el tigre

time la hora, LP; 10.1; **1.1;** el tiempo, 8.1; la vez

  at times (sometimes) a veces, 6.1; **1.2**

  at what time? ¿a qué hora?, LP

boarding time la hora de embarque, 10.1; **1.1**

departure time la hora de salida, 10.1; **1.1**

from time to time de vez en cuando, 10.2, **1.2**

full-time a tiempo completo

on time a tiempo, 10.2; **1.2**

part-time a tiempo parcial

spare time el tiempo libre, 8.1

  What time is it? ¿Qué hora es?, LP

timetable el horario, **3.1**

timid tímido(a)

tip el servicio, 4.2; la propina, **4**

  Is the tip included? ¿Está incluido el servicio?, 4.2

tire la llanta, la goma, el neumático, la rueda, **9.2;** el caucho

  flat tire el pinchazo, **9.2**

  spare tire la rueda (llanta) de repuesto (recambio), **9.2**

tired cansado(a), 6.1

to a

toast las tostadas, el pan tostado, 4.1; **7**

today hoy, LP

  What day is it today? ¿Qué día es hoy?, LP

  What is today's date? ¿Cuál es la fecha de hoy?, LP

toe el dedo del pie, **11.1**

together juntos(as)

toilet el inodoro, el váter, **7**

toilet paper el papel higiénico, 11.2; **2.2**

  roll of toilet paper el rollo de papel higiénico, 11.2; **2.2**

toll el peaje, **9.1;** la cuota

tollbooth la cabina (garita) de peaje, **9.1**

tomato el tomate, 4.1

tomb la tumba, **5.1**

tomorrow mañana, LP

  See you tomorrow! ¡Hasta mañana!, LP

tonight esta noche, 4.1

too también, 1.2

toolbar la barra de herramientas, **6.1**

toothbrush el cepillo de dientes, 11.2; **2.2**

toothpaste la crema dental, 11.2; **2.2;** la pasta dentífrica

  tube of toothpaste el tubo de crema dental, 11.2; **2.2**

English-Spanish Dictionary

to **touch** tocar, 5.1
tourist el/la turista
toward hacia
towel la toalla, 7.1; **7**
town el pueblo
town square la plaza, **8.1**
toy el juguete
track (train) la vía, 3.1
traffic el tráfico, **8.1;**
  el tránsito
traffic jam el tapón
traffic light el semáforo, **8.1;**
  la luz roja, **9.1**
track la vía, **3.1**
trail el camino; la senda, **3.2**
train el tren, **3.1**
train car el coche, el vagón, **3.1**
train conductor el/la revisor,
  3.2
train station la estación de
  ferrocarril (tren), **3.1**
to **transfer (train)** transbordar,
  3.2
transportation: means of
  transportation los medios
  de transporte, **8.2**
to **travel** viajar
tree el árbol, 2.2
trip el viaje, 10.1; **1.1**
  to take a trip hacer un viaje,
  10.1; **1.1**
trombone el trombono
truck el camión, **9.2**
true *(adj.)* verdadero(a);
  cierto(a), **6.1**
  That's true. Es verdad., 9.1
trunk *(car)* el baúl, la
  maletera, 10.1; **1.1**
truth la verdad
to **try** tratar de
tube el tubo, 11.2; **2.2**
Tuesday el martes, LP
tuna el atún, 9.2
to **turn** doblar, **9.1**
to **turn around** dar la vuelta, 9.1
to **turn off** apagar, **6.1**
to **turn on** prender, **6.1**
to **turn ... years old** cumplir...
  años
turn signals las direccionales,
  9.2
TV la tele
twelve doce, LP
twenty veinte, LP
twenty-eight veintiocho, LP
twenty-five veinticinco, LP

twenty-four veinticuatro, LP
twenty-nine veintinueve, LP
twenty-one veintiuno, LP
twenty-seven veintisiete, LP
twenty-six veintiséis, LP
twenty-three veintitres, LP
twenty-two veintidós, LP
twin el/la gemelo(a), 2.1
to **twist** torcerse, **11.2**
two dos, LP
two hundred doscientos(as),
  9.2
type el tipo, 6.1
typical típico(a)

ugly feo(a), 1.1
unattractive feo(a), 1.1
uncle el tío, 2.1
under debajo de, 10.2; **1.2**
underneath debajo de, 10.2; **1.2**
to **understand** comprender, 4.2;
  entender (ie), 8.2
unfortunately
  desgraciadamente
to **unhook** *(telephone receiver)*
  descolgar el auricular, 6.2
uniform el uniforme, 3.1
United States Estados Unidos
  from the United States
  estadounidense
university la universidad
unless a menos que
unoccupied libre, 4.2; **3.2**
unpleasant antipático(a), 1.1;
  desagradable
until hasta, LP
up: to go up subir, 7.2
upper superior
urban urbano(a), **8.1**
us *(pl. pron.)* nos
to **use** usar, 3.2

vacation las vacaciones, 7.1
vanilla *(adj.)* de vainilla
various varios(as)
veal la ternera, 10
veal cutlet el escalope
  de ternera, **10**
vegetable la legumbre, la
  verdura, el vegetal, 4.1

vegetable store (greengrocer)
  la verdulería, 9.2
vegetarian vegetariano(a), 4.1
Venezuelan venezolano(a)
very muy, LP; mucho, LP
  It's very hot (cold). Hace
  mucho calor (frío)., LP
  Very well. Muy bien, LP
view la vista
vinegar el vinagre, 4
violin el violín
to **visit** visitar, 8.2
volcano el volcán
volleyball el voleibol, 7.1
  volleyball court la cancha
  de voleibol, 7.1
vowel la vocal

to **wait (for)** esperar, 10.2; **1.2**
  to wait in line hacer cola,
  10.2; **1.2;** estar en fila
waiter (waitress) el/la
  mesero(a), 4.2, **4;** el/la
  camarero(a), **4**
waiting room la sala de
  espera, **3.1**
to **wake up** despertarse (ie),
  11.1; **2.1**
to **walk** caminar, **5.1;** andar
  to walk in a procession
  desfilar, **5.1**
to **want** querer (ie), 5.1; desear, 4.2
war la guerra
warm-ups *(clothing)* el buzo,
  11.1
to **warn** advertir (ie)
warning la advertencia
to **wash** lavar, 11.2; **2.2**
to **wash oneself** lavarse, 11.1; **2.1**
  to wash one's hair (face,
  hands) lavarse el pelo (la
  cara, las manos), 11.1; **2.1**
washbasin el lavabo, 7
to **watch** mirar, 3.2; ver, 4.2
water el agua, 4.1
  (sparkling) mineral water
  el agua mineral (con gas),
  4.2
  running water el agua
  corriente
waterskiing el esquí acuático
  (náutico), 7.1
  to water-ski esquiar en el
  agua, 7.1

wave la ola, 7.1

way la manera

    to lose one's way perder el camino

we nosotros(as)

to **wear** llevar, 3.1; *(shoe size)* calzar, 9.1; *(clothing size)* usar, 9.1

weather el tiempo, LP

    It's cold (weather). Hace frío., LP

    It's cool (weather). Hace fresco., LP

    The weather is bad. Hace mal tiempo., LP

    The weather is nice. Hace buen tiempo., LP

    What's the weather like? ¿Qué tiempo hace?, LP

Web la red, 3.2; **6.1**

    to surf the Web navegar la red, 3.2; **6.1**

Web site el sitio Web, **6.1**

Wednesday el miércoles, LP

week la semana, LP

    last week la semana pasada, 7.1

weekend el fin de semana, 7.1

weight el peso

weights: to lift weights levantar pesas, **11.1**

welcome: You're welcome. De nada., Por nada., No hay de qué., LP

well bien, LP; pues

    Very well. Muy bien., LP

well-done *(meat)* bien hecho(a), **4**

well-known renombrado(a)

well-mannered bien educado(a), 6.1

west el oeste

what ¿qué?; ¿cuál?, LP; ¿cuáles? ¿cómo?, 1.1

    at what time? ¿a qué hora?, LP

    What a shame! ¡Qué pena!, 5.1

    What day is it (today)? ¿Qué día es hoy?, LP

    What does he (she, it) look like? ¿Cómo es?, 1.1

    What's happening? What's going on? ¿Qué pasa?, 3.1

    What is he (she, it) like? ¿Cómo es?, 1.1

    What is today's date? ¿Cuál es la fecha de hoy?, LP

    what nationality? ¿de qué nacionalidad?, 1.1

    What's new (up)? ¿Qué hay?

    What size shoe do you wear (take)? ¿Qué número calzas?, 9.1

    What would you like (to eat)? ¿Qué desean tomar?, 4.2

    What time is it? ¿Qué hora es?, LP

wheat el trigo, **8.2**

wheelchair la silla de ruedas, **11.2**

when cuando, 3.1

when? ¿cuándo?, 3.2

where donde

where? ¿dónde?, 1.1; ¿adónde?, 3.2

    from where? ¿de dónde?, 1.1

which? ¿cuál?, LP; ¿cuáles?

while mientras, 5.2

white blanco(a), 5.1

who? ¿quién?, 1.1; ¿quienes?, 1.2

    Who's calling, please? ¿De parte de quién, por favor?, **6.2**

whole entero(a)

whose cuyos(as)

why? ¿por qué?, 3.2

wide ancho(a), **8.1**

wife la esposa, la mujer, 2.1

to win ganar, 5.1

wind el viento, LP

window *(store)* el escaparate, 9.1; *(plane)* la ventanilla, 10.2; **1.2**

windshield el parabrisas, 9.1

windsurfing la plancha de vela, 7.1

    to go windsurfing practicar la plancha de vela, 7.1

windy: It's windy. Hace viento., LP

wings las alitas, **10**

winter el invierno, LP, 7.2

wise: the Three Wise Men los Reyes Magos, 5.2

to wish desear, 4.2

with con

within dentro de

without sin, 7.2

woman la dama

wooden de madera

word la palabra

work el trabajo; *(art)* la obra

to **work** trabajar, 3.2; *(land)* cultivar, labrar, **8.2**

world el mundo

    World Cup la Copa Mundial

worldwide mundial

worse peor

worst el/la peor

to **be worth: It's not worth it.** No vale., 7.1

    Would that . . . Ojalá que… , **11.2**

wound la herida, **11.2**

wreath la corona, **5.1**

wrist la muñeca, **11.1**

to **write** escribir, 4.2

written escrito(a)

wrong erróneo(a)

X ray la radiografía, **11.2**

    They're taking an X ray (of him or her). Le toman (hacen) una radiografía., **11.2**

year el año, LP

    last year el año pasado, 7.1

    to be turning . . . years old cumplir... años, 2.1

    to be . . . years old tener... años, 2.1

yellow amarillo(a), 5.1

yes sí, LP

yesterday ayer, 7.1

    yesterday afternoon ayer por la tarde, 7.1

    yesterday evening anoche, 7.1

yet aún; todavía

yoga el yoga, **11.1**

    to do yoga practicar yoga, **11.1**

you tú *(sing. form.)* usted; *(pl. form.)* ustedes; *(pl. fam.)* vosotros(as); *(fam. pron.)* ti; te; *(form. pron.)* le

    You're welcome. De (Por) nada., No hay de qué., LP

young person el/la joven, 1.1

younger menor

youngest el/la menor

your *(fam.)* tu(s); *(form.)* su(s)

    It's your turn! ¡Te toca a ti!

youth hostel el albergue juvenil, el hostal, **7**

zero cero, LP

zone la zona

zoo el zoológico, **8.1**

Culture Index

Numbers in light print indicate that the cultural reference was introduced in Level 1.
Numbers in bold print indicate that the cultural reference is introduced in Level 2.

A

amigos R1, R7, **R34**, 20, 21, 23, 26, 30, 42, **42,** 52, 71, 73, **73,** 90, 103, **111,** 112, **112,** 130, 132, 133, **153, 170, 196,** 230, 239, 266, 275, 326, 370

Andes 22, **58, 59,** 78, **88–89,** 252, 265, 282, 350, 386, 387

Andorra 236

Año Nuevo 137, 143

Argentina en general, **326;** Aconcagua, **58,** 386; la bandera, 165; Bariloche, **R52, 11,** 252, 253, 339; Buenos Aires, **3, 17, 19, 33, 37,** 56, **100, 105, 113, 119, 122,** 127, **132,** 160, **161, 171, 191, 202, 213, 231, 234, 240, 244,** 264, **264,** 281, **286, 289,** 296, **299,** 310, 331, **344,** 345, 347, **355,** 361, 365; La Casa Rosada (Buenos Aires), **17,** 345; las cataratas del Iguazú, 229; el Catedral Cerro, 252; el lago Nahuel Huapi, 253; el Parque Nacional Los Glaciares, **37,** 365; el Parque Nacional Nahuel Huapi, 252; la Patagonia, **250;** Puerto Madryn, 238; Rawson, **166;** Salta, **231; La tecnología de hoy y ayer, 190; Tráfico y más tráfico, 286;** Trelew, **338**

arte la cerámica, 321; **Un día de cultura latina,** 282; *Hispanic Institute* (Nueva York, Estados Unidos), 272, 287; **Un hostal y un parador** (una estadía en un albergue juvenil en Argentina), **216;** Kahlo, Frida (pintora mexicana), 264; Museo del Barrio (Nueva York, Estados Unidos), 272; Olmedo Patino, Dolores (artista mexicana), **137;** Orozco, José Clemente (muralista mexicano), 282; Rivera, Diego (pintor mexicano), 264; *Zapatistas* de José Clemente Orozco, 283

artesanía en general, **209, 227;** canastas, **90;** tejidos, **71, 82**

aztecas 403, 405

B

baile 137, 264, 265, 405; Ballet Folklórico de México, 284

banderas 165, 185, 206

bienestar 48, 131, 192–194, 203, **324–325, 326, 327, 332, 335, 338, 339, 344,** 376; las farmacias en los países hispanos, 195, 201, 202; el hospital, **327, 334, 343; Médicos Sin Fronteras, 346, 347; Vida activa y buena salud, 344–345**

Bolívar, Simón 145

Bolivia La Paz, 21, 180; Llapallapani, 265

C

cafés y restaurantes R13, R17, **12, 102–103, 104–105, 108, 109, 100, 111, 112, 113, 115, 119, 120–122, 123, 124, 125,** 126, 127, **129,** 132, 133, 135, 138, 140, 148, 149, 152, 154, **210, 244, 253,** 285, **298, 299, 306, 318,** 340; **Restaurantes de España y Latinoamérica, 120–122; Sé lo que pedí, 124**

California Baja, **170;** Santa Cruz, 43

Camino de Santiago 218

La camisa de Margarita 406–409

campo, la vida en el en general, **228–229, 230–231, 236–237, 246, 250,** 379; Cozumel, México, **251;** Guasca, Colombia, **241;** isla Taquile (lago Titicaca, Perú), **256, 260;** la Patagonia Argentina, **250;** Puerto Montt, Chile, **254;** Riobamba, Ecuador, **238;** Salta, **231;** Santo Domingo, Venezuela, **230**

Carnaval Baranquilla, Colombia, **136;** La Habana, Cuba, **137;** Puerto Plata, República Dominicana, **134–135**

casas R2, R9, **4,** 25, 56, 57, 62, 63, 64, 69, 76, 82, 83, 109, 123, 204, 206, **295,** 332

Cervantes Saavedra, Miguel de 44, **359**

Chile en general, **44, 59, 326,** 372, 387; Arica, 61, **70, 94, 226;** la bandera, 165; el desierto de Atacama, **23, 94,** 265, 351; el lago Pucón, **226–227; La panamericana** (un viaje en carro por la carretera panamericana), **282–284;** playa de Pucón (lago Villarrica), **R46–R47;** Poconchile, 265; Portillo, **R49;** Puerto Montt, **254,** 296; Punta Arenas, 25, 50, **57,** 385; Saltos de Petrohue, **55,** 383; Santiago, 24, **203, 228–229, 230,** 275, **278,** 322; Viña del Mar, **344**

El Cid 398–401

cine 270, 274, 275, 280, 281

Culture Index

Culture Index

248, 268, 283, 326, 327, 341; Riobamba, **238**; Saquisilí, 33

educación 89; **Escuelas aquí y en Latinoamérica** (Perú), 112; **¿Quiénes trabajan?** (la vida estudiantil en Estados Unidos y en los países hispanos), 114

El Salvador San Salvador, **306**

escuela R7, R10–R11, R12, R27, R33, **R42**, 26, **28**, 32, 33, 48, **49**, 50, 88–89, 90, 91, 92, 94–96, 113, 115, 118, **133**, 142, **150, 166**, 176, 187, 190, 198, 356, 377; **Escuelas aquí y en Latinoamérica** (Perú), 112; **¿Quiénes trabajan?** (la vida estudiantil en Estados Unidos y en los países hispanos), 114

España en general, **70, 71, 298, 376;** La Alhambra (Granada), 401; Aragón, 229; Arrecife (Lanzarote), 323; Asturias, **R9, 36, 61,** 364, 389; Barcelona, **R13, R18, R31, 13, 50,** 104, **144, 148, 150,** 195, **221, 265, 298,** 300, 324, **327, 334,** 341, **345, 352,** 378; Bilbao, 188, 262–263; Burgos, **57,** 385, 399; Cádiz, **112, 120,** 171, 257; Córdoba, **87;** El Escorial (San Lorenzo de El Escorial), 397; Estepona, 90, 228, 250, **265,** 318; **Unas fiestas hispanas, 154–156;** Fuerteventura (islas Canarias), **121, 156;** Granada, **R49, 133,** 229, 308, 401; Gran Canaria, 195, 297; Guipúzcoa, 56; **Un hostal y un parador** (una estadía en un parador en España), **216, 217;** islas Canarias, 89, 195; Lanzarote (islas Canarias), **170;** Madrid, **R25, R35, 2,** 75, 84, **137;** 146, 149, **158, 159, 170,** 198, **207,**

264, 297, 301, 330, **335, 372,** 396; Málaga, **R16, R17,** 74; Mallorca, **14,** 228, 273, 342; La Mancha, 45, **264;** Marbella, 251; la Mezquita (Córdoba), **87; En un mundo tecnológico, 188;** Navarra, **202;** Nerja, **51,** 379; **La Nochevieja en España, 158;** Órgiva, 21; País Vasco, Euskadi, **372;** La Palma (islas Canarias), 7, 208; Palma de Mallorca, **R8, 215;** Las Palmas de Gran Canaria, 242, 269, **369;** el Parque Nacional de Cazorla (Andalucía), **64,** 392; el Parque Nacional de los Picos de Europa (Asturias), **371;** Picos de Europa (Asturias), **374;** los Pirineos, 236; Pradollano, 256; **Una receta latina** (el arroz con pollo), **312;** Salamanca, 216–217; San Sebastián, **R13, 103, 171,** 297; Santiago de Compostela, **216, 218, 219;** Santillana del Mar, **379;** Segovia, **7,** 335; Sevilla, **137, 182;** Tarifa, 251; Tenerife (islas Canarias), 68, **281, 303, 336;** Toledo, **123;** Valencia, **R17, 231,** 241, **311,** 322, **324–325,** 400; Vitoria, 272; Zafra, 170

familia R2, R8, R9, R12, R45, 54–55, 57, 58, 59, 60, 61, 69, 124–125, 129, 136, 228, **295, 347; Una familia ecuatoriana,** 76

ferias y fiestas en general, **134–135, 136–137, 138, 139, 143, 144, 145, 152, 154–156,**

158; el Año Nuevo, **137, 143;** Carnaval, **134–135, 136, 137;** la Cuaresma, **136;** el Cuatro de Julio (Estados Unidos), **322;** el Día de la Independencia (México), 149; el Día de los Muertos, **137, 139, 140, 141, 154–155;** el Día de San Juan (Puerto Rico), **152, 153;** la Feria de Sevilla (Sevilla, España), **137;** el festival cubano (la Pequeña Habana, Miami, Florida), **299;** el festival de la Mamá Negra (Latacunga, Ecuador), **136;** el festival de Ollantay Raymi (Perú), **137;** la Fiesta de Enero (México), **136; Unas fiestas hispanas, 154–156;** Hanuka, **143;** Miércoles de Cenizas, **136;** la Navidad, **136, 137, 141, 142, 144, 156, 162;** la Nochebuena, **142;** la Nochevieja, **158, 159; La Nochevieja en España, 158**

Fernández de Lizardi, José Joaquín 214–215

Florida Una ciudad interesante (Miami), **252;** Miami, 47, 111, 138, **252, 253, 299**

Francia la Torre Eiffel, **114**

geografía 102; de la América del Sur, **22,** 350

Guatemala en general, 33, **146, 210;** Antigua, **R1,** 24, 31, 120, 123, **125, 150,** 161, **180,** 210, 218, 224, 265, 282, 283, 304, **327;** Chichicastenango, 187, 316; Ciudad de Guatemala, **11, 15, 110,** 265, **285,** 339, 343; lago Atitlán, **212;**

Mercados indígenas (en Guatemala y Ecuador), 316; **La panamericana** (un viaje en carro por la carretera panamericana), **282–284;** San Pedro La Laguna, **174;** Tikal, **308**

Hanuka 143, 156, 157

Hemingway, Ernest 202

Honduras en general, **347;** Copán, 160, 168; Roatán, 229

hoteles y hostales 200–201, 202–203, 204, 205, 207, 211, 213, 215, 217, 221, 224, 331; Un hostal y un parador, 216

Iglesias, Enrique 47, 375

Ixtaccíhuatl 402–405

Kahlo, Frida (el Museo) 264

latinos 38; **Amigos Latinos en Estados Unidos,** 42; 164

Lazarillo de Tormes 216, 217

lenguaje en general, **109, 138, 298, 333;** comparaciones con el inglés, **R44,** 30, **46,** 95, 100, **210, 240,** 306, **340,** 374; en otras partes, **5, 8,** 23, **42,** 63, **73, 76,** 93, 97, **106,** 128, 131, 133, **142, 172, 177,** 200, **205,** 230, **232,** 235, **237,** 266, **266,** 270, 298, **301,** 302, **309,** 333, 336, 370; refranes, **19,** 39, **53,** 73, **85,** 109, **117,** 143, **150,** 177, **185,** 211, **212, 245,** 247, 279, **279,** 313, **341,** 347, 381; sufijo diminutivo, 60; tú/usted, **R15,** 35, 50

Una Leyenda mexicana: Iztaccíhuatl y Popocatépetl 402–405

literatura *La camisa de Margarita,* 406–409; *El Cid,* 398–401; *Lazarillo de Tormes,* 216–217; *Una leyenda mexicana—Iztaccíhuatl y Popocatépetl,* 402–405; *Marianela,* **368–381;** *El Periquillo Sarniento,* 214; *Don Quijote,* 44, **358–363;** *Versos sencillos,* **364–367**

literatura picaresca *Lazarillo de Tormes,* 216, 217; *El Periquillo Sarniento,* 214

Lizardi, José Joaquín Fernández de 214

Marianela **368–381**

Martí, José 365

mascotas 58, 66, 67, 73, 78, 84, 224

mayas 160, 168

Médicos Sin Fronteras 346, 347

mercados R38, 82, 116, 144, 218, **227,** 294–295, 296, 297, 302, 303, 307, 310, 316, 317, 318, **323,** 324, 326

meriendas 132, 133, 140, 142, 148, 149, 154

mexicanoamericanos 42, 199

México en general, **77, 227;** la bandera, 165; la Barranca del Cobre, **89–90;** Ciudad de México, **R5, R33, R51,** 35, **47,** 57, 126, **154,** 161, **164, 231, 249, 258, 273, 274, 276,** 284, 285, **286, 287,** 296, 309, 312, 315, 319, **326,** 375, 404, 405; Coyoacán, 264; Cozumel, **251; Unas fiestas hispanas, 154–156;** Guadalajara, 57, 67, 90, 103, **104, 115,** 130, **208, 296–297,** 307; Guanajuato, 7, 148; León, **3,** 331; Mérida, 122, 222, **298,** 317; Oaxaca, **R15, 36,** 137, 242, **327, 341,** 364; Pátzcuaro, **105, 154–155;** la península Yucatán, 228; Puebla, 71, **149, 318;** Puerto Vallarta, **R49,** 32, 228, 240; San Cristóbal de las Casas, **200–201;** San Miguel de Allende, **R20–R21, R42;** la Sierra Madre, **71, 89–90;** los tarahumara, **90;** Taxco, **231;** Tepoztlán, **R19, 105, 116,** 125, **203, 277, 298, 323; Tráfico y más tráfico, 286; Viajes ferroviarios fabulosos** (el ferrocarril Pacífico–Chihuahua), **88–90;** el volcán Iztaccíhuatl, 402; el volcán Popocatépetl, 402; Zihuatanejo, **10,** 173, 338

Miami 111; **Una ciudad interesante, 252;** parque de Máximo Gómez, **252;** la Pequeña Habana, **253;** la Pequeña Habana—la Calle Ocho, 47, **299;** Plaza de la Cubanidad, **252**

Culture Index

Culture Index

Culture Index

Chile), **228–229;** Plaza de Armas (Trujillo, Perú) 73; Plaza de la Cibeles (Madrid, España), **137;** Plaza de la Cubanidad (Miami, Florida), **252;** Plaza de la Independencia (Montevideo, Uruguay), **80, 235;** Plaza del Obradoiro (Santiago de Compostela), **219;** Plaza de las Tres Culturas (Ciudad de México, México), 404; Plaza Dorrego (Buenos Aires, Argentina), **244;** Plaza Mayor (Antigua, Guatemala), **R1;** Plaza Mayor (Madrid, España), **R25,** 149; Plaza Mayor (Salamanca, España) 216; la Puerta del Sol (Madrid, España), **158, 159;** San Juan, Venezuela, 207; Santo Domingo, República Dominicana, 38; Tenerife, 68; Valencia, España, 400; Zócalo, (Ciudad de México, México), **164,** 284, 405

Popocatépetl 402–405

Puerto Rico en general, **152, 153;** la bandera, 206; Isabela, 21; **En un mundo tecnológico, 188;** Piñones, 126; Rincón, 249; San Juan, **12, 21, 28,** 36, 142, **196,** 206, 243, **299,** 340, 349, 356; Vieques, **32, 151, 203,** 360

313, **341,** 347, 381

República Dominicana Puerto Plata, **135;** la Romana, **1,** 329; San Pedro de Macorís, 181; Santo Domingo, **R7, 3,** 20, 38, 54–55, 95, 118, 160, 331

restaurantes y cafés → cafés y restaurantes

Rivera, Diego 264

Sagrada Familia, templo expiatorio de la 148

Shakira 277

sistema métrico 305

tapas 102–103, 128

tecnología 98, **168–169, 170–171, 172, 173, 188; En un mundo tecnológico, 188; La tecnología de hoy y ayer, 190**

tejidos 71, 82, 227

Texas (o Tejas) El Paso, 31

tiempo libre 262–263

trabajo 114, **207**

tren en general, **68–69, 70, 71, 72, 73, 76, 77, 88–90, 94, 95, 132;** el Ave, **70, 75, 76; De Panamá a Colón en tren, 92;** la estación Arica–La Paz (Chile), **70;** la estación Atocha (Madrid), **71, 75;** la estación de Colón (Panamá), **92;** la estación de Divisadero (México), **90;** la estación General Belgrano (Buenos Aires), **100; Viajes ferroviarios fabulosos, 88–90**

Uruguay Colonia, **129,** 135; Montevideo, 80, 84, **235; Sé lo que pedí,** 124

Venezuela en general, **22,** 350; Caracas, **R26,** 69, **109, 265, 286, 290;** Mérida, 21, 175, 318, 326; San Juan, **R9, 190,** 207; Santo Domingo, **230; Tráfico y más tráfico, 286**

Versos sencillos 364–367

viajes y vacaciones R46–R47, 226–227, 236; **El avión en la América del Sur,** 22, 350; en avión, **1, 2, 3, 5, 11, 22, 33,** 328–329, 330, 331, 333, 339, 350, 361; el camping, **37, 42, 44, 54, 57, 58, 61, 62, 63,** 365, 370, 372, 382, 385, 386, 389, 390, 391; **Un día en una playa de España,** 250; **Domingo, día 18 de febrero** (una excursión escolar a la Ciudad de México), 284; **Julio en Argentina** (el esquí en Argentina), 252; **La panamericana** (un viaje en carro por la carretera panamericana), **282–284;** para los mochileros, **34, 35, 36, 37, 43, 45, 56, 59,** 362–363, 364, 365, 371, 373, 384, 387; **Un viaje interesante** (las líneas de Nazca), **24, 25,** 352, 353

Zapata, Emiliano 282

Culture Index

Grammar Index

possessive adjectives R9

present of **ser,** R6; of **tener,** R8; of regular verbs, R15; of **ir, dar,** and **estar,** R18; of verbs with **g** in the **yo** form, 12 (1); of **decir,** 83 (3); subjunctive mood, 304 (10) (*See also* irregular verbs; stem-changing verbs; subjunctive mood)

present participle 15 (1); with object pronouns, 244 (8)

present perfect 208 (7)

present progressive 15 (1)

preterite tense of regular verbs, R51; of **ir, ser, dar, ver,** R51; of irregular verbs with **i** in stem, 80 (3); with **u** in stem, 80 (3); with **uv** in stem, 80 (3); of **decir** and **traer,** 83 (3) (*See also* irregular verbs; stem-changing verbs; preterite vs. imperfect)

preterite vs. imperfect completed vs. repeated or habitual action, 181 (6); two past actions in the same sentence, 184 (6)

pronouns indirect object pronouns, R27; reflexive pronouns, 47 (2); after a preposition, 85 (3); **se** to express passive voice, 116 (4); direct and indirect object pronouns: **me, te, nos,** R53; **le, les, lo, los, la, las,** R53; used together, 211 (7); with **se,** 213 (7); with infinitive and present participle, 244 (8); with commands, 307 (10)

querer preterite, 80 (3); imperfect, 180 (6); future, 242 (8); conditional, 278 (9)

reflexive pronouns 47 (2)

reflexive verbs 46–47 (2); with stem changes, 50 (2) (*See also* stem-changing verbs)

saber present, R42; **saber** vs. **conocer,** R42; preterite, 80 (3); imperfect, 180 (6); future, 242 (8); conditional, 278 (9)

salir present, 12 (1); future, 242 (8); affirmative **tú** command, 276 (9); conditional, 278 (9)

ser present, R6; **ser** vs. **estar,** R25; preterite, R51; imperfect, 150 (5); affirmative **tú** command, 276 (9)

stem-changing verbs
present: (e → ie), (o → ue), and **jugar,** R33; (e → i): **freír, pedir, repetir, seguir, servir, vestirse,** 110 (4)
preterite: (e → i): **divertirse, freír, pedir, preferir, repetir, seguir, servir, vestirse,** 112 (4); (o → u): **dormir** and **morir,** 112 (4); in subjunctive mood, 339 (11)

subjunctive mood present: regular forms, 304 (10); irregular forms, 305 (10); subjunctive form used as formal (**usted, ustedes**) command, 307 (10); used as negative familiar (**tú**) command, 309 (10); subjunctive after impersonal expressions, 336 (11); after ¡Ojalá!, ¡Quizás!, and ¡Tal vez!, 338 (11); stem-changing verbs, 339 (11)

superlatives and comparatives, R44

tener present, R8, 12 (1); **tener que** + *infinitive,* R8; preterite, 80 (3); future, 242 (8); affirmative **tú** command, 276 (9); conditional, 278 (9)

time expressions used with imperfect, 146 (5); used with present perfect, 208 (7)

traer present, 12 (1); present participle, 15 (1); preterite, 83 (3)

venir present, 12 (1); preterite, 80 (3); future, 242 (8); affirmative **tú** command, 276 (9); conditional, 278 (9)

ver preterite, R51; imperfect, 150 (5); past participle, 210 (7)

Credits

The McGraw-Hill Companies, Inc. would like to acknowledge the artists and agencies who participated in illustrating this program: Michael Arnold; Bill Dickson represented by Contact Jupiter; Glencoe/McGraw-Hill; Pat Lewis; Cedric Hohnstadt; Geo Parkin represented by American Artists Rep., Inc.

Photo Credits
COVER Yoshio Tomii/SuperStock; **i** Yoshio Tomii/SuperStock; **iv** Andrew Payti; **ix** Ken Welsh; **v** Anthony West/CORBIS; **vi** (l) Glowimages/age fotostock, (r) Larry Hamill; **vii** David H. Brennan; **viii** (l) CORBIS/age fotostock, (r) Index Stock Imagery; **x** (l) Westned61/age fotostock, (r) David H. Brennan; **xi** terry harris just greece photo library/Alamy Images; **xii** Yellow Dog Productions/Getty Images, (l) (r) Andrew Payti; **xiv** (l) Glowimages/age fotostock, (r) Richard Brommer; **xv** Dynamic Graphics Group/Creatas/Alamy Images; **xvi** (l) The McGraw-Hill Companies, (r) Andrew Payti; **xvii** Getty Images; **xviii** (t) graficart.net/Alamy Images, (b) Don Tremain/Getty Images; **xx** (tl) Andrew Payti, (tr) Yvonne Cadiz, (b) Scott Gries/Getty Images; **SH1** (tl) Fotosearch, (tr) Rebecca Smith, (b) Clasos Agencia International/CORBIS; **SH2** (t) Getty Images; **SH2-SH3** BananaStock/Jupiter Images; **SH3** Andersen Ross/age fotostock; **SH4** Siede Preis/Getty Images; **SH5** Brand X Pictures/age fotostock; **SH6** Bananastock/PictureQuest/Jupiter Images; **SH20** The McGraw-Hill Companies; **SH35** (t) Andrew Payti, (c) Gabriela Zamudio, (bl) Rebecca Smith, (br) Matthew Johnston/Alamy Images; **SH42-SH43** Anthony West/CORBIS; **SH44** (tl) Fernando Fernández/age fotostock, (tr) Juan Manuel Silva/age fotostock, (bl) CORBIS, (br) Randa Bishop/Imagestate; **SH44-SH45** (c) Alan Copson/JAI/CORBIS; **SH45** (tl) Jose Fuste Raga/CORBIS, (tc) Hans Georg Roth/CORBIS, (tr) Kirk Weddle/Getty Images, (c) Alex Segre/Alamy Images, (b) Pablo Galán Cela/age fotostock; **SH46** (tl) CORBIS, (tr) Fritz Poelking/age fotostock, (c) Radius Images/Alamy Images, (bl) Andrew Payti, (br) Brian Stablyk/Getty Images; **SH46-SH47** Andrew Payti; **SH47** (t) Greg Vaughn/Alamy Images, (cl) Maria Lourdes Alonso/age fotostock, (cr) (b) Andrew Payti; **SH48** (tl) Andrew Payti, (tr) Jordi Cami/age fotostock, (cl) Keren Su/China Span/Alamy Images, (cr) Michele Molinari/Alamy Images, (bl) Frank Lukasseck/age fotostock, (br) Lori Ernfridsson; **SH49** (t) Kevin Schafer/age fotostock, (cl) Reuters/CORBIS, (cr) Panoramic Images/Getty Images, (b) OSWALDO RIVAS/Reuters/CORBIS; **SH50** (tl) nik wheeler/Alamy Images, (tr) Andrew Payti, (c) Torino/age fotostock, (bl) Kevin Schafer/age fotostock, (br) Roberto Escobar/epa/CORBIS; **SH51** (tl) Torino/age fotostock, (tr) José Enrique Molina/age fotostock, (c) Philip Scalia/Alamy Images, (b) Andrew Payti; **SH52** (tl) Woodfall Wild Images/Alamy Images, (tr) Jose Fuste Raga/age fotostock, (c) Gail Shumway/Getty Images, (bl) age fotostock, (br) Keren Su/China Span/Alamy Images; **SH53** (t) Andrew Payti, (bl) fstop2/Alamy Images, (br) Humberto Olarte Cupas/Alamy Images; **SH54** (tl) Danita Delimont/Alamy Images, (tr) James Marshall/CORBIS, (c) Gianni Dagli Orti/CORBIS, (b) Morales/age fotostock; **SH55** (tl) age fotostock/SuperStock, (tr) Stock Connection/Alamy Images, (cr) Reuters/CORBIS, (bl) Krzysztof Dydynski/Getty Images, (br) David Uribe Photography/eStock Photo; **SH56** (tl) Bill Bachmann/eStock Photo, (tr) CORBIS, (c) Gavin Hellier/Getty Images, (b) Andrew Payti; **SH56-SH57** SuperStock/age fotostock; **SH57** (t) John Arnold Images/age fotostock, (c) Klaus Lang/age fotostock, (bl) JTB Photo Communications, Inc./Alamy Images, (br) P. Narayan/age fotostock; **SH58** (tl) Anthony Cassidy/JAI/CORBIS, (tc) Robert Frerck/Getty Images, (tr) Michael Lewis/CORBIS, (bl) IML Image Group Ltd/Alamy Images, (br) David R. Frazier Photolibrary, Inc./Alamy Images; **SH59** (tl) (c) Andrew Payti, (tr) imagebroker/Alamy Images, (bl) M&M Valledor/age fotostock, (br) Abacana/age fotostock; **SH60** (tl) Brian Atkinson/Alamy Images, (tr) Scenics & Science/Alamy Images, (cl) Dorling Kindersley/Getty Images, (cr) John Hicks/CORBIS, (b) Imagestate; **SH61** (tl) Neil Setchfield/Alamy Images, (tr) James Balog/age fotostock, (bl) David Lyons/Alamy Images, (br) Ramond Forbes/age fotostock; **SH62** (tl) WaterFrame/Alamy Images, (tr) M. Timothy O'Keefe/Alamy Images, (cl) Jose Fuste Raga/CORBIS, (cr) Hola Images/Getty Images, (b) Robert Harding Picture Library, Ltd/Alamy Images; **SH63** (t) Envision/CORBIS, (c) Danny Lehman/CORBIS, (bl) Raymond Mendez/Animals Animals-Earth Scenes, (br) Richard Brommer; **SH64** (tl) Frances M. Roberts/Alamy Images, (tr) Danita Delimont/Alamy Images, (cl) Blend Images/Alamy Images, (cr) Ron & Patty Thomas/Getty Images, (b) Jon Arnold Images/Alamy Images, (inset) David R. Frazier Photolibrary, Inc./Alamy Images; **SH65** (t) AP Images, (c) Ian Dagnall/Alamy Images, (bl) Jeff Greenberg/Alamy Images, (bc) Robert Fried/Alamy Images, (br) Sylvain Grandadam/age fotostock; **R0-R1** Robert Fried/Alamy Images; **R2** (t) Laurence Mouton/age fotostock, (tc) Dynamic Graphics Group/Alamy Images, (tr) David H. Brennan, (bl) Gabriela Zamudio, (br) The McGraw-Hill Companies; **R3** Rainer Heubeck/Peter Arnold Inc.; **R4** The McGraw-Hill Companies; **R5** (t) Janine Wiedel Photolibrary/Alamy Images, (b) Andrew Payti; **R6** (t) Superstock/age fotostock, (b) Larry Hamill; **R7** (t) Alamy Images, (b) Larry Hamill; **R8** Andrew Payti; **R9** (t) De Meester, J./Peter Arnold Inc., (b) Kelli Drummer-Avendaño; **R10-R11** SuperStock/age fotostock; **R12** (tl) Larry Hamill, (tr) Andrew Payti, (bl) (br) David H. Brennan; **R13** (t) Javier Larres/age fotostock, (b) San Rostro/age fotostock; **R14** David R. Frazier Photolibrary, Inc./Alamy Images; **R15** Andrew Payti; **R16** Jeronimo Alba/age fotostock; **R17** (t) Andrew Payti, (b) J.D. Dallet/age fotostock; **R18** Xavier Subias/age fotostock; **R19** Andrew Payti; **R20-R21** Jeremy Woodhouse/Getty Images; **R22** (tl) Mike Watson Images/age fotostock, (tr) Rick J. Rudnicki/age fotostock, (cl) CORBIS, (cr) Banana Stock/age fotostock, (b) David H. Brennan; **R23** Getty Images; **R24** Michel Touraine/age fotostock; **R25** Yvonne Cadiz; **R26** (t) Getty Images, (b) Mike Watson/age fotostock; **R27** (t) The McGraw-Hill Companies, (b) CORBIS/age fotostock; **R28-R29** CHARLES W LUZIER/Reuters/CORBIS; **R30** (tl) (tr) Frederico Gil/Digital Lightsource, Inc., (b) Robert Fried/Alamy Images; **R31, R32** David R. Frazier Photolibrary, Inc./Alamy Images; **R33** Keith Dannemiller/CORBIS; **R34** (t) James McLoughlin/age fotostock, (b) Cason Ganci/age fotostock; **R35** (tl) (tr) Getty Images, (b) CORBIS/age fotostock; **R36-R37** Achim Pohl/Peter Arnold Inc.; **R38** (tl) John Powell/Alamy Images, (tr) (cr)Ann Summa, (cl) Jill Braaten/The McGraw-Hill Companies, (b) Andrew Payti; **R39** Superstock/age fotostock; **R40** Glowimages/age fotostock; **R42** Dan Gair Photographic/Index Stock Imagery, Inc.; **R43** Jeff Greenberg/age fotostock; **R44** VStock LLC/age fotostock; **R45** Steve Weinstein; **R46-R47** Ron Giling/Peter Arnold Inc.; **R48** (tl) (tr) David H. Brennan, (bl) Alamy Images, (br) ImageSource/age fotostock; **R49** (t) Getty Images, (bl) Paco Ayala/age fotostock, (br) Kerri Galloway; **R50** Steve Mason/age fotostock; **R51** Andrew Payti; **R52** (t) The McGraw-Hill Companies, (b) Andrew Payti; **R53** Andrew Payti; **000-001** Melba Photo Agency/Alamy Images; **002** (cl) Kelli Drummer-Avendaño, (t) Stuart Pearce/age fotostock, (cr) The McGraw-Hill Companies, (b) CORBIS; **003** (cw from top) Andrew Payti, (2) DAVID R. FRAZIER Photolibrary, Inc., (3) SuperStock/age fotostock, (4) Getty Images, (5) The McGraw-Hill Companies, (6) DAVID R. FRAZIER Photolibrary, Inc., (7) Larry Hamill; **004** David H. Brennan; **005** (l) Javier Larrea/age fotostock, (r) The McGraw-Hill Companies, (bkgd) David H. Brennan;

Credits

Credits

Brennan; **187** The McGraw-Hill Companies; **188** David H. Brennan; **190** (l) Andrew Payti, (r) David H. Brennan; **191** Andrew Payti; **192** (t) David H. Brennan, (b) Dynamic Graphics Groups/Creatas/Alamy Images; **193** Kerri Galloway; **194** ImageSource/age fotostock; **195** The McGraw-Hill Companies; **196** Kelli Drummer-Avendaño; **198** Suzanne Murphy/Getty Images; **199** Flat Earth Images; **200-201** Gina Martin/Getty Images; **202** (t) J.D. Dallet /age fotostock, (c) Marco Cristofori/age fotostock, (bl) Andrew Payti, (bc) Bartomeu Amengual/age fotostock, (br) David R. Frazier Photolibrary, Inc./Alamy Images; **203** (tl) Rebecca Smith; **203** (tr) (cr) Andrew Payti, (cl) Blaine Harrington III/Alamy Images, (b) Robert Frerck/Getty Images; **204** (tl) (c) (br) David H. Brennan, (tc) (tr) Andrew Payti, (bl) Yellow Dog Productions/Getty Images; **205** David H. Brennan; **206** (tl) (b) Andrew Payti, (tr) CORBIS; **207** (l) Andrew Payti, (r) age fotostock; **208** Kerri Galloway; **209** Richard Brommer; **210** Lori Ernfridsson; **211** Andrew Payti; **212** Lori Ernfridsson; **213** Alamy Images; **215** The Geoff Williamson Image Collection/Alamy Images; **216** Alamy Images; **217** Hughes Herve/age fotostock; **218** (t) Chris Howarth/Alamy Images, (b) Alan Copson/age fotostock; **219** Jose fuste Raga/age fotostock; **220** (l) Yvonne Cadiz, (r) Andrew Payti; **221** Yvonne Cadiz; **222** The McGraw-Hill Companies; **223** Noel Hendrickson/age fotostock; **224, 226** Andrew Payti; **227** IMS Communications Ltd./Capstone Design; **228-229** Jon Hicks/CORBIS; **230** (t) David G. Houser/CORBIS, (cl) Andrew Payti, (cr) Kelli Drummer-Avendaño, (b) Gavin Hellier/Getty Images; **231** (tl) Juarez Ken Welsh/age fotostock, (tr) Glowimages/age fotostock, (cl) Gianmarco Maggiolini/age fotostock, (c) (cr) Andrew Payti, (bl) Hugh Sitton/zefa/CORBIS, (br) ARCO/F Scholz/age fotostock, (tl) Bill Bachmann/Alamy Images, (tr) Courtney Brown, (c) Paco Ayala/age fotostock; **232** (b) Geoffrey Clive/age fotostock, (tl) Lemarco/Alamy Images, (tr) (c) Andrew Payti, (bl) Stuart Walker/Alamy Images, (br) Alan Howden-Argentina Stock Photography/Alamy Images; **234** (l) Keith Dannemiller/Alamy Images, (r) Andrew Payti; **235** Andrew Payti; **236** (l to r, t to b) Sean Burke/Alamy Images, (2) FRILET Patrick/age fotostock, (3) Andrew Payti, (4) Goodshoot/PunchStock, (5) Getty Images, (6) Brand X Pictures/PunchStock, (7) Getty Images; **237** (t) David H. Brennan, (b) Hubert Stadler/CORBIS; **239** Andrew Payti; **240** Andrew Payti; **241** (t) Richard Brommer, (b) Maria E. Villalta; **242** Richard Brommer; **243** Andrew Payti; **244** Picture Contact/Alamy Images; **246** Chad Case/Alamy Images; **247** Andrew Payti; **248** (t) Andrew Payti, (b) Juan G. Montanes/age fotostock; **249** (l) Andrew Payti, (r) Tono Labra/age fotostock; **250** (t) Richard Brommer, (b) Arco Images/Alamy Images; **251** M. Timothy O'Keefe/Alamy Images; **252** (t) Demmos MacDonald/Alamy Images, (b) Peter Wilson/Alamy Images; **253** James Quine/Alamy Images; **254, 255** Andrew Payti; **256** (t) Andrew Payti, (b) Richard Brommer; **257** Andrew Payti; **260** Richard Brommer; **262-263** José Fuste Raga/age fotostock; **264** (tl) Rebecca Smith, (tr) Brand X Pictures/Alamy Images, (cl) Fernando Ramirez/age fotostock, (cr) Jose Fuste Raga/age fotostock, (b) Dynamic Graphics Group/Creatas/Alamy Images; **265** (tl) Gavin Hellier/Getty Images, (tr) SCPhotos/Alamy Images, (cl) (b) Andrew Payti, (c) Xavier Subias/age fotostock, (cr) Rebecca Smith; **266** (t) Ruddy Gold/age fotostock, (b) Andrew Payti; **267** (tl) Jose Enrique Molina/age fotostock, (tr) Jennifer Doyle, (c) Simon Belcher/Alamy Images, (b) The McGraw-Hill Companies; **268** Andrew Payti; **269** (l to r, t to b) Francis Morgan, (6) (3) (2) Andrew Payti, (4) (7) Francis Morgan, (5) Michelle Chaplow; **270** (l to r, t to b) (3) (4) (5) (6) (7) The McGraw-Hill Companies, (2) David H. Brennan; **271** (tl) Image Source Ltd/age fotostock, (tr) (b) David H. Brennan; **272** (t) David H. Brennan, (b) The McGraw-Hill Companies; **273** Andrew Payti;

274 (t) (br) Andrew Payti, (bl) The McGraw-Hill Companies; **276** (t) Andrew Payti, (b) Leonardo Diaz Romero/age fotostock; **277** Andrew Payti; **278** (t) David R. Frazier Photolibrary, Inc./Alamy Images, (b) Maria E. Villalta; **281, 282** Andrew Payti; **283** Ric Ergenbright/CORBIS; **284** Andrew Payti; **285** Sylvain Grandadam/age fotostock; **286** (l) Neil Beer/age fotostock, (r) Andrew Payti; **287** Andrew Payti; **289** Robert Fried/Alamy Images; **290** Kelli Drummer-Avendaño; **291** The McGraw-Hill Companies; **295** Maria E. Villalta; **296-297** Kathy Tarantola/Index Stock Imagery; **298** (t) Robert Holmes/CORBIS, (cl) Peter M. Wilson/Alamy Images, (cr) Andrew Payti, (bl) LeighSmithImages/Alamy Images, (br) Kevin Foy/Alamy Images; **299** (tl) The McGraw-Hill Companies, (tr) Jeff Greenberg/Alamy Images, (c) Jeremy Hoare/Food And Drink Photos/age fotostock, (b) David R. Frazier Photolibrary, Inc./Alamy Images; **300** (t) CORBIS, (cr) age fotostock, (bl) (br) (cl) Alamy Images; **301** (l to r, t to b) (2) (7) (8) The McGraw-Hill Companies, (3) (4) (6) Alamy Images, (5) (9) age fotostock; **302** Kerri Galloway; **303** (t) Andrew Payti, (c) Getty Images, (b) Alamy Images; **304** Punchstock; **305** Andrew Payti; **306** age fotostock; **307** (l) Kelli Drummer-Avendaño, (r) Andrew Payti; **308** Lori Ernfridsson; **310** David H. Brennan; **311** Andrew Payti; **312** Alamy Images; **313** (l) (c) Andrew Payti, (r) The McGraw-Hill Companies; **314** Alamy Images; **315** (l) The McGraw-Hill Companies, (r) Andrew Payti; **316** (tl) Jupiterimages, (tr) Getty Images, (cl) Ken Cavanagh/The McGraw-Hill Companies, (cr) CORBIS, (bl) Getty Images; **316** (br) Getty Images; **318** Andrew Payti; **319** Hill Street Sudios/Crystal Cartier/Getty Images; **322** Punchstock; **323** Andrew Payti; **324-325** Rafael Campillo/age fotostock; **326** (t) ImageSource/age fotostock, (c) The McGraw-Hill Companies, (bl) Ben Welsh/age fotostock, (br) Robert Fried/Alamy Images; **327** (tl) Wig Worland/Alamy Images, (tr) Lori Ernfridsson, (cl) Robert Fried/Alamy Images, (cr) Andrew Payti, (b) LOOK Die Bildagentur der Fotografen GmbH/Alamy Images; **328** (tl) (b) David H. Brennan, (tr) age fotostock; **329** (tl) Getty Images, (tc) Pixtal/age fotostock, (tr) David H. Brennan, (cl) Andrew Payti, (cr) Dennis MacDonald/age fotostock, (b) Kirby Lee/WireImage/Getty Images; **330** (tl) (tc) Getty Images, (tr) Gary He/The McGraw-Hill Companies, (b) Alamy Images; **331** Andrew Payti; **332** (tl) (tc) (tr) David H. Brennan, (b) Alamy Images; **333** David H. Brennan; **334** Andrew Payti; **335** Jeronimo Alba/age fotostock; **336** (t) Andrew Payti, (b) age fotostock; **338** Andrew Payti; **339** age fotostock; **341** Andrew Payti; **343** (l) Getty Images, (r) Andrew Payti; **344** (t) Javier Larrea/age fotostock, (b) Andrew Payti; **345** San Rostro/age fotostock; **346** Doctors Without Borders/Médecins Sans Frontiéres (MSF); **347** Tina Manley; **348** (t) Getty Images, (cl) Andrew Payti, (cr) Alamy Images, (bl) Rick Brady/The McGraw-Hill Companies, (br) Getty Images; **350** Andrew Payti; **351** Kelli Drummer-Avendaño; **354** The McGraw-Hill Companies; **355** FlatEarth Images; **356** (t) Getty Images; **356-357** Ken Welsh/Alamy Images; **359** (t) Yvonne Cadiz, (b) Jack Dubois/Alamy Images; **360** PhotoLink/Getty Images; **361** Alberto Paredes/age fotostock; **362** CORBIS; **363** Andrew Payti; **364** (t) GARDEL Bertrand/age fotostock, (b) The McGraw-Hill Companies; **365** Punchstock; **366** John Pitcher/age fotostock; **367** Don Tremain/Getty Images; **368** Juan Carlos Munoz/age fotostock; **369** Philip Coblentz/Brand X Pictures/PictureQuest; **370** graficart.net/Alamy Images; **371** (t) Andrew Payti, (bl) O.Alamany & E. Vicens/CORBIS, (br) Ingram Publishing/Fotosearch; **372** CORBIS; **374** Atlantide Phototravel/CORBIS; **375** (t) Brand X Pictures, (b) Lori Ernfridsson; **376** Steve Weinstein; **379** Neil Beer/Getty Images; **blank#-SR1** Jon Hicks/CORBIS; **SR3** (l to r, t to b) (5) The McGraw-Hill Companies, (2) (4) (6) (7) Michelle Chaplow, (3) Andrew Payti, (8) Larry

Hamill; **SR4** (l to r, t to b) Michelle Chaplow, (2) (3) (6) (8) Timothy Fuller, (4) Aaron Haupt, (5) Ann Summa, (7) Curt Fischer; **SR5** (l to r, t to b) (4) Michelle Chaplow, (2) Doug Bryant/DDB Stock Photo, (3) Morgan Cain & Associates, (5) Luis Delgado; **SR5** (6) Doug Bryant/DDB Stock Photo; **SR7** (l to r, t to b) Mark Antman, (2) (5) Michelle Chaplow, (3) The McGraw-Hill Companies, (4) Steve Torregrossa, (6) Tim Fuller, (7) Creatas/age fotostock; **SR8** (l to r, t to b) Larry Hamill, (2) (3) (4) (5) The McGraw-Hill Companies, (6) Getty Images; **SR10** (l to r, t to b) (2) Larry Hamill, (3) The McGraw-Hill Companies, (4) (6) Getty Images, (5) Michelle Chaplow, (7) Steve Torregrossa, (8) Andrew Payti; **SR13** (t) Steven Ferry, (bl) (br) Aaron Haupt